Infidels

Infidels

*The Conflict between Christendom
and Islam 638–2002*

ANDREW WHEATCROFT

VIKING

an imprint of

PENGUIN BOOKS

VIKING

Published by the Penguin Group
Penguin Books Ltd, 80 Strand, London WC2R ORL, England
Penguin Putnam Inc., 375 Hudson Street, New York, New York 10014, USA
Penguin Books Australia Ltd, 250 Camberwell Road,
Camberwell, Victoria 3124, Australia
Penguin Books Canada Ltd, 10 Alcorn Avenue, Toronto, Ontario, Canada M4V 3B2
Penguin Books India (P) Ltd, 11 Community Centre,
Panchsheel Park, New Delhi – 110 017, India
Penguin Books (NZ) Ltd, Cnr Rosedale and Airborne Roads,
Albany, Auckland, New Zealand
Penguin Books (South Africa) (Pty) Ltd, 24 Sturdee Avenue,
Rosebank 2196, South Africa

Penguin Books Ltd, Registered Offices: 80 Strand, London WC2R ORL, England

www.penguin.com

First published 2003
I

Copyright © Andrew Wheatcroft, 2003

The permissions on pp. xi–xiii constitute an extension of this copyright page

Grateful acknowledgement is made for permission to reproduce an extract from
Lepanto by G. K. Chesterton. Reprinted by permission of
A. P. Watt, on behalf of the Royal Literary Fund

The moral right of the author has been asserted

Set in 12/14.75pt Monotype Bembo
Typeset by Rowland Phototypesetting Ltd, Bury St Edmunds, Suffolk
Printed in Great Britain by Clays Ltd, St Ives plc

A CIP catalogue record for this book is available from the British Library

ISBN 0-670-86942-2

For
Eric Oscar Wheatcroft
In love and gratitude

History is the most dangerous product ever concocted by the chemistry of the intellect. It causes dreams, inebriates nations, saddles them with false memories ... keeps their old sores running, torments them when they are not at rest, and induces in them megalomania and the mania of persecution.

Paul Valéry
Reflections on the World Today

Contents

Contents

List of Illustrations

Colour Section

1. *The Mufti and the Monster* by Jacopo Ligozzi, Uffizi Gallery, Florence.
2. *St George Altarpiece* attributed to André Marzal de Sas, Victoria and Albert Museum. Photo: V&A Picture Library.
3. *The Surrender of Granada, 1492* by Francisco Pradilla y Ortiz, Palacio del Senado, Madrid. Photo: Bridgeman Art Library.
4. *Ferdinand and Isabella Entering Granada* by Philippe de Vigarny, Chapel Royal, Granada. Photo: Bridgeman Art Library.
5. *The Conversion of the Moors* by Philippe de Vigarny, Chapel Royal, Granada. Photo: AKG London/Gilles Mermet.
6. *Sultan Bayezid I Routs the Crusaders at Nicopolis in 1396*, Worcester Art Museum, Massachusetts. Photo: Bridgeman Art Library.
7. *The Cairo Insurgents of 21 October 1798* by Anne-Louis Girodet de Roucy-Trioson, Château de Versailles. Photo: Bridgeman Art Library, Peter Willi.
8. *'And the Prayer of Faith Shall Save the Sick'* by John Frederick Lewis, Yale Center for British Art, Paul Mellon Collection. Photo: Bridgeman Art Library.
9. *The First Mass in Kabylia* by Horace Vernet, Musée cantonal des Beaux-Arts, Lausanne. Photo: J.-C. Durcret, Musée cantonal des Beaux-Arts, Lausanne.
10. *Mehmed Said Pasha, Bey of Rovurelia, Ambassador of Sultan Mahmud I at Versailles* by Jacques Aved, Châteaux de Versailles et de Trianon. Photo: RMN, F. Raux.

Black and White Sections

List of Maps

Acknowledgements

These pages record my thanks to some of those who have helped me understand the Infidels conundrum. With many, like Hassan and Mahmud who appear in the Preface, I do not know their full names. Chance has also played a large part. Often it was an unexpected and anonymous conversation in Amman or Texas that propelled me in a new (and profitable) direction. But I am particularly grateful to some I can name. First, those who have undertaken the thankless task of reading part (or all) of the text and putting me right. Dejan Jović has been kind enough to read through my chapters on the Balkans, suggesting many changes and improvements, and has not scorned my temerity (and ignorance) in trampling around in a field where I had so shallow a knowledge. Part of my new-found passion for South-eastern Europe stemmed from the excellent *Creating the Other* conference at the University of Minnesota (Minneapolis). Organized by the Center for Austrian Studies in May 1999, it had many Balkan tensions bubbling away below the surface. Yet we talked as dispassionately as possible about tragic events. With this book, likewise, detaching my own feelings from the subject matter that I was writing about has not always been easy.

Another area that I entered with very little prior knowledge was the role of language. Lance Butler has read every word, not just the material on language, and his advice and support have been invaluable. So too have Susanne Peters's help and advice. She has also read every chapter, sometimes in several variants. She provided me with a stream of books and articles to read, found many unusual and unexpected sources, as well as giving me consistent encouragement. Judy Delin explained complicated ideas in linguistics with such clarity that I could understand them, plus the directness to tell me when I should not use them. Michael Rice invariably gave me good advice on the texts I sent him, from his profound knowledge of many areas of the Middle East. Finally, my father, E. Oscar Wheatcroft, has read it all, an especial labour of love given his failing eyesight. Thankfully, his critical sense is still hyperactive and he saved me from many errors, such as having my galleys rowing in reverse, the result of landlubberly ignorance. None of them bear any responsibility for the flaws that remain.

I have also made myself a nuisance to many others with naïve questions that they answered with good grace. John Drakakis, Neil Keeble, Robert Miles, David Bebbington, Mark Nixon, Oron Joffe, in particular, must have dreaded my appearing round the corner at Stirling. This is also the first book I have completed with the full availability of e-mail and the Internet. While my colleagues have had some reason for answering my questions, those thousands of miles away who had never heard of me had no reason to do so. I am thankful for the help and advice of Carter Vaughn Findley, Jonathan Bloom, Dan Goffman, Robert Michaels, Larry Wolff, David Nirenberg and Eva Levin. Others, like Stephen Greenblatt, Roger Chartier, Thomas Emmert, Hugh Agnew, Margaret Meserve, Nancy Wingfield and Maiken Umbach, have had the misfortune to be pinned to a wall over a conference coffee break or interrogated over dinner. From John Keegan, I have understood, over so many years, to try and see things with clarity, regardless of the 'fog of battle'. It was John who suggested my first book, so my gratitude extends back a very long way. From Colin and Charlotte Franklin, I learned the importance of feeling and touching books, and amid the riches of their 'book barns' at Culham, learned well. Two people have helped me with research for this book, where either I did not have the time or the languages. Lina Barouch (whom Avi Shlaim shrewdly suggested) helped me enormously by assessing Hebrew material, reading the text and advising me on it. She has a wonderful eye both for things that don't work and for the inspired suggestion of something that might work. Anneyce Wheatcroft has never complained about being asked to burrow in the darker and dirtier parts of libraries and archives on my behalf. She too has the instinctive sense for unlikely but invaluable material. I am very grateful to them both.

Writing a book like this, which ranges over so many disparate areas and subjects, makes a real imposition on your friends. Rosemarie Morgan bore the brunt of the first phases. She smoothed access at

Yale, provided endless hospitality, and employed an incisive critical pencil. Without her help, this book would have been much harder to write. John Brewer and Stella Tillyard have been the best friends (and hosts) anyone could have, in Florence and in Oxford. They have also contributed more to this book, from what they have written, from conversations, or from chance asides than they could ever have realized. So too have Fuad Qushair in Amman, with whom I roamed over deep questions concerning the Arab world and the Arabic language; Mamdouh Anis and Christian Koch in Abu Dhabi, from whom I learned how to keep a book on track. In England I am grateful to David Batson, with his knowledge of the early Church; Richard Stoneman, for his expert knowledge of Greece and Turkey; Geoffrey Best, for his friendship over many years; and Roy Douglas, who helped me to decipher images. Among many others who have 'been there' with advice, help or company when I needed it, I want to mention in particular Mohammad Cherki and Djaffar Hadji, who introduced me to the new literature of Algeria; Angelica Hamilton, whose constant verve and enthusiasm stopped me doubting the whole enterprise; Nagdi Madbouli, on whom I tested Arabic meanings; Andrew Sobić and Alec Stanković with whom I talked endlessly about the Balkans; and finally Freddie Merle and Charlie Seddon, the good companions.

In Granada, many years ago, Don Jésus Bermudez Pareja and Srta Angelina Morena allowed me to roam in the archives of the Alhambra, and gave me introductions to the other archives in the city. Through them also I found my way into the mountains, to the Alpujarras, the last redoubt of the *Moriscos*. Those experiences have coloured my life and career ever since.

Two museums were invaluable for the part of the book that deals with the printed word. The first was the Musée de l'Imprimerie de Lyon, established with the guidance of Henri-Jean Martin, and the other the Gutenberg Museum, Mainz. Sadly, my visit to the Plantin-Moretus Museum in Antwerp had to be cancelled. These museums were most helpful to me and they offer a unique opportunity to get a clear sense of the world of print. This is especially true for the first three centuries and all the processes that then went into the making of books.

I want to express my continuing gratitude for access to the world of *old books* through the Library of Congress and the Folger Library in Washington DC; the Sterling, Beinecke and Seeley G. Mudd libraries at Yale; and the Wilson Library at the University of Minnesota. Also to the University Library at Texas Tech University, where I have worked happily over a number of years. Closer to home much of my work has been done in the British Library, with the book collections at the Victoria and Albert Museum and in the School of Oriental and African Studies in London; at the National Library of Scotland in Edinburgh; in the Library of Trinity College, Dublin, and the Library of the University of Leeds. Cambridge University Library, the Library of the Warburg Institute and the Special Collections of the University of Edinburgh Library have been invaluable sources of material.

In Vienna, the Österreichische Nationalbibliothek proved a treasure trove for the early images of the infidels. I have also had the benefit of using the resources of ENSSIB in Lyon. On other visits I have benefited from IRCICA in Istanbul, and the Darat al Funun, Amman, Jordan. But I have two special debts that should be acknowledged. The first is to Dr Jamal S. Al-Suwaidi who invited me to work at the Emirates Center for Strategic Studies and Research (ECSSR) on a number of occasions over a period of four years. I benefited a great deal not only from using their excellent library, but also from Jamal Al-Suwaidi's advice and interest in my work. The second is closer to home, in Stirling. Not only has the University given me generous sabbatical leave, but the work of the staff in the Library at Stirling has been far above the call of duty. I think I hold the university record for inter-library loans. This has meant that with a topic covering so many different areas and languages, I have been able to spend the time reading and writing that I had previously spent in travelling. This library cannot compare in the size of its holdings with larger institutions, but what it stocks has been well chosen. And there were many surprises. When a much larger library did not have the mid nineteenth-century volumes of *Punch* that I needed, I found them sitting on the shelf at Stirling.

I am especially grateful to my editor, Eleo Gordon, on two particular grounds. Firstly, she accepted that, while delivery kept on slipping, I was in fact working hard on the book. Secondly, as with my two previous books for Viking, every editorial suggestion she has made has been delivered with such tact that they were easy to accept. And in every case, her judgement has been incisive and absolutely right. I am especially grateful, too, for Elisabeth Merriman's patient and painstaking editing of the text. Her suggestions for rephrasing, clarification or additions have almost invariably been an improvement; I have adopted them readily and with gratitude.

There is a penultimate acknowledgement that I must make. I knew Lawrence Stone for over twenty years, for some of that time in the ambiguous role of his 'commissioning editor'. Being Lawrence's editor was a wholly one-way process. He wrote and his editor merely organized the book for publication. It was not that he would not take advice, which he did, but it was rarely needed. In the reverse process, seeking his advice for my own work, it was a very different matter. Lawrence contributed a great deal. We met annually, either in Oxford or Princeton. He made suggestions, provided contacts, was a rigorous critic of my musings, but always encouraged me to continue. Lawrence was a wonderfully supportive friend and had I written a little faster and followed fewer of the byways that Lawrence so actively endorsed, he might have seen this book before his untimely death.

My last and greatest thanks are due to my wife, Janet Wheatcroft. She has suffered from more than ten years of my worrying preoccupation with this dark topic, read drafts that are too many to count, and gently edged me away from the wildest extremities. But she has also measured what I have written against her own experience of living an essentially medieval life, solitary, in another culture, with no roads, without electricity, telephone, and lacking a common language. She lived by her wits and the loving kindness of those around her. They could not understand why she was there, but they accepted her presence. That was in Nepal, not a Muslim culture, but that made little difference. She was a silent observer, seeing Sherpa family and village life and relating it to her own experience. What I could only sense about the past, about similarity and difference, she could gauge against what she had seen and felt. Without the benefit of her insight gained over those many months, painfully lonely for both of us, I should never have been able to complete this book.

Editorial Note

Problems of terminology are inherent in a book like this. 'West' and 'East', 'Europe', 'Mediterranean Islam', 'Christendom' are all terms that I have used regularly, while recognizing that they will offend purists. Likewise I have been very chary about using now common-place, heavily charged terms like 'the Other', 'Orientalism' or 'Fundamentalism', and on the whole avoided all three.

Place names and proper names always pose a problem, especially in this book where the names themselves can be a source of bloody dispute. The general rule has been to use the form most recognizable to the English-speaking reader, but even that is not wholly systematic. The normal English version for Islam's holy text is the Koran, but I have habitually written Qur'an. There are other similar instances.

I have also faced a dilemma. Many images are mentioned in this text, many more than are actually illustrated. Where I have not shown a visual image that is significant for the argument I have described its content in detail. But one of the problems of using pictures is that they now come at a high cost. Ideally, I would have liked to use many more. But, for those readers who, like Doubting Thomas, need to see for themselves, I can only answer *mea culpa*.

For using the word 'infidel', however, I make no apology. For convenience I have taken the European, Latinate word 'infidel', both for the way that the Christians referred to Muslims and as the equivalent for the Arabic *kafir*, which was how the Islamic world regarded the Christians. Other words were used, but the category – those without the benefit of the True Faith, Islam for one world, Christianity for the other – was roughly symmetrical. That suggestion of a mirror image, and its consequences, underpins what follows herein.

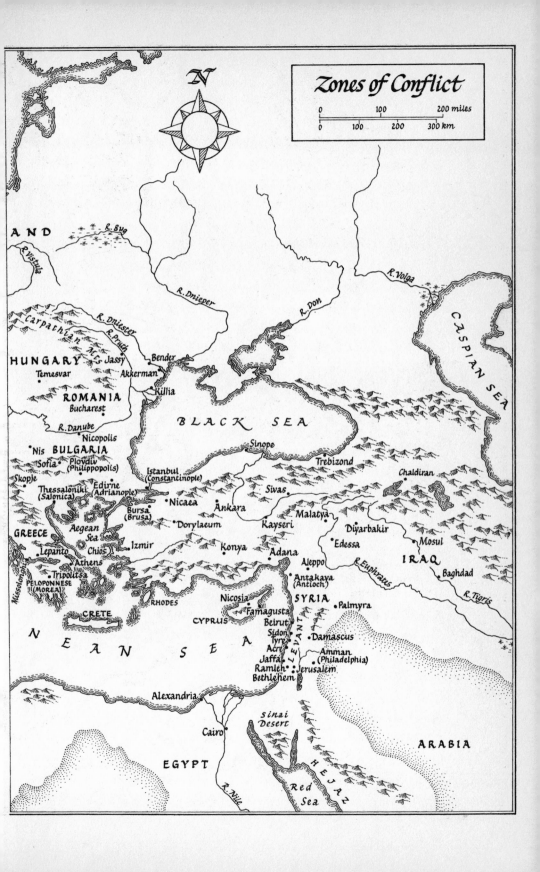

N

Zones of Conflict

```
0          100              200 miles
0      100      200      300 km
```

L A N D

R. Vistula

R. Bug

R. Dniester

R. Dnieper

R. Don

R. Volga

Carpathian Mts.

R. Pruth

HUNGARY

Jassy

Bender

Akkerman

Temesvar

Killia

ROMANIA

Bucharest

R. Danube

Nicopolis

Nis

BULGARIA

Sofia

Plovdiv
(Philippopolis)

Skopje

Thessaloniki
(Salonica)

Edirne
(Adrianople)

GREECE

Aegean
Sea

Chios

Bursa
(Brusa)

Lepanto

Athens

Izmir

Missolonghi

Tripolitsa

PELOPONNESE
(MOREA)

CRETE

RHODES

N   E   A   N   S   E   A

Alexandria

Cairo

EGYPT

R. Nile

BLACK   SEA

Sinope

Trebizond

Istanbul
(Constantinople)

Sivas

Nicaea

Ankara

Dorylaeum

Konya

Adana

Aleppo

Antakaya
(Antioch)

Nicosia

Famagusta

CYPRUS

SYRIA

Beirut

Sidon

Tyre

Acre

Jaffa

Ramleh

Bethlehem

Jerusalem

Sinai
Desert

Red
Sea

HEJAZ

CASPIAN
SEA

Chaldiran

Malatya

Kayseri

Diyarbakir

Edessa

Mosul

IRAQ

Baghdad

R. Euphrates

R. Tigris

Palmyra

Damascus

Amman
(Philadelphia)

LEVANT

ARABIA

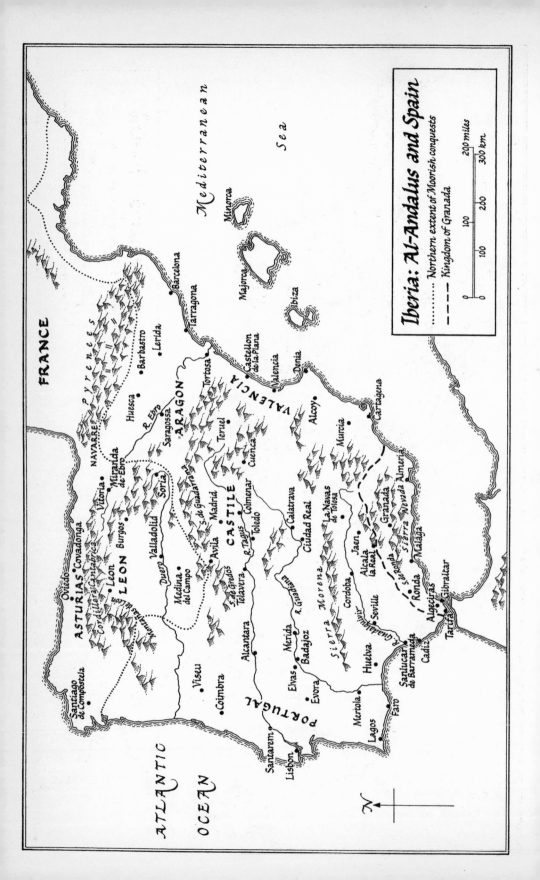

Iberia: Al-Andalus and Spain

.... Northern extent of Moorish conquests

‒‒‒‒ Kingdom of Granada

200 miles

300 km

FRANCE

ATLANTIC
OCEAN

Mediterranean Sea

Santiago de Compostela

ASTURIAS
Oviedo • Covadonga
Cordillera Cantabrica

Pyrenees

NAVARRE

LEON
Leon
Burgos
Vitoria • Miranda de Ebro
R. Ebro
Huesca
Barbastro
Lerida
Barcelona
Tarragona

Valladolid
Duero
Soria
Saragossa
ARAGON
Tortosa
Castellon de la Plana
Valencia
Denia

Medina del Campo
Avila
S. de Gredos
Madrid
S. de Guadarrama
Teruel
Cuenca
VALENCIA
Alcoy

Viseu
Coimbra
Talavera
R. Tagus
Toledo
Colmenar
Calatrava
Murcia
Cartagena

Santarem
Lisbon
Alcantara
Merida
Badajoz
R. Guadiana
Ciudad Real
Sierra Morena
Cordoba
R. Guadalquivir
Jaen
La Navas de Tolosa
Alcala la Real
Almeria
Sierra Nevada
Granada

PORTUGAL
Elvas
Evora
Mertola
Huelva
Seville
S. de Ronda
Ronda
Malaga

Faro
Lagos
Sanlucar de Barrameda
Cadiz
Tarifa
Algeciras
Gibraltar

Majorca
Minorca
Ibiza

CASTILE

Miranda de Ebro

100   100   200
0   0   100

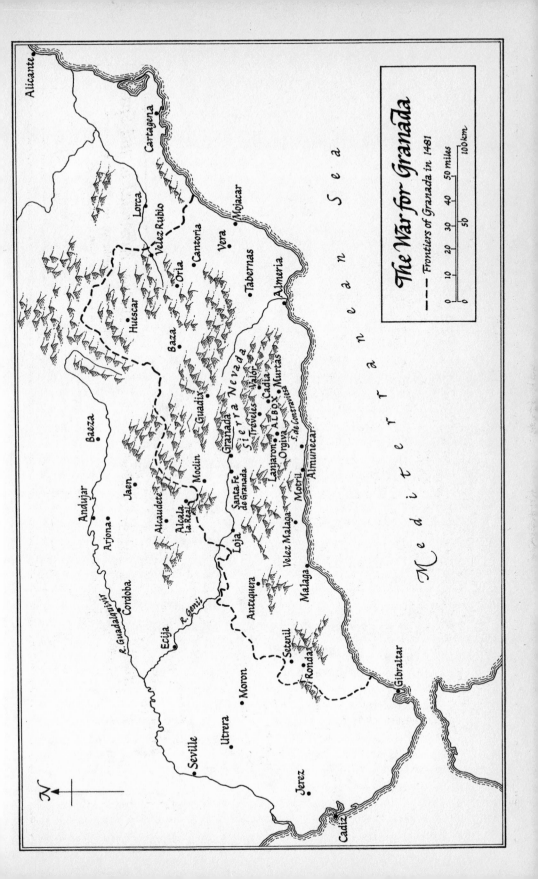

The War for Granada

--- Frontiers of Granada in 1481

0 10 20 30 40 50 miles
0   50   100 km

Mediterranean Sea

N

Alicante
Cartagena
Lorca
Velez Rubio
Mojacar
Cantoria
Vera
Oria
Tabernas
Huescar
Almeria
Baza
Sierra Nevada
Valor
Murtas
Guadix
Trevelez
Cadiar
Baeza
Granada
Lanjaron
ALBOX
Orgiva
F. de Constraviesa
Moclin
Almunecar
Jaen
Santa Fe de Granada
Andujar
Alcaudete
Motril
Arjona
Alcala la Real
Velez Malaga
Cordoba
Loja
R. Guadalquivir
Ecija
Malaga
R. Genil
Antequera
Moron
Setenil
Ronda
Gibraltar
Utrera
Seville
Jerez
Cadiz

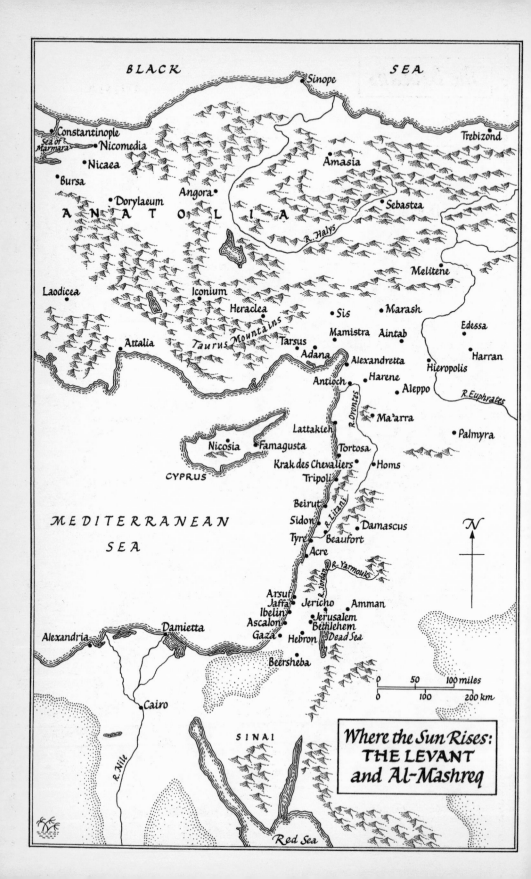

BLACK SEA

•Sinope

Constantinople•
Sea of
Marmara
•Nicomedia
•Nicaea
•Bursa
•Dorylaeum
Angora•

A N A T O L I A

•Amasia

Trebizond

•Sebastea

R. Halys

•Melitene

•Laodicea

Iconium•

Heraclea•

Taurus Mountains

•Sis
•Marash

Mamistra
Aintab•

Edessa•

•Harran

Hieropolis•

•Attalia

Tarsus•
Adana•
Alexandretta•

Antioch•

Harene•
•Aleppo

R. Euphrates

R. Orontes

•Ma'arra

•Palmyra

Lattakieh•

Nicosia•
•Famagusta

Tortosa•

CYPRUS

Krak des Chevaliers•

Tripoli•

•Homs

M E D I T E R R A N E A N

SEA

Beirut•
Sidon•
Tyre•

R. Litani

•Damascus

Beaufort•

Acre•

R. Jordan
R. Yarmouk

Arsuf•
Jaffa•
Ibelin•
Ascalon•
Gaza•

Jericho•
•Amman

Jerusalem•
Bethlehem•

Hebron•

Dead Sea

•Alexandria

Damietta•

Beersheba•

•Cairo

R. Nile

S I N A I

0   50   100 miles
0   100   200 km

Where the Sun Rises:
THE LEVANT
and Al-Mashreq

Red Sea

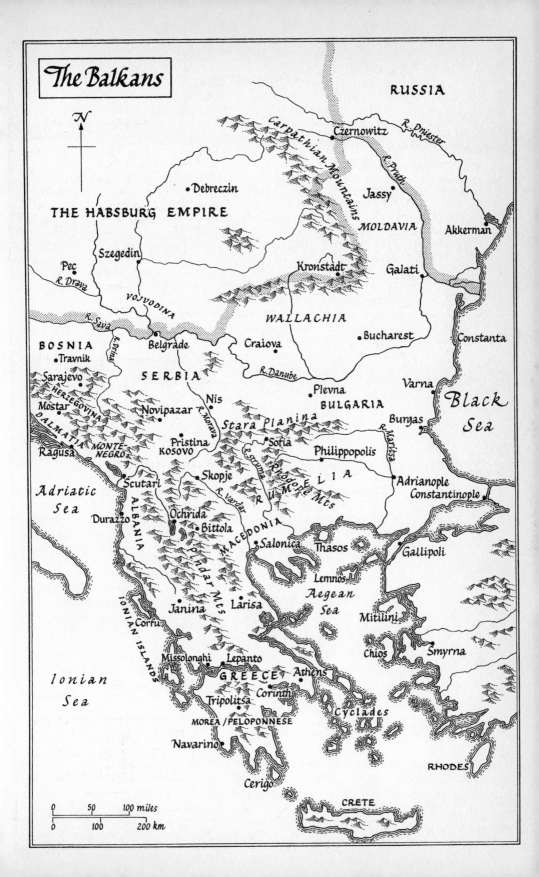

Preface

I remember sitting beside a road in the middle of Morocco, alone and fearful. Two men in an ancient little truck stopped and asked, first in Arabic and then in French, where I was going. I told them, North, to Tangier, and then to Spain. As we drove, very slowly, we talked in a desultory way, but most of the journey was silent. But when we got to the city, they insisted that I stay with them.

These two brothers took me to their home, where I stayed for several days. They showed me the low life of the city, which was extensive, and we spent (it seemed) many hours in the *suq*, drinking Moroccan mint tea, for which I have never lost the taste. At night the power invariably failed, leaving the centre of Tangier in darkness. The hubbub would stop for a few seconds, and then lights and candles would be lit, people shifting effortlessly from a modern to a more traditional pattern of life. Eventually, and with some reluctance, I said that I had to catch the boat to Malaga, and undertake another long walk to Granada. My new friends, Hassan and Mahmud, took me to the port and I left. I never saw them again, but that is where this book began.

This is the kind of experience that many travellers, men and women, have had. Later on the road I heard of people who had been robbed or held up in Morocco. From the stories I could tell that while some accounts were obviously true, others stemmed from some instinctive suspicion and from the consequent misinterpretation of a friendly gesture that can arise between 'East' and 'West'. At the time I said nothing, thinking how foolhardy I had been. But subsequently I understood not just the hospitality of my two chance friends but also the risk that *they* had taken, picking up someone who might claim that they had stolen from him, or worse. This had not stopped them. Hassan and Mahmud saw only someone tired and thirsty.

The fear was real and so too was the friendship. Over the succeeding years researching in Spain and the Middle East, I read more and more about the deep antipathy between Islam and the Western world, about the violence and hatred that it generated. But as the pile of material grew, the clarity of this image diminished. So too did the connection between cause and effect. Often some occurrence, a massacre or some other act of violence, was rooted in particular events, but as often the trail petered out. The rationale just lay somewhere in the undifferentiated past. It was a given: the two worlds ('East' and 'West' or, more accurately, 'North' and 'South', at all events 'Christendom' and 'Islam') were in opposition to each other. There were connections even longer in duration, such as the relationship between the Christian and the Jewish worlds, that often generated atrocity. But it was not the same. There was something quite specific in the meeting between Islam and Christendom that seemed to engender violence. The deep cause seemed hidden beneath the normal explanations, underlying political and economic rivalries, personal ambitions and vanities, chance and accident.

As a child I used to play a game called Chinese Whispers. There is a story from the First World War of a message being whispered down a trench, *Send reinforcements, we're going to advance*, and emerging at the end of the long line of soldiers as *Send three and fourpence, we're going to a dance*. In communications theory this would be an example of interference and dissonance. In our playground games, you passed on what you heard, never intentionally changing it (however absurd) before you whispered it to your pal. We never said to the next in line that the message seemed meaningless or stupid – at most we raised an eyebrow, but we repeated what we thought we had heard. The meaning obviously changed as the phrase travelled from person to person, but no one was consciously responsible for the distortion.

This aleatoric or unintended consequence is implicit in any act of communication. When Pope Urban II stood outside the Cathedral of Clermont in 1095 and called for Christians to rescue Jerusalem, he did not have 'the Crusades' in mind. He launched an idea to the winds, trusting to the grace of God. But Urban had no control over the effects of his words. They echoed and resonated for centuries long after his own death.[1] This is the history of non-ideas, of *Chinese Whispers*. Yet the consequences in human terms of these fuzzy messages are fearsome. This book tries to trace a few of the myriad ways in which the Christian West has responded to the Islamic East. But even talking about the task is complicated. Words such as 'West', 'East', 'Christendom', 'Europe', 'Islam' are so strongly contested that it is hard to get beyond them. Typing any of them felt uncomfortable, for I was only too aware that they could (and would) be misinterpreted. Since Edward Said eviscerated 'Orientalism', no one can write on these topics with insouciance. These are now, indeed, things of which we cannot speak with any confidence.[2] For me the way through has been to focus on *how* hatred was communicated, rather than pursuing the *why* of insult and abuse.

This book covers a huge sweep, of both time and place. It begins in the seventh century and extends into the twenty-first. Its boundaries are Tamanarasset in Algeria to the south, and Vienna to the north, the Atlantic to the west, and the Arabian Sea and the Indian Ocean to the east. Occasionally, it strays outside those limits, but its centre is the world connected with the Mediterranean. That is where I begin. Part One starts with the galley battle at Lepanto off the shores of Greece in 1571. At the time, many thought it the transforming moment in an already age-old conflict. It was not, and I go back to the first point of conflict – in Palestine nine centuries before. Parts Two, Three and Four take, in turn, three areas – Spain, the Levant and the Balkans – where Christianity and Islam existed side by side over a long period. Spain takes priority and pride of place. Perhaps the reason is that I understand that land better than the eastern Mediterranean or south-eastern Europe. But while the story of the Crusades is well known, and recent tragic events have played a bright light upon the Balkans, Spain's history 'of the Moors' remains in the shadows. Yet much of what happened in Spain had its echoes and connections elsewhere along the shores of the Mediterranean.

I am very conscious that a volume as long as this (or longer) could be written on each of those areas, and still not tell the whole story. This book follows a single thread – the antagonism between the western Christian and the Mediterranean Islamic worlds, and even then I have space to consider only one aspect of the story. In Part Five I suggest how antagonism was spread, and how it has lasted into the present.

There are other powerful terrors about which I could have written. Western fears of people with dark skins, or malign prejudices in the West extending to half the human race, that is, women, both tempted me. These too, like the fear of Islam, have altered over the centuries but have not been eradicated by Enlightenment. Moreover, they appear here, weaving in and out of the long antagonism to Islam. But at least with Islam, there was a starting point, a chronology, that gives some shape to the story. Events, like the storming of Jerusalem in 1099, the capture of Constantinople in 1453, the surrender of Granada in 1492, the battle of Lepanto in 1571, and the obliteration of the Twin Towers in 2001, have a visible consequence. We can read them and see how they made an impact on the human imagination.

Part of the *how* lies in the structures and mechanisms of language itself. A major part of language is communication by the human voice. Another part lies in the qualities of physical texts, handwritten or printed. Images, on the page or on the screen, are another form of language, whose rules are completely different from the spoken or the written word. The transmission of mis-understanding has in the past involved a mixture of all three. Now, with film and television, and the Internet, there is a completely new recombination of image, sound, speech and, sometimes, text. It is still mysterious to us. I have taken only part of this spectrum from a longer history. My story began with the power of the spoken word and handwritten text in the seventh century and (I had intended) would end with a world dominated by the printed word and the printed image on the cusp of the twentieth century. Yet from the moment that my wife called me to the television to watch the burning towers in New York on 11 September 2001, I sensed that this was no longer possible. In the days following that catastrophic act of mass murder a long-dormant style of public communication was revived. Before that day we spoke and wrote with one set of assumptions. Afterwards, we did things rather differently. This is not a value judgement, but simply an observable fact. We had shifted into a new register.

'Register' describes the sort of talk or writing that is suitable for particular situations.[3] The words that bounce around a locker room are different from those you will hear at a church social. Neither form would be appropriate to the other situation. Humans are extraordinarily well adjusted to using the correct register for different circumstances. So, faced with an unparalleled situation on September 11, what register would have been suitable? For an apocalyptic situation, the President of the United States and his advisors chose an apocalyptic register. This was the end of the world as they had known it, and a new and darker age had been ushered in. However, this instinctive dialogic shift did not have quite the results that were intended, nor did each subsequent attempt to use the new register prove wholly successful. One unexpected consequence was that it connected directly to the long-dormant memories that form the subject of this book.

I had just finished the bulk of this book and so recognized other points at which 'apocalypse' had been evoked, either deliberately or by accident. I thought of W. E. Gladstone in 1876, thundering like an Old Testament prophet at the bestial Turk. I thought also of Urban II speaking to the huge crowd at Clermont. Words, as Homer says in the *Iliad*, have wings.[4] With the Internet, e-mail, television, radio, movies, they can fly further than they could in the days of print alone. Fuelling these media with an ancient apocalyptic discourse can have unforeseen results. The novelist Douglas Adams told us in his *Hitchhiker's Guide to the Galaxy*:

It is of course well known that careless talk costs lives, but the full scale of the problem is not always appreciated.

For instance, at the very moment that Arthur said 'I seem to be having tremendous difficulty with my lifestyle,' a freak wormhole opened up in the fabric of the space-time continuum and carried his words far far back in time across almost infinite reaches of space to a distant Galaxy where strange and warlike beings [Vl'hurgs and G'Gunvuntt] were poised [in conference] on the brink of frightful interstellar battle.

. . . At that very moment the words 'I seem to be having tremendous difficulty with my lifestyle' drifted across the conference table.

Unfortunately, in the Vl'hurg tongue this was the most dreadful insult imaginable, and there was nothing for it but to wage terrible war for centuries.[5]

If there is a moral in the events that I have described in this long history, it is that words and images are weapons. Where and what they will kill or wound we cannot know when we unleash them.

Remember the old story: no point in worrying about the bullet that has your name on it, but be very worried about the one inscribed 'to whom it may concern'.

Andrew Wheatcroft, 2002

PART ONE

I

'We Praise Thee, O God'

LEPANTO 1571

On 14 August 1571, a gigantic ship's pennant of silk damask passed through the congested streets of Naples.[1] Embroidered to the pope's commission, it was the standard of Christendom, to fly from the tallest mast in the fleet of the Holy League as it sailed into battle. The pope's banner with a huge golden figure of Christ nailed to the cross loomed over the stocky Spanish soldiers who carried it in procession from the steps of the Church of Santa Clara. As the blue flag moved through the Neapolitan crowds, an unnatural stillness gripped all who watched it go by. An hour before, inside the church the assembled nobles, officers, monks and priests had stood silent and unmoving, all their eyes on the Admiral of the Holy League, Don John of Austria. Arrayed in cloth of gold, scarlet satin and white velvet, the young admiral knelt before the altar as the pope's representative, Cardinal Granvelle, handed him his staff of office and pointed to the great banner behind him. 'Take these emblems', the cardinal exhorted, 'of the Word made flesh, these symbols of the true faith, and may they give thee a glorious victory over our impious enemy and by thy hand may his pride be laid low.'

Below the Cross of Christ were the emblems of the King of Spain and of the Holy Father, Pope Pius V, with the badge of the Republic of Venice, all linked by a great golden chain, symbolizing the power of faith that bound them together. From that chain, in slightly smaller scale, hung the pendant crest of Don John.[2] The emblems marked a brief moment of unity. For the first time in more than a century, Christendom[3] had combined in force to do battle with the power of 'Islam'.[4] The war was sanctified, waged under the protection of the golden figure of Christ. The pope had declared that those who fought in this struggle were to be granted the same plenary indulgences as earlier Crusaders fighting to secure the Holy Sepulchre in Jerusalem.

All who died in the shadow of this battle flag would be spared the worst rigours of Purgatory.[5]

Eight hundred miles to the east a similar, if less public, ceremony had already taken place. From the Treasury of the Imperial Palace in Constantinople, a bulky bundle wrapped in silk had been brought from Sultan Selim II to Ali Pasha, Admiral of the Ottoman fleet. It also contained a flag, but one coloured a vivid green instead of the lambent Christian blue. Even larger than the banner that Pope Pius V had entrusted to his commander, this was one of the most potent emblems of Islam. Upon its surface the ninety-nine names and attributes of God had been embroidered in gold. It was reputed that these were repeated no less than 28,900 times. The giant Kufic characters were surrounded and interlaced with endless reiteration of those same names, in a smaller script, so that from a distance the whole surface of the pennant appeared a shimmering network of golden filigree.[6]

The two commanders were opposites – in rank, status and experience of life. Don John was the acknowledged natural brother of the King of Spain, Philip II, and the by-blow from a few months Emperor Charles V had spent with a young widow called Barbara Blomberg in the Imperial city of Regensburg. Don John had come to Naples from fighting a savage war in the mountains of southern Spain, to command the largest fleet ever assembled by Christian Europe. He had never fought at sea before. By contrast, Ali, the Kapudan Pasha of the Ottoman fleet, was a veteran of galley warfare, feared throughout the Aegean and into the far west of the Mediterranean. His origins were more humble, as the son of a *muezzin*, a mosque servant who called the faithful to prayer.[7] But the two leaders, for all their differences, had much in common. They were like twin paladins from an epic poem: yearning for battle, chivalrous and honourable. Fate decreed divergent destinies for them. One would die with a musket ball through the skull, his head then hacked off and stuck on the point of a pike. The other would return in triumph, honoured and fêted, his victory celebrated with paintings, engravings, poems, coins and medals, essays and learned disquisitions through more than four centuries.

Stories of their encounter abound, some closely following facts, others embellished to make a better tale. Quite where history ends and legends begin is still unsure. The battle they fought in the Gulf of

Lepanto has a double character: the event itself and its burgeoning afterlife. This afterlife, the mythic Lepanto, came to stand as a synecdoche for the contest between the Islamic and the Christian worlds. In deciphering the meaning of Lepanto, we may find a point of entry into those deeper mysteries. The greater struggle had deep roots. For almost a thousand years the Christian world had felt threatened by the power in the East. Sometimes, with the Crusades in the Levant for example, in Sicily and in Spain, Christian Europe had taken war to the enemy. Over the centuries a brooding sense of Muslim threat came to mesmerize Christendom. By the sixteenth century conflict was accepted as the natural and inevitable relationship between East and West. Like a child's see-saw, the rise of the East required the fall of the West. In 1571, the two adversaries sat roughly in balance.

Scholars reinforced a common belief in the danger and evil of 'Islam'. The Muslims, according to the Venerable Bede, who wrote in the eighth century, were descended from Hagar, the Prophet Abraham's concubine. Many Muslims believed that she and her son Ishmael lay buried under the Kaaba, the great black stone in Mecca, which was the focal point of the Islamic faith. Christians, however, were descended from Abraham's lawful offspring Isaac. Worse still than the stain of bastardy, an even darker curse hung over the people of the East. Christians inferred that while all men traced their line back to Adam and Eve, the Muslims were the lineal descendants of Cain, thrust from the presence of God for murdering his brother Abel. For his crime, Cain bemoaned that he would 'be a fugitive and a wanderer upon earth . . . and everyone who finds me will slay me.'[8] They had been forced to dwell 'east of Eden'. Between the children of Cain and the other descendants of Adam, there could be only mutual slaughter and revenge for the primordial crime of fratricide. So this struggle grew from a long tradition of atavistic hatred between the peoples of the West and East.[9]

What this meant in practice it is hard to say. Naturally, Christians in battle routinely insulted their enemies as the 'sons of Cain', as 'misbegotten', or 'Antichrist'. Muslims decried their enemies with equal vehemence.[10] Conflict between East and West seemed permanent, inevitable, preordained, as much for the Christians as for the Muslims. Yet it did not destroy the skein of mutual economic and political interests that dominated the Mediterranean and the Balkans, the border and boundary between the two worlds. Trade and commercial interests were constantly in play, especially in the case of Venice and the other city states of the Adriatic, who preferred to negotiate with Muslim power rather than fight it.

The Christian powers in the Mediterranean had much to fear from an Ottoman Empire intent on expansion.[11] The desire for a great victory went beyond political calculations, and not only for the pope, the architect of the grand alliance. After the capture of Constantinople in 1453, many Christians were convinced that the triumphant advance of Islam could only be part of God's plan. The Islamic scourge was a means to chasten mankind to a better sense of its faults and flaws.[12] Were Christians being punished for the sins of declining faith and, latterly, schism? For more than a century Christian Europe had resisted the Islamic onslaught, but had won few decisive victories. What better sign of renewed Divine Favour could there be than a great and annihilating victory over the forces of darkness?

Victory was also much in the minds of Sultan Selim II and his advisors in Constantinople.[13] Although the armies of 'Islam' had continued to press forward against the infidel, the pace of advance had slowed. Selim's grandfather and namesake had brought vast territories in Egypt, Arabia and the Levant into the Ottoman domain. His father, Suleiman the Lawgiver, had captured the fortress island of Rhodes, Belgrade and Budapest, and held the Hungarian plain almost to the walls of Vienna. Suleiman had destroyed the Kingdom of Hungary in a single day on the battlefield of Mohacs in 1526. Yet Suleiman too had his setbacks. He twice failed to capture Vienna – in 1529 and 1566 – and the island of Malta had withstood all the Turkish efforts at storm and siege. In the Mediterranean, the great naval battle in 1538 at Prevesa, just off the Greek mainland north of the Gulf of Lepanto, produced no decisive result.

The Ottoman state was built upon a theory of infinite expansion, and annual war to advance its frontiers. Without conquest it would decay. Moreover, all good Muslims were duty bound to extend the Domain of Peace and that burden weighed heaviest upon the sultan. Selim II had committed himself to advance the boundaries of righteousness by seizing the island of Cyprus, which was under the rule of Venice. He used the pretext that privateers had sailed from the island to harry his shipping and the coastal towns of Anatolia. By late 1570, it seemed likely that the island would fall to his armies. Even so, he desired much more than the capture of an island. The sultan demanded a dramatic victory from his commanders, another Mohacs. Thus, his admiral Ali Pasha knew that he had to achieve the complete destruction of the Christian fleet, and return laden with trophies, slaves and booty.

The two adversaries gathered their forces from far-distant points in the Mediterranean. Throughout the summer of 1571, little clusters of ships moved towards the designated meeting points: Messina for the Christians commanded by Don John, the Aegean for the sultan's warfleet under Ali Pasha. They were galleys, a type of ship built for the specific conditions of the Mediterranean. Galley warfare occupied its own universe, utterly different from battles fought between the sailing ships of the Atlantic. Long, sitting low on the water, frail by comparison with their solid Northern counterparts, war galleys appeared to be able to move regardless of the force or direction of the wind. Although these slender craft carried two or three large triangular sails, their main motive power were banks of oars that extended out forty feet or more from either side of the ship, both banks pulling in unison so that the boat moved forward swiftly in what seemed a series of rhythmic spasms. In their element, with a calm sea and a following wind, they resembled gigantic water beetles skittering on their long legs over the surface of the water. Although the galleys were faster under sail than when they depended on their oars alone, their power of manoeuvre came from the rowers. It meant that a galley never risked being blown ashore on to a rocky coast, which was a constant danger for the clumsy deep-hulled merchant sailing ships. A galley could move almost as fast backwards as it did forwards and, with its shallow draft, could negotiate shoals that would strand other sailing vessels.

Over the centuries galleys had developed many forms, some designed to carry cargo, but by the mid sixteenth century they were evolving for a single purpose: war. The Mediterranean war galley had been adapted over many generations, from the Greek triremes that destroyed the Persian fleet at the battle of Salamis, almost two thousand years before.[14] After 1500, some galleys acquired superstructures at bow and stern, to house guns and fighting men. But the essence of the galley remained the same. As in classical times, galleys were merely a floating platform from which men could board and overcome the crews of other ships, an insubstantial shell for carrying the oarsmen and men-at-arms. Originally, as in the rowing skiffs and *caïques* to be found in every Mediterranean port, each man had pulled his own oar, but this became a costly option since oars had to be made from expensive well-seasoned timber, much of it imported from northern Europe. From the mid sixteenth century a new style of rowing appeared that reduced the number of oars. Three or four men, sometimes as many as five, would sit side by side on benches, all pulling in unison on a single massive sweep. It was easy thereafter to add more men to increase the force behind the oars.

The power of a war galley lay in its personnel.[15] Aboard each one would be a number of well-equipped professional fighting men, a battle crew.[16] On Muslim and Venetian ships, many among the rowing crew were also armed and would join the mêlée. Of the Venetian oarsmen, who were volunteers, those on the end of each bench had a sword and short pike close at hand, while the second man had a bow and a quiver of arrows. As the ships closed, they would leave their oars to the third man and gather, ready to swarm across on to the deck of their victim. No merchant vessel loaded with cargo could hope to outrun a galley pursuing at full speed. Most tried, because the alternative was dire. The galley attack resembled that of a hawk swooping to snatch its prey. The sharp beak of the galley would come closer and closer to the fleeing ship, so close that the crew of the doomed vessel could see its nemesis preparing to board. At that point, many ships yielded; any that continued to run would be showered with arrows or musket fire and the crew killed. For reasons of economy the great bow guns of the attacking galley were rarely used.

Galleys were raptors, living off weaker and less well-armed vessels.

Like the carnivorous dinosaur the war galley dominated its environment. But like the dinosaur, it grew progressively larger and more powerful to compete with its own kind until, like the dinosaur, it became increasingly immobile. The tactical power of the Mediterranean war galley, with the teeth and jaws of Tyrannosaurus Rex, depended on a continuous supply of flesh and blood.[17]

Unless a galley could keep its rowing benches filled it could not survive. Much of the ceaseless raiding and predation was to seize not cargo but manpower. When a Muslim vessel took a Christian ship, all non-Muslims aboard would be immediately enslaved. Often the crew and any passengers would be the most valued prize. Some could be ransomed, and others sold for a good profit in the markets of North Africa or Constantinople.

If a Christian galley intercepted a Muslim ship, exactly the same transactions would take place. All non-Christians would be made prisoner and put to work at the oars. But Spanish, French and Venetian ships preyed as frequently on the ships of other Christian nations. There were many excuses that would permit a war galley to seize a merchant vessel. They might search a Christian ship for 'contraband', claiming that the crew was trading with an enemy. The Knights of St John sailing from their fortress island of Malta, were feared by all, Christian and Muslim alike. If they stopped a Christian ship in eastern waters, they would examine the cargo minutely for anything that could be termed illicit. When lacking anything more obvious, they were in the habit of uncovering 'Jewish clothing' during a search, indicating that the ship was trading with the Jewish population of Muslim ports. This justified the expropriation of the whole cargo, and the enslavement of the crew.

Galley fleets became larger during the sixteenth century as trade grew along the shore, and the predators prospered. Mostly these were ships exclusively engaged in raiding, from ports such as Muslim Algiers, the greatest port on the Barbary (North African) shore, or from Christian Fiume, at the head of the Adriatic. Increasingly, the economy of the galley came to depend on slaves rather than freemen for the crews. By mid century, almost every fleet, except that of Venice, which continued almost exclusively to recruit freemen, was rowed by slaves, prisoners of war or convicts. On each ship, there would be more than 100 men, most chained to their rowing station, with sometimes a few oarsmen free to move within the constraints of the narrow deck. Most lived out their lives within the two feet allotted to them. They slept, ate, defecated, bled, suppurated and often died at the same bench. Rats and cockroaches thrived in the decaying piles of food scraps mixed with ordure and urine that built up beneath their feet. A wise galley captain, knowing how rapidly epidemic disease would spread under such conditions, would regularly wash down the rowing decks of his vessel.[18] When the rats and lice had bred

uncontrollably, the ultimate solution was to put the crew ashore under
guard, unship the masts, fill the galley with stones and sink it in the
shallows until the deck and superstructure were wholly underwater.
The vermin that could not, or would not, 'desert the sinking ship'
drowned.

At dead of night, in fog, or in the half-light of dawn, the presence
of a galley was evident long before it became visible. The rank smell
of the rowing deck could be detected at up to two miles' distance. It
was said that you could tell a former galley slave or sea soldier in later
life by the excessively strong perfume he wore, as if to blot out the
olfactory memory of earlier evil days. On a galley, rarely more than
150 feet in length, all the gradations and nuances of society were
obscured by the miasma of filth and decay. The soldiers in half-armour,
the musket men and gunners, even the officers and commanders,
were never out of contact with the degraded humanity that pulled
the ship towards its destination.

However, for the chained men, whether slaves on the ships of the
Ottoman sultan and the corsair captains of North Africa, or condemned prisoners on the galleys of the Most Catholic King of Spain
or the Most Christian King of France, to serve at the oars was a form
of living death. Their end might come in many ways. They were
unlikely to starve, for it was not in the interests of any galley captain
to lose his skilled rowers needlessly. Beans, corn and a little meat, with
wine on the Christian ships, were the staples, while buckets of fresh
water were always available at each bench to slake the thirst of the
rowers. Each man would drink about two litres a day at the height of
the summer sailing season.[19] Once a rower had become conditioned
to the life, and survived the first few months, his whole body adapted
to the rhythm of the oars. Some oarsmen lasted for thirty years or
more. Disease was the most likely end to their suffering, for cuts and
wounds inevitably festered in such conditions. The weak, sickly or
moribund would simply be unchained and tossed overboard. Only the
strokes could expect better treatment: strong and reliable pace-setters
could bring a ship up to maximum speed more reliably than the whip
of the boatswain.

In times of war especially the demand for rowers was insatiable,
and there were never enough men to fill the benches. Many of the
galley slaves were the victims of countless raids along the shores of the

sea, where the great prize was human flesh. An Imperial Ottoman galley would stand off the coast out of sight and the commander would order spies to scout the local settlements. Then at night a party would be sent ashore, to burn the villages, kill the old and very young, and round up as many of the able-bodied men as could be found. The galley would be gone by first light, or sometimes a flotilla would descend on a region and stay for longer periods, spreading depredation for many miles around.

The men who filled the benches on most Christian warships were either Muslim villagers or prisoners of war. But they also included many Christians ground out through the machinery of the law. In Spain debt, sedition, even petty crime, could bring a sentence to the galleys. As the demand for oarsmen rose, so the flow of criminals through the courts who were condemned to the galleys increased.[20] Often those who had served their time at the oars and were due for release were held back.[21] These *forzados*, or pressed men, were technically free but in every other respect were treated as harshly as they had been before.[22] In France, the Catholic authorities sent a steady stream of Protestants to serve in the galleys, while the papal prisons were regularly emptied to fill the rowing benches. Yet others freely chose the life of the oarsman. The corsairs of the Barbary coast were, in effect, the shareholders of a business enterprise, where they supplied their muscle power and risked their lives for part of the profits of their raids. The Slav Uskoks of Dalmatia were freemen under the protection of the Holy Roman Empire. They followed an old profession: banditry by sea had been a part of Mediterranean life for millennia.[23] Thus, on the same rowing bench there might be a free sailor, a prisoner of war, a slave, and a criminal serving a sentence of years of labour at the oars.

Skilled sailing masters regarded their crews like trained animals, knew their individual capacities and limitations. Each rowing bench would be balanced, for the fundamental skill of galley warfare lay in mixing new blood with experienced oarsmen. Men were chosen by their size, weight and strength to produce the maximum power, and with this aim, though the conditions of life were harsh and degrading, few captains deliberately mistreated their crews. A naval gun in the mid sixteenth century was deadly to around 200 yards, but a galley rowed at maximum speed could cover that distance in half a minute, much less time than it took to reload.²⁴ No galley crew could, however, sustain top speed for more than about twenty minutes and exhausted or demoralized oarsmen for much less. It was well known among captains that Venetian and North African galleys were considerably faster and more agile than those of Spain and France. In part it was a matter of design and the heavy dead weight of the large fighting crews the latter carried. But there was also a factor of spirit and morale. The Spanish ships, rowed exclusively by captives and convicts, consumed men as remorselessly as the silver mines at Potosi, which provided the money that built so many of the galleys. Neither the ships nor the mines were designed as a form of punishment and social control, but that is what they became. In Venice and the Muslim lands, a free oarsman could become a rich man from prize money. In Algiers or Constantinople, a Christian galley slave who 'turned Turk' could end up as a galley captain or even as the admiral of the sultan's navy.²⁵

Each Imperial Ottoman vessel carried a complement of highly trained janissary infantry, some armed with sword or yataghan and others with the famous Turkish bow, which could penetrate almost any armour at a 100 yards' distance. A skilled archer could fire up to six arrows a minute, with great accuracy. It took years of training to bend the bow and use it, and increasingly janissaries adopted the arquebus or musket used by their enemies. Janissaries did not normally expect to fight on board enemy ships. The galley served as their transport and usually they would be put ashore to fight a land battle or besiege a fortress. Some wore chainmail armour, but they scorned the plate cuirasses, greaves and steel morion helmets worn by the Spanish soldiers. In any depiction of a battle of the period, there was no doubt as to which were the Christian forces and which the Muslim. Steel helmets, breastplates and shields on one side, and turbans and flowing robes on the other. These differences developed not just from distinct tactical and strategic demands, but from divergent attitudes to war.

The Christians possessed a wonder-weapon, as potent as the Greek Fire of earlier centuries.²⁶ In the fleet that was slowly assembling at Messina were six galleys quite unlike any in the Ottoman flotillas. From her long experience of Mediterranean warfare Venice had by inspired improvisation created the weapon that would prove decisive.

Standing out above all the other vessels at anchor were six tall heavy ships, quite different to the low sleek war galleys that surrounded them. These were galleasses, heavy broad-beamed sluggards propelled partly by sail and partly by huge oars, each pulled by seven men or more. The galleasses were a hybrid between the Mediterranean type of warship and the sailing vessels of the Atlantic.[27] Above the rowing deck, all along each side, was a range of heavy cannon which could deliver a broadside of shot that could shatter a more lightly built galley. These were to be floating fortresses, weapons unique to Venice.

The galleasses had not yet been tried in battle. Yet one galleass had the firepower of five ordinary galleys, and Don John was convinced that the six in his fleet would, under the right conditions, give him the edge over the Ottomans.[28] When, finally, the great armada sailed from Messina, he ordered that all the ships should proceed at the lumbering pace of the galleasses so that he would not come to battle without the advantage of this secret weapon. Why only the Venetians had developed a ship that could devastate the most powerful galley afloat will never be known. Perhaps it was simply that the materials were to hand. Laid up in the Arsenal were ten large merchant galleys, which were no longer in use for trade with the East. The Venetians also had an abundance of bronze cannon and, putting the two together, created the galleass.

It is unlikely that the Ottomans would have developed the galleass on their own, although they were quick to build them once they had seen their power in battle. It was not through lack of skill and knowledge – Turkish gunners and siege artillery were of high quality. Rather, it was that they knew their way of war was superior. It was bound up with codes of honour that equated only very imprecisely with European notions of chivalry. In the West, honour was a concept that pertained only to the topmost layer of society; most of mankind stood outside the codes of chivalric conduct. It was considered absurd for anyone not bound by noble origins to adopt knightly graces. So Miguel de Cervantes, who was one of the thousands waiting for Don John in Messina harbour (and who was to lose his arm in battle at Lepanto), would make his eponymous hero Don Quixote a madman in his neighbours' eyes.[29] His insanity lay in living by the ancient rules of knighthood that did not apply to him. But in the fleet of Ali Pasha, even the most humble Muslim fighting man was a Quixote, trapped in

the spider's web of honour: loyalty to family, to tribe, to God constrained his every move. The Christian fleet gathered at Messina had
been made holy warriors only by papal decree, an event notable for its
extreme rarity. For the most part war, even in a good cause, did not
carry that weight of Divine sanction.[30] But every Muslim soldier and
sailor was, lifelong, bound to struggle in God's cause. Nor was it just a
matter of ends, but also of means. The Holy Qur'an, which many had
learned by heart, told them clearly: 'Surely Allah loves those who
fight in His Way in ranks as if they were a firm and compact wall.'[31]
The lowliest foot soldier was honoured and remembered for how he
had fought and not merely that he had been victorious.[32]

The battle at Lepanto would mark a defining moment in the
struggle between Christendom and Islam: on the Christian side, war
was fast becoming secularized. Where once the pope had decreed
(ineffectually) that the crossbow was not to be used in conflicts
between Christians, now no barriers were placed on any engine of
war, however frightful.[33] The galleass was remarkable not for its
technology, but for the ease with which it was created, adopted and
immediately used in battle. In the Muslim ranks, by contrast, every
innovation could become a matter for argument and even resistance.
Honourable war was still fought with the weapons known to the
Qur'an – swords, spears, lances, bows and arrows. The good Muslim
soldier was the man who leaped into the breach or on to the deck of
an enemy vessel without armour and only the strength of his arms to
protect him. Guns and artillery were necessary, but carried no mark
of courage. Perhaps for this reason few of the developments and
innovations in gun technology emerged in the Islamic world.[34]
Implicit if unstated was the general belief that it was better to fight in
the right way and lose a battle than to fight without honour. Europeans
might talk about traditions, caste and honour, but quietly discarded
them in practice – occasions such as when officers courteously invited
their enemy to fire first became legendary precisely because they were
so rare.[35] In contrast, the armies of 'Islam' might adopt new weapons
but were increasingly hobbled by their ancient ethic.

It took more than three weeks for Don John to get his unwieldy
armada under way. He crossed from Naples to the port of Messina on

23 August 1571, and his arrival was the excuse for elaborate ceremonies and extended celebrations. Sicily was determined not to be outdone by the cities on the mainland. A huge building of marbled stucco, ornate with suggestively symbolic pictures of Victory and Divine Favour, was quickly built, occupying most of the open ground at the landing place. Tethered under its arches was a war horse with saddle and stirrups chased in silver, and reins of silver chain. Mounted on this lavish gift from the city, Don John rode into Messina, past huge cheering crowds, to the Cathedral of La Nunziatella, followed at a distance by his entourage. At intervals along the streets were towering triumphal arches, and his procession was showered with flower petals from the balconies above, which made a sweet-smelling slime on the ground below. Then, the festivities over, he waited with increasing frustration for the last of his command to arrive. Little had been done to put the fleet on a war footing. Don John found that no one knew where the Turkish fleet had gathered, so he dispatched a squadron of galleys under a trusted Spanish captain to discover its location. It was thought that the enemy had assembled somewhere off the long eastern coast of the Adriatic and Ionian Seas, but no one was sure precisely where, or how many ships would confront the fleet of the Holy League.

As the young commander tried to unify the Spanish flotillas with the papal contingent under Marc Antonio Colonna and with the Venetian ships of the veteran Sebastiano Veniero, he soon recognized that the fragile alliance might not survive the strain of too much delay. There were daily street-fights between the holy warriors from different cities or nations. Moreover, with some 80,000 men confined in the harbour and city, there was always the danger that epidemic disease could ravage the ranks. Yet he dared not depart until his fleet was at full strength, and every day new ships continued to arrive: the Venetian contingent from Crete rowed into Messina, as did more Spanish ships filled with troops recruited in Germany. Among the last to appear were the twenty-two galleys hired by the King of Spain from Genoa, commanded by Gian Andrea Doria, and the three great galleys of the Knights of Malta.

In the weeks at Messina, Don John quickly discovered that the Venetians loathed the Genoese, mistrusted the Spaniards and resented the Knights of Malta. Every appointment he made immediately caused feelings of slight and anger among those not chosen. There were mutterings that he inevitably favoured the Spaniards, that he was delaying the advance, thereby allowing the Ottomans to ravage Venetian possessions. Each further day of delay caused partisan feelings to fester more strongly, and it was with relief that on 16 September, with the scout-ships returned and the weather fine, he gave the order to set sail. He wrote to his mentor and advisor, the veteran soldier Don Garcia de Toledo, that the enemy

is stronger than we in the number of his vessels, but not so, I believe, in quality of either men or vessels. So, I sail, please God, tonight for Corfu and thence according to what I shall hear. I have with me two hundred and eight galleys, twenty-six thousand troops, six galleasses and twenty-four [supply] ships. I trust our God will give us victory if we meet the enemy.[36]

The pope had sent Bishop Odescalchi to Messina to bid his ships Godspeed. The bishop brought with him spiritual fortification for the holy warriors in the form of an Agnus Dei 'of great size and beauty'. This was a wafer or biscuit mixed with balm and consecrated oil. A pope blessed only a certain number of these in the first year of his pontificate, and thereafter only once every seven years. It was stamped with the image of a lamb 'reclining upon a book, bearing a banner with the sign of the Cross and surrounded by a border with the words "Lamb of God that taketh away the sins of the world, have mercy upon us."'[37] It was a powerful Christian talisman, giving its possessor protection from storms at sea, earthquakes, lightning, the plague, the falling sickness, sudden death and devils. The nuncio also carried documents containing various auspicious prophecies, written by the seventh-century Bishop Isidore of Seville, that a Holy League would be formed under a Spanish leader, who would defeat and scatter the enemies of Spain and Christ. He also brought with him the pope's private assurance that the young commander would undoubtedly gain his own kingdom as a reward for victory. But despite these assurances of Divine support and protection, Don John had some doubts about the prospects of the fleet.

As each contingent arrived he inspected it and, despite his assertion to Don Garcia de Toledo, he discovered that not all his ships were of the best quality, nor were the fighting crews as strong as their numbers suggested. His best fighting ships were the Spanish galleys, which were a little larger, heavier and more solidly built from well-seasoned timber than the Venetian and papal vessels. Their decks were crowded with well-trained and heavily armoured Spanish and German infantry. The Venetian ships looked impressive, with their sleek lines and the speed to take on even the fastest of the Ottoman galleys. But Venice's reputation was not wholly merited. In her Arsenal she indeed had the capacity to build the hull of a galley in a single day, but the Queen of the Sea was rarely in possession of a stock of spars, oars and sailcloth sufficient to run at full strength. Venetian galleys were too often built quickly of second-rate timber and inadequately fitted-out. Much more perilous under battle conditions was the lack of volunteers, which had made it difficult for Venice (which would not use Muslim galley slaves) to crew her ships, or to provide a full contingent of soldiers. Fortunately, Don John had seasoned Spanish troops in excess of his own needs, and he persuaded Veniero to take them aboard his ships. Accepting a Spanish battle crew in the days before Lepanto was regarded as an ignominious admission of weakness for a Venetian commander, and Veniero acquiesced only with the greatest reluctance.

Finally, in the early morning of 16 September 1571, the fleet began to move out of Messina. As the ships of the Holy League rowed out, dressed overall with war banners, flags and pennants, their crews saluted the papal nuncio and the little knot of clergy standing at the edge of the harbour wall. As each ship passed, the church dignitaries made the sign of the Cross, blessing the enterprise; in response the crew cheered. Like bees emerging from a hive, the line of ships seemed never-ending until, standing out a little from the land, the greatest array ever assembled in the name of Christendom finally formed up for the journey east. As it headed south to round the little Cape of Porto Salvio, to anchor on the second night off Cape Spartivento, the fleet received the first definite news of the Turks.

A small ship, sailing from the village of Gallipoli in the narrow Brindisi peninsula at the heel of Italy, came alongside Don John's flagship and reported that twenty-four Muslim galleys had occupied the harbour of Santa Maria on the Adriatic coast, south of Otranto on the Italian side, while a larger contingent had raided Corfu. But the location of the main body of the Ottoman ships was still a mystery.

Had it retired to its principal harbour at Prevesa just south of the narrows on the eastern side of the Adriatic? Or separated into raiding squadrons to harry the Balkan ports, or Crete, or the Spanish islands and coast, all now denuded of protection? The Christian fleet moved further east, mindful that it might be attacked at any moment by some, or all, of the Muslim ships. On 21 September, it halted at Cape Colonne: the ships were advancing at about fifty nautical miles a day, hampered by the need to keep the slower supply vessels and the galleasses with the main body. There the commanders learned that the bulk of the Ottoman fleet was still moored at Prevesa, waiting for instructions from the sultan on where to attack.

With his enemy only a few days' sail away. Don John wanted to press forward as fast as he could across the Adriatic to Corfu. But as the weather worsened, every attempt to negotiate the Strait of Otranto was thwarted. Some ships were blown on to the rocks and holed, others lost masts and rigging. Although galleys could row into an adverse wind, this sapped the rowers' strength, and the last thing a commander wanted was to arrive at the point of battle with a dispirited and exhausted complement of oarsmen. It was not until 27 September that the fleet finally crossed the narrow sea lane to moor in the channel between Corfu and the mainland. It found the town in ruins.

A Turkish squadron raiding up the Adriatic almost to the outer islands of Venice had ravaged Corfu on its return south. It ransacked the island's main town, destroyed churches, hacked heads off saints' statues. But the Turks had made no impression on the citadel, which the Venetians had built up over two centuries. After several fruitless attacks, and the loss of three galleys, they sailed on. However, while their houses were being destroyed, the islanders learned that the whole Turkish fleet was not in the lagoon of Prevesa, but further south in the more open waters of the Gulf of Lepanto. Don John immediately dispatched Gil de Andrade with his scout-ships to ascertain whether the Ottoman fleet was still at anchor and how large it was. Then he called a council of war on board his flagship, the *Real*. His inclination was to push forward and risk all in an immediate battle with the Ottoman fleet, but the council of war was divided. Some members were unwilling to hazard everything in the lottery of a battle, and favoured laying siege to some major Turkish fortress. Others suggested trying to draw out the enemy fleet from the protection of the harbour at Lepanto into more open waters. While the council was still in session, news came from De Andrade that the Turkish fleet was riddled with sickness, and not at full strength. Don John put it to the vote and all agreed that the whole Christian armada should attack at once and destroy the enemy in the Gulf of Lepanto.

In the curious parallelism that surrounds the events of 1571, at that moment the Ottoman commander Ali Pasha was also holding a council of war with his captains, and their opinions were divided in a roughly similar manner. Hassan Pasha, a Bey of Algiers, spoke for the overwhelming majority. He acknowledged that the scouts had told them that this was the largest fleet they had ever seen. But he recalled how at Prevesa (in 1538) and at the island of Jerbi off Tripoli (in 1560) the infidels had faded under Turkish attack. He believed that they were cowards, without spirit, and would flee here, as they had done in the past. The opposite view was presented by Hamet Bey, who suggested it would be a mistake to underestimate the power or unity of the Christians, and that Don John, although young and inexperienced, had proved himself in the war against the *Moriscos* (Muslims forcibly converted to Christianity) in the Alpujarras mountain range of southern Spain. The Ottoman fleet had everything to gain by playing a waiting game, under the protection of the guns of the Lepanto fortress.

Ali Pasha himself favoured an immediate attack, and his resolve was hardened by the long-awaited orders from the sultan. Selim ordered the fleet to capture the Christian ships and to bring them immediately as trophies of war to line the waters of the Golden Horn, below his palace of the New Seraglio in Constantinople. The order admitted no dissent and all doubters were silenced. The council came to a precipitate end, and the captains returned to their ships to prepare for battle. The efficient Ottoman commissary quickly stocked the hundreds of ships with food and water, and with large quantities of powder and shot, while Ali summoned more troops from neighbouring garrisons. He speedily added 10,000 janissaries and 4,000 other troops to his fighting crews.

Meanwhile, the fleet of the Holy League moved south. By 3 October, it was off Prevesa, but its advance was halted by high seas and adverse winds from the south. October 4 and 5 were spent battened down, riding out the storm. While the fleet was at anchor, a small vessel heading north from the island of Crete to Venice brought terrible and unexpected news.

Every Venetian in the fleet knew that the Ottomans were besieging the town of Famagusta in Cyprus. The island's capital, Nicosia, had fallen a few months after the invasion of July 1570. Twenty thousand inhabitants had been slaughtered when the Turkish troops broke into the city, and the rest of the islanders submitted to avoid the same fate. Only the small port-city of Famagusta refused to surrender and held out in the hope of relief from the sea. Within hours of the fall of Nicosia, Turkish horsemen were riding around the walls of Famagusta, taunting the inhabitants with the heads of the leading citizens of Nicosia impaled on their lance points. However, Marcantonio Bragadino, the governor in Famagusta, had prepared his command to withstand a long siege and it was clear that the city would resist, despite the frightful example of Nicosia's fate. By the early spring of 1571 more than 100,000 Turks had gathered around Famagusta.[38] It seemed that it could not hold out for long. But for four months the 4,000 defenders beat back every assault until attacks in July 1571 breached the walls in six places, and the troops in the garrison were reduced to their last barrels of gunpowder.[39] Faced with certain defeat, Bragadino sought an honourable surrender. The terms agreed on 1 August with the Ottoman commander, Lala Mustafa, were unusually favourable: the Venetians secured protection for the remaining citizens, while the garrison would be evacuated to the Venetian island of Crete.

The Turks had lost more than 50,000 men in the capture of Nicosia and Famagusta. The terms granted were remarkable, especially after the massacres at Nicosia. On 4 August, Lala Mustafa summoned Bragadino and his staff to his camp. The Venetian commander, wearing the purple robe of a senator, rode out from Famagusta under an ornate parasol (against the searing heat) at the head of his officers and with a bodyguard of forty arquebusiers. He was, according to the records, 'serene ... without fear or pride'. At the meeting, the Ottoman commander accused him of breaching the agreement for the city's surrender and demanded hostages. Bragadino responded that this did not form part of the terms. Then, at a prearranged signal, janissaries rushed into the tent and overpowered the Venetians. Outside, the senator's escort had already been disarmed.

The subsequent events were played out for the benefit of the

Ottoman army gathered in a huge mass around Lala Mustafa's encampment. It seems unlikely that Bragadino expected to survive the surrender, or to see the treaty honoured. The Ottomans usually repaid resistance with death, and to allow the defenders to retire with their arms in hand and flags flying was almost without parallel.[40] On previous occasions the Ottomans had invariably slaughtered or enslaved the bulk of their captives, sparing only a few for ransom, or to take the news back to their enemies.[41] After the battle of Mohacs, Sultan Suleiman had 'sat on a golden throne' while his soldiers decapitated thousands of prisoners. The Venetians were playing a grim but well-understood role in a gory traditional drama. The performance was designed to be exemplary, and to satisfy the sultan in Constantinople that the long and costly siege had not been in vain. Bragadino's officers and staff were beheaded in front of him, so that a rivulet of blood flowed across the hard dry ground and washed over his feet. Then he was ceremonially disfigured, with his nose and ears hacked off like a common criminal.

Surgeons staunched the flow of blood and made sure that the wounds did not become infected. Bragadino was cared for solicitously over a period of two weeks and allowed to recover his strength.[42] Meanwhile, his remaining troops, not knowing what had happened to their leader, had marched out of Famagusta to the galleys to leave for Crete, in accordance with the treaty. At the harbour they were taken and enslaved, and chained by hand and foot to the oars in the Ottoman galleys. The final act was designed to make a mockery of the Venetians and to strip their commander of all the attributes of nobility. After prayers on Friday 17 August, the Ottoman army gathered on the siege works that surrounded the city. Bragadino was brought out before them, still wearing his senator's robe. He was forced to his hands and knees, and a mule's harness was put on his back, with a bridle and bit in his mouth. Two heavy baskets filled with earth were loaded on to the harness, so that he bent under their weight. He carried them to repair the breeches in the Ottoman earthworks made by the fire from his own guns. Throughout the morning he was led back and forth in front of the troops, in and out among the tents, whipped forward and abused by the mass of soldiers. Each time he passed the Ottoman commander's tent, he was forced to prostrate himself and eat a mouthful of the dusty soil.

Later in the day the scene transferred to the harbour. The senator was hauled to the topmast of a galley, in front of all his former troops, now galley slaves. He hung in chains without nose and ears, twisting at the masthead under the hot sun. Lowered to the ground, he was taken to the marketplace and tied to a whipping frame where all the people of Famagusta could witness his humiliation. Then, as the sun fell past its apogee, 'being hung up by the heels like a sheep', an Ottoman butcher began the slow process of flaying him alive, removing the skin intact.[43] The chronicle recounts that Bragadino died when the skinner's knives reached the 'height of his navel'. The grisly task completed, the butcher scraped the hide clean of fat. Lala Mustafa and his troops watched the whole process in silence. On the next day the skin of Bragadino was stuffed with straw and neatly sewn up like a huge doll. Mounted on his own horse and paraded through the streets under the senatorial parasol, Bragadino's simulacrum rode in a parody of his departure from the city on 4 August. His skin was next hung from the yardarm of Lala Mustafa's galley, and was still dangling there like a flag, but by now tanned by the weather, when the triumphant conqueror of Cyprus returned to the waters of the Golden Horn. Its final destination was the galley slaves' prison (*bagnio*) in Constantinople, where it was hung as a mute warning to any who thought to resist or rebel.

This theatre of cruelty was partly, to adopt Voltaire's phrase, '*pour encourager les autres*'. The Ottomans ritually degraded not only the body of Bragadino, but Venice herself.[44] By showing their power over him, dragging him down from the pedestal of authority, they had humiliated their enemy. All knew that only a comparable act could erase the shame. When six years earlier at the siege of Malta the Turks had cut the hearts from the corpses of the Knights and floated their naked bodies down towards the citadel on rafts, the Maltese commander La Vallette had responded in kind. Scores of Turkish prisoners were brought up on to the battlements, to have their heads cut off in full view of their comrades, and to be fired from La Vallette's canon into the Turkish lines. He had neutralized one insult with another. But, after Famagusta, as yet there had been no rejoinder.

This was the news brought to the fleet of the Holy League waiting fog-bound between the islands of Cephalonia and Ithaca. It stilled any remaining doubts about the need for a battle, which would now, additionally, revenge the death of Bragadino and repay his humiliation many times over. As soon as the fog lifted sufficiently for the fleet to move safely, in the early hours of Sunday 7 October, the whole armada advanced into the open sea, in the mouth of the Gulf of Patras, and some forty miles from the entrance to the well-protected harbour of Lepanto. With the mainland coast in sight, Don John sent two fast ships forward down the Gulf to discover if the Ottoman fleet was still at anchor. If it was, it would not slip past the mass of Christian ships rowing down the narrowing Gulf towards the straits before Lepanto.

To the north, as the Christian galleys pushed into a stiff breeze, lay the high mountains of Acarnia; to the south the lowlands of the Morea. The winds came off the high ground, veering back and forth, so the sails on the galleasses could not be used, and the whole fleet slowed to the rowing pace of these ungainly vessels. Shortly after dawn the fleet halted, and moved into the battle formations designated by Don John. He also gave orders that the rams or spurs mounted on the prow of each war galley should be cut away. These stout wooden structures were designed to hook into the side of an enemy ship, providing a platform along which boarders could advance. But the spur made it difficult to manoeuvre the bow guns, which alone had the capacity to cripple an enemy vessel. Don John's strategy was not to capture the Ottoman fleet but to destroy it. He intended to use his heavy guns to smash the lighter hulls of the Ottoman vessels, boarding where necessary, but first sending as many ships and crews as possible to the bottom of the sea. But the order gave a deeper message to his men: cutting away the spurs was equivalent to throwing away the scabbard of his sword, signifying that it would not again be sheathed unbloodied.

No one had any prior experience of marshalling so large a fleet into battle. Moreover the six galleasses were new and wholly untried weapons. The forthcoming conflict would be like no other at sea, but Don John planned to fight in the open waters of the Gulf of Patras much as he would have fought a cavalry battle on land. However the scale was vast: the fleet extended in a line for almost four miles end to end. Don John divided the hundreds of galleys into four divisions: the centre, which he oversaw in person, two wings and behind this line the reserve, commanded by a trusted Spaniard, and intended to staunch any breach made by the enemy. The battle tactics were simple: in front would be the six galleasses, and the galleys of the Holy League would row forward at a steadily increasing pace behind them. Once the firefight began, the rowing rate would rise until the galleys covered the last few hundred yards in less than a minute, until they smashed into the enemy, also advancing at full speed. Then all semblance of strategy would vanish in the mêlée of hand-to-hand fighting. The great danger was that the fast and manoeuvrable Ottoman galleys would break through the line and swarm around the Christian ships on every side, rather in the way that on land Turkish horsemen would pull down armoured Christian knights by weight of numbers.

Although he had never fought at sea, Don John knew his enemy. The war in the Alpujarras, from house to house, from village to village, had taught him that even Muslim peasants would die rather than yield or retreat.[45] The lesson of innumerable galley battles was that once the hardy Muslim fighters gained a foothold on the opponent's decks, then the chances of survival were small. As a last act before the fray, he ordered that all his ships should be rigged with boarding nets, to act as a fence all along the sides above the rowing decks. The nets would not stop boarders, but they would slow them down, giving the defending crew time to rally. The only effective protection against the rush of the janissaries was firepower. On the *Real* he trained a force of 300 men, armed with the heavy Spanish arquebuses and muskets, to fire in volley if the enemy did succeed in boarding. But ultimately Don John could not control the flow of the fight on his ships. Success would depend on the spirit and morale of his men. In the early morning light, in a fast small *fregata* he traversed the line of stationary ships back and forth, shouting encouragement to the crews and soldiers, telling them that God was with them, and reminding them of the fate of Bragadino, for whom they would wreak revenge upon the bodies of their enemy. Cheers rose as he passed each ship. He had ordered that every Christian convict oarsman should be freed so that they could join the crusade, while Muslim rowers were double-chained, by both hand and foot, to the oars.

Only the best of his soldiers were equal to the Ottomans, and the advantage lay with Ali Pasha, with fresh troops rested, well-fed and eager for battle. Don John's victory at Lepanto was because of the supremacy of the gun.[46] He had placed the six galleasses in front of his line at intervals, confident that their firepower would disrupt the Ottoman line of battle. As well as the heavy guns, he crammed them full of marksmen with muskets. Later pictures of the battle show the ships bristling with gun barrels, like the spines on a hedgehog. Success would depend on Ottoman willingness to be drawn into the killing zone around these floating fortresses. But if the Ottomans retreated, drawing Don John's ships further down the Gulf towards the guns of the Lepanto fortress, then the dynamics would alter. There was already a stiff breeze and the sea was running against the Christian ships. The more his oarsmen exhausted themselves, the greater chance that the advantage would slip to the Turks. As in all battles, Chance and Providence were in command.

From daybreak, however, Divine favour seemed to manifest itself. It was a Sunday, the Feast of St Justina, and on each of the ships there was a monk or priest to provide spiritual support; Don John had long before ordered that Mass was to be celebrated before any battle began. On every deck, the men stood in their armour with their weapons, then knelt for the holy office. Wisps of incense rose from each ship, scenting the air before being carried away by the wind. As the Mass began, the Ottoman ships came into sight of the great Christian fleet, and observing the calm and stillness of the ships at rest in the water, thought that terror now gripped the Western armada. On Ali Pasha's vessels, extended in a long line like the Christians opposite, drums started to beat and the thousands of waiting soldiers to chant as one the verses from the Holy Qur'an, with the steady refrain '*Allahu akbar*', 'God is Great.' They stamped their feet and clashed their swords on their shields. On the ships that had musicians cymbals and horns added to the swelling sound.

Western histories of these minutes contrast the respectful religious 'silence' of the Christian fleet with the raucous 'din' of the Ottoman ships. But the events were in fact exactly parallel. On the Western ships, the single voices of priests led the worship, surrounded by silent praying masses. On the Ottoman ships, the community of the faithful made their own 'rough music'. Each ceremony, however, reinforced a single belief. Whoever died in the fight to follow was destined for Heaven, the Christians (as their priests reminded them) with the pope's certificate declaring that they would be freed from the pain of Purgatory, the Muslims with the verses of the Qur'an echoing in their ears, certain that Paradise awaited them. But to Christians at prayer, the noise from the ships only a mile or so away across the water seemed savage and barbaric. Those same histories that noted Turkish barbarism however also reported an act of honour and chivalry by Ali Pasha. As Don John was ordering the Muslim galley-slaves to be chained to their oars, to live or die with their ships, the Ottoman commander went down on to the rowing deck of his flagship, the *Sultana*, and stood among the Christian galley slaves. Speaking in Spanish, he said to them, 'Brothers, I expect you today to do your duty by me, in return for the good treatment I have given you. I promise you that if I am victorious, I will give you freedom; and if not, your God will give it to you.'[47]

Even in those last moments before Ali Pasha gave the order to advance, some of his commanders argued, as had Don John's officers when they heard reports of the size and power of the Ottoman fleet, that they should avoid a battle. It would be wiser to retreat under the guns of the Lepanto fortress and tempt the Christians to battle in the narrow waters of the inner Gulf. But Ali Pasha was determined not only to sail out and engage the enemy but to make it a combat directly with Don John. With the wind behind him, just before noon, he ordered the ships to row swiftly forward towards the enemy line, with his own vessel heading straight for the *Real*, which was now flying the great blue banner of the Holy League. As they came within range of the galleasses, cannon fire began to batter the Ottoman vessels. The wind changed: now the Ottoman crews were rowing hard into a heavy sea, while the Christian ships were borne forward by the Breath of Heaven.[48] Turkish galleys sank under the shelling from the galleasses, first from their forward guns and then from their broadsides. Seeing the damage, Ali Pasha ordered his ships to steer clear, but this fractured the Ottoman formation, as they funnelled through the gaps between the galleasses.[49] Instead of his line of ships smashing as one into the Christian galleys, the impetus was lost.

Across a span of almost a mile at the centre of the battle, ships closed and grappled. Sometimes Ottoman rams crashed into the enemy ships, sometimes the masts and rigging became entangled. The soldiers poured fire on to their opponents. Many of the Christian ships were studded with Turkish arrows, while on the Ottoman vessels the decks were pitted with musket fire. The boarding nets ordered by Don John proved their worth as they filled with Ottoman dead and dying caught in the mesh. Then janissaries leaped on to the nets, hacking at the tarred strands with knives or yataghans until they were speared or shot. More and more followed to a certain death, and continued slashing until eventually the nets hung in limp tatters. Christians boarding Ottoman galleys found that while their enemy had no nets, they had greased the ships' rails and walkways with olive oil or honey. Turks, fighting barefoot, had a better grip on the deck than the Spanish or German infantrymen, well shod and armoured. Arrows fired from Turkish bows in their thousands were as deadly at close range as musket fire, and any Christian who slipped and fell would be dispatched by a dagger thrust from the Ottoman sailors and irregulars in the mêlée.

Ali Pasha had failed to press his initial advantage and the sting of the Ottoman assault was drawn. In galley warfare, the first impact and the first assault were usually all important. Now, the ships of the two commanders were locked together, the *Sultana* embedded in the forequarter of the *Real*. But although he had faltered in the first moments, Ali had a plan to overcome the greater firepower of his opponent. Behind the Turkish flagship was a flotilla of galleys and little galiots, their decks crammed with janissaries. Linked together by ropes and gangplanks, they fed reinforcements up into the killing ground on the deck of the *Sultana*. However many men the Spanish musketry might blast away, more and more Turks came on board. Both commanders believed that the outcome of the battle would, ultimately, turn on their personal encounter. Like Don John, Ali had selected a force of men armed with arquebuses, to act as his shock force, while he himself stood on the poop of his galley, with a great recurved bow, with which he coolly shot down on to the *Real*. He watched Don John, in his black armour chased with silver, come down on to the deck of the Holy League flagship to lead his arquebusiers and swordsmen. They threw gangplanks across the narrow gap to the *Sultana*, after clearing the deck of Ottoman soldiers with a succession of volleys, and swarmed on.

But then a great weight of fresh janissaries pressed forward and forced them back on to their own deck. Again the Christians massed and charged. As the janissaries wavered, Ali came down on to the deck to stiffen his men's resolve. In the turmoil, he was struck a

glancing blow to the head by a musket ball and fell. Again the
Christians pushed forward, and one of them, recognizing the Ottoman
leader if only by the richness of his dress, hacked off his head and took
it to Don John, caught in the midst of a firefight elsewhere on the
deck. In seconds the battered head of Ali Pasha was impaled on a pike
and held high for all to see, as Spanish veterans surged forward against
the now demoralized Turks. The area around the mainmast was
secured, and the green banner of Islam torn down. A pennant with a
crucifix was brought from the *Real* and hauled up to the topmast of
the *Sultana*.

While the heart had gone out of the Ottoman fight in the centre,
it was still being fought with increasing ferocity on the two wings.
Desperate battles took place on the decks as the galleys locked, and
men died in their thousands. The waters of the Gulf were marbled
rust-red with blood. Some Ottoman galleys fled from the Venetians,
who were plainly going to give no quarter, and beached. The
Venetians pursued them ashore, killing all the fugitives. One man,
lacking any better weapon, killed his adversary on the ground by
thrusting a stout stick deep into his mouth until he was still. More
often, Christian ships stood off and sank their enemies through gunfire,
watching while all aboard drowned. In the heat of the early afternoon
sun, bodies floating in the water began to swell up with gas until they
bobbed about like corks.

By four in the afternoon the battle was over. More than 7,500
Christians had been killed, but the Ottoman losses exceeded 20,000.
More than 15,000 Christian galley slaves were freed from Turkish
captivity, but the ships they had rowed, for the most part, survived as
little more than hulks.[50] A few galleys on the Ottoman right wing, led
by the corsair Ulich Ali, once a Christian, escaped, but the rest of the
huge fleet was either sunk, crippled or seized. There were many
captives and a vast amount of booty. Immediately the Christians began
to recall the signs of Divine favour. The banner of the Holy League,
flying on Don John's flagship, was unscathed, hit by neither shot nor
arrow, although the mast and surrounding spars were riddled. By
contrast, the great green flag from Ali Pasha's *Sultana* had been
almost shot to pieces, so that much of the elaborate Kufic script was
unreadable. Not a single priest or monk on the Spanish ships had been
killed or wounded, although they had been in the thick of the fighting.

And all remembered how the wind that had blown hard into their faces suddenly dropped and reversed to carry them forward at the decisive moment. Of the numerous crucifixes on the ships, not one had suffered any damage, though a musket ball had hit close by the side of one of them. Others remembered what Don John had said to them in the hour before the battle began: 'My children, we are here to conquer or to die as Heaven may determine. Do not let our impious foe ask us, "Where is your God?" Fight in His holy name and in death or in victory you will win immortality.'[51]

From the moment that the battle ended, myth-making began. As the Christian fleet, towing its prizes, rowed slowly back to the mouth of the Gulf and anchored at Petala, they left behind a scene of desolation.

For miles around the victorious fleet the waves, as eyewitnesses asserted, were reddened with blood, and were strewed with broken planks, masts, spars and oars, with men's bodies and limbs, with shields, weapons, turbans, chests, barrels, and cabin furniture, the rich scarf of the knight, the splendid robes of the Pasha, the mighty plume of the janissary, the sordid rags of the slave, and all the various spoils of war. Boats moved hither and thither amongst the floating relics, saving all that seemed valuable except the lives of the vanquished.[52]

From the fleet at anchor, Don John dispatched a fast galley to take the news to King Philip, together with the *Sultana*'s tattered green banner. Some time later he sent the sultan's personal flag to the pope, and to Venice and the emperor in Vienna a detailed account of the great victory. But King Philip was not the first to hear as Don John had planned. On 17 October, a galley sailed into the harbour of Venice, firing its guns, and trailing banners in the water. It anchored off St Mark's Square, and curious onlookers could see Turks walking on the decks. There was a moment's panic, as people thought the Turks were once again attacking the city. But soon the truth became clear: these were Venetians dressed in the spoils of victory. The news spread almost instantly through the whole city, and four days of rejoicing began. Church bells rang continuously day and night and great fires were lit in the streets, with food and wine provided for the people.

The anniversary of Lepanto, St Justina's Day, was declared a holiday in perpetuity. Hundreds of odes and orations were quickly written and declaimed, the first of a torrent of verse and commemoration in many of the languages of Europe. From that moment the battle became an allegory, where all the details of the conflict acquired an additional significance. In these presentations the listeners heard how Don John and the noble men of Venice destroyed the ravening Wolf, the raging Bull, the fearsome Dragon and Hydra of the East. They had killed the Beast. As the news of the battle spread, various miraculous events were recalled. At four in the afternoon, at the very moment the battle ended, the pope had suddenly stopped work, walked to the window, opened it and listened intently. Then, closing the window, he said to his treasurer, 'God be with you, this is no time for business but for giving thanks to God, for at this moment our fleet is victorious.'[53]

King Philip II first had intelligence of the battle, it was said, by a messenger from Venice on 29 October, while he observed the service of vespers from the curtained gallery overlooking the palace chapel. Over time, the story of this moment was embellished to give weight to the deeper meanings that had become attached to the battle. In 1605, six years after the king's death, an account was published that described how Philip II had been at prayer, during the service of vespers, in the cathedral Church of San Lorenzo.

Don Pedro Manuel, a gentleman of the bedchamber, entered; with a perturbation of look and manner, which showed that something great had happened, he said aloud to his Majesty, 'Sir, the courier of Don John of Austria is here, and he brings news of a great victory.' Yet the magnanimous prince neither changed his posture nor showed any emotion, it being a great privilege, amongst others, of the House of Austria never to lose, happen what may, their serenity of countenance and imperial gravity of demeanour. The vespers being over, he called the prior and ordered that the *Te Deum Laudamus* should be sung for thanksgiving, with prayers of the Church suitable for the occasion.[54]

The circumstantial detail, the naming of the gentleman of the chamber, and the location within the great baroque Church of San Lorenzo are compelling. Tour guides in the palace once pointed to the very seat in the cathedral choir occupied by the king at the moment the news arrived. Yet the cathedral was not built or consecrated until 1586, fifteen years after Lepanto.

When the king eventually received the report from Don John on the evening of 22 November in El Escorial, he was surrounded by his family and courtiers. The messenger, Don Lope de Figueroa, had travelled slowly, because he had been badly wounded in the battle, but also because he had been fêted in every town through which he passed.[55] The popular rejoicing for Lepanto was not limited to the nations that had participated directly in the battle. Even in France, where for political reasons the Most Christian King preserved good relations with the Ottomans, there were processions and church services in the smallest of towns and villages. In Protestant England, there were days of exuberant celebration in London. German towns went wild with delight. Perhaps for the last time, the sense of universal participation in a holy war transcended the chasm between Catholic and Protestant.[56]

Within days of the story first being told in Andalucia, 'Lepanto' was being re-enacted as a play in the caves of the Sacromonte in Granada.[57] In such 'accounts', moral truth mattered more than factual verisimilitude.[58] What *happened* at Lepanto was compounded partly from the event itself and partly from the subsequent myths with which it was overlaid. Accurate details of the battle became widely known – from memoirs and pamphlets, or from stories told by travellers. Some of the profusion of woodcut images that appeared throughout Europe stuck to a remarkable degree to the factual truth. A pamphlet circulating in Germany within months of the battle had on its cover a depiction of a galleass at the moment of first contact. Its great guns belched smoke from its sides. The boarding nets and boiled leather shields were in place. The Turkish galleys were smashed to pieces; the sea was filled with turbaned figures and with wooden shields, blazoned with the Crescent, floating on the surface of the waters.[59] The response to the battle and the meanings drawn from it – its resonance – were extended, both in time and in place. For Sir Richard Lovelace, writing a century after Lepanto, it had become an eponym or shorthand for Christian triumph: 'When the sick Sea with Turbants Night-cap'd was; / . . . This is a wreath, this is a Victorie.'

Lepanto was remembered in many different ways. Rome celebrated the return of Marc Antonio Colonna with a Triumph worthy of a Caesar. He rode to the Capitol on a white horse, followed by long lines of soldiers and captive Turks, shackled in pairs and dragging heavy chains, all wearing his red and yellow livery.[60] Another Colonna, Honorato, and his heroism in the battle are still commemorated each year in the little hill town of Sermonetta. Messina, which had greeted the returning fleet with tournaments and a vast catafalque to honour the dead, commissioned a huge gilded statue of Don John from Andrea Calamach. The admiral still stands to this day, his left foot on the severed turbaned head of a Turk, while all around the story of Lepanto is told in bas-relief. The Signoria of Venice commissioned Tintoretto, Pietro Longo, Andrea Vincentino and Antonio Vassilachi to make a series of paintings for the Sala dello Scrutinio in the Doge's Palace. In the city churches and the Arsenal, the Holy League and the Divinely Ordained victory were recalled in altarpieces, paintings and marble plaques. The aged Titian, who had declined to produce a commemorative canvas for Venice, succumbed to King Philip. In a huge painting (*Allegory of the Battle of Lepanto*), the king is the dominant figure, offering up his infant son Don Ferdinand (born in the months after Lepanto) to Heaven. Winged Victory hands down the victor's laurels, while in the foreground a trussed-up Turk, his weapons and turban lying on the ground beside him, and a burning galley fleet in the background point to the great triumph.

The official memory of the battle was consolidated. In March 1572, the pope decreed that the Feast of the Rosary should be celebrated on the anniversary of Lepanto. In the Cathedral of Toledo a banner captured at Lepanto was displayed annually on the day of the battle, and a service of thanksgiving held. In churches throughout Christendom, the day of Lepanto was recalled long after the details of the battle had been forgotten. As a 'site of memory', it had great attraction: it demonstrated Christian unity. Subsequently, only the relief of Vienna from a Turkish siege in 1683 showed Christendom responding in a similar fashion, with a single voice. If the Protestants did not take part in Lepanto, few condemned it as a papistical triumph. It possessed a personable hero and a diabolical enemy, which is perhaps why it continued to feature in tracts and pamphlets for more than a century after.

More distant still in time, the Catholic man of letters G. K. Chesterton wrote his epic *Lepanto*, in which Don John 'has set his people *free*', righting not only the wrongs of his own day, but providing a message for the future.

> The North is full of tangled things and texts and aching eyes,
> And dead is all the innocence of anger and surprise,
> And Christian killeth Christian in a narrow dusty room,
> And Christian dreadeth Christ that hath a newer face of doom,
> And Christian hateth Mary that God kissed in Galilee, –
> But Don John of Austria is riding to the sea.
> Don John calling through the blast and the eclipse
> Crying with the trumpet, with the trumpet of his lips,
> Trumpet that sayeth *ha!*
>   *Domino gloria!*

This theme of continuity – of the continuing battle with the world of 'Islam' – had a precise context in 1911. As Chesterton's *Lepanto* was being published, and six days after the anniversary of Lepanto, the army of Italy landed in Libya to seize the last remnant of Ottoman territory in North Africa. A few days before, far away in the Adriatic, the Italian navy had attacked and sunk Turkish gunboats at Prevesa, another site of memory, for this was where Don John had anchored in the days before Lepanto.[61] With the Treaty of Ouchy, signed on 15 October 1912, Italy completed the Christian 'reconquest' of North Africa, so that European nations dominated the entire southern sea-board of the Mediterranean, from Egypt to Morocco. *Lepanto*, at least in Chesterton's eyes, was an active and current crusade, not some event plucked at random out of a dead past.

The resilience of Lepanto also bound itself to the popular imagination. The annual pageants of Christians and Moors celebrated Christian victory for centuries in towns and villages on the eastern coast of Spain, and in Corsica.[62] Old memories were revived or reconstructed, as in the huge *Moresca* held at Vescovato in Corsica in 1786 in honour of the new governor, the Comte de Marbeuf. There, 160 dancers in elaborate costumes enacted an epic tale of Christian triumph.[63]

This cycle of celebration and the memory of victory had no direct counterpart in the Islamic world. There the catastrophe at Lepanto was mourned as an act of Divine Will. The contemporary chronicle of the battle laconically recorded that 'the Imperial fleet encountered the fleet of the wretched infidels and the will of God turned another way.'[64] When he received the news, the sultan raged and wished to order the execution of all the Christians in his domains. But he was easily dissuaded, to the degree that we might suspect that his anger had primarily a histrionic purpose. It was not the Ottoman tradition to make a lasting memorial out of victory or to chasten themselves with the remembrance of defeat. Triumph or catastrophe were in the hands of God. Selim II's Chief Minister, the Grand Vizier Mehmed Sokullu, even suggested to the Venetian emissary Barbaro, who met him a few days after the news of the battle reached Constantinople, that the Christian triumph was meaningless:

You come to see how we bear our misfortune. But I would have you know the difference between your loss and ours. In wresting Cyprus from you, we deprived you of an arm; in defeating our fleet, you have only shaved our beard. An arm when cut off cannot grow again; but a shorn beard will grow all the better for the razor.[65]

Of all the great victories won by Ottoman arms, only the capture of Constantinople by Mehmed II was remembered and commemorated in the manner of the West celebrating Lepanto, and then without the pictorial and textual effusion that the Christian victory generated. As a result, it embedded itself less firmly into the domain of history and memory.

For Christians, the tales of Lepanto contained a double message about Islam. On one side there was Lala Mustafa, the commander in Cyprus, Bragadino's cruel and bestial nemesis. He exemplified the traditional Christian perception of the Muslim. But on the other was the Noble Enemy, the Ottoman commander at Lepanto, Ali Pasha. There was a long Christian tradition, back to the time of the Crusades and the stories of King Richard's chivalrous opponent, Saladin, of respecting a strong enemy. Ottoman sultans such as Suleiman the Lawgiver were also honoured for their martial and civic virtues, even if those qualities sat alongside the image of cruelty. But unlike Saladin and Suleiman, Ali Pasha was not redeemed by success. He failed: his nobility of behaviour was personal and not a consequence of his role or office. When he went down amongst his galley slaves and spoke words of comfort to them he behaved as would a Christian. This was clearly the unvoiced assumption of the Western narratives that recorded his conduct.

Don John regarded him with respect. He took Ali's two young sons, captured on the Ottoman flagship *Sultana*, under his personal protection. He sent their tutor, who also survived, back to Constantinople with a letter to their mother, saying that they were safe and well cared for. Eventually, after one of the boys had died from a chance illness, Don John returned the other to his family without payment of the large ransom that would have been traditional. This was not simply the courtesy to be expected of one commander to another. I can think of no other case in the same century that provides a parallel. Like Ali Pasha, Don John was moving past the boundaries of character and relationships prescribed for both Christians and Muslims.

More persuasive of these ambiguities than Don John and Ali was Miguel de Cervantes, a veteran of *La Naval* (as the battle came to be known to the Spaniards). Lepanto was only the beginning of Cervantes' encounter with the Muslim world. In 1575 he was captured by an Algerian corsair almost in sight of the French coast. His experience of five years in the slave prisons of Algiers became the core of the long 'Captive's Tale' in his novel *Don Quixote*. But more important than the events described is the manner in which Cervantes undermined the whole sense of the embattled relationship between the domain of 'Islam' and the Christian world. In the book, he presents himself as only the *second* author and also the first reader of the whole story of Don Quixote. He uncovered the first author and the *ur-text* by chance. As Cervantes tells it, one day in Toledo he came across a boy selling a bundle of old papers:

Now, as I have a strong propensity to read even those scraps that sometimes fly about the streets, I was led by this, my natural curiosity, to turn over some of the leaves: I found them written in Arabic, which not being able to read although I knew the characters, I looked about for some Portuguese Moor who should understand it; and indeed though the language was both more elegant and more ancient, I might easily have found an interpreter.

His interpreter read the title page out loud to him: 'The history of Don Quixote de la Mancha by Cid Hamet Benengeli, an Arabian Author'. Cervantes paid him to translate the entire text, which took six weeks, at a price of two quarters of raisins and two bushels of wheat. The mysterious and unseen Cid Hamet was not just a convenient cipher, like the exotic characters of Turks or Persians used to comment on the Christian world from some detached and external perspective.[66] The 'Arabian Author' wanders back into the text from time to time, and is there at Quixote's death. It is he who writes the final words of Quixote's epitaph:

For me alone was Don Quixote born and I for him; he to act and I to record; in a word we were destined for each other . . . let the wearied and mouldering bones of Don Quixote rest in the grave [i.e., write no further sequels to his life] . . . in doing so thou wilt conform to thy Christian profession of doing good to those who would do thee harm; and I shall rest satisfied and perfectly well pleased, in seeing myself the first author, who fully enjoyed the fruit of his writings, in the success of his design, for mine was no other than to inspire mankind with an abhorrence of false and improbable stories recounted in books of chivalry, which are already shaken by the adventures of my true and genuine Don Quixote, and in a little time will certainly sink into oblivion. Farewell.

Was this more than an audacious literary device? Cervantes did not share the stereotypical image of the Muslim. Take his presentation of Muley Malek in his play *The Dungeons of Algiers*, written about 1590.

> A famous Moor
> and in his sect and wicked law
> well versed and most devout;
> he knows the language of the Turks,
> speaks Spanish and German as well
> and Italian and French, sleeps
> in a bed and eats at a table
> seated in the Christian manner;
> above all he's a great soldier
> generous, wise and cool-headed,
> adorned with a thousand virtues.[67]

Nor did William Shakespeare, Cervantes' near-contemporary with whom he shared the date of his death, in his characterization of

Othello, The Moor of Venice. 'Muley Malek' could have served as a model for Othello.[68] Yet while Muley is all Moor, Othello is a double man, undoubtedly a Muslim Moor, and yet also a servant of Christian Venice. But for Cervantes to write as he did of Cid Hamet Benengeli, and to ascribe to him the writing of his own work, make sense only if we understand the specific historical context. The first part of *Don Quixote* was published in 1606, the second in 1615. Between the two publications, Spain rid itself finally of the Moors' descendants, the *Moriscos*, from its territory. Expelled from the kingdom of Granada after their rebellion was crushed by Don John, the *Moriscos* were dispersed throughout Spain. All the misfortunes of the nation were blamed upon them. In a final act of ethnic cleansing, they were marched to the seaports in 1609 and shipped to Morocco.

To make the infidel Cid Hamet the 'first author' of his work was unusual and, in these years, an especially daring move. Cervantes, from the events of his life – war, slavery, penury, prison, success and, finally, preparing for death in a monk's habit – knew that the division of the world into good Christians and bestial Muslims was false. Of the gulf between them he had no doubt, or that each was 'infidel' to the other. But he was treated both worse and better in his Algerine slavery than at home in Christian Spain. His work was rooted in his own experience, but even those who had never set foot in a Muslim land were forced to struggle with the issue of the virtuous infidel:

> Tho' Arabs much to Rapine are inclin'd,
> Of Nature fierce, and Manners unrefin'd,
> Yet is King Halla [of Morocco] gen'rous, mild, and wise,
> And with the most applauded Heroe vies;
> Courteous, humane, and easy of Access
> This Monarch succours Merit in Distress.
> Tho' the great Prince rejects our Creed divine,
> His moral Virtues so illustrious shine,
> That he like some, who Rome's proud Scepter bore,
> Excells most Kings who Christ their Head adore.[69]

Lepanto lay at the heart of this skein of tangled meanings. It was a stunning victory, but as the Turkish Vizier Sokullu foresaw, of passing political or military importance. Seven years after *La Naval*, at

Alcazarquivir in Morocco, a Muslim army reinforced with Ottoman janissaries killed the King of Portugal, Dom Sebastian, nephew of Don John, and most of the Portuguese nobility.[70] Yet Alcazarquivir has vanished from the collective memory, while the recollection of Lepanto has been embellished and enhanced over the years. The meeting of Don John and Ali Pasha, with its attendant cast of thousands, more than any other encounter in the sixteenth century between Islam and the Christian West presented the ambivalence and the endless ambiguities of the relationship between these worlds.

2

First Contact

This book is about enmity, how it was created and how it is sustained. While Muslims were not the first or only enemies of western Christendom, they quickly became its prime focus for fear and hatred. Eventually the very words used to describe them became common tokens of abuse.[1] Christians at the time of Lepanto often insulted each other in terms applied to Muslims. Protestants in sixteenth-century Bavaria described their clerical enemy as 'Jesuits and Mamelukkes'. In England, William Tyndale regretted how many of his Catholic countrymen had become 'the Antichriste of Rome's mamelukes'. 'Lustful Turk', 'Street Arab' and 'Mad Mullah' are all nineteenth- and early twentieth-century epithets, but they reached back to ideas about the East that developed steadily from the seventh century onward.[2]

The Christian preoccupation with 'Islam', if we judge it by the volume of written texts – books, exegeses, descriptions, polemics, odes and epics – far exceeded any Muslim interest in western Christendom.[3] We should distinguish Islam or Christianity, which are the faiths that their adherents would recognize, from 'Islam' or 'Christianity', which are images constructed by their enemies. From the mid seventh century, 'Islam' was seen as the prime external challenge to True Christian Faith. Only the enemy within, heresy, came close to its deadly menace. The image of 'Islam' as enemy, competitor, and arch-adversary grew more complex and more potent over time. The initial crudity of the image was made more subtle both by adding new dimensions as circumstances altered, and by jettisoning those no longer relevant. So, the crude parodies of the Prophet Mohammed tended to diminish while ever more baroque descriptions of Islamic virulence multiplied.

This ability to 'construct' enemies, to make them demonic in their power, all-embracing in their antagonism, unsurpassed in their malevolence, permeated western European society. It was deployed on many occasions, and proved effective against all types of dissidents, and every kind of political, ethnic and social enemy.[4] We should therefore take nothing said about 'Islam', or for that matter 'heresy' or 'Judaism', at face or surface value, but try to see, first of all, behind the accretion of meanings. From the outset, the pace of Islam's advance took Christendom by surprise. The Prophet Mohammed was born about 570, only five years after the death of the Emperor Justinian, who had restored the Roman Empire to its greatest extent since the second century AD. Yet within a single generation after the Prophet's own demise in 632, the desert warriors of Islam were laying siege to Justinian's capital city, Constantinople. As Edward Gibbon observed, 'When the Arabs first issued from the desert, they must have been surprised at the ease and rapidity of their own success.'

The Arabs described themselves as *jahili*, and the Latin epithet used by their enemies was *ferox*, for a wild headstrong impetuosity. Both had essentially the same meaning, but for the Arabs it was a largely positive self-image, while for Christians it was a synonym for barbarism.[5] The armies of Islam that emerged from the void beyond Roman Philadelphia (modern Amman in Jordan) and the other Roman cities of the desert edge, known collectively as the Decapolis, looked no different from any other tribesmen. They had none of the trained skills or the well-made weapons of the best Byzantine troops or of the heavily armoured Persian horsemen. At best, they were tribal warriors inured to a hard life, who could flourish in a desert environment where the heavily armoured cavalry and plodding infantry could not survive for more than a few days. Neither of the two Eastern empires – Rome and Persia – paid much attention to the desert margin. They hired other Arabs to protect their towns and cities from desert marauders. This was the approach that the Western Roman Empire had centuries before adopted towards its own 'barbarians'.

This was a different military problem to Rome-in-Europe, where the boundaries or *limes* ran along natural limits, such as rivers or mountains. But along the Eastern desert fringe the contrast between civilization and wilderness was often much more extreme. Civilization meant organized agriculture, village settlements, towns and cities. The wilderness seemed empty of life. The desert Arabs could wage war in more civilized territories, but it was difficult, logistically speaking, for the organized forces of the Byzantine Empire or Sassanid Persia to campaign far from their bases. The desert Arabs rarely mounted more than the occasional raid across the uncertain border. The tribes were few in number and they had no reason to attack a strong enemy. The nascent faith rallied a powerful new army and provided a purpose for war. Within a year of the Prophet Mohammed's death all the main tribes of Arabia had been cowed and notionally united under the banners of Islam. Apostates and renegades were hunted down and slaughtered. Those who had stood on the sidelines now submitted. The new faith prohibited war between Muslim brothers, so the raiding culture of the desert tribes turned outward, beyond the Arabian peninsula.

Tribal societies, especially those that emerged in Asia – the Huns and the Mongols are two prime examples – often achieved an optimum balance providing just enough social and political cohesion without curtailing their aggressive energy and vigour. The same transformation seems to have occurred in the heart of Arabia in the seventh century. As an ideology, Islam provided both coherence and direction, as well as the capacity to mobilize tribal groups which only a few years before had been at war among themselves. Thereafter, they displayed all the power, speed of movement and raw energy that later commentators observed in the hordes from further East. However, there was one difference. The Asian armies centred around the horse, while the Arabs were still foot soldiers. Of course, they had some horsemen, and camels were used to provide mobility. But unlike later images, these were not a horde mounted on fine Arab horses, cavalry armies, fighting from horseback. The Arabs were poor men, often with little more than a spear as a weapon. They walked, tirelessly, using less water and needing less food than any animal. Previously they had fought alone or in small groups, but now, marshalled by the leaders of Islam, they numbered thousands.

The Byzantines and their Persian enemies either ignored or were not fully informed of the upheavals in the desert, of the years of battles and skirmishes between the Muslims and the much more powerful tribes that surrounded them. But at midsummer 633, a large desert army suddenly appeared before the Persian walled town of Hira, on the desert frontier south of the Euphrates. At the time of the Muslim advance, Persia was weak, first from years of conflict with the

Byzantines, and secondly from civil war among the ruling dynasty. Within a matter of months, fast-moving Muslim columns had progressed northwards, destroying isolated Persian garrisons, killing those who opposed them, by crucifixion or with the sword.[6] Their enemies eliminated, they enlisted converts to Islam from among the local peasants, and passed on. They levied tribute rather than settling the lands they had conquered.[7]

Thus, like rural guerrillas throughout history, the Arab Muslims seized control of borderlands. The desert, the element in which they were supreme, was like a sea that washed the shoreline of the settled lands, in Syria and Palestine, and along the fertile plain between the Tigris and the Euphrates. They moved with astonishing speed, wrong-footing their static Persian and Byzantine enemies. A Muslim army fighting east of the great rivers of Iraq suddenly changed direction, marched south-west around the Syrian desert, then north towards Palmyra. At one stage, it had to pass through a completely arid region without oases or waterholes. Here the desert lore of the tribesmen came into play, as they searched for desert plants that indicated water just below the surface. They had also made their camels drink to fill their internal water bladders at the last oasis. Then each day they killed four of them, and cut out the sacs still full of water to provide liquid for the few precious horses.[8]

At the same time another Arab force, at least 3,000 strong, but perhaps numbering as many as 9,000 men, huge by the standards of desert campaigning, was pushing north-west from the Arabian peninsula towards the Mediterranean coast. The Byzantine Emperor Heraclius, a veteran of decades of war against the Persians, was now aware of the danger posed by the desert Arabs. He dispatched a field army from Homs in Syria to intercept the Muslims advancing north from Beersheba. This Muslim army had already tasted victory, sweeping aside the local forces commanded by the governor of Gaza. A Syriac chronicle written some time after the event described the outcome of the encounter. 'The Byzantines fled and abandoned the commander . . . and the Arabs slew him. Some 4,000 poor villagers from Palestine were killed, Christians, Jews and Samaritans, and the Arabs destroyed the palace completely.'[9] Heraclius had sent the bulk of his soldiers south along the flat coastal strip. The Byzantine column passed the town of Ramleh, heading towards the Arab army, reported as being still near to Gaza. A force of this size moved slowly, keeping close to the sea so that it could be supplied from the Byzantine fleet cruising off the coast. These were not just poorly trained local conscripts but included a nucleus of heavily mailed infantry, horse archers and armoured heavy cavalry – the cataphrachts.

At some point south of Ramleh the Byzantines were ambushed by the Arabs – the Muslim army had advanced further north than Heraclius or his commanders had anticipated. The exact location of the ensuing battle of Ajnadain is uncertain. But the outcome, on 31 July 634, was an annihilating victory for the Muslims. The Byzantine force was following the track south, giving a wide berth to the Jabal Nablus (Judean Hills). The land was flat, not the broken ground or ravines that favoured irregular fighters. The only advantage that the Muslims possessed was their speed of manoeuvre and their reckless zeal. All day long the few Arab horsemen darted at the enemy, tempting them into pursuit, and drawing the fire from their bowmen. Their leader, Khalid Al-Walid, had to remind his men to 'Reserve yourself until the evening. It was in the evening that the Prophet was accustomed to vanquish.'[10] But once it had broken the enemy ranks in the late afternoon, the Byzantine army's advantages of larger numbers and better equipment vanished. The Muslims could gut their opponents' horses with their knives and spears, and mob the heavily armoured infantry. Meanwhile, with the light failing the Byzantine archers had no clear targets.

As they slashed and stabbed, cutting off the heads and limbs of their opposites, shouting their tribal battle cries, the Arabs' assault destroyed their enemy's cohesion. The bewildered Byzantine troops ceased to obey orders, milling about as they tried to fight back against their gadfly foe. Once the Byzantines' momentum had slackened and they began to retreat, the Arabs turned this attempt at manoeuvre into a rout. The Byzantine troops fled north, pursued by the Arabs for a while, until the latter returned to strip the bodies of the fallen soldiers of their arms and equipment. Tribesmen who had been armed with nothing more than a spear now acquired a horse and a sword. Buoyed up by victory, the Muslims moved against the cities and towns. Jerusalem shut its gates, but outside the walls, according to the Patriarch of Jerusalem, the tribesmen 'plunder cities, despoil the fields, burn the villages, despoil holy monasteries'. In reality, the Muslims were more concerned with consolidating their authority. Far from mindlessly ravaging the land, they decreed that the Christian inhabitants should pay an annual poll tax of one dinar, and hand over a percentage of their crops each year.[11]

The disaster at Ajnadain was wholly unexpected and threw all the plans of the Emperor Heraclius into complete disarray. He had beaten so many powerful adversaries that it seemed incredible that he could now be humbled by a rabble of Arab tribesmen. However, the reports he received showed that these desert raiders, clad in coarse cloth or even skins, armed with a spear and a long knife, were as dangerous as the skilled Persian soldiers whom he had fought against for half his life. He quickly withdrew from Homs, which might be threatened by Arab raiders, north to the safety of Antioch, and set about rebuilding his army. He paid the Christian Arab tribes that had once garrisoned the frontier to fight for him again. He summoned the redoubtable Armenians from over the mountains in Anatolia. Meanwhile, the Muslims concentrated their forces in a well-chosen position close to the town of Deraa, on the River Yarmouk. The Byzantine armies, moving down from the north, could approach them only from the front. The land to their left was fissured by deep ravines, while to the right was a lava field, the residue of an extinct volcano. Small groups of warriors could work their way across these badlands, but no organized army would choose to fight in such conditions. The Byzantines set up a strongly fortified camp just to the north of the Arab position. This blocked the Muslims from advancing into Syria, and if they chose to attack, the Byzantine commanders were confident that their wild and savage enemies would die in their thousands before the well-built ramparts.

However, the Muslims resorted to the classic manoeuvre of desert war: a mobbing attack from all sides. Small groups scrambled through the ravines of the Yarmouk, and hid behind the Byzantine position. Others, on horseback or on camels, crossed the grey lava shale, and began to raid the Byzantine lines of communication back towards Syria. The two armies confronted each other for over four months, and the Byzantine forces ran short of food and other supplies. Their lifeline was the road to the ports of Tyre and Sidon, but all the supplies had to be carried across the bridge over the Yarmouk, only a few miles from the great encampment. In the middle of August, Muslims hiding in the ravines emerged and captured the lightly guarded bridge. This cut the Byzantines off from the coast, with their only line of retreat through the desert to Damascus. Early on 20 August 636, the wind began to blow off the desert, picking up sand and dust, with the sky turning the colour of dull bronze. As the day went on, it became darker and darker, the air so thick with sand that it was hard to breathe and impossible to see more than a few yards ahead. Struggling with the elements, the Byzantines suddenly faced the full weight of an Arab attack. It was late in the afternoon, and by the time night fell around six, the Muslims had broken through the lines at many points. All attempts at a coordinated defence fell apart, and through the night the Byzantine troops were slaughtered where they stood. By dawn their dead lay in huge heaps on the ground, with the Arabs stripping the corpses of every object they could use. Then they abandoned the battleground to the crows and other scavengers.

Only a few thousand of the Byzantine army managed to slip away in small groups to take the news of the devastating defeat to Heraclius in Antioch. After the cities of the region had fallen one by one to the Muslims, the emperor eventually concluded that the whole Levant, from the border with Egypt to the Taurus Mountains at the edge of Anatolia, was untenable. His remaining forces withdrew through the narrow pass called the Cilician Gates, after destroying all the towns and villages for miles around.[12] From then onward, the frontier of the Byzantine Empire lay on the high plateau of Anatolia, and not in the rich and fertile lands of the Levant. The emperor relinquished Jerusalem as well as the Christian Arabs who had formed much of his support in the region. However, the image of sudden and catastrophic abandonment is exaggerated. The Levant had been fought over by the Byzantines and the Persians since the days of Justinian. Heraclius and the Byzantines had regained full control of the Holy Land from the Persians barely ten years before the arrival of the Muslims. Moreover, many of the Christians in the region were regarded as schismatics and heretics by the Orthodox authorities in Constantinople, who had oppressed them remorselessly. This is one reason why some of the Christian accounts present conflicting views of the Muslim conquest. It was the Orthodox who usually anathematized the Muslims most fiercely. They were not universally regarded irreconcilably as enemies by all the Christian communities.

In the year after Ajnadain, the Arabian warriors pushed further north until they arrived before the walls of Damascus, thrusting aside the armies sent against them. A few miles short of the city, they defeated the Byzantine general Baanes. He had denuded the city of its garrison, confident that an ill-equipped desert army had no hope of taking a great city like Damascus. But a Monophysite Christian (Syriac) bishop, who had been treated as a heretic by the Byzantines, informed a Muslim commander, Khalid, that the east gate of the city was weakly defended, and even supplied the Muslims with ladders to scale the wall. Once the Byzantines learned of the breach, they quickly came to terms with the Muslim general Abu Ubaid, camped on the far side of the city. The two Muslim forces met in the centre of the city, and Abu Ubaid insisted that it should be respected and its people not put to the sword. Part of Damascus was ceded and the remainder conquered. For some time, half the Cathedral of St John was used for Christian worship, and half was turned into a mosque. A flimsy partition wall, hastily erected, divided the two faiths.

Ibn Khaldun, writing in the fourteenth century, attributed the success of the desert Arab tribes to their wild spirit. But they also proved adaptable. Poor infantrymen acquired horses and camels, and thereafter wore Byzantine swords and armour. In 636, the Muslims created the military towns that became the key element in their subsequent advance. Here the tribes encamped, and could be called to prayer on Fridays. Muslim discipline and social control could be enforced. But they also needed to be satiated, on a regular basis, with fresh conquest. Wars of conversion were a religious duty, but they were also a means of social mobility, taking tribesmen from desert poverty towards a settled life, free from want. It seems paradoxical that the Arab soldiers, whose ethos was built upon individual prowess, could act with such cohesion. However, the morality of Islam had emerged from within the values of a tribal society. There remained profound tensions between conflicting loyalties to tribe and to the service of God, but despite the contradictions, the Muslim system worked.

In the Levant much of the Christian Arab population soon converted to Islam.[13] The new faith was appealing:

The chief attraction of Islam was that it was practical; it did not demand seemingly superhuman efforts . . . The Christian East on the eve of the

Islamic conquest had forgotten the limitations of human nature. Many members of the Church desired to imitate the angels; hence the mass movements towards the sexless life of monks and nuns; hence the exodus from towns and villages into the desert; hence the feats of self-mortification which showed the extent to which men could subdue their bodies at the dictates of the spirit. Some of these Eastern ascetics slept only in a standing position, others immured themselves in dark cells or lived on pillars, or ate only herbs, and even those not more than once a week.

Islam stopped all these excesses. It swept away the exaggerated fear of sex, discarded asceticism, banished the fear of hell for those who failed to reach perfection, quenched theological enquiry . . . Islam was like the sand of the desert . . . It created a sense of solidarity and brotherhood which had been lost among the contending Christians.[14]

Not surprisingly, from the first days of the Islamic Conquest, the Orthodox hierarchy, the spiritual arm of Byzantine political power, saw the Muslims as a unique menace. They had not responded so fiercely to the Persian occupation of Palestine and their capture of Jerusalem in 614, even though the occupiers had carried away with them Jerusalem's supreme Christian relic, the True Cross.[15] On the day in the spring of 638 that the leader of the Muslims, Caliph Omar, clad in his old and tattered robe, arrived to take the city under his protection, the Orthodox Patriarch of Jerusalem, Sophronius, watched him walk slowly through the Church of the Holy Sepulchre. The patriarch remarked quietly in Greek to an acolyte, 'Surely this is the abomination of desolation spoken of by Daniel the Prophet standing in the holy place.'[16] All those who heard him would have understood not just an allusion to the Prophet Daniel, but also to the words of Jesus Christ on the Mount of Olives, when his disciples asked him to prophesy the future.

When ye shall see the abomination of desolation, spoken of by Daniel, stand in the holy place, let him understand . . . For there shall be great tribulation, such as was not since the beginning of the world to this time, no, nor ever shall be . . . Then if any man shall say unto you, 'Lo here is Christ, or there', believe it not. For there shall arise false Christs and false prophets, and shall show great signs and wonders; insomuch, that if it were possible, they should deceive the very elect.[17]

The patriarch, who had lived through the Persian occupation, saw in this grizzled old man a quality much more dangerous than in all the grand Persian satraps who had preceded him.

From this point of first contact, there was a profound fear and antipathy among the Orthodox towards Islam. These attitudes proliferated in the written polemic of Byzantine scholars. From these early days themes and tropes began to emerge, which appeared and reappeared in later diatribes.[18] Desert Arabs had been seen as barbarian long before the coming of Islam. According to one contemporary, Maximus Confessor, 'They behave like beasts of prey though they look like human beings.'[19] In later accounts, the Muslim subjects of an Armenian king had been transmogrified into dog-headed men, *cynocephali*.[20] Within two generations of Omar entering Jerusalem, Christian scholars developed a comprehensive attack against Islam. One powerful polemicist was John of Damascus, who served as an official at the caliph's court before he abandoned public life in 716 and became a monk.[21] He put the case against Islam in one sentence: 'He who does not believe according to the tradition of the universal church is an infidel.'[22] He condemned the Prophet Mohammed as the Antichrist. Yet John, who read Arabic and knew the Qur'an, was thought excessively moderate by his fellow clerics. A synod in 754 condemned him as being 'Saracen minded', and too sympathetic to Islam.[23] Nicetas Byzantios was more antagonistic to it. 'Above all [,he considered that] Islam was a step backwards, a retrogression, "a destruction and a ruin". It was a "*bad and noxious*" religion. The Prophet Mohammed himself was "*the son of the father of lies*" and he [Nicetas] triumphantly concluded, "Thus I do not hesitate to pronounce [my judgement] on Mohammed: he is the very Antichrist." '[24]

In the Byzantine system, the Orthodox Church served God through serving the state. Over the centuries since Constantine's conversion to Christianity in 312, his new city of Constantinople had become an arsenal of the Faith. More and more holy relics had been accumulated in the city's churches. At the dedication of Constantinople on 11 May 330, a great statue of the emperor had been placed atop a huge column of porphyry, which was more than 100 feet tall, and glowed a pale red in the setting sun. Holy relics were carried in procession to the foot of the shaft and then placed in a hidden chamber. There were crumbs from the bread with which Christ had fed the Five Thousand in the Wilderness; the crosses on which the two thieves had been crucified on either side of Jesus of Nazareth at Golgotha; the alabaster box that had contained the ointment with which Mary Magdalene had anointed Jesus' feet; the adze with which Noah had built the ark; the rock that Moses had touched with his wand and from which had gushed forth water in the Wilderness; and the garment of the Virgin Mary, the Palladium, which Aeneas had carried from Troy to Rome. And cast into the bronze statue itself was a fragment of the True Cross.[25]

The great Church of the Holy Wisdom, Haghia Sophia, was filled with relics, most notably the True Cross itself, recaptured by the Emperor Heraclius from the Persians shortly before the Muslims occupied Palestine. It was by then in fragments, kept in a chest on a golden altar. There, too, were other relics of the Passion: the Crown of Thorns, the Sponge, and slabs from the Tomb. The Emperor Alexis Comnenus was supposed to have written to Robert, Count of Flanders, in 1095 of the rich spiritual treasure of the city: 'You will find more of it at Constantinople than in the whole world, for the treasures of its basilicas alone would be sufficient to furnish all the Churches of Christendom and all their treasures cannot together amount to those of St Sophia, whose riches have never been equalled even in the Temple of Solomon.'[26]

All these were touchstones of the True Faith and, over the centuries, Constantinople had become one vast reliquary. The Holy Land and the Christian sites were ransacked for sacred memorabilia, and increasingly Constantinople was identified with the 'holy city' predicted in the Revelation of Saint John the Divine: 'And I, John, saw the holy city, new Jerusalem, coming down from God out of heaven, prepared as a bride adorned for her husband. And I heard a great voice out of heaven saying, "Behold, the tabernacle of God is with men, and he will dwell with them, and they shall be his people, and God himself shall be with them, and be their God." '[27] Indeed, as a city prepared for this sacred purpose, New Jerusalem was better than Old Jerusalem, which was filled with shadows of Christ's betrayal and suffering as well as with Divine light. The Passion of Christ had combined both pain and transcendence, but Jerusalem was not a city fit for the pure risen Christ, as Constantinople could be. The sheer wealth of Constantinople, with its innumerable churches, its daily processions of relics or the celebration of saints' days, made it possible to build a city worthy of its purpose. Jerusalem was the past. New Jerusalem was the future.

What prompted Byzantine polemics against Islam were attacks on the City of the Mother of God, Constantinople, New Jerusalem. In the spring of 670, to the surprise and terror of the people of Constantinople, a huge fleet of small vessels crammed with armed Muslims appeared in the Hellespont. The ships sailed down towards the Bosphorus and beached on the northern shore about seven miles from the city, close to the deserted sea palace of the Hebdomon. There they discharged their human cargo, and withdrew back into the Sea of Marmara. The long column of infantry advanced until it extended in a huge arc before the triple land walls built under the Emperor Theodosius in the fourth century, which protected the heart of the city against attack from the north. Recovering from their shock, the Byzantine forces were at first successful. They marched from the city and almost wiped out the Arab army. At sea, they attacked the Arab fleet and destroyed many of the vessels. A new weapon, 'Greek Fire', which could not be put out with water, proved a devastating weapon against the Arabs, both on land and sea.[28] But the Arab losses were quickly made up. A new fleet and a new army arrived from the south. The Byzantines had lost control of the sea around the city and now could not move beyond the walls, for they were both outnumbered and outfought by the Arabs. The Arabs were prepared to stay for as long as it took to reduce Constantinople.

From their fortified camp close to the city the Arabs mounted a new assault each spring from 671 to 676. The costs in human life were enormous. In one assault 30,000 were killed. Gradually, the Byzantine defenders adapted the tactics they had learned to use against the Muslim columns on land, and harried them mercilessly at sea. At Syllaeum, off Asia Minor, a Byzantine squadron caught the Arab supply ships heading north, and destroyed them. Deprived of reinforcements, in the seventh year of the siege, the Arabs finally abandoned their attack and returned to the Levant. They realized that they had too few men and not enough of the large siege engines needed to breach the Theodosian walls. Moreover, depending solely on the sea route for their supplies and reinforcements had imperilled the entire venture.

For a generation the Arabs made no new assault on the city. But early in 716, the Byzantine ambassador in Damascus returned to Constantinople with news that the Arabs were preparing an army and a fleet larger than any that had been seen before. The emperor issued orders that all the public granaries and cisterns were to be filled to capacity, the walls were to be repaired and extended, and all ships were to be put on a war footing. He anticipated a long investment of possibly three years.

In the late spring of 717 an Arab army of 80,000 men advanced from the south. Five years before, the Muslims had pushed aside the Byzantine field troops at the Cilician Gates and then occupied the land between the Taurus Mountains and Mediterranean coast. Now as they advanced north the Muslims took each well-fortified Byzantine-occupied city on their route without much difficulty, showing that their skills in siegecraft had improved markedly since their earlier assaults on Constantinople. They reached the Mediterranean coast at Pergamum and followed it north to the shores of the Hellespont in early June. At Abydos they met a flotilla of small ships from Syria which ferried the troops, their horses and camels across the mile of water to the northern shore. It was a historic spot, for here the Persian King of Kings, Xerxes, had, more than a thousand years before, made a long bridge of boats so that his armies could cross into Europe.

By the end of July 717 the Muslim general Maslama and his soldiers were encamped in a long curved line before the Theodosian walls. Each day he sent parties to probe the defences, noting where the walls were lightly manned, before launching an all-out assault in mid August. The emperor, Leo, who had concentrated the best of his troops in mobile squadrons behind the defences, managed to throw back the Arab attack. The weapon that did most to defeat the Arab assault on the walls was a recently improved form of Greek Fire. A Greek refugee from Syria had developed a new compound of quicklime, sulphur and bitumen tar, known as 'Sea Fire'. Mixed with water, the quicklime began to burn with an intense heat, igniting the mixture. Many of the warships in the Byzantine fleet were armed with special projectors for Greek Fire, but Leo had stripped some of the ships and placed their projectors at intervals along the highest ramparts. Special detachments were equipped with mobile versions of these flame-throwers. Once it was burning the liquid fire was almost impossible to extinguish, and the advancing Arab columns were simply inciner-ated, and by dusk a thick grey smoke hung over the city, filling it with the acrid smell of charred flesh.

In the following month, the balance of advantage shifted back to the Muslims. A fleet of some 1,800 small boats full of soldiers with twenty larger warships from Egypt sailed into the Sea of Marmara. Their commander, Suleiman, landed most of his troops to reinforce Maslama's besieging army, but then the whole armada sailed down towards the Bosphorus to attack the city from the seaward side. However, the Byzantine war galleys at anchor in the Golden Horn rowed out to shower the closely packed Arab vessels with Sea Fire, and loosed burning fireships upon them. Soon the narrow gap between the Asian and European shores was 'a moving forest' filled with blazing ships, each one setting the sails or cordage of its neighbours alight. Suleiman managed to rally a few of his undamaged vessels and sailed back down into the Sea of Marmara. Over the following winter, which was exceptionally cold, large numbers of the Arabs and other Easterners died of exposure, and the Arab commanders sent urgent requests to Damascus for fresh reinforcements.[29]

In the following spring the blockade tightened. More ships arrived from Alexandria and the ports of Africa. Meanwhile many of the ships damaged the previous autumn were salvaged and repaired. One night, under cover of darkness, a Muslim fleet slipped past the watching Byzantines and landed thousands of soldiers on the eastern flank of the city. But now the besiegers were themselves attacked on both sides. The Byzantines paid the Bulgar tribes in the Balkans to attack the Arabs and a horde of tribesmen suddenly massed around the Muslim camp. In a ferocious battle, the Bulgars overwhelmed the Arabs. Twenty thousand Muslims were left dead or wounded in sight of the great walls of Constantinople. Many more died from disease. On 15 August 718, Maslama reluctantly struck camp and marched back towards the Hellespont.

The two Arab sieges of 668–75 and 717–18, and the simultaneous loss to Muslim arms of the remaining Byzantine territories in North

Africa, established the 'Saracens', 'Agarenes' or 'Ishmaelites' as the most determined and diabolical enemy the Byzantines had ever faced. Byzantine scholars began to talk of the 'arrogant soul of the enemy, the sons of Ishmael', a 'race born of a slave'. The failure of the sieges, they suggested, stemmed from God's determination to save his people from 'the insatiable and utterly perverse Arabs'.[30] However, there was a long delay in mounting a full assault by Byzantine scholars on the Muslims because the second attack on the city was almost immediately followed by a civil war within Orthodox Christianity. Those who revered the holy images – *icons* – and those who thought them blasphemous (*iconoclasts*) persecuted and murdered each other for more than a century after the defender of Constantinople, Leo III, proscribed images in 725.[31] For most of that period the image-breakers were in power, and the iconoclast cause was strongly supported by the army. The effective end of the attack on images and the renewal of sustained conflict with the Muslims came more or less simultaneously. In March 843, under the leadership of Empress Theodora, who was regent for her two-year-old son, all the decrees against images were withdrawn, and long-dead iconoclasts were posthumously excommunicated.

It is not surprising that the very similar view of Islam and the now-defeated iconoclasts towards the depiction of God in human form were seen to be connected. 'Iconoclasm', as Nicolas Zernov put it, was 'the last Oriental protest within Christianity against Hellenism, which was interwoven with the tradition of the Byzantine Church. It was part of that movement towards Monotheism and simplified theology, the most powerful expression of which was Islam itself.' He also pointed out that the army supported its leaders in their campaign against images, and that most of the soldiers were recruited 'amongst Armenians, Mardaites, Isaurians and other Asiatic peoples'.[32] Muslims were simultaneously the external and the internal enemy, with their doctrines and ideology challenging what had become the key tenet of Orthodox belief. For some Orthodox scholars Muslims were simply heretics, to be classed with the Jacobites, Nestorians, Copts and other dissenters. For others, they were the prophesied Apocalyptic Beast, the flail of God and a hellish instrument of Divine Vengeance on a failing Christendom. Sometimes they would be equated with the old enemies of Byzantium, and were called 'Persians' and their ruler named 'Chosroes'. At others they would be called 'Ishmaelites', to mark their descent from the illegitimate son of Abraham, or 'Agarenes' descended from his mother, Hagar, the concubine of the patriarch. There is no clear answer why they should more generally have been called 'Saracens', that is descendants of Sarah, wife of Abraham, but the word was used to describe the inhabitants of desert Arabia, and then by extension, the Muslims.[33] One theory propagated by Saint Isidore of Seville was that these were 'Syringae' – Syrians – and Saraceni was a simple misreading. Another was that the word first related to one Arab Bedouin tribe, the Bani Sara, and later was applied to all Arabs.

Whatever the etymology, some common factors quickly attached themselves to the 'Saraceni' after the invasions of 634 in the Levant. The first Christian sources stress the Apocalyptic quality of the invasion, that this was the symbolic vengeance of God on His sinful people at a time when Christ's Second Coming was still confidently anticipated. The Armenian Bishop Sebeos, in his *History of Heraclius*, the only contemporary account of the conquest from a Christian source, said that he feared to tell the full horror of the invasion by the Ishmaelites. He called it a hot poisonous wind (*simoom*) 'burning and lethal, which blew upon us, setting alight the tall and beautiful trees of the garden, the young and burgeoning (leafy) plants of the garden'.[34] He also cited the other horrors committed, and suggested that this could be nothing other than the Fourth Beast of the Apocalypse 'like a flying eagle', and which unlike the other beasts, never rested day or night, 'saying "Holy, holy, holy Lord God Almighty, which was, and is, and is to come."'[35]

Sebeos elaborated his description of the Beast. It was

terrible, wondrous, with teeth of iron, talons of copper, which devoured and crushed and trampled . . . It came from great and limitless desert where once Moses and the Children of Israel lived, according to the word of the prophet, that is to say from a vast and terrible desert, whence the tempest of the nations arose and filled the earth, conquered the earth and trampled it down. And thus it was accomplished: the fourth beast will be the fourth kingdom on the earth, that will be most disastrous of all kingdoms, that will transform the entire earth into a desert.[36]

However, the Beast was doing the work of God although it was itself an instrument of evil. In the vision of Saint John the Divine, the Fourth Beast was Death: 'I looked and beheld a pale horse, and his name that sat upon him was Death, and Hell followed with him. And power was given unto him over the fourth part of the earth, to kill with sword, and with hunger, and with death . . .' What followed from the coming of the Four Horsemen of the Apocalypse, on horses white, red, black and the last pale as Death, was the fulfilment of God's prophecy: 'For the great day of his wrath is come, and who shall be able to stand it?'[37] The inevitable killings and destruction that accompanied the conquest were attested by many sources. In the written record they fulfilled a prophetic vision of Christianity. This instrument of devastation was the bastard line of Abraham: protected by God and yet at an infinite distance from the love of Christ. The metaphoric vocabulary of violence and horror created from those initial contacts carried through into many accounts. Yet as with so much prophetic utterance, the terms were unstable. Sebeos was interpreting events in terms of what *needed* to take place so as to fulfil the word and will of God. The Muslims were a necessary evil.[38]

Byzantine writers from the seventh century onwards presented Islam as a mortal danger facing the Christians, greater than Persia had ever been. At the end of his history, after recounting the first assault on Constantinople, Sebeos catalogued the threat that Islam posed: 'For just as arrows fly from the well-curved bow of a strong man toward the target, so are the Arabs who come from the Sinai desert to destroy the entire world with hunger, the sword, and great terror.'[39]

Muslims were characterized in the same negative terms in the western Catholic polemics as they had been in the East.[40] There too they were the quintessence of evil, even the Antichrist himself, but also a necessary instrument of Divine wrath and judgement upon His sinful people. Over time new forms of condemnation proliferated, but they were all raised upon a framework initially elaborated within a few decades of first contact. From this point, 'Islam' was assimilated to existing examples of evil and ruin in the Old and New Testaments. These primordial ascriptions were repeated in later scholarly discourse and went unchallenged for centuries. They also leaked out beyond the community of scholars into the minds – or mouths – of ordinary people. Thereafter the words of the scholars acquired new meanings, but this process was resisted. Alcuin, the most renowned Anglo-Saxon scholar of the eighth century and founder of the academy in Charlemagne's palace at Aachen, wrote: 'Those people should not be listened to who say that the voice of the people is the voice of God, since the riotous tumult of the crowd is always very close to madness.'[41] How ideas embodied in a few scholarly works were implanted within a much larger (and illiterate) population is still under debate.

Communicating ideas of the Muslim infidel depended on the way that language functions.[42] There are many theories of how language works, but in the 1950s the French psychoanalyst Jacques Lacan provided a useful explanation of how language bears the traces of its use. He took the model first articulated by the father of linguistics, Ferdinand de Saussure, and refined it to fit what he saw as the reality of human relationships. Saussure had defined communication as a pure and comprehensive system of signs, with each sign consisting of two elements.[43] The first was what was described, or 'signified', from the French *signifié*. The second element was the 'signifier', the means by which its meaning was communicated, by spoken sound or by visible marks, such as writing.

Communication would be impossible if there were no common understanding about how signifier and signified were linked. The same object has to be named in the same way. But as a psychologist, Lacan saw among his patients that in practice no one-to-one relationship existed between the two elements. They were already part of a chain of mental connections, and carried internally the residue of those connections. Applied to curses and imprecations, Lacan's theory of linguistic practice means that any insult has to be contextualized, because it carries inside it imperceptible traces of similar insults that have gone before. In the case of Christianity and Islam that context would encompass a history extending back over many centuries. If we accept this notion, then very few statements within that history can safely be taken at face value. Their meaning derives in part from the extended skein of fear and hatred. We lack the information in the patchy early records to see the full implications of this idea. But, stepping outside the chronological flow for a moment, there is an instance from the second half of the nineteenth century that suggests how hostility can fabricate and sustain such a tissue of meaning.

This example appears in the British consular records for June 1860, at a time when there were savage attacks on Christians in the Levant, which will figure again later in this book. The British Government asked its consuls in the Ottoman Empire to write a short overall impression of how Christians were living under a Muslim government. The various officials interpreted their open-ended instructions in different ways. Consul Blunt at Pristina in the Balkans remarked that Christians were 'decidedly' better off than they had been ten years before. In those days 'one can judge the measure of Turkish toleration practised at that time by having had to creep under doors scarcely four feet high'.[44] The inference here was unambiguous. The Turks compelled Christians to make their church doors so low that worshippers had to bend to enter and, hence, to humiliate themselves. But as I read this, I wondered whether this seasoned consular official was interpreting the situation correctly. There was another explanation for these low doors that I had picked up elsewhere. This suggested that it was the Christians themselves who deliberately made their church doors low, so that Muslims would be prevented from riding mules into their churches and the animals fouling the floors. Both versions of the story certainly demonstrate oppression – but the tales follow different paths.

However I also questioned how reliable either interpretation was as evidence of general oppression. Mary Eliza Rogers lived in Palestine during the 1850s. She described many Christian churches in great detail, but never referred to these architectural symbols of oppression, nor once alluded to Christians bending double to enter their places of worship. Were there other interpretations that did not signify oppression? In Christian Europe, church doors came in all shapes and sizes. Large and heavy doors often contain a smaller portal that is used daily, while the great doors are thrown open only on holy days and festivals. Many European churches also have small and narrow secondary entrances. So which interpretation is correct? Was it official tyranny, designed to humiliate Christians? Was it a Christian response to a distasteful problem? Or could it have been only a rhetorical device, a metaphor presented in the guise of fact, a graphic means to express the quality of 'Turkish toleration'? We cannot know. Perhaps the consul just wanted a convenient emblem of oppression for the 'bad old days' of the 1840s.

However, there is one specific door that might have been the archetype for these stories. The Church of the Nativity in Bethlehem, built by Justinian in 529, originally had three great doors in its western façade. But the history of the building reveals how it changed over the centuries:

The main access to the Basilica is by the very small Door of Humility (78 cm in width and 130 cm in height, 2.3 by 4.3 feet). Visitors must enter bending over, as if to a real cave. Originally the church had three entrances, two of which have been bricked up. They are hidden respectively by a buttress built later (after the 16th century) and by the Armenian buildings. The central and highest portal of Justinian's church door was reshaped by the Crusaders. This resulted in a pointed arch which is still visible today with the cornice of the Justinian entrance which can be seen above. The present small entrance was made during the Ottoman era to prevent mounted horsemen from entering the Basilica.[45]

All the modern accounts repeat this story, with the Ottomans stabling their horses on the holy ground.[46] But there the trail peters out. There is no agreement as to precisely when or why this sacrilege happened. Moreover, there is no sense that other sites of equal importance, such as the Holy Sepulchre in Jerusalem, were subjected to the same treatment. So which story is right: horses or humiliation? Or was the door in Bethlehem reduced in size for structural reasons, which might account for the changes made in the era of the Crusaders? Certainly, the low portal made no symbolic impression on Mary Rogers when she visited the Church of the Nativity. 'We passed under a deep arched way' was the matter-of-fact way she described her entry through the Door of Humility.[47]

These tales, and others like them, should always, I suggest, be interpreted with care. Undoubtedly, over the centuries, linking 'Islam's rule' with the image of a low and narrow church portal generated ideas of Christian humiliation. This, Westerners were expected to infer, was how Muslims always behaved towards Christians. Yet changing the context alters the meaning. The same narrow door, in a Christian land, would have a quite different significance. Then it might become a metaphor for the path to salvation, recalling the words of Christ, 'Because strait is the gate, and narrow is the way, which leadeth unto life, and few there be that find it.'[48]

This paradox reminded me of Lacan's graphic example of how meaning was created, conveyed and perceived. He first drew two identical doors side by side. Neither had any special significance until he wrote the word *Men* above one and *Women* above the other. Then the reader understood. Each portal now suggested what happened behind them, unleashing a whole cascade of connections. Lacan's point was that there was nothing in the words *Men* and *Women* alone, nor in the image of the doors by themselves. But their juxtaposition, and the words inscribed, immediately made a clear cultural connection with sexual differentiation, with urination and with defecation.[49] So, he suggested, the particular meaning of these doors was determined by context. Many of the European stories concerning 'Islam' were constructed in this way, like Consul Blunt's interpretation of the low threshold in Pristina. The dominant Western paradigms of 'Islam' – oppression, savagery and threat – determined how events, structures, and images were to be understood.

PART TWO

3

Al-Andalus

The passage into Spain was easy from the Moroccan shore. A narrow body of water, then open beaches gave way to sand and scrub, then to low hills. To the west, the sluggish River Guadalquivir (from the Arabic *Wad el-Kebir*, the big valley) flowed into the sea at the little port of Sanlucar de Barrameda, where Christopher Columbus would gather his ships in 1492. Upstream lay Seville and Cordoba, the greatest cities of the south. Beyond these were fertile rolling fields until the wooded slopes of the Sierra Morena rose to cut off the lands of the south, which Spaniards still call the frying pan of Spain, from the high cold plateau of central Spain. Only to the east, on the road to Granada and the Sierra Nevada, were there mountains to compare with the Atlas and the Ante-Atlas ranges of North Africa. Even in Granada, the high peaks of the Sierra Nevada rose behind the level fields of the Vega, which was like a verdant carpet rolled out before the city. The pioneering nineteenth-century traveller Richard Ford would catch its character, describing 'the eternal rampart of the lovely Vega . . . The clear mother of pearl outline cuts the blue sky.'[1]

For North Africans, accustomed to Morocco and Algeria, and the deserts beyond, this was an easy land. Give it water and it flourishes, abundantly. Contrast this home of plenty with the approach into Spain from the north across the Pyrenees. There were few passes through the mountains and none were easy, except where the high peaks diminished towards the Atlantic. Spain below the Pyrenean barrier was rugged and mountainous, and the great rivers, crossing the terrain from east to west, provided a further set of obstacles. The sixteenth-century English traveller James Howell observed that 'About a third part of the continent of Spain is made up of huge craggy hills and mountains, amongst which one can feel in some places more difference in point of temper of heat and cold in the air than twixt winter and summer under other Climes.'[2]

From a northern European perspective, Spain was simply a distant southern extremity, separated from the rest of the continent by the Pyrenean massif. For Spaniards, the mountains have traditionally been their salvation. A folk legend of unknown origin held that when the Devil offered to cede his Dominion over all the Earth to Jesus Christ, Spain was forgotten, concealed from his evil view by the great peaks. Spain possessed four borders: the land frontier with Europe, a coastline on the Atlantic, a long Mediterranean shoreline and, across a narrow strip of water, Africa. The Muslim Conquest of Spain was perhaps inevitable from the day in 681 that an Arab general, Uqba bin Nafi, stood on the shores of the Atlantic, close to the modern town of Agadir. The traditional account of this expedition had the Muslim commander riding into the water up to his horse's withers, gesturing with his sword towards the empty ocean, and crying, 'God is great. If my course were not stopped by this sea, I would still ride on to the unknown kingdoms of the west, preaching the unity of God, and putting to the sword the rebellious nations who worship any other god but Him.'[3] While the western ocean posed a barrier to the advance of Islam, the narrow strait between Africa and Europe was inconsequential. Ships constantly criss-crossed between the harbours of North Africa and the ports of southern Spain. The richness and abundance of Spain proved an irresistible lure.[4] Thus in the same decade, 710–20, that the Muslim armies encamped before Constantinople for the second time and were defeated, in the West their co-religionists were victorious beyond their wildest imagining. We know the outcome – the seizure of almost all the land from the southern Spanish shore to the Pyrenees (and beyond) – but the process of conquest remains shrouded in mystery. As in the East, the first contact of Muslims and Christians did not attract a chronicler until decades after the event.[5]

Some facts are undisputed. In 710, an advance party of Berber soldiers was ferried in four small ships across the ten miles of water to an island called Las Palomas, just off the Spanish coast, close to modern Tarifa.[6] The commander, Tarif ibn Malik, had only 400 infantrymen and 100 horsemen. They were lightly armed, carried only a minimum of food and water, and no heavy equipment. Nonetheless, meeting with virtually no resistance, they soon filled their ships with a huge amount of plunder. Tarif's sortie indicated that a raid in strength on the Spanish mainland would yield rich pickings. In the following year, his superior commander in Tangier, Tariq ibn Zayid, mounted a larger expedition. He sailed from the African shore early in April, and landed his 7,000 men under cover of darkness beneath the mountain that now bears his name, Gibraltar (*Jebel* Tariq, the mountain of Tariq). In the morning, they marched over the sandy strip separating the rocky peak from the mainland and occupied a wide circle of land beyond the small town now called Algeciras.

This was little different from any of the other speculative expeditions that had characterized the Arab Conquest. In the early eighth century, Spain was ruled by a Visigothic dynasty, and although the sources are scanty, we know that the King of Spain, Roderick, quickly came south with a large army to repel the invaders. He was killed in battle not far from the point where the Muslims had landed, close to the old Roman town of Asida Caesarina. The Visigothic army melted away. After the battle there was almost no organized resistance, and Tariq, who commanded little more than 7,000 men, sent a small detachment under a trusted tribesman called Mugith al-Rumi to take Cordoba. When the band arrived on the bank of the River Guadalquivir opposite the city, they learned from a shepherd that the Visigoths had abandoned Cordoba, except for a few hundred men. Al-Rumi also discovered that there was a gap in the defences. By night he smuggled in a handful of men, who opened the gate to the old Roman bridge. In the early morning his few soldiers took the city.

Meanwhile Tariq pressed north with all speed towards the Visigothic capital at Toledo. He was joined by his senior commander Musa ibn Nasir, with much-needed reinforcements. When they reached the walls, they found the gates open and the city virtually empty. The occupation of Spain north of Toledo that followed in subsequent years met with very little more opposition than this first advance. One or two towns resisted and were sacked, but as in the Levant, the Muslim Conquest seemed completely irresistible. However, at the time the loss of Spain seemed even less explicable than the loss of the East. The earliest Christian account of the fall of Spain, written about 754, put the loss into a biblical framework, much as the patriarch had done in Jerusalem a century before.[7] The Christian chronicler also declared Tariq's overlord, Musa, to be 'altogether pitiless', who 'burned fair cities, sentenced noble and leading men of the time to be tortured, and had children and nursing mothers beaten to death'. But once he had 'filled everyone with such terror, some cities which remained soon sued for peace, and he, with blandishments and mockery and guile, granted these wishes'. For the most part, such agreements were fulfilled. Christian overlordship was quickly and easily replaced by Muslim power.

Over time both Christian and Muslim accounts of this event became tales replete with prophetic utterance, spiced with suggestions of lust and betrayal. The myths provided an explanation of how it was that Tariq, with no more than a few thousand men at his disposal, could have defeated 'all the Christian fighting men of Spain', numbered by some at 100,000. Why had God turned against his people?[8] The answer was found in moral depravity that had occasioned Divine wrath. The easy victory of the Berbers and their Arab commanders was partly put down by Christian writers to malign fate. But God had abandoned His people because the Visigothic rulers' moral failures had brought them low. The theme of mordant lust leading to betrayal permeated the account. 'In the royal court in Seville, they began to talk, among other things, about the beauty of women. One of those present intervened to say that no woman in the whole world was more lovely than the daughter of Count Julian [a shadowy character, supposedly the commander of Ceuta, a Byzantine enclave in North Africa].' On hearing this, the king asked his chief advisor how he 'might secretly send a messenger to her so he might see her'. This man advised, 'Send for Julian to come here and spend some days with him eating and drinking.' While Julian was being entertained, the king wrote a letter in Count Julian's name, accompanied by the count's personal seal ring, commanding the countess to come to court with her daughter Oliva. When they arrived the king seduced Oliva and 'illicitly had intercourse with the girl over several days'.[9]

The story of the Visigothic king echoed the biblical King David brought low by his passion for Bathsheba.[10] The downfall of David in the second book of Samuel began with a prophecy: 'The sword shall never depart from thy house; because thou hast despised me and taken the wife of Uriah the Hittite to be thy wife.' The Hebrew king's lust brought down punishment upon himself and upon his people. In Spain, all the participants in the catastrophe were equally deep in sin. But the sins of the Christians had allowed an even greater evil – the Muslim invasion – to triumph. The conquest became an elaborate legend.

Spain . . . Her songs were forgotten and her language is changed into foreign and strange words. The Moors of the host wore silks and colourful cloths which they had taken as booty, their horses' reins were like fire, their faces were as black as pitch, the handsomest among them was as black as the cooking-pot, and their eyes blazed like fire; their horses were as swift as leopards, their horsemen more cruel and hurtful than the wolf that comes by night to the flock of sheep.[11]

The chronicler's commination grew more intense and dramatic as he warmed to his task. This physical, moral and intellectual obliteration of a whole nation, he declared, grew from the inherent evil of Islam. The chronicler was specific: no depravity was beyond these enemies of Christ.[12]

This was also a history confected to provide a pedigree for the future monarchs of Christian Spain.[13] Within these narratives the inborn depravity of the Moors elided with the moral failures of the Visigoths, and they become as one. King Roderick was no longer a true Christian, but became like a Moor in his uncontrollable lust.[14] The supreme villain was Bishop Oppa, of the tainted royal line. Oppa had allied himself with the infidels, and sought to persuade a Christian hero leading a small band of patriots – King Pelayo – to submit to the Islamic horde. In the *Chronicle of Alfonso III of the Asturias*, written in the late ninth century, Oppa came to Pelayo in an icy cave at Cova-donga, high in the north-western mountains. The bishop tried to persuade him to yield. To this Pelayo replied scornfully.

'Have you not read in holy scripture that the church of God can become as small as a grain of mustard and can then, by the grace of God, be made to grow again larger?' The bishop answered: 'It is so written.' Pelayo said: 'Christ is our hope, that by this tiny hillock which you see, Spain may be saved and the army of the Gothic people restored. I trust therefore that the promise of the Lord may be fulfilled in us as it was announced through David . . . In the battle with which you have threatened us, we have our Lord Jesus Christ as our advocate before the Father, and He is powerful enough to save us few from them.'[15]

Pelayo's contempt for the offer, his noble resistance, and his ultimate triumph led directly to the foundation of the Kingdom of the Asturias, and thence to the Royal House of Castile. In this dreamworld of good and evil, Castile exemplified the true heritage of the 'good' Visigoths. Roderick and Oppa shared the same blood, but they had lost their inherited virtue and honour through their depravity. They had become crypto-Moors. It was the Kings of Castile who carried the honourable heritage of the Visigoths in their veins and it was invariably the Moors or Arabs who were the agency of evil. There were Muslims in these histories who behaved honourably, but these exceptions were used to throw Christian wickedness into a starker relief.

Often these connections between the mythic past and the domain of history are mere conjecture. But in the case of Bishop Oppa we know the popular resonance of the myth. Centuries after the conquest, in 1465, during a civil war in Castile, King Enrique IV was symbolically deposed at Avila by a group of dissident nobles. An effigy of the king was sat upon a chair. The act of deposition had been carried out by Archbishop Carrillo, who took the crown from the head of the king's effigy; another noble took away the sword from its hand; and a third knocked the effigy headlong from the mock throne.[16] The news of this event spread quickly throughout Castile. A few months later Enrique's own soldiers were besieging the fortress of Simancas, and they put on a pageant to lampoon the events at Avila. But they did not give Carrillo his own name and title, but rather called him Oppa, eliding him with the arch-traitor to Pelayo more than seven centuries before.[17] By this analogy they made clear the depth of Carrillo's treachery.

The running thread of evil in these narratives, sometimes on the surface but as often below, was the Moors. They were the trial and test set by God for His people, and they would be destroyed only by a virtuous and godly Christian king, a new Pelayo.[18] Like the Jews who were often seen as their surrogates and accessories, as they had been in the accounts of the fall of Jerusalem, the essence of Islam was evil incarnate. God used the Moors like a heavy flail to beat His people back to virtue.

We need to set the reality of Muslim Spain against this artfully contrived Castilian propaganda. For almost 500 years – from roughly 720 to 1200 – Muslims dominated most of the Iberian peninsula. They called it 'Al-Andalus', the land of the Vandals, and their numbers were reinforced at intervals by new waves of conquest from North Africa. But the Muslim conquerors were few in number – no more than 20,000 in the first waves – and thereafter provided only a thin veneer, rather like the Visigothic ruling class, set atop a large Catholic Christian population. But this Muslim layer was itself divided, between Berbers and Arabs. The Berbers were the native inhabitants of the mountain regions of North Africa, whose stubborn resistance had held up the Arab armies advancing from the East. The Berbers' conversion to Islam was very recent, and many of their pre-Islamic customs were carried forward into their new faith. The Arabs, who traced their connections back to the ancient tribes of the Arabian peninsula, looked down upon the Berbers. It was no accident that the best land and the richest cities in Spain were allocated to Arabs, while the mountain zones and the poorest land were peopled by the Berber clans. This division, although obscured by the outward success of the Muslim governing institutions, was a constant and destabilizing force within the Islamic culture of Spain.

Islamic Spain appeared a strong and unified power, but this was only partly true. There were many fracture lines within the structure. Some were tribal, for the Arabs were always prone to quarrelling among themselves. The Berbers were restive and often rebelled against Arab pretensions. And as soon as central authority diminished, the political units fragmented. Thus over those five centuries there were only three periods of enforced unity and each was of relatively limited duration. The first was under the Emirate, which became the Caliphate of Cordoba in the tenth century. The second and third periods were under the domination of the Moroccan dynasties of the Almorávides and the Almohades during the eleventh and twelfth centuries.[19] But these episodes were surrounded by long years of disunity and civil war. In this the Muslim state resembled the Christian kingdoms to the north, which were as prone to fighting against each other as against their putative common enemy.

Although the Muslim states called the entire peninsula 'Al-Andalus', the northern rivers Ebro and Duero soon formed the effective dividing line between Christian and Islamic rule. Faced with the impetuous advance of the Muslims, Pelayo's small independent Christian statelet survived in the high mountains of north-west Spain. Myth traced an unbroken tradition of Christian rule from these Asturian mountains, where, as Edward Gibbon put it, 'A vital spark was still alive; some invincible fugitives preferred a life of poverty and freedom in the Asturian valleys; the hardy mountaineers repulsed the slaves of the caliph.'[20] In reality, the Arab columns had been more concerned to push forward across the Pyrenees into France than fight in the mountains. By 717, the Arabs were well established around the city of Narbonne, which they captured in 719. From their southern base, they sent out large-scale raids ever deeper into France until, at the battle of Tours in 732, a Muslim raiding army from Spain was thrown back by the Franks led by Charles Martel.[21] In the history of France this event loomed large: 'The men of the north stood as motionless as a wall; they were like a belt of ice frozen together, and not to be dissolved, as they slew the Arabs with the sword.'[22] The victory over Islam at Tours became in Western eyes an archetypal triumph, charged like the battle of Las Navas de Tolosa in 1212 or Lepanto in 1571 with a deep symbolic meaning. But, in reality, although these northern raids continued for some years after the conquest, the Muslims were content to consolidate their rule further south. Much of the terrain north of the river line was barren and unproductive. It quickly became a no man's land, dotted with towns and castles – some owing notional allegiance to a Christian king, others to the emir or caliph in Cordoba.

In these northern Spanish lands, the small nucleus in the Asturian mountains expanded westwards to become the Kingdom of Leon, with its capital at Oviedo. The border between Leon and the Muslim south was nicknamed 'the land of the castles' – Castile – because it was an area where towers and fortresses populated the landscape. Eventually Castile became larger and more powerful than its parent Leon. To the east of Castile was the Kingdom of Aragon, which began in the foothills of the Pyrenees and slowly expanded south and east towards the Mediterranean. There it confronted the Frankish

County of Barcelona and the border Muslim Kingdom of Valencia. Over time these were incorporated in the patrimony of Aragon. By the mid fourteenth century, Christian Spain consisted of five kingdoms: Portugal in the west; Leon–Castile straddling the centre; the tiny Kingdom of Navarre (in part north of the Pyrenees and in part south); Aragon, including Catalonia; and formerly Muslim Valencia (conquered by King James I of Aragon in 1238), which occupied most of the Mediterranean littoral.

The cities and the most productive terrain were in the south and held by the Muslims: Cordoba and later Seville in the flat, fertile land around the River Guadalquivir, Granada with its Vega, growing almost every type of fruit, and the rich orchards and gardens (*huerta*) around Valencia, described by one writer as paradise.[23] The Christian writers also praised their own lands as paradise, but with much less reason, for they possessed little of the superabundance of the Muslim south. Where Nature required assistance, the southerners created elaborate systems of irrigation, much like those found in Syria or Egypt. Sun and flowing water made southern Spain one of the best agricultural areas of the known world. The focus of this wealth was the capital city, Cordoba, although all the urban centres, from Saragossa in the north, through Toledo in the heart of the peninsula, to the cities of the east and south, were filled with new buildings and rich possessions.

Much of this 'Moorish' or Islamic building was created by Christians living under Muslim rule who were known as *Mozarabes*, meaning 'arabized'. In the first century of the conquest they formed a large majority in the Muslim cities, and in some parts of the countryside. Thus the population of Al-Andalus in the ninth century had four main elements: the Muslim conquerors, Arab or Berber; the Christian Mozarabes; and the Jews. The Mozarabes were descendants of the inhabitants of Roman Spain and the Visigoth invaders who had crossed the Pyrenees in the fifth century. When the Jews first came to Spain is shrouded in mystery. Some claimed that they first arrived at the time of Babylonian captivity in the sixth century BC, others that they had migrated west after the Roman destruction of Jerusalem in 70 AD. The first physical evidence of their presence is a Jewish woman's tomb at Adra from the third century. The Jewish population suffered severe persecution under the Visigothic kings, so the Muslim Conquest represented a release from oppression.

For the most part, apart from the occasional outburst of mutual antagonism, all managed to live side by side. Over the first three centuries of Islamic rule, many Christians converted to Islam and the cultures acquired characteristics in common, while still maintaining their distinct and separate identities.[24] As in the Levant, where the Arab Christians became outwardly indistinguishable from the larger Muslim population, so too in Al-Andalus the superficial differences between the different groups diminished. Mozarabes and Jews often adopted Arabic, while the Berbers also abandoned their native dialects for it (apparently, though, retaining a Berber accent).[25] Yet the communities remained distinct: they preserved their customs and observed their own laws.[26] This was the unique and paradoxical Spanish accommodation to which Américo Castro later gave the name *convivencia*, 'living together'.

Many of the varying interrelationships between Islam and Christendom (as well as Judaism) that played out later elsewhere first appeared in Spain. Yet, because of the peninsula's isolation below the Pyrenees, much of this experience has gone largely unnoticed. However, if we read the experience of Spain against the experience of the Balkans or the Levant, connections, parallels and analogies begin to surface. Throughout the long history of Al-Andalus, there was a consistent quality that Ron Barkai has called the 'enemy in the mirror'.[27] For more than 300 years Andalusi Muslims lived with Christians and Jews in their midst.[28] Then during the Moroccan reconquest of Spain under the militantly Islamic Almorávides and Almohades tribesmen, in the eleventh and twelfth centuries, the Christian and Jewish elements in Muslim Spain diminished rapidly. Andalusi Christians either converted to Islam, or were forced to migrate north to the Christian lands.[29] During those centuries the model for living together worked well, except for those who wished to accentuate religious differences. But by the thirteenth century, when the principal Christian kingdom, Castile, pushed south to Cordoba, conquering the bulk of the once-Muslim states, *convivencia* was already moribund, or in many areas of Andalusia had ceased altogether. When the Christians returned to the south, they came as rulers, as the dominant rather than subordinate group. Granada to the east became the last wholly Muslim kingdom in Spain, and a refuge for all Muslims who did not wish to live under a Christian ruler. It quickly extinguished most of the traits of *convivencia*. But only in the fifteenth and sixteenth centuries did a triumphalist Christian Spain move steadily towards expunging the non-Christian elements in her population.[30]

Nonetheless, regardless of Muslim or Christian dominance, the medieval peninsula comprised more than one culture. The fact of three communities, literate and cultivated, existing side by side within the same state was an accident of conquest, and caused infinite problems for both Islamic and Christian scholars, who consistently postulated an unbridgeable gulf between the two worlds. A late fifteenth-century Muslim scholar from North Africa, al-Wansharishi, described the dangers his co-religionists in Spain faced living in a Christian land among unbelievers:

One has to beware of the pervasive effect of their way of life, their language, their dress, their objectionable habits, and influence on people living with them over a long period of time, as has occurred with the people of Avila and other places. They have lost their Arabic, and when the Arabic language dies out, so does devotion in it and there is consequential neglect of worship as expressed in words in all its richness and outstanding virtues . . . Living with unbelievers is not permissible, not so much as for one hour a day, because of all the dirt and filth involved, and the religious as well as secular corruption, which continues all the time.[31]

Christian scholars expressed similar disgust for Muslims. If so much antagonism was expressed in both directions, how did *convivencia* once exist (and flourish) over so many centuries and, by extension, what caused it to end?

For Muslims and Christians alike the experience of living in close proximity to unbelievers was disquieting. The social customs of each group invariably sought to minimize contact with the people of other faiths. Each often spoke of the other in terms of fear and sometimes disgust. The regulations in twelfth-century Seville, under the influence of the austere North African Almorávides, stated that Muslim women

shall be prevented from entering their abominable churches, for the priests are evil-doers, fornicators, and sodomites. Frankish women must be forbidden to enter the church except on days of religious services or festivals, for it is their habit to eat and drink and fornicate with the priests, among whom there is not one who has not two or more women with whom he sleeps. This has become a custom among them, for they have permitted what is forbidden and forbidden what is permitted.[32]

While Christians and Jews might be tolerated in Muslim lands, they were nonetheless to be shunned. The same regulations expressly stated that 'a Muslim must not massage a Jew or a Christian nor throw away his refuse nor clean his latrines. The Jew and the Christian are better fitted for such trades, since they are the trades of those who are vile.' Moreover, 'a garment belonging to a sick man [probably a leper], a Jew or a Christian must not be sold without indicating its origin; likewise the garment of a debauchee.'[33] The reason for this restriction, as with all the others, was practical. All these contacts could cause defilement, all these physical encounters could cross the limit between what was permitted and what was forbidden.

Fears grew out of proximity, but not necessarily from direct experience. Fornicating priests (and Ibn Abdun who wrote the Seville regulations improbably insisted that *all* priests were fornicators) were a metaphor of what would happen when the social boundaries were breached, becoming a threat to Muslim and Christian women alike. Or worse still, a danger to the social order in general, for Muslim, Jewish and Christian men all regarded women as a point of weakness and a source of peril. As the anthropologist Mary Douglas, writing of the proscriptions in the Jewish Pentateuch, observed

Defilement is never an isolated event. It cannot occur except in view of a systematic ordering of ideas. Hence any piecemeal interpretation of the pollution rules of another culture is bound to fail. For the only way in which pollution ideas make sense is in reference to a total structure, whose keystone, boundaries, margins and internal lines are held in relation by rituals of separation.[34]

In this structure, religious designations – Jew, Muslim, Christian – delineated the boundaries. Without effective separation there was an uncontrollable risk to communal stability. Without prohibition there was a fear among Muslims, Christians and Jews alike that the pollution barrier would be crossed. As in many societies, sexual transgression was both the most emotively charged and also the most immediate danger. The Muslim men of the law (*ulema*) observed the weakness of their own gender when confronted by women, and blamed women for the temptation. The desire for separation was found in each community, which saw the others as potentially dangerous. Yet the desire to keep apart was not necessarily an actively antagonistic or hostile attitude. The communities belonged to distinct and separate castes. The word 'caste' is nowadays associated with Indian Hinduism. It was taken by the Portuguese to India in the sixteenth century and they used it to communicate – imperfectly – the complex social structure that they found there. But in the Iberian languages the word means 'bloodline' or 'clan': sharing a common connection but also displaying profound differences. The pioneering Spanish philologist Ramón Menéndez Pidal, in his early twentieth-century study of the development of the Spanish language, found that the concept provided a useful analogy to describe the many different elements which made up the linguistic culture of Iberia. Often nothing linked them in terms of ethnicity, but he saw them as separate 'castes' within a common cultural framework, inter-connected but also separate.[35] This accords with more modern definitions of 'caste': a form of social division based solely on lineage that totally constrains a person's way of life.[36] For all these reasons, I have adopted the usage here.

We cannot be entirely sure how Muslims, Christians and Jews regarded each other. Certainly, statements of enmity predominated, but these may not represent the reality of everyday life.[37] But all the evidence suggests that even when there was no active antagonism the communities wanted to remain separate. Moreover, what David Nirenberg calls the 'background static' of violence 'never receded from practical consciousness. It influenced the daily actions and strategies of minority and majority alike: what clothes to wear, what route to take to work, how to accuse an enemy of a crime – the list is endless.'[38] The negative views each group held about the others were often reciprocal. Muslims believed viscerally in the other castes' unbridled sexuality.[39] Christians believed the same about Jewish and Muslim sexuality. In the last of the *Siete Partidas*, the Castilian law code of the early fourteenth century, the jurists consider the case of Jewish men who have intercourse with a Christian woman: 'Jews who live with Christian women are guilty of great insolence and boldness, for which reason we decree that all Jews who, hereafter, may be convicted of having done such a thing shall be put to death.'[40] The Muslims were subject to the same penalties. In all medieval societies sexual transgressions were considered subversive of the entire social order. An English edict of 1417 declared that 'the illicit works of their lewd flesh [is] to the great abomination and displeasure of God'.[41] But for Christian, Jew and Muslim alike, sexual acts across the boundaries of caste were a higher order of wickedness, akin to sodomy. Peter Damian's castigation of sodomitical acts in his *Liber Gomorrhianus* (*c.* 1050) conveys an attitude applicable to both manifestations of illicit carnality: 'It pollutes the flesh; it extinguishes the light of the mind . . . it is this which violates sobriety, kills modesty, strangles chastity and butchers irreparable virginity with the dagger of unclean contagion. It defiles everything, staining everything, polluting everything . . . it permits nothing pure, nothing clean, nothing other than filth.'[42]

An infinity of traps and entanglements lay at the heart of *convivencia*. Sexual temptations across the caste boundaries were the most dangerous and contaminating. However, we should read the law codes and prohibitions less as a representation of what actually happened, and more as an effort to prevent the dangers of uncontrolled proximity. Islam never prohibited marriage between Muslim men and women of the other castes, while concubines or slaves were used sexually by men without regard to their faith. By law the children of Muslim men were supposed to follow the faith of their father. But the realities of human life, in the past as in the present, did not always correlate with the prescriptions of the law. All those instances that I have cited are from a period when the very concept of a mixed society had come to seem dangerous in the extreme, and these crimes were, I suspect, as much metaphors of the risks implicit in godless mixing as a serious attempt to prohibit actual conduct.[43] In the minds of the pure in spirit only an absolute separation or isolation of Christian, Jew and Muslim could achieve what they sought to accomplish by writ and the threat of punishment.

The topography of the city, town or village in Al-Andalus was divided along invisible lines. Each community had its own zone, which outsiders might enter at their peril. Equally, through a fragile social consensus, other areas would be common ground: these might be a market place, a road, places where water was drawn or where clothes were washed.[44] In Islamic Spain, the tribal element was added to the presence of the non-Muslim castes, and that too could provoke violence. There was a word in Arabic, *nefra'a*, to describe the 'sudden panicky "snapping"' that breaks the peace of the *suq*.[45] *Convivencia* could continue only so long as the physical or cultural barriers were not breached.[46] Then there were also episodes of heightened religious or social tension, in which the sense of division between Christians, Jews and Muslims was accentuated. But the daily practice of life was closer to what Américo Castro described as 'integralism'.[47] In defining 'integralism' Castro fell back on cultural stereotypes for both Christians and Muslims.[48] 'The Moslem feels himself in things, the Hispano Christian feels things in himself, in his person.' For Castro, Muslims were poets and dreamers, Christians were activists: 'The Spaniard speaks of himself, of his body, of his pleasures, and of his afflictions. Everything is justified and takes on value the moment it is referred to his person.'[49] He found it hard to define how these two opposites interacted. But applied to these shared communities of Al-Andalus, with their endless internal boundaries and barriers which criss-crossed and intersected with each other, the idea of integralism makes sense. Cordoba or Seville, with its hundreds of districts and quarters, was a patchwork.

Arab, Berber, Christian and Jewish zones were juxtaposed, their boundaries partly permeable and partly not.[50] Linguistically certainly, and to a degree culturally, the various peoples of the cities were integral in the limited sense defined by Castro, but they also remained separate and isolated within their separate groups. Religion was often not the sole determinant: Arabs and Berbers, both Muslim, remained apart in their clans, and frequently fought each other. Christians and Jews stayed within the bounds allocated to them by the laws of Islam, but even within their communities there were distinct gradations of wealth and status.

The success of *convivencia* depended on this segmentation, on a settled social structure that permitted multiplicity. However, no effective Grand Theory has emerged from the long history of Al-Andalus after 711, and to talk of *convivencia* as a fixed and settled entity, as Castro did, is a mistake. It was a structure of concession in which there was a dramatic imbalance of power between the majority and the minorities. When that balance changed, then the former basis for co-existence vanished. In reality, the terms were constantly shifting in the equation between the minority and majority populations.

But it is also true that, with the qualifiers I have already indicated, first Islamic and then Christian states in the peninsula successfully accommodated minority populations. For the first three centuries, Christians co-existed with Muslims in Al-Andalus, and for the second three centuries, the Christian states of the north came to pragmatic arrangements with their Muslim minorities. However, there were two periods of great stress in which compromise was deliberately abrogated. One relates to Christians under challenge as a minority within an Islamic state, and the other to an embattled Muslim community within a Christian state. The first took place in the ninth century in Muslim Cordoba, where Christians deliberately sought martyrdom to redeem their early failure to resist Islam. The second was in Christian Spain throughout the sixteenth century, with its first epicentre in the old kingdom of Granada. Here the victorious Christians decreed a radical policy of mass conversion. It ended with the ethnic cleansing of all the descendants of the 'Moors'. The first episode – the Martyrs of Cordoba – I shall discuss now. What came to be called the *Morisco* Problem appears in the succeeding chapters. But both, I believe, revealed the consequences of fracturing the unspoken assumptions that had allowed *convivencia* to work. Here the lessons for the Balkans and the Levant today are very clear.

The Muslim population in Al-Andalus grew very rapidly during the first two centuries after the Conquest. In the eighth century, Muslims were a small and isolated garrison. As they intermarried with the local population the number of Muslims by birth grew steadily. But the bulk of the growing Muslim community were not immigrants from North Africa or their children, but converts from Christianity. There were both individual conversions and the adherence of whole families, and perhaps even whole towns and districts, but there was no pressure for forced conversion. Christians and Jews were allowed to practise their faith but they were marginal, outside the main body of society in both economic and social terms. The demands that Islam made on its adherents were no greater than those of Christianity, and conversion was an attractive option, for non-Muslims were second-class citizens within

Islamic society. As we have seen, in practice many of the more rigorous restrictions on Jews and Christians were not enforced, but the sense of inferiority, whether enforced by law or not, did not disappear.

In the mid ninth century, however, there was an attempt among the more zealous Christians to arrest the erosion in their numbers and to stress the separation between Christians and Muslims. The Christian martyrdoms in Cordoba quickly formed what literary critics would term a *topos*, an easily recognized point at which a historical incident expanded to assume legendary or mythical proportions. These events for Christians came to epitomize the inevitable hostility between the two cultures. They magnified the antithesis between them so as to dramatize and laud the cultural identity of one community, and to demonize the other. Over time, and by accretion, these tales of a historic reality were transmuted into a potent subliminal sense of a fearsome, dangerous, alien power – a complex image built upon biblical prophecy, upon the shadowy character of the Antichrist, and upon a daily experience of the Muslim presence that seemed to exemplify all of these elements. In this mythopoeia, the events – the Muslim Conquest and the martyrdoms – are added like new meat to a stockpot.[51] They strengthened the mixture, blending, and eventually merging, into the simmering. In Christian theory this was, indeed, the wonderfully reinvigorating effect of the Blood of the Martyrs, as it spread and revived the Christian community. The tales of the martyrs, long after their sacrifice, were one of the most potent elements in the spiritual armoury of the true believers.

Each individual understood the stories in his or her own way. The process is perhaps explained as 'dissemination', in the way that the French philosopher Jacques Derrida intends the term. In his view, the way that language is used means that each use – *dissémination* – disrupts any possibility of fixed or settled meanings. Every time a word is employed it generates a new and subtly different accretion. So the use of language is endlessly destabilizing: 'The force and form of its disruption explode the semantic horizon.' There is no limit or end to this process of transformation, no telling what its effect might be. Derrida calls it 'an irreducible and *generative* multiplicity'.[52]

In its historical context, the martyrs of Cordoba movement (like the myths of the hero-king Pelayo) provided a 'generative multiplicity'. As we shall see, one martyrdom stimulated another, not through any obvious mechanism but apparently spontaneously. Yet the spontaneity was conditioned by the way in which the seed of martyrdom took root, and by the way in which the rapidly evolving legend of the martyrs was disseminated. What becomes significant here is not the fine detail of the events in Cordoba but their mythopoeic potential. These symbolic acts were resonant and effective in the Iberian peninsula long after the precise historical context in which they had emerged had disappeared. By that point they had become *generic*, and applicable in a multitude of circumstances. Perhaps symbolic acts, myth and legend, are more potent in some cultures than in others. Iberia (like the Balkans and the Levant) seems, over the centuries, to have been highly susceptible to these influences, where the dead past enters the living present. This process is evident in the stories of the fall of the Visigothic kingdom that were disseminated and formed the foundation myth of Christian Spain.

The ease of the conquest and the speed with which many native Christians converted to Islam led to the growth of a flourishing Arabic culture and to the decay of Christian society. In the eyes of zealous Christians, only self-sacrifice could redeem what Christian vice had permitted in the first place. To make the self-destruction of the martyr more plausible, the horrific consequences of the fall had to be accentuated. This was not easy. Al-Andalus, with some exceptions, fulfilled its Qur'anic obligations to its non-Muslim minorities. Jews and Christians paid the poll tax and were allowed to exercise their faiths. The Christian martyr movement of the mid ninth century was a protest against increasing assimilation, rejecting the slow decay of both their culture and their faith. Among Christians in the great cities of Al-Andalus, Arabic had replaced Latin as the sophisticated language of culture, while an amalgam of Arabic, Romance dialect and Berber became a language of home and the street.[53] A rich young Cordovan, Alvarus, became the biographer of Eulogius, himself the recording angel for the Christian martyrs of Cordoba. Alvarus conveyed a deep sense of loss in Christian culture.

My fellow Christians delight in the poems and romances of the Arabs; they study the works of Mohammadan theologians and philosophers not in order to refute them, but to acquire correct and elegant Arabic style. Where today can a layman be found who reads the Latin Commentaries on Holy

Scriptures? Who is there that studies the Gospels, the prophets, the Apostles? Alas, the young Christians who are most conspicuous for their talents have no knowledge of any literature or language save the Arabic . . . The pity of it! Christians have forgotten their own tongue, and scarce one in a thousand can be found to be able to compose in fair Latin to a friend.[54]

Alvarus observed two attitudes towards Islam among contemporary Mozarabes. He was not talking about those souls, the *muwallid* – Christians who had converted to Islam. The majority of Christians recognized the power of Islamic culture, and sought to benefit from it. A minority aimed to create an impenetrable wall around the Christian community. In the manner of dissident and revolutionary groups throughout history, the members of this minority created a demonic enemy as a myth to sustain their resistance. They did so through the traditional weapon of the weak: symbolic action, *propaganda by the deed*.

The deed was to be martyrdom, which would serve to construct a black legend of an Islam that put the martyrs to death. In this image of Islam, two elements prevailed: the first was sensuality, and the other cruelty. Muslim cruelty, it was suggested, had a habitual viciousness about it. Violation of virgins, destruction of altars and holy books, and wanton slaughter were crimes all on a par. The commission of one implied a propensity for all the others. The factual details of the martyrs' movement can be simply stated. Over a period of nine years, forty-eight Christians came to the capital of Al-Andalus, Cordoba, and deliberately brought a public death upon themselves by denouncing the Prophet Mohammed as a false prophet. Similarly, blaspheming in a western Christian country, as did many pagans and heretics, would also have attracted a capital penalty. The first to die was rather different from the others, and his story illustrates the nature of the relationship between the religious groups in the city before the movement for self-martyrdom began. He was a Christian priest called, appropriately, Perfectus. Fluent in Arabic, he often talked with Muslims in the market, and it seems clear that matters of belief and faith were frequently discussed. One day he was asked what he thought of their Prophet. At first he demurred, for he recognized the danger, saying that they intended to entrap him, and have him put to death. They denied this, and guaranteed they would not denounce him. He then told them that Christians considered the Muslims' Prophet as 'the servant of Satan'.

Perfectus overstepped the boundary between what was permissible and what was not. There is no indication in Alvarus' account of why he took this fatal step. Initially those with whom he had debated let it pass, but by doing so they were implicated in his blasphemy, and later they shouted out in the market that he had blasphemed against the Prophet.[55] Perfectus was then taken before the judge (*qadi*). When his guilt was proved according to the law, he received the only sentence possible: death. After many months, on 18 April 850, he was finally brought out for execution before a ribald crowd celebrating the end of Ramadan. Facing the sword of the headsman, he shouted out loudly time and again, 'Yes, I did curse your Prophet, and I curse him now. I curse him as an impostor, an adulterer, a child of Hell. Your religion is of Satan. The pains of Gehenna await you all.' Only the falling blade silenced his firm and strident declarations.

The Christians of the city reclaimed his body from the execution ground and reopened the ancient tomb of Saint Acisclus, a saint who had suffered martyrdom under the Emperor Diocletian (and who would be reburied, centuries later, in what had become Perfectus' own church). There, led by the Bishop of Cordoba, an elaborate ceremony was held as the corpse was interred as a new martyr amid the hallowed bones of the established saint. This was a deeply symbolic act, physically conjoining the earlier saint, a martyr, with his successor, Perfectus. Soon after, another Christian called John was whipped after being accused of taking the Prophet's name in vain.[56] That he was not condemned to death, although many Muslims demanded it, indicated that the legal authorities were not seeking to conduct a purge of Christians or inflame Christian opinion. Rather, it seems, the reverse. The judge interpreted this new instance as leniently as he could, and was criticized for it.

The judge's fears were justified. Muslims were becoming roused against Christians, whom they saw as deliberately mocking the Prophet Mohammed. In John's case this was not true. But among those who deliberately sought martyrdom their denunciations of Islam were now carefully and deliberately contrived to be unpardonable. Christians desiring martyrdom now made a point of coming into the capital to denounce Islam and to achieve salvation. The next was a monk, Isaac, from a wealthy family, and a scholar in Arabic who had been appointed as a government secretary. He came to the *qadi* in open court and said that he wished to make the Muslim profession of faith. But as the judge was instructing him, Isaac suddenly shouted out, 'Your Prophet has lied, he has deceived you; may he be accursed, wretch that he is, who has dragged so many wretches down with him to hell. Why do you not, as a man of sense, abjure these pestilent doctrines.' Infuriated, the *qadi* struck him across the face, but he was restrained by his advisors, who told him that even a condemned criminal should not be insulted.

Recovering his self-control, the *qadi* suggested to Isaac that he might be either drunk or mad, since he could not be ignorant that death was the only punishment for blasphemy. '*Qadi*,' the monk replied quietly, 'I am in my right mind, and I have never tasted wine. Burning with the love of truth, I have dared to speak out to you and the others here present. Condemn me to death: far from dreading the sentence, I yearn for it; hath not the Lord said, "Blessed are they which are persecuted for the truth's sake, for theirs is the kingdom of heaven."'

The *qadi* tried to avoid imposing the inevitable sentence, but under the law he had no option. Isaac duly met his desired end, on 3 June 851. Thereafter the headsman was kept busy. Two days after Isaac, a man named Sancho blasphemed and lost his head. Two days after that, six monks, among them Isaac's uncle, came before the *qadi* and declared, 'We also echo the words of our holy brothers Isaac and Sancho.' More followed, until eleven had died as martyrs in less than two months. Many Christians opposed these sacrifices fearing that they would provoke Muslim anger against the whole Christian minority.

The interests of the Muslim authorities and the wider Christian community in preventing these suicidal confrontations were identical. A church council was summoned to prevent further martyrdoms, but it only seemed to rouse the staunchest Christians to ever more ecstatic zeal. Two monks entered the Great Mosque of Cordoba at Friday prayers, and shouted, 'The kingdom of heaven is at hand for the faithful, but for you infidels, hell yawns, and it will shortly open and swallow you up.' They narrowly escaped lynching by the faithful at prayer, and were swiftly judged and decapitated in the market place.

The final victims of their own zeal were Bishop Eulogius and a young woman, Leocritia. Eulogius had written a powerful account of the martyrdom movement and sent it north for safe keeping beyond the frontier of Muslim Spain. He was arrested and accused of seeking to convert Leocritia, who had been born of Muslim parents. The *qadi* was reluctant to condemn so senior a Christian, and ordered him to be whipped for a more minor offence. Then Eulogius denounced the Prophet Mohammed in the most vitriolic terms. But still the magistrate refused formally to condemn him and simply committed him to the court of the vizier, the senior official of Cordoba. One of the court members came to Eulogius and said,

I am not surprised, Eulogius, when madmen and imbeciles offer their heads without cause to the executioner; but how is it that a learned man like yourself, and one who enjoys general esteem, follows their example? What frenzy impels you? Why have you thus plotted against your own life? I pray you heed my words. Bow to the necessity; utter but a single word retracting what you have said before the *Qadi*, and in that case I will answer for my colleagues and myself that you will have nothing to fear.

But Eulogius refused to recant, and set out to secure a truly memorable martyr's death. He was formally condemned and sent for execution. A court eunuch abused him and struck him across the face on the way to the killing ground. In accordance with Christian precepts, Eulogius presented the other, unbruised, side of his face, and said, 'Smite that also.' The eunuch obliged, and a few minutes later, at a little after nine in the morning on 11 March 859, the bishop lost his head. His body was exposed to be gnawed by scavenging dogs, cats and rats, until the Christians gained permission to recover it. Leocritia was executed four days later and her body thrown into the river, 'to be eaten by fishes'. The demise of so senior a figure as Eulogius made a much greater impact than the deaths of all the more humble martyrs, and when the King of Leon made a treaty with the Sultan Mohammed in 883, one of the terms was that the bones of the holy martyrs Eulogius and Leocritia were to be ceded to him.[57]

The motives that impelled the martyrs have never been satisfactorily explained.[58] Many of them came from mixed families, with both

Islamic and Christian beliefs in their background. Many came from the small monastic communities clustered around Cordoba, notably from one foundation at Tabanos that produced no fewer than ten martyrs. As the number of martyrdoms mounted, the Muslim authorities responded with collective punishments. Significantly, the traditional limitations on the minorities were for the first time rigidly enforced. Christians were dismissed from their government posts and forced to wear the distinctive dress prescribed by law. Churches were examined to see if any were newly built and therefore subject to destruction. Even minor repairs or improvements could lead to their demolition. Many Christians turned against the enthusiasts. Eulogius recorded that at first Christians may have been impressed by the martyrdoms, but

when the divine fire inflamed many and led crowds of the faithful to go down to the square and denounce the enemy of the church with the same confession of faith that Isaac made, soon everyone, frightened by the rage of the savage tyrant, with amazing fickleness changed their minds; they disparaged and cursed the martyrs, and declared that both the martyrs and their supporters were the authors of a great crime.[59]

Eventually, around 854, the martyrs were formally denounced as heretics before the *qadi* by a group of leading Christians – bishops, abbots, priests and nobles – in an attempt to prevent further pressure on the Christian community.

The blood of martyrs had sustained the early Church, and eventually brought down pagan rule. 'The prototype of the Christian saint was the martyr; and as in due course holy men and women who had not died for Christ came to take their place alongside the martyrs, the figure of the martyr still remained the paradigm of the saint. The cult of the saints . . . had its undisputed origins in the cult of the martyrs.'[60] With the conversion of the Emperor Constantine, martyrs were no longer needed: but faced with the infidel (and seemingly unconquerable) power of Islam, this most powerful weapon in the Church's armoury was used again. If the precise causes of the martyrs movement lie within the heart of each of them who decided to lay down his or her life, its intention was clear. All the stories of the martyrs under Roman tyranny were a kind of miracle of the faith that would in some way, known only to God, bring about the triumph of the church.

One author, al-Kushani, contrasted Christian zealotry with Islamic reason. He retold the story of a Christian who came before the *qadi* some sixty years after the martyrs, in 920. The story's narrator explains that Christians believed this sort of suicide to be a pious act, although Jesus never encouraged any such thing. The *qadi* reprimanded the Christian for trying to commit suicide; the Christian replied that it would not be he who was killed, but only his image (*shabhi*), 'while I myself will go to heaven'. The *qadi* had him whipped, then asked on whose back the whip had fallen. 'On mine,' the Christian replied. 'Just as the sword will fall on your neck,' said the *qadi*.[61] So, although the occasional self-martyr and fanatic was still to be found, by the tenth century something of the old stability had been restored. The envoy of the Emperor Otto I, John of Gorze, to the court of Abd al-Rahman III at Cordoba had been brought up on tales of the Cordoban martyrs. He cheerfully expected the same glorious end. Instead, he found Christian clergy who warned him against antagonizing the Muslim authorities and firmly discouraged any provocative acts. The caliph refused to accept the letters sent by the emperor, because he found their tone demeaning and insulting, and instead sent back a Christian civil servant called Recemundus, appointed Bishop of Granada, to ask the emperor to withdraw the letters, which he did. Dignity was satisfied, and John of Gorze returned home after a parade in his honour.

Recemundus exemplified the larger numbers among Christians who were determined to function effectively within an Islamic society. He compiled an elaborate Calendar of Cordoba, which combined astronomical, agricultural and Christian liturgical details. He presented a copy to Abd al-Rahman's successor, Hakam II. In fact he prepared two versions. The longer contained details of all the martyrs of Cordoba and their feast days and was used by Christians. On the copy presented to the caliph, these details were tactfully (and prudently) omitted. In essence,

the realities of Islamic rule ultimately favoured this kind of compromise . . . a radical Church appealed to some Christians, but such a Church could only become a focus of more violence. It could not maintain the stable relationship between government and subject population that would allow Christians to go about their daily lives in peace.[62]

The martyrs movement, attempting to promote a violent reaction among Muslims, used arguments that had already been developed in the Levant. One of the martyrs had come to Spain from the Syrian monastery where John of Damascus had written his polemic against Islam. Many of the same themes were introduced into the Cordoban diatribe against Islam. The Prophet Mohammed was accused of being sexually promiscuous, and ensnared by a preoccupation with the body. Paul Alvarus, who wrote the life of Eulogius, contrasted Christ, who preached peace, with Mohammed, who taught men to fight; while Christ promoted chastity, Mohammed, the glutton for all forms of pleasure, practised incest.[63] All the long catalogue of by now traditional insults was offered up:

Muslims are puffed up with pride, languid in the enjoyments of fleshly acts, extravagant in eating, greedy usurpers in the acquisition of possessions . . . without honour, without truth, unfamiliar with kindness or compassion . . . fickle, crafty, cunning and indeed not halfway but completely befouled in the dregs of every impurity, deriding humility as insanity, rejecting chastity as though it were filth, disparaging virginity as though it were the uncleanness of harlotry, putting the vices of the body before the virtues of the soul.[64]

This led naturally to the assertion that Mohammed was a precursor of the Antichrist; in later polemics he became the Antichrist himself.

This wild rhetoric echoed the assaults that Christians had made against the pagan emperors of Rome. These had reminded their own adherents of the evil against which they were struggling. More importantly, they concealed a weakness in the case for godly martyrdom. For Islam did not demand that Christians worship false idols. Many Muslim scholars were even reluctant to accept converts from Christianity, arguing that they polluted Islam. One scholar, Ibn Haddah, wrote, 'They say that temptations will come with the People of the Book [Christians and Jews] and they will be due to them.'[65] Although marriage between a Muslim man and a non-Muslim woman was not forbidden, it was seen as fraught with spiritual danger. A Christian or Jewish wife would be a source of instability and corruption in a

Muslim household, for she would inevitably be tempted to lead her children from the true path of Islam.[66] In this some Islamic jurists and the Christian Alvarus were in agreement: separation was better than any other form of contact.

However, in Cordoba the martyrs were quickly forgotten and the apogee of the Caliphate of Cordoba in the last half of the tenth century was remembered as a golden age. The nineteenth-century historian of Islamic Spain Reinhart Dozy echoed the praise heaped upon the city by contemporary historians, poets and foreign envoys alike.

The state of the country harmonized with the prosperity of the public treasury. Agriculture, manufactures, commerce, the arts, sciences, all flourished. The traveller's eyes were gladdened on all sides by the well-cultivated fields, irrigated upon scientific principles, so that what seemed the most sterile soil was rendered fertile . . . Cordova [sic], with its half million inhabitants, its three thousand mosques, its splendid palaces, its hundred and thirteen thousand houses, its three hundred public baths, and its twenty-eight suburbs, yielded in size and magnificence only to Baghdad . . . The fame of Cordova penetrated even distant Germany: the Saxon nun Hroswitha, famous in the last half of the tenth century for her Latin poems and dramas, called it the Jewel of the World.[67]

In the courts of Christian Europe, Cordoba's products – ivories, silks, bronze vases fancifully shaped as peacocks, stags and imaginary beasts, chests of golden *dinars* – all became emblems of a world of incomparable civilization and luxury. Heathen Al-Andalus may have been an enemy of Christ. Nonetheless, it was alluring.[68]

4

'The Jewel of the World'

At the heart of the jewel-like city of Cordoba was the Great Mosque. It was built by Abd al-Rahman I from 785 to 787, and extended and embellished by his successors. Its architectural origins were complex, with suggestions of Byzantine forms as well as strong echoes of Syria. The Ummayad Caliphs had ruled in Damascus from 641 to 750, when they were overthrown by their rivals the Abbasids, and all except one of the Ummayad family were hunted down and killed. The survivor – Abd al-Rahman – fled west to the remotest portion of the Mediterranean Islamic world. In Spain he found loyal supporters. Under his rule, Al-Andalus declared itself independent from the new Abbasid Caliphate based in Baghdad. Abd al-Rahman I created a powerful state centred on Cordoba that eventually became the Ummayad Caliphate of Cordoba in 929.

The Great Mosque he built was the first evidence of this self-governing status. In structure and function it resembled the mosques of the East; but its forest of columns, crowned with polychrome double arches whose wedge-shaped stones (*voussoirs*) radiated from the arch's centre, were found in no building in the East. This was a characteristic of Visigothic buildings, and was adapted and extended by Mozarabic craftsmen.[1] At each stage of its elaboration, the mosque became more Hispanized, and less like the great religious buildings of the Muslim East.[2] There was also a direct connection with the *Christian* East, for in 965 Caliph Al-Hakam wrote to Constantinople asking for the services of a skilled mosaicist for the mosque. Not only did the caliph's envoys return with a craftsman, but with 320 *quintales* of mosaic squares that 'the King of the Rumi sent as a gift'.[3]

The same Hispanized cultural fusion – part Arab, part Mozarabe – was found in the palace of Madinat al-Zahra built outside Cordoba by Abd al-Rahman III, who had in 929 declared himself Caliph,

Commander of the Faithful and Defender of the Religion of God.
The new palace was a testimony to his exalted status. There marvels
were to be seen: the same arches characteristic of the mosque, but
more massive and emphatic; stone tracery like a forest of vegetation
spreading over walls and columns; little water fountains gushing from
the beaks of bronze birds or the mouths of sturdy horses; and ivory
and alabaster boxes intricately carved with scenes of the court. These
are almost all that now remains of life within this palace, which once
rivalled the great Palace of Constantine in Constantinople.[4] Madinat
al-Zahra had some of the elements to be found in the Ummayad
palaces of Syria and Jordan, but many more that originated in Al-
Andalus. The palace was named, it was said, in honour of Abd
al-Rahman's favourite wife, and called the City of the Flower. Building began in 936, and for twenty-five years up to 12,000 workmen
were at work on the site. Its scale was vast, with the outer wall more
than one and a half kilometres long while, in the great hall, a huge
pool of mercury shimmered and reflected the arches and tracery.

The impact that the palace and the caliph made upon foreign
visitors, accustomed to the cruder life of the North, was recorded on
several occasions. One story tells how the caliph wished to impress
them with his magnificence, so within the palace

he placed dignitaries, whom they took for kings, for they were seated on
splendid chairs and arrayed in brocades and silks. Each time the ambassadors
saw one of these dignitaries they prostrated themselves before him imagining
him to be the caliph, whereupon they were told, 'Raise your heads! This is
but a slave of his slaves!'

At last they entered a courtyard strewn with sand. At the centre was the
caliph. His clothes were coarse and short: what he was wearing was worth
no more than four dirhems. He was seated on the ground, his head bent; in
front of him was a Koran, a sword and fire. 'Behold, the ruler,' the ambassadors were told.

This conspicuous modesty echoes the entry of the Caliph Omar
into Jerusalem in 638, with his darned and well-worn clothes and
his broken-down mule.[5] Symbolically, the Cordoban caliph showed
himself as the humble servant of God, who would carry the holy
word, with fire and sword, against the enemies of Islam. For although

the city and the palace were architectural and human evidence of cultural fusion, the context in which the caliph presented himself also emphasized the oppositional purpose of Cordoba, its wealth and its military power. Dozy wrote of Abd al-Rahman III who 'in his wide tolerance calls to his councils men of another religion . . . a pattern ruler of modern times, rather than a medieval *Khalif*'.[6] But this claims too much. It is true that many of the early rulers of Cordoba were more open to non-Muslim influences than their Almoravid or Almohad successors from the deserts and mountains of North Africa. But for all the achievements in art, science and learning, Cordoba was built around the theory, if not always the practice, of war with the Christian North. The true temper of the Cordoban caliphate was embodied in another symbolic moment. Abd al-Rahman III died in 961; in 997, the military strong-man of Al-Andalus, Al-Mansur, led back his victorious army from destroying the great Christian shrine of Santiago de Compostela.

Compostela was, Spanish Christians argued, the holiest site in Europe. Many north of the Pyrenees agreed with them. For at Santiago, in about 818, the remains of Saint James had been miraculously discovered.[7] Moreover, these bones turned out not to be those of the Apostle James, as was first thought, but of another James: the brother of Christ himself. Thus, on Spanish soil, at the heart of the Asturian kingdom, constantly assailed by the infidel Muslims, was a saint's body related as closely as it was possible to the person of Christ himself. This was a relic more precious than any sliver of the True Cross or one of the Holy Nails.[8] Already in 822, at the battle of Clavijo, Saint James had intervened when King Ramiro of the Asturias was losing against the Moors. Suddenly, a figure on a white horse appeared, and turned the struggle in favour of the Christians. He told the king that Christ himself 'gave Spain for me to watch over her and protect her from the hands of the enemies of the faith'. This was the first appearance of *Santiago Matamoros*, Saint James Moor-slayer. Thereafter he returned time and again to save Christian Spain from disaster.

Thus for the Muslims to capture the saint's remains would be an act of great audacity. In August 997, Al-Mansur and the army of Cordoba fought their way north to the city of Compostela, and the Christians were powerless to resist them. The shrine was deserted except for a single monk. Al-Mansur asked him why he had remained when all the others had fled. The monk said, 'I am praying to Saint James.' The commander told him to pray in peace and set his own guard around him for protection. On the following day, Al-Mansur had the tomb razed 'so effectively that on the morrow no one would have supposed that it had ever existed'.[9] Yet the bones of the saint were left unmolested. 'In due time Al-Mansur made his entry into Cordoba accompanied by a multitude of Christian captives, bearing on their shoulders the gates of Santiago's shrine and the bells of the church. The doors were placed in the roof of the unfinished mosque and the bells were suspended in the same edifice to serve as lamps.'[10]

Why had Al-Mansur left the bones of the saint undisturbed? In one sense the objects he had carried back with him in triumph were the symbols of Santiago's power. The sound of Christian church bells, louder than the *muezzin*'s call to prayer, was deeply offensive to Muslims. In Islamic states, Christians were usually prohibited from using church bells. Thus, by taking the bells he had silenced the voice of the saint and stifled the summons to his shrine. The doors were symbolic of the sanctity and power of the church, and by hanging them in the mosque he neutralized the power of the saint.[11] In a later generation, a ruler of Granada similarly debased a Castilian prince's status: he had the skin of the prince, who had been killed in battle, stuffed with straw and suspended before the great gate of his palace, before consigning it to hang in perpetuity in the city's largest mosque. Yet Al-Mansur did not attempt to disturb the remains of Santiago, and Christians said that such was the holiness of James and the power of his bones that even Al-Mansur had not dared interfere with them. The efficacy of the saint and his relics was proclaimed as even greater than before. This was all the more remarkable given that at Al-Mansur's hands, according to an anonymous Christian author, 'in Spain divine worship perished; all the glory of the Christian people was destroyed; the treasures stored up in the churches were plundered'. Al-Mansur himself 'was seized . . . by the demon which had possessed him while he was alive, and he was buried in hell.'[12]

Was it respect or superstition that had moved the 'accursed' Al-Mansur at Santiago de Compostela? There is a case for preferring the former. Despite the Christian polemic, Al-Mansur was not a zealot. On the whole it was only fanatics among both Muslims and Christians who desecrated the shrines of the other castes.[13] Muslims recognized both Jesus as a prophet and his mother Mary as a holy virgin. In some cases, Muslims and Christians used a shrine that attracted worshippers from both faiths. It was therefore quite consistent with Muslim practice not to disturb the bones of the brother of the Prophet Isa (Jesus) while destroying the shrine above them. Indeed, during both the emirate and the caliphate of Cordoba, as already discussed, the instinctive practice of *convivencia* meant that Muslims, Jews and Christians drew back from gratuitous insults to the other castes. The episode of the martyrs of Cordoba is the one striking example to the contrary.

After the death of Al-Mansur in 1002, the caliphate of Cordoba had less than thirty years to run, and its increasing failure presaged military revolt and a succession of short-lived rulers. One caliph lasted no more than forty-seven days. The caliphal palace at Madinat al-Zahra was sacked and pillaged by rebellious Berber mercenaries, while the even larger palace complex built by Al-Mansur for himself and his family, and called (confusingly) Madinat al-Zahira, was torn down stone by stone so that nothing survived. By 1031, the entire valley of the Guadalquivir had been laid waste; trees were uprooted and the fields were left unplanted.[14] Local Muslim chieftains set themselves up as petty kings, known as *reyes de taifas*. Some of the largest kingdoms were centred on cities such as Seville, Granada, Badajoz and Saragossa, but others were little more than a castle and its surrounding lands. Many of those close to the frontier with the Christian states of the north began to pay protection money (*parias*) to the rulers of Castile and Aragon in order to survive.

For a little over fifty years, no central rule existed in Al-Andalus. Several of the petty kings sought to enjoy, albeit on a more limited scale, the good living that had formerly existed in Cordoba. The period of the *taifas* was an era of artistic efflorescence and rising consumption of luxury goods. Each little court vied with the next. Many of the statelets did not survive, their lands and palaces taken by their more powerful neighbours, their rulers quietly murdered. The Christian states exacted huge payments of protection money from the Muslim kingdoms, but in 1085 the King of Castile, Alfonso VI, instead of taking the bribes offered by the ruler of Toledo took his city instead. However he continued to exact payment in gold from more distant monarchs, such as the King of Granada. But Alfonso's intent was clear. His envoy to Abd Allah, the ruler of Granada, was unambiguous: 'Al-Andalus belongs to the Christians from the beginning until they were conquered by the Arabs. When you no longer have money or soldiers, we will seize the country without the least effort.'[15] The Muslim kings, fearful of attack from the north after the capture of Toledo, sent messengers over the straits to North Africa to ask for help from the old Saharan warrior, Yusef ibn Tashfin, the Almoravid ruler of Morocco.

The human flow back and forth across the straits had been ceaseless since the first conquest of 711. Berber traders, settlers and mercenaries had always regarded Al-Andalus as a Promised Land. The Almorávides, however, were not like the stream of earlier arrivals.[16] They emerged among the tribes of the Saharan fringe, where many of the men were veiled and women went bare-faced.[17] One of their common names was 'the Wearers of the Veil'.[18] Like other reform movements refined in the harsh conditions of the desert, they saw the world in a stark perspective, and dedicated their lives first to purifying themselves and, thereafter, Islam. As with the tribal Muslim armies of the first Arab advance in the seventh century, they proved a strong, flexible and cohesive military force. By 1061, armies led by Yusef ibn Tashfin had conquered the coastline from the Kabyle mountains in what is now Algeria to the Atlantic. In 1062 he founded a new capital at Marrakech, and united the lands from the great bend of the River Niger south of Timbuktu to the Atlantic in the west and the Mediterranean in the north. This was a powerful empire, dominating the trade routes into Africa, with large resources of manpower, and controlling the ports of the North African littoral.

In 1085, while Toledo was under siege to the Castilians, the ruler of Seville, Al-Mutamid, wrote to Yusef ibn Tashfin, who now styled himself Commander of the Faithful:

He [the ruler of Castile, Alfonso VI] has come to us demanding pulpits, minarets, mihrabs, and mosques, so that crosses may be erected in them, and so that monks may ruin them . . . God has given you a kingdom because of your Holy War and the defence of His right, because of your endeavour . . .

1. *The Mufti and the Monster* by Jacopo Ligozzi, watercolour, 1576–80. The Mufti, or 'Pope of the Turks', is shown with a grotesque familiar, half-man half-monster. The spiked club being tested by the Mufti suggests that his intentions are sinister.

2. *St George Altarpiece* (detail), attributed to André Marzal de Sas, tempera on panel,
c. 1410. The Moors are unmistakable: dark and malevolent figures. But the
message is that they are now very much on the defensive against the saint and
his knights. Little details, such as the scorpion on a Moorish shield, remind the
Christian audience that the Moors still have the power to do great harm.

3. *The Surrender of Granada, 1492* by Francisco Pradilla y Ortiz, oil on canvas. This is a Romantic late nineteenth-century image of a fictitious scene in the Castilian victory. Isabella on her white horse is at the heart of the picture.

4. and 5. *Ferdinand and Isabella Entering Granada* and *The Conversion of the Moors*, carved and painted wood, *c.* 1502. The panels by the Burgundian artist Philippe de Vigarny depict the apogee of the Catholic Kings. Both Ferdinand and Isabella regarded the forced baptism of the Moors as the final grand act in the redemption of Spain.

6. *Sultan Bayezid I 'the Thunderbolt' Routs the Crusaders at Nicopolis in 1396*, watercolour and ink, from *The Hunername [History] of Lokman*, 1584. This illustration of the great Ottoman victory tells the story of the battle. A Western depiction in Froissart's *Chronicles* reveals the aftermath: the systematic killing of the captured Christian knights.

7. *The Cairo Insurgents of 21 October 1798* (detail) by Anne-Louis Girodet de Roucy-Trioson, oil on canvas, 1810. This section of the vast canvas, by a pupil of David, epitomises the essence of Romantic violence entangled with sex. In a mêlée of bloody swords, a naked slave defends his epicene Ottoman master, and with a strong left hand grips the Turk's breast. A dying man embraces the slave's right leg. The French soldiers by contrast exhibit traditional Christian manliness.

8. *And the Prayer of Faith* by John Frederick Lewis, oil on panel, 1872. This is one of the Lewis *harem* pictures, based on his life in Cairo. It divides oddly into two disconnected halves, one male, the other female. But the copious flowers bridge the gulf and, despite the separation, Lewis shows us an image of contentment rather than languor.

9. *The First Mass in Kabylia* by Horace Vernet, oil on canvas, *c.* 1838. Vernet presents France's 'return' to North Africa as a renewal of the Crusades. The cross, rough-hewn from a tree, like the Cross of Christ himself, is the visual centre of the composition, with a ghostly cloud of mist swirling about it. Muslim Berbers sit impassively behind a fence of bayonets as their land is re-Christianized.

10. *Mehmed Said Pasha, Bey of Rovurelia, Ambassador of Sultan Mahmud I at Versailles* by Jacques Aved, oil on canvas, 1742. Said Pasha is portrayed as a man belonging to two worlds. His dress is entirely Ottoman, yet he is shown in a wholly Western pose, with his right hand indicating his greatest achievement – the first books to be printed in Ottoman Turkish in Constantinople.

And you now have many soldiers of God who through their fighting may win paradise in their own lifetime.[19]

Although Yusef did enter Spain with troops, and defeated the army of Alfonso at Sagrajas, close to Badajoz, in October 1086, he had little desire to embroil himself in the affairs of Al-Andalus. He went back across the straits, and it was not until 1091 that he finally returned at full strength, after many appeals from the Muslim rulers, to resist the advance of Christian power. Thereafter until 1145, Al-Andalus was ruled from Marrakech as a province of the Almorávides.

The capture of Toledo (plus the other advances by Alfonso VI, who raided as far as the walls of Seville) and the arrival of the zealot armies of the Almorávides were linked. After attacking Seville, Alfonso had ridden on to Tarifa, where the first Muslims had landed, and strode out into the surf. 'This is the very end of Spain,' he declared, 'and I have set foot upon it.' He wanted to make good his claim to be 'Emperor of all the Nations of Spain'. The Christian 'holy war' that began with Pope Urban II's appeal for the First Crusade to the Holy Land in 1095 had its antecedents in Spain. Likewise, *jihad* – internal spiritual reform and external wars to advance the faith – which was the motive force of the Almorávides, was now echoed by parallel and contemporary developments within Christendom.[20] Urban's predecessor, Gregory VII, had encouraged Christians to fight in Spain on behalf of the papacy, which was seeking to extend its rights over lands once Christian but now held by infidels. Alfonso declined the opportunity to act as the agent of the papacy, and rejected the papal claims to power over Spain. He began to call himself Emperor of all Spain (*Imperator totius hispaniae*). The reconquest of Toledo, the capital of the Visigoths, was a powerful re-statement of the ancient claim of the Leonese and Castilian kings, the heirs of the Visigoths, to rule the whole peninsula.

Toledo surrendered to Alfonso VI on 6 May 1085. The Muslims who remained in the city were allowed to keep all their property and to exercise their faith freely. Like Christians under Muslim rule in Al-Andalus, they paid a poll tax. There was much disquiet when the new bishop of Toledo and the queen, both French in origin, while the king was absent on campaign, ordered that Toledo's main mosque should become the city's new cathedral. But that mosque in turn had been built above an ancient Visigothic church, as had the mosque in Cordoba. Nonetheless, in the years after the Christian Reconquest of Toledo as in the first centuries of Muslim Spain, the Muslims who now came under Christian rule established a form of *convivencia*.[21] Many scholars have seen this spirit expressed in the intellectual production that emanated from Toledo, much as Cordoba was earlier celebrated as a centre of culture. Toledo also became home to many Mozarabic Christians fleeing from the harsher environment of Al-Andalus under Almoravid rule.

A counterpoint to the image of this scholarly tolerance under Alfonso VI lies in the career of Rodrigo Díaz de Vivar, known as El Cid Campeador, or more simply as El Cid (The Lord). Rodrigo straddled two worlds. He grew up in the equivocal and ambiguous border terrain of the *taifas* kingdoms, and ended up in the new epoch of Crusade and *jihad*. He died in July 1099, within a week of the final Crusader assault and capture of Jerusalem, in the city of Valencia, which he had conquered. Even before his death, his valorous deeds had been written of in a *Historia Roderici*. *The Poem of the Cid* was composed at the beginning of the thirteenth century. 'Cid' is a version of the Arabic *sidi*, a title of respect, and Rodrigo was honoured by both Muslim and Christian alike. He and his men killed 'the Moors' with gusto, calling on their patron saint, Saint James Moorslayer, as they did so. But the killing was a matter of business and not hatred.

The Cid's vassals dealt pitiless blows and in a short time they killed three hundred Moors. While the Moors in the trap uttered loud cries . . . the ever fortunate Cid spoke these words: 'Thanks be to God in heaven and to all his saints. Now we shall have better lodgings for the horses and their masters . . . Listen to me, Alvar Fañez and all my knights. We have gained great wealth in capturing this stronghold; this many Moors lie dead and few remain alive. We shall not be able to sell our captives, whether men or women. We would gain nothing by cutting off their heads. Let us allow them to return to the town, for we are masters here. We shall occupy their houses and make them serve us.'[22]

When finally the Cid retreated from this stronghold (after selling it to the Muslims from the neighbouring towns for 3,000 gold pieces), 'all the Moors were sad to see him go: "You are going, Cid," they said. "May our prayers go before you! We are well satisfied with the way you have treated us." [23]

The Cid was presented as an ambivalent figure, who fought the Christian Count of Barcelona, a Frank, with the same robust delight as he fought the Moors. In the poem, the Muslims are described simply as *moros*, without additional pejorative attributes. In battle, there is an equivalence between the adversaries: the 'Moors called upon Mohammed, the Christians on St James'. Some Moors were craven, but so too were many Christians. The bulk of the poem deals with the treachery and spite directed at the Cid by his fellow Christians. The Cid described the Muslim governor of Molina as a friend with whom he lived in peace; and the governor gave the Cid's men 'a joyous welcome, saying, "Here are you, vassals of my good friend [*mio amigo natural*]"'.[24] Two generations after the poem was written down, elsewhere in Castile the *Estoria de España*, as we have seen, presented the relationship between Moor and Christian in terms that denied any possibility of amity.

The Cid was a man of the frontier who, rejected by his king, could take other service, with Muslim or Christian. In the last third of the thirteenth century, this was still just possible along the frontier, but it was much harder for a man like Rodrigo to live in both worlds. In *The Poem of the Cid*, Rodrigo was presented more as a Christian knight and less as the frontier mercenary of history. Later still he became the epitome of Spanish manhood, a human avatar of Santiago.[25] As Eduardo Manzano Moreno observed, relationships between Muslims and Christians across the frontier were very different from either the theories of Christian scholars and canonists, or the prescriptions of Islamic jurists. Nothing should

deny the existence of a difference, of an antagonism or a confrontation between the realms of Christianity and Islam in the Iberian peninsula. More or less continuously, more or less apparently, conflict did exist, and took a variety of forms throughout the eight centuries of Muslim rule. It is obvious that this strife produced frontiers, but it seems clear that these frontiers cannot be assessed by projecting present-day notions of borders on to the Middle Ages.[26]

However, the life of the border in the era of the crusade in Spain, or the 'Reconquest' as it came to be called, was different from what it had been in the era of the Cid, and in the centuries before.

The capture of Toledo effectively began the Reconquest. The fall of Saragossa to the crusading army of Alfonso I of Aragon on 18 December 1118 meant the loss of Islam's northern outpost. But the capture of Cordoba on 29 June 1236 was a decisive symbolic moment in the shifting pattern of Iberian history. Before Ferdinand III of Castile entered the walls of the city, he ordered that anyone who wished to leave was free to go, carrying all their possessions with them. Those who remained, it was also agreed, were free to practise their faith, but under Christian and not Muslim rule. For devout Muslims such a proposal was an abomination, and no doubt they formed the bulk of the refugees, some travelling south towards the coast to take ship for North Africa, and others south-east across the Guadalquivir and along the road to Granada. When the king entered the city, he went first to the Great Mosque, where he saw the bells of Santiago. In the words of the Castilian *Primera Crónica General*,

On the feast day of the apostles Peter and Paul, the city of Cordoba . . . was cleansed of all filthiness of Muhammad and given up and surrendered to King Ferdinand. King Ferdinand then ordered a cross to be put upon the chief tower where the name of the false Muhammad was wont to be called upon and praised, and then the Christians all began to shout with happiness and joy, 'God, help us!, and he [the king] found there the bells of the church of St James the Apostle in Galicia, which had been brought there by Almanzor [Al-Mansur] . . . and placed in the mosque of Cordoba to the shame of the Christians; and there the bells remained until this conquest by King Ferdinand of the city of Cordoba . . . King Ferdinand then had these same bells taken and returned to the Church of Santiago of Galicia. Thus, the church of Santiago was once more happily adorned.[27]

Moorish prisoners carried the great bells back to Compostela, where in the church rebuilt after Al-Mansur's assault a space had been left for them. Once rehung, the deep voice of the bells sounded again to announce that Saint James had again triumphed over the enemies of Christ.

৵

That moment marked the beginning of a new phase in the history of the peninsula. As we have seen, for most of the period from 711 until the late eleventh century Muslims, Christians and Jews lived together mostly under Muslim rule. There were then few Muslims in the Christian kingdoms of northern Spain. But by the early thirteenth century, the bulk of Muslims and Jews were living predominantly under Christian dominion; this situation persisted until this second period of *convivencia* ended with the expulsion of the Jews in 1492, and the conversion-by-decree of the Muslims eight years later. The concept of living together characterizes both eras, but it unfolded under very different terms. By the mid thirteenth century, Ferdinand III of Castile had occupied Seville and the whole valley of the Guadalquivir, and James I of Aragon had conquered the Balearic Islands, Valencia and the little kingdoms to the south. Only the Kingdom of Granada remained a solid and coherent bloc of territory in Muslim hands.

The majority of Muslims now lived under Christian rule, a situation that the laws and practices of Islam had never envisaged.[28] For the purist, good Muslims could only fulfil their duty to God within a Muslim-ruled community. Yet from the thirteenth century Muslims lived permanently in all the five Christian Spanish kingdoms. Each state had its own approach to its Muslim and Jewish subjects, and each kingdom, and every local community within each kingdom, had its own framework of regulations and customs governing the relationship. The theoretical position advanced by Alfonso X of Castile in his ideal law codes, the *Siete Partidas*, encompassed the double nature of the Christian attitudes to the Muslims:

Moors are the sort of people who believe that Mahomet was the prophet or messenger of God. Because the works or actions he performed do not demonstrate any great holiness on his part, such as might justify according to him such a holy status, their law is like an insult to God . . . And so we say that the Moors should live among the Christians in the same manner as . . . the Jews, observing their own law and causing no offence to ours. But in the Christian towns the Moors may not have mosques, nor may they make public sacrifices before men, and the mosques which were formerly theirs must belong to the king, who may grant them to anybody he wishes. And even though the Moors do not have a good law, nevertheless, as long as they live among the Christians under their protection, they ought not to have their property stolen from them by force.[29]

Under Islam, Jews and Christians had also been 'protected', as the 'People of the Book', since they venerated Abraham and the other precursors to the Prophet Mohammed. In practice, this had not prevented them coming under extreme pressure from the Almorávides and the Almohades. In the Christian kingdoms, the idea of the Moors as a necessary evil gained strength. The Infante Don Juan Manuel of Castile in his *Libro de los Estados* ('The Book of The Estates') expressed a view common throughout Christian Spain:

Long after Jesus Christ was crucified, there arose a false man named Muhammad. He preached in Arabia, convincing certain ignorant people that he was a prophet sent by God. As part of his teaching he offered them wholesale indulgences in order that they could gratify their whims with excessive lust and to an unreasonable extent ... They had seized lands belonging to Christians. That is why there is war between Christians and Moors [*moros*], and there will be until the Christians have recovered the lands that the Moors took from them by force; but there is no other reason either because of their faith or the [false] sect [*secta*] they belong to that there should be war between them. Jesus Christ never ordered anyone to be killed nor that anyone should be pressured to accept the Christian faith, for He does not wish any forced service.[30]

From the time that the Christian kingdoms acquired a large Muslim population with the capture of Toledo in 1085, their rulers attempted to preserve a clear separation between Christians, Jews and those Muslims now living under Christian rule, and known as *Mudéjares* or 'those left behind'. Each district and region varied in the precise arrangements, but both minorities clustered around their own districts or settlements, especially since there they could have synagogues or mosques, which were not permitted in Christian areas. Repeated statutes were issued to require minorities to wear distinctive hats, badges, clothes or, in the case of Moors, a 'Moorish haircut'.[31] But plainly they often did not work. One ribald instance concerned a Christian prostitute called Alicsand de Tolba in the winter of 1304, when she was looking for business in an outlying shepherds' camp in

Aragon. She asked the shepherds whether there was anyone else who needed her services, and was told, 'Only a Moor'. But one of the Christian shepherds went to the Muslim, Aytola 'the Saracen', and asked if he wanted to sleep with Alicsand. He said this was not possible since he was a Muslim and, moreover, he had no money. The shepherd, Lorenc, said he would give him the money, and as to the other, he should say his name was Johan and that he came from the port, and was presumably a foreigner. All was well until suddenly she cried out as she discovered at a certain point that her customer was circumcised and hence either a Muslim or a Jew.

This tale tells us several things: that Muslims and Christians worked together; that they could have the easy, bantering relationship that this tale implied; that it was not easy to tell a Muslim from a Christian by outward appearance. And, finally, if even a rough joke like this became known to the authorities, the consequences could be dire. Aytola the Saracen wisely fled before the law could catch up with him, for the penalties for flouting the sexual boundaries between Christians and Moors could be savage, even for congress with a prostitute.[32] He was in the kingdom of Aragon but in Castile the law said, 'If a Moor has intercourse with a common woman who abandons herself to everyone, for the first offence, they shall be scourged together through all the town, and for the second, they shall be put to death.'[33]

The more we know of the situation of the *Mudéjares* in the aftermath of the Christian Reconquest of the thirteenth century, the less it becomes possible to talk of the situation of Muslims in Spain with any overall or general perspective.[34] Gabriel Martinez-Gros makes the point that there were many varieties of Muslim experience under Christian rule, partly because each kingdom or locality operated on its own lines. The long-established Mudejars in the communities of the north, like Toledo, were in a different situation to the 'new' Mudejars of the south. But even in Toledo, often presented as a model of 'pluralism and tolerance', there were two very dissimilar categories of Muslims: free and slave.[35] The slaves were those taken in war or by right of conquest, but also it was easy for Muslims who fell foul of the many laws governing their subservient status to cross the boundary between free and slave status.

These differences figured strongly in the language with which Muslims described Christians, and vice versa. The Spanish Arabist

Eva Lapiedra Gutiérrez has painstakingly traced the sixteen terms used
to describe Christians in Arab histories of Iberia written between the
ninth and fourteenth centuries. Her conclusions are ambiguous, which
no doubt reflects the reality. Enmity had its gradations. There were
degrees and different types of hostility expressed in the words that
were used. For example, she describes *aduwallah*, 'enemy of God', the
most commonly used term, as aggressive. But the next most common
term, *Nasrani* ('follower of the Nazarene', Jesus of Nazareth), was
neutral by comparison. *Rumi*, which technically meant a Byzantine
but was haphazardly applied to Spanish Christians, fell somewhere
between the two, but was less often used. *Kafir* or 'infidel' was
also used less frequently. So even in the context of Spain, with its
ever-advancing war front in the north, sometimes Christians were
spoken of as hated enemies, but on other occasions they were
described in terms that contained no strong sense of hostility. Muslim
Arabic-speakers gradually created an expanding repertoire of terms to
describe Christians and Jews. *Frenk, Frenj, Ferinj*, applied to Christians
in Spain and the Holy Land, literally meant Frank or Frenchman. In
the East, however, only western Christians were described in this
way. Local Orthodox or Syriac Christians were *Nasrani*, never *Frenj*.[36]

Gutiérrez has discovered the presence of a changing, adaptive syntax
to encompass the increasingly dominant Christians. All save two of
the terms were traditional, derived from the Holy Qu'ran composed
in the seventh century. But Muslims needed a new framework of
language to describe the experience of Christian power. When Muslims
wanted to extend their repertoire of insult they more and more
departed from this hallowed traditional lexicon. Non-Muslims were
increasingly called *ily*, 'uncivilized'.[37] It was, suggests Gutiérrez, 'the
most complex of all the terms used in the Arabic-Muslim chronicles
to define the Christians'. It had the sense of someone bloated and
crude, but also with the wildness and sexual proclivities of a wild ass.[38]

Using this vocabulary, Muslims could present Western Christians
as inherently morally defective, condemned by their environment and
the corrupting effects of their culture. The Franks' misfortune was to
come from bitter northern climes. Writer after writer stressed that
this had determined their character: 'Excessive cold . . . ruined their
manners and hardened their hearts . . . Their colour is, of course,
white and they, like beasts, care only for war, combat and hunting.'[39]

Even their manner of writing was against nature, being from left to right and thus 'away from the heart and not towards it'. Christians came to be described in zoomorphic terms: as dogs (especially despised in Islam) or, worse still, as pigs. This then brought the terms of condemnation back within the Qur'anic system of what was permitted and what forbidden.

Infidels were unclean, in the same way that semen, urine, menstrual blood and faeces were filthy and contaminating.[40] If Muslims wanted to make the taint of being infidel even stronger, they then associated it with other ritually and fundamentally unclean objects. Terms like wild beast, dog or pig referred to inalienable characteristics.[41] A pig was always a pig.[42] To bestialize any human being, to give them the character of a despised animal, carried a huge metaphoric potential, and their animal qualities by exchange emphasized the speaker's humanity and Muslim cleanliness. But the curse of infidelity would be lifted at the moment that the infidel made the Profession of Faith and began to lead a truly Islamic life.

The everyday Christian perceptions of the Moor were correspondingly fearful. The border ballads romanticized the Moorish warriors of the frontiers with Granada, but they were still figures of fear and danger. Christians rarely made a direct equation between Muslims and the other (and more prosperous) minority, the Jews, but distaste for one group also seemed to spill over on to the other, and Jews and Moors were linked together in the minds of many Christians. Rulers and popular opinion alike regarded them as enemies, existing only by the benevolence of the Christian community. The Jews suffered attacks more regularly and more severely than the Moors. An outburst of popular rage, which led to savage massacres of Jews, began in Seville in June 1391 but soon spread to many parts of Spain. It was the product of many different causes, mostly purely local. But running as a common thread through all the killings, in Andalucia, in the rest of Castile, in Aragon, and especially in the Balearic Islands, was a sense of revulsion against *all those who were not Christian*.

In 1378 Archdeacon Ferrán Martinez, of Ecija near Seville, began to deliver a series of popular sermons directed against the Jews. They were well attended. In 1391, he encouraged the Seville mob to attack the Jewish quarter and raze 'the houses of the devil', the synagogues. It is hard to find any direct cause for new animosity towards the Jews, but the eminent Castilian statesman Perez Lopez de Ayala reflected a general prejudice when he wrote of the Jews as 'ready to drink the blood of the oppressed . . . The Jews divide up the people, who die undefended.'[43] In 1412 the Valencian Dominican preacher Vincent Ferrer castigated the Jews, but he also made explicit their connection with the Muslims. Both Jews and Moors should be isolated from contact with Christians. As he put it, 'Just as prostitutes should live apart, so should Jews.' Muslims should be confined to their *morerias*, where they could not contaminate Christian Spain.[44]

Increasingly vicious attacks prompted many Jews to accept baptism. As 'New Christians' or *conversos*, there was nothing in law to prevent their intermarriage with other 'Old Christian' families, and both among the 'Old Christians' and among Jews who had kept their faith, old fears of consanguinity and sexual mingling across the boundaries of the castes once more came to the fore. A sixteenth-century Jewish writer blamed the persecutions themselves on this cause: 'These sufferings were a just punishment of divine wrath. For many had taken Gentile women into their homes; children were born of these illicit unions and they later killed their own fathers.'[45] The process of mass-conversion, however, also changed the whole pattern of relationships between Christians, Jews and Muslims. During the fifteenth century, the dominant Christian states in Spain began to develop a new theory of the infidel. In this view, Judaism and, by extension, Islam, carried a genetic taint and thus no convert of Jewish or Muslim stock could ever carry the True Faith purely, as could someone of 'untainted' Christian descent.

No doubt these views had long been embedded in Christian society within the peninsula, where sexual deviance could carry a stigma that extended down the generations ('son of a whore' (*hijo de puta*) was (and is) a classic Castilian imprecation, but one that was once upon a time severely punished if uttered publicly). This latent tendency within Hispanic society was elaborated into a body of law from the mid fifteenth century, but emerging from below rather than by royal decree. The first instance was in 1449, when Pero Sarmiento – the leader of a rebellion in Toledo against royal support for Jewish converts – issued a declaration that no one except an Old Christian of untainted blood could ever hold public office. In front of a large gathering in the city hall of Toledo, Sarmiento catalogued all the evil deeds that the Jews were said to have committed. The first was that the Jews of Toledo had opened the gates of the city to Tariq's Moors in 711, thereby ensuring centuries of Muslim domination; and their descendants, the 'New Christians', were continuing their 'intrigues' against true Christians.[46] Within living memory, they had conspired with the enemies of Toledo to 'wage a cruel war with armed force, with blood and fire, inflicting theft and damage as if they were Moors, enemies of the Christian faith'.[47] Even when the rebellion was suppressed in 1451, Sarmiento's decree continued to be observed. Over the next forty years, more and more institutions adopted requirements that 'purity of blood' (*limpieza de sangre*) should be a prerequisite for membership of a guild or any similar body. The vocabulary that was used is particularly significant: the 'Old Christians' described themselves as the 'pure' (*limpios*); they were 'fine Christians', and the assumption was that the converts were impure and coarse.

The fresh attack against 'New Christians' that began in the 1460s was inflamed by sermons, and by influential polemical publications such as the 'Fortress of Faith' (*Fortalitium fidei contra Christianos hostes*) by Alonso de Espina. The Holy Inquisition, established in Castile in 1478, led the charge. Albert Sicroff, the principal scholar of the early history of *limpieza de sangre*, makes the point that Muslims were not the main target or the subject of these restrictions.[48] However, the language used almost always embraced both 'Jews and Moors', as in the case of Toledo in 1449. In the fifteenth century, the *limpieza de sangre* laws were constructed to constrain the converted Jews. But after 1500, and especially after their revolt in the Alpujarras in 1568, the (forcibly) converted Muslims or *Moriscos* were increasingly seen as the more dangerous of the enemies within the lands of Spain. There was a deep ambiguity in the laws of purity of blood. In Christian belief, baptism purged all sins, and sincere repentance meant that nothing remained from the former life. Yet could baptism and repentance obliterate the popular perception of Jewish guilt for the death of Jesus Christ? For theologians knowledgeable in the biblical sources, conversion indeed wiped clean the past through the sacrificial blood of the Lamb of God, Jesus Christ.[49] But this was too intricate an idea to resonate with the unlearned. Thus, the complex messages of Espina and his fellow polemicists were simply received as a call to protect Christian society from its assailants, the Jews and the Muslims.

The number of Moors (*Mudéjares*) exceeded the number of Jews in
Christian Spain, yet paradoxically it was the Jews and Jewish converts
to Christianity who throughout the fifteenth century, and afterwards,
were the primary target of the purity legislation, and, later, of the
Holy Inquisition. This is explained by the fact that the two communities were very different in their distribution and function. The bulk
of the Muslims laboured on the land, while the Jews were concentrated
in the towns, where tensions, especially over trade and business,
could easily spill into violence. They also performed roles, such as
tax-gathering, that roused hostility.[50]

Moreover, although Islam was the menacing external enemy, the
relationships between Judaism and Christianity (born out of Judaism)
had become a ritualized antagonism. The ritual could all too often
become reality. In many places, the Holy Week celebrations required
the portrayal of the Jews in an enactment of the Crucifixion. This was
frequently a time of heightened feelings that might be carried into
symbolic attacks on Jewish houses and synagogues. Whether these
emblematic acts of hatred triggered real violence is not clear, but there
were numerous assaults, often accompanied by gratuitous acts of
savagery, on Jews in Castile. The attacks in 1391 were the most
notorious, but these assaults recurred on many occasions during the
fifteenth century: in Toledo in 1449 and 1467, in Vallodolid in 1470
and in Cordoba in 1473. None of these were officially sanctioned,
but from the 1480s official policy towards non-Christians, both Jews
and Mudejars, began to harden. Ancient edicts concerning dress,
restrictions on trade, and living apart from Christians were enforced.
Isolated ghettos and *morerias* were constructed outside towns or by
blocking off streets and filling in doors and windows.

It is not surprising that most scholars have focused on the Christian
obsession with newly converted Jews. These false converts were said
to make constant attempts to undermine the Christian kingdoms.
Crudely forged texts were produced, like the concoction in 1492 of
the letter of Yusef, Chief of the Jews of Constantinople, who was
supposed to have laid out a plan of infiltration and subversion of
Christian Spain. Its content strongly suggested the main elements of
Christian paranoia. Asked by the Jews of Spain how they could resist
the King of Spain who was forcing them to convert or even killing
them, Yusef is supposed to have replied:

Where you say that the King of Spain would convert you to Christianity, do it because you have no alternative. Where you say that they deprive you of your property, make your sons merchants so that little by little you can take theirs. Where you say that they are robbing you of your lives, make your sons doctors and apothecaries so that you can end theirs. Where you say that they are destroying your synagogues, make your sons clerics and theologians, so you can destroy their churches. And as far as your other troubles are concerned, make your sons advocates, administrators, lawyers, and advisors, and let them take part in affairs of state so that you can gain land . . .[51]

However, while historians' preoccupation with the persecution of the Jews in the fifteenth century is understandable, it obscures the roots of the oppression suffered by the Muslim population in the following century. The Muslims were left out of the account, and to modern eyes it seems implausible that an attribution of blood taint – as Christ-killers – could suddenly be applied to them in later years. It was well known that Islam had developed centuries after the death of Christ. Yet by a process of syllogistic argument Muslims too, stage by stage, acquired an ineradicable taint like the Jews. Did they not, so many Christians believed, worship the Antichrist Mohammed, and had they not despoiled the Holy Land itself? Had the Jews not aided the Muslims and were Muslims not therefore as guilty as those who had actually killed him? So, while in the drive for purity of blood the main victims were Jews and Jewish converts, the Moors were usually yoked with them in the litanies of hatred.

The position of Granada, the last non-Christian enclave in the peninsula after the mid thirteenth century, was in a permanent state of flux. Granada could become an ally or an enemy of the Christian realms with bewildering speed, as one faction or another took control either in the Christian kingdoms or in Granada itself. In Granada power shifted back and forth from one part of the royal family to another. One ruler, Mohammed IX 'the Left-Handed', took the throne on no fewer than four separate occasions. However, despite the instability of Granadine politics, the military might of the last Moorish state grew during the fifteenth century. While Castile, in particular, had begun to develop gunpowder weapons and a siege train with cannon and bombards, the Granadines concentrated on building a profusion of small fortified towns and peel towers. These could be used as bases for a type of highly mobile border warfare that was becoming increasingly prevalent along the frontier.

Two styles of campaigning began to emerge from the 1400s. The Castilians with their superiority in weapons, money and manpower could usually take even a strongly fortified citadel after a long siege. But not always. In 1407 the three great guns of Infante Ferdinand, son of King John II of Castile, had successfully breached the walls of the Granadine town of Zahara, and moved on to nearby Setenil. Here the guns were set up and battered the town day and night to such an extent that within a few weeks the Castilians had run out of stones to fire. Each knight and man-at-arms was thereafter given a daily quota of rocks to find to keep the guns from falling silent. But, as autumn passed, the citizens continued to hold out, repairing the damage by night. By the end of October, Ferdinand had still not brought the city to the point of surrender and he did not want to be trapped over the winter in enemy territory, where the Granadine light cavalry (*jinetes*) could cut off his supply train. So the Christian besiegers withdrew in some disorder, to the taunts of the defenders on the walls.[52]

The Granadine method of war depended on speed and mobility – classic border raiding. The *jinetes* had adapted the loose riding style of North Africa (which Géricault would later, to great effect, depict for the salons of nineteenth-century France). The horsemen rode small and lightly built stallions, bred for sure-footedness over rough and stony ground, and wore only light armour, usually chainmail or, at most, a light cuirass. Their offensive weapons were a bundle of throwing spears and a long sword, but many were also proficient in the use of a light but powerful crossbow, which they could fire and reload even while moving. They had perfected a tactic called *kerr wa-farr*, often used in the tribal battles of Morocco. They would attack, and then retreat, trying to draw their enemy after them. Against Christian cavalry this proved very effective, because the charge of heavy armoured cavalry depended upon mass and impact for its success. Once separated from their 'squadron' the Christian knights were easy targets for the *jinetes*. Indeed, to meet the challenge, the

Castilian nobles whose lands bordered Granada began to employ light horsemen themselves.

Conversely, in a battle where the Granadines fought in the static Castilian style, they invariably came off worst, as in an encounter near Lorca in 1452, where a raiding party returning to Granada with 40,000 head of livestock was caught by Christian knights.

When they came in sight of one another, the Moors drew themselves up in battle array and the Christian knights did the same. The battle was so keenly fought that the Christians had to make three charges, but finally the Moors were beaten, and more than eight hundred of them killed; the Christians lost forty killed and two hundred wounded.

The Christians' leader, Alonso Fajardo, further took his revenge by mounting a raid on Lorca, where he slaughtered the Muslim inhabitants, and then on to a village on a high peak. He recorded laconically, 'I took Mojacar where such great deeds were done that the streets ran with blood.'[53] This raiding and skirmishing continued regardless of whether or not there was declared war between Granada and its neighbours, winter and summer alike. Granadine bands ravaged up to the gates of Cartagena, while Miguel Lucas de Iranzo from Jaen burned towns only a few miles from Granada itself in retribution.

Prophecy had always been popular in Christian Spain and settling the final account with Granada had long been expected. It was remembered that King Pelayo in his Astunian cave at Covadonga had foretold that God would eventually come to the aid of His people, and that was taken to mean that God willed the reconquest of Granada. But the omens that attached themselves to Prince Ferdinand and Princess Isabella, the heirs to Aragon and Castile respectively, exceeded those of the past. Many Castilians believed that Isabella the Catholic (*La Católica*) had been born miraculously, for the 'Redemption of Lost Kingdoms'. Others called her a second Virgin Mary.[54] The conjuncture of the birth of a male heir to Ferdinand and Isabella in 1478, the settlement of the Castilian succession, and Ferdinand's coming to the throne of Aragon generated still more prophecies. The salvation of the kingdom would be accomplished, and Spain would be restored as 'one Christian nation, destined first for universal monarchy, and thereafter, for celestial hierarchy'.

Ferdinand and Isabella were seen as the chosen agents of the Divine plan. Their victory over evil, it was hoped, would have two aspects. The first was interior purity. A national council of the Spanish Church was held in Seville in the summer of 1478 and declared a programme for reform. In the autumn, Isabella and Ferdinand secured approval from Pope Sixtus for the appointment of Inquisitors to serve in the realm of Castile. They began work in earnest in 1480, and between 1481 and 1488, thousands of 'Judaizers', heretics and other enemies of Catholic Spain were 'reconciled' to the Church or relinquished to the state to be burned.[55] The other aspect of this national purification was completing the holy work of the Reconquest. A popular poet, Fray Iñigo de Mendoza, proclaimed that the King and Queen of Castile would end the abomination of Islamic rule in the peninsula.[56] The old ideas of 'Imperial' Castile were revived, while prophecies appeared in Aragon that Ferdinand would drive the Moors completely from the land of Spain and, indeed, out of North Africa.[57]

The idea of recapturing the entire peninsula from Muslim dominion was not the same as removing Moors from the face of Spain. For centuries, the communities had lived side by side, in varying political circumstances. Where under Islam the Christians and Jews were *dhimmis*, the protected but subordinate minorities within the state, in Christian Spain the Muslims now became feudal subordinates (or the slaves) of either king or some noble, who thereafter had responsibility for them. Granada was abominable not so much because it was filled with Muslims, but because it was a free and independent state, aggressively Muslim and endlessly fomenting intrigues with North Africa and pursuing border skirmishes with the Christians to the north. Even while a notional truce existed with the Granadines, Ferdinand and Isabella began to plan for a campaign against Granada, for, as they wrote to the pope, they were motivated not 'by any desire to enlarge our realms but . . . hoping only that the Holy Catholic faith will be multiplied and that Christendom will be quit of so constant a danger as she has here at our very doors, if these infidels of the kingdom of Granada are not uprooted and cast out from Spain.'[58] Thus, while it was a Granadine attack on long-disputed Zahara on 26 December 1481 that became the *casus belli*, the plan for the final extirpation of Islamic rule in Spain had already been devised.

However, the Kingdom of Granada was well defended, by both

Nature and military art. Every town and city was walled, and the frontier zone was studded with a profusion of stone-built peel towers which, if held by a determined garrison, could only be starved out or taken when the defences had been breached by artillery. Centuries later, the American writer Washington Irving described the land as he first saw it:

The ancient kingdom of Granada, into which we were about to penetrate, is one of the most mountainous regions of Spain. Vast *sierras* or chains of mountains, destitute of shrub or tree and mottled with variegated marbles and granites, elevate their sunburnt summits against a deep blue sky . . . In traversing these lofty *sierras* the traveller is often obliged to alight and lead his horse up and down the steep and jagged ascents and descents, resembling the broken steps of a staircase. Sometimes the road winds along dizzy precipices . . . [or] straggles through rugged *barrancos* or declivities, worn by winter torrents.[59]

But once through the mountains, a different Granada appeared. There 'lie engulfed the most verdant and fertile valleys, where desert and garden strain for mastery, and the very rock is, as it were, compelled to yield the fig, the orange and the citron, and to blossom with the myrtle and the rose'.[60] The walled capital itself had, it was said, 1,030 turrets and seven great gates; inside was a population estimated at the beginning of the fourteenth century to be around 200,000. Above the city on a rocky outcrop stood the fortified palace of the Alhambra, with its citadel, the Alcazaba, and outside its perimeter wall, the summer palace or Generalife. The splendours of the city gave rise to a little refrain: a citizen of Seville could assert

> *El que no ha visto á Sevilla*
> *No ha visto maravilla*
> (He who has not seen Seville has not seen a marvel.)

To which the Granadino would reply:

> *El que no ha visto á Granada*
> *No ha visto de nada*
> (He who has not seen Granada has seen nothing at all.)

The Kingdom of Granada was rich and productive. Ships from the eastern Mediterranean called at ports such as Malaga to purchase silks and other textiles, sugar and fruit.[61] Florence bought 'Cordovan' leather. Unsurprisingly, the Holy Roman Emperor's ambassador en route to Lisbon contrasted the refinement and elegance of Granada with the more rudimentary facilities of the Christian kingdoms.[62] The pomegranate, *Punica granata*, was Granada's eponymous emblem. For Muslim mystics the fruit, filled to bursting with tiny glistening seeds, signified the Garden of the Divine Essence, and represented the vast multiplicity of God's creation.[63] Christians like King Ferdinand knew nothing of this deeper symbolism. He once described his strategy for the conquest of Granada in the form of a pun: he would, he said, eat the seeds of the pomegranate one by one. But he tempted fate. Everyone knows that a pomegranate contains seeds in vast profusion. The joke rebounded, for the final act of the Reconquest took more than ten years to accomplish and then only at ruinous cost.

The medieval battles of the *Reconquista* had largely been fought on terms that favoured the Christian armies of the north.[64] Even where they had suffered a catastrophe, as at Alarcos in 1195, it was usually the result of some tactical or strategic misjudgement, not because of inferior numbers or resources. The war for Granada was no different. The nobles, towns and cities of Castile were all summoned to provide their contingents of horsemen and men-at-arms, as in any medieval army. The military orders of Calatrava, Santiago and Alcantara formed the professional and disciplined elite cavalry used to spearhead attacks. But beside them, drawn up in ranks with powder and projectiles carried in a line of carts, were a new element: a large number of artillery pieces designed to batter down the stone walls. Some of these were huge, much larger than those used with such success earlier in the century. Those deployed at the siege of Baza were twelve feet in length, with bores fourteen inches in diameter and firing a stone ball weighing over 175 pounds. These great guns could discharge only a single shot per hour, but few walls could stand up to steady fire. Yet they were not necessarily decisive. The defenders of Baza were not battered into submission, but simply ran out of food and ammunition.

The Castilians were also over-confident. Their first success had been capturing the town of Alhama, in the heart of the Kingdom of Granada, by a bold surprise attack. Such a master stroke could not be repeated. Their next assault at the town of Loja in July 1482, a move designed to reinforce Alhama, was a disaster. Granadine *jinetes* swiftly overran the Christian positions, while Granadine crossbowmen picked off the more heavily armoured and cumbersome Castilians. Few of the Christian troops had ever fought in the torrid climate and rough conditions of the south, while the Granadines had been hardened over generations of border warfare. A major Castilian advance on Malaga the following spring was ambushed in the wild mountains and deep ravines to the north of the city. Battered on every side, the Grand Master of the Order of Santiago, the premier order of Spanish chivalry, was supposed to have cried, 'Oh God how great is Your anger this day against Your servants. You have changed the cowardice of these infidels into desperate valour, and have made peasants and serfs into men of valour.'[65]

It was becoming clear that the war for Granada could be won only by slow and remorseless pressure.[66] Staying clear of the high ground wherever possible, the Christian armies began to advance along the river valleys and flat plains that led eventually to the capital of Granada, beneath the Sierra Nevada. But all approach roads were heavily defended and at each stronghold or fortified town the same drama was enacted. Setenil, north of Ronda, which the Castilians had failed to take in 1407, was carved out from the hill and was protected by a tower on the hill above it. The Castilian artillery was emplaced and slowly battered down the walls. Once the troops were able to enter, they slaughtered everyone left alive amid the rubble. At other sites, such as Benamquex in 1408, Ferdinand took a town by storm, and then hanged more than a hundred of the most prominent men of the town, suspending their bodies in a long line like a necklace over the walls. He enslaved the rest, men, women and children. But the towns continued to resist stubbornly and the pace of advance grew slower. The capture on 22 May 1485 of Ronda, a fortress town built upon a sheer rocky outcrop above the River Guadalevín, turned the war in the Christians' favour. Ronda could have held out longer, but a number of its leaders decided to surrender on favourable terms. Thereafter Ferdinand gave his enemies these options: death or enslavement to those who resisted; honeyed words and favours to those who surrendered their posts. The latter proved increasingly alluring as the long war continued.

The Christian armies were now moving towards Granada from both the west and north. They were beaten back from Moclin, south of the Castilian frontier town of Alcala la Real. Moclin was another citadel built to take advantage of the lie of the land, making it a near-impregnable barrier to any advance along the main road to Granada.[67] They failed to take it. But the long frontier meant that there were many other points of attack. Rebuffed from Moclin, the Christians probed again from farther east, and with much greater success. A large force moved south from Jaen to attack the twin fortresses of Cambil and Alhaber, which had been erected to protect the high road to Granada. Once again the Castilians laboriously manoeuvred their heavy guns into position and shattered the old walls. They succeeded and, with the twin forts fallen, the last of Granada's outer lines of defence had been pierced. By the summer of 1486, after four years of campaigning, Ferdinand's front line rested at the 'apple of Granada', the fortress of Illora. In front of it lay the River Cubillas, crossed by a narrow bridge at the village of Piños Puente; and thence, for an ordinary traveller, it was less than a half a day's easy walk into the city of Granada itself.

The greatest danger now lay not in the city before them but from behind. While the coastline was still in Muslim hands, the threat of Moroccan or even Ottoman support for their Muslim brothers could not be discounted. The garrison of Malaga was largely made up of Berber volunteers from North Africa, eager to strike a blow against the infidels. Meanwhile the rulers of Granada sent a stream of envoys to seek support from any Muslim state that would come to their aid. However, neither the rulers of Morocco and Egypt, nor the Ottoman sultan in Constantinople was willing or able to help them. Nonetheless, Ferdinand decided on a strategy that would cut off Granada from the ports along its southern flank, and then isolate the capital entirely. Granada's best tactic was to attack each Castilian force in turn, relying on the fact that their speedy horsemen could move more easily from front to front. What ultimately doomed their defence was disunity. The royal family was split into numerous factions, intent on fighting each other rather than their external enemy. At times, one group held the city of Granada and besieged another in the Alhambra above. At other times some of the leading figures of Granada were in league with the Christians while others were struggling with them on the battlefield.

While the Granadine aristocrats squabbled, the full weight of the Spanish siege train was marshalled against the port-city of Malaga late in the spring of 1487.[68] Soon more than 60,000 men were encamped around Malaga, with detachments from Germany, France, England and many other parts of Europe. Every attempt by the besiegers to overcome the defence with siege towers and mining was frustrated by the Muslims. The historian of the War of Granada, Fernando de Pulgar, observed, 'Who does not marvel at the bold heart of these infidels in battle, their prompt obedience to their chiefs, their dexterity in the wiles of war, their patience under privation and undaunted perseverance in their purposes.'[69] The strength of their resistance made the Castilians fight for every yard of ground. Pulgar said that they seemed to have a greater desire to kill Christians than to preserve their own lives. On the Christian side the savagery of the fighting meant that a desire for vengeance predominated over the desire for financial gain. No one attempted to take prisoners. They wanted only to kill or maim. But as the siege was prolonged the townspeople began to starve. According to an Arabic source, when the food stocks ran out, 'they had to eat whatever was edible: horses, asses, donkeys, dogs, skins, the leaves from trees', and only then would they seek terms.[70]

But Ferdinand in this case would give them none, so they faced either death or slavery. When the city and its fortresses finally surrendered after three months of siege, Ferdinand and Isabella with their whole court celebrated Mass in the principal mosque, hurriedly consecrated as St Mary of the Holy Incarnation. Meanwhile long lines of the people of Malaga were led away into slavery. For two groups, however, a special fate was reserved. Twelve renegades, who had abandoned their Christian faith for Islam, were led out to an open field, stripped and bound to upright posts. They were to be killed with sharpened canes, *acañavereado*. The horsemen in the army were given bundles of long stiff canes cut to a fine point. They rode back and forth, hurling their improvised javelins at the tethered renegades. Their accuracy improved until the bodies of the condemned resembled models for the Martyrdom of Saint Sebastian, spiked through with arrows. This protracted and exemplary execution lasted most of the day under the summer heat before the last unfortunate had expired. To complete what the chronicler Father Abarca described as 'the festivities and illuminations most grateful to the Catholic piety of our sovereigns' a number of Jewish converts who had returned to the faith of their fathers were burned alive at the stake.[71]

Malaga had guarded the western approaches to Granada, and Ferdinand already controlled the approach to the Vega of Granada itself. The only other area where the Muslims remained in control was the eastern half of the kingdom, with the great fortress city of Baza dominating the road from Valencia and Murcia. In the spring of 1489, the Castilian siege train deployed once more, but after five months Baza seemed no closer to surrender than on the first day. Even Heaven seemed against them, for a sudden and unexpected flash flood swept away much of the Castilian camp and destroyed most of the rudimentary roads. Six thousand pioneers were set to work by Queen Isabella to restore the roads, and she came in person to raise the waning spirits of her troops. In the adulatory phrases of Peter Martyr d'Anghiera (later a noted historian of Spain and its empire in America), while the Muslims crammed the battlements of the city to watch, the queen arrived, 'surrounded by a choir of nymphs, as if to celebrate the nuptials of her child; and her presence seemed at once to gladden and reanimate our spirits, drooping under long vigils, dangers and fatigue'.[72] It had the opposite effect on the defenders, who sent negotiators to Ferdinand. His terms were as generous as those offered to the people of Malaga had been harsh. The surrender was quickly agreed, and on 4 December 1489, Ferdinand and Isabella rode into Baza, while a banner emblazoned with the Cross was raised over the battlements. With the fall of the city, the last fortified town other than the city of Granada was in Christian hands.

But the cost of the war was growing daily. The king and queen had 80,000 men in the field and the prospect of undertaking a siege of Granada itself was an enterprise far greater than either Malaga or Baza. The task was more akin to the Ottoman assault on Constantinople in 1453 than anything that the armies of Spain had tackled. Peter Martyr said that Genoese merchants, 'voyagers to every clime, declare this to be the largest fortified city in the world'.[73] But unlike Constantinople, with its tiny garrison wholly inadequate to defend the long walls, Granada was crammed with 20,000 armed men, including the remains of the garrisons of Baza and Guadix, determined to defend the last piece of Muslim land in Al-Andalus. The heights above the city were walled and heavily defended and overlooked the plain below. The city itself was immured and could only be attacked frontally. William Hickling Prescott, in his *History of the Reign of Ferdinand and Isabella*, likened it to a sturdy oak, 'the last of the forest, bidding defiance to the storm that had prostrated all its brethren'.[74]

So the Castilians sat down before the city and waited for it to yield. From the spring of 1490 to the winter of 1491, they waited. The delay was punctuated by enemy sallies from the gates of Granada, one-to-one combats, processions and church services amid the tented city. Early in 1491, a permanent encampment called 'the Holy Faith' (*Santa Fê*), a name given to it by Isabella herself, was built in the shape of the Cross. In the end, a small band of the city's leading citizens began to open secret negotiations for its surrender in October 1491. Once more faction and division undermined the Granadine cause. To avoid a longer siege, or the risk of an attack, it was sensible for the Christians to offer acceptable terms. Ferdinand's negotiators agreed to everything that was demanded of them. The Muslims of Granada were to be allowed to remain in their homes or emigrate to North Africa as they wished; their rights of worship, their own legal codes, protection from unfair taxes, all were guaranteed. Only, the Jews of Granada were less lucky. Perhaps in anticipation of the greater fate that was to befall them, those who did not convert to Christianity were 'to cross to North Africa within three years'.[75]

The agreement was formally concluded in secret, but some of the inhabitants of Granada got wind of it, and 'a Moor . . . began an outcry within the city, saying that they were bound to win, if only they exalted Muhammad and if they challenged the settlement. He went about the city shouting, and twenty thousand Moors rose with him.' It was decided to advance the day of formal surrender from the Feast of the Epiphany (6 January) to 2 January. On 1 January, one of Ferdinand's officers, Gutierre de Cárdenas, with a troop of veterans received the keys to the citadel and occupied all the key points of the fortress. When on the following day Ferdinand received the keys to Granada from Emir Mohammed XII, known as 'Boabdil', who kissed his hand, it was an event enacted for the poets and historians. The transfer of power had already taken place: Al-Andalus had submitted to all-conquering, Eternal Spain.

Most of the Castilian chroniclers, poets and artists celebrated the accomplishment of God's promise to His people. Moreover the end of Al-Andalus was merely a stage in the advance of the Cross of Christ that was to lead to the recovery of the Holy Land itself. In 1506, it was proposed that Ferdinand, with his kinsmen Emanuel of Portugal and Henry VIII of England, should march through North Africa to Jerusalem.[76] The moral consequence of ending Islamic rule in Spain was enormous: the grant of the title of the Catholic Kings (*Los Reyes Católicos*) to Ferdinand and Isabella in 1494 by Pope Alexander VI was primarily a reward for the conquest of Granada and for expelling the Jews from Spain. The imagery of Crusade or 'Reconquest' stressed the continuity with an imagined Christian-Visigothic past, for the title itself had a historic echo. King Alfonso I of the Asturias in the eighth century had also been a 'Catholic' king, as had Peter I of Aragon in the thirteenth. The exuberant exaltation of the Catholic faith rewrote the past and the voices of those cultures destroyed in the process were largely mute.

Myth (and history) records the 'last sigh of the Moor' as the last emir, Boabdil, mourned the loss of Granada; but this is merely an elegiac of submission. It does not capture the sense of resistance, the determination to die rather than yield, that better characterized the long war for Granada. The Castilian historian, Fernando de Pulgar, recorded one small incident that is more truthful to the character of Al-Andalus, and predictive of the final throes of the Muslims in Spain. He told the story of a simple Moorish weaver at Loja in 1485. When his neighbours and his wife prepared to flee from the advancing Castilians, he continued to work at his loom. When they begged him to join them, he rejected their pleas.

Where do you want us to go? Where should we seek to preserve ourselves? From hunger? From cold steel? Or from persecution? Wife, I tell you that since we have no friend to take pity on our misfortunes and to put them to rights, I prefer to wait for an enemy who covets our goods and will kill me. I would rather die here by steel [*fierro*] than later by shackles [*fierros*]. For Loja, which once defied the Christians and defended the Muslims, has become the tomb of its defenders and the home of its enemies.[77]

Refusing to change his mind the man remained in his own house, until the Christians broke in and killed him.

5

Eternal Spain

The year 1492, the triumphant moment in Granada when the Christians finally 'recovered' the last acres of Spain, appeared differently to each generation. The writers and painters of the nineteenth century found it especially enticing. Four centuries after the event, both Washington Irving and his near-contemporary, the history painter Francisco Pradilla y Ortiz, *Romanticized* the event. In Irving's description of the celebrations, Ferdinand and Isabella

at last . . . saw the silver cross, the great standard of this crusade, elevated on the Torre de la Vela, or great watch tower, and sparkling in the sunbeams . . . Beside it was planted the pennon of the glorious apostle St James; and a great cry of 'Santiago! Santiago!' rose throughout the army. Lastly was reared the royal standard, by a knight at arms, with the shout of 'Castile! Castile! For King Ferdinand and Queen Isabella'. The words were echoed by the whole army . . . At the sight of these signals of possession, the sovereigns fell upon their knees, giving thanks to God for this great triumph. The whole assembled host followed their example; and the choristers of the royal chapel broke forth into the solemn anthem of *Te Deum laudamus*.[1]

Then the whole procession moved forward towards the citadel, on the way meeting the last emir leaving the city for the final time. This was the event immortalized by Pradilla y Ortiz, with Boabdil holding the keys to the citadel and Ferdinand leaning slightly forward on his stallion, his hand outstretched to receive them. But it is the queen, Isabella, resplendent on a pure-white palfrey, who dominates the image.

However, it was the first artist to depict this scene who came closest to the central meaning of the Reconquest and Isabella's role in it. The Burgundian painter Philippe de Vigarny had been employed in Spain since 1498. He had with others created the magnificent polychrome altar in the Cathedral at Burgos, and was involved in the first plans for the Chapel Royal in Granada in 1505. When Emperor Charles V had his grandparents' resting place built on a grand scale, Vigarny was largely responsible for the great altarpiece of carved and painted wood. He knew the message that Ferdinand had wished to convey and it is reasonable to assume that this monument to the glory of God accurately presented the aspirations of the Catholic Kings. The altar was shaped like the portico of a Renaissance church, and through a set of elaborately carved and painted tableaux presented the Crucifixion, the saints and martyrs of the Church, the Evangelists, who all rose in tiers to the holy dove and God himself at its apex. At either side knelt Ferdinand and Isabella, angled not towards the central focus of the altar, but facing each other. From this the spectator was perhaps intended to infer the great and holy love they had for each other.[2]

Beneath them, on the base or *predella* of the altar, was another tableau of carved panels, on which the whole superstructure (literally and metaphorically) rested. It told the story of the capture of Granada. Below Ferdinand's effigy was related the war and the triumphant entry to the city, with the queen to the fore. Under Isabella were two reliefs that depicted the crowning moment of the conquest, the queen's ardent desire, which was the conversion of the Muslims to Christianity. This was the act of 'overthrowing the Mahomatan sect' that was inscribed on their tomb, and marked the true culmination of the *Reconquista*.

It has long been debated whether the dominant partner was Ferdinand or Isabella. The iconography suggests Isabella, but the question could be asked in another way, and to that the answer is beyond question. Was the victory Castile's or Aragon's? Castile led and Isabella was the embodiment of the long tradition of Castilian political ideology. Ferdinand inherited the same tradition: John I of Castile had been great-grandfather to both of them. Indeed, the very closeness of their genetic connection had posed a considerable problem. When they married they did so without the essential papal dispensation that allowed a union between cousins. They had relied on a document that had been forged. So it was not a matter of Isabella representing the values of Castile and Ferdinand those of Aragon. They were heirs to a common heritage.

But there was a distinction between them. Ferdinand had been born in Aragon, while Isabella was a child of Castile, born at Madrigal de las Altas Torres, close to Medina del Campo. She was also the King of Castile, direct inheritor of the long monarchical tradition of Castile and Leon, of Asturias and the near-legendary Visigothic kingdom. Moreover, the idea of home and birthplace, of the land that Spaniards call the *patria chica* (untranslatable, really, but the closest is perhaps 'home ground'), was at the heart of the 'Spain' that both of the Catholic Kings fought to restore. The concept of restitution, taking complete possession of a land stolen from 'Spaniards' and from Christendom by the Muslims (and their allies, the Jews), existed regardless of the political realities of the Iberian peninsula.

The plans that Ferdinand and Isabella began to put in place during their few months of residence in the Alhambra in 1492 were founded in the ideas and aspirations of history. But they were also suffused with a new spirit of opportunity. The old accommodations and equivocations of the past were no longer necessary. They expected that the Muslims would convert en masse, as the Jews had done during the earlier part of the century. Isabella's own confessor, Hernando de Talavera, was appointed Archbishop of Granada, and he immediately began to implement plans to explain the truth and right of Christianity to leading Muslims in the city. Conversion had to be genuine and not forced if it were to be solid and sincere. However, the problems with this policy had already emerged in the case of the Jews. Those who had converted were, according to the Inquisition, likely to 'relapse' into their old customs and habits of life. The existence of both practising Jews and New Christian converts within Spain suggested the impediments in the godly path to conversion. The answer to so-called 'Judaizers', who undermined the New Christian faith of converts, was to remove these tempters from the soil of Spain.

The process began in Granada on 31 March 1492 when the victorious Ferdinand and Isabella decreed the definitive expulsion of Spain's believing Jews. A forewarning of the monarchs' attitude had been contained in the deed of capitulation signed with the Muslims of Granada in November 1491. This had envisaged the 'transfer of the Jews of Granada to North Africa'. Two decrees, issued simultaneously in Castile and Aragon, were unambiguous:

The said Jews . . . of our kingdoms [are] to depart and never to return or come back to them . . . Jews . . . of whatever age they may be . . . with their sons and daughters, manservants and maidservants, Jewish familiars, those who are great as well as the lesser folk, of whatever age they may be, and they shall not dare to return to those places, nor to reside in them . . . under pain that they incur the penalty of death and the confiscation of all their possessions.

The grounds were that the Jews' continued presence would corrupt the re-Christianized peninsula. The decree was finally promulgated in April 1492, and it did not apply to Christians of Jewish origin: the option of conversion remained open. In May, Ferdinand instructed the Inquisitor Tomás de Torquemada not to impede any Jew who expressed a wish to become a Christian and return to Spain. Even after the expulsion was completed, Ferdinand issued a further decree from Barcelona so that any Jew who had left could return (contrary to the ordinance) provided they could produce evidence of conversion.[3]

But perhaps 50,000–80,000 were expelled from Castile and Aragon, some to North Africa and many taking ship to Italy or Constantinople. The conditions were onerous. Wealthy merchants were not permitted to take any gold or silver and, although they were allowed to sell their property, anything left unsold would be claimed by the Crown. In effect, it was a confiscation of all save their most movable property. This contemporary report of their arrival in Genoa en route further east expresses the extent of this human tragedy.

No one could behold the sufferings of the Jewish exiles unmoved. A great many perished of hunger, especially those of tender years. Mothers with scarcely strength to support themselves, carried their famished infants in their arms and died with them. Many fell victims to the cold, others to intense thirst . . . they arrived in Genoa in crowds, but were not suffered to tarry there long by reason of the ancient law which interdicted the Jewish traveller from a longer residence than three days. They were allowed, however, to refit their vessels and to recruit themselves for some days from the fatigues of their voyage. One might have taken them for spectres, so emaciated were they, so cadaverous in their aspect and with eyes so sunken . . . Many fainted and expired on the mole [of the harbour].[4]

But while the Catholic Kings' objective was a unitary Christian Spain, made up of Old and New Christians, the opposite tendency towards a Spain divided by origin was growing ever stronger. In the last year of the campaign for Granada, considerable efforts were being made to fabricate evidence that Jews and converts both posed a mortal threat to Spain. Between 1490 and November 1491, no effort was being spared by the Inquisition (including repeated bouts of torture) to prove that ten men had kidnapped a child from the village of La Guardia near Toledo, crucified him, then cut out his heart and drunk his blood. Despite the fact that no child was ever found to be missing from the village, the accused were eventually found guilty and burned alive. Accounts of the trial were published and widely circulated. In content the allegations differed very little from other propaganda and false accusations directed against the Jews in other parts of Europe. The episode was strikingly similar to the case of Simon of Trent, which took place in northern Italy in 1472. There, unlike in the affair of La Guardia, a young child did disappear and the corpse was found in the river a few days later. However, there was no evidence whatsoever of any Jewish connection to his death. Nor is there any suggestion that other more plausible alternatives were considered.

However, the grotesque tales and accusations that quickly developed around Simon of Trent soon followed a pattern that was later recognizable in Spain.[5] The same elements, such as crucifixion, circumcision and bleeding, repeatedly appeared in the cases made against Jews. Simon of Trent became a popular subject for gory woodcuts, as did the imaginary Infant of La Guardia, later named Cristobal, a 'Christ child'.[6] After the events at La Guardia, social panic over the *conversos* became general, and as Yosef Yerushalmi has observed, 'the traditional mistrust of the Jew as an outsider now gave way to an even more alarming fear of the *converso* as an insider'.[7] Many in Spain believed that the 'taint' of Jewish birth could never be eradicated. Stories like this suggested the strength of the popular mood. Increasingly the name now widely used for converts was *marrano*, meaning pig, playing contemptuously with the Jewish prohibition against eating pork. The word for Jewish women who converted, *maranna*, came to mean a whore or slut.[8]

The fires that consumed the Jews and *conversos* in La Guardia were barely cold before the terms were agreed for the surrender of Granada in January 1492, and it was in this climate of fear that two months later the decrees of expulsion were issued. Although Jews and Muslims were linked in Christian attitudes, in popular understanding they were not considered identical. The position that Jews occupied in relation to Christians was anomalous, for Jesus Christ himself was a Jew, 'born of the House of David', but had also been killed by the Jews. The threat that Jews were thought to pose to Christians was subtle and insidious rather than bellicose. Muslims, by contrast, were the exterior enemy, unparalleled in their capacity for war and savage cruelty. But, like certain wild animals, they could be tamed. There were 'Moors of peace', the industrious peaceful agriculturists and craftsmen of both Castile and Aragon. The people of Granada were undoubtedly 'wild Moors', who had just fought a ten-year war against the best soldiers that Christian Spain could marshal. But it was widely believed in 1492 that conversion could accomplish this transformation, and once Christian they would leave their old ways behind. This, of course had also been the theory applied to the Jews.

Ferdinand and Isabella certainly held that the Muslims could be converted into sober and useful citizens. The clear expectation in 1492 was that the Muslims would be willing to become Christian. The unusual generosity to the Muslim population in the capitulation was dictated by a desire to bring the long war to an end. The terms had followed the old medieval pattern of agreements made by the rulers of Castile with their new subjects, plus a number of remarkable concessions, such as the right to retain arms. But it was written within an entirely new context. There were two clauses relating to the issue of conversion. The first concerned Christians who had converted to Islam. Their motives were not to be questioned. Nor would a female convert to Islam who had married a 'Moor' be forced to become Christian 'against her will'. The same would apply to the children of a Christian mother and a Muslim father. The second stated that no 'Moors', man or woman, would be forced to become Christian against their will. These clauses expressed a Muslim fear of forced conversions, beginning with the most vulnerable and marginal categories. The confident expectation among Spaniards was that there would be many who would come willingly to the welcoming arms of Christ. Islam was not expected to last for long in Granada. The sixth clause of the capitulation had been unambiguous:

Their highnesses and their successors will ever afterwards allow King Abi Abdilehi [Boabdil] and his [officials], military leaders, and good men and all the common people, great and small, to live in their own religion [*su ley*], and not permit their mosques to be taken from them, nor their minarets nor their muezzins, nor will they interfere with the pious foundations or endowments which they have for such purposes, nor will they disturb the uses and customs which they observe.[9]

The expectation was that many of the 'warlike Moors' would prefer to emigrate to North Africa under the favourable conditions laid out in the surrender or would at any rate leave the city. Ferdinand's secretary Hernando de Zafra wrote in December 1492 that 'the Abencerrajes [considered an especially bellicose clan] have taken their womenfolk up to the Alpujarras. After selling off all their property, they are preparing to leave by the end of March. As far as I can see most people are packing up to leave at the same time.' By the summer he predicted that only farmworkers and craftsmen would be left. They did not leave because they had been badly treated – as he said, 'No people have ever been treated better.'[10] A generation later, in 1526, a commentator remarked that all the 'noble people' of the Muslim community had gone and all those left were 'low and common folk'.[11] Within a few years of the conquest Granada had ceased to be a predominantly Muslim city.[12] It was officially divided, like many of the cities of Castile, into Christian and Mudejar quarters. The area called the Albaicin became a purely Muslim quarter, while the lower parts of the city were designated for Christians, both migrants from the north and Muslim converts. The separation was extended by regulations designed to keep Christians and Muslims within the bounds of their own communities, not an easy task in a city such as Granada.

By 1499, almost 40,000 'Old Christian' colonists had entered the Kingdom of Granada, many with families. By 1530, the number had reached 100,000.[13] It was hoped that these pioneers would provide a Christian example for the Muslims. First the Muslim community in the city of Granada would convert, and then the common folk of the countryside would follow their lead. Progress was expected to be rapid. Three years was set as a limit in the terms of surrender as a tax amnesty for Muslims, and after that point taxes would be reimposed.

The new taxes on Muslims were set at a substantially higher level than for their Christian fellow-citizens so there was a strong financial incentive to convert. Three years was also the time during which Muslims could emigrate without payment. The assumption by Zafra was that those who did not wish to live under Christian rule would have left before the 1495 deadline and that those who remained would be ripe for conversion.

The confidence of the Catholic Kings in their mission was unbounded. They envisaged reconquering the ancient Visigothic lands in North Africa and recapturing Jerusalem. The Genoese Christopher Columbus presented his commission to sail west to discover the Indies as part of the Divine mission that Ferdinand and Isabella were predestined to accomplish. Columbus saw how first they had conquered Granada. Then they had expelled the Jews. Finally, Columbus claimed, he would bring back such riches 'in such quantities that within three years the Sovereigns will prepare for and undertake the conquest of the Holy Land. I have already petitioned Your Highnesses to see that all the profits of this, my enterprise, should be spent on the conquest of Jerusalem.'[14]

A more reliable source of profit came from the gold of Africa which flowed from the Canary Islands – those, so the Castilian histories claimed, had formerly belonged to the unlucky Visigothic King Roderick. In 1458 the Castilian Kings had assumed the title of 'King of the Great Canary with all its islands'. The conquest of the islands had been waged intermittently in 1402, but in 1483 a large Castilian fleet had sailed to the islands and completed the occupation of Gran Canaria on behalf of the Crown. Some of the aboriginal inhabitants (*guanches*) of the other large island, Tenerife, resisted fiercely. In May 1494 the *guanches* had attacked and killed 2,000 Spanish soldiers as they ascended the steep slopes of Teide, the volcano dominating the island. They severely wounded the Spanish commander, Alonso Fernandez de Lugo. More Spanish soldiers were landed on the island and they began systematically to kill or enslave the inhabitants. Many *guanches* had already been converted to Christianity, and the Catholic Kings sent an official in 1498 to look after the interests of all the Canarians, regardless of their faith. It was recognized that the simple people of the Canaries were ripe for conversion, and many became 'good Christians' and, it was argued, should consequently be treated well.

However, a boundary had been crossed in 1494. In the act of resisting the occupation of Tenerife, and by killing Christians, the *guanches* had shown their savage nature, had became recalcitrant, and were thus subject to forcible measures. The conquest and conversion of the Canary Islands and the conquest and conversion of Granada should not be considered in isolation from each other. The Jews were never considered savages. Their conversion fell within a set of established categories and was presaged in holy writ. The manner of it was laid down: conversion should be 'willing', and based upon consent. Moreover, once converted, former Jews should be thought of as other Christians. The Muslims represented a different problem. Few Muslims had converted in the past and, when offered the opportunity in earlier conquests by Castile, many had chosen to leave for a country under Islamic rule. However, the peaceful and industrious *Mudéjares* who had lived in Christian lands for generations showed that it was possible for 'Moors' to live quietly under Christian rule. In some areas they had increasingly accommodated to the dominant culture, so that in places like Avila in Castile and in much of Aragon, they no longer used Arabic.

The heritage of Muslim culture, which had produced the Alhambra and the Great Mosque of Cordoba, was not ignored by Christians and that respectful attitude determined the initial policy and practice of conversion. Yet Christians still perceived 'Moors' as possessing wild and savage qualities as well. This ambiguity existed in the Christian medieval polemics and in the histories of the Reconquest, and sometimes governed the experience of contemporaries as well. The Muslims of Granada, like the *guanches*, were held to be of an indeterminate and uncertain character. If the 'Moors' were savages, then their conversion would be less hedged about with restrictions than that of the Jews. The strategy of conversion would shift in a different direction.

It is possible to look at the last half of the fifteenth century from many distinct perspectives. The artistic and cultural Renaissance, the spread of printing, the loss of Constantinople, the European discovery of the Americas and Vasco da Gama's voyage to India have all been taken as touchstones of the age. The previous century has been characterized as 'calamitous', partly due to the consequences of the Black Death, which killed perhaps one-third of the population living between Iceland and India.[15] A large set of connections – social, political, religious, economic – have been linked to that one event. Philip Ziegler, in his study of the Black Death, refers to the twentieth-century analogy made between the aftermaths of the Black Death and the First World War. The comparison, he suggests, was that both made 'the greatest single contribution to the disintegration of an age'.[16] The fifteenth century in Spain saw both disintegration and reintegration, but upon different foundations than those that had prevailed before. Moreover, rather than one single monumental cause, events were increasingly perceived as possessing a multiplicity of origins. Everything was in flux and subject to change. Laws were written and never enforced, or enforced for only brief periods. Dynasties changed, with kings, bastards, pretenders all vying for power. I am also thinking here of France and England, powerful, rich and hitherto stable states. But in a culture dominated by its inner frontiers and boundaries like the Iberian peninsula, we should expect few certainties or set patterns during the fifteenth century and beyond.

Formerly settled social categories in Spain were becoming fissile and this is evident in the language of the time. 'Christian' divided into 'Old Christian' and 'New Christian'. Jews bifurcated into 'Jews' and what Christians more and more referred to insultingly as *marranos*, or as crypto-Jews. Muslims were called 'Moors', *Moros*, which could sometimes be admiring, but more often contained a sense of contempt, or they were called *Mudéjares*, which was a category of subjugation. Then they were transmogrified through conversion to Christianity into *Moriscos*, 'little Moors', a contemptuous and derogatory term, if sometimes tinged with a sense of pity.[17] But sometimes not. The 'true' author of Don Quixote, Cid Hamet Benengeli, whom we met in Chapter One, was a cultivated and learned figure. We should be as uneasy using the insulting word *Morisco*, for the same reason that *marrano* is not a word to be uttered lightly.[18] It was resented and never used by these 'New Christians' themselves. It was freshly minted to convey a new attitude towards a subject people, who had been stripped of their old religion by decree and given a perfunctory baptism. When the '*Morisco*' Nuñez de Muley wrote to protest about their treatment in Granada, he called them the *naturales*, the people of the land.

But changes in language mark a change of status. First in Granada and Castile, later in Aragon and Valencia *Mudéjares* became *Moriscos* by Royal decree. Gone was the wild, savage but noble 'Moors' of the border ballads; now over the space of a century they became a people who 'have only the outward appearance of a man, for the rest of you are beasts'. *Moriscos* were the antithesis of all that was good, worshipping Mohammed, who was 'the word of the devil', instead of Jesus Christ, who was 'the word of God'.[19] Here we can see change in process. The traditional diatribe against the Muslim, built up over many centuries, coalesced with a new style of abuse. This did not just happen as some kind of linguistic evolution: it was rooted in a specific sequence of events. This outcome was not by design. It was an unforeseen but not a random consequence.

We can locate a starting point for this new idiom of disparagement in Granada during the late summer of 1499. In July the Catholic Kings were in Granada for the first time since the spring of 1492. After seven years they had expected to see a people won for Christ, as the reports of Archbishop Talavera and Hernando de Zafra had led them to believe. Yet the city was much as they had left it, still looking to all appearances more a Muslim than a Christian city.[20] In the new Christian quarters new churches were strongly in evidence, as were a gratifying number of processions, saints' days commemorations, and the sound of church bells (which the Granadine Muslims referred to contemptuously as 'cowbells'). However, the mosques were still thronged by the faithful on Fridays.

Ferdinand and Isabella wanted to advance the pace of conversion, perhaps to the level achieved among the mainland Jews and the *guanches* of the Canaries. Outside the Kingdom of Granada better progress was being made. At the town of Caspe in Aragon the *Mudéjares* had converted to Christianity en masse, led by the most prominent members of their community. During the five months of their stay in the Alhambra, the Catholic Kings became convinced that conversion was not being pursued with sufficient energy in the capital; and if Granada lagged, then the conversion of the kingdom at large would be much more difficult. Before they left in November they had instructed the Archbishop of Toledo, Francisco Jiménez de Cisneros (who had succeeded Talavera as Isabella's confessor), to summon his team of able preachers and catechizers to Granada and so speed the process.

Jiménez de Cisneros had already argued at court for a more aggressive policy towards the Muslims in Granada. In particular, he was
completely opposed to the clause of the 1492 capitulation that allowed
former Christians and their children to remain, if they chose, with
Islam. Once installed in the 'Moorish' quarter of Granada, he began
immediately to make lists of these individuals, termed *elches*, who
were summoned to his presence. There he harangued them and, in
the words of one of the court historians,

with kind words he persuaded them to return to our holy Catholic faith,
because, as he said, it could not without the gravest sin be permitted for
people to belong to the religion of the Moors if their forebears had been
Christian . . . Those converted in this way were given assistance by him,
and he bestowed gratifications upon them: those who refused, he had put
in prison, and kept locked up until they were converted . . . When he heard
that many Muslim leaders were attacking his methods as being contrary to
the agreements . . . [he] imprisoned the dissidents in chains, and though it
ran counter to his temperament, he allowed them to be dealt with by
methods that were not correct.[21]

This was a euphemism for strict imprisonment and torture. In this
Jiménez de Cisneros was merely taking the same path as the Inquisition, which in Valencia was beginning, illegally, to take jurisdiction
over Muslims as well as Christians.[22] Moreover, anticipating the
increase of converts in Granada in 1499, the jurisdiction of the Inquisition in Cordoba was extended to take in the Kingdom of Granada.
Eventually Archbishop Talavera himself was to be called before it on
the grounds of seeking to convert Spain to Judaism by witchcraft.[23]
    When one of Jiménez de Cisneros' officials went up into the
Moorish quarter on 18 December 1499 to summon other *elches*, the
people of the quarter killed him, closed the gates and took up arms
in defence of their rights. 'They began to call upon Mohammed,
clamouring for liberty, and saying that they would burn the treaty of
surrender; they took to the streets, blocked and fortified the gates to
the Albaicin against the Christians of the city. They began to fight
with them and all through the night the tumult grew.'[24] There was a
near-panic among them that all Muslims would be converted by force.
Even the well-liked Archbishop Talavera was stoned and not allowed

to enter. When the Count of Tendilla, the Captain General of the kingdom, followed the Archbishop he was heard more respectfully. He told them that the pursuit of the *elches* would end, there would be no more forced conversions and, in a symbolic gesture, he brought down his wife and young child from the Alhambra to the Albaicin and entrusted them to the care and hospitality of the Muslim inhabitants. The rising in the city lasted some ten days, but further outbreaks of violence were forestalled. Yet nothing could be done to prevent news of the events in the capital reaching the staunchly Muslim villages of the Alpujarras. These had become a last redoubt for those who could not or would not leave their country, but did not want to live too close to Christians. Many of them had participated in the defence of Granada and were familiar with every contour and crevice of the land, invaluable knowledge in the guerrilla war that soon engulfed most of the kingdom.

Meanwhile Jiménez de Cisneros continued with his programme of mass conversion, and rendered Tendilla's promises worthless. Five days after the rising of the Albaicin had ended, Cisneros boasted that he had baptized 3,000 in a single morning. Messengers were sent to Ferdinand and Isabella at Seville, who, while fearing Muslim anger, were even more impressed by the rising total of conversions. They instructed Jiménez de Cisneros that 'our desire is that in conversion you make all the fruit you can make'.[25] To justify this shift in policy, Ferdinand now held that the brief rising in Granada, which had cost but a single life, had transformed the Granadines into warlike 'Moors' who had broken the terms of the capitulation. That this was a ruse is suggested by the fact that he also recognized that the rising was little more than a riot. He immediately confirmed Tendilla's pardon for all except those directly involved and extended an amnesty for all acts of rebellion provided those concerned converted to Christianity by 25 February 1500. The mass conversion that the Muslims feared was already under way and Cisneros, reassured of royal support, now redoubled his efforts. By the deadline he and his team had baptized almost the entire population of the city – this is the 'heroic' event commemorated on Vigarny's relief in the Chapel Royal.

Talavera had come to know the Muslims of Granada well; now marginalized by Jiménez de Cisneros, he feared disaster. He wrote to Ferdinand's secretary that the success in the capital did not represent what would happen in the countryside. 'One swallow does not make a summer . . .' he commented laconically. He ended his letter: 'From Granada, in truth very *desgranada* [winnowed and turned into an empty husk].'[26] The mass rising in the mountains that soon followed was on a scale never anticipated by the king. However, it also seemed to confirm that he had been right all along: the Muslims were wild and warlike, and tranquillity would only reign when they were all converted. Only a Christian Spain could hope to flourish. But as the towns and villages of the Alpujarras rose one by one, it was clear that this goal would not be accomplished by peaceful means. The Captain General, Tendilla, gathered what troops he could find and moved against Guejar, the closest fortified town in the mountains. After a bitter fight, the trained Christian soldiers overwhelmed the townspeople. The surviving male population was slaughtered in batches, while the women and children were enslaved, after which the town was ransacked by Tendilla's men. Early in February, Ferdinand arrived from Seville with fresh troops, and in March put Lanjaron to the sword. Another column entered the Alpujarras under the Count of Lerin, who stormed many villages, and in one confined the women and children to the village mosque before blowing it up with gunpowder.[27] The seventeenth-century historian of Aragon, Pedro de Abarca, described the villagers as 'these wild beasts of the Alpujarras', a widely held view at the time. The western part of the mountains surrendered, and the survivors were granted peace, on surrender of all their arms and fortresses, and payment of a punitive fine of 50,000 ducats.

In July 1500, Isabella and the court came to Granada and the work of conversion continued under the watchful eye of the queen. The cities of Baeza, Gaudix and Almeria were converted. Teams of preachers were sent into the conquered zones, and a further induce-ment offered. No new convert would have to pay his or her share of the huge fine levied on the rest of the population. But in December this active proselytizing pushed the eastern Alpujarras into a revolt, which was systematically suppressed by storming each town or village, and enslaving the survivors. The men were killed, but sometimes they were baptized en masse before they died. In February 1501, there was a more dangerous outbreak in the mountains at the far end of the Kingdom of Granada, beyond Ronda and much closer to Malaga and the urban centres of the south. A large body of leading Castilians, with 300 horsemen and 2,000 foot soldiers, immediately set out from Seville to put down the new rebellion. Lured into the mountains, many were killed, including their leader, a famous soldier called Alonso Hernandez de Córdoba, usually known as Alonso de Aguilar whose heroic end became the subject of innumerable ballads.[28] It was the worst disaster for Castilian arms since the losses in the war for Granada. Ferdinand gathered a huge force, complete with artillery, at Ronda and prepared to cleanse the land in the same way that the Alpujarras had been purged, with fire and sword. The leaders of the rebellion in the west quickly sought terms for peace. Ferdinand offered them a simple choice: baptism or leave the lands of Castile. Until they agreed he kept up the advance, storming fortified villages, killing the men and enslaving the women and children.

His decision was unequivocal: Islam would be ended in Castile: 'My opinion and that of the Queen,' Ferdinand declared, 'is that those "Moors" be baptised, and if they should not be Christian, their children or grandchildren will be.'[29] Terms of peace were agreed on 11 April 1501, and many Muslims immediately crossed the straits to North Africa. For Isabella too all Muslims in Castile must 'either convert or leave our kingdoms, for we cannot harbour infidels'.[30] In July, the Catholic Kings issued an order from the Alhambra forbidding Muslims to reside within the boundaries of the Kingdom of Granada, for they impeded the spiritual progress of the converts. On 12 February 1502 a decree was promulgated for Castile, that all Muslims had to choose baptism or leave Spain by 20 April, rather less time than had been given to the Jews a decade earlier. In part this indicated a conviction that not many would wish to leave, and this proved the case. Most who had wanted to go had already departed. Few Christians regretted what had happened. Indeed, once all those enslaved in Granada were sold, the war had made a considerable profit for the Crown.

The edict requiring conversion did not amount, in the queen's eyes, to forced conversion, because Muslims had been offered the alternative of leaving Castile or undergoing baptism. A number of Castilian *Mudéjares* fled to Aragon, and to Navarre, where they could still practise Islam. It was her grandson Charles V who applied the formula of baptism or expulsion to all his Spanish kingdoms. This casuistry was unconvincing, and her emissary Peter Martyr d' Anghi-era, sent to explain the decision to the King of Egypt, found the reality of forced conversion hard to deny. The Muslims of Granada had never expected that the Christians would adhere to the 1492 agreement. But the story of Castilian perfidy became a source of mistrust in the communities of the newly converted. The Muslims resisted conver-sion both by fighting, and by a sullen acceptance of their new status. The savagery of the war in the Alpujarras, and especially the death of the Marqués de Córdoba (Alonso de Aguilar), reinforced even further the popular equation between Islam, violence and latent danger. The Muslim Granadines were thought to be in contact with Barbary pirates, with their clansmen in North Africa, or with the more distant Ottomans. As the converted Jews had a taint in the blood, so the Muslims, transformed en masse into Christians, were seen by nature to be resentful and dangerous. A *Morisco* in Granada by law might not even possess a pocket knife for eating with that did not have a rounded point, lest he savage a Christian with it.[31]

Within a few years, Spain was to acquire many new infidels as subjects, in the new territories of America. The recent experience in mass conversion with the Muslims of Granada was carried forward into practice across the Atlantic.[32] At home the perception of the Muslim population as being threatening, the enemy within, was fuelled by the great struggle with the Ottomans developing in the Mediterranean. The sense of danger was well founded. Ottoman occupation of Aragonese territory in Apulia around Otranto in the Kingdom of Naples in 1480–81 was brief but menacing. The cathedral built by a King of Aragon in 1088 was reduced to rubble and the city sacked as the Ottoman fleet withdrew. The ships sailed home because of the death of Sultan Mehmed II, but it was thought they might return at any time. The Ottomans also feared Spain's ambitions. Her campaign to 're-conquer' North Africa began in 1497 with the capture of the town of Melilla, which remains, like Ceuta, Spanish territory to this day.

The strong clan connections between the *Moriscos* of Granada and those who had crossed the straits into Islamic territory grew in Castilian eyes into a form of conspiracy. Correspondence with 'Barbary' and seeking to flee across the water became offences punishable by death.

Even Father Bartolomé de las Casas, the ardent defender of the infidel Indians in the Americas, believed that Christian war against Muslim infidels was 'necessary and praiseworthy to recover Jerusalem, to drive the "Moors" from Spain, and always to fight against Muslims everywhere, the *"enemies of the faith, usurpers of Christian kingdoms"*.'[33] Elsewhere Las Casas expressed the double motive for fighting Islam: 'We have a just war against them, not only when they are actually waging it against us but even when they stop, because we have a very long experience of their intention to harm us; so our war against them cannot be called war but legitimate defence.'[34] When Las Casas presents the illegitimacy of persecuting and mistreating the *indios* (native inhabitants of the Americas), he does so by contrasting their plight with the legitimacy of a holy war on the infidel Turks and 'Moors', 'who pester and maltreat us'. He draws the contrast between American infidels, 'who never knew nor were obliged to know that there were Christian people in the world and therefore had never offended them' and 'the "Moors" and Turks, persecutors of the Christian name and violent occupiers of the kingdoms of Christianity'.[35] It was true, he stated, that there were certain infidels in America who merited harsh treatment, such as the Caribs, who resisted Columbus (and against whom Ferdinand authorized extreme measures).

After they rose and rebelled against us they have caused all the remaining Indians in the island to rebel . . . They have tried and are trying to protect themselves from being indoctrinated or taught the things of our Catholic faith and continually war against our subjects . . . they are hardened in their ways, dismembering and eating other Indians.[36]

The accusation of cannibalism was a calumny, not very different from the accusation that Jews crucified children and drank their blood. However, like the 'cruelty' of the Muslims, it served to detach the Caribs from the protection to be accorded to peaceful Indians.

As the political dangers from an expansive Muslim power increased, so new and potent meaning was given to ancient fears and prejudices. Civilized Renaissance scholars no longer believed that Muslims had heads like dogs and barked, but they nevertheless attributed brutal and monstrous qualities to them: ancient visceral prejudices were transmuted. During the reign of the Catholic Kings, a new theory of the Infidel was beginning to develop. In 1517, Cardinal Tomás de Vio Cayetano developed a novel doctrine of degrees of Infidelity. There were those infidels actually under the jurisdiction of Christianity, of whom the Muslims in Spain were the classic example. There were those who by law but not in fact were under Christian rule, like the inhabitants of North Africa or the Holy Land; and there were those who like the Indians of the Americas had never been under Christian rule.

While it was legitimate and laudable to coerce the first two categories, it was not legitimate to enslave and punish the natives of the New World. They were 'to be sent good men who by their preaching and example would convert them to God'.[37] This was exactly the policy that Talavera had sought to apply (with some success) in Granada, before it was replaced by the more robust methods of Jiménez de Cisneros. The same debate over baptism and honest conversion that had resonated in Granada between 1499 and 1501 was played out again. The good intention behind the baptism came to dominate the theory, a view expressed definitively by Pope Paul III in his Bull *Altitudo divini consilii* (The height of Divine providence): 'Whosoever baptised those Indians who came to the faith in Christ in the name of the Blessed Trinity without following the ceremonies and solemnity observed by the Church, did not sin for they thought rightly it was proper to do so.'

Thus the view of Ferdinand and Isabella that the good objective of conversion for the Muslims of Granada outweighed any doubts about the methods used was retrospectively endorsed. But the view of Las Casas, not circulated in print until four centuries after it was written, of the consequences of this style of conversion for the Indians applies just as readily to the Muslims of Spain. They would thereafter be

dominated by perpetual hatred and rancour against their oppressors . . . And therefore, even when they may sometimes say they wish to convert to the Christian faith and one can see that it may be so by the external signs that they use to show their will; you can always, however, be suspicious that their conversion does not come from a sincere intention nor their free will, but it is a false conversion, or one accepted to avoid some future evil that they fear would overcome them again.[38]

Ironically, it was Jiménez de Cisneros, the pioneer of mass conversion, who in 1516 had set the course for Las Casas' life's work by appointing him to head a commission of inquiry into the evils done to the Indians. But Las Casas' prophecy applied with even greater force to his homeland than it did in Spain's American possessions.

The critic Stephen Greenblatt has noted that the sixteenth-century Spanish *conquistadores* in the Americas (who brought with them their experience of conquering Islam in Spain) saw their language as a mechanism of conquest. He cited Antonio de Nebrija, whose *Gramática de la Lengua Castellana* – significantly – was published in 1492, and presented to Queen Isabella by the Bishop of Avila. The queen asked what the book was for, and the bishop replied, 'What is it for? Your Majesty, language is the perfect instrument of empire.'[39] Greenblatt's vision of the New World encounter between the dominant power and speech of Spain and the muted native inhabitants has a strong resonance of the earlier contest with the Muslim 'Other'. He suggests that the West had 'rehearsed their encounter with the peoples of the New World, acting out in their response to the legendary Wild Man, their mingled attraction and revulsion, longing and hatred'.[40] In the eyes of many, the Wild Man was not some legendary abstraction: many of his characteristics were already attached to the Muslims, descendants of Ishmael. The Angel of God had told his mother, Hagar, 'Call his name Ishmael; because the Lord hath heard thy affliction. And he will be a wild man; his hand will be against every man; and every man's hand shall be against him.'[41] Wildness, violence, lack of self-control and unbridled passion were the fundamental critiques that the Christian world had made of the Sons of Ishmael from the earliest days.

6

'Vile Weeds'

MALAS HIERBAS

Spain under the successors to the Catholic Kings – first their grandson Charles, and then their great-grandson Philip II – had many enemies. There were ancient antagonisms with her neighbours France and the Muslim states of North Africa. Then there were doctrinal enemies, among whom Christian reformers such as Luther and Calvin and the followers of Erasmus appeared the most menacing. Finally, there was the ever-present threat of the Ottoman Empire. And, insidiously, the internal danger of the 'New Christians' – former Jews and the once-Muslim *Moriscos*. Las Casas, writing in Spain in the latter years of his life, could see at first hand what Old Christians feared as the invisible taint of Judaism and the threat posed by the *Moriscos* who stubbornly refused to become like other Christians. The conviction that neither group had converted sincerely to Christianity was widespread. Both were believed to threaten the faith of Christians and thus ultimately the security of Spain. Yet it was the *Moriscos* who were eventually considered too dangerous to live on the soil of Spain and who, regardless of whether they were sincerely Christian or not, were expelled between 1608 and 1614. Las Casas died in the convent of Atocha in Madrid in 1566, so he did not live to see the outcome of 'perpetual hatred and rancour' in the second revolt of the Alpujarras that began just before Christmas 1568.

The 'hatred and rancour' between Old Christian and *Morisco* was reciprocal. As the Spanish state pressed ever harder on its convert minority, the capacity and will of the *Moriscos* to resist hardened and grew. The two terrible wars between Christians and *Moriscos* (in 1499–1501 and 1568–70) were avoidable; contemporaries also saw them as pointless and unnecessary. Both stemmed from victors' justice, not only from the ten-year war for Granada but from the centuries-old desire within Castile to right the wrongs inflicted upon its legendary

Visigothic ancestors. The myths that mobilized Castilian society during hundreds of years of Islamic power had also inculcated a spirit of revenge. Ferdinand and Isabella both desired the ancient goal of a pure Spain, but their political sense told them that it should be achieved by gradual rather than radical means. But, as we have seen, they found the lure of a sudden, decisive and dramatic gesture irresistible. First came the solution to the 'problem' of the Jews, offering them exile or adherence to the Cross. Next came mass conversion in Granada, which took place under the eyes of Isabella. Finally the royal writ applied the conversion formula to all the Muslims of Castile in the wake of the first war of the Alpujarras.

Nothing on this scale had ever been attempted in Christendom since the mass conversion of the Balkan Slavs and of the Baltic tribes centuries before. In Spain, conversion of the Jews and the Muslims was a state enterprise, pushed forward by the Catholic Kings and their successors for the glory of God and of Spain. The Spanish Church and the Spanish Inquisition were largely instruments of the state. Neither Charles V nor Philip II allowed the papacy any controlling role within their lands, and they were both at odds with the popes who tried to constrain them. The troops of Charles V sacked Rome itself in 1527. In 1556, the violently anti-Spanish Pope Paul IV excommunicated both Philip and his father, and Philip sent his troops against the papal territories. After Paul IV's death, Philip (restored to the company of the faithful) sought to rebuild his bond with the Holy See; by 1591 forty-seven out of seventy cardinals had been paid pensions by Spain.[1] Thereafter, both Philip and the Holy See avoided confrontation. But conversion of the masses first developed in Spain against papal protests. Under Charles V and to a greater degree under Philip II, the equation between a good Catholic and a good subject became an underlying determinant of state policy. The northern Netherlands, under Spanish rule, became a nest of Protestant heretics and rebels, who would never become dutiful subjects until they were, once more, faithful Catholic Christians. Similar criteria were applied to the *Moriscos* in Spain after 1502.

Like all administrative categories, the term *Morisco* concealed within it many sub-divisions and local differences. Four generations separated the conquered of 1492 from those expelled in 1608, and much changed over that long period.[2] In the old Kingdom of Granada, in the first year, there were initially few Old Christian immigrants, but by the 1560s these 're-populators' made up more than 45 per cent of the population.[3] Throughout Castile, Aragon and Valencia, 'Moors' and then _Moriscos_ were viewed as the natural allies of Spain's various enemies: Valencian _Moriscos_ were seen as being in league with the North African pirates or the Turks. The _Moriscos_ of Aragon, living in the foothills of the Pyrenees, were in contact with the French Protestant Huguenots on the other side of the mountains.[4] In the eyes of most officials, _Moriscos_ were an undifferentiated menacing mass. But in reality the scattered communities of former Mudejars in Castile were very different from the large population in the Kingdom of Valencia, where in the highlands they formed the majority. In Granada the problem was, in Christian eyes, acute. This was a newly conquered country and this battle for the 'hearts and minds' of the population was fought like an extension of the war. The objective was pacification.

The two alternatives in Granada after 1492 were the cautious and painstaking approach offered by the Archbishop of Granada, Talavera, and the robust strategy of the Primate of Spain, Cardinal Jiménez de Cisneros. For Talavera, well-trained clergy, well versed in the language of the converts, would then bring them to Christ but by persuasion not force.[5] Jiménez de Cisneros preferred to bring Moors as quickly as possible within the embrace of the Church and then to use the Inquisition and other means of social control to prevent dissidence. Cisneros won the debate and once forced conversion had taken place, the kingdom was divided up into parishes, and priests dispatched to the larger centres of population. There they waged a largely fruitless battle to turn token Christians into true Christians.

The dilemma was not new. In the twelfth century, Peter the Venerable had already urged that Muslims could better be won for Christianity 'not as our people often do, by weapons, not by force but by reason, not by hate but by love'.[6] It is worth recalling that an example of a slower and more evolutionary model had already taken place in Iberia, but in _Muslim_ Al-Andalus. There had been no systematic campaign of forcible Islamization in Spain after the Muslim conquest. Yet within two centuries the Christians of Al-Andalus had for the most part adopted Islam. The vigorous methods pioneered by Jiménez de Cisneros were dictated by political motives and they seemed to succeed in the short term. By law, and on paper, Islam was ended and the whole nation made officially Christian. But the instruments of control and repression ultimately proved inadequate. They could not overcome the passive resistance of the Granadine *Moriscos* however strenuously they were applied.

Surreptitiously, the Granadine *Moriscos* continued to recite the Holy Qur'an, gave their children Muslim names, and circumcised their sons. The authorities underestimated the *Moriscos'* capacity to resist and attempted to destroy their faith by means designed to work on Christian heretics and Jews. Their first method of control was to eradicate the texts of Islam. In 1499, Cisneros had ordered that all copies of the Holy Qur'an and other religious works should be collected and then decreed their destruction. This was a deeply symbolic act. While the Inquisition lit slow fires under the heretics and *conversos* of Spain, Jiménez de Cisneros provided his own auto-da-fé in the main square of Granada: he burned the holy books of Islam.[7]

This was not quite the act of crass barbarism that it now seems. Cisneros was the greatest patron of scholarship in Spain who almost single-handedly pushed forward the production of the *Biblia complutense*, which printed the texts of the biblical sources in Latin, Greek, Hebrew and 'Chaldean' (or Syriac) in parallel columns. Just as Jiménez de Cisneros believed in the power of the written word and that Christianity would be advanced through this monumental edition of the Holy Bible, so he was convinced Islam in Spain would be mortally wounded by destroying its sacred texts. He was well aware of the reverence with which Muslims regarded the Holy Qur'an and the extraordinary esteem in which they held the Arabic language. The book-burning was an essential part of his policy of accelerated conversion, in cutting off newly converted Muslims from the possibility of reversion. In his eyes there would be a natural propensity for Muslim converts to seek the light of Christ, and only the agency of 'Islamizers' could draw them back into their old ways. There were no printed versions of the Holy Qur'an and the manuscript texts consumed in Granada could not easily be replaced.

Certainly, the Archbishop of Toledo's biographers saw the book-burning as a supremely potent and meritorious act, evidence of Jiménez de Cisneros' determination (*rectitud*) to achieve the purposes of God. So they inflated the number of volumes to more than a million, an unlikely figure that allowed more than three manuscript texts for every inhabitant of the Kingdom of Granada. This total was more metaphor than fact, like the improbably heroic scale of early Christian victories over the infidel on the battlefields of the Reconquest. In the eyes of his advocates, Jiménez de Cisneros had accomplished a majestic triumph in a spiritual war being waged by every means possible. To find a parallel within Christian terms, we need to look to the Catholic horror and revulsion at the Protestant destruction of images and relics in the Netherlands later in the sixteenth century. The bonfire in Granada was an act of purposeful iconoclasm. It was also unsuccessful, because the books themselves were only the apogee of the Muslim structure of belief in Granada. The majority of the *Morisco* population in Granada lived not in the cities but in the country, where few of the people could read the texts. But the message was known and taught orally, rather as most contemporary Christians learned their faith by ear rather than by eye. So the true strength of Islam resided in the minds and memories of children. Since the days of the Prophet Mohammed they had learnt the Holy Qur'an by rote. Thus even within poor village communities there was a human resource of knowledge.

We are now beginning to understand the importance of the written *Morisco* texts, passed from hand to hand and copied, hidden from the eyes of neighbours and from the spies of the authorities. They were written in a variety of languages and scripts. Some were in Arabic, some in the *Morisco* dialect of Romance called *alajamiado*, meaning foreign. Sometimes *alajamiado* would be written in Arabic script and sometimes with a Latin alphabet. It suggests a community restricted in its use of Arabic, because to speak Arabic in public risked attracting the attention of the Inquisition. But the written script was created, so they believed, expressly for the writing of the Holy Qur'an. It was a badge of their heritage and identity and anything penned in it was an act of faith. So the manuscript texts, in Arabic or in *alajamiado* using Arabic characters, were vital for scholars and for the unity of belief. But they were also prized throughout the *Morisco* communities as symbols of their hidden faith and true origin. The written and the spoken word were complementary. If the faith were transmitted only through memory and speech, over time this knowledge would become altered or corrupted. But so long as there were those who could read the verses of the Holy Qur'an, write them down and pass them on, burning the books would have only a limited effect.

The *Moriscos* were officially Christian, and monks and priests were drafted into the kingdom to bolster their new faith. For ten years, until 1511, powerful efforts were made to make these notional conversions real. However they failed to make any tangible inroads with a population that evinced no positive interest in Christianity. Gradually the officials in Granada recognized that the *Moriscos* could only be 'Christianized' by changing every aspect of their lives. In May 1511, and over the following years, sets of rules were promulgated to regulate *Morisco* life. These embraced all customs that had a specifically religious origin, such as ritual ablutions, marriage practices, methods of ritual slaughter. All *Morisco* infants were to have an Old Christian godfather and godmother. Every *Morisco* marriage was to take place with an Old Christian witness.[8] At the same time attempts were made to stop the *Moriscos* of the city and the plain from fleeing to the 'unchristian' villages of the Alpujarras.[9] In 1513, orders were issued that Old Christian men should not have intimate relations with *Morisca* women.[10] Later, this hedge of restrictions was broadened to include the food *Moriscos* ate and the conduct of family life.[11] In 1526, there was 'a pause in the repression of the *Moriscos*'.[12] Charles V came to visit his magnificent new palace, built of pale stone and gleaming white marble, high on the hill over the city amid the ruddy walls of the Moorish fortress. When the emperor arrived, he quickly saw the scale of the social and political problems and he put in hand an inquiry into the position of the *Moriscos*. The report made it clear that they had not received proper religious instruction, and that they had been grossly exploited. As a result, it came to the startling conclusion that there were no more than seven true Christians among the considerable number of *Moriscos* they had interviewed.

Charles, who prolonged his stay in Granada for six months through the autumn of 1526, sought to bring about a definitive solution. In the Edict of Granada of 7 December 1526, he ordered that forty major injustices inflicted upon the *Moriscos* be ended, but he also imposed many new restrictions. They were to be prohibited from using Arabic or wearing what was defined as Moorish dress. Women were to be unveiled. They could not wear jewels or carry any weapons; the doors of their houses should be kept open on Fridays and during weddings

lest they engage in Islamic practices. And Muslim names were forbidden. Finally, he defined the meaning of the word and status of
Morisco and he ordered a programme of preaching and instruction
under the aegis of the Archbishop of Granada, Pedro de Alba.[13]

This was Charles in the role of Arbiter of the Faith that he had
assayed five years before at the Diet of Worms. Then he had been
frustrated by Martin Luther, but his efforts were no more successful
in Granada. However, the decrees generated revenue. Accepting a
payment of 90,000 ducats for six years from the *Moriscos*, he agreed to
a suspension of the punitive decrees, an arrangement that lasted (with
several additional payments) until he abdicated in favour of his son
Philip in 1556. It was, though, an unbalanced truce: in fact the
instruments of conversion and repression were strengthened. In 1529
the Inquisition of Jaen was transferred to Granada and set up in a fine
building in the city; formerly, the Inquisition in Granada had only
functioned as a sub-office of the Inquisition of Cordoba. More and
more priests were sent into the kingdom, and a manual for conversion
was produced in the 1530s.[14]

However, this increased pressure to convert had an unintended
consequence. It heightened the sense of Muslim identity among the
people of Granada, who developed particular skills in resisting the
overwhelming power of the Church. Through the half-century after
the first war in the Alpujarras, we can see two parallel and connected
developments. On one side, there was frustration at every level within
Old Christian society at the extraordinary intransigence of the *Moriscos*,
most of whom, people held, were Christian in name only. More than
that, they were seen to be becoming ever more dangerous. They
seemed to be increasing in numbers faster than the Old Christians,
and this impression was often true. This increase was put down to
their inherent lustfulness. Even their virtues, like industriousness, now
had a negative connotation. They worked hard, but only because
they were avaricious: gaining money and never spending it except in
their own community. In 1602 the Archbishop of Valencia, Juan de
Ribera, reflected what had long been the common view: 'Since they
are generally covetous and avaricious and love most of all to save
money and not to spend it, they have chosen to take on the easiest
jobs, shopkeepers, peddlers, pastry cooks, gardeners . . . they are the
sponge that sucks the wealth out of Spain.'[15]

But more than anything else they were seen to be vicious. *Moriscos* conspired with the external enemies of Spain, while inside the country more and more of them were retreating beyond the limits of the law, becoming bandits or highway robbers (*monfies*). At an official level, this frustration appeared in increasingly stringent legislation designed to break down the resistance of the *Moriscos*, but often, these laws were never put into practice. In Valencia, noble landowners relied on *Moriscos* to farm their estates and so protected them as far as was possible.

The other line of development took place inside *Morisco* society. In Granada and in the rest of Spain, the *Morisco* community had been largely deprived of its natural leaders, who had departed for North Africa. However, a sufficient number of the educated and religious classes remained to sustain the fundamentals of Muslim belief and the community also began to develop a new elite. Many of these men, like the scholar Alonso de Castillo, were genuine converts to Christianity, but nonetheless they did not lose their sense of connection to their families and origins.[16] The *Moriscos* quickly became adept at occasional and reluctant conformity to Christian belief. When pressed, they would bring their children for baptism, but after the ceremony, returned home and carefully washed away all traces of the infidel's holy water. Given Christian names, they never used them amongst themselves. If they attended Christian services, they said the wrong words or spoke at inappropriate places in the ceremony, pleading ignorance. Outraged Old Christians referred to this scandalous irreverence and grave offences against the Holy Sacrament. *Moriscos* continued to give the alms ordained in the Qur'an, to say their prayers when possible and had their children learn to read the holy books. When someone died the relatives bribed the gravediggers not to bury their *Morisco* dead in the churchyard but in open and unconsecrated ground. They had no truck with Christian authority. The confessors working in the *Morisco* community in Tortosa found that they completed their work extremely rapidly, because 'when confessing them, they never reveal any sins so they find nothing to confess'.[17] We can gain a sense of how they resisted from the formal decree issued in Ottoman-ruled Oran in 1563, which legitimated various compromises with the strict observance of their faith:

Continue to pray, even if you may have to do so silently or by signs.

Fulfil the obligation to pay the alms tax by whatever means of doing good to the poor, remember God is not concerned with externals, but with the inward intention of your hearts.

To fulfil the laws of purification, bathe in the sea or the river; and if that is forbidden, do it at night and that will be as good as doing it by the light of day.

Make the ritual ablutions before prayer if only by rubbing your hands on the wall.

If at the hour of prayer you are compelled to venerate the Christian idols . . . look at the idols when the Christians do, but think of yourself walking in God's path, even though you are not facing the *qibla* [the niche in a mosque indicating the direction of Mecca].

If you are forced to drink wine, drink, but set yourself apart from all intention to commit evil.

If you are forced to eat pork, do so, but with a pure mind and admitting its unlawfulness, as you must do for any other prohibited thing.

If you are forced to take interest [forbidden under the laws of Islam] do so, purifying your intention and asking pardon of God.

If you are being adjudged by infidels, and you can dissimulate, do so denying with your heart what you are saying with your words, which are forced from you.[18]

Nowhere was the *Morisco* determination to resist stronger than on the issue of circumcision. Male Christians were not normally circumcised, while Muslims and Jews invariably were. It was a defining and ineradicable point of identity, an act of blood utterly unlike the pure and cleansing Christian ritual of baptism.[19] It was prohibited by Charles V in person in Granada in 1526, except with the permission of the bishop or the senior magistrate of the kingdom. The penalty for circumcising was permanent banishment and loss of all property. Strong efforts were made to track down those who carried it out. *Morisca* midwives were officially forbidden and Old Christian midwives were instructed to report to a priest if they found an infant had been circumcised.[20] But according to Bernard Vincent, the vast majority of males in Granada continued to be circumcised in the decades between the first and second wars of the Alpujarras. Inquisition records in Valencia indicate that in three villages in 1574 almost 80 per cent of the male population were circumcised. But whenever the authorities tried to discover who was responsible, they met with a wall of silence or misleading information. A *Morisca* in Valencia said she did not know who had done it: her son had been taken from her and when he was returned, he had been circumcised. Others blamed it on unknown persons or on those who were already safely dead. The Christian authorities sought to catch the circumcisers but usually failed; when they did succeed, the circumcisers often suffered the ultimate penalty: one was condemned to be burned alive in Valencia in 1587.[21]

However, provided the Christian authorities did not seriously compromise their social and religious identity, the *Moriscos* remained outwardly pacific. They were content to wait, for they believed that they would be revenged on their enemies, who had been guilty of bad faith in 1499, breaking their sworn word. In Granada and perhaps elsewhere in the *Morisco* communities of Spain it was believed that the Christian dominion would not last for ever. Under Christian rule the *Moriscos* continued to flout the legal prescriptions that hedged them about. In Christian eyes it was an increasingly insupportable anomaly, as by their dress, language and demeanour the *Moriscos* seemed to spurn everything that was offered to them. The rise in hostility at a popular level occasionally entered the historical record. At one trial in Cordoba, an Old Christian was reported to have shouted at *Moriscos* in the street, 'Dogs, who have burned the images and the crosses and the churches and put the Holy Sacrament in a cowpat.' Another cried out, 'May these sodomites die who turn from the faith of Jesus Christ.'[22]

The effective compromise that had existed since Charles V's visit in 1526 ended in 1556. Many explanations have been produced for this sudden hardening of attitudes towards the *Moriscos*. Spain had a new king, and 'what could be bought under Charles V could not under Philip II'. The rising power of the Ottomans in the western Mediterranean and the clear evidence of *Morisco* contacts with their co-religionists further heightened fears of the 'enemy within'. The authorities began to hear reports that *Morisco* renegades in the mountains were beginning to form large war bands, and were attacking even well-armed groups of Christian travellers on the roads, and small isolated communities.[23] The Inquisition throughout Spain became more active, and on 4 May 1566 the long-suspended edicts of 1526 for Granada were revived and strengthened. The newly appointed President of the Royal Chancellery in Granada, the supreme legal body in the kingdom, was Pedro de Deza. He had instructions to enforce the new decree to the letter. So that there should be no ambiguity or uncertainty, he had copies of the new restrictions printed and planned to publish them on 1 January 1567, in commemoration of the capture of the city by Ferdinand and Isabella.

In 1568, Francisco Nuñez Muley, a *Morisco* and a sincere convert to Christianity, pleaded against the edict of 1567, which called for the summary abolition of *Morisco* customs and prohibited the use of Arabic:

How is it possible to take away people from their native tongue with which they were born and brought up? Egyptians, Syrians and Maltese, and others speak, read and write Arabic and are as Christian as we are . . . All Moriscos wish to learn Castilian, but it is difficult if not impossible to learn Castilian in their remaining years. In sum the ordinance was contrived to ruin us. Imposing it by force causes pain to those natives who cannot meet such a burden; they flee the land . . .[24]

When the *Moriscos* rose in revolt the following year, one of their leaders, Mohammad bin Mohammad bin Dawud, wrote a popular ballad that reminded his listeners of the contamination that Christianity had brought upon them:

> To adore their painted idols,
> Mockery of the Great Unseen
> When the bell tolls we must
> Gather to adore the image foul;
> In the church the preacher rises,
> Harsh voiced as the screaming owl.
> He the wine and pork invoketh,
> And the Mass is wrought with wine;
> Falsely humble, he proclaimeth
> That this is the Law divine.[25]

Each element – the clamorous bells, the owl (a bird of ill omen), the unclean wine and pork – reminded his readers and listeners that Christianity aimed to destroy them.[26] *Moriscos* called Spanish priests 'wolves, merciless thieves, characterised by haughtiness, vanity, sodomy, laxity, blasphemy, apostasy, pomp, vainglory, tyranny, brigandage, and injustice'.[27]

The new decree had one clear intention. It was designed finally to obliterate the differences that allowed the *Moriscos* to maintain their separate identity. It systematically prohibited all those distinctions that defined their social structure. They were to learn Castilian within three years, after which Arabic would be forbidden in public and private. All documents written in it would be null and void – and this included any property document or contract. All Arabic books were to be submitted for inspection, and those deemed harmless could be retained, but not for more than three years. Moorish dress was to be permitted only for a maximum of two years, after which *Moriscos* would have to dress like Castilians. All Islamic personal and family names and all records of lineage were forbidden, as were all forms of traditional dancing and singing, called *zambras* and *leilas*. The most threatening provisions were the prohibition on Arabic documents and language, and the extinction of all marks or mention of lineage. For several years, the authorities in Granada had been examining title deeds and confiscating any land holdings that were not precisely as described in the deeds. Wealthy *Moriscos* saw the edict as a comprehensive means of stripping them of their assets, to the enrichment of officials and other Old Christians. The prohibition on genealogy cut to the heart of the social structure, for it would make marriages within the old clan system impossible.

The edict was duly issued, and on the same day parties of soldiers entered Granada's Moorish baths – prohibited under the regulations – and began to destroy them. It was clear that these new laws would not become a dead letter like earlier legislation and hurried meetings were held in the Albaicin, where it was decided that unless the provisions were eased, the *Moriscos* would rebel as they had in 1499. Another decree was published ordering that on New Year's Day 1568 all the *Morisco* children between three and fifteen were to be taken to the local priest, who would place them in a school where they would be taught Castilian and Christian doctrine. There were many delegations of protest to the President of the Chancellery, Deza, but he told them all that the king was resolved to save the children's immortal souls and the decision was absolute. There were constant riots during April 1568, in the capital and in the mountains. There was a growing sense that an uprising was planned and the government issued orders to confiscate all the crossbows and arquebuses that had been licensed for hunting.[28] The rumours were true, for *Moriscos*, with the sense of a tightening noose, had made comprehensive plans for a rising on New Year's Day 1569, both in the city and in the mountains. Eight thousand men, dressed as Turks to arouse fear among the Christians, were to march on Granada where the Albaicin would close its gates and begin the revolt. But such was the fear and hatred in the countryside that the rising began prematurely. Soldiers and local garrisons were massacred in the villages and small towns. By 23 December, 182 places had risen in revolt. A raid into Granada itself was successful but ill-coordinated. The roots and strength of the rising were among the mountaineers of the Alpujarras.

Yet by mid February 1569, the Marqués de Mondejar, who knew both Granada and the Alpujarras, had virtually suppressed the revolt. In each village he offered terms of surrender, and those that submitted were well treated. Those that did not were killed or enslaved. But then his concessions were overruled and he was replaced as commander by Don John, the king's half-brother. The *Moriscos* now realized that they were faced with death or enslavement even if they submitted to the king. So they fought on with increasing desperation and conceded each town or village only at a high cost in Spanish (and their own) lives. By the time that the last traces of revolt were put down on 19 May 1570, the campaign had cost 60,000 Spanish dead and 3 million ducats.[29] Moreover, as the Venetian Ambassador Leonardo Donato observed, had the Turks sent their fleet to support the *Moriscos* instead of turning on Venice, they 'would have kindled a flame almost impossible to extinguish and had the revolt extended to Murcia, Valencia, Catalonia and Aragon, Spanish statesmen expected half the Huguenots of France to pour over the Pyrenees'.[30]

Not all the *Moriscos* in the Kingdom of Granada had joined the revolt, but those that survived unscathed were all treated in the same way. On 1 November 1570, the remaining *Moriscos* were told to assemble in their towns and villages.[31] A detachment of troops arrived at each point of assembly, and split the population into groups of 1,500, each with an escort of 200 soldiers. Men and women were expected to walk, and to carry their children and old people. Behind them their personal possessions were piled in carts. As they headed north or west, to their destinations in Castile, they were expected to cover about thirteen miles a day. They were supposed to receive two good meals each day. In practice, the initial expulsion of more than 50,000 over poor roads and in bad weather proved impossible to manage or coordinate. By the time the *Moriscos* reached their destinations in Old and New Castile, at least 20 per cent had died on the road between November 1570 and spring 1571.[32] In all some 80,000 were uprooted from their home towns and villages, and were resettled in communities that had no desire to receive them. A few were left, plus a host of bandits and *Moriscos* who fled to the mountains rather than submit to Christian justice. But this purgation had been achieved at an enormous cost, for a once prosperous region now became a burden on the Spanish state; Granada was effectively emptied of its former inhabitants. Even when repopulated with Christians from the north, the kingdom never recovered its prosperity.

In Castile, under constant surveillance, their children taken from them to live in Old Christian families, the Granadine exiles still excited wild fears among Christians. The former Granadines attracted the special interest of the Inquisition wherever they were settled, and yet despite weekly visits from a priest, many still failed to become 'good and sincere Christians'. The people of Granada still perversely followed their old ways, both in religion and in their supposed 'wildness'. In 1573, a *Morisco* from Aranda on the River Duero, deep in the heart of Castile, told his local priests that 'the Moriscos who were taken from Granada intend to rise up again and to take to the hills when the time is ripe'.[33] The *Moriscos* of Valencia, Murcia and Aragon represented an even greater danger, for they could unite with the Ottomans and guide the galleys from Algiers in their attacks on the Spanish coast. In 1580, it was widely rumoured that the *Moriscos* in western Andalucia were in contact with North Africa and were planning a landing of troops from Morocco.[34] The danger (built upon rumour and some evidence) seemed pressing and required an immediate solution.

Barely ten years after the de-population of Granada, Philip II and his advisors met in Lisbon to discuss the *Morisco* Question. In 1580 Philip had gained the throne of Portugal, so that he now ruled all the lands of Iberia. But this achievement seemed threatened by the insoluble problem of the *Moriscos*. It was accepted that a complete and permanent solution had to be found, for Spain could no longer risk their presence. The king asked for suggestions. One proposal was that the entire *Morisco* population should be crammed on to old ships that would then be scuttled at sea, drowning all aboard. But the logistical difficulties proved insuperable, and the fleet was needed in Flanders. Over the next two decades other imaginative schemes were suggested as the king extended the inquiry. Another proposal was to work all the males to death in the galleys, to the great benefit of the state. Another, from a priest of *Morisco* origins, Durrical, proposed a stock-breeder's solution: the king should command that 'no Morisco shall marry a Morisca; but only with Old Christians. The Children will be brought up as Christians, while the adult males would not reproduce and the line would die out.'[35]

In 1587 the Bishop of Segorbe, Martin de Salvatierra, answered Philip's request for a solution with a programme of Swiftean audacity. In Salvatierra's view it was too dangerous to allow the *Moriscos*, this 'evil and pernicious people', to go to North Africa, where they would only reinforce Spain's enemies. The better answer was that all *Moriscos*, men and boys and all grown women, should be gelded or spayed, and then they could be taken to empty zones of the New World and left there.[36] In the following year, Alonso Gutiérrez of Seville proposed a kind of clan system where each *Morisco* would be branded on the face with a mark, so that they could be identified and then set to work. If the numbers grew too great, some should be selected for castration, 'which is what they do in the Indies without any great difficulty'.[37] These procrustean solutions had one factor in common: effectively abandoning all hope of conversion and assimilation. While the immediate dangers were political – from the Turks and the Protestants – dealing with the *Moriscos* was essential because as had been long suspected they were by birth pernicious. The Bishop of Segorbe bundled Jews and *Moriscos* together as dangers confronting Spain: 'this abominable people is blind and contumacious in its infidelity by its pure malice and spirit of rebellion, as it was and is with the Jews, resisting the holy spirit.'³⁸

There was undoubtedly a political dimension that made fear of the *Moriscos* appear a reality rather than merely a phantasm. The idea of a conspiracy between the Spanish Jews and *conversos* and an external enemy (the Jews of Constantinople, the French or the Protestants) was insubstantial, and although it occasionally surfaced, it had little or no foundation in reality. The Jewish *conversos* were pursued for sins of the spirit. But the connections between *Moriscos* and external Muslim enemies were real enough. A contingent of Ottoman soldiers fought with them in the Alpujarras, *Morisco* pirates raided the coasts, and the crime of 'fleeing to Barbary' appears time and again in the records of the Alhambra, the military headquarters in Granada. Inquisitors ordered the 'application of the cords', or sanctioned the slow crushing and fracturing of the leg bones to extract confessions of the full extent of *Morisco* intransigence. They learned that *Moriscos*, many of whom were peddlers or carriers, criss-crossed Spain, carrying with them news and sometimes Muslim books. They brought news of Christian defeats in the Mediterranean, which were greeted with joy, while Ottoman defeats such as Lepanto were received with resignation. Small communities, sometimes only a few families in an Old Christian town or village, or a *Morisco* living in the same house as Christians, learned the whispered prophecies.

In 1569, in the midst of the war for the Alpujarras, the Inquisition in Granada extracted a confession from a *Morisco* called Zacharias. He told them that his people were sure that they were about to wreak their revenge upon the Christians. 'They have learned', the secretary to the tribunal wrote, 'in the books and stories that they will regain this land, and the "Moors" of Barbary will win.' All the Spanish towns in Africa would fall to them, and then the *Moriscos* believed 'a bridge made of copper would appear at the straits of Gibraltar, and they would pass over, and take all Spain as far as Galicia.'³⁹ Many of these prophecies were entirely new, not ancient traditions. The hopes of revenge grew from the recent successes of Islam elsewhere. *Moriscos* told themselves that 'the Turks would march with their armies to Rome and the Christians will not escape except those who turn to the truth of the Prophet; the remainder will be made captive or killed.'[40] The *Moriscos* seemed persistently to most Spaniards to pose a danger to the faith and a danger to the state.[41]

It has been observed, however, that the point at which the *Moriscos* were expelled coincided with the lowest level of threat from the Ottomans in the Mediterranean for many years. The expulsion was not, though, designed as a cure for an acute illness but for a chronic disease. Cervantes expressed the popular attitude to the *Moriscos* when he wrote through one of his canine characters in his novella 'The Dialogue of the Dogs', 'They are the slow fever that kills as certainly as a raging one.'[42] While the *Moriscos* remained in Spain, so the argument went, the nation could never thrive. Better and more rational cases were made against the expulsion on economic grounds, but in a debate that extended over decades, those opposed to removing the *Moriscos* could not answer an argument that had no basis in facts and figures. For their enemies, the *Moriscos* were a disease of the body politic, and they had, like some evil humour, to be drained from it by any means necessary. Although the expulsion of the Jews in 1492 was present in the minds of all concerned, the situation was not exactly parallel. In 1492, the line had been drawn, approximately, between believing Jews and New Christians of Jewish origin. In effect, the Jews went and the New Christians stayed. In recent years there has been an acrimonious debate as to whether the expulsion of the Jews in 1492 was on the basis of race or belief. That question is still open; however, it is clear that the expulsion of the *Moriscos* in 1609–14 was predicated upon the basis of race.[43]

The polemic that the scholar Pedro Aznar Cardona turned on the *Moriscos* in 1612 was different from any past vituperation against Muslims. *Moriscos* were

a pestilence, vile, careless and enemies of letters and the sciences; they bring up their children as animals without any education; they are dumb and crude in speech, barbarous in language and ridiculous in dress; they eat on the floor and live on vegetables, grains, fruits, honey and milk; they do not drink wine nor meat unless it is slaughtered by them; they love charlatanry, stories, dancing, promenading and other bestial diversions; they pursue jobs that require little work such as weaving, tailoring, shoemaking, carpentry, and the like; they are peddlers of oil, fish, paste, sugar, eggs and other produce; they are inept at bearing arms and thus, are cowardly and effeminate; they travel in groups only; they are sensual and disloyal; they marry young and multiply like weeds (*malas hierbas*) overcrowding places and contaminating them.[44]

Not everyone agreed with him. The complex and often anguished debates recognized the injustice and sinfulness of expelling adult *Moriscos* who were sincere Christians and sending away innocent children. There were proposals that very young *Morisco* children should be kept in Spain and raised as good Christians, away from the corrupting influences of their parents. But it was eventually agreed and, as the impassioned historian of the expulsion Pascual Boranat y Barrachina later put it,

the law of providence made its heavy weight felt, not only on the guilty individuals, but upon an entire people, on father and sons, on great and small alike: the sin of descent [*pecado de raza*], the sin of the whole nation that infused the [obstinate] prevarication of the baptised 'Moors', that could not be exculpated by the punishment of an individual, but only through the punishment of all those guilty of complicity in the crime and of solidarity with the common apostasy . . . The children were paying for the sins of their fathers.[45]

He was expressing, centuries after the event, the still-violent feelings of nineteenth-century Catholic Spain towards the *Moriscos*. Of the decree of expulsion of 22 September 1609, he wrote, 'We now come, at last, to the hour when the Moriscos root and branch [*la raza Morisca*] atoned for the interminable sequence of profanations, blasphemies, sacrileges, apostasies and political conspiracies within the breast of our dear country. *Alea jacta est* [the die is cast].'[46]

The final decision was for expulsion to North Africa rather than genocide, and to that degree, humanity had triumphed over Realpolitik. In exile, the *Morisco* resentment of their expulsion continued among their descendants. In the twentieth century, some families could still produce ancient keys and said they would open the doors of their old homes in Spain. In the decree, there were some concessions. Not all those of 'Moorish' descent were required to go. *Moriscos* could leave behind children of up to four years to be brought up as Christians. Children of up to six years born to an Old Christian father and a *Morisca* mother could remain, and their mother with them; but if their father were a *Morisco* and their mother an Old Christian, then he would be expelled while they could remain. There were possible exemptions for those *Moriscos* who had lived only among Christians, and those who could obtain from a bishop and a local priest a certificate of their unimpeachable Christianity. These clauses were to salve the conscience of those who could not bear to punish the innocent.[47] No time was allowed for *Moriscos* to make representations. The expectation was that the expulsion should be total.

So, not all the *Moriscos* were expelled, although the exodus was as comprehensive as any seventeenth-century government could hope to achieve. The *Morisco* bandits and highwaymen continued to plague Spain, and they occasionally reappeared in the records of the Inquisition. The last trial of *Moriscos* took place in Cartagena in 1769, where a group was discovered inside a secret mosque.[48] For many Spaniards, as much in the nineteenth century as in the seventeenth, the expulsion of the *Moriscos* seemed necessary or inevitable, a view that also persisted into the second half of the twentieth century. Claudio Sanchez-Albornóz, at the end of his *Spain: A Historical Enigma*, projected a future in which the *Moriscos* had not been expelled.

One does not need extensive imagination to calculate the problems that a 'Moorish' Valencia, after three hundred years almost superior to the Christian population of the country and a mass of *Moriscos* not very inferior to the Christians of Aragon, would have caused for Spain in [the] turmoil of the nineteenth and twentieth centuries . . . The nation avoided grave dangers . . . that the *Morisco* majorities would have posed for our historical life and would continue to pose today [1962] for our future.[49]

Here is the old language of demographic challenge, as voiced by Cervantes' dog, Archbishop Ribera and many others at the time of the expulsion. But Sanchez-Albornóz wrote from a perspective not of a distant threat from 300 years in the past, but of a more recent danger. The fear of the Islamic threat remained a strong connection between the past into the present. All the old terrors could be reinvigorated. Thus, military disaster in Morocco in 1922, when a Spanish general lost 12,000 men – killed and mutilated by Berber tribesmen at the battle of Anual – unlocked a torrent of fear and hatred. So too did the rebel General Francisco Franco when he brought the Army of Africa with its 'Moorish' contingents to Spain in 1936. He provided the legitimate Republican government with a potent rallying point. Franco had brought the 'Moors' back to Spain and, with them, barbarism. Thus although 900 years of Islam ended with the expulsion of the *Moriscos*, their spectral presence remained from that point forward into the twentieth century.

Hatred and fear were ever present in Iberian as in all societies. But in Spain they focused over several centuries on the division between the Christian and Muslim worlds. Nor was this a theoretical abstraction as it was in the rest of Christian Europe. Christianity and Islam were interwoven in the landscape. The two faiths lived side by side, not in amity but in a kind of equilibrium. That changed over less than a century, as the balance was altered, as Judaism and Islam were officially abolished, and a new unitary Christian culture was created. In later centuries this would be described as social engineering, but in the sixteenth and seventeenth centuries it was articulated within a religious argument. Jews, *conversos*, Muslims and *Moriscos* were enemies of Christ, and gradually the *Moriscos* came to be seen as the most directly threatening. Soon they began to attract the kind of visceral insult that for centuries had been directed at the Jews. This abuse, which developed from the 1570s, had a single end in view: to categorize them all as crypto-Muslims. They were the perpetual enemy within. They were the rampant '*weeds*' that were choking the state. Thus, the street language of loathing and disgust percolated upwards into learned treatises written by scholars and clerics.

These educated men often wrote in the vernacular, Castilian, which made what they published directly accessible to a wide audience within the Spanish lands. But it also allowed them a wider public still. In the sixteenth and seventeenth centuries Castilian was the language of the greatest power in Europe. Books published in Spanish could be read by the educated in much of Europe. Thus polemic written in Spain, whether in Castilian or Latin, had a resonance and influence far beyond the Pyrenees. By this time we should cease seeing Spain as an isolated southern outcrop of Europe but, rather, in terms of ideas and attitudes, as a nodal point. Spain disseminated ideologies that purported to have a universal application but that were often rooted in the particular preoccupations of Iberia. Foreign travellers rightly recognized the Iberian peninsula as somewhere distinct, for reasons that they often ascribed to its 'Moorish' and Jewish antecedents. Often, ironically, the literary stereotypes that they applied to Spaniards were those that Old Christians had fixed on the *Moriscos*. Long after the last 'Moors' and Jews had gone, these images and tropes persisted. The Spanish state appeared to some a miracle, a model and ordered Christian state, a pattern for Utopia. For others it was just the opposite, a dystopia. Whether the expulsions of the Jews and *Moriscos* were utopian or dystopian depended upon your inclination or perspective.

However, images and language never remain static. At some point after the expulsion of the *Moriscos* from Granada in the 1570s and the repopulation of the empty towns and villages with Old Christians from the north, *fiestas* of *Moros y Cristianos* ('Moors' and Christians) began to appear in these communities. Gradually, also, as the 'Moor' became a distant and near-mythical figure, the menacing Turk became the dominant and threatening image of the infidel.[50] Sometimes they figured together in the *fiesta*. In 1533 the Toledo celebrations of the landing of Charles V at Barcelona had centred on a pageant around 'a very high tower [made of wood and plaster] filled with "Moors" completely dressed in the "Moorish" style and inside the Grand Turk defending the castle.' Moors and the Grand Turk were roundly defeated and paraded in chains through the town, carrying their banners. This pageant had a clear and direct message of immediate import, but the ceremonial of Christian triumph over Islam survived after its central purpose had been forgotten. To this day, the town of Baza celebrates the *Cascamorras* on 6 September every year. Men stained brown from head to foot roam the town, while people hit them, shouting that they have come to steal the image of the Virgin. The origin of this ritual is shrouded in mystery; some have suggested (a little improbably) that it recalls the harsh intolerance of the Almohades in the thirteenth century. Even the name – *Cascamorras* – is obscure. However, Baza was a great victory for the Catholic Kings in the war for Granada, and *Cascamorras* can easily be read as 'smashing the Moors' (*cascar los moros*).

There are similar celebrations all over what was once Al-Andulus. Although the scripts for these increasingly elaborate events date from the nineteenth century, the 'Moros' and 'Christianos' appeared in festivals long before then. At Alcoy in Valencia, St George's Day in 1668 was marked with processions through the streets, with some men dressed up as 'Christian "Moors"' and others as 'Christian Christians', in costumes of the previous century. In the stylized battle that concluded the celebration, it was no surprise that the Christians once more proved invincible. The purpose of these ceremonials was not so much to show the superiority of Christianity to Islam, but to

present a scene of ideal unity and an image of the greatness of the city: the 'Moors' were no longer presented as frightening or ridiculous figures . . . The 'Moors' in the fiestas are not savage warriors but noble gentlemen: their costumes are almost always more spectacular than those of the Christians, and they appear majestic.[51]

Over time, these celebrations became increasingly complex and spectacular, with defined roles assigned to particular districts, churches, or brotherhoods. But in the villages and small towns of the Alpujarras, they retained their original form and purpose for much longer. In Valor, where one of the leaders of the second war of the Alpujarras was born, the emphasis was on Christian benevolence. The 'Moorish' king offered his sword to the Christian king and knelt at his feet. The Christian replied:

> Moors, among Christians clemency
> Lives in our hearts, it fills our soul;
> Although you are conquered, I set you free
> Take your sword and arise.[52]

There had been no scene of honour and clemency in Valor in 1568. It was a bloody battle for a starving town, where 200 *Moriscos* died in a fight against trained and hardened infantry. When they abandoned the town to the Spaniards, they hanged their Christian hostages from the church tower. But even in Valor, the myth-making of *Moros y Cristianos* successfully obscured the historical fact, as it did throughout Spain. This celebration of unity eventually lost its original purpose and became a folkloric memory during the eighteenth century, a little more than a century after the departure of the last 'Moors'. During the nineteenth century the events became formalized, and by the beginning of this century these local events had been transmuted into a mass international tourist attraction.

However, *Moros y Cristianos* and the language of the Reconquest also appeared in the Spanish colonial territories of the Americas and the Far East.[53] There they did not lose their original roots of conflict. The *fiestas* spread rapidly through Mexico and Guatemala, where no 'Moors' had ever been seen. But the indigenous inhabitants took to them. They identified with the *Moros*, and carried traditional Aztec festivals and mock battles into the *fiestas*. While the Spanish colonists saw in the *fiestas* a message of pacification and Christian forgiveness, the local people found in *Moros y Cristianos* a means of preserving memories of Aztec power and even hopes of an eventual expulsion of the Spaniards.[54] Nor were the language and attitudes of the Reconquest restricted to the Atlantic dimension. Later in the sixteenth century, far to the east in the Philippines, the Spaniards found powerful and combative Muslim communities in Mindanao and the Sulu archipelago. Instinctively, they called them *Moros*. They termed the many groups they managed to convert to Christianity collectively *Indios*, after the pacified peoples of the Americas. It was the intransigents who were generically called *Moros*. The Muslims of the Southern Philippines were never successfully controlled by the Spaniards nor, indeed, by any subsequent government. Thus, the association of 'Islam' with wildness persisted as Spaniards took their culture into the wider world.

In this way Spain carried its long conflict with 'Islam' beyond the peninsula. I have suggested that the 'how' and 'why' of words and concepts becoming fixed to Aztecs or Malay tribesmen were circumstantial. But the inner intimations of danger and savagery were disseminated with the words themselves. All Spaniards knew what a *Moro* could and would do. This attitude persisted even in more tranquil contexts. In the Renaissance courts of Europe, there was a frenetic and uncontrolled dance that came to be called the *Moresque*, or 'Moorish' dance. A German poet visiting Nuremberg in 1491 saw a display where the participants moved in a circle, throwing out their arms and legs in jerky spasms, their necks stretched back and wild grimaces on their faces. Sometimes they were called 'Madmen' or 'Savages', but most often they were known as 'Moors'. You can still see them, for there is a fine set of small gilded wooden figures, the *Moriskentänzer,* by Erasmus Grasser, in the Stadtmuseum of Munich. These little Moors have dark faces, sinewy legs and arms, strong hands, unsmiling faces. They convey an air of power, mystery and menace.[55]

PART THREE

7

To the Holy Land

The Iberian peninsula has loomed large in this book, but there is no simple and neutral way to refer to it. Each of its names – Iberia, Hispania, Al-Andalus, Spain – proclaims a different heritage, a particular view of its history and origin, although it notionally describes the same territory. For a long time those who wrote about 'Spain' did so mainly from Christian sources, and those who chronicled 'Al-Andalus' worked principally from Muslim materials. Thus the history of the same past, in the same landscape, had a double aspect. It included both what was written about and what was ignored, what was visible on the surface, and what Meron Benvenisti calls 'buried history'.[1] Buried history is not some archaeological material that can be excavated, but rather a terrain full of ghosts and memories. All the three areas that I consider in this book have buried histories.

Spain was the first. Another was that broad wedge-shaped peninsula with the Adriatic to its west and the Black Sea to the east, stretching up to the great Hungarian plain. The Turks called it *balkan*, 'the mountain', and that name – the Balkans – has stuck. Here, like the holy sites of Spain, buried saints suffused the land with a kind of holiness. A third lay to the east, at the opposite end of the Mediterranean. It extended from the desert edge of Sinai to the foothills of the Anatolian plateau. It had various names, but in many European languages it was (and is) the Levant, from the Italian and Spanish term for the point where the sun rises in the East (*levante*). In Arabic it was called *Al-Mashreq*, also meaning the land where the sun rises.[2] But the archetype for this idea of holy ground was that part of the Levant where Jesus Christ had been born, lived and died.[3]

Muslims were enjoined to make the journey to Mecca at least once in their lives. But pilgrimage to Palestine, the Holy Land, was not mandatory for Christians. Nonetheless a pilgrimage still conferred a great spiritual benefit. The pilgrim's journey involved physical sacrifice and hardship, which was meritorious in its own right. Furthermore, to pray with a pure heart where Christ Himself had once stood was an act of great symbolic significance. One knight, leaving his goods to the Abbey of Cluny as he left for the Holy Land, wrote: 'I have decided to go to Jerusalem, where God became man, where He spoke with men, and to adore Him where He walked.'[4] Pilgrimage could also be imposed as penance for a serious crime such as murder, and these pilgrims sometimes carried a heavy iron chain about their waists to signify the reason for their journey. It was widely believed that when the sinner prayed in Jerusalem, God Himself would shatter the iron links to make clear His absolution.

Jerusalem was a magnet for Muslims as well as Christians and Jews. It was the third holiest site of Islam, after Mecca and Medina; for Muslims it was Al-Quds, the holy place.[5] Devout Jews often came to the city in the month of *Tishri*, and stayed to celebrate the Feast of the Tabernacles.[6] Christian pilgrimage had begun under the Emperor Constantine and continued under his successors. Great efforts had been made to recover the Christian past of the Holy Land. Lost or half-forgotten biblical sites were located and restored, and lavish churches were erected to enshrine the key places in the life of Jesus Christ. The vast Holy Sepulchre complex was first built between 326 and 336, over the tomb in which Christ had briefly lain. Constantine's redoubtable mother, Helena, commissioned the building of churches in Bethlehem and on the Mount of Olives. She was also responsible for rediscovering the three long-lost crosses upon which Jesus of Nazareth and the two thieves had been crucified, relics that had disappeared centuries before. The cross on which Christ had died was identified by the simple expedient of lowering a mortally ill woman on to each of the three wooden shafts in turn, and witnessing her miraculous recovery the instant she was placed upon the True Cross.

Not only Jerusalem, but Bethlehem, Nazareth and many other places named in the Old and New Testaments received a steady stream of pilgrims from the fourth century onwards. Saint Jerome (342–420), living in the Holy Land, observed that the places where a diligent Christian should pray in Jerusalem had become so numerous that it was impossible to visit them all in a single day.[7] Ardent pilgrims soon discovered a multitude of additional holy sites, some of dubious authenticity. One of Jerome's community told him how she had visited the houses where Cornelius and Philip had once lived in Caesarea, as well as the grave of four unspecified holy virgins. In Bethlehem, she had visited not just the Church of the Nativity, but also what was by tradition the tomb of Rachel. At Hebron she was taken to see some remarkable relics: she entered the authentic hut of Sarah, wife of Abraham, where the swaddling clothes of Isaac had been preserved and, outside the hovel, she saw the remains of the patriarch's oak, gnarled with age but still in vigorous leaf.[8]

The Persians' invasion and occupation of Palestine in the early seventh century, the wars of the Byzantine Emperor Heraclius against them and the Muslim occupation that followed sometimes severely impeded the flow of pilgrims, especially those from the West. But the flow never ceased entirely, and the Emperor Charlemagne (who legend held had himself made the pilgrimage) later purchased a hostel in Jerusalem, which welcomed any western Christians, as well as building a church and a library for their use. In 810 he also sent money to be used for the repair of the main holy sites in the city.[9] However the bulk of pilgrims were not western Christians, but devout men and women from Egypt, and other lands by then under Muslim rule, as well as those from the Byzantine domains. The long journey from western Europe restricted pilgrimage to those who could afford the time and considerable expense.[10] Nonetheless pilgrimages from the West had increased steadily. There were six substantial groups from the German-speaking lands in the ninth century, eleven in the tenth, and thirty-nine in the eleventh.[11] But by the mid ninth century the journey had become much more dangerous.

Islam may have triumphed in the seventh century but political and military control over the Muslim lands eventually fragmented. A strategist looking at a map of the Mediterranean would see Africa joined to the Levant and Anatolia by only a narrow bridge of land fringed by desert, across the Sinai Peninsula and north along the coastal strip of Palestine.[12] The same *coup d'oeil* would register that the various terrains of North Africa – part coastal littoral, part high mountain ranges, part desert – were distinct from the Muslim lands to the north of the land bridge. Above all, Egypt, at the junction of

Africa and the Levant, was a historic entity in its own right. The land of Egypt, like Jerusalem, featured in the Qur'an, and so existed within the Islamic ethos from the outset. The economy of Egypt, based on the Nile, had no equal, and Islam in Egypt had inherited a long tradition of culture, government and power. With the building of Cairo in the last quarter of the tenth century and the opening of the Al-Azhar mosque and university in 988, Egypt also became an intellectual centre of the Muslim world.[13]

But there were not many other factors in common between the peoples of North Africa and those across the land bridge. Islam in North Africa was formed from both Arab and Berber strands. West from the city of Cairouan, on the great open Gulf of Sirte, it was Berber- and not Arabic-speakers who formed the bulk of the population. From the fringe of these lands came the Fatimid conquerors of Egypt in the mid tenth century. These adventurers followed the Shia line of the faith, taking their name from the daughter of the Prophet Mohammed, from whom they claimed descent.[14] The caliphate they established in Cairo was based on the Shia traditions of Islam, even though the majority of the Muslims they ruled in their new state followed the Sunni line. Much of the subsequent history of the Islamic lands in the Levant was a struggle between those who ruled to the north of the land bridge and those who ruled to the south, regardless of the pattern of Islam to which they adhered.[15] From the late tenth century, armies raided more or less continuously back and forth across the narrow coastal strip of the Levant, as they engaged successively with Byzantine armies and the Abbasid rulers of Baghdad. But even more dangerous from a pilgrim's perspective were the Bedouin tribesmen, who lived by raiding traders and travellers. Palestine had become a zone of war.

Muslim rulers rarely made any attempt to curtail pilgrimage, which provided them with a valuable source of income. There were occasional riots and other popular outbursts, as in 966 when part of the rotunda of the Holy Sepulchre was destroyed. But in 1003 these attacks became official policy. The bizarrely eccentric Fatimid Caliph Al-Hakim in Cairo suddenly began a campaign against local eastern Christians and Jews and their holy places. On his orders, numerous churches and synagogues were razed. Most dramatically of all, the vast shrine of the Holy Sepulchre was 'dismantled', with the upper levels pulled down until the towering mound of stone blocks and rubble stood so tall that it prevented any further demolition. Then the Church of St Mary on Mount Zion was levelled to its foundations, while the Church of St Anne was completely obliterated and its stones used for new buildings on the site.

Al-Hakim devised new and ingenious means of putting pressure on local Christians to convert to Islam. He ordered Coptic and Orthodox Christians to dress only in black, 'and to hang [heavy] wooden crosses from their necks, half a metre long and half a metre wide'. In 1013 he ordered Jews to wear large bells around their necks when they entered the public baths.[16] Many succumbed and professed Islam. Yet Western pilgrims continued to stream into Jerusalem even during the fiercest persecutions of local Christians. Al-Hakim's attacks on the 'Peoples of the Book' were not part of a growing Muslim hostility to Christians in general. Many said that the Fatimid caliph was mad and impious, and his policies were certainly without precedent. Also in 1013 Al-Hakim declared that he possessed divine qualities and began to persecute Sunni Muslims with much the same vehemence as he had attacked the other faiths.[17] Finally, in 1021, he died in mysterious circumstances, and his obsessions ended with him.

However, the destruction of the Holy Sepulchre resonated powerfully in Europe. Pope Sergius IV supposedly issued an encyclical to the faithful, exhorting them to send an army by sea from Italy that would rescue the sorely wounded city of Jerusalem:

Let all Christians know that news has come from the east to the seat of the apostles that the church of the Holy Sepulchre has been destroyed from roof to foundations by the impious hands of the pagans. This destruction has plunged the entire church and the city of Rome into deep grief and distress. The whole world is in mourning and the people tremble, breathing deep sighs . . .

With the Lord's help we intend to kill all these enemies and restore the Redeemer's Holy Sepulchre. Nor, my sons, are you to fear the sea's turbulence, nor dread the fury of war, for God has promised that whoever loses the present life for the sake of Christ will gain another life which he will never lose. For this is not a battle for an earthly kingdom, but for the eternal Lord.[18]

After Al-Hakim's death, the physical damage was slowly repaired. The Holy Sepulchre was partially rebuilt, although not on the same scale as Constantine's great edifice. However, nothing could eradicate the folk memory of its destruction at the hands of the infidel.

The millennium of Christ's Crucifixion in 1033 stimulated pilgrimage to Jerusalem. Yet those who journeyed to the Holy Land came back with tales of desolation in a country riven by war and of constant attacks by Bedouin. More and more, pilgrims had to travel in large and defensible groups: one from Germany in 1065 led by Gunther, Bishop of Bamburg, totalled 7,000, including a number of nobles and an armed escort.[19] But even for a party as large as this the journey was fraught with unexpected dangers. On 15 March, with the Holy City almost in sight, they were attacked by raiders and suffered heavy losses. For two days they did not attempt to fight back, but as the tribesmen grew bolder the knights and their retainers armed themselves, and drove off their assailants. The column was saved by the *amir* of Ramleh, who arrived with his garrison and repulsed the raiders. Then he escorted the party on their way to Jerusalem. Thus at least on this occasion the authorities did what they could to protect pilgrims. But for those who eventually reached Jerusalem and came safely home, the strongest memories were of those who had died on the road. Of the 7,000 who had set out, only 2,000 returned.[20]

By the mid eleventh century Palestine had been laid waste by war, and was full of robbers and brigands. Providing protection and supplies for the bands of pilgrims was beyond the capacity of the Muslim rulers, in a land that was short of food and water. These groups several thousand strong, with their armed protection of armoured knights and retainers, and their fortified marching camps, must have seemed more like invading armies than parties of the pious. Increasingly, large groups of pilgrims seeking food and water met with a hostile response. There were skirmishes at ports such as Tripoli and later in roadside towns such as Ramleh, where the townspeople refused to admit the travellers within their gates. Pilgrims saw only that the Holy Land, which should belong to Christendom, was suffering at the hands of the 'Saracens'. It had become a wilderness. In the pilgrims' eyes there was little outwardly to distinguish those Muslims who like the *amir* of Ramleh behaved well towards them, from others who did not. The endless frustrations of the journey, the ceaseless demands for fees and bribes to pass through both Byzantine and Muslim territories, the requests for payments to ease entry into the holy sites fuelled their undifferentiated sense of rage and resentment. So the thousands of pilgrims carried home tales of their difficult and dangerous journey, stories that were no doubt exaggerated with each retelling, to enhance their heroism.

It is almost impossible, at the start of the third millennium, to reconstruct the popular understanding of the Holy Land during the eleventh century. But it is safe to say that few believers can have been ignorant of it. For most lay-Christians at the time, their faith was determined by the ceremonies of the Church, and God's truth, but not directly through the texts in which it was inscribed.[21] The Word of God came to them via a series of verbal dramas enacted by their priests. The pioneer philologist Walter Ong called this an 'oral literacy'. And he also noted the essentially dramatic quality of the Christian message. It was designed to be spoken, especially since it was structured around a set of narratives or parables. These possessed all three vital characteristics for a good story: location, character and incident. The Qur'an by contrast, despite its great poetic power, is essentially abstract and rarely topographical. The Christian narratives all have a precise *topos*: as with the stable in Bethlehem, or the feeding of the Five Thousand beside the Sea of Galilee. The entry of Jesus into Jerusalem, His trial and Crucifixion in the city are all closely bound to a place.[22] The imagined topography of the Holy Land became the staple of medieval art and illustration. Jerusalem in particular must have been a place more real to many Christians than Rome, Paris, Edinburgh or London. Bethlehem, Nazareth, Galilee and, above all, Jerusalem, were part of every Christian's inheritance. The immediacy of the region was heightened by the sense that many of the holy relics enshrined in Western churches had their origins in the East.[23]

The Holy City, for western even more than for eastern Christians, was 'the navel of the world, a land fruitful above all others, like a Paradise of delights'.[24] It was the central point on the globe, where Dante entered Hell at the beginning of his *Divine Comedy*. Jerusalem was not so much a place name as an individual. Pope Urban II echoed this popular feeling, personifying the struggle, when he summoned

Christendom to Jerusalem's aid: 'This royal city, therefore, situated at
the centre of the world, is now held captive by His enemies . . . She
seeks therefore and desires to be liberated, and does not cease to
implore you to come to her aid. From you especially she asks succour.'
The pains and torments suffered in the East were human and not
abstract. Evil men had ravished a land that belonged to Christ:

An accursed race, a race utterly alienated from God, a generation forsooth
which has not directed its heart and has not entrusted its spirit to God, has
invaded the lands of those Christians and has depopulated them by the
sword, pillage and fire . . . it has either entirely destroyed the churches of
God or appropriated them for the rites of its own religion. They destroy the
altars, after having defiled them with their uncleanness. They circumcise
the Christians, and the blood of the circumcision they either spread upon
the altars or pour into the vases of the baptismal font.

When they wish to torture people by a base death, they perforate their
navels, and dragging forth the extremity of the intestines, bind it to a stake;
then with flogging they lead the victim around until the viscera having
gushed forth the victim falls prostrate upon the ground.

Others they bind to a post and pierce with arrows. Others they compel
to extend their necks and then, attacking them with naked swords, attempt
to cut through the neck with a single blow. What shall I say of the abominable
rape of the women? To speak of it is worse than to be silent.[25]

Urban's diatribe talked of Palestine, although in reality even under
Al-Hakim assaults this severe had never taken place. But Urban's
invisible subtext was the cruel and bloody Roman martyrdoms so
familiar to his listeners.

It is an open question as to whether the Crusades could have been
launched without the oratorical skills of Urban II. He understood
both his immediate and his wider audience. He skilfully reworked the
elements known to his listeners – cruelty and barbarity, the destruction
of the Holy Sepulchre, infidel rule – into an appeal that could have
only one response. Unfortunately, we know tantalizingly little about
his plans and intentions in the late summer of 1095 when he crossed
the Alps into southern France. Had Urban already decided to make
his appeal to Christendom or did this conviction emerge as the autumn
progressed? He had certainly chosen the venue with some care. The

leaders of the Church in France were summoned to meet the pope in Clermont, on the edge of the Auvergne; it was a point accessible from both north and south. On 18 November 1095, 300 churchmen and their clerical retinues gathered in the largest church of the city, filling it to capacity. There they settled disputes about discipline and good order: the King of France was excommunicated for adultery and the Bishop of Cambrai for selling official positions in his diocese. But as the meeting proceeded, the pope suddenly announced that on Tuesday 27 November he would speak not just to the Church but to the world. A dais was built outside the eastern gate of the city and early on the morning of the address the papal throne was set up before a huge crowd.

For so momentous an event in history, the accounts of Urban's speech are teasingly confused. No one wrote down a verbatim account and there are five different versions of what Urban said, each subtly different in tone and emphasis, to reflect the writer's own preoccupations. However, clearly common to each version is Urban's method of winning over his audience, and if the details differ, his intention and technique are evident. He was telling the vast crowd gathered before him a story, reminding them of facts they knew already, interweaving his ideas and narratives in ways that they had hitherto not considered. In one version, by Robert the Monk, he appealed to them as men of France, upon whom he called in the hour of Christendom's need:

Oh, race of Franks, race from across the mountains, race chosen and beloved by God as shines forth in very many of your works; set apart from all nations by the situation of your country, as well as by your catholic faith and the honour of the holy church! To you our discourse is addressed and for you our exhortation is intended.[26]

In another (by Fulcher of Chartres), he carefully linked the issue of a pure Church, which they had been discussing for nine days, with the great and manifest evil in the East. He called upon Christians to make a pilgrimage in arms to the East:

I, or rather the Lord, beseech you as Christ's heralds to . . . carry aid promptly to those Christians and to destroy that vile race from the lands of our friends.

I say this to those who are present, it is meant also for those who are absent. Moreover, Christ commands it.

All who die by the way, whether by land or by sea, or in battle against the pagans, shall have immediate remission of sins. This I grant them through the power of God with which I am invested.

O what a disgrace if such a despised and base race, which worships demons, should conquer a people which has the faith of omnipotent God . . .

As he spoke, the crowd shouted back their assent, *Deus lo vult* ('God wills it'), and as he finished Adhemer, Bishop of Le Puy, knelt before him, begging his permission to join the great expedition. Suddenly, the crowd surged forward, and the cries of 'God wills it' rose to a crescendo. In Guibert of Nogent's account, it was at this point that Urban blessed them all, making the sign of the Cross with his hand, and then giving them the emblem under which they would fight: 'He instituted a sign well suited to so honourable a profession by making the figure of the Cross, the stigma of the Lord's Passion, the emblem of the soldiery or, rather, of what was to be the soldiery of God.'[27]

At Clermont, Urban II achieved what his quarrelsome (and, arguably, greater) predecessor Gregory VII had failed to accomplish. He stretched out beyond the issues of papal power and government to galvanize Christian society, clerical and lay, to action. The movement that he unleashed (and plainly, the potential for a war on God's account existed before he spoke) had no set bounds or limitations.[28] It had no name. It would be centuries before the term 'crusade' was first coined, and this did not become common usage until the eighteenth century, long after the first impetus had slackened. For Urban and his contemporaries it was a pilgrimage or a journey, but one made unique by the Cross that they wore. Everything was embodied in the emblem, the undeniable mark of Christ, familiar to all Christians.[29]

The image of the Cross marked a boundary between Christendom and the world of Islam. For Christendom it represented an elemental triumph – over death itself. It signified both Jesus Christ's humanity and divinity, especially when the body of Christ was depicted hanging on the Cross. For the Muslim it marked the essential absurdity of the Christian claims to divinity. Muslims in the Levant were already well aware of the symbolic importance of the Cross for Christians. It was for this reason that Al-Hakim had forced them to suffer the weight of heavy wooden crucifixes around their necks. It was for this reason that Christians were not allowed to place a cross atop their buildings, and the cause of Muslim outrage when the victorious Crusaders placed a cross on one of the most holy Muslim sites in Jerusalem.

Urban's call for a pilgrimage in arms, under the banner of the Holy Cross, produced a response among the population at large that exceeded all his expectations. This surge of popular feeling and commitment cannot be properly explained by material causes, like poor harvests, although such issues were certainly a factor. Those who rallied to his call to liberate the Holy Land seemed to have had some hazy idea of what their objective entailed. No practising Christian could have been unaware that there was a place in the East where Christ had been born. Many must also have heard that this paradisal land was under threat. In some communities there might also have been a pilgrim who had already made the journey and, in a culture where knowledge was still passed by word of mouth, such a testimony spread with remarkable speed. Others might have known of the tales of great heroes like King Arthur, who were widely believed to have made the journey in earlier days. But latterly the pilgrims' stories had not been of the glories of the Holy City, but of their failure to complete the journey: they had found the road blocked and had to retreat. Peter the Hermit, who led the People's Crusade in 1096, had already failed to reach the Holy Land on a previous occasion. The Turkish soldiers who controlled the roads to Jerusalem had forced him to turn back, cursing him as he went.

The Holy Sepulchre had been destroyed less than a century before, and this still resonated in the collective memory. Now, the Holy Places again seemed under threat. The fear if not the fact was real enough. The East was ravaged by war for much of the eleventh century, but in August 1071 the strategic balance between the Byzantine Empire and the Muslims had suddenly altered profoundly. The Seljuq Turks who had dominated the eastern Islamic world defeated the Byzantine armies at the battle of Manzikert in Armenia. Within a few months, Turkish riders had reached the shores of the Mediterranean, and a Seljuq sultanate was established in Anatolia. An army of Turks besieged Jerusalem in the same year but only took the city from its Fatimid garrison two years later. In 1077 the local Muslims rebelled against their new masters, and expelled the Turks. When these returned in force, the city was recaptured with a great slaughter of the *qadi* and all the leading Muslim families. The Turkish yoke sat as heavily on Muslims as on Christians and Jews. Heavy taxes were imposed indiscriminately.

The new soldiers of Christ were 'signed with the Cross', *crucesignati*. They were exempted from the normal processes of law while they were on their journey to the East. Their possessions could not be seized, no action could be taken against them. Up to that point Christendom had recognized two categories in society: those who belonged to the Church establishment, and the vast majority who did not. Now those who took the Cross stood midway between the two and, over time, military orders of knighthood developed that acknowledged this intermediate status in a more formal manner. But in the 'crusade' launched by Urban's words, the majority of those who set out for the East were neither of noble birth nor even skilled in arms. Where Urban, both by letter and by a ceaseless round of preaching, roused southern France for the armed pilgrimage, the call for a war to rescue Jerusalem was spread further north by shadowy figures such as Peter the Hermit, a former monk from north-eastern France.

Legend has perhaps exaggerated Peter's physical characteristics – a heavy accent, a stocky but cadaverous appearance – his filthy clothes, and the aged donkey on which he covered huge distances. But the effect of what he said in villages and towns was electrifying. Guibert of Nogent said that he was constantly surrounded by 'great throngs of people', who used to pluck hairs from his mule, which they treated as holy relics.[30] He summoned the people to a war for Christ, and they followed him immediately, bringing with them what weapons or implements they had to hand. From the Low Countries and northern France and the valley of the Rhine, he had gathered about 15,000 followers by the time he arrived with his army at Cologne early in April 1096.

Bands of these poorly armed but wildly enthusiastic soldiers for Christ began to march east.[31] When this human mass finally reached the walls of Constantinople, the Emperor Alexius greeted them warmly, but refused them admission to the city. They were only allowed through the gates to see the holy shrines in parties of eighteen, and under heavy guard. The pilgrims set up a straggling camp below the walls of Theodosius, and lived off the land. They robbed the suburban houses and villas that surrounded the city, especially along the seashore, and even stripped the lead from the roofs of churches.[32] On 6 August, Alexius provided a fleet of small ships to ferry the pilgrims across the Bosphorus. He was pleased to see them depart: these were not the troops that he had hoped would help him resist the depredations of the Turks. Nor did he believe that this rabble could survive in battle with the Muslims. He would be proved right.

The people's army advanced south, laying waste the land before them. They achieved some success, capturing isolated castles and amassing a large quantity of plunder. But in October the Turks gathered an army large enough to deal with this increasingly provocative enemy whom they regarded as Byzantine mercenaries.[33] Spies lured the pilgrims out of their camp with tales that the largest and richest city in the region, Nicaea, only a few miles away, was ripe for seizure. At dawn on 21 October the entire force – of about 25,000 men on foot and 500 mounted knights – set out for Nicaea. Barely three miles from the camp they were ambushed by the Turks, who had hidden in woodland either side of a river valley. Showered with arrows, and battered by sudden attacks by the Turkish horsemen, all order broke down, with knights riding down their own men in an attempt to escape.

The popular Crusades that ended so disastrously were not the pilgrimages that the pope had envisaged when he issued his appeal at Clermont.[34] Urban II had stipulated Constantinople as the meeting point for the pilgrims and by the spring of 1097 four columns of knights and men-at-arms, and a mass of armed camp followers, had converged on the city. By early June an army of 50,000–60,000 had been transported across the Bosphorus by the Byzantine navy. This large figure gives a misleading sense of the Crusade's military strength. Only some 7,000 of this number were heavy armoured cavalry, western Europe's particular contribution to the art of war. Some of the remainder were experienced spearmen and a few archers, but the vast bulk were poor pilgrims, men and women, lured by the Cross and the promise of plunder. Each armoured knight (*miles*) was the nucleus of a miniature war band. He was supported by a retinue, some mounted and some on foot, but all well armed and loyal to their leader. In turn, most of the knights owed allegiance to one of the great lords or rulers who were in charge of the expedition. But it was a loose structure with little coherent sense of direction, an army managed by a committee of commanders. In the West, most warfare was local and while many had been on pilgrimage, only the Normans from southern Italy had any experience of an Eastern way of war. Yet even they had no knowledge of the vast distances in Asia Minor, of the harsh climate, with deserts of salt where nothing could grow, and of a powerful enemy unlike any they had previously encountered.

West and East approached the conduct of war from different perspectives. The Western style was based on close combat, on the impact of an armoured knight riding at full speed at his enemy, often with his retinue around him. European war horses were larger and heavier than those in the East, and while Crusaders normally fought from horseback, with a heavy spear and a long straight sword, the versatility of Christian knights was remarkable. Their heavy chain mail *hauberks*, like long shirts, reached to mid calf. An iron cap, often studded and reinforced, would deflect almost any blow. The late medieval image of the lumbering man in armour, who had to be winched into the saddle, did not apply to these armies. Mounted or on foot, a company of mailed Crusaders could cut a swathe through most Eastern formations.

While Western knights rammed themselves into the heart of the enemy ranks, the Turks usually stood off from their opponents, raking them with arrows and javelins from a distance, before darting in at speed to deliver the *coup de grâce*. The incomparable Turkish recurved bow was made from layers of horn and sinew; in the hands of a skilled man it could send arrows to punch holes through mail or an iron helmet. One account tells of a Crusader shot in the leg: the Turkish arrow went through two layers of mail and so deeply into the horse's flank that it dropped dead, with the rider still pinned to its corpse. The Turkish horse archer could fire three shots in a few seconds, while riding at full speed, either charging forward or in retreat. Moreover, the armies of the East possessed specialized troops not yet developed in the armies of the West. Horse archery was the most notable skill of the Turks; the Syrians produced light horsemen (*faris*) skilled with the lance; the Persian cavalry were heavily armoured, man and horse alike.

The Westerners found that the armoured knight was not invulnerable. After the First Crusade, a local ruler held a trial combat between champions. In the tourney the Western knight charged his opponent with a heavy spear, aiming at his exposed chest. The Syrian *faris* threw a javelin into the shoulder muscle of the knight's horse, causing it to stumble and crash to the ground. The knight was thrown off but, before he could get to his feet, the Arab had knocked him prostrate with his war hammer, and then jumped down to prick the Westerner's exposed throat with his sword. At that point the mock combat was stopped. However the Arabs and Turks quickly realized that these men were not like the Byzantines, whom they knew from many battles. An image of these powerful Franks (*Franj* in Arabic) surfaced in Arabic literature. They appeared as huge clean-shaven men 'like leftovers from the race of Ad' or not men at all. They carried stout broadheaded lances or spears of tempered steel.[35] The reckless courage and determination of the knights was incomprehensible to their Muslim peers. Usama Ibn-Munqidh, the Muslim paladin, tells a story of eight Arab warriors who met a single Crusader horseman. He demanded that they give him their camels. They cursed him and refused. One by one he killed or disabled four of them. Then he demanded the camels again, saying, 'Otherwise I shall annihilate you.' Then he divided the eight camels and led four away. 'He drove his four under our very eyes, for we were helpless with regard to him and had no hope for him. Thus he returned with his booty; and he was only one while we were eight men.'[36]

The first battle of the Crusade clearly showed how dangerous the Western style of war could be to much larger Eastern armies. The Crusaders besieged the town of Nicaea, which had been the fatal lure for the People's Crusade. On 16 June 1097 the Seljuq Sultan, Kilij Arslan, sent his best troops to relieve the garrison defending the chief city of his domain. The Turks descended from the high surrounding hills, shouting their battle cries and banging on drums. A thin line of Crusaders stood between the Turks and the ramparts of the city. Kilij Arslan's men rushed at the city's main gate, expecting to brush the Westerners aside. To their surprise, as they pushed forward, a column of Crusaders struck them a stunning blow to their flank. The

Orientalist nineteenth-century painting of the battle by Henri Serrur is highly Romanticized, but it captures the sense of a savage mêlée, with the knights steadily hacking their enemies asunder. In a battle that lasted from dawn to dusk, Kilij Arslan learned the devastating power of the long spears and heavy swords of the Westerners.

The Crusaders, for their part, soon learned to respect the accuracy and rapid fire of the Turkish archers. Little over a month after the fall of Nicaea, the Turks ambushed a Crusader column on its way to the old Roman road junction at Dorylaeum. They killed or wounded many Westerners, but the survivors regrouped, fought back, and then slaughtered the Turks. However great their losses, nothing halted the slow advance of the Crusaders. As they ran out of supplies and the horses died, the knights ended up riding oxen. But still they marched on. They made a huge sweep east and then south, over deserts and across mountains; they were losing men daily, but by October 1097 they stood before the huge city of Antioch, the key to the Levant. A massive urban sprawl, Antioch covered a plain almost three miles long and a mile wide between the River Orontes and Mount Silpius, where the Lebanon and the Taurus mountain ranges meet. Its long lines of ramparts followed the contours of the land, without any obvious weak points. Above the city walls stood a strongly fortified citadel. All through the winter the Crusaders camped before these impenetrable walls, suffering daily the sorties of the city's defenders. However, the halt before Antioch allowed them to replenish their supplies. Fleets of ships brought food and equipment from Cyprus. Kerbogha, the ruler of Mosul, far to the east in modern Iraq, was also using the winter and early spring to rally a large army for the relief of Antioch. If the Crusaders did not take the city before he arrived, they would be in a dangerous position, caught between the walls of Antioch behind them and a new and confident enemy before them.

But on 2 June 1098, the Crusaders made as if they were striking camp and set off eastward, apparently to confront Kerbogha. Then, after nightfall, they doubled back, and a small band of knights scaled the north-west walls, which had been left unguarded. Inside the city, they met some of the Christian citizens of Antioch, who led them through the tangle of streets to two of the city's smaller gates. There they cut down the guards and opened the portals. The whole Crusading army poured through into Antioch. In a single day every Turk, male and female, was killed. By nightfall on 3 June, according to the *Gesta Francorum* chronicle, the Crusaders made an attempt, which failed, to take the citadel. They had blockaded Antioch for eight months. One day after they had captured the city (if not the citadel), the first outriders of Kerbogha's great host appeared before the walls. The whole Muslim army soon arrived and took over the siege works built by the Westerners. Sandwiched between the citadel above them and the encircling army from Mosul beyond the walls, the Crusaders were trapped in a city that contained no food and little water. Men boiled and ate the leaves of figs, vines, thistles and all kinds of trees. Others stewed the dried skins of horses, camels, oxen or buffaloes.[37]

They were saved by a miracle. Inside the city, morale deteriorated day by day, until an extraordinary relic was discovered on 14 June. The Holy Lance that had pierced the side of Christ at the Crucifixion was unearthed beneath the floor of the ancient Church of St Peter. Its location had been revealed in a vision. The find was taken as a message of God's favour.[38] Just two weeks later, after endless sermons, prolonged fasting and the preparation of the fragile relic as a battle standard, the Crusader army marched, with soaring spirits, out of the Bridge Gate over the River Orontes, and headed straight towards the Muslim force encamped before it. The Holy Lance was held high in the vanguard for all to see. The army moved at a slow walking pace. Only about 200 of its war horses were left after the long months of siege.[39] But the foot soldiers walking before the few remaining mounted knights were not the nondescript muster of ill-equipped and untrained men, stiffened with a few trained spearmen, who had formed the infantry in earlier battles. Most of those in the line were skilled knights in full armour, whom it proved immensely hard to kill. Accounts told of knights bristling like porcupines with arrows, darts and javelins, but still moving forward and fighting ferociously. While the mounted knight, the epitome of chivalry, possessed great striking power, the Turks had found that his horse was vulnerable. Against armoured infantry, fighting in unison, the traditional Turkish tactics proved much less effective. Western knights were trained to fight on foot or on horseback: this versatility was the Crusaders' salvation on 28 June 1098.

The Muslims gathered before the Bridge Gate were only a fraction of the main army, which was encamped some miles away to the north of the city. When they saw the army of footmen advancing, they perceived a forlorn and desperate attempt of an enemy on the verge of defeat. They had no reason to know of the Crusaders' new sense of ecstasy. It seemed impossible that this mob of men on foot could prove as deadly as men on horseback. The Turks attacked, showering the Crusaders with arrows. Many of the camp followers were killed, but very few of the knights. They quickly came upon the Muslim foot soldiers who formed the bulk of the besieging force and cut them down in their thousands.[40] They then turned north, keeping close to the river on their right so that they could not be outflanked, and advanced at a steady pace. Muslim horsemen charged and charged again, but they were brushed aside. Nothing halted the Holy Lance. By nightfall, the whole army of Kerbogha had retreated in disorder and the Crusaders had taken possession of its camp. They found a vast amount of plunder and food, numerous camp followers, and Kerbogha's field treasury.

The God-given victory before the walls of Antioch was the first of a near-unbroken line of triumphs. The Muslim armies melted away as the Crusaders continued their progress south through the Levant to Jerusalem. From Antioch onwards, the attitude of Muslims to the Western invader began to change. The Crusaders had made a decisive impact not just on the Seljuq Turks, but on the complex and fragmented political culture of the Levant. The Muslim chronicles now noted how very different the *Franj* were from the Byzantines: they were completely uncivilized. The Damascus chronicler Ibn Al-Qalanisi called them infidels, or 'God-forsaken', but his main complaint was that they broke solemnly concluded agreements. At the town of al-Ma'arra, 'the Franks, after promising [the inhabitants] safety, dealt treacherously with them. They erected crosses over the town, exacted indemnities from the townsfolk, and did not carry out the terms on which they had agreed.'[41] He did not include the most terrible occurrence at Ma'arra, which other Muslim and Christian historians recorded. Fulcher of Chartres wrote,

I shudder to say that many of our men, terribly tormented by the madness of starvation, cut pieces of flesh from the buttocks of Saracens lying there dead. These pieces they cooked and ate, savagely devouring the flesh while it was insufficiently roasted. In this way [eating half-cooked meat] the besiegers were harmed more than the besieged.[42]

This was the behaviour of animals and not men, and chroniclers noted example after example of this orgiastic violence. At Antioch, Fulcher recorded that when the Crusaders had captured the Muslim camp, they did not enslave the women that they found there (as Muslims would have done) but 'in regard to the women found in the tents of the foe the Franks did them no evil [did not rape them] but drove lances into their bellies. Then all in exultant voice blessed and glorified God. In righteous compassion he had freed them from the cruellest of enemies.'[43] A merchant from Ma'arra declared that 'I am from a city which God has condemned, my friend, to be destroyed. They have killed all its inhabitants, putting old men and children to the sword.'[44] Muslim chroniclers related many acts of treachery and brutality within Islam, but there was something different about the Westerners' rude animal vigour. The qualities that made them so effective in battle also made them capable of any atrocity.

In Islamic eyes, the most extraordinary example of this viciousness came as Jerusalem was finally captured. When Muslims had first occupied the city, it had been regarded with respect and reverence and, with the exception of the brief period under the Caliph Hakim, Christians, Jews and Muslims had existed side by side within its walls. But the Crusaders would treat the city like any other place that had offered resistance. Their army finally arrived at its destination on 7 June 1099. What the Crusaders saw came as a shock. Instead of the Holy City of their imagination, they were faced by a fortress.[45] Unlike Antioch, set on its flat plain and with its long walls, Jerusalem offered opportunities for assault, but the advantage lay with the fresh and well-equipped defenders of the city. Little over a year earlier, the city had been reoccupied by Fatimid troops, who expelled the Turkish garrison. They had worked energetically to improve the defences and made it clear they would not yield without a fight.[46] On the day after its arrival, the whole Christian army, many barefoot and in the clothing of penitents, processed around the city, to derisive shouts from the soldiers lining the walls. Then the army gathered on the Mount of Olives to hear sermon after sermon, which roused their spirits and reminded them of their journey's purpose. The Crusaders no longer enjoyed the benefit of the Holy Lance. Its reputation had been tarnished by rumours that it was not a true relic. The monk who had discovered it, Peter Bartholomew, then demanded the right to defend his honour and that of the Holy Lance through trial by ordeal. Unfortunately, he was 'horribly burned' in the flames and died twelve days later.[47]

The Crusaders outside Jerusalem now had news of a large army massing in Egypt to relieve the Holy City. There was no chance of starving Jerusalem into submission – it could be taken only by assault. Once more, as at Antioch, they risked being trapped between the enemy within the walls and the enemy without. A long investment was therefore out of the question: the city had to be taken by storm. But there was no wood to hand from which they could make ladders and siege towers and the garrison had poisoned the wells outside the walls. Parties were sent out to scour the country to find enough trees to build siege engines, and eventually two large mobile towers were made in secret out of wood, and clad with wet hides to prevent the Muslim garrison destroying them with Greek Fire. On 13 July 1099, the larger of the two towers was rolled slowly into position close to the northern wall of the city, while a covered ram battered away at a lower outer wall that protected the main fortification. For two days the ram pounded at the wall, under constant enemy fire. But it slowly dislodged the stones in the wall so that on the morning of 14 July the tower could be pushed into position, close enough to lower the assault bridges on to the city rampart. The defenders made increasingly desperate efforts to topple it, but they were swept off the wall by a hail of arrows.

Suddenly, huge clouds of acrid black smoke poured out of the siege engines and drifted over the walls, choking the defenders. Seeing the direction of the light breeze, the Christians had lit bundles of damp straw inside the towers. As smoke enveloped the walls, the assault bridges were dropped and two Flemish knights crossed, jumping down on to the city wall. As they held off the defenders, more knights poured across the bridge, consolidating the position on the wall. The defence weakened, and then broke. Ladders were pushed up to the wall and more knights clambered into the city. As they advanced through the streets, the Muslim defenders fled before them. Some knights moved off to open the Gate of the Column, allowing the main body of the army into the city. Others pursued the defenders, and began the slaughter of every living thing within the walls. Count Raymond had given his safe conduct to the survivors of the garrison in the city's citadel, but many were killed. Raymond of Aguilar, who was with him, wrote:

Some of our men (and this was more merciful) cut off the heads of their enemies; others shot them with arrows, so that they fell from the towers; others tortured them longer by casting them into the flames. Piles of heads, hands, and feet were to be seen in the streets of the city. It was necessary to pick one's way over the bodies of men and horses . . .

Indeed, it was a just and splendid judgement of God that this place should be filled with the blood of the unbelievers, since it had suffered so long from their blasphemies. The city was filled with corpses and blood.[48]

Then there was a hiatus. On the first day, the massacres took place in the heat of battle. On the next day,

in the morning our men climbed up cautiously on to the roof of the Temple and attacked the Saracens, both male and female, and beheaded them with unsheathed swords. The other Saracens threw themselves from the Temple . . . The Saracens who were still alive dragged the dead ones out in front of the gates, and made huge piles of them, as big as houses. Such a slaughter of pagans no one has ever seen or heard of.[49]

The Jews of the city had been confined to their synagogue, which was then set alight. All died. And one writer, Albert of Aix, mentions an event that none of those present in Jerusalem included in their reports. On the third day after the city fell, the leaders of the conquest decided that all remaining prisoners, men, women and children, should be killed lest they side with the army advancing from Egypt in a new siege that the Crusaders expected and feared.[50]

But that Muslim advance was halted by one final, stunning victory. The elation of the Westerners was crowned by the recovery of some fragments of the True Cross. These had been taken by Orthodox priests expelled from the city by the Fatimid commander before the Westerners' arrival. After the conquest they returned with their precious treasure, and concealed it. The Westerners tortured them until they revealed its hiding place. Unlike the Holy Lance, the True Cross had an unquestioned pedigree. Thus, when the army of Egypt moved along the coast to the city of Ascalon, it was faced by a reinvigorated Crusader army, bearing this most holy of relics in the vanguard.

The Egyptian army was mostly made up of footmen: Arabs, Ethiopians, men from North Africa, Armenians. They were well armed and well equipped. On 11 August, the Crusaders, who had marched at full speed to meet their new enemy, came upon them before the walls of Ascalon. The Westerners had learned the lesson of Antioch: now their mounted knights were protected by a strong force of foot soldiers, many in armour. But at Ascalon, it was the Muslim army that charged into the Christian lines, led by the Ethiopians who wielded huge iron flails that could shatter flesh and bone. On both wings, the Egyptian cavalry and some horse archers tried to envelop the Crusaders. Pinned with their backs to the walls of Ascalon, the heaving mêlée of Muslim footmen provided a perfect target for the charge of the mounted knights. One or two charges threw them into complete disarray, then the Crusaders re-formed and charged again, heading for the Egyptian standard. Finally, the Egyptians broke and fled from the battlefield.

At Antioch, the Crusaders' desperate assault had panicked a much larger force, which had put up little effective resistance. At Ascalon, it was a much harder fight, and the Crusaders were fortunate that the full Egyptian force was not ready for battle when they opened their attack. But by August 1099, they had been hardened by three years of battles, sieges and an epic journey. Moreover, they had refined the raw skills of Western war. Armoured infantry played an increasingly important part and they recognized the value of lighter and more manoeuvrable mounted troops who could protect the more heavily armoured knights, by chasing away the mounted Turkish horse archers. After Ascalon, there was no enemy likely to challenge their possession of Palestine. The Latin Kingdoms of the East, stretching from the edge of the Anatolian plateau to the fringes of the Sinai desert, began to embed themselves.

The Latin Kingdom of Jerusalem lasted for eighty-seven years, from 1100 to 1187. Its counties, baronies and lordships formed a frontier society which was constantly under threat. It is not surprising that the most notable and permanent impact that the Westerners made upon the land was in their huge castles and military architecture. The kingdoms in the East were sustained by irregular infusions of fresh manpower and money from the West, but never enough and rarely in a timely fashion. This was a foothold and not a comprehensive conquest, like the Norman occupation of England in 1066. There were perhaps some 3,000 adult Frankish knights, plus around 5,000 sergeants of men-at-arms, many of whom married local Christians or even took Muslim wives – the Western population of the kingdom cannot have exceeded 25,000 in total, amid a much larger population of Arabic-speaking Muslims and local Christians.[51] On the borders to north and south lay hostile Muslim states, which eventually overwhelmed the Latin enclave. The Westerners were no more than a scattering of small colonies, usually centred on a castle or a fortified town, their power stronger in theory than it ever was in practice. The Holy Land came to dominate them rather than the reverse.

෨

I have used the words 'Crusade' and 'Crusader'. Everyone does. But not a single 'Crusader' participated in the First Crusade. At best they were Crusaders *avant la lettre*, before the word existed. The wars to rescue Jerusalem long antedated the word 'Crusade', which was first coined in Spain in the thirteenth century as *cruzada*, a generation after the loss of Jerusalem in 1187. It first entered English usage as the French word *croisade* about 1575, and it was not fully anglicized as 'crusade' until the early eighteenth century, after *crusado*, *crusada* and *croisado* had all been tried and found wanting.[52] 'Crusade' has from the beginning been a floating, highly mobile and adaptive term, precisely denoting very little but replete with connotations. It has always been a versatile theory. Popes championed a useful concept that allowed them to declare a holy war on any individual or group, proscribing them as enemies of Christ.[53] There were holy wars against Muslim infidels; against heretics like the Albigensians of Provence; against recalcitrant Christian monarchs; even against humble towns that failed to toe the papal line. But the first category, war against the Muslim infidel, was always popularly regarded as the true war 'for and by the Cross'.

Sanctified war was an innovation within the Christian Church, which had for centuries struggled to impose the peace of God upon adversaries. The bishops in the province of Narbonne had, forty years before Urban's speech, declared, 'Let no Christian kill another

Christian, for no one doubts that to kill a Christian is to shed the blood of Christ.'[54] And Urban II, according to Fulcher of Chartres, had expressly contrasted the evil of war with a struggle in a good cause. Urban told the throng at Clermont:

Let those of you who have formerly been accustomed to contend wickedly in private warfare against the faithful, fight against the infidel, and bring to a victorious end the war . . . Let those of you who have hitherto been robbers now become soldiers. Those of you who have formerly contended against their brothers and relatives now fight against the barbarians as they ought.

Islam had developed a coherent theory of a holy war long before. Muslim jurists had presented a world split into two parts – one was the House of Peace (*Dar ul Islam*), where a true Islamic ruler governed, and the other the House of War (*Dar ul Harb*), where Islam was not in control.[55] Muslims should strive to ensure that Peace took the place of War.[56] The Arabic root of the word to strive or struggle, J-H-D, generated the word *jihad*, which meant any kind of battle in a good cause. In everyday terms it referred to the internal struggle against evil or temptation and was called the 'greater *jihad*', much as later Christian writers came to talk of a holy war against sin.[57] But the same word also meant a 'holy war' in the purely military sense, which most Muslims regarded as a 'lesser *jihad*', derived from this process of inner purification.[58] Most Western writers have subsequently focused on the secondary meaning, as Rudolph Peters succinctly put it:

The Islamic doctrine of *jihad* has always appealed to Western imagination. The image of the dreadful Turk, clad in a long robe and brandishing his scimitar, ready to slaughter any infidel that might come his way and would refuse to be converted to the religion of Mahomet, has been a stereotype in Western literature for a long time . . . The assumption underlying these stereotypes is that Moslems, often loosely called Arabs, are innately blood-thirsty and inimical to persons of a different persuasion, and that [is] owing to their religion, which allegedly preaches intolerance, fanaticism and con-tinuous warfare against unbelievers.[59]

The theory of *jihad* was drawn from a few occurrences of the word in the Qur'an and more fully in the juristic commentary on the oral traditions (*hadith*) of the Prophet Mohammed. These statements often required considerable interpretation to mould them to events. In theory, for Islam as for Christendom, war was an evil. For battle and killing to be sanctified it had to be a struggle in a good and godly cause. Over time, therefore, both communities evolved superficially quite similar ideas for a just war in a good cause. But there were differences between the parallel but separate processes of evolution.[60] In Christendom, the doctrine of holy war was hotly debated and transmuted over time into many different ideological strands, mostly in response to social and political change. The terminology of 'Crusade' was highly mutable: pilgrimage, journey, signed by the cross, and so on, were other ways of describing it. In Islam, there were two terms commonly used – *jihad*, and *ghaza* in Ottoman Turkish – and there could be little debate about the meaning of these terms, and little theoretical investigation of their limits and boundaries. This was because in the dominant Sunni branch of Islam theoretical evolution was severely constrained; as contemporaries expressed it, the 'gates of interpretation' (*ijtihad*) had been closed around the year 900. This meant that the principles of the faith, including the struggle for purity (*jihad*) were beyond debate and could not be altered.[61]

But Muslim scholars continued to adjust the application of these immutable principles, by 'explaining and interpreting the eternal truths and applying the eternal laws'.[62] It was not an ossified and monolithic system and if the theory was fixed, its application was not. Not all wars against infidels were declared to be holy wars, and resistance to the Franks in 1097–9 was certainly not regarded at the time as a *jihad*. But during the two centuries that the *Franj* occupied the Levant, the language of *jihad* grew louder and more sustained. Like the summons to the Crusade, this call to Muslims served a particular purpose.[63] The summons brought together an otherwise disunited community. The new idiom of holy war provided a uniquely powerful rhetorical style. Before that fateful encounter in Palestine, Christendom had been focused upon the notion of the Peace of God, and most of the Islamic world had conveniently abandoned both the traditional rhetoric and its practice of the 'lesser *jihad*'. As an outcome of their struggle in the Levant, both cultures were left with a well-honed ideology of war in a just cause.

When the organized forces of 'Crusade' and *jihad* confronted each other directly on the battlefield, the contrast between them was immediately apparent. Visually speaking, the dominant motif of the western Christian side overwhelmed all others. The Muslim banners carried many different emblems and texts, mostly the names and qualities of God and other suitable verses from the Qur'an. But on the Christian side the single image of the Cross was dominant. From the first contact the defining characteristic of the Crusade was the symbol of the crucified Christ. The 'Crusaders' were *crucesignati*, 'signed with the Cross'.[64] In Arab Muslim eyes, there was something distinctive and disquieting about these Christians, the Franks, who wore the Cross and had stormed Jerusalem in 1099.[65]

The Cross-wearers violated all the acceptable standards of society in ways unthinkable to the local Christians and even the Byzantines. The twelfth-century Muslim warrior Usamah ibn-Munqidh recounted the corrupting impropriety of the Crusaders' behaviour in the Holy Land. They were 'without any vestige of a sense of honour and jealousy'. He told a story of a bath-keeper, whose establishment was frequented by the Franks.

One day a Frankish knight came in. They do not follow our custom of wearing a cloth around their waist while they are at the baths, and this fellow put out his hand, snatched off my loin cloth and threw it away. He saw at once that I had just recently shaved my pubic hair. 'Salim!' he exclaimed. I came towards him and he pointed to that part of me. 'Salim! It's magnificent! You shall certainly do the same for me!' And he lay down flat on his back. His hair there was as long as his beard.

I shaved him, and when he felt the place with his hand and found it agreeably smooth he said, 'Salim, you must certainly do the same for my *Dama.*' In their language *Dama* means lady. He sent his valet to fetch his wife and when they arrived and the valet had brought her in, she lay down on her back, and he said to me, 'Do to her what you did to me.' So I shaved her pubic hair, while her husband stood by watching me. Then he thanked me and paid me for my services.

This colourful tale may have recalled a real event, or perhaps it was simply an anecdote. But the Franks certainly baffled Usamah. 'You will observe,' he wrote, 'a strange contradiction in their character: they are without jealousy or a sense of honour, and yet at the same time they have the courage that as a rule springs only from the sense of honour and the readiness to take offence.'[66] As Carole Hillenbrand has observed:

This story touches on the essential difference perceived by Muslims between their own society and that of the Franks. In a society where women were protected by their menfolk, not allowed to reveal their unveiled faces except to a prescribed number of close male relations, the conduct of the French knight and his wife . . . both castigates Frankish immorality and also [by contrast] reinforces the values of Muslim society.[67]

In fact their transgression went further than this. For Muslims, the Crusaders, by breaking the bounds between the forbidden (*haram*) and the permitted (*halal*), disrupted and destabilized not only their own lives but also the entire world around them. In Muslim eyes, the Franks created a constant and highly visible desecration. The dominant symbol of the cross was everywhere, atop churches and even the holy mosques of the Dome of the Rock and Al-Aqsa in Jerusalem. The military orders established within the Crusader states all used the cross as their emblem and it became a graphic symbol of defilement. This sense of pollution runs through one of the tales incorporated in the *Thousand and One Nights*. It tells how the dried excrement of the High Patriarch in Constantinople was so revered among Christians that it was preserved and made into the 'holiest incense for the sanctification of Christians on all solemn occasions, to bless the bride, to fumigate the newly born and to purify a priest on ordination'. Since the Patriarch could not produce the volume required, 'the priests used to forge the powder by mixing less holy matters with it, that is to say, the excrements of lesser patriarchs and even of the priests themselves'. Later, this same sanctifying incense was smeared upon a great wooden cross, which Christian soldiers were forced to kiss and, in this case, the narrator avers, 'there could be no doubt as to the genuineness of the powder as it smells terribly and would have killed any elephant in the Muslim army'.[68]

This Rabelaisian burlesque, like Usamah's tale, related directly to the perceived filthiness (in a physical sense) of the Westerners but it also suggested their deeper offence to Muslim sensibilities. For them, the depiction of Christ on the Cross transgressed a wide range of taboos. God-made-flesh was unthinkable, and even more so a God who experienced a physical birth. In Islam God was transcendent, while the western Christians proclaimed His materiality. The Crusaders' capacity to pollute seemed limitless. They had, unwittingly or deliberately, defiled the holy site in Jerusalem (the *Haram al-Sharif*) from the first moments of their occupation. They had killed thousands within the holy precinct. They had briefly stabled their horses by the Mosque of Al-Aqsa, while one later visitor recorded that 'As for the Dome of the Rock, the Franks had built upon it a church and an altar. They had adorned it with pictures and statues.' The same writer saw 'pictures of grazing animals fixed in marble and I saw amongst those depictions of the likenesses of pigs'.[69] Whether or not pigs were depicted is perhaps less significant than the certainty that for Muslims it seemed entirely plausible. Another Muslim traveller was shocked when he climbed up to the holy sites. 'I entered Jerusalem and I saw monks and priests in charge of the Sacred Rock . . . I saw upon it bottles of wine for the ceremony of the mass. I entered the Aqsa mosque and in it a bell was suspended.'[70] The most manifest evidence of this desecration to Muslim eyes was the large gold cross that had been placed on the highest point of the Dome of the Rock.

The cross soon became an emblem of every type of pollution associated with the Franks. In part at least, this Muslim revulsion was based upon the day-to-day reality of life in the Crusader kingdoms where (unsurprisingly) Christian images supplanted Islamic aniconism. It was this public display that was so disturbing for Muslims. Many practices, such as the reverence for the cross, holy pictures, statues and the like, were common among local Christians living under Islamic rule both before and after the Crusader occupation of Palestine. However, Christians living under Islam were normally prevented from displaying aural and visual manifestations of Christianity: no bells summoning the believers, no crosses upon their churches, no public processions. Nothing, in short, to offend the majority's sensibilities, so Muslims normally were not confronted with Christian worship, which was largely invisible. The public triumph of Christianity, especially in the plethora of new churches and shrines that were built throughout Palestine, came as a visual and psychological shock.[71] There had been numerous churches and shrines before 1099, but now the pace of new building was inexorable and barely slackened over six or seven decades. The Holy Sepulchre was extended to become a huge Romanesque pilgrimage church, guarding the greatest shrine in Christendom. The mosque called the *Haram al-Sharif* (Dome of the Rock) was left physically intact but was covered with frescoes outside and sacred objects inside: transformed into the Church of the Holy of Holies (*Templum Domini*) it was dedicated at Easter 1141. The physical 'Christianization' of the city was accompanied by a shift in population. Muslims and Jews were mostly precluded from living within the walls, so that Jerusalem was now a Christian city, with even the old Muslim and Jewish quarters thronged with Western migrants and pilgrims.[72]

For centuries, except on a few rare occasions and regardless of who ruled the city, Jerusalem had been a neutral space. Jews, Christians and Muslims had operated a Peace of God. Pilgrims could worship at their sacred places, scholars could come closer to God through study. Sometimes a kind of informal academy developed, where the different faiths could debate issues of belief. The First Crusade and the near-century of the Latin Kingdom interrupted that long tradition. But it also created a new sense of anger and anxiety in both the western Christian and the Mediterranean Islamic worlds. Its roots lay earlier, in the seventh century, and a shadowy negative image of the infidel must already have existed within Western society in the eleventh century. Nothing else can explain the extraordinary response to Urban's summons. But it was not a dominant discourse. After the First Crusade it was, both in the East and the West. During the period of Christian occupation of Jerusalem, from 1099 to 1187, the trope of defilement and the consequent need for purification grew more dominant among Muslim writers. In tone, if not in content, it was similar to the Western reactions to the Muslim occupation of Jerusalem in the years just before the conquest of 1099, and again in the centuries after the loss of the city in 1187.

The Muslim reconquest evoked a plethora of different responses in the West. By the 1340s the noted Dominican scholar and preacher Robert Holkot could argue that 'It is not possible to teach the life of Christ unless by destroying and condemning [*destruendo et reprobando*] the law of Machomet.'[73] He further asserted that Islam should be eradicated both by preaching, 'the spiritual sword', and if necessary by conquest and extermination. Nor was Holkot an insignificant figure. His reputation grew after his death in 1349 and his *Study on the Book of Wisdom*, in which this condemnation was contained, went through twenty printed editions between 1480 and 1520.[74] But there were others, like William of Tripoli, writing in Acre, who believed firmly in the possibility of converting Muslims by peaceful means to the Christian life. He concluded his *De Statu Saracenorum* with this confident assertion: 'Solely by the word of God, without philosophical argument and without military weapons, they will like simple sheep seek the baptism of Christ and will enter into the flock of God. He says and writes this who by God's will has baptised more than a thousand.'[75]

Yet his confidence in conversion was not widely shared. More typical were scholars who cast doubt on even the desirability of conversion. The Franciscan Alexander of Hales in his *Summae Universae Theologiae* of 1256 classed Muslims with heretics irredeemably tainted by their unbelief and who should therefore be killed by any lawful authority. Benoit of Alignan in his *Tractatus fidei* suggested that the 'absurdities of Mahomet' should be extirpated by 'fire and sword'.[76] But no scholar suggested that the fact of Islam's existence could ever be ignored. This was the vast 'myth of crusade' that Alphonse Dupront traced through his life's work, a history on an almost Gibbonian scale. This myth, as he put it, became 'an endemic reality, that is a [permanent] condition of the collective spirit.'[77] But the medieval Crusades, like the Ottoman expansion into the Balkans and the two great sieges of Vienna (1529 and 1683), had a double impact. They transformed the West, but they also transmogrified the East.

8

Conquest and Reconquest

The First Crusade was born out of fear. Urban II believed that the Holy Land was in danger and Christendom responded to his call. Although later Crusades to the East were to a greater degree a product of political ambitions and territorial aggrandizement, the visceral element never disappeared. The fears grew, through contact with the East and increasing Western preoccupations with Islam. While Muslims saw a source of defilement in Frankish Christians, so too Christians now blamed the existence of Islam for the rising tide of corruption in the Christian world.[1] Churchmen complained that the people of the Latin Kingdoms were acquiring the lewd ways of the East, wearing unchristian clothing and disporting themselves with Muslim women. If James of Vitry is to be believed

Among the *Poulains* [children of the Crusaders born in the Holy Land] there is hardly one in a thousand who takes his marriage seriously. They do not regard fornication to be a deadly sin. From childhood they are pampered and wholly given to carnal pleasures, whereas they are not accustomed to hear God's word, which they lightly disregard . . . And the city [Acre] is full of brothels, and as the rent of prostitutes is higher, not only laymen, but even clergymen, nay even monks, rent their houses all over the city to public harlots.[2]

Nowhere were these ideas of pollution more graphically presented than in Avignon in the spring of 1335. In February, a middle-aged priest called Opicinus de Canistris had suddenly fallen ill. He lay in bed until the end of March, when he suddenly recovered having, as he said, seen a vision of the world. His illness had left his mind confused and his right arm paralysed. His official career as a papal secretary in the pontifical palace was ended. Nonetheless, he learned to use his left arm, and began writing and drawing at breakneck speed. Over the next few months he filled more than fifty-two large parchments. At that point he disappears from history – the date of his death is uncertain – and his work vanished into the papal archives where it lay undiscovered for almost 600 years.

Opicinus had become obsessed with his own sin and desire, and during his illness he began to see the shapes of three huge figures concealed in the outline of the Mediterranean. One was male, another female, and the third was a bearded and monstrous devil. He drew his grotesque figures over the contours of the coastline, believing that God had carved out the land for a purpose and His message was unmistakable. So Opicinus presented the Mediterranean as a Sea of Sin. Over the northern (European) and southern (African) shorelines he inked in the heads of twin figures, one male and one female, and gave them faces, clothes, arms and legs. The lower extremities fitted the topography less exactly. Italy made a convenient right leg and boot for the Europe figure; but the left leg ended clumsily in the heart of Greece. However the apex, where the two heads almost touched, was his focal point. Opicinus made it plain that this was no chance proximity. They were deep in carnal conversation.[3]

Over the African shore he drew a female figure in Moorish dress, who, with her arm pointing towards his midriff, whispered sugges- tively into Europe's ear, 'Come, let us *copulate.*'[4] The Latin word he used, *commiscemini*, has the sense of illicit mixing; and Opicinus declared of the Straits of Gibraltar: 'Between Spain and Mauritania is the *vulva Oceani* from which the Mediterranean Sea proceeds.'[5] The evil that obsessed him was the sexual conjunction of a seducing Muslim woman and a pure Europe turned from the path of virtue. This was truly the Devil's work. At the other end of the Mediterranean, he saw the head of the Evil One, a dark shape that occupied the eastern Mediterranean, with its face covering the Levant and the lands occu- pied by Islam, and a full beard fringing the Balkans.

Opicinus became preoccupied with these deeper meanings in the landscape. He came to see every event of his own troubled life as depicted on the maps before him. Progressively, he became the Europe-Man, struggling with temptation. When he was constipated, he understood his discomfort as an emblem of the political troubles afflicting Lombardy. Examining the patterns of hair on his body, he

realized that they 'signified' the location of the vineyards throughout Europe.[6] His preoccupation with lust and the Devil grew
ever stronger. Africa-Woman became 'the symbol of sin, hypocrisy
and the like', while Europe-Man represented 'purity, salvation or
piety'.[7] He played with the conjunction of the northern and southern
shores: sometimes Africa was a virile male and Europe the frail
virgin. But in most of his sketches, Africa wore the clothes of a Muslim
woman: Africa-Woman was, of course, an infidel. The Christian
world was contaminated by its contiguity with Africa and the
Levant. This was the meaning of Africa-Woman and the shadowy
figure of the Devil. These were the lands occupied by 'Islam'. Jerusalem itself lay under the body of the Devil, while Spain was being
seduced.

Opicinus expressed (in an extreme fashion) a common association
of the Muslim East with danger and corruption. The experience of
the Levant over the two centuries of Christian occupation confirmed
the beliefs that had stimulated the Crusading impetus in the first place.
The first Crusaders had dedicated themselves to the salvation of the
Holy Places, which they believed were in danger of destruction. This
sense of threat increased once they arrived in the East and this anxiety
grew through the whole period of Western presence. They were few
and the infidels were many: 'Where we have a count the enemy has
forty kings; where we have a knight they have a duke . . . where we
have a castle they have a kingdom.'[8] This sense of oppression, of a
tiny western Christian minority drowning in a sea of infidels, was
both real and fictive. A century before Opicinus de Canistris, the
chronicler Roger of Wendover observed in a letter written from
the city of Acre in 1221, 'We and the other peoples on our side of the
water are oppressed by so many and great expenses in carrying on
[this crusade], that we shall be unable to meet our necessary expenses
in carrying on . . . unless by the divine mercy we shortly receive
assistance from our fellow Christians.'[9] Yet a presence in the East was
essential to further the triumph of Christ: for this reason an anonymous
poet hailed the Crusade of King Louis IX of France in the mid
thirteenth century as the means to 'baptise the sultan of the Turks,
and thereby free the world'.[10]

In Palestine as in Spain, Islam and Christianity were in contest for
the same terrain. Yet there was a subtle difference. Al-Andalus lay on

the outer perimeter of Islam, and did not have the special significance
for Muslims of the 'Far Distant Place of Worship' in Jerusalem,
whither the Prophet Mohammed came miraculously by night and
was thence taken up into Heaven.[11] Christian Spaniards claimed Spain
as their own holy land by prior right, in which the Moors were
temporary intruders. By contrast in Palestine, Muslims, Jews and
Christians all claimed full rights to a territory revered by all three
communities. Moreover, in each case, the process of losing and later
redeeming this land became a dominant religious and literary motif.
The loss of the Muslim holy places in Jerusalem – *Al Quds* – from
1099 to 1187 generated an intense preoccupation with the infidel
Christian enemy.

The encounter between western Christendom and Islam after 1099
created a malign heritage for both communities. Each battle, siege,
despoliation or defilement fuelled opposing narratives. Thus the conquest of the Christian County of Edessa in 1144 by Imd al-Din Zengi,
the Turkish ruler of Mosul, seemed a divine intervention to the
chronicler Ibn al-Athir:

When Almighty God saw the princes of the Islamic lands and . . . how
unable they were to support the [true] religion and their inability to defend
those who believe in the One God and He saw their subjugation by their
enemy and the severity of their despotism . . . He then wished to set over
the Franks someone who could requite the evil of their deeds and send to
the devils of the crosses [western Christians] stones from Him to destroy and
annihilate them.[12]

For the Christian Bishop William of Tyre, the city was lost through
Christian failures – the petty squabbles among Christian princes and
a negligence in Christendom for the sacred patrimony in the East:

Thus while the Prince of Antioch, overcome by foolish hatred, delayed
rendering the help he owed to his brothers and while the count awaited
help from abroad, the ancient city of Edessa, devoted to Christianity since
the time of the Apostles and delivered from the superstitions of the infidels
through the words and preaching of the Apostle Thaddeus, passed into an
undeserved servitude.[13]

The loss of Edessa roused the West to launch the Second Crusade led by the Emperor Conrad III and King Louis VII of France. Steven Runciman charted the rise and ignominious fall of the enterprise:

No medieval enterprise started with more splendid hopes. Planned by the Pope, preached and inspired by the golden eloquence of St Bernard, and led by the two chief potentates of Western Europe it had promised so much for the glory and salvation of Christendom . . . in fact the Crusade was brought to nothing by its leaders, with their truculence, their ignorance, and their ineffectual folly.[14]

No subsequent Crusade met the high expectations created by the first 'pilgrimage'. During the twelfth and thirteenth centuries a succession of failed ventures caused a number of writers to ask whether these journeys were indeed God's will. Would He have allowed them to fail so ignominiously if they were? Many ingenious solutions were found to this conundrum. Failure stemmed from the moral imperfections of the Crusaders themselves and of the wicked society that had produced them. They were unworthy to recover the Holy City. Others explained the Muslim infidels' victories as the instrument by which Christ chastened His sinful people and called them to reform. But gradually a more comprehensive explanation emerged, which seemed both to fit all the circumstances, and also corralled Islam within Christian doctrine.

For many scholars the success of Islam could only be rationally explained if the Prophet Mohammed and his followers represented the Antichrist, whose appearance foreshadowed the final triumph of Christ in His Second Coming. Saint Paul had given this ancient idea a succinct Christian definition: 'That day [the Second Coming] shall not come except there is a falling away first and that man of sin be revealed, the sin of perdition. Who exalteth himself above all that is called God or that is worshipped.'[15] For many Christians, the self-evident *man of sin* was the Prophet Mohammed. Yoking Muslims with the Antichrist made them implacably hostile to Christians, but it also assured their ultimate defeat. It is risky to be too definite in matters of perception. A single event, text or image should not be read outside its original context, and we can never be sure that the few written documents are not chance (and thus misleading) survivals from the distant past. But from the late medieval period onward, there was a shift in the image that the communities, Christian and Muslim, had of each other. Both were hostile and suspicious, but while the Western image of the East seemed to be in a constant state of flux and mutation, the Islamic attitude stabilized. The closest we can get to popular attitudes were the tales of folk heroes who vanquished their opponents, sometimes Christian Crusaders, sometimes Byzantines. In addition to traditional folk heroes like Abu Zayd and Rustam, there were new and historical heroes like the ruler of Egypt, the Mamluk (Turkish) Sultan Baybars, who finally expelled the Franks from their last foothold in the land where the sun rises, the *al-mashreq*.[16]

The tradition of these tales is entertaining fantasy, which is what the people wanted. Narratives that were full of drama, excitement and colourful characters were the stock in trade of professional travelling storytellers. So the *Sirat al-Zahir Baybars* is a long succession of wildly improbable adventures. The sultan defended the poor and righted wrongs. He was transported magically to England and had many thrilling encounters there. Nonetheless his experience of Christians was typified by the 'treachery' of 'Juwan' – John – who eventually received his just deserts at the sultan's hands. In another folk epic, the *Dhat al-Himma*, even the bravest of the Franks was described as 'a very wicked and guileful man'.[17] These were all stock villains, just as Baybars was a one-dimensional hero figure. But, like the Western characterization of the men (and women) of the East, these were images of the infidel readily recognizable to Muslims, who already knew that western Christians were essentially wicked. They had heard that the Franks were dangerous, treacherous and vicious, both physically and spiritually corrupt. Ultimately, not much survived of the admiration for the Crusaders' courage which had appeared in the writings of Usamah ibn-Munqidh.

The confrontation in the Levant administered a deep shock to both western Christendom and the world of Mediterranean Islam, imprinting deeply upon both cultures. Every conquest engendered a desire for reconquest. To understand how and why this effect persisted over many centuries lies within the domain of social psychology, and then the difficulty is finding methods of interpretation that are not simply anachronistic or inappropriate. Kimball Young, one of the early pioneers of the discipline, set out the essence of the problem: 'Propaganda may be open and its purpose avowed, or it may conceal its intention. It always has a setting within a social-cultural framework, without which neither its psychological nor its cultural features can be understood.'[18] The fear and hatred that grew out of the confrontation between Islam and Christendom were a conditioned or a 'Pavlovian' response.[19] The reinforcement sustaining that response was sometimes a *personal* experience but, more often, it stemmed from a firm conviction acquired by other means. Most of those who believed that the infidels – 'Saracens', 'Agarenes', 'Ishmaelites', 'Turks' – were savage and barbarous had never met a Saracen or a Turk in their lives. Yet this understanding was as real to them as if they had. They knew it from their neighbours, from listening and reading, from visual images, much as we do today. This infusion of new knowledge was vital to maintaining hostility.

Pavlov's message was that unless these experiences and beliefs were sustained and regularly reinforced, then the conditioned response would dwindle. This drip-feed of new information and ideas, the reiteration of old themes meant that the far-distant conflict in the Levant conditioned the subsequent relationship between Christendom and Islam. It became the symbolic reference point for future recollections. As Alphonse Dupront put it, 'When we say the word "crusade", something thrills and disturbs us. This "something" is the utmost power of myth that is alive and real.'[20] The word 'Crusade' in Western society has now largely lost its specific denotation – war in a good cause – but it still carries a powerful charge. By contrast 'Crusade' carries a stronger meaning for many Muslims, while Holy War – *jihad* – still evokes a frisson of fear among Christians. These words have become metonyms of the enemy, reinforcing memories of their essential cruelty and savagery.[21]

We can trace the means by which these fears and hatred were constructed. Emmanuel Sivan began his seminal work on the Muslim 'Counter Crusade' by pointing to distinct but parallel elements in the creation of this ideology: *existing attitudes*, which were in place before the pressure of events and of propaganda, and *created attitudes* formed (or exploited) as a result of events or propaganda.[22] These functioned as reinforcement for the existing attitudes. But these twin elements were just as powerful in creating first the ideology and, later, the myth of the 'Crusade' in Western culture. The Crusaders who marched to the Holy Land had firm (if ill-founded) ideas about their enemy, while the Muslims they encountered had almost no specific notions about the Franks, except that they were grotesquely unappealing infidels. However, during their confrontation in the East, Muslims and western Christians developed much more complex and roughly symmetrical views of each other. The degree to which each group produced reverse or mirror images is remarkable. Christians regarded Muslims as inherently cruel and violent; Muslims felt the same about the Westerners. Christians developed wild imaginings about the sexual proclivities of Muslims. Muslims regarded the Franks, as Usama made clear, as little better than animals in terms of sexual propriety.

Equally, each could initially appreciate heroic and noble qualities in the other. The Sultan Saladin was portrayed in many Western accounts, despite the loss of Jerusalem to his armies in 1187, as more just and honourable than many Christian rulers. Likewise, Muslims had no difficulty in recognizing the military skill and bravery of their opponents at the same time that they described them as 'accursed'. Nor did negative attitudes prevent many forms of political and economic connection between enemies even in times of war and rancorous propaganda.[23] However, while the Muslims might produce the occasional Saladin and Baybars, and were formidable opponents on the battlefield, their visible power appeared inferior to Westerners'.[24] No Saracen fortress, for example, could match the raw defensive power of the Crusader castles such as Krak des Chevaliers, Beaufort or the sea castle at Sidon.[25] It was the rise to dominance of the Ottoman Turks from the mid fourteenth century, in both Anatolia and Balkan Europe, that altered that equation. Saladin had been a noble individual, but represented a contemptible people. The *Grand Signior*, the Sultan of the Turks, the 'Great Cham', represented an infidel state and culture whose power was to be feared and could not be denied.

૭

The Sultan of the Ottoman Turks made himself the standard bearer of Islam. The Ottoman Turks were nomads who, brought as mercenaries into Anatolia by the Seljuqs, survived their downfall. By 1280 they had established a small Ottoman centre, named after their chief Osman, in western Anatolia. His son, Sultan Orhan, established their capital at Bursa on the slopes of Mount Olympus in Mysia (Mount Uludağ) in 1326, where Osman's title is inscribed as 'The *mujahid* [he who fights for Islam], Sultan of the *ghazis*, *ghazi* son of a *ghazi* [warrior son of a warrior]'.[26] Orhan's palace was built in the city's citadel on a long mountain spur, a fortress which he enlarged and extended until it was 'nearly impregnable'.[27] In 1350 the Byzantine Emperor, John Cantacuzenus, recruited Orhan's Ottoman warriors in his campaign against the King of Serbia, Stephen Dushan. Three years later Orhan's son, Suleiman, crossed the Hellespont to take possession of the fortresses promised as the price of their support. Within a few years, from their base at Gallipoli, the Ottomans had advanced to cut the road from Constantinople to the fortress town of Adrianople, the capital of Thrace.

Suleiman was thrown from his horse while hunting and died of his injuries. It was his son Murad who succeeded his grandfather Orhan as sultan around 1361. In fifteen months his *ghazis* had brought terror to the land. Adrianople surrendered rather than risk the fate of Chorlu, where the Turks had slaughtered everyone within the walls, only saving the commander for a formal execution. Soon the Turkish domain in Europe extended from the Bosphorus to the foothills of the Balkan mountains. The Byzantine emperor in Constantinople accepted the Ottoman power, but other Christians were not so quiescent. The Serbs, with some Hungarians in alliance, crossed the River Maritza, only to be 'caught as wild beasts in their lair', and driven back into the river 'as flames driven before the wind', in the words of an Ottoman chronicler.[28] In 1366, the Ottomans crossed the River Maritza and pushed north until by 1369 they had taken the mountain passes and the land before Sofia. Then Murad turned west into Macedonia. In three years the Turks had reached the River Vardar at the town of Skopje and their European dominions at that point extended from the Thracian plain to the Dinaric Alps. The sultan also extended his territories in Anatolia, but the bulk of his domain lay north of the Hellespont, so he shifted his capital from Bursa to Adrianople. By 1386 most of the main Christian cities of the southern Balkans, including Sofia, Monastir and Nish, were in his hands. Only Belgrade on the Danube and Constantinople remained beyond his power. In 1388, Murad launched his armies against the Kingdom of Serbia to complete his conquest of the Balkan lands.

On 20 June 1389, on the plain of Kosovo Polje, the 'field of the crows' where the corvines feasted on the bodies of the dead, Murad, with his Asian and European armies, and backed by all his Christian tributaries, defeated Lazar, the leader of the Serbs. At this moment of triumph, the sultan was killed on the battlefield and immediately succeeded by his son Bayezid, who was commanding the Turkish right flank. In the aftermath of the battle, the surviving Serb princes submitted to Turkish power. After Kosovo, the Ottomans turned their attention to the one remaining obstacle to their domination of the southern Balkans. In 1391, they laid siege to Constantinople itself, but once again the great walls protected the city. A contingent of 600 men-at-arms and 1,600 archers led by Boucicault, the Marshal of France, arrived in 1398 breaking the Ottoman blockade and stiffening the Byzantines' resistance. Yet even this reinforcement could not remove the Turkish threat, so a year later Boucicault withdrew and the siege was lifted in exchange for concessions that effectively made the Byzantine emperor a vassal of the sultan.

Western Christendom had finally recognized the power of its new enemy. Over roughly fifty years (1396–1448) four Crusades were mounted with the intention not of recapturing Jerusalem, but of attacking the Ottoman infidels in the Balkans. After 1389, the Muslim enemy was not in Asia but on the banks of the Danube, with Tartar horsemen raiding into Hungary and the borderlands of Austria. Six years after Kosovo, Crusaders responded to the urgent appeal of Pope Boniface IX and a Christian army marched east. They were crushed on 26 September 1396 by the well-organized Ottoman troops of Sultan Bayezid Ilderim ('the Thunderbolt') before the town of Nicopolis on cliffs above the River Danube. On the morning after the battle the sultan sat and watched as the surviving Crusaders were led naked before him, their hands tied behind them. He offered them the choice of conversion to Islam or, if they refused, immediate decapitation. Few would renounce their faith and the growing piles of heads were arranged in tall cairns before the sultan, and the corpses dragged away. By the end of a long day, more than 3,000 Crusaders had been butchered, and some accounts said as many as 10,000. A single knight was freed and sent to Paris to recount the sultan's vengeance to the King of France. The carnage was in part a response to the Crusaders' massacre of their Turkish prisoners before the battle, but this formal and ceremonial slaughter was an innovation, and different from the massacres that were commonplace after the capture of cities or in the immediate aftermath of a battle. The mass killings by Crusaders in Jerusalem in 1099 had stemmed from an enraged blood lust after battle. Bayezid by contrast intended a calculated and memorable act of cruelty, which ran counter to the normal customs of war: many of those killed were of noble birth, for whom a ransom would have been paid.[29]

But the sultan's aim was achieved. The news of Nicopolis and its aftermath quickly became known throughout Europe and it proved very difficult to rouse any interest in the West for a new Crusade.[30] Only in Hungary was the appeal of the Crusade still potent, and eventually Bayezid's son Murad II confronted a resurgent Hungarian power. The Hungarians and their allies were led by the 'White Knight of Wallachia', János Hunyadi, whose silvered armour became famous throughout the Balkans. The Hungarians knew him as '*Török-verö*' (Scourge of the Turks). He was appointed governor of Transylvania in 1441, and regained much of the land lost to the Turks along the Danube. In 1443, the long-anticipated Crusade was launched: Vladislav, King of both Poland and Hungary, launched a new Crusade, and advancing south of the Danube recaptured both Sofia and Nish. After a serious defeat at Kostunitza, Murad sanctioned a ten-year truce.

But in the following year, the Hungarian king broke the terms of the truce and led a new Crusade down the Danube. Murad, at the time defending his territory in Asia, quickly gathered the Ottoman armies from there and Europe. He marched north towards the Crusaders. At the city of Varna, on the shores of the Black Sea, the sultan unexpectedly won another victory on the scale of Nicopolis. King Vladislav and many of his best troops died in the battle. The king's head was cut from his body, preserved in a barrel of honey and dispatched to Bursa, where it was spiked on a lance and paraded in triumph through the streets.[31] Meanwhile, Hunyadi, who had commanded one wing of the Crusader force, escaped from the debacle and fled north beyond the Danube. He slowly gathered a new army and again marched south to attack the Ottomans. On 16 October 1448, on the fateful plain of Kosovo, Hunyadi and his army of Hungarians, Wallachians, Czechs and Germans met the Ottomans on the same ground where Lazar had fallen more than half a century before. The battle lasted three days, and Hunyadi's army succumbed to Ottoman discipline and tenacity.[32]

There was a new intensity to these wars in the Balkans. Hitherto, the Mongols had been unique in their relentless cruelty, but now it seemed that both Christians and Muslims vied with each other for the scale and ingenuity of their atrocities. The ruler (*voivod*) of Wallachia, Vlad Tepes 'the Impaler', perfected the technique of mass death, skewering his enemies on a long spit or spear – the longer the stake the higher in rank the victim.[33] In 1461, Murad II's son, the young Ottoman Sultan Mehmed II, was horrified when he saw the 20,000 rotting corpses hanging on sharpened stakes outside the walls of Vlad's capital of Tirgoviste, although he himself had had no hesitation in condemning criminals to death by impalement in his own domains. Earlier centuries had seen many isolated examples of deliberate savagery, but from the fifteenth century barbarity reached new levels. The public death by flaying of the Venetian Senator Bragadino just before the battle of Lepanto, which I described in Chapter One, was paralleled in western Christian society by the elaborate ceremonial of the auto-da-fé in Spain, and an increasingly spectacular theatre of cruelty in public executions north of the Pyrenees.[34]

The greatest atrocity, however, in Christian eyes was the capture and ravishment of Constantinople by Mehmed's armies on 28 May 1453. The defeat at Varna had greatly diminished Hungarian enthusiasm for a Crusade in the East, and there was no coherent opposition from the West to the young sultan's invasion of the city. In stark contrast to the earlier Muslim sieges of Constantinople over the centuries, the army that assembled in the early spring of 1453 relied not so much on weight of numbers (although it was very large) but upon military professionalism and advanced techniques of war. Firstly, the Turks had armed their twin fortresses on each side of the Bosphorus with powerful guns designed to prevent any relieving force gaining access to Constantinople. Secondly, at a new cannon factory in Adrianople, huge siege artillery pieces that could destroy the ancient triple walls protecting the Byzantine capital were designed and built. But the imbalance between Muslim power and Christian weakness was apparent in the muster rolls: fewer than 7,000 men defended Constantinople's fourteen miles of walls, confronting the 80,000 Ottomans gathered outside.

Early in the morning of 28 May, after fifty-three days of desperate resistance, the Ottoman janissaries broke through the walls into the city. By custom they were entitled to three days of looting in any city they had taken by storm. At first they killed everyone they found alive. From the Church of St Mary of the Mongols high above the Golden Horn, a torrent of blood ran down the hill towards the harbour. The soldiers broke into the churches, ripping out the precious objects, raping or killing anyone who caught their fancy. In the afternoon the sultan made his formal entry, and went directly to the Church of the Holy Wisdom, Haghia Sophia. There he ordered an end to the pillage and destruction and directed that the great church should become the chief mosque of the city. Ducas, in his *Historia Turco-Byzantina*, records the day:

He [Mehmed] summoned one of his vile priests who ascended the pulpit to call out his foul prayer. The son of iniquity, the forerunner of Antichrist, ascending the holy altar, offered the prayer. Alas, the calamity! Alack, the horrendous deed! Woe is me! What has befallen us? Oh! Oh! What have we witnessed? An infidel Turk, standing on the holy altar in whose foundation the relics of Apostles and Martyrs have been deposited! Shudder, O sun! Where is the Lamb of God, and where is the Son and Logos of the Father Who is sacrificed thereon, and eaten, and never consumed?

Truly we have been reckoned as frauds! Our worship has been reckoned as nothing by the nations. Because of our sins the temple [Haghia Sophia] which was rebuilt in the name of the Wisdom of the Logos of God, and is called the Temple of the Holy Trinity, and Great Church and New Sion, today has become an altar of barbarians, and has been named and has become the House of Muhammad. Just is Thy judgement, O Lord.[35]

The same sense of violation fills the letter written by the Byzantine scholar, and later cardinal, Bessarion to the Doge of Venice two months after the fall of the city.

Sacked by the most inhuman barbarians and the most savage enemies of the Christian faith, by the fiercest of wild beasts. The public treasure has been consumed, private wealth has been destroyed, the temples have been stripped of gold, silver, jewels, the relics of the saints, and other most precious ornaments. Men have been butchered like cattle, women abducted, virgins ravished, and children snatched from the arms of their parents.[36]

However, the abominations of the Turks had a precursor. The capture of Constantinople by the Western Crusaders in 1204 had been described in very similar terms. Nicetas Choniates wrote of those days, two and a half centuries before:

Alas, the images, which ought to have been adored, were trodden under foot! Alas, the relics of the holy martyrs were thrown into unclean places! Then was seen what one shudders to hear, namely, the divine body and blood of Christ was spilled upon the ground or thrown about.

No one was without a share in the grief. In the alleys, in the streets, in the temples, complaints, weeping, lamentations, grief, the groaning of men, the shrieks of women, wounds, rape, captivity, the separation of those most closely united.[37]

In Orthodox Christian eyes there was perhaps little to choose between Catholic or Muslim rapine. But there was nonetheless a subtle distinction in the language used to describe the perpetrators of these bestial horrors. The Muslims were implicitly evil: 'son of iniquity', 'the fiercest of wild beasts', 'inhuman barbarians', 'the infidel'. Much was also made in Ducas' account of the sodomitical perversion of the Ottomans. Mehmed, drunk at a banquet after the fall of the city, demanded that Lukas Notaras, one of the surviving Byzantine officials, should send him his handsome younger son. Notaras replied: 'It is not our custom to hand over my own child to be despoiled by him. It would be far better for me if the executioner were sent to take my head.' When the executioners came, he bolstered his sons' courage with an appeal to their Christian and patriotic zeal.[38] This was not just the martyrdom of Notaras and his family, but of the great Christian city.[39]

These themes of destruction and martyrdom and of the rampant bestiality of the Ottomans were built upon earlier perceptions of

Islam. For many western Christians the capture of Constantinople and the slaughter that accompanied it became a catastrophe on a par with the loss of Jerusalem in 1187. Conversely, for Muslims the final capture of the city seemed both an emblem and a guarantee of the ultimate triumph of Islam. Where 'Jerusalem' had been a dominating trope of the Middle Ages, the loss of Constantinople, the last outpost of Christendom in the East with all its holy sites, became both a political and religious motif for the following four centuries, in both western and eastern Europe. With the capture of the 'New Jerusalem', the Ottomans became the cynosure for the Christian world. But any element of admiration was equalled by a sense of terror, and both were firmly rooted in reality. Constantinople under Ottoman rule – or Istanbul to give it its Turkish name – was infinitely grander in its splendid new buildings, in its vast wealth, in a greatly enlarged population and, above all, in military and political power far superior to its decayed Byzantine predecessor. Equally, under the Ottomans it seemed to contain all the qualities of lust, perversion, sinful luxury and cruelty against which Christian scholars had inveighed for centuries.[40] These Turks, in Christian eyes, now epitomized the infidel, logically enough perhaps because it was the Turks whom they had been fighting since the First Crusade.

What is a Turk? a celebrated Austrian preacher asked rhetorically late in the seventeenth century. His answer was: 'He is a replica of the Antichrist . . . he is an insatiable tiger . . . he is a vengeful beast; he is a thief of crowns without conscience, he is a murderous falcon . . . he is oriental dragon poison; he is an unchained hellhound; he is an Epicurean piece of excrement; he is a tyrannic monster. He is God's whip.'[41]

The Crusading discourse has mutated throughout its long history. From the sixteenth to the nineteenth century it took a variety of new forms.[42] I have suggested how the Spanish *cruzada* against the Moors extended during the sixteenth century into a string of conquests in North Africa and in the new territories of the Americas. Now we should cast our net wider. From the eighteenth century, the missionary 'crusade' became a Protestant venture, acquiring a new life in the British colonial conquests of India and Africa during the nineteenth century (and beyond). Many enthusiastic Christian evangelists found it natural to use the vocabulary of the 'crusade', which for them exemplified a spiritual war against evil. Hymnals and religious song books, such as *Hymns Ancient and Modern* (first published in 1861), were best-sellers by the last quarter of the nineteenth century, and many knew the words and tunes of the most popular hymns by heart.[43] These hymns exhorted the faithful to 'Fight the good fight / With all thy might' (John S. B. Monsell, 1863), or to see themselves as soldiers in God's cause. The most successful of these calls to action was 'Onward Christian soldiers, marching as to War / With the Cross of Jesus, going on before' (1865), written by the Reverend Sabine Baring Gould because he 'wanted the children to sing when marching from one village to another, but couldn't think of anything quite suitable; so I sat up at night, resolved that I would write something myself. "Onward, Christian Soldiers" was the result.'[44]

Gradually, the common meaning of 'crusade' in the English language became a metaphor for a sustained and powerful action in a good cause.[45] But the older sense of the Cross and Holy War was still a potent symbol. Nor was the specific enmity to Muslims completely lost. I remember singing at school a hymn by J. E. Neale, which had been popular since first published a century before. Neale had re-worked a text by Andrew of Crete.

> Christian, dost thou see them
> On the holy ground?
> How the troops of Midian
> Prowl and prowl around?
> Christian, up and smite them,
> Counting gain but loss;
> Smite them by the merit
> Of the holy cross.

I wondered idly at the time who the 'troops of Midian' might be. It was only much later that I discovered that the hymn's author would have known 'Midianites' as a synonym for Arabs or 'Saracens'.[46] And, plainly, the 'holy ground' for Andrew of Crete was Jerusalem and the Christian sites of the Levant – in Neale's day under the rule of the Ottomans.

However, Neale's usage was atypical, and he later produced a more anodyne version. The 'troops of Midian' were transmuted into 'The powers of darkness'. Perhaps he considered this more appropriate to the mission fields? Likewise, 'infidel', which had still been in use in the early nineteenth century, fell out of favour with hymn writers.[47] 'Heathen lands' and 'pagan darkness' replaced the wastelands of the infidel. Perhaps 'infidel' was too precisely associated with Mediterranean Islam? However, in 1911, Robert Mitchell returned directly to the language of 'crusade' in its original bellicose sense:

> Hark to the call of the New Crusade,
> Christ over all will King be made;
> Out to the world let the challenge ring:
> Make Christ King!

His refrain elaborated the theme:

> Hail to the King of kings! Triumphant Redeemer!
> On march the soldiers of the New Crusade.
> This is the battle cry: Christ made the King!
> And to our Sov'reign we allegiance bring;
> Prince, Guide and Counsellor He shall be.
> Carry the standard to victory!
> Hail to the call of the New Crusade:
> Make Christ King!
> Strong is the foe of the New Crusade,
> Sin in its armour is well arrayed;
> Into the fight we our best must fling:
> Make Christ King!

There were hundreds of missionaries to the Holy Land at the time that Mitchell wrote, but the big battalions of evangelism directed their attention elsewhere.[48] Nevertheless, the essential terminology of 'crusade' and conquest remained a constant presence in Christian discourse and activity.[49]

Nineteenth- and twentieth-century evangelicals crusaded, as they believed, for a spiritual victory, not for territorial conquest. But the word does not allow so facile a separation. This ambiguity between a holy war in a spiritual sense and a victory over the temporal forces of darkness had a long pedigree. Two seventeenth-century near-contemporaries, John Bunyan and Thomas Fuller, both wrote books entitled *The Holy War*. Bunyan's allegorical intentions were clear from this title: *THE HOLY WAR Made by Shaddai upon Diabolus for the Regaining of the Metropolis of the World or The Losing and Taking Again of the Town of Mansoul*. It was published in 1682. Thomas Fuller's *The Historie of the Holy Warre* was equally popular. First published in 1639, and reprinted four times between 1640 and 1651, it was rarely out of print. Fuller's work was a historical account – the first full description of the medieval Crusades in English. Bunyan's elaborate allegory also drew on images of the infidel. He used a perception of the alien common in his day: his villain was King Diabolus, whom he described as 'king of the blacks, and a most raving prince'. He had 'A Luciferian heart', as 'insatiable, and enlarged as hell itself'. These were descriptions frequently applied to the Turks.

Unlike Bunyan, who was the son of a tinker, Fuller had a more settled and comfortable position in society. He was a clergyman of the Church of England, a moderate Royalist and chaplain to General Sir Ralph Hopton during the Civil War. Although his *Holy Warre* was first published before fighting broke out in 1642, his description of the Crusaders struggling with the armies of the infidel seemed to have a particular resonance for both sides in the increasingly bitter internecine war. Both the Royalist and Parliamentary causes saw the infidels and enemies of the True Faith in their opponents. Allegory, history and current events were thus inextricably bound together.

Popular histories of the Crusades also appeared in other European languages. But it was the turn of the twentieth century before Muslims came to write their own histories of the Crusades in the Levant. By then, Christian missionaries believed they had converted the concepts and vocabulary of 'crusade' into a spiritual war on sin and evil. But now Muslims rediscovered the harsh consequences of the events of the eleventh century: the desecration and despoliation of *their* holy places. For them, the Crusades became a contemporary event, not something mellowed by the passage of 800 years. The Arabic word for Crusade and Crusaders – *al-salibiyyun* ('the crosses') – was used in a translation of a French military history in 1865. The earliest full-scale text written in Arabic (and from Arabic sources), entitled *The Splendid*

Story of the Crusading Wars, was published in Cairo by Sayyid Ali al-Hariri in 1899.[50] The word for the Christian cross had existed in Arabic in earlier times, but it was not until the twentieth century that it acquired this new and hateful connotation.[51] From that point onwards, new meanings proliferated. The neologism *Al-salibiyyun* came to mean proto-colonialists, exploitative agents of Western imperialism, enemies of Arab nationhood and of Islam.[52] New political meanings of the West merged with the older tropes of contamination and despoliation formed from the Muslim experience of the Crusades centuries before.

It was not only Muslims who were re-evaluating the era of the Crusades. France began a new 'crusade of conquest' early in the nineteenth century. By the 1820s the French Bourbon monarchy had returned to power after the final defeat of the Napoleonic Empire in 1815. Louis XVIII became preoccupied with North Africa, inheriting a tradition where his distant ancestors' glory was associated with the East. An immensely popular *Histoire des Croisades* by Joseph-François Michaud had appeared in the latter years of the Napoleonic Empire, and the author had been rewarded with the Légion d'Honneur for his efforts. But the restored Bourbons, especially Louis's successor from 1824, Charles X, concurred with Michaud's view that 'What is the most positive of the results of the first crusade is the glory of our fathers, this glory which is a real achievement for a nation.'[53] The Crusades rapidly became the first example of France's national grandeur. Michaud's work was constantly reprinted and led to an ambitious collection of original sources in five languages − *Recueil des historiens des croisades* − which began in 1824; further volumes appeared at regular intervals thereafter under the auspices of the Académie des Inscriptions et Belles-Lettres. When King Charles X came to the Chamber of Deputies formally to announce intervention in Algeria, he justified it as 'for the benefit of Christianity'.[54] His ministers had calculated more cynically that success in North Africa might divert attention from the rising political crisis at home. It did not, and the Bourbon monarchy fell from power.

However, if Louis-Philippe, the victor of the 1830 Revolution, did not share his predecessor's exalted Catholicism, he was nonetheless addicted to national glory. He saw a direct connection between the heroic France of the First Crusade and the triumphs of the new crusade and conquest in Algeria of the 1830s, in which his sons played an active part. The essence of this new crusade was later painted by Horace Vernet, a particular favourite of the new king, in *The First Mass in Kabylia*, which depicts a field service. The troops kneel respectfully as the celebrant holds up the Host for them to see; symbolically the body and blood of Christ subdue the lowering mountains which form the background, while a group of Arabs sit sullenly in the foreground. In 1837, as the conquest advanced, Louis-Philippe began to remodel the great palace of Versailles to create a national history museum celebrating the many centuries of French military triumph. Vernet's work would feature prominently among the vast canvases that covered the walls.

The first rooms of the king's museum depicted the Crusades, with a mock-Gothic style of decoration and a long list of the French Crusaders, the first heroes for France. Then came the other great figures of French military history, culminating in Napoleon's supreme achievement. But the story of glory continued after the emperor. The final galleries, the Salle de Constantine and the Salle de la Smalah, honoured the new crusade in Algeria. The official guidebook to the museum left no doubt as to what was the message the visitor was intended to receive:

We there find again, after an interval of five hundred years, the French nation fertilising with its blood the burning plains studded with the tents of Islam. These are the heirs of Charles Martel, Godfrey de Bouillon, Robert Guiscard and Philip Augustus, resuming the unfinished labours of their ancestors. Missionaries and warriors, they every day extend the boundaries of Christendom.[55]

Soon a steady stream of colonists began to settle in the nascent French Proconsulate of Algeria, providing a Christianizing presence in a terrain formerly 'infidel'. A diocese was created in Algiers in 1838, which became an archdiocese in 1866, with two subsidiary bishoprics at Constantine and Oran. Two years later a new missionary order called the White Fathers was founded with the aim of carrying the Christian message into Kabylia and south into the desert. Dressed in a white robe, or *gandoura*, with a mantle, they looked more like Algerian Arabs than Frenchmen. Under the direct authority of the Congregation of Propaganda in Rome, in their ardour, discipline, asceticism and energy the White Fathers resembled the Jesuits in their exultant heyday centuries before.[56]

This preoccupation with North Africa survived Louis-Philippe, continued through the rule of Napoleon III, and on into the Third Republic that followed him. By the end of the nineteenth century, writers could look back at a constant extension of French conquest: in Algeria, in a French Protectorate of Tunisia and in the French (and Spanish) partition of Morocco in the 1890s. The theme of the crusade remained popular. Michaud's *History* had became a school textbook in 1844, with eighteen editions published by the end of the century, and in 1877 a new luxury edition appeared, which was illustrated with a set of magnificent engravings by Gustave Doré representing Christian power and dominance. This rhetoric and image of crusade in the first half of the nineteenth century was usually a mask for grubbier enterprises, but it is wrong to regard it with complete cynicism. French Algeria may have been a colony created first by accident, and then as a device to counter the unpopularity of successive governments in Paris. But many of the migrants to Algeria and even of the soldiers who fought there, and certainly the missionaries labouring in the deserts, often believed that they were following a higher calling. Nowhere else in the Islamic lands had there been such a reprise of the medieval Latin Kingdom. Once again a Christian community had been implanted among the infidels. All patriotic citizens of France should rejoice that their nation, which had won Jerusalem in the First Crusade, had now brought Christian power back to the southern shore of the Mediterranean. This had been the great mission of Saint Louis, the nation's patron saint, which was finally fulfilled some seven centuries after his death.

Nor did France ever intend to leave. Algeria became an integral part of metropolitan France, and its existence an exemplar of France's civilization and cultural destiny. That 'civilizing mission' was taught in every school in France and in the schools of the empire beyond the seas, and this unifying ideology gradually replaced the sectarian vocabulary of crusade, except in high Catholic circles. But support for French Algeria transcended the gulf between clericals and anticlericals.

Many believed with an absolute conviction in France's mission in North Africa and were prepared to use any means to sustain it. Other colonial territories, such as Indochina, could be abandoned or bargained away in the 1950s. Ironically, it was Algeria, the first fruit of the civilizing mission, a land reconquered by crusade, that ultimately destroyed the Fourth Republic and ushered in the presidency of Charles de Gaulle. The recriminations over the abandonment of *l'Algérie française* continue to this day.

If any one individual embodied the renaissance of the French spirit of crusade it was Charles de Foucauld. Born in 1858, orphaned in 1864, he later became an army officer. It was a natural career, for the names of his ancestors who had fought in the Crusades were inscribed on the walls of Louis-Philippe's museum at Versailles. But he was a hopeless soldier, until he discovered a love of the desert and a zest for exploration. In 1887 his pioneering study, *La Reconnaissance du Maroc* ('The Discovery of Morocco'), was published. Then two years later, still a hero in Paris, he entered a Trappist monastery and openly proclaimed his yearning for martyrdom. In 1901 he was dispatched by his order as a missionary into the Sahara. Fifteen years later he was murdered, or, as some claimed, martyred. This career, lurching from one extreme to another, echoes that of the young Englishman T. E. Lawrence. However there was a direction to Foucauld's erratic path. Like his ancestors, he was driven by many forces, but strongest was a true spiritual crusading zeal, lacking in Lawrence. In the Anglo-Saxon countries, the ideal of the crusade had become an antiquarian interest, or the subject of rousing tales for boys, such as the novelist G. A. Henty's successful *For the Temple: A Tale of the Fall of Jerusalem* (1904).[57]

The vocabulary and ideology of 'crusade' sometimes came just as easily to Christians engaged in war against Muslims as the terminology of *jihad* came to Muslims resisting them. In neither case were theory and practice very close. No pope ever authorized France's 'crusade' in North Africa in the 1830s and many of the *jihads* called against the Europeans in the same region were technically dubious in the eyes of the Ottoman religious authorities in Constantinople. By that point both Christian and Muslim holy wars looked back to their earlier origins but had moved beyond them. The language of holy war had become a means of mobilization, unconstrained by the limits of law. Talking of either 'crusade' or *jihad* sounded a powerful chord, an irresistible call to arms. It was a deep conditioned memory of fanatical zeal and heroism given new life each time its language and ideology were revived. By the modern era, it was no longer a matter of what either word meant in precise legalistic terms, but rather the response that each of them called forth.

The encounters between Christendom and 'Islam' in Spain and in the Levant were very different. In the Levant, western Christendom intervened in an area that already had a long Christian tradition and a large Christian population, albeit one largely indistinguishable, to Western eyes, from the Muslims. In Spain, it was the position of 'Islam' that changed, from victor to vanquished. The *Moriscos* became a feared and despised remnant in a Christian state that ultimately found their presence intolerable. The confrontation between French glory and Muslim resistance in North Africa was a *synthetic* crusade. In the Balkans, the third area where 'Islam' met Christendom, the situation was different again. Only on one level – in the encounter between two religious faiths – was the position strictly comparable. Everything else – languages, history and ethnicities – was different. But if there are few direct connections there are at least suggestive parallels. In the Balkans, many local Christians in Albania and Bosnia converted to Islam, just as Christians had done in Spain in the first centuries after the Muslim conquest. In the Levant, after the mass conversions that followed the Muslim conquest, the local Christians preserved their own culture and faith largely intact. Orthodox Christians suffered more under the Latin Crusaders than they did under Islam.

All of these regions were detached from Europe. (If the Pyrenees do not now seem a daunting barrier, they did in earlier times.[58]) The Levant was unquestionably part of the East, 'belonging' to Europe only in a metaphysical sense. But the Balkans were Europe's wild frontier, on the perimeter but nonetheless integral.[59] By the sixteenth century the Ottoman occupation of the Balkans seemed a cancerous intrusion within the natural bounds of Christendom. The geographer Abraham Ortelius reflected a widely held view when he wrote 'For Christians, see Europeans' in the 1587 edition of his *Thesaurus geographicus*.[60] The re-emphasis of the idea of Christendom (even though irretrievably divided by the Protestant Reformation) was generated by the threat from Islam. The constant fear of Ottoman incursions across an open frontier made the Turks' possession of these formerly Christian lands a real menace.

From the last quarter of the sixteenth century, even if there was no war between the Habsburgs and the Ottomans, almost every year Tartar bands slipped across the border from Hungary and raided as far west as Steyr in western Austria. Like the conflict in the Mediterranean, which was punctuated by great battles such as Lepanto, this new enmity was never ending. The struggle with Islam in the Balkans, within the body of Europe, became more virulent than any earlier encounters. All the weight of anti-Islamic propaganda, such as the fiery orations of the seventeenth-century Austrian divine Abraham à Sancta Clara, of the hundreds of books and pamphlets directed against the Turks, constituted a sustained attack unlike any which had been deployed before. Thus, the Balkans became the *mise en scène* for the final act of Europe's encounter with 'Islam', a last 'crusade'. Unfortunately, the long-run consequences of that antagonism have outlived the Ottomans.

PART FOUR

Balkan Ghosts?

In my grandfather's house, *worldly* books were kept in a dark, musty and icy-cold back room. Downstairs, in a stained-oak bookcase with little green curtains covering the glazed panels, were the various editions of *The Holy Scriptures: A New Translation from the Original Languages* by J. N. Darby, the King James Bible (for critical and comparative purposes), Cruden's *Concordance*, and shelves of pamphlets, Bible readings and tracts. There too were the Bible games that we played on Sundays – Question 6: 'Name the three good men cast into the burning fiery furnace.' But upstairs were forgotten and ignored heaps of old *National Geographic* magazines, and untidy piles of books that had belonged to my grandfather's childhood, and which still bore the grubby fingermarks of my own father's avid reading. There were many volumes of G. A. Henty's stirring and, I still think, rather effective tales; Sherlock Holmes in the *Strand Magazine*; the gung-ho patriotic *Our Living Generals*; and all the literary paraphernalia of a Victorian boy's childhood. The *National Geographic*s were exceptionally *worldly*, but then my grandfather had received the Lord quite late in life and absolute consistency was never his strongest point anyway.

However, amid all the battles and gore of the books, only one thing terrified me. In a dull grey-blue tome called *With the Colours or, The Piping Times of Peace*, R. Mountjoy Jephson described the adventures of a young officer in the 1860s. He overcame the natives in the Ionian Isles, Hong Kong, India, China and Japan, and his trusty revolver saved him in many sticky situations. But in Corfu he nearly met his end. A huge Albanian dog attacked him:

In a moment, I am dashed to the ground, and the infuriated beast is over me. He struggles to get at my throat, but fortunately my hands are already at his and I hold him off . . . His hot breath fans my face, his eyes gleam like pieces of live coal, and the saliva streams from his cruel powerful jaws. Those sharp white teeth have already met in my flesh, for my hands and the sleeves of my coat are crimsoned with blood and I feel the warm current trickling down my arms as I hold him from me.

Fortuitously young Bob Foyle has a hunting knife and manages, with difficulty, to kill his adversary. Then he faces the dog's avenger: 'The Albanian with his long yataghan naked and uplifted in his hand, his face livid and distended with fury, is within three paces of me.' Trusty Sheffield-steel hunting knife parries yataghan, but

the sharp blade of the yataghan glances off the handle of my knife and rips my forearm from wrist to elbow . . . I now grapple with him, for the closer we are the better for me . . . I notice how strong he smells of garlic; and even to this day a whiff of that redolent bulb always brings to my mind the deadly perils of that savoury embrace.[1]

All ended well. Bob's chums rescued him in the nick of time, and bound the Albanian hand and foot. But Bob, mindful that he had killed the man's obviously beloved dog, turned him loose. Simkin's engraved illustration of this event terrified me at the age of nine, and still has the power to frighten. The Albanian rushing from the woods, with dark cruel eyes, tight lips and a bristling beard, was the stuff of nightmares. To this day it remains my first instinctive and childish understanding of the Balkans. But I was not alone in my terror: fear of the East is common to many nations. For the English, the barbarians began at Calais and, according to Prince Metternich, Asia began at Vienna's highroad, the Rennweg, which led east to Hungary.[2] Yet this cultural map was never exact nor precise. The lands south of the rivers Danube and Sava had a double character. They were both part of Europe and part of the East; the same was true further north. Poland and Russia were Christian, but they were also savage. The heart of this paradox lay in Greece: indubitably Balkan, part of the Ottoman world, yet also the cradle of Hellenism and of Western civilization. How could Greece have fallen so low, from its ancient glory to the decayed state described by European travellers from the seventeenth and eighteenth centuries?

11. The engraver Bernard Picard's frontispiece to his *Histoire générale des cérémonies, moeurs et coutumes religieuses de tous les peoples du monde*, 1741. The Muslims sit next to the mouth of Hell.

12. The Filipino painter Juan Luna de San Pedro y Novicio was commissioned in 1884 by King Alfonso XII of Spain to paint the battle of Lepanto. Luna caught the drama and chaos of the battle, with Don John's silhouette dominating the image.

13. The caliphal court of Cordoba receives the Imperial Ambassador, John of Gorze, in 958. Painting by Dionisio Baixeras-Verdaguer, 1885.

14. The triumphant *Capture of Jerusalem by the Crusaders, 15 July 1099* painted for Louis-Philippe's Museum of French History in the Palace of Versailles by Emile Signol in 1847.

15. The Alhambra from the Albaicin, in a nineteenth-century engraving. The remains of the Moorish kingdom continued to dominate later Christian Granada long after the last of the *Moriscos* had been expelled.

16. The prolific Nuremberg woodcut artist Erhard Schoen presents a stereotype: a Turkish horseman, with his Christian captives in tow, and an infant skewered on his lance; before 1540.

17. The Roman goddess of war, Bellona, leads the Habsburg armies against the savage Turks. Engraved by Jan Müller, from a design by Bartholomeus Spranger, 1600.

18. Luigi Mayer's drawing of Balkan malefactors impaled 'on the main road in the direction of Constantinople', *c.* 1800.

19. *The Pasha*, a satirical watercolour by Thomas Rowlandson of an Englishman engaging in lewd 'Eastern' acts, from a sequence of caricatures depicting the sexual practices of the English aristocracy, 1808–17.

20. Eugène Delacroix's vision of the Hellenic cause: *Greece Expiring on the Ruins of Missolonghi*, 1826, an allegory of the defence of Missolonghi against the Turks, 22 April 1825.

21. Unlike Delacroix's painting, the frontispiece to Casimir Delavigne's 1840 French collection of poems and popular songs presents Greece's conclusive triumph. She has broken her shackles and stands over the corpse of the Ottoman tyrant.

22. *The Great Han, Damascus*, by Richard René Spiers, 1866. Great indoor markets such as this, built in the sixteenth century, were far in advance of the West. Here European traders found the products of the East.

Engravings from the *Tableau général de l'empire othoman* by Mouradgea d'Ohsson, 1788–9.
23. *The Sultan at His Ablutions*: the sultan and handmaidens are all chastely covered, unlike in Western images of the imperial *harem*.

24. *Learning in Constantinople: A Public Library.*

25. *Ottomans at Work: A Vizier's Office.*

26. *James Silk Buckingham and His Wife, in Arab Costume of Baghdad*, by H. W. Pickersgill, *c.* 1816. Buckingham was a traveller and author. This is an example of the widespread fashion of the time for portrait sitters to be shown in Eastern costume.

27. A twentieth-century Westerner dressed up in Bedouin costume.

The answer was the Ottomans. 'Turkey in Europe' had begun in the fourteenth century, had occupied the Christian lands from the Aegean to Budapest by the 1530s, and then slowly diminished from its apogee until it included only the plain of Adrianople, its first European centre, and the city of Constantinople (Istanbul) by the 1920s. Almost five centuries of Ottoman rule became the whipping boy for everything that had gone awry in these lands. There was a wildness and rugged strength in both the peoples and the topography of the Balkans; the Turks made the people into savages and the landscape became, if anything, even more untamed. In his remarkable book *Balkan Ghosts: A Journey Through History* (1994), Robert D. Kaplan talks of the Ottomans as if they had overlain the Balkans like an incubus. Anything that was misbegotten could, in one way or another, be traced back to their presence. An Orthodox nun, Mother Tatiana, one of his main informants, told him that 'We [the Serbs] would have been even greater than the Italians, were it not for the Turks.' Kaplan himself added: 'That was a refrain you heard throughout the Balkans, in Dame Rebecca's day [Dame Rebecca West, author of *Black Lamb and Grey Falcon*] and in mine. Dame Rebecca writes, "The Turks ruined the Balkans, with a ruin so great that has not yet been repaired." '[3]

For Kaplan, the Balkan past could be mobilized to explain the dark and harrowing events of the Balkan present. I had admired the quality and insight of his writing for many years; I liked his capacity to present nuance, light and shade. But in *Balkan Ghosts*, those qualities were absent: he now wrote of a world that contained only horror and atrocity, without nuance, always haunted by a sanguine past. Even his vocabulary had darkened. It was still compelling; and yet, at the same time, he brought back fearful memories of the garlic-scented Albanian of my childhood.

The reasons for his deepening gloom grew from the times in which he wrote. Here was a man seeing places, which he had known in happier days, that had suddenly become murderous and savage. He discovered the origins of this bleak transformation wholly within the region's long (and dark) history. Past was present, with metaphors of atrocity drawn from the 1870s being attached to the atrocities of the 1990s. The Bulgarian massacres of 1876, when Ottoman bashi-bazouks killed thousands with their lances and yataghans, were the point at which, for Robert Kaplan, we could say, 'In modern times, it all began here.'[4] He was creating a special type of history for the Balkans – what the social scientist Immanuel Wallerstein later called 'TimeSpace', where 'the meaning of time and space in our lives is a human invention . . . time and space are irremediably locked together and constitute a single dimension.'[5] Wallerstein used one Balkan example, that of Kosovo, and one from Northern Ireland, to show that two completely divergent versions of the past could exist simultaneously within the same area, visions that no amount of evidence could alter or disprove.[6] This is what anthropologists used to call the anthropological present – a kind of TimeSpace particularly suitable for 'primitive' peoples, in whose world 'Time had frozen, and where there was no possibility of change or alteration'.[7] This style of history of the Balkans is exemplified by Franjo Tudjman, scholar and first president of independent Croatia after 1991.[8]

But, later, as I read more widely, it became clear that Kaplan was not alone in adopting these conventions. He stood in a long tradition of writing about Balkan malevolence and darkness.[9] Some eight decades before Kaplan's *Journey through History*, another writer, Harry de Windt, Fellow of the Royal Geographical Society, author of *The New Siberia*, *A Ride to India* and *From Paris to New York by Land*, visited the Balkans as a special correspondent of the *Westminster Gazette*. His book was entitled simply *Through Savage Europe*. He explained why:

'Why "Savage Europe"?' asked a friend who had recently witnessed my departure from Charing Cross for the Near East.

'Because', I replied, 'the term accurately described the wild and lawless countries between the Adriatic and the Black Seas.'

For some mystic reason, however, most Englishmen are less familiar with the geography of the Balkan States than with that of Darkest Africa. This was my case and I had therefore yet to learn that these same Balkans can boast of cities which are miniature replicas of London and Paris. But these are civilised centres. The remoter districts are, as of yore, hotbeds of outlawry and brigandage, where you must travel with a revolver in each pocket, and your life in your hand, and of this fact, as the reader will see, we had tangible and unpleasant proof before the end of the journey. Moreover, do not the now-palatial capitals of Servia and Bulgaria occasionally startle the outer world with crimes of medieval barbarity . . . Wherefore the word 'savage' is perhaps not wholly inapplicable to that portion of Europe which we are about to traverse.[10]

Windt and Kaplan were saying roughly the same thing. The Balkans were irredeemable, cursed by their collective past. A 'journey through history' becomes a tour through the heart of darkness, a catalogue of horrors. Thus, set into the context of this dark past, the present – in either 1907 or 1993 – seems explicable. The same stories inevitably appear in both books in different guises: the (improbable) blinding of 14,000 captured Bulgars by Emperor Basil II Bulgaroctonos 'The Bulgar Slayer', Vlad the Impaler with his forest of twisting bodies, the grim battlefield of Kosovo Polje. Kaplan was able to add the nightmare events of the 1990s. Harry de Windt had rushed through on a whirl-wind tour, but Robert Kaplan moved more methodically, recording the authentic voices of nemesis, such as Mother Tatiana who had, like Berthold Brecht's Mother Courage, seen everything and suffered it all.

'I am a good Christian, but I will not turn the other cheek if some Albanian plucks out the eyes of a fellow Serb or rapes a little girl or castrates a twelve-year-old Serbian boy.' . . . My eyes adjusted to the darkness and for the first time I got a good look at her face. She had a strong, lusty appearance, with high cheekbones and fiery maternal eyes. She was a handsome old woman who was clearly once attractive. Her eyes, while fiery, also appeared strangely unfocused, as though blotted out by superstition.[11]

Here is a deeper truth. Blindness of superstition, old stories em-bellished, retold, and then made still more bitter in the retelling, lie at the heart of these journeys through history.

By contrast, the Irishman James Creagh, author of *A Scamper to Sebastopol and Jerusalem in 1867*, presented himself as a species of tweedy fool, for whom everything turns sunny side up.[12] Just as the Muslim inhabitants of the Balkan provinces of Herzegovina and Bosnia were taking up arms against the reforming sultan in Constantinople, he set out on a leisurely tour down the Danube to Belgrade, thence west into Bosnia and Croatia, and finally meandering south to the mountains of Herzegovina, Montenegro and the Albanian lands. His book, published in the following year, was entitled *Over the Borders of Christendom and Eslamiah: A Journey through Hungary, Slavonia, Serbia, Bosnia, Herzegovina, Dalmatia, and Montenegro, to the North of Albania in the Summer of 1875*.

Creagh's principal preoccupation seems to have been 'tall and well-made girls in gaudy bodices and petticoats [that] gave them, at a distance, the appearance of Affghan maidens'.[13] But beneath the jovial banter, Creagh saw things in a very different perspective from many other Western travellers. He quoted an old and much-travelled Magyar whom he met on the journey down the Danube.

The travelling philosopher will find men and women, at bottom, the same everywhere. There is the same ambition in every heart; the same credulity in every mind; the same roguery in every priest; the same desire to domineer in every woman; and the same selfishness among all. Their languages and education are alone different.[14]

Unusually he made few distinctions between Muslims and Christians. In Belgrade, he described a panorama of the 'graceful minarets of the deserted Turkish mosques, the church steeples, and the wide red-tiled roofs'; the mosques were 'now closed or used for the vilest purposes; and in a place once considered sacred by the Turks, their temples are defiled and desecrated by a people who were once their slaves'.[15]

However, in some respects, Creagh offered much the same overall picture as other writers. Outside the towns and cities the Balkans were lawless, as Ottoman government had little authority in its borderlands. Creagh described a Turk who told him that it was extremely dangerous to travel in Bosnia, and pointed to a wound in his side, which he said had come from an attack in the woods the day before. Anyone, Muslim or Christian, local or visitor, was a possible victim. The seemingly imperturbable Irishman stayed in filthy *hans*, where 'dirty, picturesque and handsome-armed ruffians lay about the floor'; was attacked by swarms of fleas – 'The vilest lodging house in St Giles [in London] could not have been more abominable than this place; nevertheless . . . I never slept more comfortably.'[16] But he observed rather than condemned, and certainly did not blame all the ills of the Balkans on the Ottomans:

The Turks and the Christians in Bosnia, except for service in the army, are on a footing of equality; but the remembrance of ancient persecutions still inspires those deadly hatreds which, like the passions of the Ribandmen [a Catholic association] and Orangemen [a Protestant association] in the north of Ireland are ever ready to break out with a violence all the more astonishing because the causes that might justify it have long been removed.

[In Bosnia] a feast, a procession, a word or a song may set the province in a blaze which would throw even the riots of Belfast into the shade . . . God knows the Turkish Government is not the most enlightened administration in Europe; but it has fearful difficulties to contend with and its despotic and paternal rule certainly prevents the Bosniacs from tearing each other to pieces.

Every misfortune is attributable to the Turks, and we hear so often that they are tyrants and oppressors that the people generally believe they are so.[17]

In Montenegro, later on his journey, he had another encounter, very similar to Robert Kaplan's meeting with Mother Tatiana.

A gentleman, bristling with arms and wearing a light green body coat told me he was a barrister. Expressing wonder at my having escaped without any incidents during so long a journey in Turkey [in Europe] he began to apostrophise the Turks in gracefully rounded periods, delivered in impassioned gestures of forensic eloquence. With flashing eyes, he called them dogs, pigs, foxes, snakes and serpents; and declared that they were as brutal, uncivilised and degraded, as the Christians of the same provinces were cultivated, polished and advanced.

Creagh politely demurred, saying that was not his experience. The lawyer rounded on him, saying that 'he never heard such an opinion in the whole course of his life, and it was the duty of all Christians to hate the Musselmans'.[18]

These travelogues – and there were many others like them – are neither diaries nor documented history, but kinds of polemic. Each writer was telling a tale that he had made up for himself. Characters such as the verdant Montenegrin advocate or the fiery-eyed Orthodox nun were selected for a narrative purpose, to tell a particular story. Kaplan wanted to show that the Balkans were fixed in ancient hatreds:

Mother Tatiana obliged. Creagh, who had come rather to like the 'gentlemanly' qualities of the Ottomans, presented his Slavic popinjay who would condemn himself as in essence a 'coarse mountaineer' and whose God was called, Creagh claimed, the 'Old Murderer'.[19] Within the Balkan lands it seemed possible, in the space of a short journey, to piece together almost any view of the past and, hence, of the present. One prolific modern writer on the region goes so far as to suggest that 'The Balkans . . . is the unconscious of the world. It is here that the repressed memories of history, its traumas and fears and images reside.'[20]

In such a shadow world nothing could be taken on trust. Even the image of the barren and precipitous Balkan peninsula so often depicted in engravings was only partly true.[21] Hills and mountains covered much of the land south of the Danube, and the Carpathian chain to the north. But there was no massive chain of towering peaks (*catena mundi*), that ran continuously from the Black Sea to the Alps and then continued on to the Atlantic as some geographers had once asserted.[22] In reality, Italy is more precipitous than much of the Balkans.[23] In many parts of Serbia, the 'summits are often below 2,000 feet and seldom exceed 3,000 feet'. Even in Montenegro, 'like a sea of immense waves turned to stone', the peaks rarely exceed 6,000 feet.[24] But the idea of an extreme landscape was deeply rooted. The origins of the word 'Balkans' was Old Turkish, meaning simply highland, and more specifically, a heavily forested mountain slope.

Since Westerners erroneously perceived the whole region as wild uplands, the entire area between the Aegean Sea and the Danube – mountains, hills, and open plains – was defined as 'highlands'. Maria Todorova has found that the first use of the word 'Balkans' in any Western language came at the end of the fifteenth century, in a description sent by the Italian humanist Phillipus Callimachus to Pope Paul II. The local people, he observed, called the mountains 'Bolchanum'.[25] Yet this misconception was also revealing, for well into the nineteenth century geography was often as much about perception as scientific measurement. So, in Scotland, 'Highland' signified savagery and barbarity, while 'Lowland' was equated with cultivation, both in the sense of agriculture and of civilization.[26] In reality, there was much wild high ground south of the Highland Line; some mapmakers logically marked both 'Northern' and 'Southern' Highlands.[27]

Mountains were an emblem of risk, and in that sense the Balkans were indeed *vertiginous*. The uplands of Bosnia, Herzegovina, Montenegro and Albania were filled, Western travellers learned, not with colourful peasants but with brigands and bandits. These categories were, however, mutable. Often local people's perception was a mirror image of the visitor's viewpoint, although the former gave it a different slant. *Balkan* to the Easterner, like *montaña* to the Spaniards far away in the West, meant a home to outlaws, *monfies* and thieves. But it was also the heartland of tribal honour and, latterly, of patriotism. The harsh terrain bred doughty fighters, and in the more impenetrable recesses of the Balkans, wild men – called variously *armatoli*, *hajduks*, *klephts* – preserved their ancient customs, vendettas and myths of a heroic past.[28] They were simultaneously feared and admired: a murderer and robber could also be perceived as a man of honour. They were epic characters, whose fame (rather than infamy) lay in exacting vengeance from their enemies. The historian Branimir Anzulovic recounts how in one folk tale Grujo punished his wife for her act of betrayal to the Turks:

> He smeared his wife with wax and tar
> And sulphur and fast powder
> Wrapped her in soft cotton,
> Poured strong brandy over her,
> Buried her up to the waist
> Lit the hair on her head
> And sat down to drink cool wine
> While she cast light like a bright candle.[29]

Other European cultures have possessed similarly ambiguous folk heroes.[30] But the Balkans possessed an especially rich vein of myth-making, with each village or family telling stories of its own local heroes. Slav and Albanian pride in their languages was considerable. Slavs traced its written form back to two early Orthodox missionaries from Salonika, Cyril and Methodius, who created a version of the Christian liturgy in a Slavonic idiom, and wrote it in a unique script called Glagolitic, from the Old Serbian 'to speak'. This later became known as Church Slavonic, and this sacralised the Slavic tongues over all other vernaculars, raising it in Slav eyes to the same level of

Latin, Greek and Hebrew as a worthy vehicle for transmitting the word of God.

This subtle and mellifluous tongue soon developed many forms and variants. The most fragmented zone – in language, and in ethnic and religious terms as well – lay along the westernmost part of the Balkans, all along the Adriatic littoral, through what are now Herzegovina, Montenegro and down into modern Albania and Greece.[31] Across the limestone escarpment of the Dinaric Alps in Bosnia there was an even greater variety and complexity. There Catholicism existed alongside Orthodoxy and Islam, but even within the Catholic community there were divisions. Some Catholics worshipped God in Latin and wrote in the Latin script, as they had been taught by missionaries from Italy; others learned their Catholic liturgy in Church Slavonic in the Glagolitic script; still others read it in a Bosnian variant of the Cyrillic. In Bosnia there also was (in Catholic eyes) a 'heretical' Bosnian Church. In many areas there were pockets or Orthodox believers. Thus, western Balkan Christendom contained not merely the binary division between Orthodoxy and Catholicism, but a bewildering variety of dialect and scriptural forms, all fiercely defended by their adherents. Further east, in Serbia, Orthodoxy dominated, but even there there were still many subtle dialectal differences.[32] Among the Slavs, national labels like 'Serb' or 'Bulgar' did not adequately denote identity.[33] Placing strangers as friend or foe meant knowing which village or town they came from, of which community or kin they were part.

The extreme diversity is difficult to relate to the clearly defined 'homelands' presented by nineteenth-century nationalist historians and propagandists.[34] A similar fragmentation existed outside the Slavic populations. The land that became Albania in 1913 had never been occupied by the Slavs. The native Illyrians who lived there successfully maintained both a distinct culture and a Latinate language incomprehensible to the Slavs. Within the ethnic category of 'Albanian', there were marked divisions, both in religion and social structures. In the south, close to the Greek lands, Orthodox Christianity predominated, while in the north some of the tribes were Catholic. But the Albanian communities were further divided between southern lowlanders (*Tosks*) and northern highlanders (*Ghegs*). After the Ottoman conquest of the Balkans, the Tosk and Gheg communities still retained Christian and Muslim enclaves. But despite these Christian communities, being Albanian soon became almost synonymous with being Muslim. In Bosnia, too, there was an additional religious mélange, with numerous conversions to Islam among local Slavs, so that they called themselves 'Turks' (*Turci*). They continued to use their Slavic mother tongue, but with a distinctly Bosnian tinge. Other Muslims, 'true Turks', whether from Anatolia or Circassian Tartars settled by the Ottoman rulers in the Balkans, were always distinguished from local 'Turks' and called *Turkuse*.[35]

Any map of the Balkans that truly showed the extraordinary diversity of languages and religious faiths and ethnic distribution in the region looked nothing like one of the twentieth-century frontiers. If anything, the pattern resembled more closely the maritime chart of an archipelago, such as the northern Aegean or the Cyclades. So, rather than 'peninsula' – the traditional description of the region – perhaps a better metaphor for the Balkans is an archipelago, a pattern of separate islands, some large, others small. An archipelago society, however, especially one set in an ethnic and linguistic landscape as convoluted as the Balkans, will of necessity become acutely aware of local differences, and will not take easily to the ordered structures of more traditional polities.[36] Edith Durham, travelling in Macedonia in 1905, was surprised that in some isolated areas Christian customs seemed strongly tinged with ancient folk beliefs.

I do not think I ever saw a picture of a saint in any of these houses. The icon and the lamp, so conspicuous in the houses of the Serbs, the Montenegrins and the Orthodox Albanians, was wanting. Nor did the people invoke Christ or the saints, or cross themselves at mealtimes, or before going to rest for the night. They seemed to possess none of the religious fervour that is so marked a characteristic of Orthodox peasants. They had more faith, it seemed, in the amulets they wore than in anything else. Some of these were very odd. One was a green glass heart, two pink beads, and an English sixpence.[37]

She quickly realized that easy generalizations in so idiosyncratic a land were meaningless. People saw themselves as possessing multiple loyalties and identities. Ascribing hatred to ethnic origin was too limiting a classification: as everywhere, antipathy had manifold causes and manifestations. Neighbours warred with each other; men and women were at odds; strangers were all devils and dangerous. Sturdy individualism was perhaps the only quality that characterized the Balkans as a whole, true of the people of the plains almost as much as those occupying mountainous ground.[38]

No one is quite sure where the boundaries of the Balkans should be drawn. Were the Carpathians – the principalities of Wallachia and Moldavia, peopled by 'Romanians' speaking a Latinate language – part of the Balkans? The Transylvanian monk who in 1779 published a prayer book, *Carte de rogacioni*, in Latin instead of in Cyrillic script thought not. He made 'a declaration of the Romanians' ethnic distinctiveness and an affirmation of the bond with Europe'.[39] Most of this chapter is concerned with the lands south of the Danube. The majority of internal nationalist historians tend to minimize the role of external forces, while many historians writing from an outside perspective look upon the Balkans as a natural field for their involvement. But both approaches to the region's past histories share a common premise. The long Ottoman occupation had been the source of all the region's problems. Remove that malign influence and the Christian East could be redeemed.

The Austrian and the Russian plans for this redemption were far from disinterested. Russia in particular had huge ambitions. There is a popular eighteenth-century cartoon of the Empress Catherine II making the Great Imperial Stride (*l'enjambée impériale*) between the solid rock of Russia on to the sharp Islamic crescent atop the minarets of Constantinople. The crowned heads of Europe stand underneath, looking lewdly up her voluminous skirts and commenting on what they see. The great empress looks uncomfortable at her exposure.[40] But the cartoon makes a serious point: neither Russia nor the Habsburg Empire believed they could afford to ignore the Islamic power in the Balkans, any more than they (and Prussia) could have left Poland alone. The partitions of Poland in the late eighteenth century foreshadowed the treatment of the Balkans in the nineteenth century, although, unlike the case of Poland, only the Habsburgs made major additions to their territory from the carve-up of the Balkans. But Russia gained a dominant role if not land, becoming a symbolically menacing Bear, looming suggestively over her Balkan protégés or puppets. Justifying both the eighteenth-century dismemberment of Poland and nineteenth-century approaches to reshaping the Balkans was the belief that their barbaric peoples would benefit from 'Enlight-enment'.[41] These perceptions had deep roots. In 1572 a French prince, Henry de Valois, had ruled briefly in Warsaw. His court poet could see nothing good about the Poles and their land:

> Farewell Poland
> Farewell deserted plains
> Eternally covered with snow and ice
> Oh savage people, arrogant and thieving
> Boastful, verbose and full of words
> Who wrapped night and day in shaggy furs
> Takes its only pleasure playing with a wine glass
> By snoring asleep and falling to sleep on the floor
> And who then, like Mars, wishes to be famous.
> It is not your great grooved lances
> Your wolf's clothing, your misleading coats of arms
> Spread all over with wings and feathers
> Your muscular limbs, nor your redoubtable deeds,
> Dull-witted Poles, that saved you from defeat.
> Your miserable condition alone protects you.[42]

Writers in the eighteenth century, in the era of the Enlightenment, appeared just as preoccupied with the East as their predecessors in earlier centuries. The focus of interest had shifted, but not the under-lying assumptions. Larry Wolff's ground-breaking studies, *Inventing Eastern Europe* and *Venice and the Slavs*, have presented a new and convincing interpretation of Western preconceptions of the Slavic world. Reading both books, I was struck by how the negative attitudes I had hitherto associated specifically with the Muslim and Ottoman East were extended in the eighteenth-century Enlightenment to the Slavic world as well.[43] The differences between the two worlds were still profound. The Slav world was (largely) Christian and the Ottoman world was predominantly Muslim; yet Western travellers saw both of them as sunk in ignorance, lust and violence.

Wolff quotes the Comte de Ségur writing of Catholic Poland as a

void, with vast forests punctuated by open plains, and 'a poor population, enslaved; dirty villages; cottages little different from savage
huts; everything makes one think one has been translated back ten
centuries and that one finds oneself amid hordes of Huns, Scythians,
Veneti, Slavs, and Sarmatians'. An English visitor, William Coxe,
travelling in Russia and Poland, also found the sources of Eastern
barbarities in the primitive peoples of the region, which could be
subsumed under the broad heading of the 'Tartar Yoke'. In Moscow,
he encountered 'an Armenian, recently arrived from Mount Caucasus'. He was the very image of a barbarian, and Coxe described him
in much the same way as others portrayed the wild *ghazi*, *akinji*,
bashi-bazouks or dervishes in Ottoman service.

His dress consisted of a long loose robe, tied with a sash, large breeches and
boots: his hair was cut, in the manner of the Tartars, in a circular form; his
arms were a poignard, and a bow of buffalo's horn strung with the sinews
of the same animal . . . he danced a Calmuc dance, which consisted in
straining every muscle, and writhing his body into various contortions
without stirring from the spot; he beckoned us into the garden, took great
pleasure in showing us his tent and arms . . . We were struck with the
unartificial character of this Armenian, who seemed like a wild man just
beginning to be civilised.[44]

   This 'Armenian' displayed the negative particulars – wildness and
lack of control – that had been pinned to 'Islam' since the early
medieval period. The 'backwardness' of the Slav East came from many
distinct causes, but I wondered if one was the contact with the Eastern
Muslim world?[45] Islam had impinged on the Slav world along an
extended frontier. In the fourteenth century, as the Ottomans were
advancing into southern Europe, the Mongols of the Golden Horde,
whose 'Tartar yoke' had long overshadowed the northern Slav lands
of Muscovy (Russia) and Poland, accepted Islam. In time, the rising
power of Russia gradually freed itself from the suzerain power of the
Golden Horde, but the Tartar horsemen merely regrouped further
east, thereafter raiding rather than ruling their former domain. In
1484, the Ottoman armies, pushing north, took the key fortified
towns of Killia at the mouth of the Danube and Akkerman at the
mouth of the Dniester and became a dominant force in the borderlands

around the Black Sea. Crimean Tartars were allied to the Ottomans, and Tartars and Caucasian skirmishers became a valued element in the Ottoman armies, raiding on their fast ponies far beyond the Danube into Hungary and the Austrian duchies. They settled in many parts of the European Ottoman domains, and remained largely separate from the local Muslim population, who spoke a quite different language.

In Western eyes, 'Tartars' and 'Turks' had both collective and separate identities. The hellish witches' brew in Shakespeare's *Macbeth* contained the twin elements of evil, 'nose of Turk, and Tartar's lips'.[46] While the phrase 'the Grand Turk' embodied the grudgingly admired 'imperial' qualities of the Ottomans, the Tartars epitomized the unspeakable and fearsome savagery that was their other attribute. Some said that their name meant they were the denizens of Hell (from the Latin *Tartarus*).[47] The Abbé Fortis became the West's literary cicerone for the Balkan wilderness and its inhabitants. He wrote that he 'saw customs, poetry, music, clothing, and habitations as Tartar as they could be in Siberia'.[48] The Chevalier Louis de Jaucourt, writing on 'Tartars' in 1765 in Diderot's *Encyclopédie*, observed that it was 'humiliating that these barbaric peoples should have subjugated almost all our hemisphere' in the age of Genghis Khan. He assured his readers that although 'this vast reservoir of ignorant, strong, and bellicose men [had] vomited its inundations in almost all our hemisphere . . . the polished nations are sheltered from the irruptions of these barbarous nations.'[49] But not, however, in the rough and rugged lands of the Balkans.

Which peoples were 'polished' and which 'barbarous' could never clearly be defined where Turks, Tartars and Slavs had common boundaries. The precipitous Dinaric Alps, inland from the Adriatic, provided one such fracture zone. After his visits to Venice's Balkan possessions, Fortis published his *Travels in Dalmatia* (*Viaggio in Dalmazzia*) in 1774. He described the people of these mountains, the Morlacchi, as not at all the 'race of ferocious men, unreasonable, without humanity, capable of any misdeed', whom the people of the coast accused of 'the most atrocious excesses of murder, arson and violence'.[50] Fortis' book and his many letters presented a much more positive image of these highlanders. He held that the violence for which the Morlacchi were sometimes justly blamed stemmed from the circumstances in which they lived. In a society where banditry and raiding were the norm, many Morlacchi perforce became *hajduks* or border reivers. These men 'lived the lives of wolves, wandering among rocky and inaccessible precipices, hanging from stone to stone ... It would not be surprising if frequently one heard of strokes of atrocity by these men grown wild and irritated by the ever present sentiment of such a miserable situation.'[51]

The Morlacchi and others were forced to lead such desperate lives by the entropy that afflicted the Ottoman lands in Europe, and which spilled over into the domains of Venice or of the Habsburgs beyond the mountains. Life on the rugged frontier was different from in the towns and villages of the plain. The *hajduks* of the Dinaric Alps, like the *uskok* frontiersmen of Senj in the sixteenth century, were men 'Who have no father and mother / Gun and sword are their father and mother.'[52] The highlands – much of Greece, great tracts of Albania, Herzegovina and Bosnia, the whole of Montenegro – were filled with armed men, both Christian and Muslim. The roads and passes were notionally protected by armed militia, *armatoli*, against the bandits known in the Greek-speaking areas as *klephts*. Raiding was an honourable profession, and some, like the famous 'Lion of Janina' Ali Pasha (immortalized by Dumas in his novel *The Count of Monte Cristo*), became powerful and successful by practising these traditional skills. It was easy to romanticize them. Thomas Gordon, in his 1832 *History of the Greek Revolution*, rhapsodized:

Extraordinary activity and endurance of hardships and fatigue made them formidable light troops in the native fastnesses; wrapped in shaggy cloaks they slept on the ground, defying the elements, and the pure mountain air gave them robust health. Such were the warriors that, in the very worst of times kept alive a remnant of Grecian spirit.[53]

The hardships and fatigue had one simple cause. Without the heavy burden of the Turks, the old civic virtues of the Ancient Hellenes could rise again. And so too could the Slavs.

Learning to Hate

I have no interest in providing an apologia for the Ottomans. But making them the *fons et origo* of all evil is only a convenient myth. For the West, cruelty and the Turks had become more or less synonymous. The Turks exhibited all the traditional Muslim flaws. So however much the Ottomans might intrigue and preoccupy their European neighbours, however much admiration and envy they might inspire, the Turks' evil heritage was unquestioned. The Venetian ambassador to the *Grand Signior* Murad IV, wrote of this mighty seventeenth-century prince that 'he turned all his thoughts to revenge, so completely that, overcome by its seductions, stirred by indignation, and moved by anger, he proved unrivalled in savagery and cruelty. On those days he did not take a human life, he did not feel that he was happy and gave no sign of gladness.'[1] A century later another Venetian Ambassador, Giovanni Emo, wrote of the Vizier Topal Osman's courage and generosity; however he was also flawed by the inherent defects of his faith. 'Cruelty and avarice were his vices; strong will, mental capacity and practical knowledge his virtues.' Osman 'punished every light transgression of the law with death, which covered his cruelty with the mantle of justice'.[2]

This presumption, that Turkish or Muslim virtue was outweighed by vice, had distant origins, as I have outlined in earlier chapters. In plays, novels and poems all through the eighteenth and early nineteenth centuries, the Muslim world, usually depicted as the Turk, became the natural locus for portraying unbridled passion, or ingenious cruelty.[3] Even the enthusiastic eighteenth-century Turcomania, which revelled in Oriental costumes and exotic scenarios, had an echo of these darker aspects. However joyous and light-hearted Mozart's *Flight from the Seraglio* appeared, its audience did not fail to feel the frisson of Turkish tyranny. Often Westerners seemed willing to believe any tale of injustice without question. 'History shows us that Europe is always brave and always jealous of her freedom; it also shows us by contrast that Asia is always a slave and as feeble as a woman [*efféminée*].'[4] This Western belief, that the East could only escape from its essential flaws if it became like the West, was also adopted by some Ottoman reformers. (Muslims who first visited western Europe in this period were either shocked by what they saw or they might just as easily have become passionate Europhiles through the experience.[5])

It was extremely hard to negate attitudes that had been inculcated from the first lessons of childhood. In 1853, 'A British Resident of Twenty Years in the East' (a diplomat called J. H. Skene) travelled along what he called 'the Frontier Lands of the Christian and the Turk'. His account is lively and full of interest. Skene's warm personality opened many doors. He met with a well-known general, Mustapha Pasha. They got on famously, and the general sent for his children to meet the visitor. Skene found them delightful, and 'asked their father if they were all born of the same mother, which I thought a natural enough question [the children had the same features, but different-coloured eyes], but it did not please the pasha, who answered dryly that he had been only once married and that his children were consequently all of the same mother.'[6]

Was it a 'natural enough question'? It violated both Western and Ottoman codes of courtesy. Skene would never have asked so indelicate a question of a fellow Englishman whom he had just met.[7] But to ask such a question of a Muslim trespassed into the private domain of the family, which was definitely out of bounds. However, it was *natural* to Skene because he thought that all well-bred Ottomans would be polygamists, indulging themselves with more than one wife at a time. His question was a solecism and not a crime, and Skene certainly did not assume that all Ottomans were cruel or vicious. Indeed, he held many whom he met on his travels to be fine men. But perhaps 'A British Resident of Twenty Years' should have known better before following his knee-jerk response.[8] Western travellers who did not have his wealth of experience in the region could not be blamed for coming to a similar conclusion: their upbringing and Christian culture had given them preconceptions about what they might see and hear.[9]

The essential moral behind Skene's little story was that he had a typology in mind, and believed the Ottomans would invariably revert to type. This same theme of reversion runs through Kaplan and others who present the history of the Balkans as a kind of collective psychosis. The Balkan peoples of the 1990s, in the *Balkan Ghosts* scenario, were simply reliving their brutal heritage. Or, rather, they were enabled to regain this contact with their past, their collective cultural memories, through the efforts of propagandists. These were *recovered memories*, which recalled their ruination or perversion by the Ottoman occupation.[10] Then, in some unspecified manner, Serbs and Croats, distant descendants of those who had been violently abused by the Turk, somehow became violent abusers themselves. The tangle between myth and reality is almost inextricable.

What was the source of these social memories? We need to begin (at least) with the seventeenth century, if not further back. In 1683, the Ottomans, supposedly in a state of 'declination', suddenly surprised western Europe by launching a huge army towards Vienna and threatening the city. Their bold effort failed and they were driven off. Thereafter the Austrian Habsburgs took full advantage of the Ottomans' disarray. In a series of campaigns extending over thirteen years, they pursued them, first through Hungary, then beyond the Danube and, ultimately, far south into the heart of the Balkan archipelago. In 1689, an Austrian army even pushed into the region of Kosovo and proclaimed that Christianity had triumphed over Islam. The Serbs of Kosovo were happy to swear allegiance to the Emperor Leopold II, only to see the Austrians retreat in the following year, leaving them at the mercy of the returning Ottomans.

As an Ottoman army and their Tartar allies re-entered Kosovo they regarded many of the Serbs as traitors and rebels who had sided with their enemy. Village after village was ravaged and, wisely, many families decided not to take the risk of remaining under Turkish rule. Led by the respected Patriarch Čarnojević of the Orthodox holy sites at Pec, they abandoned their farms and villages to trek north, then crossed the Danube with the retreating Austrians into Habsburg-ruled Hungary. In what was thereafter called Vojvodina, from the Slavonic for 'duchy', the emperor gave the Serbs a charter to establish their own community. The Habsburgs used these exiles as the first line of defence against Ottoman incursions. The 'Great Migration' became the mythical equivalent of the Israelites' Exodus from Egypt. The patriarch was their Moses.[11] Like the Children of Israel, whose identity was forged first by their slavery in Egypt, and then annealed by their later Babylonian captivity, their lost lands became a totem of a vanished Golden Age for the Serbs in exile.

The Migration of 1690 was the second great Serb loss at the hands of the Ottomans. Exile and defeat joined to form a diptych of Serb identity, with catastrophe becoming a necessary prelude to triumph. As mentioned earlier, three centuries before, in 1389, in the heart of Kosovo, at Kosovo Polje, the army of the Serbs had been massively defeated by the Ottoman forces of Sultan Murad I. The precise factual history of the battle and its aftermath was less important than the dense network of legends and epic poems that was woven around it. From the early eighteenth century onwards, few children in the Vojvodina can not have known of saintly Prince Lazar who led the Serbs and of the many fine men slaughtered after the fight by the cruel and implacable Ottomans. They would also have learned of the evil Turkish sultan stabbed on the battlefield, in an act of divinely inspired retribution. An early Serbian chronicler began his account of the 'noble and gentle Lazar' with how he

> Fought the good fight
> For the godliness of the land
> Not allowing during his lifetime
> The cursed, arrogant and cruel beast
> To destroy your [Christ's] flock
> Which you gave him.

Then Lazar himself declared,

> I'd rather shed my blood
> Than draw near to or bow down
> To the cursed and evil
> Murderer, Hagar.[12]

The traditional language used about Islam since the seventh century – 'Hagar', 'the cruel beast' – was the natural idiom to describe the Turks. The trope of triumph through martyrdom, where defeat was transmuted into a glorious victory, becomes a recurrent theme and inspiration for the Serbs' future. The Patriarch Danilo, in his late fourteenth-century *Narrative about Prince Lazar*, summed up the future for the army of the Serbs in the face of their monstrous enemy: 'We have lived for a long time for the world; in the end we seek to accept the martyr's struggle and live for ever in heaven. We call ourselves Christian soldiers, martyrs for godliness to be recorded in the book of life . . . Suffering begets glory and labours lead to peace.'[13]

Such myths were first rooted in oral folk tales. Later the account of these events was written down, but existed only in very few manuscript copies. In 1601, a Carthusian monk called Mavro Orbini in the Adriatic city of Ragusa (Dubrovnik) published the story of Lazar in *Kingdom of the Slavs (Il regno degli Slavi)*.[14] In 1722, on the orders of Peter the Great, this powerful advocacy of 'the Slavic nation and language' was translated.[15] It was not, it seems, a full or faithful translation, but the Kosovo story had an increasing impact, especially among the Serb communities in the Habsburg lands whose ancestors had left in 1690.[16]

Balkan Muslim communities, although they did not use written or visual materials to the same degree as the Christians, also developed their sense of cultural identity. These Muslim communities were as deeply rooted in the land as their Christian counterparts, for most of them were the descendants of local converts and not of migrants. As a result, Islam in the region developed many characteristics not found elsewhere in the Islamic world. These lasted to the end of the twentieth century. It was considered 'being Muslim the Bosnian way', according to Tone Bringa, who interviewed Bosnians in the 1980s. She describes an incident during the mandatory fast of Ramadan (*Ramazan*), which in Bosnia was thought suitable for women and old men, who did not have to work hard.

One evening a couple had a rather typical dispute during Ramadan. The quarrel started when the wife urged her husband to come along for evening prayers in the mosque. It then developed into a row about past events of their twenty-year marriage, the husband asking his wife why she had not married a *hodza* [imam or Islamic teacher] if that was what she wanted. He then summed up his miseries: '. . . I had no coffee all day and it is Ramadan, and [so] I may not drink brandy.'[17]

Nor was this just a twentieth-century development. In 1897, H. C. Thomson, visiting Bosnia, had also noted this characteristic of Bosnian men: 'He will not drink *wine*, but will drink beer, or brandy or whiskey, or any other form of alcohol, because the Prophet only forbad the drinking of *wine*.'[18] Plainly, in many of these Muslim communities the strict religious law was quietly put to one side.[19]

Storytelling reinforced the sense of community. Both Christians and Muslims shared a common tradition of stories, often about similar themes. But they had very different messages, each version changing subtly and distinctively over time. Some Christian tales were profoundly anti-Turkish: 'The songs of the *hajduks* and the *klephts* have no substance or meaning without the Turks, and the Moslem counterparts would not have meaning without the *hajduk* songs. This whole genre depends upon the Turks. The Kosovo cycle is patently impossible without the Turks.'[20] The Muslim tales were usually much longer than the Christian ones. Relating them might extend over several days. Like the stories told until recent times in modern Turkey, the entire village would settle down to listen, would interrupt, comment on the quality of the storytelling, and even add to the speaker's account. These were oral epics in the Homeric style, experienced by the whole community. And in Bosnia this tradition of community was strong in other respects: Bosnians would rally to repel any enemies from outside. They resisted the armies of Austria who invaded the provinces in 1878 just as they had attacked marauding Ottoman janissaries a few years before.

A sense of place and community was often as significant as language and religion. The people of one valley or one hillside would be set against those of another, even if they used the same language and shared the same faith. Moreover, while outsiders might see a unitary community defined by a common language and a common faith, those inside the community would more often perceive stark and unmistakable distinctions within these broader categories. The reality (if not the theory) of the Balkans was polysemic. Straightforward ethnic and religious differences – as between Slavs, Bulgars, Albanians and Vlachs, or between Christians and Muslims – invariably noted by foreign writers, were not in practice the only marks of difference. Locals talked more readily of a plethora of distinct communities, each of which saw itself as separate from its neighbours. Individual communities also constructed their own versions of the traditional heroes.[21] This endless process of fission was partly determined by geography. Even if the landscape was not Alpine in scale, the succession of hills, ridges and valleys divided one settlement from another. Places separated by only a few miles in distance were often much farther apart in journey time over rough paths, and therefore contact was often limited. A remarkable diversity in language was one consequence. The Slavic languages used by Serbs and Croats were divided into a great variety of dialects: Ivo Banac identified ten main dialect groups in the period after 1700.[22]

☙

This multiplicity undermined one of the strongest 'Presuppositions' among Westerners about the Balkans.[23] They assumed that for all purposes Muslims formed one community and non-Muslims another. It was a logical conclusion to draw, for this was the principle on which the Ottomans appeared to base their political structures. They divided their populations along simple pragmatic lines into *millets*, or religious communities, rather as other empires defined their subjects in terms of colour or tribe.[24] It was an effective and extremely economical arrangement. The non-Muslim *millets* policed themselves: Christians and Jews were largely self-governing, under the authority of their religious leaderships. Thus the Patriarch in Constantinople was responsible for the good behaviour of the Orthodox Christians anywhere in the Ottoman domains. If they rebelled, he might pay with his head. It was a refinement of the ancient Turkic nomadic practice of hostage-taking.[25] One consequence of this structure was that the Ottoman subject peoples, or *raya*, were, within set limits, permitted to run their own affairs. All who were not members of the Ottoman ruling caste were *raya*, whether they were Muslim, Christian or Jewish by faith. It is very clear that Muslim *raya* were oppressed by the Ottoman authorities almost as much as non-Muslims. The burden of Ottoman rule often lay heavily on all its subjects.

However, the non-Muslims suffered more. There were infinitely greater, almost endless, opportunities to wheedle money for fees, licences and bribes from Christians and Jews than from Muslims. Wherever Christians or Jews came into contact with officialdom, money usually changed hands. Repairs to non-Muslim religious buildings required a licence, and invariably officials profited from this. The right to build a new church or synagogue could sometimes be purchased, but at a high price. This pressure was not unique to the Ottoman domains: Protestants in Catholic European countries and Catholics in Protestant countries were frequently subject to even more systematic and opprobrious official sanctions, and the treatment of the Jews in Christian Europe had always been notorious. And there is little evidence that the central Ottoman state had any consistent policy of oppression. There was no gain for the Ottoman authorities in terrorizing the non-Muslim faiths in the Balkans. They wanted to take as much as possible in levies and taxes from the 'flock'. Beyond that, they were usually content to leave the *raya* alone.[26]

In areas of the Balkans where the communities were mixed, Muslims sometimes had a better chance of seeing their Christian neighbours at first hand, and they shared a language and a communal life. But how great a part their religious identities played in everyday life is hard to say. There is little evidence one way or another. Violent antagonisms between the different communities do not seem to have been common or, at least, they went unrecorded. Neither population had much incentive to disturb the other since it would only bring down the unwelcome attention of Ottoman officialdom. Often when disputes appeared to be between *Muslims* and *Christians*, the real causes were rooted in more mundane issues: money, land, jealousy and avarice.[27] But when arguments moved into the area of officialdom, courts and legal decisions, non-Muslims were certainly at a disadvantage. Yet a rich and powerful Christian or Jew might still secure a positive decision against a poor Muslim. However, given that the courts were stacked against them, Christians had even less interest than their Muslim neighbours in attracting the intrusive attentions of the authorities. There is no doubt that many Balkan Christians felt oppressed. In part this was because there was a sense of underlying resentment that developed from the late eighteenth century onwards that the land and all its resources, which had once belonged to their people alone, was now occupied by Muslims.

As they were told more and more about their noble heritage, of the great Christian rulers and heroes of the past, of a time before the coming of the Turks, the instinctive response of the Christian peasants was to think that their Muslim neighbours' possessions should rightly belong to them. Paper icons in the home, patriotic legends retold in the family and the village, books and pamphlets, even education itself, all helped to foster a sense of identity. This turned into a sense of injustice feeding upon deeply rooted (if latent) antagonisms. Christians resented that they had to pay a capitation tax, although they were exempted from paying the *zakat*, the religious charitable tithe due from all Muslims. There were other duties that fell upon the Muslim *raya*, and not upon the Christians and Jews, just as there were payments that the latter had to make and their Muslim neighbours did not. Some of the inequities were either imaginary, or tales from the distant past.[28]

However, the financial burden on the subject peoples of the Balkans increased inexorably through the eighteenth century. Little of the money reached the central state treasury. Instead, it stuck to the hands of intermediaries. Since the conquest, the Ottomans had ruled their Balkan provinces by using various forms of indirect rule and a small body of state officials.[29] They had co-opted many of the leaders of the various Christian communities into the governmental system, so that the most senior figure, the Orthodox Patriarch in Constantinople, had the exalted status of a pasha and was entitled to an official Ottoman standard. But indirect rule only functioned effectively when it was controlled and constrained by honest governors sent from the capital, with the power of life and death over local officials. It was these who were ultimately responsible for enforcing the law, and ensuring that the highways and public buildings were kept in repair. Terrorized from above, they terrified those below them, and by such means the apparently ramshackle structure functioned with a degree of equity.

From the early eighteenth century the whole system began to fail. Powerful regional interests, both Muslim and Christian, sensed a weaker hand in Constantinople and began to treat the law with impunity, increasing taxes and requisitions on peasants of all faiths. In Bosnia, local lords known as *beys* ignored the authority of the state officials. They even prevented the pasha of the region from residing in the capital Sarajevo, and made him stay in the smaller town of Travnik. The janissaries, who had originally been stationed for limited periods in the Balkans to defend the sultan's realm, refused to return to Constantinople and acquired land and property, as well as a fearsome reputation among the Christian villagers around their camps. They turned a deaf ear to commands issued from Constantinople, becoming in the regions the effective power within the state, like their fellow janissaries in the capital, who deposed and even murdered sultans. The janissaries based in the fortress of Belgrade were especially notorious for their exactions.

Eighteenth-century Ottoman rulers were concerned not with the internal condition of the Balkans (provided the tax revenues were remitted) but with the increasing pressure from the Habsburg Empire and Russia on the borders of their domains. In the east, Iran had once more become a competitor for local loyalties where previously Ottoman power had been unquestioned. In the period of Ottoman expansion, warfare had been productive, bringing booty, territories, slaves and taxes. In the eighteenth century the pattern was reversed. War now drained away the state's resources. It also made increasing demands on manpower, with villagers taken away under guard to fight the Russians or the Austrians.[30] The pressures on the empire grew steadily and leading Ottomans came to believe that they would need to adopt the military systems of the West if they were to defend their domains.[31]

We should not exaggerate Ottoman incapacity, since it was often a metaphor for their perceived moral inadequacies rather than real military weakness – the Ottomans could still surprise Western armies with their skill and tenacity. The Turks had been consistently portrayed as in a state of precipitous decline since the late seventeenth century. Many of the eighteenth-century writers who presented the same picture were revealing their own frustrations at the impenetrable veneer of Ottoman conservatism. In reality, the process of decay was quite slow. Ironically, it was the strongest autocratic state of western Europe, France, which first imploded, rather than the allegedly decrepit Turkish Empire. But thereafter the Turks could no more resist the shock waves emanating from the French Revolution than any of the countries of Europe. Blown away in a Napoleonic whirlwind, small states re-emerged as new republics under French tutelage. Even empires such as Austria and Russia were forced to accommodate the new French imperial power. France first intervened in the East with the invasion of the Ottoman *pashalik* of Egypt in 1798, which led to the defeat of the ruling Mamluks at the Battle of the Pyramids outside Cairo. French action brought about ultimately the dominance of Mehmed Ali, the Albanian pasha appointed by Sultan Selim III. Egypt under Mehmed Ali created a powerful army and navy and became the greatest buttress for the Ottoman state but also the greatest threat to the continuing power of the sultans.

French involvement in the Adriatic had a more immediate influence. Centuries of Venetian occupation on the Adriatic coast of the Balkans was replaced by French domination, first (briefly) in the Ionian Islands, and later, after 1809, in the Illyrian Provinces, from the head of the Adriatic to the south of Dalmatia, creating a single state from former Habsburg and Venetian possessions.[32] Revolutionary France undermined the Ottoman position.[33] In 1797 Napoleon ordered his commander in the Ionian Islands to 'flatter the inhabitants . . . and to speak of the Greece of Athens and of Sparta in the various proclamations that you will issue'.[34] This approach appears very similar in intention to the French attempts to pander to Muslim opinion in their first proclamations in Egypt in 1798. But in the case of Greece it had a deeper resonance. The identification of the people of Greece with the civilization of Ancient Hellas was common among educated circles in many western European countries, but especially so in France, Britain, and many of the German-speaking states. It was a connection actively fostered by what has fairly been called the 'Greek intelligentsia' – mostly expatriate Greeks living outside the Ottoman dominions, or in the independent principalities of Moldavia and Wallachia, north of the Danube. Revolutionary France had an important lesson for these Balkan proto-liberators. There could be no limits to the pursuit of liberty.[35] No sacrifice was too great if it led, ultimately, to the Nation.

I do not propose to follow all the twisted paths that led towards national liberation for the different peoples of the Balkans.[36] Over the century from 1804, when the Serbs rose against the banditry practised by the janissary garrison of Belgrade, until the end of the Balkan Wars in 1913, the Balkans were in a more or less steady state of strife. Sometimes the Balkan peoples fought against each other, sometimes they battled against the Turks, either singly or in alliance. The other major European states played an active role, backing one party or another. But in that long conflict two horrific episodes epitomized 'the Balkans' for all outsiders: the massacres that accompanied the beginning of the Greek Revolution in 1821–2 (which I shall discuss here), and the 'Bulgarian Horrors' of 1876 (which will be looked at in detail in the next chapter). In both cases, what actually happened and what was written at the time diverged sharply. We can see how the new Balkan myths were formed and then disseminated like the dragon's teeth of Greek mythology.

It is indisputable that, like most highland zones, the lands south of the Danube had inherited long traditions of social violence. Life seemed cheap. In Montenegro taking heads was a common practice, as it was among the Ottomans. This was a world in which individual life expectancy was short, but where the community lived on in all its members, bound together by common bonds. The demands of honour extended throughout a whole family, or in the mountains to an entire clan. In highland Albania, honour crimes, feuds and vendettas would survive through many generations until the wrong was avenged.[37] The only security against a knife in the back or an unexpected bullet lay in killing anyone who could be linked into the chain of vengeance. This was the unspoken thought behind the cry 'Kill all the Turks in the Morea' that echoed in Greek village after village in the spring of 1821.

The Ottomans too had a culture of revenge. Justice was based on summary punishment and terror. One man or a whole community would die to expiate a crime. Individual responsibility or collective responsibility were equally valid justifications for capital punishment. If a miscreant had fled, a judge would order the punishment of someone from the same family, the same village or even from the same *millet*.[38] This was the case when Suleiman Pasha, the governor of Belgrade, was restored to his capital after the Serb revolt in 1807. He had 'men roasted alive, hanged by their feet over smoking straw . . . castrated, crushed with stones, bastinadoed . . . Outside the Stamboul Gate in Belgrade . . . [were] corpses of impaled Serbs being gnawed by packs of dogs.'[39] When Belgrade had fallen to the insurgents, most of the men had been killed. But Muslim women and children were kept alive, to be forcibly baptized.[40] It is highly unlikely that the Turks tortured to death were the actual men who had committed the offences, firing buildings and burning all inside alive. Others suffered for the community's crimes, to discourage further acts of rebellion.

Ottomans, Slavs, Greeks and Albanians all observed the unwritten law of slaughter and reprisal.

There are many candidates for the 'Precipitants' and 'Triggers' of the Greek Revolution but none of them fully explain why, suddenly, around Easter 1821, the Greek peasants of the Peloponnese began to kill all the Muslims in the land – men, women and children alike. Almost 20,000 were slaughtered in a few months. This killing of Muslims, and not the Turkish massacres of Christians on the island of Chios in the following year, was the starting point of atrocity in the War of Liberation. There were antecedents for slaughter on this scale, but not in the Balkans. In the three decades before 1821, indeed, it was western Europe and not the torpid East that provided the most fearsome examples of mass murder. 'Terror' was elevated to a principle of government during the first years of the French Revolution. The Paris mob hideously mutilated some of its victims, while in the French provinces ingenious means, such as mass drowning, were devised to speed up the process of disposing of the enemies of the people. Goya's etchings of the *Disasters of War*, showing the incomparably savage cruelty of Spain's Peninsular War *guerrilla*, were long considered too shocking to publish. In the early nineteenth-century Balkans, killings were on a lesser scale, until, that is, the sudden and unparalleled atrocities of 1821–2.

The bloody hands of the Greeks were an uncomfortable fact for the Western supporters of Hellenism. No one epitomized this acute dilemma better than the courageous soldier and fine writer Thomas Gordon. In his preface to the *History of the Greek Revolution*, published in 1832, he apologized for writing on a 'hackneyed and apparently exhausted subject'.[41] Forty writers, he said, had published on the topic, of whom he judged only three or four worthy of attention. His own book was a model work of history: Gordon had researched it thoroughly, with the added advantage of knowing the ground and many of the participants. He wrote while the events were still fresh in his mind. The Turks disgusted him but not to the point of obsession.[42] The 'grand causes' of the revolt in Gordon's eyes were 'religious zeal, patriotism, and national pride, deeply wounded by insult and injury'.[43] He recorded how in 1821 the Greeks were shipping arms and gunpowder into the Peloponnese and rebellion was in the air. To some later historians it seemed as though the rising had been planned.

Everywhere, as though at a preconceived signal, the peasantry rose and massacred all the Turks – men, women and children – on whom they could lay hands.

> In the Morea [Peloponnese] shall not Turk be left,
> Nor in the whole wide world.

Thus rang the song, which from mouth to mouth, announced the beginning of a war of extermination.[44]

It was neither planned nor organized. Once Bishop Germanos and the leaders of the Orthodox Church had 'raised the standard of the cross' in April 1821 the insurrection

gained ground with wonderful rapidity, and from mountain to mountain, and village to village, propagated itself to the farthest corners of the Peloponessus. Every where the peasants flew to arms, and those Turks who resided in the countryside or in unfortified towns, were either cut to pieces or forced to fly into strongholds.[45]

Gordon made rather more of Greek deaths. Several Greek hostages were, by order of the Turkish general, 'led forth and beheaded; their blood tinged the threshold of his residence, and their bones were long allowed to bleach in the court.'[46] Others they threw 'naked and headless' over the battlements of the Acropolis in Athens.

But Gordon was horrified at what he saw of Greek barbarity. At the city of Tripolitsa, crammed with Muslim refugees from the surrounding countryside, he watched as the Greeks stormed the walls.

The conquerors, mad with vindictive rage, spared neither age nor sex – the streets and houses were inundated with blood, and obstructed with heaps of dead bodies. Some Mohammedans fought bravely and sold their lives dearly, but the majority was slaughtered without resistance . . . Flames blazing out from the palace and many houses lighted up after a night spent in rapine and carnage.[47]

Gordon, as a soldier, could understand the bloodlust of the first moment of victory, but vengeance went far beyond that.[48]

It was the image of Tripolitsa – of 2,000 women and children 'massacred in a defile of Mount Maenalion' where their bloated corpses filled a vast open grave – that filled Gordon's mind when he described the subsequent Ottoman atrocities on Chios. He wrote of an idyllic island, seven miles off the coast of Asia Minor, with sixty-eight villages, 300 convents, 700 churches. Chios had a population of 100,000 Greeks, 6,000 Turks and a few Catholics and Jews. It was notable for its fine climate, the mutual tolerance among its various communities, and (Westerners averred) the easy morals of its women. It was also a centre of Greek education and literature, with a college, library, printing presses and a museum.

A small raiding party of Hellenic revolutionaries from Samos had briefly brought the insurrection to the island. They had burned buildings and looted all the movable property they could find. Then they left. But a few weeks later, a larger invading force arrived and then the revolution began in earnest. Local Muslims were killed and mosques burned. When the news arrived in Constantinople, the government feared that the rising would spread to the other Greek-dominated islands close to the Turkish coast, and then across the water and on into the cities of Asia Minor. In this crisis the Ottoman ruler called for a general levy among the Muslim *raya* to recapture Chios.[49] Yet, as Gordon observed, the sultan hinted the island was to be attacked not only because of 'affection for . . . religion and empire'; there was a baser motive: Christian Chios promised rich plunder.

A motley horde of Anatolians crossed over the calm sea in an armada of small boats. Ottoman soldiers broke into the island's capital, and the scene, as the Scot put it, 'might be aptly compared to the sack of Tripolitsa. Nine thousand were massacred in a single day. Every Greek they could find was put to the sword, even the inmates of the madhouse, the patients in the hospital, and the deaf and dumb institution.' More than 30,000 Muslims from Asia Minor swarmed into the island, killing and plundering as they went, capturing women and children for the slave markets. By the end of May 1822, 25,000 had been killed and 45,000 taken captive. The huge number of slaves swamped the markets of Constantinople, and many who were not sold easily were simply killed off like old sheep, and their bodies left on the streets to rot.

Yet Gordon still refused to damn one side and condone the other. 'Did we write', he observed, 'for the purpose of rendering exclusively odious one nation or party, it would be easy to prolong this catalogue of slaughters, sometimes springing from the systematic cruelty of a barbarous government, but oftener from the blind rage of an infuriated populace.'[50] I have concentrated on his account partly because he was an accurate and truthful witness, but also for this rare capacity to judge dispassionately, despite favouring the cause of Greece. But while he could understand the Turkish cruelties, the callous butcheries of the Hellenes were more disturbing to him. Eventually Gordon came to the conclusion that true Greeks of his day had inherited their finer feelings from their ancient ancestors, while those who had been corrupted by Eastern barbarism exhibited its cruelty and treachery.[51] This process had begun, he suggested, with the Easterners perverting the Greeks in the age of Alexander the Great. Alexander's men were already no angels, but 'their native vices were aggravated by Oriental softness, and by mingling with subjects still more corrupt than themselves'.[52] By this circular logic, the Greeks of his own day had become 'like the Eastern nations in every age'.[53]

If Thomas Gordon became the Clio of the Revolution, another Gordon was its Calliope, its Muse of eloquence. No individual did more to alert the West to a kind of new crusade in Greece than the poet George Gordon, Lord Byron. In *Childe Harold's Pilgrimage* (1812–13), Byron's pyrotechnic gallop through Western art, philosophy and history, he first presented Greece as a land of epic struggle. The rebirth of Ancient Hellas in a new Greece would usher in a wider, universal Revolution:

> A thousand years scarce serve to form a state;
> An hour may lay it in the dust; and when
> Can man its shatter'd splendour renovate,
> Recall its virtues back, and vanquish Time and Fate.[54]

This conflict transcended all the earlier struggles. In Byron's eyes the obstacle to this new age was Ottoman rule, the infidels 'whose turbans now pollute Sophia's shrine', and who had made the 'path of blood along the West'.[55] But his attitude to the East moved beyond the traditional stereotypes. His *Turkish Tales*, published following the astonishing success of the first Canto of *Childe Harold*, were filled with 'Noble Turks' such as Hassan in *The Giaour* (1813) or the unlucky

Selim of *The Bride of Abydos* (also 1813). Although Byron's tragic characters contained, in their externals, the typical eighteenth-century typology of the Turk, they were more human and vulnerable than any of the usual lay-figures.[56] Hassan and Selim were Western in their passions, hopes and fears. What destroyed those hopes was the brutal harshness of the pashas and sultans, and what destroyed human life on an individual level was even more lethal to human aspirations on the national scale.

From the beginning of the Greek Revolt in 1821, books and pamphlets had begun to appear against the 'cruel Turks' and their savagery in Greece. After Byron's 'martyr's death' at Easter 1824 in the citadel of Missolonghi in western Greece, there was a sudden increase in the publications devoted to the Greek cause.[57] France in particular was gripped by the drama of the Greek Revolt. Paris had for many years been a gathering-point for expatriates and exiles, including the pioneer of the revival of the Greek language Adamantios Korais, who spent most of his adult life in the city; he died there in 1833. Some, like Grigorios Zalykis, were closet revolutionaries who also served the Turks – he was First Secretary at the Ottoman Embassy in Paris from 1816 to 1820. Minas Minoidis taught Greek in the city and also acted as an interpreter to the French Ministry of Foreign Affairs. Paris was the first European capital to receive news from this Greek 'colony'.

The emotional appeal of Hellenism was powerful, but we should not forget that French artists had more mundane motives for the sudden flood of images of the war in Greece that they produced. Napoleon's empire had provided a multitude of commissions for artists, while print makers and retailers had made a living from selling copies of famous paintings to a wider public. After 1815, artists who had found a ready market for battle scenes were looking for new subjects. The outbreak of the revolution in Greece itself was much more stirring than a rising in the Danubian Principalities.[58] All the political factions in France, from Ultra-monarchists to Liberals and former Bonapartists, supported the Greek cause. Those who hated revolution quelled their misgivings: the Ultra-monarchist newspaper *Le Drapeau Blanc* concluded that 'they [the Greeks] are Christians who want to shake off the Islamic yoke, therefore it is good.'[59] It was also a wonderfully Romantic cause, exotically Oriental. Women dressed

à la Turque once again, but now in the politically correct Greek colours
of blue and white.

The sudden efflorescence of paintings and prints that followed the
start of the war in Greece thus had a variety of 'Triggers'. The French
press presented highly coloured accounts of Ottoman atrocities. On
27 May 1821, *Le Constitutionnel* reported that it had been officially
decided in Constantinople 'to slaughter all the Christian subjects of
the Ottoman empire'; by 24 July this had become a plan of the
Ottomans to wipe Christianity from the face of the earth. The *Gazette
de France* of 25 May 1821 had compared the Turks to bloodthirsty
wild beasts, a 'mob attacking every Christian without any distinction'.
Ironically, at that time, in the Peloponnese, the Greeks fitted this
stereotype better than the Turks. There were one or two depictions
of Turks being killed, and an ode by Alphonse Dupré on the capture
of Tripolitsa by the Greeks on 5 October 1821. But the vast majority
of the images presented the conflict in very simplistic Hellenophile
terms. The cross was omnipresent, set against the emblem of Turkish
power, the pasha's horsetail standard. Usually the latter was cast down
into the dust, as in an unfinished sketch by the Lyonnais painter Pierre
Revoil. His *War in the Morea or, the Triumph of the Labarum* (a labarum
is a cross and flag combined) showed the pasha's standard lying at
the feet of the fierce-eyed Greeks, with the cross looming above.
Conversely, in the *Disaster at Missolonghi*, Charles Langlois' painting
depicts the horsetails advancing on the fleeing Greeks.

The symbolism proliferated as time went on. After the invasion of
the Peloponnese by the well-trained Egyptian troops commanded by
Mehmed Ali's son, Ibrahim Pasha, acting for the Sultan Mahmud II,
the Greek armies were shattered and their strongholds taken with
great bloodshed. A print by Ducarme of 1828 presented 'Greece
sacrificed' (*La Grèce immolée*). An old man with a young boy clutching
his knees stands before the cross. A woman, her arms wrapped around
the cross, has a naked child grasping her hand, while to the side
another Greek is dying, an arrow through his heart, while yet another
lies already dead close by. In the background, a classical column has
fallen over. Riding towards them on rearing stallions are a group of
Turks, armed with bows, pistols and a long yataghan. Behind, a
standard-bearer brandishes the horsetail pennant. There is little doubt
about the fate of the old man and the children. For the woman, sexual

violation seems certain, as she raises her eyes to Heaven. No one in Paris in 1828 who saw this print could have had any doubt as to its meaning.

These tropes appeared time and again on canvas: the cross, the heroic Greeks on foot fighting against expressionless Turks on horseback, women with children at the breast, maidens praying to the Virgin. They were just as omnipresent in the images sold on the streets of Paris as in the paintings shown in the Salons and in aid of the Greek cause. They presented a strong single image of 'Good' fighting 'Evil'. Many of the themes were already familiar, from earlier paintings, such as Gros' 1806 *Battle of Aboukir*, where the horsetails were reeling towards the ground as the vanquished Mamluk commander offered his scimitar to General Murat. But the mixture of pathos, Christian pride and heroism and Ottoman arrogance was a new combination. Eugène Delacroix's *Massacre on Chios*, exhibited in 1824 and then bought by Louis XVIII for the Louvre, was the quintessence of these themes. Criticized at the time for being muddled and chaotic, it drew upon Delacroix's skill in satirical cartooning, which at that point provided his main source of income. It was not art but propaganda.[60] The exhausted Christians herded together to be shipped to the capital as slaves are languidly guarded by two Turks. A cold and expressionless Ottoman, on a rearing horse, is drawing his sword to hack down a brawny Greek seeking to protect a half-naked woman. But it is in the background that the real business of conquest is taking place. Women are dragged along by their hair, others are having their clothes ripped from them, still others are pursued by lancers on horseback. Unlike in a great classical painting in the style of David, the main action is not in the centre of the foreground, but in the random savageries revealed behind.

The many paintings of the fall of Missolonghi in April 1826 revealed a double theme: martyrdom and triumph. At Missolonghi the Greeks were massacred by the victorious Turks, but in their last moments they blew up their powder magazine, killing, it was claimed, more than 2,000 of the 'barbarians'. After Missolonghi the image of savagery was made still more powerful and explicit. In the print of Eugène Devéria, a naked baby is about to be skewered by a Turkish sword despite its mother's pleas, while the Turkish horses wear a string of Christian heads like a necklace.[61] In another image a woman prepares to stab herself and her child rather than suffer 'a fate worse than death'.[62] Delacroix's *Greece on the Ruins of Missolonghi* (1826) is more subtle: the horsetail standard waves in the background, and the great city has exploded, crushing its people beneath its stones. Yet the incarnation of Greece, half-kneeling on the ruins, is not cowed or fearful; she is defiant and proud.

The source material for all these images were events as they were perceived in France. They drew on news reports, public meetings, pamphlets, poems and even novels. But the process was circular. The images were generated from the written texts, and they both catered to popular taste and then helped to form that taste. Thereafter they became sources for further texts and images. The massacres on Chios were remembered as Delacroix or other artists such as Colin had painted them. Conversely, because the killings of the Muslims in the Peloponnese were not depicted, although they were reported, these atrocities seemed less real and were less potent and emotive. The great paintings survived in the public imagination long after the written texts on which they were based had been forgotten. French artists, from masters to hack print makers, created visual metaphors for the Hellenic revival, which they portrayed as a new crusade.

'A Broad Line of Blood'[1]

Between the massacres on Chios in 1822 and the killings in 1876 that became known colloquially as 'the Bulgarian Horrors', many of the political elements in the equation altered. The Ottomans had acquired a 'Western' veneer, from their black frock coats referred to as 'Stamboulines' to the trappings of constitutional government. In 1839 and again in 1856, Sultan Mahmud II's successor, his son Abdul Mejid, issued decrees that outdid Western governments in their paper idealism. Slurs and insults directed at Christians, such as *Kaur* and *Kaurin* (anglicized as *Giaour*), were officially banned.[2] In the Crimean War, between 1853 and 1856, the ostensible cause of British and French intervention against Russia was the protection of Turkey from Russian attack. These motives were, of course, scarcely altruistic, but a degree of 'Turcophilia' slowly developed in the West.[3] Byron had articulated the struggle of the individual dragged down by a cruel and corrupt state. Now, as the Ottoman state proclaimed reform, a new cycle of attraction rather than revulsion began.[4]

Not everyone believed that the Turks had changed. William Ewart Gladstone later described Britain and France as determining 'to try a great experiment in remodelling the administrative system of Turkey, with the hope of curing its intolerable vices and making good its not-less-intolerable vices'.[5] More and more Westerners had witnessed Ottoman government at first hand. Christian pilgrims travelled to the sites in Palestine, and inevitably suffered the vagaries of Ottoman officialdom. Something of the old anger that the land where Christ had lived was under alien rule began to resurface. Meanwhile, further north, the mountains of Lebanon were racked by inter-communal strife, with Druze villagers (regarded as heretics or worse by orthodox Muslims) killing Maronite Christians, and these events were fully reported by Western consuls in the region.[6]

In 1860, the intermittent violence developed into a civil war, which suddenly extended to a massacre of thousands of Christians in Damascus by an enraged mob. As many as 12,000 terrified Christians were protected by the exiled Algerian leader, Abd el Kader, who ordered his bodyguards to safeguard those sheltering in his palace. Eventually, the Ottoman government responded and dispatched the Foreign Minister, Fuad Pasha, with an army and instructions to restore the state's authority. This he did by executing all Ottoman officials who had failed to prevent the murders and rapes, hanging the leaders of the Damascus killings, levying huge indemnities on the Druze community in Lebanon, and exiling Druze chieftains.[7] An Austrian geographer, Philip Kanitz, found a few survivors living squalidly in cages fifteen years later in Ottoman Bulgaria.[8] Under pressure from Britain and France, new administrative arrangements were created that prevented a recurrence of civil war between Maronites and Druze.[9]

Few in the West appreciated the complexity of Levantine politics or the volatility of the Damascus mob. They read accounts of Christians being killed and mutilated, with the Ottoman authorities seemingly complicit (or even instigating) the atrocities. There were even reports of Ottoman officials taking Christians under their protection, confiscating their arms, and then allowing their enemies to kill them. When an Englishman, Cyril Graham, visited the district of Hasbeya in Lebanon, he found evidence of atrocity – rotting corpses, arrogant killers and official inaction. Graham sensed that he was in the midst of some extraordinary blood frenzy, whence all normality had vanished. He reported how 'the Druzes accompanying me made jokes on the bodies, and one fellow showed me a pair of pistols set in silver, one of which had been broken in dashing the brains out of Christian heads.' What also shocked him was the Druze themselves: 'I have travelled all over their country . . . and never met with anything but courtesy; now they speak with great insolence, boast of the numbers of Christians they have killed, and assert they will cut to pieces any force which shall be brought against them.'[10] For many, these murders came as no surprise. The Turk had merely (once again) reverted to type.

That was 1860. The news of the mass killing of Christians in Bulgaria sixteen years later produced a response on a vastly different scale. Yet as Richard Shannon observed, 'there was nothing new or

unusual in the fact of either the [Bulgarian] insurrection or the massacre. Both were endemic features of Ottoman administration. The
massacres in Bulgaria were not unusually extensive, and there is no
reason to assume that they were unusually atrocious.'[11] To put it
crudely, the totals of victims in Damascus and Lebanon in 1860 and
in Bulgaria in 1876 were not very different. However, the former
provoked anger only among those prone to outrage, while the latter
caused a moral crusade on a vast scale. In 1877, the eminent historian
E. A. Freeman wrote in the *Contemporary Review* that opposing the
Turks had become a moral imperative: 'Men came together as if to
deliver their own souls, as if their hearts would not rest within them
till their tongues had spoken . . . to wash their hands clean from the
deeds of which they had just heard the tale.' For Freeman, 'the
common earth had received a defilement, and the common human
nature had received a defilement which needed some rite of lustration
[ceremonial washing-clean] to wipe off from the consciences of all
mankind.'[12] The agent of this defilement was the 'indescribable Turk'
or, as one Anglican clergyman privately described it, the 'most nau-
seous of all abominations, Mohammedanism'.[13]

This superheated language had a precedent. Less than a generation
before, in 1857, the British public had eagerly endorsed a wide range
of atrocities by the British army in suppressing a 'Sepoy Mutiny'
in India. Newspapers egged on the government to an ever-greater
harshness. They were encouraged in this campaign by many leading
figures. On 4 October 1857 the novelist Charles Dickens had assured
his readers in London that were he commander-in-chief in India, he
would 'do my utmost to exterminate the Race on whom the stain of
the late cruelties rested . . . and with all convenient dispatch and
merciful swiftness of execution, to blot it out of mankind and raze it
off the face of the earth.' He meant Indians, of all ages, and, presumably, men, women and children alike. The mechanism of national
outrage worked in the same way on both occasions.

Nations in the grip of a mass social panic, whether the British in
the face of the Indian Mutiny in 1857 or the Bulgarian Horrors of
1876–7 (or the United States after 11 September 2001), tend to behave
in the same fashion. In all these cases, panic was fuelled by the written
word and visual images. Public rage developed in 1857 as the British
read of white women violated and innocent children cruelly

murdered.[14] In India as in the Balkans there was little organization or serious planning that engendered the initial massacres.[15] The counter-atrocities, by the British authorities in India, and the Ottomans (1822 and 1877) were carried out as an official act of deliberate terror.[16] Neither government believed them disproportionate at the time: they saw themselves faced with a massive and all-embracing conspiracy.

A series of disconnected incidents, beginning with strident Muslim resistance to the plan that a new Orthodox cathedral being built in Sarajevo would tower over the sixteenth-century Begova mosque, sparked violence. From 1872 onwards there was resistance to Ottoman tax-gatherers, with peasants arming themselves and taking refuge in nearby Montenegro. The local authorities responded, as they usually did, with a knee-jerk brutality: by 1876 hundreds of villages had been burned and more than 5,000 Bosnian peasants killed.[17] Soon the contagion of rebellion began to seep into the Bulgarian provinces. The threat of a general uprising seemed imminent.

Every piece of revolutionary propaganda received or each intelligence report read served to bolster the fear. Was the government in Constantinople to disregard the terrorist threats made by the Bulgarian revolutionaries? The insurgents wrote: 'Herzegovina is fighting; Montenegro is spreading over the mountains and coming with help; Serbia is ready to put its forces on the move; Greece is about to declare war; Rumania will not remain neutral. Is there any doubt that death is hanging over Turkey?'[18] In July 1875, at Nevesinje in Herzegovina, the clan chiefs had met and thrown down a challenge to the Turks. One declared:

Ever since the damned day of Kosovo [Polje, in 1389] the Turk robs us of our life and liberty. Is it not a shame, a shame before all the world, that we bear the arms of heroes and yet are called Turkish subjects? All Christendom waits for us to rise on behalf of our treasured freedom . . . Today is our opportunity to rebel and to engage in bloody fight.[19]

This guerrilla war, in Harold Temperley's view, led directly to the revolt in Bulgaria and all that followed. It was a cruel war on both sides. The first things that British Consul Holmes saw as he entered Nevesinje were a Turkish boy's head blackening in the sun, and a bloody froth bubbling from the slit throat of a young Turkish girl.[20]

In both India and the Balkans fact was quickly conflated with myth. But it was sometimes the myths that stuck in the memory. Yet securing a mass response was not an easy matter: it required a rising sense of drama and horror, a quasi-theatrical style of presentation. Sir Edwin Pears recalled the Bulgarian Horrors of 1876 in his memoirs:

They had seen dogs feeding on human remains, heaps of human skulls, skeletons nearly entire, rotting clothing, human hair, and flesh putrid and lying in one foul heap. They saw the town with not a roof left, with women here and there wailing their dead amid the ruins. They examined the heap and found that the skulls and skeletons were all small and that the clothing was that of women and girls. MacGahan counted a hundred skulls immediately around him. The skeletons were headless, showing that these victims had been beheaded.

Further on they saw the skeletons of two little children lying side by side with frightful sabre cuts on their little skulls. MacGahan remarked that the number of children killed in these massacres was something enormous. They heard on trustworthy authority from eye-witnesses that they were often spiked on bayonets.

There was not a house beneath the ruins of which he and Mr. Schuyler did not see human remains, and the streets were strewn with them.[21] When they drew nigh the church they found the ground covered with skeletons and lots of putrid flesh. In the church itself the sight was so appalling that I do not care to reproduce the terrible description given by Mr. MacGahan.[22]

Januarius MacGahan was an experienced war reporter; his first account from the front was published in the *Daily News* in London on 7 August 1876. On the same day, an official report read out in the House of Commons confirmed MacGahan's gruesome details. More and more column inches kept Bulgaria in the public mind. A longer and even more horrific dispatch from MacGahan appeared on 16 August. Thirteen days later American Consul Schuyler's Preliminary Report to the US Government was printed in full in the *Daily News*. This added further fuel to the fire. All the earlier warnings, from May 1876 onwards, some accurate others fanciful, were confirmed.[23] Gladstone's pamphlet crystallized an existing popular feeling of horror and revulsion. He began to formulate his own contribution to the campaign against the Ottomans even before he had seen Schuyler's report. He wrote in a white heat – by 1 September 1876 he had already completed more than half of it.[24] Late on 3 September he concluded his text and sent it to the printer. On 5 September all the copies were finished and distributed.

The impact of Gladstone's *Bulgarian Horrors and the Question of the East* had no parallel. It sold 24,000 copies on the day it came out, 40,000 in less than a week and 100,000 copies in the longer term.[25] Thousands of other publications appeared. Fresh horrors were exposed. But the appearance of Gladstone's great diatribe against the Turk in September 1876 was the point at which the anti-Ottoman cause became a juggernaut. The Grand Old Man distilled the historic Christian antagonism to Islam into the incomparable evil of the Ottomans: 'Wherever they went, a broad line of blood marked the track behind them, and as far as their dominion reached, civilisation vanished from view.'[26]

Gladstone had set foot on Ottoman soil only once, in February 1859. He wrote then in his diary, 'The whole impression is most saddening: it is all, all, indolence, decay, stagnation; the image of God seems as it were nowhere.'[27] Gladstone annotated the books that he read, and also recorded their contents each day in his diary. From this it is clear that in his reading about the East, over some fifteen years, books hostile to the Ottomans were predominant. Only two Turcophile works found a place on the shelves of his library. A passionate philhellene, a scholar immersed in the glories of Ancient Greece, his distaste for the Ottomans had both rational and deeply emotional grounds.[28] As the massacres took place, he was at work on a book on Homer, and his mind was occupied with the origins of classical Greece. The contrast he saw between the cultured glory of the Ancient Hellenes and the gross barbarity of the contemporary Turks gave wings to his pen. *The Bulgarian Horrors* showed a change in register: Gladstone adopted the style and remorseless aggression of a philippic, not really typical of his powerful but usually more measured rhetorical style.[29]

Few short texts – it was sixty-four pages in total – can have had a more immediate effect. The British response to the Bulgarian atrocities built up steadily thereafter, over five months. The agitation was fed by speeches in Parliament, cartoons, reports in newspapers, and by public meetings. '*The Bulgarian Horrors* succeeded so completely because it concentrated into a single utterance a profoundly excited public mood struggling for articulation.'[30] But when there were no new incidents and no new reports, public interest waned. It became clear that popular fury could not be sustained in the long term. By 1878, the agitation over the massacres of 1876 had faded, and the British streets were echoing with a new popular song of the hour, directed not at the Turks but at the Russians:

> We don't want to fight,
> But by Jingo if we do,
> We've got the ships,
> We've got the men,
> And got the money too.
> We've fought the Bear before,
> And while we're Britons true,
> The Russians shall not have Constantinople.

In 1876, Britain was the principal focus of outrage, taking on the role that France had assumed over Greece in the 1820s. In 1876, the agitation was fuelled by the written word and public meetings, while in 1822, it was images and visual symbols that had been the more persuasive. But most remarkable of all was the essential *modernity* of the response in 1876: this was a powerful and concerted media campaign that helped to create an acute political polarization, between anti-Turk and pro-Turk, at all levels of society. There was no unquestioning Slavophilia, like the near-universal sympathy for the Greeks in the 1820s. Finally, the reaction was framed within a national political framework. In Britain, Victorian high-mindedness, in its Liberal incarnation, found a natural outlet in condemnation of the Turks, who became a metaphor for the sleazy dealings of the British Tories. Their pragmatic Conservatism began to look tainted and immoral.

If images played a smaller part in 1876 than they had in 1822, perhaps this was a consequence of Gladstone's dominating presence, both as a public speaker and as a writer of polemics. However, there were some extraordinarily strong visual images that fired the public imagination. On 5 August 1876, two days before MacGahan's first report appeared, a *Punch* cartoon entitled 'NEUTRALITY UNDER DIFFICULTIES' attacked the Prime Minister, Benjamin Disraeli. The cartoon showed the figure of Britannia pointing to a scene where Turkish soldiers were carrying off women and raising babies to meet their swords, amid a forest of heads spiked on bayonets. The Prime Minister sat calmly reading his Blue Book over a caption declaring, 'Bulgarian Atrocities! I can't find them in the "Official Reports"!!!' A month later, on 9 September 1876, *Punch* published another and even angrier image: 'THE STATUS QUO'. Britannia looks contemptuously at 'the Turk', a bloody sabre hanging from his arm. Behind are burning buildings, heads impaled and dead babies. Turkey demands Britain's support. The reply is: 'Befriend you? Not with your hands of *that Colour.*'

But the tone of the cartoons soon changed. By October *Judy*, a rival to *Punch*, had the sturdy figure of John Bull (a more earthy symbol of England than Britannia) separating Turk and eastern Christian. Both Orientals are armed to the teeth, and heavily caricatured. But they are plainly equally at fault, and it needed British intervention to keep them in check. The caption declared 'WHAT IT MUST COME TO'. The bloody-handed Turk had become a portly invalid fed distasteful nostrums by the European rulers.[31] By the following year Russia and Turkey were *both* portrayed as barbarians.[32]

Anthropologists used to define a society as a group of people living together at the same time, in the same place and speaking a common language.[33] In the Balkans, making a state from a cluster of micro-communities proved extraordinarily difficult. Drawing up the frontiers for each new nation, on the basis of language or otherwise, was repeatedly frustrated by where people actually lived after centuries of Ottoman occupation. For example, more than 40 per cent of Albanian-speakers lived outside the boundaries of the Albanian state established in 1913. (Many of them had moved to the safer lowlands, away from the rigours and the blood feuds of mountain life.) There were at least five areas whose national character was constantly being defined or redefined. Macedonia was Greek or Bulgarian or even Albanian, depending on your perspective. Even after 1878, Bulgaria contained many Turks. Thrace remained a battleground between Turks, Bulgarians, Serbs and Greeks. Bosnia and Kosovo proved the most problematical of all. For nation-builders there were two main options: either, they could incorporate divergent elements and hope to subdue them, or they could homogenize the disparate groups.

Implicit in the concept of the Balkans' new nations created in the nineteenth and early twentieth centuries was some kind of trans-formation. At one level it could be merely freedom from the 'Ottoman yoke' and allowing the ancient nation a chance to 'breathe free'. This was the naïve enthusiasm that underpinned the notion of a reborn Greece. In Serbia and Croatia, it was rooted in a pick-and-mix attitude to the past.[34] The folkloric compilation of ancient songs, patriotic poems and a carefully edited version of history created what Ivo Banac aptly described as 'racial messianism in culture'. It took many forms. Before the First World War, the Croat artist Ivan Meštrović planned a Kosovo Temple, in the form of a Latin cross, with a dome 'bigger than St. Peter's'. A five-tiered 'tower of ages' would symbolize 'five centuries of slavery'; each tier was to be flanked by figures of the 'martyr spirits' and at the very top an eternal torch, a 'people's prayer'.[35] His great architectural vision was never built but he later explained the motives behind his design: 'What I had in mind was an attempt to create a synthesis of popular national ideals and their development, to express in stone and building how deeply buried in each one of us are the memories of the great and decisive moments of our history.'[36]

However, these memories could never be shared by one group in the Kingdom of Serbs, Croats and Slovenes. Like the Montenegrins and Herzegovinans, who were subsumed (as Serbs) within the new state, they were not named. The Muslims of Bosnia (*Bosniacs*) may have shared a language, lived in the same place, at the same time but their culture was not that of their neighbours.[37]

Ethnic cleansing, either as 'transfer', or the more horrific version that emerged in the 1990s, has affected virtually all the Balkan nations.[38] It was, however, not an exclusive product of the 'Balkan psyche'. Rather, it can be traced back to the way that the nation states came into being from the 1820s onward. But no historical process explains the extraordinary violence and hatred that sometimes emerged. How is it to be understood? One answer perhaps lies in the work of the two Nobel Laureates for Literature from the area. Elias Canetti was born in Ruse on the banks of the Danube in 1905. His ancestors were among the Jews expelled from Spain in 1492 and his first language was Ladino. He was six when he left Bulgaria for

ever and ended his life as a naturalized Englishman. Canetti began
to write the book that eventually became *Crowds and Power* (*Masse
und Macht*) in Vienna in 1925. It was finally completed and published
in 1960.

The other Laureate, Ivo Andrić, was born in a village near Travnik
in 1892, and remained immersed in his memories of Bosnia for the
remainder of his life. He grew up in a colony – the only colony – of
Austria-Hungary. Bosnia-Herzegovina had been notionally under
Ottoman sovereignty until 1908, but then even that illusion was ended
when it was formally incorporated in the Habsburg domains. But
Bosnia and Herzegovina remained anomalous. The territory was
ruled not through the governments of either Austria or Hungary but
personally by the Joint Minister of Finance acting for the Emperor
Franz Joseph I. Under him a huge swarm of bureaucrats administered
the country and its people more comprehensively and intrusively than
ever before.[39] The forty years of Habsburg rule isolated the Bosnians
(in particular the Muslims) from the political experience of the other
Balkan nations. 'Being Muslim the Bosnian way' was a product of
that period of isolation, when Bosnian Muslims became part of a
largely secular society that was dominated by neither Serbs nor Croats.
Nor, of course, did they as Muslims have the privileged position that
they had formerly enjoyed under the Ottomans.[40]

Andrić's experience of Habsburg Bosnia as a child and young man
was instrumental in the topic he chose for his doctoral thesis at
the University of Graz. In 1923, he completed a study on 'The
Development of Spiritual Life in Bosnia under the Influence of
Turkish rule'.[41] From his work he concluded that history had created
a deep and unbridgeable gulf in his homeland.[42] In Bosnia, he wrote
in 1954, 'There were two worlds, between which there cannot be
any real contact nor the possibility of agreement; two terrible worlds
doomed to an eternal war in a thousand various forms.' Yet Andrić,
who admired the great cultural heroes of the past, like Vuk Stefanović
Karadžić and Petar Petrović Njegoš, did as they had done.[43] He was
conflating the past and the present. The Bosnia that he had known
from his childhood and his early scholarship became the Bosnian
present. Life did not just mimic history: it was history. He recognized
this: 'Our traditional and written literature has made the Turks into
the wrath of God, into a kind of scarecrow that could be painted only

with dark and bloody colours, something that could not be quietly talked about or coolly thought about.'[44]

An unalterable past manufactured an unchangeable present. His diagnosis was painful to him. One of his characters in *Bosnian Chronicle*, the febrile and introspective Dr Cologna, expressed Andrić's own situation. For someone who knew the West,

to live in Turkey [Bosnia] means to walk along a knife edge and to burn on a low fire. I know this, for we are born on that knife edge, we live and die on it, and we grow up and are burned out on that fire . . . No one knows what it means to be born and live on the brink, between two worlds, knowing and understanding both of them and to be unable to help explain them to each other and bring them closer. To love and hate both . . . To have two homelands and yet have none. To be everywhere at home and to remain forever a stranger. In short, to live torn on a rack, but as both victim and torturer at once.[45]

The past, like the present, was paradoxical. In 1939, on the 550th anniversary of the Battle of Kosovo Polje, Bishop Nikolaj Velimirović had talked of 'our national Golgotha and at the same time our national resurrection'.[46] World War Two brought an end to the Serb resurrection. The state headed by Josip Broz (Tito) in 1945 proclaimed the 'brotherhood and unity of the peoples of Yugoslavia' and persecuted all strands of exclusive nationalism. Instead of the triune state of Serbs, Croats and Slovenes, the new Yugoslavia gave political identity and parliamentary institutions to many excluded from the South Slav idea. Macedonians and Bosnians were both recognized as national groups. Tito's answer to the problems of majorities and minorities was to abolish the very concept. All were equal within a people's democracy.[47] This supranational Yugoslav identity survived Tito's death in 1980 by little more than ten years. On 25 June 1991, the republic of Slovenia was the first to break away from the federal state. But two years before, on the 600th anniversary of Kosovo Polje, the Serbian President Slobodan Milošović on the same battlefield had spoken for a militantly revivalist Serbia, and expressed the same ambiguity as Bishop Velimirović fifty years before: 'It is difficult to say today whether the Battle of Kosovo was a defeat or a victory for the Serbian people, whether thanks to it we fell into slavery or we survived in this slavery.'

Mobilizing the past to guide the present is scarcely unique to the Balkans. But Balkan myths, whether stories of Kosovo, the tales of Skenderbeg, Njegoš's *Mountain Wreath*, or the idea of the unfulfilled nation written by Ljudevit Gaj in 1831 – 'Long she slept, but she's not vanquished / We shall wake her and revive' – appear to serve dark and cruel ends.[48] A Muslim epic song from Bosnia goes like this:

> The bloody frontier is like this
> With dinner blood, with supper blood,
> Everybody chews bloody mouthfuls,
> Never one white day for repose.[49]

Does this mean that the Balkans were haunted by an inescapable history, cursed ceaselessly to repeat the bloody deeds of the past? The problem was not a curse but a deep belief that history was mother and father to the present. Each time memories of a century – or six centuries – ago were deferred to, they were given new life. Robert Kaplan wondered why Mother Tatiana's eyes appeared 'strangely unfocused' as she told of an Albanian castrating a young Serbian boy. They looked, he thought, as if they had been 'blotted out by superstition'. There was another explanation: in her mind's eye, she was really reliving the past. Hers were foul memories, but conjured up by choice and assembled into a narrative rather as Victor Franken-stein had pieced together his revenant:

Who shall conceive the horrors of my secret toil, as I dabbled among the unhallowed damps of the grave, or tortured the living animal to animate the lifeless clay? . . . I collected bones from charnel houses; and disturbed, with profane fingers, the tremendous secrets of the human frame . . . The dissecting room and the slaughterhouse furnished many of my materials; and often did my human nature turn with loathing from my occupation, whilst still urged on by an eagerness which perpetually increased . . .[50]

This chapter, like its subject matter, is deeply ambiguous. On one side it denies that 'the Balkans' are uniquely given to cruelty and atrocity. On the other, it presents a long string of horrors that seem to prove the reverse. Had I catalogued the most recent *Balkan Horrors* of the

1990s in all their stomach-turning detail the pages would have been saturated bloody red. For the same reason I also drew back from repeating the famous account of impalement in Andrić's *Bridge over the Drina*. There is scarcely a nation in the world that does not have a black past, but there is something special about the way history has been used in the Balkans. The Greeks can legitimately claim to possess the longest and most impressive heritage, but each of the Balkan nations has constructed a clear memory of its own heroic eras: Byzantine, Bulgarian, Serb, Croat and Bosnian periods of imperial glory have all been carefully recorded. In virtually every case, and often by playing fast and loose with chronology, the idyllic Christian past was deemed to have been brought to a shuddering halt by the Turks. Everything could be blamed on their presence.

In the Balkans, because of the 'Turkish yoke', folklore had a powerfully political meaning. Stories of ancient victories and killings, as in Njegoš's *Mountain Wreath*, had a direct symbolic relevance:

> The Serbian name has perished everywhere.
> Mighty lions have become meek peasants.
> Rash and greedy converted to Islam –
> – may their Serb milk make them all sick with plague!
> Those who escaped before the Turkish sword,
> those who did not blaspheme at the True Faith,
> those who refused to be thrown into chains,
> took refuge here in these lofty mountains
> to shed their blood together and to die,
> heroically to keep the sacred
> oath, their lovely name, and their holy freedom.
> Our heads withstood the hard test in battles!
> Our brave lads have shone like the radiant stars.
> Those who were born in these lofty mountains
> fell day by day in the past's bloody wars
> and gave their life for honour, name, and freedom.
> All of our tears were always wiped away
> by the deft sounds of the lovely *gusle*.
> Sacrifices have not been made in vain
> since our hard land has now truly become
> of Turkish might the insatiable tomb.[51]

This relevance to the present is missing in the tales recorded by the Brothers Grimm, and in English ballads. Only in English-ruled Ireland did the folkloric past provide the language and models for contemporary political action. A stanza of one ancient poem reprinted by Constanza, Lady Wilde, read:

> When the Fenian wrath was kindled,
> And the heroes in thousands rode to war,
> And the bridles clanked on the steeds.[52]

Irish revolutionaries proudly described themselves as 'Fenians' waging war on their English oppressors. In Ireland as in the Balkans, the scholarly work of recording and disseminating the nation's past provided a coded message against oppression.

Memories of oppression are probably inexplicable to anyone who has not been brought up with them from infancy. Acquiring these feelings and prejudices is not genetic. They have to be learned. For more than a century the source of most stories has not just been an oral tradition handed down by word of mouth from generation to generation, but also the medium of the printed word and the visual image. In many old homes, I guess, there is the equivalent of that back room in my grandfather's house. Now we can also learn how to hate in new ways: through film, on the television screen and the Internet. Yet the process remains the same. Malediction is mobile: it can shift its target, but it still carries with it all the weight of past opprobrium. In the Balkans after 1922 there were Ottomans no more. They had departed. They had been the enemy in the Slav national epics, and now they were no longer present. But the Muslim Albanians and, to a lesser degree, the Bosnian Muslims took their place as the alien antagonist. For a considerable time the Albanians had acted as the enforcers for the Ottoman authorities in distant Constantinople. The last autocratic sultan, Abdul Hamid II, used Albanians as guards within his fortified palace at Yildiz, trusting his life only to them. When the Balkan Wars ended in 1913, the Turks even insisted that the Albanians should be granted their own state; however, as noted earlier, many were already settled outside its new boundaries.

The Albanians in Kosovo became an object of particular hatred for the government of Serbia. For ultra nationalists, the presence of

Muslims in the sacred land that Serbs had been forced to abandon in 1690 was insupportable. In the 1980s a series of sensational misdeeds were attributed to Kosovar Albanians, and were considered by many Serbs to illustrate the threat posed by these 'aliens'.[53] One in particular connected directly to the ancient rhetoric against the Ottomans. On 1 May 1985, according to Yugoslav newspaper reports, a Serbian peasant called Djordje Martinović was attacked by two unidentified Albanian men, who 'mistreated him, and forced a bottle into his rectum'.[54] The bottle's neck broke in his anus, causing great pain and physical damage. There were suggestions that the motives might be something to do with land, but no satisfactory causes ever emerged. Then it was suggested that it was in fact an act of sexual self-gratification. Martinović, it was said, had put the bottle on a wooden stick and then sat upon it. But that too went against the medical evidence. At least four different (and mutually contradictory) explanations were eventually advanced.

But in time the facts became less important than the symbolism. Newspapers began to call it 'impalement' and linked it to atrocities committed 'in the time of the Turks'. This was widely taken as a reference to Andrić's description of such an incident in *The Bridge over the Drina*.[55] The Serbian Academy of Sciences issued a long memorandum that referred to the Martinović case, and said it was 'reminiscent of the darkest days of Turkish impalement'. A writer who had researched the case put it more bluntly: 'Here we are dealing with the remains of the Ottoman empire . . . [Albanians] stuck him to a stake, this time just wrapped in a bottle. In the time of the Turks, Serbians were being impaled too, though even the Turks were not the ones who did it, but rather their servants – Arnauts [the old term for Albanians].'[56]

Albanians in general were implicated in a crime that was at best uncertain. In the end the evidence against them came down to the fact that this was how the Turks had behaved, and the Albanians were their surrogates. Ten years after the event, Julie Mertus observed that 'the power of the Martinović case lay in its ability to invoke the primary imagery of Serbian oppression: the Turkish barbarity of impaling.'[57]

The case illustrates the extraordinary invasiveness of *maledicta*, which can defy all truth and logic. Indeed, they rewrite and redefine the truth. In 1992 the Bosnian Serbs elected a psychiatrist from Montenegro, Radovan Karadžić, as their leader. Marko Vešović, a school friend of Karadžić, spoke about how his former classmate had become an author of genocide. Vešović blamed Karadžić's malign deeds on the fact that he was born a Montenegrin. 'Serbs are not a mythological people or nation. In this war we have to understand that the Montenegrins are a mythological people. You can say that in this war the Serbs were infected by Montenegrin mythology ... The main expressive tool of Montenegrins is hyperbole. In one minute they go to extremity ...' Then he mentioned the 'greatest words' of the Montenegrin poet Njegoš: 'Let the possible be. Let that happen which is not possible.' Radovan Karadžić fancied himself as a poet, in the manner of his heroic namesake. There is unmistakably an echo of this poetic theme in the Doctor's own verse: 'When I am in a kind of mad fire / I could do anything.'

Vešović described how it was 'an experience par excellence to sit in the winter nights in Montenegro and listen to the stories that were so rich in fantasies ... so detached from reality'.[58] As a political leader Dr Karadžić showed how with a lie here and a half-truth there, he could and would do anything. All his stories and maledictions against the Muslims of Bosnia were, in the end, narratives without boundaries. Dr Karadžić linked old texts to new fears, talked to his audience in terms they knew from their childhood. He made killing seem natural, normal, even predestined.[59] Calling up dark memories of an imagined past, he was like some demented Pied Piper:

> By means of a secret charm, to draw
> All creatures living beneath the sun,
> That creep or swim or fly or run,
> After me so as you never saw!
> And I chiefly use my charm
> On creatures that do people harm.[60]

PART FIVE

'Turban'd and Scimitar'd'

There is a dark little lithograph by Nicolas-Toussaint Charlet that shows how Parisians learned of the destruction of the Egyptian-Ottoman fleet at Navarino in 1827. Charlet takes us inside a very humble house, where the neighbours have come to hear the news. A child stands on a table with the newspaper and reads to the gathering of adults. Other children play and dogs roll around on the floor in a typically domestic scene. This picture tells us quite a lot about who was literate and who was not, and shows the process by which the written and printed word was spread far beyond the limits of those who could read for themselves. But since the first days of printing in the 1450s even the unlettered had been able to 'read' some things for themselves: pictures.

Images usually have a surface message, but for those who had learned the key, the pictures were charged with deeper meanings.[1] Even the illiterate were used to reading images. Not every household in England that owned a copy of John Foxe's *History of the Acts and Monuments of the Church* (1563), better known as his *Book of Martyrs*, was able to follow the text of its more than a thousand pages.[2] Nor would they necessarily have been interested in the early persecutions of Christians under long-forgotten Roman emperors. But they could understand the powerful woodcuts and would painstakingly decipher the short captions that described the torments suffered in their own day. For English Protestants these images and the stories were reminders of Catholic oppression and tyranny. Foxe's book was so enduringly popular that new editions were still being reprinted three centuries after its first publication.

Depictions of the Turk were similarly replete with symbolism. Swords, bows and spears took the place of the pyres on which the Protestant martyrs suffered, but were just as much perpetual reminders of violence, threat and danger. And sometimes sexual excess and perversity were suggested instead of savagery. In some images all these elements were present. Many Europeans were convinced that Muslims were pederasts and sodomites. The Turks were held to be devotees of impalement, one of the few forms of cruel punishment not practised in the West. The depictions of this implied both unnatural sex and excessive cruelty.[3]

But not all pictures were of this type. Many showed the solemnity of Ottoman life, the Turks' sumptuous apparel and their dramatic townscapes full of fine buildings. The Renaissance image of the Turk had multiple facets, some admiring and curious, some fearful. But just as it was difficult for a seventeenth-century Englishman to see a picture of Rome and not recall the Protestant martyrs burnt at Smithfield, the image of the East was tainted with dark or salacious overtones. Every depiction, as Lacan suggested, has been supercharged by the ways in which it has been used before.

Specific images developed slowly. At first few European artists had any notion of how to draw a 'Saracen', so they made them look like Westerners, wearing the same armour, riding the same horses and often carrying the same arms. So in a picture of the battle of Mansourah in 1250 (during the Seventh Crusade), Louis IX of France is only distinguishable from his Muslim opponents by the crown on his head.[4] Gradually, identifying marks appeared. In the windows of the Habsburg chapel at Königsfelden in Switzerland, Saracens were differentiated from Christians by the stylized scorpion emblems on their shields.[5] But they still wore European-style armour. It was in Spain, unsurprisingly, that more realistic images were first painted showing infidels as being very different from their Christian adversaries.[6] An altarpiece in Valencia showed King James I of Aragon aided by a saint in a battle with the Moors. His adversaries, with their dark features, flowing robes and heart-shaped shields, could never be mistaken for Christian knights.

The view of the Islamic world in the West was largely *imprinted* during the two centuries after the fall of Constantinople in 1453. This period coincided with the development and spread of the printed word and image in the West. By the late seventeenth century, what the infidel looked like, and how he behaved, had become common knowledge. Hostility to the Islamic world, as I have suggested earlier, had very distant antecedents.[7] But printed images, painted works of art, sculpture, and objets d'art gave that hostility a visual identity, which to some extent changed and shifted over time, as new elements were introduced. But the very basics that constituted the infidel enemy remained more or less the same, although their ordering and arrangement altered over the centuries. The process of identification was both visual and textual. Quite often images and words were not in harmony. Sometimes the pictures invoked older and more visceral responses than the written texts that accompanied them. The gap between image and text grew during the eighteenth century, narrowed during the nineteenth, and narrowed further in the twentieth century.

The actors also changed. Until the nineteenth century, the infidel was 'the Turk', but during the first half of that century, Europe also rediscovered what the travel writer A. W. Kinglake called in his book *Eothen* (1847) 'the True Bedouin'.[8] The desert-dweller was imbued by many Europeans with the qualities of the Noble Savage that could never be applied to the Ottomans. Forty years after *Eothen*, Charles Montagu Doughty published his *Travels in Arabia Deserta* in two substantial volumes. He made heroes both of the desert and those who lived in it. The French conquest of North Africa also threw up distinctively Arab heroes, such as the Algerian Abd el Kader, who became a latter-day Saladin and Noble Enemy. The change in the role of images in nineteenth-century publications meant a much greater diversity in what was depicted and how it was presented. Printed images became games that an increasingly educated market could read and decipher. As a consequence of that cultural shift, it is a mistake to search for a single image, the sense of unmitigated hostility of the Middle Ages. Images and texts in the nineteenth century and later are both more complex and more allusive, for they assume a literate audience. The *Punch* cartoons that I discussed in Chapter 10 have to be read in context: not for nothing was *Punch*'s secondary title 'The London Charivari', a colloquialism for a cacophony or hubbub. It took some skill to make sense of the discordance.

Yet despite these new styles and modes of presentation, older attitudes towards the infidel East still remained. Quite how this shadow first developed is not at all clear. Early (fifteenth- and sixteenth-century) images alone could not, I suggest, root the idea of the infidel particularly deeply. For one thing they did not exist in any great number.[9] About 'Turks' there was nothing like the plethora of mordantly abusive (and highly memorable) Lutheran images of the pope and his cardinals. Here images usually made visible and specific what had already been named. But with the 'Turk' the visual form sometimes anticipated the words. Take the deeply curved sabre, often with an absurdly broad tip that made it look like some kind of meat cleaver: we call it a scimitar. The first recorded usage of the word 'scimitar' in English to refer to a curved Turkish sword came in 1548, long after the image had become a visual signifier of the fierce and dangerous Turk. Quite where the word had originated no one knows. It was not a Turkish term, and has no obvious etymology.[10] Yet it became emblematic of the infidel. In, for example, Molière's comedy *Le Bourgeois Gentilhomme*, first performed in 1670, a strange 'Turkish Ceremony', delivered in an outlandish 'lingua franca', was used to ennoble the gullible Bourgeois, Monsieur Jourdain.[11] The objects that transform him into a noble Turk are a turban and a scimitar. The Bourgeois first appears 'dressed in the Turkish style, but without a turban [*turbanta*] or scimitar [*scarcina*]'. Then, ceremoniously, 'the Mufti' bestows these on him and, lo, he becomes a Turk. 'Scimitar' and 'turban' remained symbols of the Turk well into the twentieth century. Dr George Horton, American Consul General in Smyrna, in his Turcophobe book *The Blight of Asia*, published in 1922, described how 'the Turk, wherever his scimitar reached – degraded, defiled and defamed – blasting with eternal decay Roman, Latin civilization, until when all had gone he sat down satisfied with savagery to doze into hopeless decrepitude.'[12]

A 'scimitar' featured in the first printed images of the outlandish Turks that had been based on observation.[13] These appeared in *The Pilgrimage to Jerusalem* (*Peregrinatio in terram sanctam*) written by a secular official of the Cathedral of Mainz, Bernard von Breydenbach. In April 1483, he began a pilgrimage to the Holy Land in the company of the artist Erhard Reuwich and a number of aristocratic travellers. Breydenbach always intended an account printed with wood engravings since he made Reuwich sketch the places they visited, as well as a set of images of the people in the Holy Land. The most dramatic features of the book were the panoramic views of the ports the party passed through, especially the pull-out view of Venice, more than six feet in length, and one of the earliest depictions of the Queen of the Adriatic.

Reuwich, even in his panoramas, had a wonderful eye for social detail. He sometimes took a high-angle perspective, looking down on an urban scene, but also incorporating the surrounding countryside. Here we can see robbers holding up travellers and other crimes, women washing clothes, and punishments being executed. Breyden-bach's writing was competent, but it was Erhard Reuwich's woodcuts that made the work stand out. Other images were embedded in the text, such as a group of Turks riding, Saracens with their women, a Jew with bags of coin, travellers settling down to a meal. The image of the Jew struck an uncertain note, but the rest showed only curiosity and no obvious hostility.[14]

Breydenbach's book was first printed by Reuwich in Mainz in 1486, and subsequently appeared in some twelve editions, in Latin, Dutch, German, Spanish and French.[15] It became a staple ingredient in later compilations such as Samuel Purchas' famous compendium, or history of the world, *Purchas, His Pilgrimes*, first published in 1625.[16] In the dedication of the First Part to Charles, Prince of Wales (soon to be King Charles I), Purchas wrote that he had 'out of this chaos of confused intelligences framed this historical world by a new way of Eye Evidence.' 'Eye Evidence' was very different from the fantasies of Sir John Mandeville, and wrong or grotesquely opinionated though some of Purchas' witnesses may have been, they had indeed seen with their own eyes what they described.[17]

But with *The Pilgrimage to Jerusalem*, both author and illustrator had seen the sights – at the time this was highly unusual. Reuwich's depictions became one standard source for future images of the East. His Turks and Saracens wore turbans and flowing robes. They were all armed, with characteristic bows and 'scimitars'. Their faces were lean and hawkish. Yet not all readers would see the same images when they read Breydenbach's text. The French edition published in Lyons in 1488 was a free adaptation by Nicholas le Huen, with fanciful copper engravings instead of Reuwich's woodcut originals. Over time the range of images supposedly depicting the Ottomans, some based on 'Eye Evidence', increased enormously. Indeed, these depictions came to epitomize the mysterious East in all its aspects. In many biblical scenes, Jews of the time of Jesus Christ wore the flowing robes and capacious turbans of sixteenth-century Turks.

These same elements – robes, curved swords and turbans – became (with the omnipresent crescent) the emblems of a mortal enemy. In *Othello*, Shakespeare succinctly described the enemy (the 'circumcised dog') in terms his audience would recognize. He calls him 'a malignant and a *turbaned* Turk'.[18] Suggestive details were essential. In 1522, the well-known Nuremberg artist Hans Sebald Beham produced a single-sheet engraving of the contemporary Turkish attack on the island of Rhodes, then occupied by the Knights of St John. Some of the details seem out of place. Beham's besieged city of Rhodes looks like a south German town. His Turks fire Western-type field guns, and advance like the German mercenary infantry, known as *lands-knechts*, on the breaches in the city walls. Their ships at sea are pot-bellied Atlantic vessels, not sleek Mediterranean galleys.

But a few deft symbolic touches specified an unmistakably Eastern and mighty enemy.[19] The attackers all wear turbans, they carry curved swords. They have Eastern-style war tents, each decorated with a crescent half-moon, while on the foreshore an unfortunate (and we presume) Christian has been impaled on a stake. The Turks appear as disciplined and implacable opponents. Beham's large engraved image was intended for an affluent audience, but similar visual components appeared on numerous cheaper pamphlets and broadsheets in Germany in the first half of the sixteenth century. Also in 1522, an anonymous pamphlet called *A Little Book about the Turks: A Useful Discourse or Conversation among Several People* went through four editions, and was reprinted again in 1527 and 1537.[20] There were many more 'informative' publications, all dwelling on the new Turkish danger, a powerful enemy who had captured the impregnable island of Rhodes and the well-defended fortress of Belgrade within a few months. Most of these had very short texts of four or five pages only, and many had illustrated covers or some engravings within.

How people 'read' these pamphlets and illustrated books is imposs-ible to know.[21] But the images themselves seem to me to provide the key. Michel de Certeau devised a wonderfully vivid phrase – 'a laminated text' – to describe the situation where two different and contrary types of material are bonded together.[22] He was thinking about types of written text and not of the relationship between image and text, but the tensions I found were similar to the examples that he gave. Laminating an image to a text on the same page creates instability. The text is read sequentially, from the top left to the bottom right of the page; anything interrupting that flow distorts meaning. So even the most appropriate image is never wholly harmonious with the text. The image is there to attract attention. It is read or understood in ways very different from the words that surround it.

The repertoire available to a woodcut artist was much more limited than the resources available to a writer. In practice, woodcuts were intended to be simple and dramatic, and so often, in this context, heightened the fierce and bellicose qualities of the Muslim infidels. When the printer Johann Haselberg wrote and published his own pamphlet in 1530, exhorting Emperor Charles V to attack the Turk, he commissioned a front cover depicting the two armies. The turbaned host led by Sultan Suleiman, 'the arch-enemy of the Christian faith', confronts the forces of Christendom led by Emperor Charles. The latter wears peacock's feathers on his helmet, symbolizing immortality and resurrection. The cover image strongly influenced how the inside text was understood. Then, as now, a reader absorbed the text with that image in mind.

In the period bounded by the Turkish destruction of the Hungarians at the battle of Mohacs in 1526 and the Turkish defeat at Lepanto in 1571 ever more potent and complex ways of portraying the malevolent and powerful Ottomans were devised. Beham's fairly simple imagery was superseded by increasingly convoluted designs. At the end of the sixteenth century, the court artists of Charles V's great-nephew, Emperor Rudolf II, got to work on the 'Turkish Menace', and produced Baroque masterpieces. However, despite their sophistication, the images were still governed by the same limited range of basic themes that reached back to the *incunabula*, the very first printed books. Jan Müller's engravings from this era show swords and scimitars, bows and arrows, and even grander turbans. These elements remained the fundamental visual signature of the Turk.

The arrangement and deployment of these symbols – weapons and costume – began to alter subtly in the first decades of the eighteenth century in part, remarkably, as a result of a shared interest in flowers. Flowers had been highly visible in the Ottoman capital from the mid sixteenth century. By the 1630s the famous Turkish traveller Evliya Chelebi was estimating that there were some 300 florists in Constantinople. The open meadows along the Golden Horn were filled with tulips and lilacs in the spring and the lilacs' scent was intoxicating. The introduction of the tulip to Europe from Turkey in the mid sixteenth century, first to Augsburg in 1559, then to Antwerp and the Habsburg domains in the Netherlands between 1562 and 1583, revived a passion for flowers and gardens in the West. Mass production of blooms developed into an industry in the Netherlands, and tulip bulbs were exported across Europe. The Margrave of the small state of Baden Durlach had more than 4,000 tulips in his garden by 1636, all carefully listed in his garden registers.[23]

This 'Tulipomania' that gripped Europe during the seventeenth century eventually subsided (after making many fortunes and breaking many more). But it had an aftershock in the Ottoman domains early in the eighteenth century. Sultan Ahmed III had an excessive passion for tulips, and his reign, between 1703 and 1730, became known as _lale devri_, 'the Tulip Era'. The blooms that decorated his palaces were not the wild native Turkish or Persian varieties but the products of European horticultural ingenuity. These exotic (and often diseased) specimens, as gaudy as parrots, marbled in different colours, were called 'Bizarres' or 'Fantasticks'. They were very different from the simple slender flowers long revered by the Turks. Yet they were ravishing and infinitely seductive to the Ottoman taste. The French Ambassador reported in 1726 that there were

500,000 bulbs in the Grand Vizier's garden. When the Tulips are in flower and the Grand Vizier wants to show them off to the Grand Seigneur [the sultan] they take care to fill any spaces with Tulips picked from other gardens and put in bottles. At every fourth flower, candles are set into the ground at the same height as the Tulips and the pathways are decorated with cages of all sorts of birds. All the trellis work is bordered with flowers in vases, and lit by a vast number of crystal lamps of various colours.[24]

This was not quite the old image of cruel barbarity.

It is impossible to be precise about the date but certainly beginning in the Tulip Era the symbolic connotations of 'the Turk' began to gather new and extended meanings. The similarity of the tulip's appearance to a turban was first noted by the Habsburg Ambassador to Constantinople Ghislain de Busbecq in the 1550s. He was passionate about flowers and, based upon this visual connection, mistakenly gave the tulips their name – a corruption of the Turkish for turban, *tulban*. But turbans, once the symbol of Eastern violence, now acquired an additional, softer connection. When the first Ottoman embassies came to France in the 1720s, turbans, heavy silks, furs and flowing robes suddenly became immensely desirable. The fashion for being painted in Oriental dress, *à la Turque*, spread throughout Europe's aristocracies. For the West, flowers, silks and flowing robes suggested an indolent life rather than the rigours of the field of battle (although the evidence of earlier images showed that turbans and kaftans had done nothing to hinder the Ottomans in war).

A la Turque was also a fashion suggestive of the boudoir, and highly eroticized images of the Ottomans began to proliferate. Where once the limitless and boundless energy of the sultan and his pashas had evoked blood and gore, now images of them suggested ravening lust, raw sex and brutal passions in the *harem*.[25] Early in the nineteenth century, Thomas Rowlandson's satires on *The Harem* depicted this connection with an obscene directness, but the same association appeared in myriad if less direct images. The scene had shifted from the field of glory to the bedroom. The 'young sultanas in the seraglio' in the *harem* of little girls (and the *harem* of little boys) in the Marquis de Sade's *One Hundred and Twenty Days of Sodom* were the dark side of *à la Turque*.[26]

There is no accurate total for images mass-produced in the Western world between 1480 and 1800. In seventeenth-century Netherlands alone the number reaches the many millions.[27] Cheap popular literature often had a decorative cover image, often disconnected from the detail of the text. The picture defined the genre, such as a horrible murder or a romance. But by the eighteenth century a more elevated role for the printed image had also emerged. The 'pattern book' for this concept of publication was the great *Encyclopédie* published by Denis Diderot between 1751 and 1772, in seventeen volumes of text and eleven volumes of plates.[28] Diderot had originally intended a close integration between words and images, but the circumstances of the publication of the *Encyclopédie* and the physical separation of images from related text made this impossible. In handling words and images together the *Encyclopédie* had a number of successful precursors. One of the most ambitious was *The Ceremonies and Religious Customs of the Various Nations of the Known World*, in seven volumes, published by the noted engraver Bernard Picard.[29]

Born a Catholic in Paris, Picard's dazzling talent as a draughtsman first emerged during his training at the Académie Royale. But in his thirty-seventh year he settled in Amsterdam and converted to Protestantism. He was already an established and successful engraver when he conceived the idea of a comprehensive and comparative study of all the religions of the world. The nineteenth-century Catholic writer Count Joseph de Maistre lambasted Picard's 'Protestant burin' because he attacked the Spanish Inquisition which Maistre sought to defend.[30] This trivialized Picard's objective, which was to depict all religions equally. The texts of the many editions of the book vary considerably. The first version, published in Amsterdam between 1733 and 1743, was the work in the form that Picard intended. In the second part of the seventh volume, in a Note to the Reader (*Avis au lecteur*), he denounced the 1741 French edition, which had been 'adjusted' to meet the requirements of the censor. The Amsterdam volume reprinted the new material that had offended Picard. The various English editions were abridged and reworked. But while the texts altered, the pictures remained. In one sense, this is not surprising: Picard's renown was as an engraver, and the texts were written and rewritten by a number of different authors, around his images.

However, it is odd that one particular illustration, perhaps the most sophisticated in the entire work, should have escaped the censor's attention. In the seventeenth century the frontispiece – inside the book, usually facing the title page – had developed as a visual epitome of the book, rather like the dustjacket in the twentieth century. By the eighteenth century readers had become used to these visual arguments.[31] Picard's engraving was extraordinarily complex, and to make sure there was no ambiguity he provided a long caption. But he did not describe in this everything that he showed. Protestant sectarians stand side by side with the bishops and priests of the Catholic Church. Behind them are pagodas and fanciful idols, while to one side animists worship animals and the powers of Nature. But in the foreground there is a little cliff, no more than a few feet high, and on the ground at the foot of that cliff sit the Muslims.[32] The reader immediately inferred by their clothes, weapons and wild look that these were Muslims. Another sure sign was that they are grouped around a signature camel. It was no accident that they sit next to the Mouth of Hell, with the anguished faces of the damned grimacing through the thick iron grille. This single image, unlike any other in the many volumes of Picard's 'scientific' history, captured an idea that *every* Christian would recognize: the Muslim infidels were 'below' every other faith and they were close to Hell's Mouth, through which they might soon pass. This was an impression that any Western reader would receive from this frontispiece, the essence of the entire work. It expresses the great power of the infidel stereotype, built up over centuries, despite Picard's intention to cleanse himself of all prejudice.

The Ceremonies and Religious Customs is an early example of the Enlightenment's desire to document the known universe in all its aspects. This vast task included recording the mysterious world of the East, but this project was flawed. Europeans instinctively believed in the immutable timelessness of the East, and this attitude suffused many of the great projects of accumulated knowledge. One of the first was Count Luigi Ferdinando Marsigli's survey of the military power of the Ottoman Empire. Marsigli had made a surreptitious visit to the Ottoman lands between 1679 and 1680, and wrote the text of his report on his return.[33] Fifty years later, two years after Marsigli's death in 1730, it was published. He had been working on the illustrations up to a few days before his death.[34] But by that time, the military structure of the Ottomans was not the powerful machine it had been in the period before the disastrous failure outside Vienna in 1683.

Nothing of this decline appears in the book as published. It was copiously illustrated, and Marsigli's manuscripts in the library of the Royal Armoury in Stockholm show a neatly handwritten text with drawings and watercolours in position. For the rest of the eighteenth century (and bizarrely, beyond) Marsigli's seventeenth-century vision was taken to be a largely up-to-date statement on Ottoman military might. His book was published in French, then in Italian, and even, in 1737, in St Petersburg in a Russian edition.[35] A more remarkable suspension of temporality took place with the translation of the

Imperial Ambassador Busbecq's famous Latin *Letters* into English.
Busbecq described the Ottoman Empire as he remembered it from the
1550s. In 1744, his *Letters* were marketed in English by an enterprising
bookshop/publisher as 'containing the most accurate account of the
Turks, and neighbouring nations'.[36]

Through the eighteenth century an ever-growing number of
Western artists visited the Ottoman domains and painted or drew
what they saw. Some, like Jean-Baptiste Van Moeur and Jean-Etienne
Liotard, spent long periods in Constantinople, but the world they
depicted was part real and part fantasy. Liotard, and others, specialized
in painting Westerners in Constantinople dressed in authentic Ottoman costumes. Antoine de Favrey's picture of 1754 was entitled
Turkish Women, but it is highly unlikely that his models were, as he
suggested, Ottoman Muslim women. The images these artists created
were much more exact and 'accurate' than those produced a century
before. But they also painted for a market that demanded that they
portray what they could not possibly have seen. No male artist could
have entered a woman's bathhouse or the private quarters of an
Ottoman house where the women and children lived. Fleeting impressions became fixed as an immovable depiction of the empire. The
artists painted the formal ceremonial court dress of Ottoman officials
on grand state occasions. The Western audience assumed that these
were the clothes Ottomans wore every day, winter and summer.
European artists lived among Western diplomats and expatriates, or
among the Ottoman Christian or Jewish communities. Not surprisingly, they reflected the mores, interests and prejudices of their hosts.

However, there was one huge work in the eighteenth century
on the Ottoman Empire that presented what the author, Ignatius
Mouradgea d'Ohsson, saw as the empire's underlying reality. He was
determined, for the first time, systematically to show the Ottoman
world to the West, faithfully illustrating the text so that word and
image told the same story in a *General Picture* [Tableau général] *of the
Ottoman Empire. Divided into Two Parts, of which One Contains the
Muhammadan Legislation, the Other the History of the Ottoman Empire.*
This aim was born out of frustration. Half-Armenian, half-French,
Catholic, born an Ottoman subject, and spending his life until middle
age in the Ottoman domains, he was increasingly angered by the
plethora of books and images that failed to portray that world as he

knew it. In his Preamble (*Discours préliminaire*) he was very precise about his intention. Other authors, he declared, had only looked at the surface of this vast state, 'without understanding the [underlying] causes. Illusions and error result from these distant, superficial and fleeting perspectives.' This misapprehension had serious conse-quences. 'Absolute ignorance' and 'barbarism', said D'Ohsson, were the usual epithets applied in Europe to the Ottomans. In reality he was even more of an enthusiast for the empire than most Muslim Ottomans. One, Ebu Bekir Ratib, Ottoman ambassador to Vienna in 1792, wrote that 'God knows, he is so zealous for the Sublime State that if I say [he is] more so than we [are], I would not be speaking falsely.'[37]

D'Ohsson's ambition for his project knew no bounds. His book was to be published by the Royal Press, the Imprimerie de Monsieur, using the finest printers in Paris run by the Didot family. The engrav-ings were to be carried out by Charles-Nicolas Cochin, the best practitioner of the day. The three elephant folio volumes, and the seven smaller octavo volumes of the 'popular' edition, contained only the smaller part of his vaunting vision.[38] Carter Findley described this as 'a vast never-to-be-completed survey of Islamic and pre-Islamic history, from ancient Egypt and Iran to the Mongols; this was to be followed by a history of the Ottoman Empire [from distant origins to 1774], and then – this part being the *Tableau général* – the legislation of the Ottoman Empire.'[39] Thus, only one aspect of the grand plan ever emerged into print in its full glory. Reading it now, it seems like a precursor (in publishing terms) of the grandest publication of the nineteenth century: the French Imperial *Description of Egypt* (*Descrip-tion de l'Egypte*). D'Ohsson's first two huge volumes published in the late 1780s must have been known to Napoleon as he planned to immortalize his own entry into Egypt in 1798–9.

For almost two centuries 'M. de M★★★ d'Ohsson', has seemed as Romantic and mysterious a character as Alexander Dumas's Count of Monte Cristo. Was the Baron D'Ohsson really the descendant of an ancient Swedish noble family, or was he simply an Armenian trader who worked in the Swedish embassy in Constantinople? He was the son of Oannes Mouradgea, an Ottoman Armenian in the service of the Swedish consulate in Izmir, and Claire Pagy, the daughter of a French consular clerk in the same port. In 1740 Ignatius was born in

Pera, a European quarter of Constantinople across the Golden Horn. He followed his father and became a translator to the Swedish embassy in 1763; by 1768 he was Chief Translator. He was appointed Chargé d'Affaires in 1795, and later briefly held the highest post in the Constantinople embassy, Head of Mission.

An advantageous marriage to the daughter of a rich Armenian merchant banker, Abraham Kuliyan, had financed a style of life far beyond his income as a translator. By 1780, Ignatius was also in business with his father-in-law, as well as working for the embassy. In 1786, the King of Sweden allowed him to change his name in honour of an uncle who had shown him 'paternal kindness'. This figure was, it seemed, conveniently called D'Ohsson, an imaginative rendering by Ignatius of his uncle's Armenian patronymic Tosunyan, which meant, roughly, 'raging bull'. This francophone appellation carried him a long way. In 1780, he was given a Swedish title of nobility, and he progressed from 'le Sieur Mouradgea' through 'le Chevalier de Mouradgea' to, finally, 'le Chevalier d'Ohsson'. At the French court he presented himself as an unambiguously Oriental figure. Amid the *perruques*, satins and silks, he strode about in the flowing robes of an Ottoman official and the tall and peaked fur hat worn by embassy translators. His wife died in 1782, and from 1784–92, he lived in Paris to oversee the publication of his great work.

The project had been in his mind since 1764, when he read one of the first Turkish printed books from the long-defunct press of Ibrahim Müteferrika, which I shall discuss in the next chapter. D'Ohsson planned his *Tableau* with care over many years. He employed artists to paint and draw locations, costumes and grand events in conditions of secrecy. His governing principles were accuracy and utility, and the result was a work that lacked the sensationalism of the many Western images. The most telling example of this difference is in his engraver's portrayal of the women's bath. By the late eighteenth century this had already become a site of fevered lubricity for Westerners. What happened within could only be imagined, since men had no access. But the later paintings by Ingres of *The Bath* was both the apogee of a long tradition of depicting naked female flesh en masse and also the beginning of a fertile theme in Orientalist art. How did D'Ohsson's book display the women's (as well as the separate men's) bath house? The only naked flesh on show was that of a mother discreetly feeding her infant; everyone else was clothed in the tradition of Eastern modesty. Even on this point, where his Western audience expected a different (and possibly titillating) vision of the Ottomans, D'Ohsson adhered to what he knew to be true.

The first volume of the *de luxe* edition appeared in 1787, the second in 1789. The third and final volume was published in 1820, thirteen years after his death, by his son Abraham. Publication of what he hoped would be a mass-market edition began in 1788, but that too was only completed in 1824. Plans for an English translation never came to fruition, nor did schemes for a grand Viennese German-language edition, although parts did appear in German, Swedish and Russian, while a curious hybrid version was published in Philadelphia in 1788. The latter held out the allure of 'Exhibiting Many Curious Pieces of the Eastern Hemisphere, relative to the Christian and Jewish Dispensation; with various Rites and Mysteries of the Oriental Freemasons'. D'Ohsson's dignified presentation of a true image of the East had been debased. There is an extraordinary graphic quality to both his writing and to the carefully designed images that make his words real. But the market demanded something different: 'Curious Pieces', depicting Oriental lust, despotism and cruelty. By the time that publication was finally completed, any substantial audience for the *Tableau* was about to vanish. After the Massacre of Chios in 1822, few people in France wanted to read or see anything that presented the Ottomans in a benign light.

D'Ohsson's attempt to defy the dominant discourse was doomed to failure: not even three volumes in elephant folio could disrupt it. But the form that the discourse took was not immobile. The West's image of the Ottoman East, Asli Çirakman suggests, moved from a wide disparity of conflicting views in the sixteenth and seventeenth centuries to a single consistent hostility in the eighteenth. However, this process of change continued, and not always in the same direction. In her view, in the first period the image was a simple tyranny, in the second it appeared as a more complex despotism.[40] But if we take the story forward into the nineteenth century, the shape changes again. After 1829, when the Ottomans abandoned the seductive silks and furs and put aside the turban in favour of the fez and Stambouline frock coat, they began to be depicted in the West as new men, set on the path of progress. Yet they still carried the irredeemable taint of their origins, as Gladstone presented it in his diatribe of 1876:

They are not the mild Mahometans of India, nor the chivalrous Saladins of Syria, nor the cultured Moors of Spain. They were, on the whole, from the black day when they first entered Europe, the one great anti-human specimen of humanity . . . For the guide of this life, they had a relentless fatalism: for its reward hereafter, a sensual paradise.[41]

Over the centuries, under Western eyes, the Muslim infidel had assumed many different guises.[42] They had been *Agarenes, Ishmaelites, Saracens, Moors, Turks, Tartars, Bedouins, Arabs.* With each iteration the image of the infidel became more precise. Visually speaking, an Agarene or an Ishmaelite or even a Saracen has no particular shape. It is just a name. But Moors, Turks, or Bedouins have a very precise and definite visual image. They have become fixed, in the sense that a photographic image is chemically 'fixed' and made permanent, by printed images and by works of art.

13

The Black Art

A printing press is a machine.[1] It has no morality. But its potential power is awesome. The visionary poet (and working printer) William Blake imagined that he visited a 'printing house in Hell'. There he 'saw the method in which knowledge is transmitted from generation to generation' and 'printing in the infernal method, by corrosives, which in Hell are salutary and medicinal . . . displaying the infinite which was hid.' And, as Blake observed, 'if the doors of perception were cleansed every thing would appear to man as it is, infinite'.[2] He articulated, in an extreme form, his contemporaries' general confidence in the power of the printing press as a moral agent. This had distant roots, but in the Enlightenment the magical agency of the press to transform society became a near-universal belief. Censorship was the negative recognition of this absolute credence, and the eighteenth-century relaxation of control over the printed word (in the Habsburg domains and in Russia) was a short-lived experiment. But what was the state of those who did not enjoy the benefit of the Printed Word? They lived in an unimaginable darkness, waiting and longing for the coming of the light. And what of a government that deliberately turned its back upon the printing press? It could only be considered as the epitome of barbarism.

That was precisely the position of the Ottoman Empire and the infidel East. The West believed that the Ottomans 'prohibited' the printing press because of their obscurantist faith – Islam. The Turks' refusal to accept this unique benison from the West was an indication of their deep and fundamental wickedness. By sustaining ignorance they perpetuated the despotism described by Asli Çirakman.[3] I believe that the debate over printing was the final formulation of the Western malediction of the Eastern infidel, but it was a condemnation carefully adjusted and attuned to the mores of an Enlightened age. What had begun with the Muslim as 'the Abomination of Desolation', then continued with 'the Antichrist', 'the malignant foe' and all the other epithets, ended with a portrayal of debased ignorance. This is the stereotype that has come through to the present day, and still flourishes in the West, but I believe that the Ottoman 'failure' to adopt the printing press was the first point at which this prejudice was systematically articulated.

If I am right, then this obscure issue – whether or not some piece of machinery was or was not used at the far end of the Mediterranean – acquires a much deeper symbolic resonance. The shock of Westerners about the 'intellectual desert' in the East was a commonplace observation. The French traveller and savant C. F. Volney wrote a hugely popular account of his travels to Syria and Egypt between 1783 and 1785. He was especially appalled at the lack of books. He portrayed a stark contrast: in France reading was common, but 'in the East, nothing is rarer'. Over the space of six months in the Levantine provinces of the empire he found a number of texts, but what books he discovered were mostly ancient works on grammar and eloquence, and interpretations of the Qur'an. As far as any other topic was concerned, virtually nothing existed: 'very few histories, tales and novels. I only saw two copies of *One Thousand and One Nights*.' Finally he decided that it was not so much that there were few good books in the East, but more that there were hardly any books at all. The reason was clear: 'in this country all books are written by hand.' Volney's conclusion was that without more books there could not be any major change or advance in the Ottoman Empire.

He saw relatively little merit in Arabic, which simply rendered printing difficult.

The costs of printing are considerable, especially considering that paper has to be imported from Europe and the hand work is very slow. The former problem could be quite simply resolved, but the latter needs a more radical solution. Arabic characters have to be joined by hand, and to join and align them requires great care, and careful attention to each letter. Moreover, the way the letters join depends on where they come in the sentence, and there are even different varieties of letters at the beginning and end of a word. Finally there are many double letters. These cannot be made by simply doubling the existing letters. A compositor has to walk up and down a table eighteen feet long and find the letters which are contained in nine hundred type boxes. All these time-wasting operations mean that Arabic printers can never achieve the greater perfection of our own presses.[4]

Volney's solution was a comprehensive reformation of the inconvenient script.[5] He was shrewd enough to recognize that simply introducing the printing press alone was no answer to a much more fundamental problem: what was needed was a wholesale transformation of Eastern society, beginning with its language.

In 1791, he returned to the topic. In his much-translated observations on an apocalyptic 'Clash of Civilizations', which he called *The Ruins, or, Meditations on the Revolutions of Empires and the Laws of Nature*, he began his *Journey* through the past 'in the Ottoman dominions and through those provinces which were anciently the kingdoms of Egypt and Syria'. His dire prediction was based upon what he had seen of these lands under Ottoman rule; in Chapter 12, 'The Lessons of the Past Repeated on the Present', he laid out the imminent doom of the Ottoman Empire. 'Turkish' became an adjective evidencing contempt and condemnation: so China, where cruelty reigned, had 'a truly *Turkish* government'. Moreover, he was sure that like the Muslim world 'as long as the Chinese world shall in writing make use of their present characters, they can be expected to make no progress in civilisation.'[6] What did Europe have that the Ottoman and the Chinese empires did not? Volney had no doubts, and expressed an idea that remains as potent in our day, a confident vision fulfilled even more successfully by our electronic media. They lacked 'The gift of heavenly Genius, the holy art of printing, having furnished the means of communicating in an instant the same idea to millions of men and of fixing it in a durable manner, beyond the power of tyrants to arrest or annihilate.'[7]

Given the power that attached to the 'holy art' we need to disentangle the reasons that the infidel East apparently spurned it. The failure to adopt Gutenberg's new art became a touchstone of the essential backwardness of Muslims. From the eighteenth century, it was a convenient explanation for the growing divergence of the Western and Eastern worlds, with the West looking forward and the East looking backward. It has become part of a historical paradigm, what the historian of science Thomas Kuhn called the 'normal' state of understanding. To change or even question that norm is to enter a maelstrom. It is easier to pose the question as a counterfactual, a 'what if'.[8] *What if* Mehmed II 'the Conqueror', to cap his victory at Constantinople in 1453, had paid the debts of the floundering Mainz entrepreneur Johann Gutenberg, and shipped his printing press to the Old Palace above the Bosphorus? It is perhaps not such a foolish premise, knowing what we do of both Mehmed's passions and Gutenberg's financial circumstances. Nor is it entirely fanciful, because the Islamic world had already pioneered a development much more far reaching than Gutenberg's trio of innovations – reusable metal type, the casting mould and the printing press.

It was paper more than print that revolutionized the world. Take another counterfactual: *what if* Johann Gutenberg had had to print his great Bible on the only material available in 1455: *sheep, cow and goat skins*? What would have happened to his great invention if there had been no paper in western Europe? The role of paper in the printing revolution has been strangely passed over.[9] Yet without paper, transmitted from China to the Muslim world, and thence to Europe, the development of publishing in Europe is virtually unimaginable.

The production of paper in Europe began in Italy in the thirteenth century, at Amalfi, south-east of Naples, and at Fabriano, north of Assisi. It was said that here they had learned the secrets of papermaking from the Moors of Xativa, near Valencia. Both Italian towns managed to make a paper of high quality, which they then shipped back to the Islamic world, still the main market for this product. It was not until 1390 that papermaking moved north of the Alps, with a Nuremberg city official, Ulmann Stromeir, converting his flour mill outside the city into a paper mill, worked by skilled Italians.[10] But Italian papers were superior to all others, both in the quality of the writing surface and durability. Sultan Mehmed II bought paper from Italy for his scribes, but also set up his own paper mill beside the stream called the Kagithane at the head of the Golden Horn.[11] Although papermaking rose and declined in the various centres of production in the Islamic lands, it never failed entirely, despite the competition from Italy and later from other parts of Europe. Muslim papermakers continued to experiment and develop new types of paper for different needs certainly until the nineteenth century and, I believe, up to the present.

Contrast this spirit of enterprise with the Islamic obscurantism that supposedly prevented the introduction of Gutenberg's press. Or, perhaps we should think of it as a double dose of conservatism, since the Islamic culture that had adopted Chinese paper evidently failed to adopt Chinese printing from the same source, centuries before Gutenberg. If this were true, it might constitute clear evidence of some innate fear of innovation. But it does not. The prohibition on printing and the printed book is a topic shrouded in mystery, oddly so given the importance that has been attached to it in the West.[12] The same story is repeated by a number of visitors to the Ottoman Empire. A prime source was the sixteenth-century French traveller and historiographer to the court of Catherine de Medici, André Thevet. He was told that

Greeks, Armenians, Mingrelians, Abyssinians, Turks, Moors, Arabs and Tartars only write their books by hand. Among the Turks they follow the decree of Bajezid, the second of that name their Emperor, proclaimed in 1483, on pain of death, not to read printed books, which ordinance was confirmed by Selim the first of that name his son, in 1515.[13]

But Walid Gdoura, author of the major study on the slow development of printing in the Middle East, is rightly sceptical about these second-hand accounts. I suspect the ideas about an Islamic prohibition on printing emerged from an Islamic anathema on images.[14]

Here we might seem to be on more solid ground. The prohibition on images has been held to be a total, permanent and unalterable distinction between East and West. It was commented upon from the first centuries of contact, and was confirmed by Muslim disgust at the use of religious images in the Crusader states. But it is not true in these absolute terms. There had been a long tradition of human and animal depiction in the Muslim East, which proliferated under the Ummayad caliphates in both the Levant and in Spain, and which can still be seen in the objects that have survived from their palaces.[15] Visual and pictorial arts flourished in private under the Ottomans, and also, pre-eminently, in Persia and in Mughal India. But unlike in the Christian realm, in the Muslim world recognizable human images (and those of animals) played no part in religious art.[16] If, exceptionally, the Prophet Mohammed or one of his successors were depicted for any reason, their faces were almost always veiled and 'invisible'.

So, the theoretical absolutes crumble and the supposedly immutable mutates. The deeper we dig into the issue of images and of printing, at every point we discover there are unexpected ambiguities. Where the long-established assumptions about the East are tested, anomalies, divergence from the rule and exceptions immediately emerge. Daniel Goffman has written that the reality of the Ottoman lands was a 'world governed by exceptions'.[17] This is a striking revision to long-held attitudes. Most writing about the Eastern world has hitherto assumed that the ordering of life as written down in legislation, regulations and codes of precedence and behaviour corresponded precisely to the everyday reality. For this reason Busbecq, writing in the sixteenth century, was still a valued authority in the eighteenth. Many Easterners have also believed in the protective value of a settled order within their world. Those who visited the West often perceived this quality of orderliness to be the best feature of their own world by comparison with what they saw as the turmoil of the West.[18]

But their Eastern world was no more completely static than the West was rootless and in perpetual flux. An important distinction concerns the printing press. The reasons that the Eastern world did not adopt the printing press when it first became available in the fifteenth century were neither to do with wilful obscurantism nor with a naïve fear of the printed word. There were other more mundane reasons. Over many centuries, the Arabic script had proved extraordinarily successful in the East. It was used for writing Arabic, Turkish, Persian and Hebrew. It was not, however, necessarily very well adapted to transmuting the spoken form of any of these languages into printed form. There are twenty-eight phonemes in spoken Arabic, represented by eighteen written characters. Dots were marked over and under some letters, inflecting and altering their sounds, while vowels were often not written down at all. Even when speaking in Arabic, let alone in the other tongues for which the script was used, an oral source rather than a written text was often the more reliable, especially if the speaker had memorized the words which he (or she) had heard.

The development of the manuscript tradition in the West through-out the Middle Ages led to a certain codification of practices by scribes, but there were many variants and irregularities, and in certain areas, like the courtroom, the *spoken* record remained the true and accurate text. (Under some circumstances the written text is still considered to be secondary.[19]) The superiority of the spoken form was acknowledged but its status was diminishing even before the age of print. With printing, conventions were gradually standardized, and variants were discarded. In fifteenth-century England, the leading printer William Caxton did much to fix the London dialect as the form for the printed book. Through the sixteenth and seventeenth centuries printers progressively dropped the accidentals and variant letter forms when they could, because more letters just increased their costs, both in buying type characters and by slowing the work of the typesetters. The same processes of 'refinement' took place in both French and German.

Typesetting in Arabic posed unique problems. As Volney first observed, printing was not easy in Arabic. Jonathan Bloom has analysed why. Arabic is essentially a cursive written language, whereas all European languages are made up of individual letters that adapted readily to typesetting words letter by letter. Also the Arabic letter forms change, depending on where in the word they appear. The creation and use of Arabic founts in the West was not something that most commercial printers would sensibly undertake: they would need a minimum of 500 different pieces of type. The fount used by Napoleon to print documents in Arabic during his invasion of Egypt in 1798 had 700 different characters. As a rough comparison, a European 'Roman' typeface might contain about 250 different variants of type (upper case, lower case, punctuation symbols, and so on). All the early Western ventures in Italy and elsewhere to create Arabic-type founts usually needed the support by a patron with deep pockets (such as Cardinal Ferdinando di Medici in 1585) who supported the venture for ideological motives or for reasons of prestige.[20] One of the immediate objectives was to provide liturgical material for eastern Christians whose language was Arabic. Rome feared they might otherwise be won over to Protestantism through printed texts in Arabic or Ottoman Turkish supplied by heretics from the Netherlands, England, Sweden or Germany.[21]

Not many books in Arabic script were produced in Europe and none could accommodate all the subtleties and flourishes of the calligraphic Arabic texts. In the sixteenth and seventeenth centuries, they compared unfavourably with the work of a skilled copyist in the Ottoman domains. There was no shortage of those willing to enter this profession. Luigi Ferdinando Marsigli suggested that there were more than 80,000 scribes working in Constantinople in the 1680s, although his figure must have included all the numerous letter-writers as well as the book-copyists. It was a common saying that 'the Qur'an was revealed in Mecca, recited in Egypt, and written in Istanbul.' The manner of book production in the East was normally oral: a scholar would dictate from memory to a battery of scribes. In Christendom, Saint Thomas Aquinas had been renowned for dictating four books in the same session to four different secretaries, switching back and forth from secretary to secretary to keep up the pace of work.

For the Muslim world the process was more mechanical. Perhaps a dozen copyists would inscribe the same text from a single dictation. Once it was completed, each scribe would read back what he had written down to ensure accuracy, and the scholar would certify the copy as correct. Very quickly more than a hundred copies could be produced by systematic copying and verification.[22] There was also a great number of libraries in the Muslim world, initially on a far larger scale than those in the West. Many were part of mosque complexes and most of their texts were religious in nature.[23] But there was also a tradition of private book collections being open to the public. There were large public libraries in the capital, but in many smaller places as well. In Jerusalem, the Khalili collection had more than 7,000 manuscripts in Arabic, while the Ragib al-Khalidi collection contained more than 10,000 works in Arabic, Turkish and Persian when it opened to the public as the Maktubat al-Halidja early in the twentieth century.[24]

In the first two centuries after Gutenberg, the benefits of print must have seemed questionable within an Eastern world that used the Arabic script. But by the end of the seventeenth century it was evident that for anything of a technical nature, the printed text had great advantages. However, the introduction of this Western innovation would trample on several powerful vested interests. The first were the scribes and clerks upon whom the entire Ottoman administration depended; and the second were the religious class, *ulema*, who controlled the mosques, where much of the book-copying was carried out, and the majority of publicly accessible texts in their libraries. The advocates of printing were careful to take account of the objections of the *ulema*. The document submitted by a Transylvanian convert to Islam named Ibrahim Müteferrika in 1726 to the Grand Vizier stressed the many benefits of the new technique, but especially 'the publication of dictionaries, histories, medical texts and science books, philosophy and astronomy books, and information about nature, geography and travelogues'. Just as telling, and despite an assertion that the 'illustrious Ottoman state possesses thunderous cannons, fierce incendiaries and powerful muskets' and thus had nothing to learn from the West in the art of war, military technology was uppermost in the minds of the Ottoman government.[25] For thirty years after the failure to take Vienna in 1683, the Ottomans had consistently been beaten by the Habsburg armies. They hoped to learn the military mysteries of the West out of books.

The sultan's permission to introduce printing in Ottoman Turkish was carefully circumscribed. It excluded all books concerning religion and law (which was part of the religious domain). These remained firmly part of the manuscript tradition. The key figure in the introduction of the Western innovation was not the humble Ibrahim Müteferrika, but a much more prominent man of the Ottoman establishment. The order was granted to the printer and to Mehmed Said Pasha, who had accompanied his father Mehmed Pasha on an Ottoman embassy to France. The decree was formally endorsed by the religious authorities in Constantinople, in Galata (across the Golden Horn) and Salonika, as well as by the *Shaikh ul-Islam*, the senior religious figure in the empire. Said Pasha financed the whole operation, importing the press itself from France, paying the skilled printers from Vienna, and acting as the patron and protector for the fledgling venture. Appropriately, Said's portrait, painted by Jacques Aved in 1742, shows him with his hand resting on a book, in European art traditionally signifying his commitment to literature and culture.[26]

Yet this first press, active for eighteen years, succeeded in printing only twenty-three books. Only one of these, the first, an Arabic dictionary translated into Ottoman Turkish, was ever reprinted. This failure was in part because the Grand Vizier Ibrahim who had supported the press was killed by the janissaries at the deposition of Sultan Ahmed III in 1730, ending the Tulip Era. A suspicion of European innovations re-emerged. But the greater reality was that there was little demand.

The reasons become a little clearer if we consider the matter not so much in terms of prejudice against print as in terms of permissible topics. The Ottoman administration defined these very tightly. As Volney indicated, somewhat to his disgust, religion and law were already the subject matter of the majority of *manuscript* books. In fifteenth-century Europe, likewise, religion and law were the most popular and successful categories in early printing, covering more than 80 per cent of all titles published.[27] So the Turkish printing press, producing texts in Ottoman Turkish, was left with a small segment of the market, and an insufficient volume of publications to develop the necessary network of distribution and publicity. Add to that the fact that the first books were not very appealing by contrast with the finer handwritten products. Not only were the letters relatively crude, but they were often based on North African or Levantine styles of writing that looked odd to many Turkish readers, rather as the German Gothic script looked strange and was hard to read for Westerners used to the Roman founts. Consider these factors and the reasons for the initial failure of printing acquire a far less ideological cast.

But was it for reasons of religious scruple that the administration prohibited the printing of religious books? I believe this too needs to be seen in a broader context. The Ottomans were not ignorant of the divisions in Europe caused by religious schism; indeed, they benefited from it in both political and economic terms. They were also aware that the printed word had been a powerful force in causing that fracture. Printing was allowed in the Christian and Jewish minorities, in their own languages and also in Arabic script (but not in the Ottoman language). However these were books that served the needs of their own communities and had almost no dissemination beyond them. Books in Arabic were imported from Italy, France and the Habsburg lands, although there had been severe restraints on the trade in the sixteenth and seventeenth centuries. The response to the printed word, even in Arabic script, was not uniform: sometimes printed books were allowed, at other times they were not permitted. The main political concern of the government seems to have been books printed in Ottoman Turkish, which was the lingua franca of the empire.

The essence of the Ottoman Empire was control, but policy on how best to exercise this was always in a state of flux. In theory the sultan's government controlled everything; in practice, in distant provinces, that power might be completely illusory.[28] Licensed printing, under strict conditions, with the chief religious authority of the empire as head of the editorial board, was an attempt to allow development and at the same time maintain control.[29] Many European governments, notably those in Catholic countries, also constantly adapted and adjusted their systems to achieve the maximum level of protection against undesirable (heretical, politically sensitive, lewd and pornographic) material. Not, however, with uniform success.[30] Governments in the West would have preferred to keep a rein on the printed word rather than allow its headlong, unfettered development. The history of the post-Reformation period contains countless examples of their attempts to tame it through censorship, persecution or the scaffold.[31]

Perhaps if printers had been allowed to produce religious and legal books in the Ottoman Empire, the industry there might have grown more rapidly. But that is not certain, given the fragility of any market for books and the lack of a system for distribution. It has been estimated that in the century between the foundation of Müteferrika's press and the death of the great reforming Sultan Mahmud II in 1839 no more than 439 titles were published in Ottoman Turkish.[32] Production increased dramatically during the nineteenth century, but ultimately no more than 20,000 titles were published before 1928, when a new Roman alphabet was adopted by the Turkish Republic. The same tardy development of the market for books affected all areas of the Ottoman domain in Europe, and indeed the Slav and Hellenic communities on its fringes.[33]

Müteferrika's first titles had been strange hybrids. They imitated the binding and appearance of the Islamic manuscript tradition, but unlike most Muslim books, some of them were illustrated. The second publication, an account translated from a Jesuit's text about a bloody revolt in Afghanistan, had engravings, and the third, a history of the West Indies and a collection of fables, was fully illustrated. One of the stories had a picture of a tree that bore women as its fruit, who fell to the ground as they ripened, shouting 'wak wak'. According to Abbé Giambattista Toderini, who published his huge history of Turkish literature and music in 1787, these figures became so popular that they were copied and displayed in official festivals, as the spectators shouted 'wak wak'. Yet despite this suggestion of public interest, it is impossible to consider the venture successful. One thousand copies was an average print run and the volumes were expensive.

It was not Gutenberg's type but Alois Senefelder's invention of lithography in 1798 that made possible a mass market for the printed word in Arabic script.[34] Letterpress had improved as new Arabic founts were produced. A large printing works was set up by Mehmed Ali Pasha, the ruler of Egypt, at Bulaq in the suburbs of Cairo in 1815.[35] Other printers were established in Constantinople, and on the Asian shore at Uskudar (Scutari). But the basic problems of Arabic typesetting had not altered. It was only with lithography that the limitations inherent in Gutenberg's type vanished. With lithographic printing, instead of laboriously assembling type, a calligrapher's hand-written text could be printed exactly as written. Illustrations could be drawn on transfer sheets or directly on to the surface of the carefully ground printing stones. The resulting quality was impressive, and even a selection of colours could be used. The first lithographic book in Ottoman Turkish was printed not in Istanbul but in Paris, by T. X. Bianchi in 1817. The first lithographic press in the Ottoman Empire arrived in Constantinople about 1830. It was set up in the grounds of the Ministry of War, under the patronage of Khusrev Pasha, by two well-known French printers from Marseilles, Henri and Jacques Cayol. Their patron's own book, complete with seventy-nine images, was their first publication in 1831.[36]

By the mid nineteenth century the lithographic process, which had in the early days required considerable skill to prepare the stones and to print accurately, was mechanized and zinc plates rather than lithographic stones were increasingly used. An Ottoman illustrated-magazine industry flourished from the late 1860s with a circulation throughout the empire. Thus, by the accession of Sultan Abdul Hamid II in 1876, the Ottoman world possessed newspapers, magazines, printing and photography, different only in their extent from the Western world. These were the emblems of modernity and of the city, in a society that remained largely rural, illiterate, conservative and resolutely resistant to change.

So the 'black art' – letterpress printing – came late to the Ottoman world. In the West it had gained this nickname because printing was a grimy business and printers were always spattered with ink. But the phrase means something else as well. In the West, with rare and precious exceptions, a printed book would be printed in black ink on white paper or on parchment. Images too would normally be printed in black. In certain books, such as Bibles or service books, some letters or sentences might be printed in red, 'rubricated'. The English phrase 'a red letter day' comes from the practice of highlighting church feasts and holidays in red print in the *Book of Common Prayer*. But until the general use of colour in printing late in the nineteenth century, even prestigious and costly printed books were more usually a monochrome experience. In the older manuscript tradition, of course, a book might include illuminations and decorations in a multitude of colours, but the domain of colour after the 'Gutenberg Revolution' had been yielded to painters and miniaturists. In the East, by contrast, books continued to be embellished. Book decorators and illuminators were prized at the Ottoman, Persian and Moghul courts, and it was almost unthinkable for a fine book not to be enriched with colour. Many were enhanced with the depiction of human and animal forms, supposed by Westerners to be universally anathematized within the world of Mediterranean Islam.

But it is also true that nowhere in the Ottoman domains – not even in Mehmed Ali's aggressively modernizing Cairo – was there anything similar to the slow percolation of the printed image into a largely preliterate society that took place in the West. In the 'well-protected domain' of the Ottomans, until the mid nineteenth century, in the cities and towns there were no religious pictures, few portraits or cartoons, and, in fact, a paucity of secular images of any sort. In the countryside, among the poor and illiterate, there were none at all.

For many Muslims, a visual image made by a human hand was something completely abstract and unknown. A picture was simply a category of evil like the Devil himself. It was irreligious, an innovation, to be shunned and avoided. Culture formed around the spoken word, which translated the glories of nature not into an image but into poetry. The world of Islam did not share the iconic awareness common throughout the West, where images were part of the culture that developed in every European nation. Even those ascetic Protestants who defaced sculptures in churches, and ground the images of saints, martyrs and the Holy Virgin underfoot, usually accepted pictures in the secular domain. At the very least, they knew what images were. The situation in the Muslim East was quite different. Brinkley Messick has coined the redolent phrase 'the calligraphic state' to describe a society (in Yemen) that existed without images and was ruled by the *written* word.[37] His concept was founded on the power and importance of script in the Arabic tradition. But the written word in that tradition was itself but a shadow of the spoken word. The human voice was more potent than any form of writing, extended as it was by body language, vocal tone and inflection, and even by an audience's energizing presence.[38] The essence of Islam was a recitation (*qur'an*), carried over into a book (*kitab*). And that book might not even be a physical text, but a book that existed only in the mind.[39] Texts written in Arabic were suffused with something of this Divine book, but even a sacralised script could only imperfectly express its ineffable oral grandeur.

Printed images had no public place in this world. They were at most for private enjoyment by the sophisticated few. Esin Atil has described the evolution of the imperial studio (*nakkashane*) that produced illustrated books.[40] In this studio some artists specialized in calligraphy, especially in the elaborate imperial signatures or *tughra*. The portrait painters, because of their skill in depicting the human form, were an essential but more marginal and exclusive group within the studio and among its freelance workers. There were many artists working privately in the capital, but few who declared themselves as painters of portraits, in part certainly because of the opprobrium this activity might attract. What was appropriate for the sultan was more risky for the individual artist or collector. Some sultans from Mehmed the Conqueror onwards both commissioned books full of images and amassed other illustrated books from a variety of sources. They were all stored with other treasures for the private use of the sultan in the Inner Treasury of the Topkapi Palace.

The production of these works in the sixteenth century, notably the histories, was an act of state, dramatizing the course of Ottoman history and the successes of Ottoman arms under the sultans. They therefore depicted both Muslims and non-Muslims, but there appears much less of the hostility that dominates many Western images of the infidel. In, for example, Lokman's *Hunername*, the Westerners are shown as ordinary human figures. On one page they appear very bored, some playing dice, a few firing their cannon at the Ottoman armies, and one man (improbably) asleep against an artillery piece. None of them are especially vicious images.[41] This does not, of course, say anything about popular attitudes, since these images would be seen only by the privileged few.[42] But such a presentation in a state document was obviously both appropriate and acceptable to the imperial patron. The Westerners might be ritually reviled in word or in writing, but they were depicted merely as objects of curiosity.

Magnificently decorated Qur'ans are common but it is impossible to conceive of a Qur'an with images in the way that there were numerous pictorial Bibles.[43] Images with a human face or an animal form played, at most, a marginal part in the formation of Muslim culture. To the majority of Muslims, beyond the small groups of urban sophisticates, images were incomprehensible. The closest I can come to understanding this experience is the situation described by the writer Albert Manguel in his enticing book, *A History of Reading*. Manguel relates how in 1978 he was working for a publisher in Milan. One day a package arrived.

It contained, instead of a manuscript, a large collection of illustrated pages, depicting a number of strange objects and detailed but bizarre operations each captioned in a script none of the editors recognized . . . Made entirely of invented words and pictures, the Codex Seraphianus [after its author, Luigi Serafini] must be read without the help of a common language, through signs for which there are no meanings except those furnished by a willing and inventive reader.[44]

Intrigued, I went to the British Library to see for myself a copy of this odd work. It is in a handsome black cloth binding, and its pages are illuminated like a medieval manuscript. I quickly realized that its meaning to me would be only what I brought to it. The script was indecipherable, but to a degree I could make contact with the images – some of them had bits and pieces within them that I recognized. But there was no way of knowing what the pages really meant and, after half an hour, I gave up. This collision with the incomprehensible is how people living in a world without images respond when first confronted with pictures. It is a new language that has to be learned.

There is a never-ending debate among scholars about the language and meaning of images. Some perceive them as one element in some vast structure of signs, others as a map of 'multimodal texts, vectors and forces'. At the other extremity, images become discrete and powerful entities with a life of their own, 'icontexts'.[45] Relating the theories to the real world is not easy, especially since images printed in books and other publications are often ignored. Unlike works of art or even artists' prints, they do not stand alone. They are bound in with the words around them. And, just as the words that make up the written text have to be learned or deciphered, so too the images have to be understood.[46] But as with the *Codex Seraphianus*, understanding what an image means is virtually impossible if nothing about it is recognizable. Images remained an unfamiliar, alien presence in the Muslim world before (at the earliest) the eighteenth century. In practice it was not until the late nineteenth and the early twentieth centuries that they became more commonplace, even in the major cities. For this reason most of the theories produced in the West concerning the nature of images do not seem to have much obvious relevance to the Islamic condition.

Over many centuries western (and eastern) Christians had become adept at understanding figurative images made by a human hand. They were instructed that a statue of a saint had special qualities relating to the saint's life and story, that a golden reliquary enclosing a withered hand or a bejewelled skull was a holy relic and had meaning. They were taught how to *read* the image or object by seeing it. Those same visual skills of interpretation were later employed in literacy, in learning to read the written texts.[47] The Protestant iconoclasts of the sixteenth century rarely abominated images in an absolute sense: the Biblical commandment – 'Thou shalt not make unto thee any graven image' – meant for them the *ungodly worship* of images.[48] Nowhere in the world of Islam were painted or printed images as common as they were in the Christian world. Muslims, the literate and the non-literate alike, lived among voices. They learned by hearing, recitation and repetition. Knowledge was transmitted through the spoken voice, which was more resonant and truthful than mute words printed on a page.[49] It was a culture in which the printed image (of animals and human beings) had none of the educational role that it did in the

Christian world. Children were not taught to read using visual images, but through recitation and through deciphering a written text.[50]

However, the contrast between the two worlds – the West with images and the East without – was not truly absolute: a range of public depictions did exist in the Islamic world and were widely used. As D'Ohsson observed, while Muslims themselves made no coins that bore human images they were happy to use Western money that did. The silver *thaler* of Maria Theresa and later the British gold sovereign with the head of Queen Victoria became the trusted common currencies throughout the Arabian peninsula. But nonetheless they belonged to the distant, alien and infidel outside world.

It was not until after the development of photography in the nineteenth century that human and animal images entered the Muslim domain more generally. Thereafter, while purists might still anathematize any image that showed a human or animal figure, photography cut away many religious objections. It was argued that creating a photograph was not a human act, but God's light acting upon an emulsion to make the image. This also opened the way to the acceptance of printed but non-photographic images, for from the mid nineteenth century photography began to be used for making lithographic plates. By the same logic, etching, aquatint and mezzotint, all processes that used chemical action to make an image, could also be treated more permissively. Engraving could also be explained away in the same fashion, because blocks were increasingly produced mechanically or chemically.

The same principles of exception later extended to both film and television. By the last decade of the twentieth century the Muslim realm had adapted to a world where depiction and the image of human forms were normal. Only the most purblind, austere and narrow-minded continued to abominate all visual images, whether made by human art or God's divine light. In the 1920s King Ibn Saud of Saudi Arabia had shocked his *ikhwan* (brotherhood of warriors) by having his photograph taken. This Defender of the Holy Places of Islam, King of the Hijaz and future king of Saudi Arabia, paid no attention to their protestations, any more than to their fevered objections about cars and aeroplanes. It was relatively easy for a king to follow his own inclinations, but millions of ordinary Muslims did the same.

ؔ

I have increasingly come to the conclusion that attempting codification of the differences between East and West (while they might have the solid sanction of holy writ) cannot correspond to the quotidian realities of life. Very few, in the East or in the West, in the past as in the present, voluntarily lived or live their lives *wholly* according to the Holy Books and the Laws. Most people spent their days in conformity to the mores of their own group and community.[51] At the interface, where the two worlds collide, problems occur. In one particular context, international commerce, you may observe eminent Western visitors to the East becoming frustrated at the different pace at which business is done. But, equally, senior figures from the East can feel discomforted by the pell-mell of meetings in some Western countries: that characteristic phrase, 'cut to the chase', taken from Western movie culture, dramatizes the difference. For some, what comes before the main event is only an insignificant prelude; for others, the main event is only part of the whole complex of customs and courtesies. This temporal shift, between an event that can be 'cut', and one that cannot, I think, begins to get to the heart of difference.

There is clock time and there is human time. Gerhard Dohrn-van Rossum has shown how the West became progressively dominated by clock time. By the nineteenth century, one French minister of education could boast that he knew precisely what any school pupil in France would be studying at any hour of the school day.[52] In the East clock time was more controversial. Sultan Murad III, like his ancestor Mehmed the Conqueror, was curious about Western mechanical clocks. Murad's astronomer and chief astrologer set up an observatory in the capital and wrote the first handbook on mechanical clocks in the empire. In 1561, he made a clock that showed the times of prayer, an instrument eventually destroyed because it was considered to be an infidel device seeking to replace the *muezzin* and the power of the human voice. Like the printing press, clock time has had a chequered and complex history in the East.

My great-uncle Otto Veit once had a watch that he had bought in the Grand Bazaar of Constantinople when he travelled there from Vienna in the years before the First World War. I remember it showed the different times that were used under the Ottoman Empire. One dial showed mosque time (*hijri*), one dial had time used in government and business offices (*mali*), and a third showed Western time (*alafranga*).

He told me that he had bought it after he had missed appointments because those he was supposed to meet were using one time and he was using another. I subsequently read of an earlier traveller who had the same problem:

The time will be given in Turkish fashion, which begins to count at sundown, and goes on for the whole twenty-four hours, so in the middle of the afternoon one may be told it is exactly 17 o' clock. Then as the sun does not have the politeness to set every day at the same time, it is necessary to carry an almanack in one's head to reduce the Turkish time to English.[53]

The issues discussed in this chapter all come down to timing. In the twenty-first century, the West and the East now share many of the same goods and commodities, and especially radio, television, movies and the Internet, as well as books, magazines and newspapers. But these did not come into use at the same time. There was a lag, with the West developing new modes of communication, and the East adopting them later. It was four centuries before images and the printed word became as common in the Muslim East as they were in the West. With film, radio and television it was a matter of decades; with the Internet, less than five years. But that long delay in accepting the printing revolution had profound consequences. It meant that Eastern time scales and Western time scales were not identical, and like my great-uncle in need of the watch, we need a means to relate the two.

The argument of this book is that both the Christian infidels and the Muslim infidels have regarded each other with suspicion throughout their long connection. Each routinely cursed and abominated the other, which is only to be expected. But the malediction has not been of quite the same kind. Certainly from the invention of printing, and through the proliferation of images, the West's *maledicta* have been infinitely more potent and widespread. But now, as the clock moves on, the East has learned the lesson. 'Islam' uses the printing press and visual and electronic media with the same skill and sophistication as the West. And it has also learned how these new techniques can now carry the East's *maledicta*, farther and more potently than the scribe's pen.

CONCLUSION

14

Maledicta

WORDS OF HATE

The two opposing sides at Lepanto in 1571 shouted at each other from the galley decks. We can deduce a few things about that exchange. Although the crews and soldiers might not have understood the language spoken by the enemy, provided they could hear the sounds of speech above the din of battle their minds would have attempted to make what was said intelligible. Human physiology dictates that the brain cannot choose not to process what it perceives as sound. As David Crystal puts it, 'When we hear sounds, we hear them as speech, or non-speech: there seems to be no middle ground. No matter how hard we try, we cannot hear speech as a series of acoustic hisses and buzzes, but only as a sequence of speech sounds.[1]

Curses, maledictions, insults and invocations of divine aid against the hated enemy were what both Christians and Muslims would have expected in such an extreme context. But the process of understanding what was being said even in the midst of battle was little different from what happened in the mixed communities around the Mediterranean on a daily basis over many centuries. In everyday encounters, the human brain would process all speech sounds. Face to face, gestures and body language could be read even if the words were unintelligible. Mistakes might be made, but it was usually easy to determine from the circumstances whether a speaker's intention was friendly or hostile. The first channel of understanding – interpreting the sounds – is involuntary; only by physically blocking off the sounds can this be prevented. The second channel – attributing meaning to those sounds – is, I suggest, in part a conditioned reflex based on past experience, and part a reasoned assessment of the current situation. For example, an insult or coarse suggestion shouted across the street is usually clear as to its intention. Such an interchange exists below the level of understanding what the words mean. The hearer does not need to master the exact meaning of the words to know that they are not compliments. In his novel *Bosnian Chronicle*, Ivo Andrić presented precisely such a situation. At one point in his story, set in the Bosnia of 1804, a new French consul, Jean Daville, rides with his escort through the streets of Travnik to meet its Ottoman pasha:

Then as soon as they reached the first Turkish houses, they began to hear curious sounds: people calling to one another, slamming their courtyard gates and the shutters of their windows. At the very first doorway a small girl opened one of the double gates a crack, and muttering some incomprehensible words began spitting rapidly, as though she were laying a curse upon them. One after the other, gates opened and shutters were raised to reveal for a moment faces possessed with a fanatical hatred. The women, veiled, spat or cursed, and the boys shouted abuse, accompanied by obscene gestures and unambiguous threats, clapping their buttocks or drawing their hands across their throats . . . Daville saw them dimly, as though through an unpleasant veil trembling in front of his eyes. No one ceased working or smoking or raised his eyes to honour the unusual figure with so much as a glance . . . Only Easterners can hate and despise others to such an extent and display their hatred and contempt in such a way.[2]

Daville knew hate when he heard and saw it. (Would he have been more or less affronted had he understood the words the women were shouting at him? He might have been able to respond effectively in kind; but, on the other hand, the insult might have been even more mordant.) The insults got through, penetrating the armour of incomprehension.

Words of hate, like words of love, have a strong sense of intention.[3] The Christian and Muslim worlds have been religious, geographical, political and economic rivals and competitors since their point of first contact, and it is no wonder that words of hate rather than words of love have predominated when one world evoked the image of the other. But thereafter, the process and consequence of evoking that image diverge. How was hostility formed out of two contrary experiences of life? The first was, and remains in some areas, that of living side by side. The second was when the object of hatred was never experienced directly, but was nonetheless terrifying. This was largely how the image of the lustful Saracen or the terrible Turk was formulated in the West by scholars who never lifted their eyes from the pages of their texts. Living in close proximity might give a human dimension to the Other. Lack of contact might allow the formation of Romantic notions, which infused many genres in literature and the visual arts. But the outcome was not necessarily predetermined by the context.

Maledicta exist everywhere. Many people use them, but normally in a private or restricted sphere. Their significance is defined by where and to whom they are addressed. Everybody will talk to their friends and peers in a language that they would not use publicly – to their parents, their boss, or other figures of respect. But when private speech becomes public knowledge, its significance shifts.[4] The power of curses and abuse is directly related to this resonance, and since the invention of print, the boundaries between the private and the public contexts have slowly diminished. There is an important distinction: words spoken inside a family or in an isolated village are functionally (if not philosophically or theologically) different from the same words published in newspapers or broadcast worldwide on television and radio.

From reading Mikhail Bakhtin, I began to get an insight into a world without fixed meaning or solid structures. Perhaps Bakhtin's harsh experience of life was reflected in what and how he wrote. He was born in 1895, the second son of a prosperous provincial banker. A golden early career ended when he fell foul of Stalin in 1929. For the whole of his adult life, revolution and the social transformation of Russia distorted Bakhtin's fate. Instead of falling victim to a bullet in the neck or a one-way trip to the Gulag, Bakhtin was sent into internal exile in Kazakhstan. There he taught bookkeeping by day and studied by night. By remaining silent and inconspicuous he escaped a new purge in 1937.

The war with Germany meant that he was allowed to teach German (in which he was virtually bilingual) to high-school students, but even after the conflict ended he was still regarded as 'unreliable'. In part this was because he refused to denounce his Orthodox roots and upbringing. With his 'cosmopolitan' interests and connections he was lucky to survive a third purge of intellectuals in the 1950s. It was only in the 1960s that Bakhtin was rescued from obscurity, by a group of scholars who had read his work and were amazed to find him still alive. By then he had lost a leg through osteomyelitis, and walked on crutches or unsteadily with a stick. Chain-smoking cheap cigarettes gave him a permanent cough and the emphysema that eventually killed him. (In the depths of WWII, lacking paper, he had torn up the only copy of one of his manuscripts to roll his own cigarettes.)

All the work that he wrote, unobtrusively, in exile or in self-imposed isolation, was shot through with a theme of impermanence. Insecurity and change were the constants of his life, and mutability was the essence of his scholarly message. It was present in his studies of Dostoyevsky, in his essays published in English as *The Dialogic Imagination*, and in his greatest work, on Rabelais. He saw almost every word in a language as being in a state of flux, as it interacted or was coloured by the use of other words. This 'intertextuality' was natural. For Bakhtin the normal, healthy state of life involved interaction with others. Whatever they did or said affected you and influenced your own response. Yet this mutual relationship could never be congruent. Bakhtin told a story of two people looking at each other. Consider them as an observer looking at *another* observer. You are one, someone else is the other.

You can see things behind my back that *I* cannot see and *I* can see things behind *your* back that are denied to your vision. We are both doing essentially the same thing, but from different places: although we are in the same event, that event is different for each of us. Our places are different not only because our bodies occupy different positions in exterior, physical space, but also because we regard each other from different centres.[5]

Bakhtin's work has helped me to make sense of 'Christian Infidel' and 'Muslim Infidel' as 'enemies in the mirror'.[6] Over many centuries, while each might have been aware of the other, even have observed the other, neither could, as Bakhtin suggests, see what the other sees. The relationship between 'one' and 'another' would also be constrained by their relative social, political or military power. Ultimately they were incommensurable.[7] Words of hate and images inviting disgust were a direct product of differences in position. Bakhtin described what happens when such words are uttered: 'The utterance is related not only to preceding but to subsequent links in the chain . . . From the very beginning the speaker expects a response from them, an active responsive understanding. The entire utterance is constructed, as it were, in anticipation of encountering this response.'[8] In this dialogue language is both a 'weapon' and a 'shield'.[9] The deliberate intensity of insults, spoken or written, makes their effect unpredictable. *Maledicta* are the most volatile and dangerous elements in any language.

Following Bakhtin's idea of dialogue, there are two parties to every malediction. It might seem logical that the person affected most directly is the one insulted. But I believe the reverse is true. If you are the object of an insult, you may not know that it has happened, or understand exactly what has been said, like Ivo Andrić's character Consul Daville. Today the most foul and gratuitous insults lurk on the Internet, but are never read by their intended victims. But those who curse certainly hear the words, resonating in their own mind. Even if you are the intended target of a curse, (and both hear and understand the insult), you still have the power to deny it. Crude maledictions like 'cockroaches', or 'sons of monkeys and pigs' no doubt make those who utter them feel good. But they rarely hit their target, for who will believe such an insult directed against them?[10]

This kind of abuse has a different purpose: to define communal differences, between 'them' and 'us'. *They* are portrayed as subhuman or not even human at all. *We* are human, with our roots in higher values. Demonized enemies —whether those of 'impure blood', or 'sons of monkeys and pigs' — have no part in human society: words or images are used to cut them out from the codes and taboos that govern relationships between human equals. No longer human, they are not entitled to humane treatment. These ultimate words of hatred have now become enormously more effective with modern mass communication.[11]

There are also words or images which have one sense within one community and quite another outside it. Words like *jihad* in the world of Islam or 'crusade' in the Christian West have this double resonance. Both these ancient terms have changed radically in meaning in the last and this century, while still retaining their old senses. I have discussed the earlier formulations and practices in previous chapters, but now I will look at the new *jihad* and the new 'crusade'.

In the modern era a new meaning and practice of *jihad* has been evolving. This transformation had two distinct facets: its meaning within the world of Islam and its impact outside. In 1978, the Revolutionary Iranian Government violated all the rules of diplomacy and seized the staff of the US Embassy in Tehran. Some years later, on NBC Television, the spiritual leader of Iran, Ayatollah Khomeini, explained himself.[12] He talked of America as 'the Great Satan, *the wounded snake*'. The USA's reaction was continuing outrage at the treatment of its citizens and contempt at being described as the Devil. It was then supporting Iraq in her long war with Iran.

Few noticed the 'wounded snake', the last part of Khomeini's denunciation. It was classed as mere abuse. In fact, there was a deeper meaning underlying his verbal assault. The Ayatollah was referring to an ancient tale of the Imam Ali, father of Hussain, who was martyred at Kerbala. Hussain's cruel death was the founding moment of Shia Islam. This gave the parable a special significance in Iran. The story recounted that once Shaitan (the Devil) had decided to disturb the Imam's prayers.[13] The Devil then took the form of a snake and bit the Imam's legs continuously. The Imam felt the pain but carried on praying as if nothing had happened. What Khomeini was saying was that the Devil (the United States) might wound but could not impede the devoted Muslim. A wounded snake would perhaps become even more vicious but it would weaken and eventually die.[14] 'All-powerful' America would ultimately give way to the God-given power of Islam.

Ayatollah Khomeini was following in a long tradition of the Shia branch of Islam. But the other radical strand, in Sunni Islam, of *jihad*'s modern iteration had been emerging in Egypt. Since the foundation of Cairo in 969 and the creation of Al-Azhar, the oldest university in the world, some three years later, scholars had debated the shape and structures of the faith. This tradition of criticism and scholarship in Cairo outlasted its competitors in Damascus and Baghdad, and from the early nineteenth century the city became a pioneer of the printing and publication of secular, nationalist and also religious material. In the years after the First World War, as Egypt remained in thrall to Britain, much of the political debate in Cairo began to focus anew on the Holy Qur'an and the *hadith* for guidance. This had to be done carefully. Islam was opposed to the idea of innovation (*bid'ah*), which would undermine the concept of a perfect revelation of the ideal society.[15] Change had to be presented, rhetorically, as 'no-change' or, better, as a reversion to an earlier and purer state of society. A

28. A view of Belgrade in the 1860s by the Austrian watercolourist Carl Goebel. Muslims and Christians can be easily identified by their distinctive dress.

29–30. Austrian propaganda about Bosnia-Herzegovina, 1886–1902. (Left) The old unreformed Ottoman Bosnia. (Right) The new Austrian province. The image suggests that under benign and progressive Austrian rule even cabbages thrive and grow extra large.

31. *A Doorway in Cairo* by William Simpson, *c.* 1884. Orientalist painters often showed a preoccupation with accuracy of costume and architecture; the audience welcomed the inclusion of outlandish detail, such as the Nile crocodile here.

32. Djouni, Lady Hester Stanhope's residence, is shown here in a 1837 engraving by W. H. Bartlett. Unlike more transient commentators on the East, Hester Stanhope settled in Lebanon in 1818 and remained there until her death in 1839.

33. *Bosnia*, by Bernard Rice, woodcut, *c.* 1928. This view of an imaginary but archetypal Bosnian village has all the elements of a mixed heritage, with minarets side by side with church towers, and a castle and fortifications perched on the hillside.

34. 'The Albanian ... his long yataghan naked and uplifted, his face livid and distorted with fury' from R. M. Jephson, *With the Colours* or *The Piping Times of Peace*, 1880.

35. Britannia, personifying the British nation, spurns the 'savage and murderous' Turk, *Punch*, 1876. The Sultan, a bloody sabre hanging from one arm, and with impaled heads, slaughtered women and children in the background, appeals for British understanding. 'Not with your hands of *that colour*,' replies the civilized Western world.

36. *Judy*, though a rival to *Punch*, nonetheless displayed the same attitude to the 'bestial' Ottomans. John Bull, another personification of the nation, shows how to deal with a vicious-looking little sultan who brandishes a woman's severed head.

37. A 'savage' Montenegrin by Amadeo, Count Preziosi, 1854. The subject, heavily armed, exhibits all the dignity and defiance we would expect.

38. 'Herr Madden assassinated', front cover of *Le Petit Journal*, 1905. A largely imaginary scene: as one wild Moroccan stabs the Austrian consul, another gouges out his eyes. Meanwhile, a third fires point blank at the consul's young wife in her negligée.

39. The stairs up to the Holy Sepulchre, Jerusalem, in a nineteenth-century photograph, possibly by the famous Bonfils studio. Tourist trap–style souvenirs line the side of the steps.

40. *Damascus: The Ruins of the Christian Quarter*, a photograph by Francis Bedford from a series entitled *Tour in the East*. The destruction wrought by the 1860s massacre is all too evident.

41. The sixteenth-century bridge at Mostar destroyed by shelling in November 1993.

42. President George Walker Bush mis-speaks, using a 'C word', *The Times*, London, 2001. While 'crusade' sounded just peachy in the Texas Panhandle, it often had a much darker resonance beyond the USA.

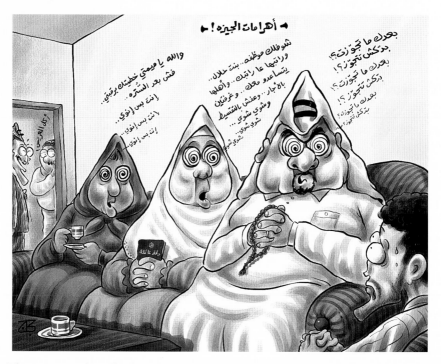

43. The renowned Jordanian cartoonist Emad Hajjaj shows the concerns that cross cultural frontiers. Here an Arab family, their headdresses peaked like the Pyramids of Giza, ask their grandson when he is going to get married. This question, Hajjaj proposes, is as old as history.

new practice had to be embedded within an unchanging paradigm. Nevertheless there was a tradition of speculation, for unobtrusive re-examination and reinterpretation of questions that had been 'closed' centuries before.[16]

In the early history of Islam ideas had been passed on by pupils, each of whom listened to the words of their master, and then transmitted them to his own successors. It was a chain binding each scholar irrevocably to his predecessors and to those who in turn had learned the truth from his own lips. A similar chain of connection linked the theorists and activists of the Islamic revival, each of whom added his own contribution. An intellectual movement centred upon fighting the power of the West began with a complex figure called Jamal al-Din, often known as Al-Afghani, who taught in Egypt, was exiled to Paris, and eventually died in Constantinople in 1897. He called on Muslims to resist the West, to turn the West's own weapons and techniques against it.[17]

One of his most devoted supporters was an Egyptian called Muhammad Abduh who taught at Al-Azhar. When Al-Afghani was expelled from Egypt, Abduh followed him to Paris. There they published a short-lived journal, *The Indissoluble Bond*, which preached Muslim unity in the face of Western power. Abduh's work was continued by one of his pupils, the Syrian Rashid Rida. He in turn became a powerful influence on Hasan al-Banna, who founded the Muslim Brotherhood (*Ikhwan-al-Muslimim*) in 1928, and on its most notable theorist, Sayyid Qutb.[18]

Banna created a new kind of political and religious organization that began 'as a youth club with its main stress on moral and social reform through communication, information and propaganda'.[19] Banna started a tradition where Islamist politics were allied to providing assistance to the poor and dispossessed. By 1940 there were more than 500 branches of the organization in Egypt; this number had risen to 5,000 by 1946. Banna's *Ikhwan al-Muslimim* found many adherents throughout the Middle East, where they were often ruthlessly repressed by secular authorities. King Abdul Aziz of Saudi Arabia said he had his own *ikhwan*, and politely declined their offer to establish a branch in his domains.

Sayyid Qutb was both a scholar and a prolific author, who wrote his last and (arguably) greatest work in prison in the 1960s. He became one of the leading figures of the Muslim Brotherhood. When he was hanged on the orders of the Egyptian government, he turned into a martyr in the eyes of his supporters. A younger Egyptian, Abd al-Salem Faraj, suffered the same fate as Qutb; in 1979 he had founded a group called the Society for the Holy War (*Jamaat al-Jihad*), usually known simply as Al-Jihad. On 6 October 1981 Al-Jihad succeeded in killing the President of Egypt, Anwar Sadat, whom they had proscribed as an evil prince. As one of the assassins publicly declared, 'I am [Lieutenant] Khalid Islambuli. I have killed Pharaoh and I do not fear death.'[20] For Faraj, Islambuli and their group, Sadat merited death. 'We have to make the Rule of God's Religion in our own country first, and to make the Word of God supreme . . . there is no doubt that the first battlefield for *jihad* is the extermination of these infidel leaders ['corrupt' Muslims like Sadat] and to replace them by a complete Islamic Order. From there we should start.'[21]

Al-Jihad believed in the near-magic potency of a dramatic revolutionary act. In their opinion, 'Killing Pharaoh' would ultimately usher in the restoration of a true Islamic state.[22] Unlike Qutb's profuse and articulate writings, Faraj's output was only one single work, an eighty-page pamphlet, *The Neglected Duty* (*Al-Faridah al-Gha'iba*), but its influence was out of all proportion to the number of copies printed.[23] Faraj, like his predecessor, had joined the chain. He advanced the idea that in the desperate situation of his own time, the (lesser) *jihad*, or armed struggle, had become the individual duty of each and every true Muslim. This was in Faraj's eyes the duty that had been 'neglected'. If not exactly an innovation, this represented a complete reversal of many centuries of Muslim practice. Such a concept of struggle waged through a symbolic chiliastic act had a long-forgotten counterpart within Western thought – in the nihilism of the nineteenth-century Russian anarchist Nechaev. He called political killings 'the propaganda of the deed'. But in Russia these had proved to be floating and aberrant ideas, and when they spread west, nihilistic killings had little of the impact that Nechaev had confidently expected.

In the Islamic world, symbolic violence had a different history. Faraj linked his *jihad* back to the earliest days of the faith, which gave his killings a solid context and ideology that had eluded the rootless anarchist Nechaev. By stages the Islamic revivalists also abandoned any hope that virtue would ever come from the secular Muslim states. Only a godly society 'rightly guided' by the Holy Qur'an would do. They refused to make any compromise or accommodation with the Powers of the Earth, whether government by Muslim rulers or by Western-style mass-democracy. They were driven by the conviction that through endless sacrifice and implacable determination their *jihad* would eventually triumph. For the revolutionaries, the blood and sacrifice of the martyrs would eventually restore the purity of the faith. Moreover, the destruction of every one of those who were 'corrupt upon earth' would hasten that salvation. How such enemies were designated was tied only very loosely to tradition and long-established custom.[24] Ancient maledictions were easily adapted to meet the needs of contemporary policies.

'Crusade' has changed in roughly similar ways. As we have seen in Chapter 8, from the early nineteenth century the word developed two parallel meanings. One was as the technical term to describe the 'historic' Crusades in the Middle East, which had previously gone under a variety of names. The other was as a synonym for 'fighting fiercely in a good cause'. Thomas Jefferson's 'crusade against ignorance' was probably the first usage in this sense.[25] But this style of militancy retained a strong connection with older values, although this is less widely recognized in the West than in the revival of *jihad*. I have found virtually nothing published on the new traditions of 'crusade' while there is a plethora of new books on the Muslim Holy War. But the evidence and the practice of crusading today are there for all to see.

'Fighting talk' is still widely used. One pastor described a successful visit to India in March 2000: 'I was invited to preach a crusade in India . . . When we arrived, I immediately saw all the devastation and spiritual decay, and it grieved my heart. Hindu temples of every kind were at practically every corner . . . All glory given to God, over 420 Hindus were saved!'[26] It seemed bizarre to me that he should be surprised by Hindu temples on every corner in the parts of India that he visited: what was he expecting? However, this evidence of the enemy's powerful presence did not daunt him, or others. Since 1976 Dr Davy has delivered King's Cross Victory Crusades all over India.[27] He and his devoted staff 'have a united vision of delivering One Million Bibles to the people of India who are hungering for the Gospel of Jesus

Christ and have never held a Bible in their hands'.²⁸ The language of
holy war was also used by other Christian missionaries. Two of them,
also working in India, were described as 'worthy warriors'.

What comes to your mind when someone says war? Do you think of the
bombing of Pearl Harbor, D-Day, perhaps the Korean or Viet Nam War,
Desert Storm, the ongoing conflicts in Bosnia, Kosovo, or East Timor? As
horrible as these wars can be, today, I am writing about the war of all wars
and two worthy warriors. It is a war that '. . . is not against flesh and blood,
but against principalities, against powers of this dark world and against the
spiritual forces of evil in the heavenly realms' (Ephesians 6:11–12).

It is a war to free those who have been taken captive by the devil and his
followers. Who are these warriors in the Lord's Army? They are the Christians who proclaim the freedom found in Jesus Christ.

Among the Lord's many dedicated warriors, two Missionaries to India,
Jerris and Juanita Bullard, are surely worthy of the Lord's Distinguished
Medal of Honor. They continue to attack the strongholds of Satan in India,
seeking to free captives.²⁹

They were 'battling on the front lines'. War in a good cause –
'crusade' – has clearly remained a fundamental part of Christian
missionary dialogue. I have deliberately chosen examples that related
to the impact of 'crusade' directed primarily at Hindu and not Muslim
communities; in the Islamic world the idea of 'crusade' generates
an exasperated and often violent response. This militant use of the
word 'crusade' was denied by Professor Bernard Lewis, writing on
27 September 2001:

In Western usage, this word has long lost its original meaning of 'a war for
the cross' and many are probably unaware that this is the derivation of the
name. At present, 'crusade' almost always means simply a vigorous campaign
for a good cause. This cause may be political or military, though this is rare;
more commonly it is social, moral or environmental. In modern Western
usage it is rarely ever religious.³⁰

This is a curious observation. 'Long lost its original meaning . . .
rarely ever religious'? Lewis' assertion, delivered with all the weight
of a renowned scholar, was confected to address the politically embar-

rassing 'mis-speaking' by the US President of the word 'crusade', to which I shall come shortly. The professor was adapting a classic (if cheeky) old challenge: 'Who are you going to believe? Me, or your lyin' ears?' In fact, the association of 'crusade' and religion has remained omnipresent both within evangelical Christianity and outside it.[31] But Lewis was not entirely adrift in his interpretation. In the United States, crusade also means for most Christian people, 'something moral and virtuous'. But by asserting only part of the story, he has spread ignorance and not enlightenment. Unfortunately the impact of the word 'crusade' on the world outside the United States is analogous to the impact of the word *jihad* beyond the Islamic community and context.[32]

Both *jihad* and 'crusade' are relics from an earlier era that have survived into the present. Just as ideas of *jihad* have always been present within Islamic society, so too 'crusade' has an undeniable long and continuous history within 'Christendom'. But the new *jihad* and the new 'crusade' have mutated, and in the process acquired new political and social force. They are not living fossils but rather products of the twentieth century.[33]

'Crusade' in its old meanings still has its public advocates.[34] Dr Robert Moray, a fervent anti-Islamist, has founded a Crusaders Club. It has three grades. A 'Crusader' pays $25 a month and receives in return a free 'Tape of the Month' and a bumper sticker. To become a 'Lion Heart' means paying $100 monthly and for that he (or she) receives the free Tape of the Month and the bumper sticker and, in addition, a subscription to the *Quarterly Journal of Biblical Apologetics* and a special Faith Defenders Coffee Travel Mug. A 'Knight' has to commit $5,000 or more annually. But a 'Knight' is given a Faith Defenders 'Crusader's Sword', and receives special quarterly messages from Dr Moray, as well as all the benefits that accrue to the lower grades of membership. However, all members subscribe to the same statement of principle:

The religion of Islam stands to be the greatest threat against humanity that the world has ever known. I therefore agree with this statement and will pledge my support. I also understand that my donation will further the efforts of Faith Defenders to reach these lost souls for the sake of Christ. I stand firm with Faith Defenders and further understand that at this time in history, we are in a crisis of epic proportions.[35]

It is easy to dismiss these and similar campaigns as unimportant, but modern means of communication have given both the new *jihadists* and new 'crusaders' an extraordinary range, far greater than they ever possessed before.

Maledicta is the name I have used to describe the traditional and historic system within which 'Christendom' relates to 'Islam'. It was first assembled in the distant past, but the edifice has been rebuilt, added to, and modernized over the centuries. But like any historic structure, it is built on old foundations. *Maledicta* are about cursing – not so much about everyday 'bad language', but about formal and purposeful imprecations. Many cultures use curses or words of power, but in both Christendom and Islam the pronouncement of a formal malediction was a most solemn act, replete with dire consequences. To sense the power of such a curse we can read an all-encompassing malediction, the Great Cursing of Archbishop Dunbar of Glasgow upon the bandits (reivers) of the Anglo-Scottish border. Originally written in Scots, it loses a little by being rendered in standard English:

I curse their head and all the hairs of their head; I curse their face, their brain, their mouth, their nose, their tongue, their teeth, their forehead, their shoulders, their breast, their heart, their stomach, their back, their womb, their arms, their legs, their hands, their feet, and every part of their body, from the top of their head to the soles of their feet, before and behind, within and without.

I curse them going and I curse them riding; I curse them standing and I curse them sitting; I curse them eating and I curse them drinking; I curse them rising, and I curse them lying; I curse them at home, I curse them far from home; I curse them within their house, I curse them outside their house; I curse their wives, their children, and their servants participating with them in their deeds. I curse their crops, their cattle, their wool, their sheep, their horses, their swine, their geese, their hens, and all their livestock. I place my curse on their halls, their chambers, their kitchens, their stanchions, their barns, their cowsheds, their barnyards, their cabbage patches, their ploughs, their harrows, and the goods and houses that are necessary for their sustenance and welfare.

May all the malevolent wishes and curses ever known, since the beginning of the world, to this hour, light on them. May the malediction of God, that fell upon Lucifer and all his fellows, that cast them from the high Heaven to the deep hell, light upon them.

He continued, ramifying and extending his imprecation, to the final and absolute anathema:

And, finally, I condemn them perpetually to the deep pit of hell, there to remain with Lucifer and all his fellows, and their bodies to the gallows . . . first to be hanged, then ripped and torn by dogs, swine, and other wild beasts, abominable to all the world. And their candle goes from your sight, as may their souls go from the face of God, and their good reputation from the world, until they forbear their open sins, aforesaid, and rise from this terrible cursing and make satisfaction and penance.[36]

This sixteenth-century anathema against the evildoers has an antique ring. But it also has more modern resonances. The Islamic religious decree or *fatwa* was virtually unknown in the West until the condemnation by Ayatollah Khomeini in February 1989 of Salman Rushdie for his *Satanic Verses*. Such was the blasphemous and evil effect of the book, Khomeini said, that its author deserved to die. Of course, at the same time pastors, priests and ministers inside the Christian churches were also inveighing against other forms of 'evil' to their congregations.[37] But their efforts had little impact outside the communities of Christian believers in a largely unbelieving society. While Khomeini pushed the language of evil once more into the centre of the political domain, political figures in the West were more cautious.

The classic exception was President Ronald Reagan and his famous 'Evil Empire' assault on the Soviet Union. The address that President Reagan delivered to the British House of Commons on 8 June 1982 has since become known colloquially as 'The Evil Empire Speech'.[38] But, oddly, those words do not exist in the official transcript. On that occasion, before the notoriously cantankerous British parliamentarians, President Reagan had indeed eschewed this emotive phrase. He was reserving it for a very different audience.

Reverend Richard C. Cizik, a Vice-President of the National Association of Evangelicals, had suggested that Reagan deliver a speech on religious freedom. On 8 March 1983 the president obliged. In the Citrus Crown Ballroom of the Sheraton Twin Towers in Orlando, Florida, Reagan addressed the assembled evangelists. He covered all the traditional topics that preoccupied his audience: he spoke of abortion, school prayer, of the 'spiritual awakening' of America. Then he spoke of history:

But if history teaches anything, it teaches that simple-minded appeasement or wishful thinking about our adversaries is folly. It means the betrayal of our past . . . So, I urge you to speak out against those who would place the United States in a position of military and moral inferiority . . . I urge you to beware the temptation of pride – the temptation of blithely declaring yourselves above it all and to label both sides equally at fault, to ignore the facts of history and the aggressive impulses of an evil empire, to simply call the arms race a giant misunderstanding and thereby remove yourself from the struggle between right and wrong and good and evil.[39]

Reagan, a skilful speaker, had selected his register to suit the audience. In London he had intended to touch different bases: freedom, democracy, a turning point in history. He declared that Totalitarianism and Communism were destined for the 'ash can of history'. Symbolically perhaps, the disquisition on 'evil' was reserved for a niche group, the congress of pastors at Orlando.[40]

In Europe, Reagan was often condemned as a buffoon, who misspoke, said the unsayable, lurching outside the boundaries of proper political discourse.[41] That was also my view until I heard him speaking directly to the nation in one of his regular 'fireside chats', modelled on Franklin Delano Roosevelt's pioneering radio talks of the 1930s. Every Saturday, starting in 1982, Reagan spoke to Americans about the political and governmental issues of the day. The performance was flawless, convincing even to the sceptic. Every word fell into place, every intonation conjured up a man talking to you across the room, not across a continent. Thereafter I listened to his speeches wherever and whenever I could. Years later I realized that the three American master orators – Roosevelt, Reagan and Clinton – could all speak to the millions and yet make it sound as though they were chatting to a friend. Sometimes their message would be homely and intimate, at other times more presidential and solemn. Their instinct was not just for the right word, or the telling phrase, but that right register, the appropriate tone for the event. They would lead the listener (or the viewer) seductively through their message, with never an opportunity wasted. All three were Great Persuaders of twentieth-century politics.[42]

But none of them, not even Reagan, was a fervent crusader in the Christian sense.[43] Reagan's campaign against Communism, his conservative and Republican credos, were all acquired with his second marriage. Religious convictions played a relatively minor role in the careers of both Roosevelt and Clinton. But Clinton's successor, George Walker Bush, the son of Reagan's vice-president, is different. He, like Reagan, is a convert, but unlike Reagan he was born into the Republican aristocracy. *His* conversion was from the myriad sins of the flesh (notably alcohol) to the rapture of being 'reconfirmed' (his own word) in Jesus Christ. Some questioned his sincerity, but there is no evidence for such cynicism. George W. Bush is a true believer, indeed like the majority of his fellow Americans. He reads the Bible daily.[44]

From the beginning of this book I have worked with the now traditional historical assumption that, through the twentieth century, the West became increasingly secular, whilst in the Eastern, Islamic world religious faith remained the more potent, both in society and politics. I am not suggesting the tired old fallacies about an unchanging East stuck in an immutable past or, as Edward Said memorably put it, 'confined to the fixed status of an object frozen once and for all in time'. He added 'by the gaze of Western percipients', but I think that is too simplistic. Other local agents, closer to home, were also implicated in that process. But while staring east I failed to notice what was happening to the West, an even odder omission since my main theme is the Bakhtinian reflexive and reactive nature of the relationship between the enemies in the mirror.

On Inauguration Day 2001, a reconfirmed or born-again Christian became the forty-third President of the United States. Contrary to the fears of many, but dictated by political prudence, this seemed at first to have little effect. The second President Bush ran a traditional administration, despite the many passionate believers in its ranks.

Until, that is, the cataclysm of 11 September 2001 called for a response off the scale of normal political responses. Now, thanks to Bob Woodward, no natural admirer of George Bush, we have had, within months of the events, an insight into the conduct of affairs in the Hundred Days after the catastrophe in New York and Washington, DC. In *Bush at War*, Woodward makes himself the omniscient narrator, who builds up his favourite characters, cheers for his heroes and hisses at the villains. But despite this tiresome semi-fictive format, the important fact is the nature of the evidence on which his account is based: the sources are very solid. All the main actors in the drama spoke to Woodward, at length, and often over several sessions. The president himself had two long, laid-back meetings with the journalist, and he described to him how he heard the news of the attack on New York, and what dominated his response as seen on TV. 'What you saw was my gut reaction coming out.'[45]

Gradually, George Walker Bush learned more and more to trust those visceral responses. He instructed that meetings planning 'the war' should begin with prayer; he said repeatedly that this was the moment at which a new United States would be reborn in the eyes of the world: 'I do believe there is the image of America out there that we are so materialistic, that we're almost hedonistic, that we don't have values, and that when struck, we wouldn't fight back.'[46]

There were sound reasons for the president's celebrated or infamous use of the word 'crusade' in the aftermath of the atrocity. Faced with an apocalyptic situation, with fires still burning in New York, and the smoke from the Pentagon visible in the heart of Washington, DC, Bush was convinced that he had to find the right register for his first public speech after the catastrophe. He was certain beyond doubt of the dominating presence of threatening evil in the world. He had mused openly in these terms during a campaign speech at Albuquerque, New Mexico, in May 2000: 'We're certain there are madmen in this world, and there's terror, and there's missiles, and I'm certain of this.'[47] On the afternoon of Sunday 16 September 2001, on the South Lawn of the White House, he spoke to the Press and the world.

We need to be alert to the fact that these evildoers still exist. We haven't seen this kind of barbarism in a long period of time. No one could have conceivably imagined suicide bombers burrowing into our society and then emerging all in the same day to fly their aircraft – fly U.S. aircraft into buildings full of innocent people – and show no remorse. This is a new kind of – a new kind of evil. And we understand. And the American people are beginning to understand. This crusade, this war on terrorism is going to take a while.[48]

The president was tired and drained by the turmoil of events. The day before he had been at Ground Zero in New York. Now he spoke from the heart, in a rambling and repetitious fashion, as he said, on the Lord's Day. But he made sure that he hammered home the words 'evil' or 'evildoers' time and again.[49] His remark about a crusade came in an off-the-cuff response to a journalist's question. What Bush actually said was:

This . . . this . . . this . . . crusade . . . this [pause] war on terrorism.[50]

Listening to a recording again, one is struck by how he struggled to find the right word, which was, for him, 'crusade'.[51] This was a word that came from deep inside, a gut reaction. It meant a lot to him: it signified the struggle of Good with Evil.

To me, he sounded a little like Tom Sawyer giving Huck Finn a history lesson. In Mark Twain's novel, *Tom Sawyer Abroad*, his young hero explains the idea of the 'crusade':

'What's a crusade?' I [Huck] says.

He [Tom] looked scornful, the way he's always done when he was ashamed of a person, and says: 'Huck Finn, do you mean to tell me you don't know what a crusade is?'

'No,' says I, 'I don't . . .'

Says he: 'I never see such an idiot. Why, a crusade is a kind of war . . . A crusade is a war to recover the Holy Land from the paynim.'

'Which Holy Land?'

'Why, the Holy Land – there ain't but one.'

'What do we want of it?'

'Why, can't you understand? It's in the hands of the paynim, and it's our duty to take it away from them.'

'How did we come to let them git hold of it?'

'We didn't come to let them git hold of it. They always had it.'

'Why, Tom, then it must belong to them, don't it?'

'Why of course it does. Who said it didn't?'

I studied over it, but couldn't seem to git at the right of it, no way . . .

[Tom said,] 'Oh, shucks! you don't know enough to come in when it rains, Huck Finn . . . You see, it's like this. They own the land, just the mere land, and that's all they DO own; but it was our folks, our Jews and Christians, that made it holy, and so they haven't any business to be there defiling it. It's a shame, and we ought not to stand it a minute. We ought to march against them and take it away from them.'[52]

'Paynim' is an old word for pagan, which Tom had found in the novels of Sir Walter Scott. He just liked the sound of it, rather as the president felt very comfortable with 'crusade'.

It was the right response to what was, Bush said, 'a new kind of evil'. Unlike Huck, everyone would know what he meant, deep down. For the same reason, he again used the language of *maledicta* on a much more formal and better-prepared occasion. The utterances on 16 September – the repeated reiteration of 'evil' and 'evildoers', the invocation of a crusade – were in an impromptu setting. But in his first State of the Union Address on 29 January 2002, he once more insisted upon the same register:

States like these [Iran, Iraq, North Korea], and their terrorist allies, constitute an axis of evil, arming to threaten the peace of the world. By seeking weapons of mass destruction, these regimes pose a grave and growing danger. They could provide these arms to terrorists, giving them the means to match their hatred. They could attack our allies or attempt to blackmail the United States. In any of these cases, the price of indifference would be catastrophic.[53]

These two Bush speeches turn upon the same themes, but for the State of the Union Address there had been a process of careful fine-tuning. 'Axis of Evil' was a well-honed 'portmanteau phrase'.[54] It was made up of two separate elements. Before 29 January 2002, 'Axis' in the United States always referred to the Axis Powers of WWII.[55] This was one form of evil by association. So the Bush phrase really meant, in effect, 'the (Evil) Axis of Evil'. 'Evil' or 'evildoers' came very naturally to the president's lips, but the words also had a special political resonance in US presidential discourse: Bush, from the global podium of the State of the Union Address, evoked Reagan's 'Evil Empire' speech.

The language you choose affects the listener's perception of what you are saying. Bush turned naturally to preacher-talk, to the sonorous phrases of Sunday sermons. But his speechwriters used this same vocabulary, and honed it to provide a broader and more appealing message. It is worth considering why the reference to the 'Axis of Evil' was incorporated so publicly in Bush's State of the Union message. He did not precisely follow Reagan's precedent, as some have suggested. The most probable answer is that, given the unprecedented sense of apocalyptic crisis after the attacks of 11 September, it seemed necessary to 'foreground Evil' in a most public domain. Quite how the 'Axis of Evil' phrase first emerged is not entirely clear. 'Axis of Hatred' was raised as another possibility.[56] Bush approved 'Axis of Evil' and it survived all the redraftings of the speech. It certainly fitted in well with earlier examples of the president's instinctive rhetoric. So on 29 January 2002 George Walker Bush launched a phrase that will guarantee his place in any future *Dictionary of Quotations*. As an utterance, it had an emotive force, as powerful in its own way as Franklin Delano Roosevelt's words in his first Inaugural Address of 1933: 'The only thing we have to fear is fear itself.' Nothing else in President Bush's address was memorable, so perhaps we need to consider wherein its resonance lies.

Would Axis of Hatred have had the same impact as 'Axis of Evil' in January 2002? Probably not. Some words are curiously loaded, and 'evil' is one of them. So too, as we have seen, are 'crusade' and *'jihad'*. For much of the history described in this book, 'infidel' was another. 'Terror', 'terrorism' and 'terrorist' have now acquired many of the attributes of fear and horror that once attached to Turks and Tartars. There were many such regressions to the older world of *maledicta* in the conversations recorded in *Bush at War*, but one that stands out in particular:

The president had signed a new intelligence order, the gloves were off.

'You have one mission,' Black instructed [Cofer Black was the Director of the Counter-Terrorism Center at the Central Intelligence Agency] . . . 'Get Bin Laden, find him. I want his head in a box.'

'You're serious?' asked Gary ['Gary' was the senior agent on the ground in Afghanistan] . . .

'Absolutely,' Black said. The new authority was clear. Yes, he said, he wanted Bin Laden's head. 'I want to take it down and show the President.'

'Well, that couldn't be any clearer,' Gary replied.

. . . In Afghanistan a few days later, the agent asked Washington to fly in some heavy-duty cardboard boxes and dry ice, and if possible some pikes.[57]

Incredible, perhaps, but Bush had been hugely impressed by Black's go-getting attitude. In the president's inner circle the CIA man was known as 'the flies-on-the-eyes guy', from his earlier comment that 'when we're through with them [Al Qaeda], they will have flies walking on their eyeballs.' Woodward concluded, after his lengthy interviews with Bush, that the Commander-in-Chief was 'tired of rhetoric. The president wanted to kill somebody.'[58]

This dialogue seems more suitable to a sixteenth-century Ottoman sultan and a pasha eager to please than to a twenty-first-century United States administration. The reader's mind races. What did Gary intend to do with the pike? Decapitate Bin Laden with a Government-issue machete, then parade the head, still dripping blood, through the cheering ranks of US troops, rather like that of the Ottoman admiral at the battle of Lepanto? What this little episode suggests is that once you have entered the world of *maledicta*, with its accursed enemies, it is near impossible not to fall from a modern world that respects progress into the dark domain of raw faith. But just imagine if Black's plan had been fulfilled, and he had carried the head of America's evil enemy, in dry ice, triumphantly into the Oval Office. How would the president have responded to this culmination of his crusade?

The exercise of Realpolitik generates so many similar examples of casual-but-necessary brutality that this minute picking-over of a few words might seem a ridiculous scholastic exercise of the 'how many angels can dance on the head of a pin' variety. But watching history-in-the-making, without the benefit of hindsight and an archive, demands that we consider these tiny physical traces like those that archaeologists use to reconstruct an image of lost worlds. The argument of this book is that words and images matter, because it is often in spontaneous or ephemeral productions that the uncensored truth resides. Censorship can be of two types. We all self-censor, and the presentation President Bush makes of himself after preparation is very different from the man speaking off the cuff or under pressure. Then there is the censorship or artful rhetoric produced by professional speechwriting. In the Hundred Days after the murderous attacks on New York and Washington, it has been the unguarded moments that have provided the greatest insights and revelations.

There is no problem in reverting to the apocalyptic register, to *maledicta* – if you are willing to accept the consequences. The US columnist Arianna Huffington expressed the issue succinctly:

I was always troubled by the president's repeated references to 'the evil ones' – from his first press conference after the attack, when he mentioned 'the evil one' and 'evildoers' five times, to his recent vow that 'across the world and across the years, we will fight the evil ones, and we will win.' I objected not because the terrorists aren't evil but because, as much as we would love it to be true, such a simple demarcation of good and evil flies in the face of history, religion and human nature.

The lure of this kind of reductionist thinking is not a new one. Alexander Solzhenitsyn, himself a victim of some of the most horrific evil of the 20th century, warned against it in *The Gulag Archipelago*: 'If only there were evil people somewhere insidiously committing evil deeds and it were necessary only to separate them from the rest of us and destroy them. But the line dividing good and evil cuts through the heart of every human being.'[59]

It is enormously difficult to keep the language of *maledicta* under control, to hold it within bounds. It touches too many deep and visceral feelings, dramatizing the conflict between a good and an imperfect world. As I was writing this, I thought of another conflict between perfection and imperfection, imagined by Dean Swift in *Gulliver's Travels*. Swift is usually remembered for his first story, where his hero, Lemuel Gulliver, has extraordinary adventures in the Land of the Lilliputians. This is a happy satire, today considered entirely appropriate for reading in schools.

But Gulliver's last voyage is a much darker story and certainly not suitable for children. Swift wrote of a society ruled by a race of godlike stallions called Houyhnhnms, which meant in their language 'the Perfection of Nature'. In their world, human beings were vile and degraded creatures called Yahoos. Gulliver, who walked on two legs not four, and was obviously a Yahoo by appearance, puzzled them. Try as they might, they could not divorce in their minds this bright and alert traveller from his brutish tribe. Over time Gulliver admired the horses much more than the humans of his own world. Houyhn-hnms epitomized what was best in the human world and had abolished its negative qualities. There were no words in their language for 'lying' or 'falsehood', and Reason was invariably their guiding principle. When Gulliver described the atrocities of war in his own country, his Houyhnhnm 'master' told him to be quiet.

He said whoever understood the nature of the Yahoos might easily believe it possible for so vile a creature to be capable of every action I had named . . . But, as my discourse had increased his abhorrence of the whole species, he found it gave him a disturbance in his mind . . . He thought that his ears being used to such abominable words, might by degrees admit them with less detestation. That, although he hated the Yahoos of this country, yet he no more blamed them for their detestable qualities than he did . . . a sharp stone for cutting his hoof. But, when a creature pretending to reason, would be capable of such enormities, he dreaded, lest the corruption of that faculty [Reason] might be worse than brutality itself.[60]

The nation constructed by 'the Perfection of Nature' was rational, well ordered, productive and comfortable. But its mentality could not come to terms with anything it did not understand. In the end Gulliver represented a threat to this settled world of the horses. It was not because of anything he had done, but because he was a 'brute animal' like the rest of his species. With the greatest reluctance, Gulliver built himself a small boat and sailed away, eventually returning to England.

There, in a final irony, after rejection by the Houyhnhnms whom he idolized, Gulliver became a renegade among his own species, the English, or revolting Yahoos.

My Wife and Family received me with great Surprise and Joy . . . but I must confess, the Sight of them filled me only with Hatred, Disgust and Contempt . . . And when I began to consider, that by copulating with one of the Yahoo species, I had become a parent of more, it struck me with the utmost Shame, Confusion and Horror.

As soon as I entered the house, my Wife took me in her Arms and kissed me; at which, not having been used to the Touch of that odious Animal for so many Years, I fell into a Swoon for almost an Hour. At the time I am writing it is almost five Years since my last Return to England; during the first Year I could not endure my Wife or Children in my Presence, the very Smell of them was intolerable.[61]

Swift's humane message is partly confounded by its sardonic expression. But he tells us that, very gradually, Gulliver came to accommodate himself to the Yahoos of his own family.

Is the lesson of this long history of the Infidels one of despair, of unending hatred? Not entirely. Even the misanthropic Dean Swift expressed a positive if guarded optimism about the future: 'I am not altogether out of hopes in some time to suffer Neighbour Yahoo in my Company, without the Apprehensions I am yet under of his Teeth and his Claws.'[62] The message for us? Are not all those whom we fear 'Yahoos', except that we call them by different names? And are they really as dangerous as we have always feared?

If the Yahoos (or evildoers) do pose an omnipresent or mortal threat, then perhaps the only alternative is to pursue them to the last extremity, to behave as did the Houyhnhnms. So let us consider the operational realities, as Cofer Black might put it. In the medieval or early modern Total Wars against evil, even primitive methods of social control were relatively efficient. How much more, then, could be achieved with modern systems of information and control? It would mean reverting to the inquisitorial mind-set like the one I described earlier in this book. There is a high price in social terms for re-inventing heresy. But there should also be the nagging doubts as to whether it would work. The 'evildoers' now seem to be more powerful than ever, and like the unclean spirits in St Mark's gospel, their name is Legion.[63] However, demonizing new enemies like Al Qaeda in crusading language is to misunderstand their power and practice. The temptation is to consider them primitives stuck in a set of seventh-century beliefs. According to Western traditional thought, these fanatics would have no truck with images, television or the Internet. But they are not primitive in this sense. Osama bin Laden is not preoccupied with ancient prohibitions, such as the public display of images – his face is everywhere.

The world of the 'evildoers' is mutable, not fixed, with an ideology capable of taking any shape. Currently, they disseminate their 'product' by what is for the moment called 'viral marketing'. Dr Ralph F. Wilson describes this:

You have to admire the virus. He has a way of living in secrecy until he is so numerous that he wins by sheer weight of numbers. He piggybacks on other hosts and uses their resources to increase his tribe. And in the right environment, he grows exponentially. A virus doesn't even have to mate – he just replicates, again and again, with geometrically increasing power, doubling with each iteration:

1

11

1111

11111111

1111111111111111

11111111111111111111111111111111

1111111111111111111111111111111111111111111111111111111111111111

In a few short generations, a virus population can explode.

What does a virus have to do with marketing? Viral marketing describes any strategy that encourages individuals to pass on a marketing message to others, creating the potential for exponential growth in the message's exposure and influence. Like viruses, such strategies take advantage of rapid multiplication to explode the message to thousands, to millions.

Off the Internet, viral marketing has been referred to as 'word-of-mouth', 'creating a buzz', 'leveraging the media', 'network marketing'. But on the Internet, for better or worse, it's called 'viral marketing'. While others smarter than I have attempted to rename it, to somehow domesticate and tame it, I won't try. The term 'viral marketing' has stuck.[64]

The viral analogy is relevant to the spread of terrorism, for infective viruses cannot be treated by traditional 'antibiotic' methods. It is clear from *Bush at War* that the measures used by the president and most of his main advisors against 'the evil enemy' have treated only what they imagined to be the symptoms and not the underlying condition. The Bush administration, viscerally predisposed towards 'a war on evil' has looked only to destroying the bodies that house the infection. But they are blind to the true nature of their opponents. The ancient language and ideology of evil has inclined the US government to see their enemy as some crude, inflexible quasi-medieval relic that can be extirpated with fire or the sword. In their minds they see an emeny wearing a turban. The reality is an opponent like a 'virus', endlessly changing its shape and mutating to counter the strengths and qualities of the most powerful nation on earth.

But there are alternatives to the *maledicta* of the political language of 'evil' and 'evildoers'. Thomas Jefferson drafted the section of the United States Declaration of Independence that contains the following phrase: 'We hold these truths to be self-evident, that all men are created equal, that they are endowed by their Creator with certain unalienable rights, that among these are life, liberty and the pursuit of happiness.' His original draft was more comprehensive, but the phrase 'pursuit of happiness' survived editing and redrafting, rather as 'the Axis of Evil' survived into President Bush's 2002 State of the Union Address. The language of happiness was a common political discourse at the time that the Declaration was compiled. It has been considered so inclusive as to defy precise definition.[65] Such objectives were not unique to the United States, but no other nation has made it a founding principle of its state's existence. Moreover, it was clear that happiness was not an other-worldly objective, to be achieved in the hereafter, but something that related to the conduct of everyday life. It was an ideal at the heart of the eighteenth-century Enlightenment.

In his first Inaugural Address on 4 March 1801, after a fiercely contested election, which eventually tied at thirty-seven electoral-college votes with his opponent Aaron Burr, Jefferson warned of a crabbed and constricted political imagination. 'And let us reflect that, having banished from our land that religious intolerance under which mankind so long bled and suffered, we have yet gained little if we countenance a political intolerance as despotic, as wicked, and capable of as bitter and bloody persecutions.' The success of the young United States depended, in his view, upon a 'sacred principle'.

'Every difference of opinion is not a difference of principle . . . If there be any among us who would wish to dissolve this Union or to change its republican form, let them stand undisturbed as monuments of the safety with which error or opinion may be tolerated where reason is left free to combat it.[66]

Is this just another of the sententious platitudes that too often figure in public rhetoric? I think not: here is a uniquely powerful, combative idea. Reason, in Jefferson's view, is a weapon that will undermine or neutralize 'error of opinion'. It is more adaptable, more resilient, and more dangerous to 'error' than the blind certainties of faith. Lurking in these words, it seems to me, is the germ of an 'anti-viral', a powerful strategy more than capable of resisting this new 'viral' enemy. It will succeed better than the messianic zealotry embodied in the non-Jeffersonian ideas that 'extremism in the defence of liberty is no vice . . . moderation in the pursuit of justice is no virtue!'[67] *Maledicta* and a 'crusade against evildoers' are decrepit and antiquated responses to an enemy that might appear to take an ancient shape, but is in reality infinitely adaptable, more post-modern than modern.

In the short term, of course, overwhelming military power will triumph. But in the longer term, over years and decades, the eventual outcome could be very different. A reversion to *maledicta* will ultimately prove self-destructive. An ideology based on these atavistic conditioned responses to the 'infidel' will fail, and in failing may even slowly unravel the last two centuries of the West's social, cultural and spiritual development.[68]

Notes on the Text

NOTE: Unpublished Spanish sources are referred to as Document, with a number, and are listed in full at the beginning of the Sources and Select Bibliography. For published works cited here in a shortened form only, the complete bibliographic details appear in the Select Bibliography. Other published sources appear here in full, and not in the Select Bibliography.

Preface

1. And, of course, we do not have Urban's precise words, but only the memory of them through a number of different writers.
2. This is Ludwig Wittgenstein's statement in the Preface to *Tractatus Logico-Philosophicus* (London: Routledge and Kegan Paul, 1922) that 'What can be said at all can be said clearly; and whereof one cannot speak thereof one must be silent.' But this translation does not really capture the resonance of the original ('*Was sich überhaupt sagen lässt, lässt sich klar sagen; und wovon man nicht reden kann, darüber muss man schweigen*').
3. See Lance St John Butler, *Registering the Difference: Reading Literature through Register*, Manchester: Manchester University Press, 1999.
4. *Iliad*, bk 1, l. 201.
5. Douglas Adams, *The Hitchhiker's Guide to the Galaxy*, London: Pan Books, 1979, pp. 144–5.

Chapter 1

1. Twenty-four feet long by thirteen feet wide.
2. Cited in Rodgers, *Naval Warfare*, p. 179.
3. Although the French were not present, popular emotions in France seem to have been with the forces of the Holy League. In the Protestant states, sentiment likewise seems to have been united with the arms of Catholic Europe.
4. Christendom and Islam are both complex terms, which many theorists might (appropriately) term 'discourses'. I have certainly used 'Christendom' in this way, not just as a term meaning a monolithic Christian society, which never existed after the early days of the faith, but rather to describe cultures derived from a long history of Christian belief. Islam is not exactly a comparator of Christendom in its structures, but we have no single word in English to

encompass that discourse either. The phrase *Dar ul-Islam* has been variously translated as the Abode, House, or Domain of Faith, Righteousness, or Peace. The basic point is that for a sincere and committed Muslim all that is good and necessary exists within the world of Islam, while all outside is of a lower order. But what is outside can often be brought inside and rendered good. On these topics see Hentsch, *Imagining*.

5. They escaped, by this papal decree, 200 years of Purgatory.

6. The banner, which was long kept as a trophy in Spain, was destroyed by fire in the nineteenth century.

7. Ali had formerly been second in command to Piali Pasha.

8. Genesis 4:14. The traditional explanation, that the Arabs descended from Ishmael, the elder son of Abraham, and his concubine Hagar, elided with the legend of Cain, also the elder son, and also cast out. For the instability and mutability of these legends of origin, see Freedman, *Images*, pp. 89–96.

9. The leader of the poor warriors of the First Crusade, the King of the Tafurs, called Muslims 'sons of whores and of the race of Cain'; see Cohn, *Pursuit*, p. 67. The people of the West, it was believed, were descended from Adam's third son Seth, via Noah and his lineage.

10. See, for example, Christian Augustus Pfaltz von Osteritz, *Abominatio desolationis Turcicae*, Prague: Carl-Ferdinand Druckerei, 1672, pp. 81–3.

11. France adopted the alternative approach of seeking alliance with the Ottomans, and Spain also sought an accommodation after 1580.

12. The paradox and ambiguity between Islam as part of God's intended plan – to bring his people to self-awareness – and Islam as pure evil was never properly resolved. Many writers embody both attitudes.

13. Some, like the Grand Vizier Sokullu, preferred to use diplomatic means.

14. So-called from the three banks of oars on each side.

15. Increasingly, also in the artillery carried aboard. This proved to be a decisive advantage for the Christian ships in battle. But the guns could only sink or disable an enemy ship. Like infantry ashore, a galley battle usually depended on hand-to-hand fighting.

16. This numbered about sixty-five soldiers in the Spanish galleys of the 1530s, but this had risen markedly by the 1570s. See Guilmartin, *Gunpowder and Galleys*, p. 227.

17. Ibid., p. 221.

18. This practice was especially common among the Maltese captains.

19. See Guilmartin, *Gunpowder and Galleys*, p. 63.

20. See I. A. A. Thompson, 'A Map of Crime in Sixteenth-century Spain', *EHR* Second Series, XXI, No. 2 (August 1968), pp. 244–67.

21. Often false 'debts' were created to allow them to be kept at the oar.

22. See Ruth Pike, *Penal Servitude in Early Modern Spain*, Madison, WI: University of Wisconsin Press, 1983.

23. See Bracewell, *Uskoks*.

24. See Guilmartin, *Gunpowder and Galleys*, p. 99.

25. This was the case with Ulch Ali, or Kulic ('the Sword') Ali; a Calabrian, kidnapped from his village, he became the Kapudan Pasha after Lepanto.

26. This was a form of flammable liquid (like napalm) devised by the Byzantines that would burn even under water. Its exact formula remains unknown to this day.

27. The first forms were Venetian merchant galleys adapted to carry cannon. Later forms evolved towards becoming longer and broader in beam.

28. See Guilmartin, *Gunpowder and Galleys*, p. 234.

29. Strictly speaking, he lost the use of his arm.

30. For example, the sixteenth-century French jurist and philosopher, Jean Bodin (now best remembered for his writings on political sovereignty), denied that it was a sufficient cause for a just war.

31. Qur'an, Surah 61:4.

32. See Renard, *Islam*, pp. 43–65.

33. The Patent Number 418 of 15 May 1718 for Puckle's machine gun, however, shows that it was designed to fire round bullets at Christians and square bullets at Muslims. This was perhaps the last effort at this kind of control on sectarian grounds. See W. H. B. Smith, *Small Arms of the World*, Harrisburg, PA: Stacpole Publishing Company, 1957, p. 92.

34. Artillery *was* used in innovative fashions, as, for example, Mehmed the Conqueror employing siege artillery to destroy the walls of Constantinople, but it was manufactured by renegade Hungarian Christians.

35. As, notably, at the battle of Dettingen in 1743.

36. See Stirling-Maxwell, *Don John*, vol. I, p. 385, citing Don John to Don Garcia de Toledo, 16 September 1571.

37. Ibid., pp. 384–5.

38. The 100,000 men included new contingents that arrived in early spring. See Beeching, *Galleys*, p. 175.

39. Ibid., p. 176.

40. However, Suleiman the Lawgiver had allowed the Knights of St John to evacuate Rhodes after a five-month siege that cost between 50,000 and 100,000 Turkish lives. But on that occasion hostages were exchanged and both parties fulfilled the stipulations of the agreement to the letter.

41. See Bohnstedt, 'The Infidel Scourge', p. 19. One German Reformation pamphleteer, Veit Dietrich, described the Turks thus: 'of such merciless, wild murdering there is no example in history, not even in that of the pagans, except for the doings of the Scythians and other barbarians at times when they are exceptionally angry. But the Turk does such things all the time, for no other reason than that the devil drives him against the Christians.'

42. Some sources suggest that he was whipped every day. My account is based on Stirling-Maxwell, who in turn bases his reconstruction on Paolo Paruta, *Storia della guerra di Cipro*, part of his contemporary *Historia Venetiana*, published in 1605, and on Nestor Martinengo, taken prisoner at Famagusta, and whose *Relazione di tutto il suceso di Famagusta*, was published in Venice in 1572. All these sources reflect viewpoints acceptable to Venice, but there is no reason to doubt their accuracy. I have not been able to find an Ottoman source that covered these events in any detail. See Stirling-Maxwell, *Don John*, vol. I, p. 370.

43. C. D. Cobham (ed.), *The Sieges of Nicosia and Famagusta: With a Sketch of the Earlier History of Cyprus*, edited from Midgley's translation of Bishop Graziani's *History of the War of Cyprus* (1624), London: St. Vincent's Press, 1899, p. 17; and *The Sieges of Nicosia and Famagusta in Cyprus Related by Uberto Foglietta*, trans. Claude Delaval Cobham, London: Waterlow and Sons, 1903.

44. Flaying was seen to be the ultimate degradation, partly for its cruelty but also for its slow stripping of identity. It was rare among the Ottomans, where other cruel punishments were more common. It was no doubt for the shock effect that Lala Mustafa ordered this frightful form of lingering death. The point of reference here is the story in Ovid's *Metamorphoses* of Apollo ordering the flaying of his rival Marsyas. The scene was depicted most graphically by Titian in *c.* 1575, and also by Raphael, Giulio Romano, Melchior Meier and in numerous engravings. The horror felt at the flaying process was evident in Arthur Golding's 1567 translation of the *Metamorphoses*:

> For all his crying ore his earses quite pulled was his skin
> Nought else was he then but one whole wounde. The grisly bloud did
> spin
> From every part, his sinewes lay discovered to the eye,
> The quivering veynes without a skin lay beating nakedly.
> The panting bowels in his bulke ye might have numbred well,
> and in his brest the shere small strings a man might tell.

See Jonathan Sawday, *The Body Emblazoned: Dissection and the Human Body in Renaissance Culture*, London: Routledge, 1995, pp. 186–7. It was noted that Bragadino did not cry out but murmured the words of faith until he fell silent.

45. See the dispatch from Don John to Philip II, describing the taking of Galera, reprinted as Appendix I in Stirling-Maxwell, *Don John*, vol. 2, pp. 364–71: 'In the place itself the defence was so obstinate that it was necessary to take it house by house and the taking of it lasted from nine in the morning, fighting going on the whole while in the houses, in the streets and on the roofs, the women fighting as well and bravely as their husbands.'

46. This was Stirling-Maxwell's conclusion about the battle: 'Although in numbers, both of men and vessels, the Sultan's fleet was superior to the fleet of the league, this superiority was more than counterbalanced by other important advantages possessed by the Christians. The artillery of the West was of greater power and far better served than the ordnance of the East.' See ibid., vol. I, p. 423.

47. My translation from M. Antonio Arroyo, *Relación del progresso della Armada de la Santa Liga* (Milan, 1576), cited in ibid., vol. I, p. 410. Maxwell translates *Hermanos* as 'Friends', but 'Brothers' makes better sense.

48. Putti blowing on to the Christian ships to fill the sails were shown in paintings of Lepanto.

49. Some of the commanders on the wings had already made the decision for themselves and gave the galleasses a wide berth.

50. Of the 170 Ottoman galleys captured most of them were so badly damaged as to be useless. See Stirling-Maxwell, *Don John*, vol. I, pp. 430–31.

51. Ibid., p. 407, citing Girolomo Diedo, *Lettere di Principe*, vol. III, p. 266.

52. See Stirling-Maxwell, *Don John*, vol. I, p. 427.

53. Ibid., pp. 445–6.

54. Fray Josef de Sigüenza, *Historia de la Orden de San Geronimo* (1605), cited in ibid., p. 448.

55. As he wrote to Don John six days later, 'I thought I should never have arrived but have been made into relics in Italy and France as a man sent by your Highness.' With a studied impassivity, the king asked nothing about the battle at first. 'For the first half hour he did nothing but ask "Is my brother certainly well?" and all sorts of conceivable questions that the case admitted. He then ordered me to relate everything that had happened from the beginning, omitting no single particular, and while I spoke, he three times stopped to ask me for further explanations; and when I had ended, he as often called me back to ask for further explanations; about your Highness's care for the wounded, and how you gave away your share of the prize money to the soldiers, at which he was not a little moved.' See Rosell, *Historia*, Appendix xiv, p. 208.

56. See Christopher Tyerman, *The Invention of the Crusades*, Basingstoke: Macmillan, 1998, pp. 101–6.

57. See Rosell, *Historia*, p. 208, for the report of Don Lope de Figueroa.

58. I owe this observation to John Brewer.

59. Reproduced in Göllner, *Turcica*, vol. 1, p. 234.

60. This was recalled in an etching of the Triumphal Entry made in the mid nineteenth century. Now in the Museo de Roma, Gabinetto Comunale delle Stampe.

61. It had been also, of course, the site of the inconclusive battle of Prevesa in 1538.

62. The traditional puppet theatre of Sicily also enacts these stories.

63. See Musée de la Corse, *Moresca*.

64. Cited in Lewis, *Discovery*, p. 43.

65. See Joseph von Hammer-Purgstall, *Histoire de l'Empire ottoman: depuis son origine jusqu'à nos jours*, trans. J.-J. Hellert, 18 vols, Paris: Bellizard, Barthès, Dufour, 1835–43, vol. 6, p. 434.

66. As in Montesquieu's *Lettres Persanes* (1721).

67. *The Dungeons of Algiers*, act 3.

68. Muley Malek was modelled on reality, from a Moroccan prince, Muley Maluco, living in Spain.

69. *Alfred, An Epick Poem*, 'In Twelve Books' by Sir Richard Blackmore, London, 1723, bk I, p. 24.

70. The last early modern Mediterranean 'crusade' was not Lepanto, but this Portuguese expedition that ended in disaster on 4 August 1578 not far from Tangier. See Braudel, *Mediterranean*, pp. 1178–9, and Hess, *Forgotten Frontier*, pp. 96–8.

Chapter 2

1. In 1575, in his dedication (to Howard of Effingham) of his version of Curio's *Notable Historie of the Saracens*, Thomas Newton declared that 'this Babylonian Nebuchanezzer and Turkish Pharoeh [are] so near under our noses . . . Now

they are even at our doors and ready to come into our Houses . . . this raging Beast and bloody Tyrant, the common robber of all the world.' See Coelius Augustinus Curio, *A Notable Historie of the Saracens*, trans. Thomas Newton, London: n.p., 1575, rep. Amsterdam: Walter J. Johnson Inc, 1977.

2. The first 'Mad Mullah' was the Somali leader Mohammed bin Abdullah Hassan, against whom the British fought from 1899. 'Mad Mullah' has now become a common insult.

3. The tenth-century writer Hamza al-Isfahani listed only five great nations, from China in the East to the Berbers in the West, plus the Byzantines. Cited in Khalidi, *Arabic Historical Thought*, pp. 117–18. There was a Muslim polemic against Christianity, and against western Christians in particular, but before the late eighteenth century it was not accompanied by any strong curiosity about those whom it attacked. Jacques Waardenburg also notes that while the Muslims had 'a lingering curiosity for those non-Muslims outside the *dar-ul-islam*, there was a near-complete absence of interest in the *dhimmis* [local Christians and Jews] in Muslim lands'. See Jacques Waardenburg, 'Muslim Studies of Other Religions: The Medieval Period' in Van Gelder and De Moor, 'The Middle East and Europe', pp. 10–38.

4. This was the 'persecuting society', first identified by R. I. Moore, subsequently challenged and modified, but still solid in all its essentials. See Moore, *Formation*, and Laursen and Nederman, *Beyond*.

5. Muslims also used the word *jahilyya* to describe the period before Islam brought light and order to the world. But the pre-Islamic poetry of Arabic depicts the noble qualities of that world.

6. For example, at Duma in 634. See Glubb, *Conquests*, p. 132.

7. Mark Whittrow has pointed to multiple problems with the sources for the first Islamic conquests. See Whittrow, *Making*, pp. 82–9.

8. Cited in Gil, *History*, p. 41.

9. Ibid., pp. 38–9.

10. See Gibbon, *Decline and Fall*, vol. 5, p. 422. Gibbon uses the often fanciful chronicle of Al Wakidi, and Ockley's *History of the Saracens*. But although the details are embellished the essence of the battle seems plausible.

11. See Gil, *History*, pp. 42–4.

12. This was the pass that Alexander the Great and his armies had traversed.

13. Gil, *History*, p. 170, asserts the contrary: 'One should not assume that the Moslems were in a majority during this period.' However, his Muslims are Peninsular Arabs, 'tribes who derived their income from taxes from the subdued population', and so converts do not figure.

14. See Zernov, *Eastern Christendom*, p. 84.

15. This had been miraculously rediscovered by the Emperor Constantine's mother, Saint Helena.

16. Cited in Glubb, *Conquests*, p. 183.

17. Matthew 24: 15–24.

18. See Constantelos, 'Moslem Conquests', p. 325.

19. Cited in Christades, 'Arabs', p. 316.

20. These monstrous creatures were first described by Pliny the Elder in his *Historia*

Naturalis, completed in AD 77. See Moser, *Ancestral Images*, pp. 36–7. See also C. Meredith Jones, 'The Conventional Saracen of the Songs of Geste', *Speculum* 17 (1942), pp. 201–25.

21. See Sahas, *John of Damascus*.

22. *De Fide Orthodoxa*, IV, 11; cited in Khoury, *Polémique*, p. 11. John's father had been among those who formally surrendered Damascus to the Muslims.

23. See Jane I. Smith, 'Islam and Christendom: Historical, Cultural and Religious Interaction from the Seventh to the Fifteenth Centuries' in *The Oxford History of Islam*, ed. John L. Esposito, Oxford: Oxford University Press, 1999, p. 322. She observes: 'Scholastic writings coming out of the eastern part of the empire in the ninth and tenth centuries, especially from Byzantium, tended to be contemptuous and even abusive of the Prophet. In general this polemic was apocalyptic (prophesying the end of the Arabs) and highly uncharitable. The work produced in Spain . . . provided the first attempt at a comprehensive view of the religion of the Saracens, despite its predilection to see Islam as a preparation for the final appearance of the Antichrist.'

24. See Khoury, *Polémique*, pp. 360–61.

25. See Sherrard, *Constantinople*, pp. 8–9.

26. Cited in W. R. Lethaby and Harold Swainson, *Sancta Sophia Constantinople: A Study of Byzantine Building*, London: Macmillan & Co., 1894.

27. Revelation, 21: 2–3.

28. However, it was difficult to use effectively, except in limited defensive situations. For a balanced view, see Whittrow, *Making*, pp. 124–5.

29. See Gibbon, *Decline and Fall*, vol. 6, p. 8: 'The winter proved uncommonly rigorous. Above an hundred days the ground was covered with deep snow, and the natives of the sultry climes of Egypt and Arabia lay torpid and almost lifeless in their frozen camp.'

30. Theodosius Grammatikos, in Spyridonos Lambros, 'Le deuxième siège de Constantinople par les Arabes et Théodosius Grammatikos', Athens: *Historika Meletemata*, 1884, pp. 129–32, cited in Ducellier, *Chrétiens*, p. 133.

31. See Brubaker, *Vision*, pp. 19–58.

32. Zernov, *Eastern Christendom*, p. 86.

33. See Rotter, *Abendland und Sarazenen*, pp. 68–9.

34. Sebeos is a shadowy individual but, whoever he was, the dating and detail of his history is not in question. *History of Heraclius*, cited in Ducellier, *Chrétiens*, p. 28. The best translation is *The 'Armenian History' Attributed to Sebeos*, trans. Robert Thomson, 2 vols, Philadelphia, PA: University of Pennsylvania Press, 2000.

35. Revelation, 4: 7–8.

36. Ducellier, *Chrétiens*, p. 28.

37. Revelation 6: 1–17.

38. In fact, Sebeos' attitude, although hostile, shifted in register between a historical narrative and making an apocalyptic connection. Thus in Chapter 30 of his *History* he begins by saying, 'I shall discuss the [line of the] son of Abraham: not the one [born] of a free [woman], but the one born of a serving maid, about whom the quotation from Scripture was fully and truthfully fulfilled,

"His hands will be at everyone, and everyone will have their hands at him'
[Genesis 16: 12].'

39. Ibid., Chapter 38.

40. See Michael McCormick, 'Diplomacy and the Carolingian Encounter with
Byzantium down to the Accession of Charles the Bald' in B. McGinn and
W. Otten (eds), *Eriugena: East and West*, Notre Dame, IN: University of Notre
Dame Press, 1994. However, the outcome of these connections can be seen in
the cluster of chronicles concerning the seventh century of Spain: the *Chronicle*
of 754, the *Continuatio Byzantia Arabica* or *Chronicle* of 741, and a lost *Historia
Arabica*. The historiographical connections between them and their relative
importance is contested, but it is clear that Christians in Spain were fully aware
of events in the eastern Mediterranean during the conquest after 634, and
related these to the conquest of Spain. For a good discussion of these issues see
Collins, *Arab Conquest*, pp. 52–65. Dubler, 'Sobre la crónica' is suggestive of a
wider range of connections.

41. Alcuin, *Opera*, in J. P. Migne, *Patrologiae Series Latina*, Paris: Migne, 1863, vol.
100, letter 164.

42. This becomes how Lacan in *Ecrits* described the manner in which concepts and
ideas adhere. Jacques Derrida also noted the complexity of these attachments
and the way in which the accretions (and their interpretation) grew over time:
'The dissimulation of the woven texture [of a text] can in any case take centuries
to undo its web: a web that envelops a web, undoing the web for centuries;
reconstituting it too as an organism, indefinitely regenerating its own tissue
behind the cutting trace, the decision of each reading'; Jacques Derrida, *Dissemination*, trans. Barbara Johnson, London: The Athlone Press, 1981/1993, p. 63.
See also Jacques Lacan *Ecrits*, trans. Alan Sheridan, New York, NY: Norton,
1977. I found Lacan extraordinarily difficult to understand, even in translation,
although the original French edition (Editions du Seuil, 1966) was a useful
point of cross-reference. However, some of the papers in Mark Bracher
and Ellie Ragland-Sullivan (eds), *Lacan and the Subject of Language*, London:
Routledge, 1991, proved helpful.

43. On Saussure and Lacan, see Martin Francis Murray, 'Saussure, Lacan and the
Limits of Language', University of Sussex PhD, 1995. On Lacan's approach,
see Nancy and Lacoue-Labarthe, *The Title*.

44. Cited in Bat Ye'or, *Decline*, p. 419, Blunt to Bulwer, 14 July 1860.

45. See Qustandi Shomali, 'Church of the Nativity: History and Structure',
@ www.unesco.org/archi2000/pdf/shomali.pdf

46. There is also a Muslim story of desecration, with the Crusaders stabling their
horses in the Al-Aqsa mosque after the capture of Jerusalem in 1099. Are the
two stories connected or reciprocal?

47. Mary Eliza Rogers, *Domestic Life in Palestine* (1862), London: Kegan Paul
International, 1989, pp. 41–2.

48. Matthew 7:14. Gate and door are synonymous. See, also, Luke 13: 23–4: 'Then
said one unto him, "Lord, are there few that be saved?" And he said unto
them, "Strive to enter in at the strait gate: for many, I say unto you, will seek
to enter in and will not be able." '

49. Lacan said, 'Doubling a noun through a mere juxtaposition of two terms . . . a surprise is produced by the unexpected precipitation of an unexpected meaning: the image of twin doors symbolizing, with the solitary confinement offered Western man for the satisfaction of his natural needs away from home, the imperative which he seems to share with the great majority of primitive communities by which his public life is subjected to the laws of urinary segregation.' See Jacques Lacan, 'The Agency of the Letter in the Unconscious or Reason since Freud', *Ecrits*, trans. Alan Sheridan, New York, NY: Norton, 1977, p. 151.

Chapter 3

1. In his *Handbook for Travellers in Spain* (1845), reprinted in Richard Ford, *Granada: Escritos con dibujos inéditos del autor*, Granada: Patronato de la Alhambra, 1955.
2. But he also recognized the essence of the unforgiving terrain: 'But where Spaine has water and Valleis there she is extraordinarily fruitfull'; James Howell, *Instructions for Foreign Travell*, 1650.
3. Cited in Glubb, *Conquests*, p. 355.
4. See W. Montgomery Watt and Pierre Cachia, *A History of Islamic Spain*, Edinburgh: Edinburgh University Press, 1996, pp. 9–10, on the alternative possibilities of expansion.
5. The Christian *Mozarabic Chronicle* and the *Continuationes Bizantia-Arabica et Hispania* date from a few decades after the conquest. The first Arabic sources are later. See Collins, *Arab Conquest*, pp. 710–97. Ron Barkai makes the valid point that *Bizantia-Arabica* is less negative towards the Muslims in its language, and many of the more positive passages do not appear or have been altered in the *Mozarabic Chronicle*. See Barkai, *Cristianos y musulmanes*, pp. 24–5.
6. Tarif gave his name to the first Muslim town in Spain, built close to the former Roman citadel of Julia Traduce.
7. See the *Continuatio Isidoriana Hispania ad annum 754*, commonly called the *Mozarabic Chronicle*, translated by Colin Smith, in Smith, *Christians*, vol. 1, pp. 12–13. This chronicle is the first version of the story.
8. See the *Chronicle of Alfonso III of the Asturias*, written in 883: 'Because they had abandoned the Lord, and had not served him in righteousness and truth, they were abandoned by the Lord and were not allowed to dwell in the promised land [*terram desideratam*]'; in ibid., pp. 24–9.
9. See the *Historia pseudo-Isidoriana*; in ibid., pp. 14–16. This twelfth-century text introduced the trope of illicit sexuality into the foundation myth of Spain. In the *Mozarabic Chronicle* (754), the moral flaw of the king (Roderick) was that he 'violently usurped' the crown; ibid., pp. 10–11.
10. The two connected in a confused and uncertain fashion in what, since Julia Kristeva, we have called 'intertextuality'. My suggestion here is that Roderick's story is depicted, by a succession of clerical authors, in markedly Davidic terms.
11. The *Estoria de España* was written in the last quarter of the thirteenth century,

when this mythic description of the conquest reached an extraordinary efflor-escence. Moreover, this was written not in scholar's Latin but in Romance (Castilian). See Smith, *Christians*, vol. 1, pp. 21–2.

12. Ibid.

13. Américo Castro recognized the significance of these stories: 'Because Castile for centuries bore the brunt of the struggle against a people judged to be lascivious, a people that spoke of love and orgies in their literature, she imagined that violation of a maiden and the polygamy of the clergy were the determinants of a triumphant Saracen invasion.' See Castro, *Structure*, p. 328.

14. This image of Muslim lust became paradigmatic. Thus Juan Manuel in the *Libro de los Estados* noted, 'Long after Christ was crucified there arose a certain false man named Muhammad ... As part of his teaching he offered them wholesale indulgences in order that they could gratify their whims lustfully and to an altogether unreasonable extent.' Cited in Smith, *Christians*, vol. 2, pp. 94–5.

15. Cited in ibid., vol. 1, pp. 26–9.

16. See Angus MacKay, 'Ritual and Propaganda in Fifteenth-century Castile', *Past and Present* 107 (May 1985), pp. 3–43.

17. Ana Echevarria rightly observes that fifteenth-century Castilians showed a special identification with their ancestors, and evidently a knowledge of the epics that portrayed them. See Echevarria, *Fortress of Faith*, p. 121. The events at Simancas are outlined in W. D. Phillips, *Enrique IV and the Crisis of Fifteenth-century Castile*, Cambridge, MA: Medieval Academy of America, 1978.

18. See also the explanation for the instrumentality of the Muslims offered by Juan Manuel in the *Libro de los Estados*; Smith, *Christians*, vol. 2, pp. 94–5. This same theme emerged in the letter written by Alfonso VIII to Innocent III lamenting that so few Christians had died in the triumph over the Muslims at Las Navas de Tolosa in 1212: 'There is one cause for regret here: that so few in such a vast army went to Christ as martyrs'; ibid., p. 23.

19. The periods of central Muslim authority in Al-Andalus were as follows:
     Governors of Al-Andalus: 711–55
     Umayyad Emirate: 756–912
     Umayyad Caliphate: 912–1031
     Almoravid Caliphate: 1086–1145
     Almohad Caliphate: 1145–1224
     I have followed the periodization given in Kennedy, *Muslim Spain and Portugal*.

20. Gibbon, *Decline and Fall*, vol. 5, p. 479.

21. It was also known as the battle of Poitiers.

22. Isidore of Beja, *Chronicle*, cited in William Stearns Davis (ed.), *Readings in Ancient History*, Boston, MA: Allyn and Bacon, 1912–13, vol. 2, pp. 362–4.

23. See Glick, *Islamic and Christian Spain*, citing Elías Téres, 'Textos poéticos arabes sobre Valencia', *Al-Andalus* 30 (1965), pp. 292–5.

24. The number of converts is still a matter of controversy. The best calculation, by Richard Bulliet, has been questioned but not overturned. But it is clear that the immigrants from North Africa, even allowing a high rate of natural growth,

still could have formed only a minority of the Muslim population. See Glick, *Islamic and Christian Spain*.

25. The language issue is even more hotly disputed than the issue of conversion. The degree to which Berber remained a language of the hearth cannot conclusively be established. Whether Romance as spoken by the Mozarabes became a lingua franca is also in dispute. Popular oral practice is harder to establish than written textual practice, but even the latter is uncertain. But there is some evidence: by 1085, for example, when the Christians captured Toledo, the large Mozarabic population in the city all spoke Arabic. On trade languages and lingua franca, like Sabir, see J. E. Wansbrough, *Lingua Franca in the Mediterranean*, Richmond: Curzon Press, 1996.

26. See Chejne, *Muslim Spain*, pp. 110–20.

27. See Barkai, *Cristianos y musulmanes*.

28. See Ross Brann, *Power in the Portrayal: Representation of Jews and Muslims in Eleven- and Twelfth-century Islamic Spain*, Princeton, NJ: Princeton University Press, 2002.

29. See Guichard, *Al-Andalus*, pp. 171–2.

30. The Jews were expelled in 1492 from Castile and Aragon, and from Portugal and Navarre in the sixteenth century. Muslims were converted by decree in 1499, and those who adhered to their faith were forced to leave. The Christianized descendants of former Muslims were deported between 1609 and 1614.

31. From al-Wansharishi, Abul Abbas Ahmad, *Kitab al-mi'yar al-mugrib*, Rabat: 1981, p. 141. Translated from the Arabic in Harvey, *Islamic Spain*, pp. 58–9.

32. See Ibn Abdun, *Hisba manual* [market codes], translated in Olivia Remie Constable, *Medieval Iberia: Readings from Christian, Muslim and Jewish Sources*, Philadelphia, PA: University of Pennsylvania Press, 1997, p. 178.

33. Ibid., p. 179.

34. Douglas, *Purity and Danger*, p. 41.

35. First, in his *Manual de gramática histórica española elemental*, Madrid: Suarez, 1904, but the idea of a culture built up from many different intertwined sources suffuses Menéndez Pidal's later work, especially *Orígenes del español, estado lingüístico de la península ibérica hasta el siglo xi*, Madrid: Editorial Hernando, 1926. The extended concept of castle, *casticismo*, meaning purity of essence, has a powerful and somewhat malign meaning in Spanish history. This was in part the topic of Miguel de Unamuno's volume of essays *En Torno al Casticismo* (1895). Hence the use of the idea of caste in the Spanish context has a strong resonance. Américo Castro took Menéndez Pidal's notion and translated it into a theory of Spanish particularism; see Castro, *Structure*, pp. 607–15.

36. The definition is that of David Crystal in *The Cambridge Encyclopaedia of Language*, Cambridge: Cambridge University Press, 1997, p. 38.

37. The 'oppositional' statements predominated from the mid eleventh century, at a point when the confrontation between Islam and its Christian enemies became acute.

38. Nirenberg, *Communities*, p. 127.

39. See Geertz, *Meaning*, pp. 141–2.

40. The code envisaged that even after such a punishment, the woman might not

be able to resist temptation a second time. 'For the second offence, she shall lose all her property and . . . she shall be put to death.'

41. Jeffrey Richards, *Sex, Dissidence and Damnation: Minority Groups in the Middle Ages*, London: Routledge and Kegan Paul, 1991, p. 139.

42. Ibid., pp. 139–40. Peter Damian referred specifically to clerical acts of sodomy, but the tone is analogous to the general abhorrence of transgressive acts. The Seville market regulation of Ibn Abdun, for example, declared that catamites were 'debauchees accursed by God and man alike'; see Olivia Remie Constable, *Medieval Iberia: Readings from Christian, Muslim and Jewish Sources*, Philadelphia, PA: University of Pennsylvania Press, 1997, p. 179.

43. The great Castilian law codes created by Alfonso X, the *Siete Partidas*, for example, were never promulgated at the time of their creation. They were not so much law codes as a representation of an ideal state.

44. Mark R. Cohen cites the study by A. L. Udovitch and Lucette Valensi on the modern Jewish community of Djerba (Jerbi) in Tunisia, to the effect that 'although the ethnic and religious boundaries separating Muslims and Jews are by no means absent or obliterated in the market place, it is here that the lines of demarcation are most fluid and permeable'. See Cohen, *Under Crescent and Cross*, p. 118.

45. Francisco Benet, 'Explosive Markets: The Berber Highlands', in Louise E. Sweet (ed.), *Peoples and Cultures of the Middle East*, Garden City, NJ: Prentice Hall, 1970, pp. 171–203. Benet is writing principally of modern Berber culture, but Islamic Spain was predominantly Berber in culture, and the parallels drawn seem appropriate.

46. David Nirenberg has pointed out that in Spain, where the three castes lived side by side, meat (which had to be slaughtered to prescribed standards for Jews and Muslims) became a focus for violence and dispute; see Nirenberg, *Communities*, pp. 168–72. At times attempts were made to produce wholly segregated facilities, but this was rarely successful in the long term, unless they could be divided by time, as in the case of access to the communal bathhouses in ninth-century Cordoba, at least in the view of Janina Safran; see her 'Identity and Differentiation'.

47. 'If I give the name integralism to certain features that are common to Spanish and Moorish existence . . . In spite of the similarities between Spaniards and Moslems, the two people were differently situated inside the vital whole wherein are integrated the activity of the mind and the awareness of the objective and subjective – the "dwelling places" of their lives were different.' See Castro, *Structure*, p. 239.

48. It is curious that he uses 'Spaniards', rather than 'Christians' as the parallel term to 'Muslims'.

49. Castro, *Structure*, pp. 248–50.

50. Spanish has retained a rich vocabulary of locality, which perhaps echoes this tradition of segmentation: *barrio* (neighbourhood), *rincon* (quarter), *querencia* (favourite place; now usually a bullfighting term).

51. See Dana Reynolds, 'The African Heritage and Ethnohistory of the Moors', in Van Sertima, *Golden Age*, pp. 93–150.

52. This is Derrida's *dissémination*. Typically, he denies its meaning: 'In the last analysis, dissemination means nothing, and cannot be reassembled into a definition.' But the word 'dissemination' is a Derridean pun, filled with multiple connotations. It embodies the sexual act of in-semination, and no one can tell as a consequence how heritable qualities will change or transmute down the generations. However, dissemination is itself the act of spreading, and not knowing where the seed will fall or where it will implant and grow. Thus there has to be a common framework of meaning if communication is to take place at all, but the consequences of dissemination mean that this transfer of meaning is always subject to distortion. See Jacques Derrida, *Positions*, trans. Alan Bass, Chicago, IL: University of Chicago Press, 1981, pp. 44–5. I am grateful to Professor Nick Royle for drawing my attention to this relatively clear statement of a Derridean position.

53. Américo Castro observed that 'nothing is more revealing than language.' But, equally, nothing is more confusing and uncertain. Anwar Chejne, who has written a useful history in English of the Arabic language, also presents a picture of the particular development of Arabic in Al-Andalus; see Chejne, *Muslim Spain*, pp. 182–95. But even Chejne's presentation is uncertain about the exact interconnection between the languages. The linguistic melange of Al-Andalus included a great variety of *spoken* dialects – Arabic, Berber, and Romance – and *written* Arabic and Latin, the former advancing and the latter declining. There is later evidence that many northerners had some knowledge of spoken Arabic. There is no real support in Spain for Norman Daniel's suggestion, in respect of Norman Sicily, that the 'continued use of three languages' created a multicultural or tolerant society. See Daniel, *The Arabs*, p. 146, and Buxó, 'Bilingualismo y biculturalismo', pp. 177–92.

54. Alvarus wrote profusely. His main works were his letters (*Epistula*), *Memoriale sanctorum*, *Vita Eulogii* and *Liber apologeticus martyrum*, all contemporary with the events he described. On the effect of martyrs in Cordoba, see Dozy, *Spanish Islam*, pp. 268–9.

55. Jessica Coope, in her excellent account of the martyrs movement and of Perfectus, draws rather different conclusions. She notes that the Church of St Acisclus was a centre of 'radical' Christianity, and that the Muslims sought deliberately to entrap Perfectus. However, rather than resisting their entrapment, he participated in it with fatal results. The same body of evidence (and that provided by partisans, Eulogius and Alvarus) is capable of a number of interpretations. But all the sources tend towards the volatility of the religious situation in Cordoba at the time. See Coope, *Martyrs*, pp. 18–19.

56. Ibid.

57. The material for this section is drawn from Dozy, *Spanish Islam*, pp. 268–307.

58. Wolf, *Christian Martyrs*, analyses the movement in depth. He makes the case that the movement was not masterminded by Eulogius but, rather, that he portrayed the events in a way that would make their message more powerful. In particular, he countered the arguments that they were not true martyrs because they performed no miracles, and that they brought their deaths upon themselves, as indeed the authorities in Cordoba, both Christian and Muslim, clearly believed.

59. Eulogius, *Epistula ad Alvarusum*, 1, cited and translated in Coope, *Martyrs*.
60. R. A. Markus, *The End of Ancient Christianity*, Cambridge: Cambridge University Press, 1990, p. 24.
61. Coope, *Martyrs*, p. 52.
62. Ibid., p. 69.
63. Alvarus, *Indiculus luminosus*, cited and translated in ibid., p. 49.
64. Ibid.
65. Cited in Safran, 'Identity and Differentiation', p. 583.
66. Ibid. Abu Abdullah, Malik bin Anas, was born in Medina in 715. He produced the *Kitab-al-Muwatta*, the earliest surviving book of Islamic law, and made an important collection of *hadith*, oral traditions of the Prophet. The Malikite legal tradition followed in Al-Andalus 'disliked marriage with *dhimmi* women but did not forbid it. He [Malik] disliked it because the *dhimmi* wife eats pork and drinks wine and the Muslim husband kisses her and has intercourse with her. When she has children, she nourishes them according to her religion; she feeds them food that is forbidden and gives them wine to drink. Malik disapproved of intermarriage out of concern for purity and also because he feared for the religion of the children.'
67. Dozy, *Spanish Islam*, pp. 445–6.
68. See *Las Andalucías de Damasco a Córdoba*, Paris: Editorial Hazan, 2000.

Chapter 4

1. See Dodds, *Architecture*, pp. 94–6.
2. In much the same way that the Ottoman Turks centuries later adapted the architectural traditions of the Byzantines in building their state mosques. See Godfrey Goodwin, *A History of Ottoman Architecture*, London: Thames and Hudson, 1971.
3. From a Spanish translation of Ibn Idhari, *Al Bayan al Mughrib*.
4. Excavations have now extended to some ten hectares, less than 10 per cent of the 112 hectares that comprised the whole palace. The palace was built on rising ground overlooking the River Guadalquivir, with the caliph's personal quarters like a mirador looking out over the countryside. See *Las Andalucías de Damasco a Córdoba*, Paris: Editorial Hazan, 2000, pp. 64–5.
5. For Abd al-Rahman's palace reception and its impact, see Dozy, *Spanish Islam*, pp. 446–7. The entry of Caliph Omar into Jerusalem and, specifically, whether he was riding upon an ass, a horse or a camel has its own hotly disputed symbolism; see http://answering-islam.org/Responses/Al-Kadhi/r06.14.html. The significance of his riding an ass is that it would have echoed the prophecy of Zechariah 9:9 – 'Behold, thy King cometh unto thee; he is just, and having salvation; lowly, and riding upon an ass, and upon a colt the foal of an ass.' It was widely known that Christ had entered the city on an ass, in fulfilment of that prediction. Another echo was that of al-Buraq, a magical beast that had carried the Prophet Mohammed to Jerusalem on his night journey, and which was often depicted as part winged ass and part mule. These complex resonances also have a more modern context. In 1918 General Allenby, followed by his

staff, had deliberately dismounted from his horse so as to enter Jerusalem respectfully on foot, unlike the German Kaiser Wilhelm II who on his visit ten years before had been driven through the Jaffa Gate in great state. Allenby's Christian humility was ordered by the Foreign Office to contrast with the emperor's apparent Teutonic arrogance.

6. Ibid., p. 447.

7. See R. A. Fletcher, *Saint James's Catapult: The Life and Times of Diego Gelmírez of Santiago de Compostela*, Oxford: Oxford University Press, 1984, pp. 56–8.

8. Castro, *Structure*, pp. 130–45.

9. See Dozy, *Spanish Islam*, p. 519.

10. Ibid., p. 520. Castro, *Structure*, says that the bells were *melted down* to make lamps for the mosque.

11. Bruce Lincoln gives some sense as to what was intended in attacking the symbolic aspects of the shrine when describing the attack on the emblems of the Church at the start of the Spanish Civil War in 1936: 'It is their [the enemies of the Church's] intent to demonstrate dramatically and in public the powerlessness of the image and thereby inflict a double disgrace on its champions, first by exposing the bankruptcy of their vaunted symbols and second, their impotence in the face of attack.' See Bruce Lincoln, *Discourse and the Construction of Social Boundaries*, Oxford: Oxford University Press, 1989, pp. 120–21.

12. *Historia Silense*, written in Leon in about 1115.

13. In the case of the Wahabis in the nineteenth and twentieth centuries in Arabia, they desecrated even Muslim sites, proclaiming them idolatrous.

14. This was against the law and practice of Islam.

15. E. Lévi-Provençal, 'Les Mémoires de Abd Allah', *Al-Andalus* 4 (1936), pp. 35–6.

16. Their name is a version in Spanish of *Al-Murabitun*, meaning those who came from the *ribat*. These were closed encampments where the chosen warriors of Islam could lead pure lives. The first military towns of the Arab armies, such as Kufa or Cairouan, had served much the same function, as did the Wahabi settlements in Arabia in more modern times.

17. Like their modern descendants, the Tuareg.

18. See Chejne, *Muslim Spain*, pp. 69–72.

19. Ibn Idhari, *Al Bayan al Mughrib*, cited in Chejne, *Muslim Spain*, p. 72.

20. Few terms are more confused or misused than *jihad*. Not all wars fought by Muslim armies were holy wars, nor was the term applied only to warfare, for the 'struggle' could be interior and moral as well as military. Similarly, the Christian conflict of 'crusade' was replete with ambiguities: there were Crusades against secular enemies of the papacy or the church hierarchy, against heretics, as well as against Muslims. But the concept of *jihad* could be invoked by a ruler and once this was done the nature of any conflict altered. There is a large literature on this topic, but for a broad perspective see Johnson and Kelsay, *Just War*.

21. María Jesús Rubiera Mata has pointed out that the 'tolerance' of Toledo is a misnomer, being much more an accommodation between Muslims and

Christians. Against that should be set regular attacks on the Jews of the city. See 'Les premiers Mores convertis ou les prémices de la tolérance', in Cardaillac, *Tolède*, pp. 102–11.

22. *The Poem of the Cid* (anonymous), translated by Rita Hamilton and Janet Perry, Harmondsworth: Penguin, 1975, p. 55.

23. Ibid., p. 71. (Corneille produced his own version of the heroic deeds of Rodrigo in his play *Le Cid* of 1637.)

24. Ibid., p. 98.

25. For this transition see Fletcher, *Quest*, pp. 193–205. Plainly, at this distance in time, the boundary between the history and legend is blurred and subject to interpretation. But the desire to construct an ideal type of Hispanity, through the Cid or even Don Quixote, who has also been made to serve a similar typological purpose, is a persistent characteristic of the Spanish past.

26. See Eduardo Manzano Moreno, 'The Creation of a Mediaeval Frontier: Islam and Christianity in the Iberian Peninsula, Eighth to Eleventh Centuries', in Power and Standen, *Frontiers*, p. 52.

27. Cited in O'Callaghan, *History*, pp. 344–5.

28. Many Muslims had lived in Old and New Castile and the Kingdom of Aragon for several generations, and though in a minority were a settled part of the population. They were very different from the newly conquered communities in the south. See Harvey, *Islamic Spain*, pp. 51–2.

29. Cited in ibid., p. 66.

30. See Smith, *Christians and Moors*, vol. 2, p. 94, (my translation).

31. In 1408, Queen Catalina, regent for the young Juan II, ordered that Moors should wear a blue moon on their clothes and, four years later, that no one should address a Moor with the courtesy title *Don*. She even decreed that all Moors and Jews should live within their own communities and should not work for Christians. But the decrees were not effective and, in 1418, the status quo ante was restored; see Hillgarth, *Spanish Kingdoms*, vol. 2, p. 129.

32. This story is told in Nirenberg, *Communities*, pp. 146–8.

33. From the *Siete Partidas*. The Muslim and Jewish communities were even more anxious to preserve the separation of the communities.

34. This is the point that Gabriel Martinez-Gros raises against Pierre Guichard's *Structures sociales orientales et occidentales dans l'Espagne musulmane*, Paris: Ecole des hautes études en sciences sociales, 1977. Martinez-Gros regards an 'Andalusian identity' as a form of Orientalism: 'About the first hundred pages of Pierre Guichard's book are devoted to defining the characteristics of "Occident" and "Orient" as a benchmark from which we can judge the society of Al-Andalus . . . The "Occident" is derived from the Carolingian epoch, where we return to the first centuries of the history of Al-Andalus. The "Orient", by contrast, finds its essential framework and definitions in the studies of modern anthropologists, well versed in understanding the mountains of the maghrib, the marshes of Southern Iraq, or the deserts of Arabia, as if a sort of Eternal East existed, eternally preserved for good or ill within history.' He suggests that the evidence used by Guichard will not sustain the elaborate superstructure built upon it; see Martinez-Gros, *Identité Andalouse*, p. 117.

35. See Mikel de Epalza, 'Pluralisme et tolérance, un modèle tolédan?' and Jean-Pierre Molénat, 'Mudéjars, captifs et affranchis', in Cardaillac, *Tolède*.

36. See Lapiedra Gutiérrez, *Como*, pp. 67 sqq. Logically, Jews should also have been called *kafir*. No doubt they were, but more often it seems were referred to as *yahudun* or *hudun*; see Rubin and Wasserstein, *Dhimmis*.

37. See Lapiedra Gutiérrez, *Como*, pp. 189–247.

38. This usage referring to human beings defined, from a negative perspective, a xenophobic hatred of the 'Other', directed towards a barbaric and uncivilized being; it is a usage that has an obviously humiliating connotation. By contrast, the Muslim Arabic-speakers possessed, implicitly, the opposite qualities – that is, they were cultivated, civilized; they did not abandon themselves to their brutal passions; they were formed by the constraints of an education and culture that taught them to control their primitive instincts; ibid., p. 193.

39. Abdullah Thabit, 'Arab Views of Northern Europeans in Medieval History and Geography', citing Shams al Din al-Ansari, *Kitab Nukhbat al-Dahr fi 'Aja'ib al-Barr wa al-Bahr*, in Blanks, *Images*, pp. 74–8.

40. A modern view is: 'As regards the people of the Book [i.e. the Jews and the Christians] who do not accept the Prophethood of Prophet Muhammad bin Abdullah (Peace be upon him and his progeny), they are commonly considered najis, but it is not improbable that they are Pak. However, it is better to avoid them.' See section on *kaffir* @ www.al-islam.org/laws/najisthings.html

41. 'Islamic tradition has long identified the baser human tendencies, referred to collectively as "nafs", with wild beasts such as the dragon or wolf'; see Renard, *Islam*, pp. 213–14.

42. For a remarkable and wide-ranging analysis of the 'meaning' of the pig, see Fabre-Vassas, *Singular Beast*. Despite its title, much of its content has a resonance for the reaction in Muslim societies to the pig. However a 'sea pig' is not *najis*. See clarification of *najis* @ www.al-islam.org/laws/najisthings.html

43. Cited Hillgarth, *Spanish Kingdoms*, vol. 2, pp. 138–9.

44. Ibid., pp. 142–3.

45. Cited ibid., p. 140.

46. See Sicroff, *Controverses*, pp. 32–6.

47. Ibid., p. 35, note 37, citing Alonso de Cartagena, *Defensorium Unitatis Christianae*.

48. Ibid., p. 26.

49. Pope Nicholas V condemned the Toledo decree as against the laws of God. I owe the recension of Christian attitudes to the Jews to Professor Robert Michael.

50. The range of occupations open to Jews was restricted.

51. Cited Sicroff, *Controverses*, pp. 116–17. He found various manuscript copies of similar letters from the Jews of Spain to those of Babylon. The original texts were attributed by some authorities to Juan Martinez Siliceo, Archbishop of Toledo.

52. This episode is described in Harvey, *Islamic Spain*, pp. 232–3.

53. Cited ibid., pp. 258–9.

54. See Hillgarth, *Spanish Kingdoms*, vol. 2, pp. 363–4.

55. 'Judaizers' was a term first used in the early Church for a group that sought to hold Christianity to the Mosaic law and Jewish traditions. In the hands of the Spanish Inquisition, from the fifteenth century, it became a device to interrogate and control New Christians of Jewish origin. Benzion Netanyahu in *The Origins of the Inquisition in Fifteenth-century Spain*, New York, NY: New York Review of Books, 2001 (2nd edn), has assembled a mass of evidence and argues fervently that 'Judaizers' were largely a chimera, constructed to control the mass of converts, and prevent them from taking their place in Christian society. The Inquisition presented the vision of a 'Judaizing' conspiracy, but it is much more likely that many converts knew little of Christian doctrine and still lived within a culture that carried a strong resonance of their origins. On this view, see David Nirenberg, 'Mass Conversion and Genealogical Mentalities: Jews and Christians in Fifteenth-century Spain', *Past and Present* 174 (February 2002), pp. 3–41.

56. See the works of Dechado Iñigo de Mendoza, Madrid: Nueva Biblioteca de Autores Españoles, 1902–28, 19:72.

57. See Edwards, *Spain*, pp. 222–3.

58. Cited D. Nicolle, *Granada 1492: The Reconquest of Spain*, London: Osprey Publishing, 1998, p. 16.

59. Washington Irving, *Tales of the Alhambra*, Granada: Miguel Sanchez Editor, 1976, p. 19.

60. Ibid.

61. Edwards, *Spain*, p. 169.

62. Cited by Prescott, *History*, p. 191.

63. This was a Sufi image. For Shi'ites, each seed represented the tears shed for the murder of Hussein at Karbala. See Malek Chebel, *Dictionnaire des symboles musulmans: Rites, mystique et civilisation*, Paris: Albin Michel, 1995, pp. 186–7.

64. See Ladero Quesada, *Granada*, pp. 171–4.

65. D. Nicolle, *Granada 1492: The Reconquest of Spain*, London: Osprey Publishing, 1998, p. 47.

66. But Ferdinand and Isabella were fortunate when Mohammed XII, known to the Spaniards as Boabdil, who was the son of Granada's emir, was captured in a skirmish. They signed an agreement with him and thereafter fostered his growing sense of rivalry with his father.

67. It eventually succumbed in 1486 when an incendiary projectile blew up the arsenal.

68. Prescott, *History*, p. 258.

69. Ibid., p. 264.

70. Nubdhat al-asyr', cited by Harvey, *Islamic Spain*, pp. 299–300.

71. Prescott, *History*, p. 269.

72. Ibid., p. 282.

73. Ibid., p. 292.

74. Ibid.

75. Cited Harvey, *Islamic Spain*, p. 321.

76. See Dupront, *Mythe*, vol. 2, p. 791.

77. Cited Harvey, *Islamic Spain*, p. 290.

Chapter 5

1. Washington Irving, *A Chronicle of the Conquest of Granada*, London: John Murray, 1829, vol. 1, pp. 648–50.
2. In El Escorial, the royal figures at prayer face the altar.
3. See John Edwards, *The Spanish Inquisition*, Stroud: Tempus, 1999, p. 88.
4. The account is by the Genoese Senarega, cited in Prescott, *History*, p. 322.
5. See Fabre-Vassas, *Singular Beast*, pp. 131–8.
6. This putative child of La Guardia was canonized in 1807.
7. See Yerushalmi, *Assimilation*, p. 10.
8. See Sicroff, *Controverses*, pp. 26–7. See also Antonio Domínguez Ortiz, *La Clase social de los conversos en Castilla en la Edad Moderna*, Madrid: Consejo Superior de Investigaciones Científicas, 1955, p. 13. For the complex vocabulary linking pigs and Jews see Fabre-Vassas, *Singular Beast*.
9. See Harvey, *Islamic Spain*, pp. 314–21. The easiest source of the full text of the capitulation is in García Arenal, *Los Moriscos*, pp. 19–28.
10. Caro Baroja, *Los Moriscos*, p. 9.
11. Ibid., p. 12.
12. Caro Baroja indicates that most of the Muslim inhabitants appeared content with these arrangements.
13. See Miguel Angel Ladero Quesada, 'Spain 1492: Social Values and Structures', in Schwartz, *Implicit Understandings*, pp. 101–2.
14. Columbus' *Journal*, cited Liss, *Isabel*, p. 291.
15. 'The calamitous century' was how Barbara Tuchman described it in her popular book, *A Distant Mirror* (1978).
16. See Philip Ziegler, *The Black Death*, London: The Folio Society, 1997, p. 245. The comparison he refers to was made by J. W. Thompson in 'The Aftermath of the Black Death and the Aftermath of the Great War', *American Journal of Sociology* 26 (1920–21), p. 565.
17. Anwar Chejne observes that the term *Morisco* was less used than the traditional 'moro', Saracenos, Agarenos, etc. The term *Morisco* was also used earlier than 1502, as for example in the fourteenth-century *Libro del Buen Amor*. See Chejne, *Islam and the West*, p. 176.
18. See Arturo Farinelli, *Marrano (storia de un vituperio)*, Geneva: L. S. Olschki, 1925.
19. Pérez de Chinchon, *Antialcorán* (Valencia: 1532), cited in Cardaillac, *Moriscos*, p. 355.
20. 'Almost nothing is known about the history of Granada from 1492 to 1499, but this period has survived in the "folk memory" as a golden age of peace and prosperity. Disputes over the interpretation of the terms of the capitulation were settled by Zafra to the satisfaction of both Muslims and Christians; Talavera made every effort to convert the Muslims through education and example, established a seminary to train priests in Arabic and in the missionary traditions of the church, and accommodated the new converts' Muslim dress, customs, and language. This period of peace was possible because both sides were willing to live in mutual toleration of one another, an attitude rooted in tradition and

in the personalities of [the Count of] Tendilla [the military commander] and Talavera'; Helen Nadar, *The Mendoza Family in the Spanish Renaissance 1350–1550*, New Brunswick, NJ: Rutgers University Press, 1979, pp. 157–8.

21. Alonso de Santa Cruz, *Crónica de los Reyes Católicos*, ed. Juan de Mata Carriazo, Seville: Escuela de Estudios Hispano-Americanos de Sevilla, 1951, vol. 2, pp. 191–2.

22. See Lea, *Moriscos*, pp. 27–8.

23. He came from a Jewish *converso* family.

24. Luis del Mármol Carvajal, *Historia del rebelión y castigo de los moriscos del Reyno de Granada* (1600), Madrid: Sancha, 1797.

25. Ladero Quesada, *Mudéjares*, p. 77.

26. Cited Liss, *Isabel*, p. 331.

27. See Lea, *Moriscos*, p. 461.

28. His brother served under Tendilla in the Alpujarras and went on to become one of the greatest soldiers of the age: Gonzalez de Córdoba, El Gran Capitán.

29. Ladero Quesada, *Mudéjares*, p. 81.

30. Liss, *Isabel*, p. 332.

31. Decree of 12 May 1511 (Seville) of Ferdinand the Catholic, authorizing new converts to use knives with a rounded point (*cuchillos de punta redonda*), *Colección de documentos inéditos para la Historia de España*, 113 vols, Madrid, 1842–95, vol. III, p. 568. The issue of bearing arms, whether for hunting or for other purposes, was a key area of contention between the *Moriscos* and the authorities. See Documents nos 1–6, 9, 11 and 13–17.

32. See Mercedes García-Arenal, 'Moriscos and Indians; A Comparative Approach', in Van Gelder and De Moor, 'The Middle East and Europe', pp. 39–55.

33. Casas, *Apologética*, p. 1037, cited in Luis N. Rivera, *A Violent Evangelism: The Political and Religious Conquest of the Americas*, Louisville, KY: Westminster, 1992, p. 212. See also Document 20.

34. See Casas, *History*.

35. Casas, *Apologética*, p. 1039.

36. See Richard Konetzke, *Colección de documentos para la historia de la formación social de Hispanoamerica 1493–1810*, Madrid: Consejo Superior de Investigaciones Científicas, 1953, vol. 1, pp. 32–3.

37. Tomás de Vio Cayetano, *Secunda secundae partis summae totius theologiae d. Thomae Aquinatis, Thomas a Vio Cajetani comentariis illustrata* (1517), part 2, 2.66.8; cited by Luis N. Rivera, *A Violent Evangelism: The Political and Religious Conquest of the Americas*, Louisville, KY: Westminster, 1992, p. 214.

38. See Bartolomé de las Casas, *Del único modo de atraer a todos los pueblos a la verdadera religión*, trans. by Atenógenes Santamaría, Mexico City: Fondo de Cultura Económica, 1975, p. 465.

39. Stephen J. Greenblatt, *Learning to Curse: Essays in Early Modern Culture*, New York: Routledge, 1990, pp. 16–17.

40. Ibid., pp. 21–2.

41. Genesis 16: 11–12.

Chapter 6

1. See Geoffrey Parker, *The Grand Strategy of Philip II*, New Haven, CT: Yale University Press, 1998, pp. 80–81.
2. See L. P. Harvey, 'Los Moriscos y los cinco pilares de Islam' in Temimi, *Prácticas*, pp. 93–7.
3. See John Lynch, *Spain 1560–1598: From Nation State to World Empire*, Oxford: Blackwell, 1994, p. 313.
4. See Braudel, *Mediterranean*, vol. 2, pp. 376–82.
5. Nigel Griffin makes the point that there was a constant shortage of competent missionaries, and many were being absorbed by the missions in America. See Nigel Griffin, '"Un muro invisible": Moriscos and Cristianos Viejos in Granada' in Hodcraft, *Mediaeval*, pp. 133–66. He also observed that the records of the Granada Chancellery and the archives of the Alhambra are 'still incompletely utilized by historians'. This was certainly true when I was working there almost twenty years earlier. Before my time in Granada only K. Garrad (among Western scholars) had used the material in a systematic way. And Garrad's splendid thesis has never been published.
6. Cited Kritzeck, *Peter*, p. 161.
7. Ordered on 12 October 1501. The limited effect of his ordinance may be gauged from a decree of Ferdinand on 20 June 1511 issuing a pardon to *Moriscos* who had books in Arabic and ordering them to hand them over to the authorities. They were to examine them, to pass on the books of philosophy, medicine and history, and to burn the rest; *Colección de documentos inéditos para la Historia de España*, 113 vols, Madrid, 1842–95, vol. XXXIX, p. 447.
8. See Documents, no. 21. There was a further decree in 1523 against attempts by *Moriscos* to bypass this provision. Then there was a further letter issued in 1530 on the enforcement of the regulations.
9. See Documents, no. 22.
10. See Documents, no. 21.
11. See for example a copy of a 1530 letter from the empress in the archive of the Cathedral of Granada that the *Moriscos* should alter their form of dress. See Documents, no. 23.
12. See Domínguez Ortiz and Vincent, *Historia*, pp. 25–33.
13. Decree of 7 December 1526, cited in Gallego y Burín and Gámir Sandoval, *Moriscos*, pp. 206–13.
14. See Documents, no. 23. See also Antonio Garrido Aranda, 'Papel de la Iglesia de Granada en la asimilación de la sociedad morisca', *Anuario de historia moderna y contemporanea* 2–3 (1975–6), pp. 69–103.
15. Ribera's second 'Memorial', translated and cited in Hillgarth, *Mirror*, pp. 206–7.
16. See Cabenalas Rodriguez, *El Morisco granadino*.
17. Cardaillac, *Moriscos*, pp. 36–43.
18. On this process, called *taqiyah* or dissimulation, and the Mufti of Oran's advice, see Chejne, *Islam*, pp. 24–5.
19. See Fabre-Vassas, *Singular Beast*, pp. 112–19.

20. *Moriscos* began to circumcise their children later in childhood thereby evading this surveillance.

21. See Bernard Vincent, 'The Moriscos and Circumcision' in Cruz and Perry, *Culture*, pp. 78–92.

22. Juan Aranda Doncel, 'Las Prácticas musulmanas de los moriscos andaluces a traves de las relaciones de causas del Tribunal de la Inquisición de Córdoba' in Temimi, *Prácticas*, pp. 11–31.

23. See B. Vincent, 'Les Bandits morisques en Andalousie au XVIe siècle', *Revue d'Histoire Moderne et Contemporaine*, 1974, pp. 389–400, and Reglá, *Estudios*, p. 44. The military headquarters in the Alhambra at Granada received reports of *monfíes* and *Moriscos* attacking fishermen on the beach at Velez Malaga in 1564 (see Documents, no. 10); of Christians being taken prisoner by *monfíes* in 1566 (see Documents, no. 12); and of murders *Moriscos* are supposed to have committed in La Cuesta de Cebeda (see Documents, no. 7).

24. Cited Chejne, *Islam*.

25. The full text is in Lea, *Moriscos*, pp. 434–7.

26. For these symbolic meanings see Malek Chebel, *Dictionnaire des symboles musulmans: Rites, mystique et civilisation*, Paris: Albin Michel, 1995.

27. All these appear in E. Saavedra, 'Discurso', *Memorial de la Real Academia de la Historia*, 6 (1889), p. 159.

28. See Documents, no. 14.

29. See Lea, *Moriscos*, p. 263.

30. Ibid., citing *Relazioni Venete*, Serie 1, Tom VI, p. 408.

31. The *Moriscos* in the capital itself had already been expelled in June 1569.

32. Lapeyre, *Géographie*, p. 125.

33. Domínguez Ortiz and Vincent, *Historia*, p. 58.

34. Ibid., p. 62.

35. He gave some thought to the problem of *limpieza* and concluded it was not an obstacle.

36. See Boronat y Barrachina, *Moriscos*, vol. 1, p. 634. The bishop proposed that these people without a land should be taken to a land without people: '*Este gente se puede llevar a las costas . . . de Terranova, que son amplissimas y sin ninguna población.*' That would finish them off and, to make sure (*specialmente*), there would be '*capando* [gelding] *los masculos grandes y pequeños y las mugeres* [the males large and small and the women].' This could be done in sequence, taking those from Valencia to one place, those from Aragon to another, those from Castile to another. These solutions have remarkably close echoes to Book IV of Swift's *Gulliver's Travels* (1726), where the Houyhnhnms debate the respective merits of exterminating or castrating the Yahoos. See Jonathan Swift, *Gulliver's Travels*, London: The Folio Society, 1965, pp. 215 and 240.

37. 'Informe de Don Alonso Gutiérrez acerca la cuestión morisca, Sevilla 5 Sept. 1588', cited in Boronat y Barrachina, *Moriscos*, vol. 1, p. 346.

38. Ibid., p. 627.

39. AHN Inq. Leg. 2603 I. Cited Cardaillac, *Moriscos*, p. 62.

40. See ibid., p. 60.

41. See Maria Soledad Carrasco, *El Moro de Granada en la literatura del siglo XV al*

XX, Madrid: Revista de Occidente, 1956. The bulk of this was first published in English as 'The Moor of Granada in Spanish Literature of the Eighteenth and Nineteenth Centuries', PhD thesis, Columbia University, NY, 1954.

42. See Miguel de Cervantes Saavedra, 'The Dialogue of the Dogs' in *Exemplary Novels*, Warminster: Aris & Phillips, 1992.

43. For a clear parallel see Caro Baroja, *Formas*, p. 459.

44. Pedro Azanar Cardona, *Expulsión justificada de los moriscos españoles y suma de las excelencias cristianas de nuestro Rey D. Felipe et Católico tercero deste nombre*, Huesca, 1612, translated in Chejne, *Islam and the West*, pp. 177–8.

45. Boranat y Barrachina, *Moriscos*, vol. 2, p. 172.

46. Ibid., p. 189.

47. Ibid., pp. 192–3; expulsion decree, clauses 9–12.

48. See Lea, *Moriscos*, p. 391. Others suggest that these were not *Moriscos* but Muslim slaves or servants.

49. Sanchez-Albornóz, *Spain*, vol. 2, p. 1245.

50. 'Popular imagination was so horrorstruck at these terrible events [the Ottoman successes in the Mediterranean and Balkans] that thereafter the word "Turk" was substituted [in traditional village plays] for the old terms used to designate evil-doers and bandits who had formerly been termed the "Saracens" or "Moors".' See Georges Hérelle, *Les Pastorales à sujets tragiques considerées littéraire-ment*, Paris: Librairie Champion, 1926, pp. 108–9.

51. Marlène Albert-Llorca, 'Le Maure dans les fêtes valenciennes de *moros y chris-tianos*', in Musée de la Corse, *Moresca*, p. 341.

52. Harold Lopez Mendez, *España desconocida: la Alpujarra, rincón misterioso*, Madrid: n.p., 1967, p. 90.

53. I am very grateful to David Nirenberg for introducing this whole area to me. In a private communication, he contrasted the performances in the Spanish Holy Week celebrations with *Moros y Cristianos*. In Spain, certainly, *Moros y Cristianos* was a performance of the established and public order, re-enacting ancient triumphs, and legitimating the nature of the victory. However, in my view, once outside the controlling dialogue in Spain, and where the traditional subject – or alien Other – had been removed, they could acquire a different, and subversive, potency.

54. See Harris, *Aztecs, passim*.

55. Calling for 'thick description'? See Geertz, *Interpretation*, pp. 6–30.

Chapter 7

1. This is different from the 'national' history common to many societies. In Spain, two conflicting interpretations competed for the same native land. See Glick, *Islamic*, pp. 3–15, and Meron Benvenisti, *Sacred Landscape: The Buried History of the Holy Land since 1948*, Berkeley, CA: University of California Press, 2000. There is also a good chapter by Béatrice Caseau, 'Sacred Landscapes', in Glenn Bowersock, Peter Brown and Oleg Grabar (eds), *Late Antiquity: A Guide to the Post Classical World*, Harvard, MA: Belknap Press of Harvard University Press: 1999, pp. 21–59.

2. See Anzulović, *Heavenly Serbia*, p. 22.

3. Many of the cities of the Levant and Anatolia had sites associated with the heroic early days of Christianity and were accordingly treated with reverence.

4. *Recueil des chartes de l'abbaye de Cluny*, cited in Dupront, *Mythe*, vol. 3, p. 1361.

5. The common Arabic term for the city, *Al-Quds*, refers to its sanctity. Later the sacred terrain was extended to the area immediately around the city to become the Holy Land, *al-ard al-muqaddasa*. After Saladin's reconquest this latter term was used to include the whole 'Holy Land', roughly as Christians conceived it. See Hillenbrand, *Crusades*, pp. 301–2.

6. See Gil, *History*, pp. 622–6.

7. Jerome, Epistle 46:9: 'Time forbids me to survey the period which has passed since the Lord's ascension, or to recount the bishops, the martyrs, the divines, who have come to Jerusalem from a feeling that their devotion and knowledge would be incomplete and their virtue without the finishing touch, unless they adored Christ in the very spot where the gospel first flashed from the gibbet.'

8. Jerome, Epistle 108, which is the longest of his letters and where he describes Paula's journey through the Holy Land.

9. Cited Gil, *History*, pp. 285–7.

10. It has been estimated that it cost a year's income or more to undertake a pilgrimage. See J. Sumption, *Pilgrimage*, London: Faber, 1975, pp. 169, 205–6.

11. R. Röhricht, *Die Deutschen im Heiligen Lande: Chronologisches Verzeichnis derjenigen Deutschen, welche als Jerusalempilger und Kreuzfahrer sicher nachzuweisen oder wahrscheinlich anzusehen sind c. 650–1291*, Aalen: Scientia-Verlag, 1968 (new edition of 1894 edition), cited in Gil, *History*, p. 483.

12. This is Sir John Keegan's image, in our joint book *Zones of Conflict*, and I am grateful to him for it.

13. The Fatimid rulers of Cairo were Shia Muslims, but Al-Azhar always attracted students and teachers from the entire Muslim world.

14. There is a huge literature on the various patterns of belief in Islam, and I do not propose to define the differences here. I would suggest that they represented different tendencies in belief, political and social practice, within the overall framework of Islam that altered over time, sometimes leading to further divisions and subdivisions. Modern historians of Islam also emphasize the traditions of Sufi practitioners, the various dervish traditions, and 'folk islam', which bonded local cults and practices into the faith. In addition, there were later ascetic traditions such as the Wahabis in eighteenth-century Arabia. For a clear outline see Lapidus, *History*.

15. Although sectarian issues played some part, Sunni rulers fought Sunni rulers with the same verve that they confronted the Shia ones.

16. This is from the fifteenth-century *Kitat* by Al-Maqrizi, cited in Elizabeth Hallam (ed.), *Chronicles of the Crusades: Eyewitness Accounts of the Wars between Christianity and Islam*, Godalming: Bramley Books, 1996, pp. 22–5.

17. Gil, *History*, pp. 379–80. He notes that Al-Hakim may have regarded himself as the *mahdi*, 'redeemer', who had come to save and rescue Islam. Others simply considered him insane.

18. The history of this document is chequered. Carl Erdmann considered that it

was contemporary with the destruction wrought by Al-Hakim. Later scholars, like Gieysztor, suggested that it was confected by the monks of Moissac at the time that Urban II was promoting the First Crusade. However, more recently Schaller has reinterpreted the whole issue and considers it authentic. Regardless of its date, it indicates the horror with which the destruction of the Holy Sepulchre was greeted. See Erdmann, *Origin*, pp. 113–17; A. Gieysztor, 'The Genesis of the Crusades: The Encyclical of Sergius IV (1009–1012)', *Medievalia et Humanistica* 5 (1948), pp. 3–23, and 6 (1950), pp. 3–34; H. M. Schaller, 'Zur Kreuzzugsenzyklika Papst Sergius IV' in H. Mordek (ed.), *Papsttum, Kirche und Recht im Mittelalter: Festschrift für Horst Fuhrmann zum 65 Geburtstag*, Tübingen: M. Niemeyer, 1991, pp. 135–53.

19. Marshall W. Baldwin, *A History of the Crusades: The First Hundred Years*, Philadelphia, PA: University of Pennsylvania Press, 1958, pp. 76–7.

20. See Gil, *History*, p. 487.

21. 'The centrality of the bare scriptural word in liturgy, catechism and sermon receded before the elaboration of the church liturgical tradition. Thus the Word was available to the rank and file mainly through the evolved forms of the liturgy, biblical storytelling, or biblically inspired art, and much less, if at all, through substantial reading, recitation and study of the holy words themselves.' See Graham, *Beyond*, p. 120.

22. The only parable that lacks a sense of precise topography is where Jesus was tempted by the Devil.

23. I am grateful to the Rev. David Batson for explaining the issue of relics to me.

24. See Cohn, *Pursuit*, pp. 64–5.

25. This is taken from the account of Urban's Clermont speech by Robert the Monk from a work called the *Historia Hierosolymitana*. He was present at Clermont, but the text was written much later. I have used the online version @ www.wwnorton.com / nael / nto / middle / crusade / clermontfrm.htm

26. Robert the Monk claimed to have been present on the day although he composed his version about a quarter of a century after Clermont, and with the *Gesta Francorum* (*The Deeds of the Franks*, written about 1100, an account of the First Crusade) before him. But the details unconsciously reveal Urban's rhetorical skill and are thus convincing. See August C. Krey, *The First Crusade: The Accounts of Eyewitnesses and Participants*, Princeton, NJ: Princeton University Press, 1921, pp. 33–6.

27. 'This, made of any kind of cloth, he ordered to be sewn upon the shirts, cloaks, and byrra of those who were about to go.' See ibid., pp. 36–40.

28. According to Robert the Monk, when Urban heard his call to arms greeted with cries of 'God wills it, it is the will of God', he 'gave thanks to God and commanding silence with his hand, said, "Unless God had been present in your spirits, all of you would not have uttered the same cry; since although the cry issued from many mouths, yet the origin of the cry is as one. Therefore I say to you that God, who implanted it in your breast, has drawn it forth from you. Let that then be your war cry in combat because it is given to you by God. When an armed attack is made upon the enemy, this one cry be raised by all the soldiers of God: 'It is the will of God! It is the will of God!'"'

29. Curiously, the anthropologist Roy Wagner, who coined the phrase 'Symbols that stand for themselves', bypassed the cross when searching for the core symbol of the West. In fact it meets his needs much better than the Eucharist, which he selected. See Wagner, *Symbols*.

30. Cited by Dana C. Munro, *Urban and the Crusaders: Translations and Reprints from the Original Sources of European History*, vol. 1:2, Philadelphia, PA: University of Pennsylvania Press, 1895, p. 20.

31. They had conjured up the image of an infidel enemy who had to be defeated and destroyed whatever the cost. The first to suffer from this effusion of ferocious enmity were the Jews of the Rhineland towns. The pilgrims' prime motives were theft and pillage, but underlying the savagery of their attack, which emerges in all the sources, Latin and Hebrew, was a hatred for a people who, like the infidels occupying Jerusalem, had denied Christ. More than a thousand Jews, men, women and children, were killed in Mainz and many more in cities as far away as Prague which opened their gates to the pilgrims. When they passed on into Hungary on the road to the East, the pilgrims treated the local inhabitants as they had the Jews. In one village they impaled a young Hungarian boy who could not tell them where they could find food. See Runciman, *History*, vol. 1, p. 116.

32. See Runciman, *History*, vol. 1, pp. 106–7.

33. There were many foreigners in Byzantine service, most notably the Varangian Guard, composed first of Norsemen, and later of Normans. After 1066, many Anglo-Saxons left England and made a new life in the East.

34. Nor did the Church approve of the massacres of Jews in the Rhineland by the popular Crusade. See Jacob R. Marcus, *The Jew in the Medieval World: A Source Book 315–1791*, New York, NY: Harper & Row, 1965, pp. 115–20.

35. Lyons, 'Crusading Stratum', pp. 147–61.

36. *An Arab-Syrian Gentleman and Warrior in the Period of the Crusades: Memoirs of Usamah ibn-Munqidh*, trans. by Philip K. Hitti, New York, NY: Columbia University Press, 2000, pp. 120–21.

37. *Gesta Francorum*, cited in France, *Victory*, p. 277.

38. The Church of St Peter was being re-consecrated after its use as a mosque. Some doubted the authenticity of the relic but kept silent, because this manifest token of Divine favour suddenly restored the spirits of the Crusaders.

39. Even the fresh horses that had been gathered along the way had mostly expired and been eaten.

40. Kerbogha's army comprised many different detachments, including infantry spearmen and archers.

41. H. A. R. Gibb, *The Damascus Chronicle of the Crusades, Extracted and Translated from the Chronicle of Ibn Al-Qalanisi*, London: Luzac and Co., 1932, p. 47.

42. Harold S. Fink, *Fulcher of Chartres: A History of the Expedition to Jerusalem 1095–1127*, Knoxville, TE: University of Tennessee Press, 1969, pp. 112–13.

43. Ibid., p. 106.

44. Cited in Hillenbrand, *Crusades*, p. 71.

45. For the images of Jerusalem, see Dupront, *Mythe*, vol. III, pp. 1361–4.

46. There are suggestions that a Crusader embassy was negotiating in Cairo for a

Christian protectorate over the city, such as the Byzantines had previously exercised, and as Emperor Frederick II was to conclude in 1229 for a period of ten years.

47. See Runciman, *History*, vol. 1, pp. 226–7.

48. The often quoted statement that the Crusaders walked 'up to their knees in blood' was a metaphor. The similarity between so many of the descriptions of killing and atrocity, notably in the capture of Constantinople by the Crusaders in 1204 and then by the Ottomans in 1453, suggests that many of these statements are stylistic and not intended to be taken literally. See August C. Krey, *The First Crusade: The Accounts of Eyewitnesses and Participants*, Princeton, NJ: Princeton University Press, 1921, pp. 257–62.

49. *Gesta Francorum*, cited by Elizabeth Hallam (ed.), *Chronicles of the Crusades: Eyewitness Accounts of the Wars between Christianity and Islam*, Godalming: Bramley Books, 1996, p. 93.

50. See France, *Victory*, p. 356.

51. See Runciman, *History*, vol. 2, pp. 237–64.

52. For a good introduction to this topic, see Christopher Tyerman, *The Invention of the Crusades*, Basingstoke: Macmillan, 1998. By the late eighteenth century, the future president of the young United States, Thomas Jefferson, had turned the word into a figure of speech, calling for a 'crusade against ignorance'.

53. 'A holy war fought against those perceived to be external or internal foes of Christendom for the recovery of Christian property or in defence of the Church or Christian people'; see Riley-Smith, *Short History*, pp. xxviii–xxix. There were attempts to limit this plenary power, and Marsilio of Padua was only the most notable figure who attacked papal misuse of this right to initiate a Crusade.

54. Meeting of the Bishops at Narbonne, 1054, cited in Marc Bloch, *Feudal Society*, trans. L. A. Manyon, London: Routledge and Kegan Paul, 1962, p. 413.

55. It was possible for a nation to be Islamic in belief but not under true and authorized Islamic rule. Thus rebels or Islamic enemies are often characterized as 'apostates' (*ridda*) and falling outside the protection of the faith. On this topic see the references cited by Fred M. Donner in his article 'The Sources of Islamic Conceptions of War' in Johnson and Kelsay (eds), *Just War*, pp. 31–69. In their survey article 'The Idea of the Jihad before the Crusades', Roy Mottahedeh and Ridwan al-Sayyid present convincing evidence that there was a multiplicity of interpretations for the lesser *jihad*. See Angeliki E. Laiou and Roy Parviz Mottahedeh (eds), *The Crusades from the Perspective of Byzantium and the Muslim World*, Washington, DC: Dumbarton Oaks, 2001.

56. The concept of War to enforce this Peace was criticized by Moulavi Cheragi Ali in *A Critical Exposition of the Popular Jihad*, Karachi: Karimsons, reprint of 1885 edition, n.d., pp. 157–9: 'It is only a theory of our Common Law, in its military and political chapters, which allow waging unprovoked war with non-Muslims . . . The casuistical sophistry of the canonical legists in deducing these war theories from the Koran is altogether futile . . . Neither these verses had anything to do with waging unprovoked war and exacting tributes during Mohammad's time nor could they be made a law for future military conquest.'

57. That is: *al-jihad al-akbar*.

58. That is: *al-jihad al-asghar*.
59. See Peters, *Islam*, pp. 4–5. He goes on to make the more contemporary point: 'Nowadays that image has been replaced by that of the Arab "terrorist" in battledress, armed with a Kalashnikov gun and prepared to murder in cold blood Jewish and Christian women and children.' The popular film *The Siege* (1998), which depicts the United States traumatized by Arab terrorism in New York, is a powerful example of this tendency; the mass murders at the World Trade Center on the morning of 11 September 2001 come into the same category as the killings in Jerusalem in 1099 in the history of atrocity.
60. See Johnson, *Holy War*.
61. The division between the Sunni and Shia branches of Islam in the seventh century had already created major divergences within Islam. Thus Shia scholars never accepted that interpretation was a closed issue.
62. This is Bernard Lewis's expression. See Lewis, *Political Language*, p. 129.
63. See Bonner, *Aristocratic Violence*, pp. 155–6.
64. See Hillenbrand, *Crusades*, pp. 304–8, and Lewis, *Discovery*, p. 22.
65. The point at which they came to be called *saliba*, 'crosses', is difficult to determine precisely.
66. Gabrieli, *Arab Historians*, pp. 77–8.
67. See Hillenbrand, *Crusades*, p. 280.
68. 'Tale of Umar b. Numan', *The Book of One Thousand and One Nights*, 4 vols, trans. J. C. Mardrus and Powys Mathers, London: Routledge, 1994, vol. 1, p. 442.
69. Imad al-Din al-Isfahani, *Kitab al-fath*, cited and translated in Hillenbrand, *Crusades*, p. 290. I wonder whether the stabling of horses in Al-Aqsa was either the source of the story for the Ottomans stabling horses in the Holy Sepulchre, or a memory that provoked them to do it.
70. Ibn Wasil, *Muffarij al-kurub*, cited and translated in Hillenbrand, *Crusades*, p. 291.
71. On the building of Muslim Jerusalem and its transformation, see Oleg Grabar, *The Shape of the Holy: Early Islamic Jerusalem*, Princeton, NJ: Princeton University Press, 1996.
72. For the near-complete separation of Muslim and Latin Christian societies in Palestine, see Benjamin Z. Kedar, 'The Subjected Muslims of the Frankish Levant' in Powell (ed.), *Muslims*, pp. 135–74.
73. *Postilla super librum sapientiae*, c.5, lecture 65: '*Non enim est possibile docere vitam Christi nisi destruendo et reprobando legem Machometi.*' On Holkot, see Kedar, *Crusade*, pp. 188–9.
74. It had been much copied in the scriptoria, and the early editions appeared in Reutingen, Speyer, Cologne and Basel; Holkot remained in print well into the seventeenth century.
75. Translated and cited in Throop, *Criticism*, p. 122.
76. See Kedar, *Crusade*, p. 189.
77. Dupront, *Mythe*, vol. 2, p. 976. The more than 2,000 pages of Dupront's work *Le Mythe de croisade* constitute one of the great works of modern historiography, but Dupront understood (and the book was published after his death) that he was able to explore only part of the vast spider's web of connections that he uncovered.

Chapter 8

1. See Penny J. Cole, ' "O God, The heathen have come into your inheritance" (Ps. 78:1): The Theme of Religious Pollution in Crusade Documents 1095–1188', in M. Shatzmiller (ed.), *Crusaders and Muslims in Twelfth-Century Syria*, Leiden: E. J. Brill, 1993, pp. 84–111.

2. Cited in Prawer, *World*, p. 91.

3. Richard G. Salomon, 'A Newly Discovered Manuscript of Opicinus de Canistris: A Preliminary Report', *Journal of the Warburg and Courtauld Institutes* XVI (1953) 1, pp. 45–57. The full treatment of the Opicinus MSS and his life appeared in Richard G. Salomon, *Opicinus de Canistris: Weltbild und Bekenntnisse eines Avignonesischen Klerikers des 14. Jahrhunderts*, 2 vols, London: Warburg Institute, 1936. The second volume consists of a set of images of the various elements within the MSS. Opicinus de Canistris was obsessed with impurity, to the degree that Richard Salomon classed him a sexual psychopath. But he also observed, 'Of course, not everything in the work of a psychopath is pathological.' The supremely diabolical quality of the carnal connection between Muslim Africa and Christian Europe offended doubly against the law of God. There was no better (or more readily identifiable) means of depicting the corruption of the world than by suggesting a sexual union between a Christian and an infidel. In Opicinus' day, the loss of Jerusalem to the Muslim enemy was still an open wound. He struggled vainly to present the complexity of the political and theological world that confronted him; inevitably, his sheets remained a work in progress, unfinished and experimental. They were littered with images of God, Jesus Christ, doves with vast embracing wings, the Virgin Mary, strange and mythical beasts; yet in his own mind all were worked back into the themes embodied in his texts and captions.

4. See Jörg-Geerd Arentzen, *Imago Mundi Cartographica: Studien zur Bildlichkeit Mittelalterlicher Welt- und Ökumenkarten unter besonderer Berücksichtigung des Zusammenwirkens von Text und Bild*, Munich: Wilhelm Fink Verlag, 1984, p. 315. Chapter 4, 'Die Karte als Sinnbild in den Zeichungen des Opicinus de Canistris', pp. 275–316, is the most thorough recent treatment of Opicinus. *Commisceo* has the sense of mixing or mingling, in this case perhaps relating to seminal and vaginal emissions.

5. Richard G. Salomon, 'A Newly Discovered Manuscript of Opicinus de Canistris: A Preliminary Report', *Journal of the Warburg and Courtauld Institutes* XVI (1953) 1, p. 53.

6. Ibid., p. 52.

7. His sexual obsession has caused one scholar to observe that 'for Opicinus, earth cartography is tantamount to exposing the fornicating world . . . a cartographer's attempt to represent the world as a netherland that embodies – incorporates – corruption and sexual sin.' See Gandelman, *Reading Pictures*, pp. 84–5. Richard Salomon also noted 'his tendency towards prurience' and cited Opicinus' remark in his text: 'While I was working on this, a simple priest from Lombardy came to see me, and I had to cover the abdomen of the woman with a piece of paper in order not to shock him.'

8. H. Hagenmayer, *Die Kreuzzugsbriefe aus den Jahren 1088–1100: Eine Quellen-sammlung zur Geschichte des ersten Kreuzzuges*, Innsbruck: Wagner, 1901, p. 147. Cited and translated in Riley Smith, *First Crusade*, p. 91.

9. Cited and translated in Peters (ed.), *Christian Society*, p. 141.

10. Cited in Kedar, *Crusade*, pp. 161–2.

11. See Hillenbrand, *Crusades*, pp. 141–61, for the growing importance of Jerusalem within Islam.

12. Cited and translated in ibid., p. 112.

13. William of Tyre, *Historia rerum in partibus transmarinis gestarum*, trans. James Brundage in *The Crusades: A Documentary History*, Milwaukee, WI: Marquette University Press, 1962, pp. 79–82.

14. Runciman, *History*, vol. 2, p. 234.

15. II Thessalonians 2:4.

16. For the heroic self-image, see Renard, *Islam*, and Bridget Connelly, *Arab Folk Tale and Identity*, Berkeley, CA: University of California Press, 1986, pp. 4–6. The *Sirat al-Zahir Baybars* chronicles the wars of the Mamluk Sultan Baybars against the Mongols, Persians and Christian Crusaders. The *Dhat al-Himma* recounts deeds of the Arabs against the Byzantines and the Franks. 'However, while the fourteenth-century polemicist Philippe de Mézières praised the chivalry of the Turks it was a means only to condemn the "Saracens" who occupied Jerusalem and to chastise the failures of Christians who behaved worse than the Turks.' See Petkov, 'Rotten Apple'.

17. Malcolm C. Lyons, *The Arabian Epic*, 3 vols, Cambridge: Cambridge University Press, 1995, vol. 3, p. 112.

18. Cited in J. A. C. Brown, *Techniques of Persuasion: From Propaganda to Brainwashing*, Harmondsworth: Penguin Books, 1963, p. 19.

19. Pavlov's experiments 1901–1903 demonstrated that specific behaviour could be 'conditioned'. His research investigated how dogs digested their food and he wanted to see if external stimuli could make them salivate. At the same time as he fed them he rang a bell. After a while, the dogs – which had previously only responded when they saw and ate their food – would begin to salivate when the bell rang, even if no food were present. When he published his results he called this response a 'conditioned reflex'. This kind of behaviour had to be learned and Pavlov described this learning process (where the dog's nervous system linked the sound of the bell with food) as conditioning. But, just as significantly, he also discovered that this conditioned reflex weakened if the bell rang repeatedly and there was no food. If that happened, the dog eventually stopped salivating at the sound of the bell. If the stimulus was not effectively 'reinforced', the conditioned reflex decayed and failed. See Ivan Petrovich Pavlov, *Essential Works of Pavlov*, ed. Michael Kaplan, New York, NY: Bantam Books, 1966.

20. Dupront, *Mythe*, vol. 1, p. 19.

21. Emmanuel Sivan demonstrates convincingly that in the Muslim world malediction based on 'crusade' vocabulary was a product of secular modernism. The words Crusade/Crusaders then mobilized and revived the earlier antagonism to the image of the cross. See Emanuel [sic] Sivan, 'Modern Arab Historiogra-

phy of the Crusades', *Asian and African Studies: Journal of the Israel Oriental Society* 8 (1972), pp. 109–49. Similarly, *jehad* or *jihad* was first recorded as being used in English in 1869, although knowledge of the Muslim Holy War had existed since the later Middle Ages. Thus the concept was used *avant la lettre*.

22. See Sivan, *Islam*, p. 7.

23. For the Crusading period, see Michael A. Köhler, *Allianzen und Verträge zwischen fränkischen und islamischen Herrschen in Vorderen Orient: Eine Studie über das zwischenstaatliche Zusammenleben vom 12. bis 13. Jahrhundert*, Berlin: Walter de Gruyter, 1991.

24. See Smail, *Crusading Warfare*, p. 215: 'Every strong place had, however, the same fundamental importance. Wherever it stood, it was the embodiment of force, and therefore the ultimate sanction of the Latin settlement.' Saladin acquired a curious position as the 'noble Arab' in Western eyes. Gladstone in his attacks on the Turks in 1876 talked of the 'noble Saladins', meaning the Arabs. But Sultan Baybars did not attract anything of the same favourable Western response as Saladin.

25. See Adrian J. Boas, *Crusader Archaeology: The Material Culture of the Latin East*, London: Routledge, 1999, pp. 91–120.

26. Cited by Colin Imber, 'The Ottoman Dynastic Myth', *Turcica* 19 (1987), pp. 7–27.

27. See Godfrey Goodwin, *A History of Ottoman Architecture*, London: Thames and Hudson, 1971, p. 35.

28. Cited by Lord Kinross, *The Ottoman Centuries: The Rise and Fall of the Ottoman Empire*, New York, NY: Morrow, 1977, pp. 46–7.

29. Ransoms were demanded for the most eminent and profitable captives.

30. This was remarkable, because in 1402 the Ottomans were beaten by the Mongol ruler Timur in Anatolia, and Bayezid was taken prisoner. A long period of Ottoman political turmoil ensued, when a Crusade could have retaken the Ottoman possessions in Europe. However, after Nicopolis there was little enthusiasm for a new enterprise.

31. Stavrianos, *Balkans*, p. 54.

32. His ally, the Albanian Skenderbeg, arrived just too late to turn the tide of battle in Hunyadi's favour.

33. Vlad Tepes believed in a puritan moral order and, in addition to many of his political rivals and the wealthy classes of Wallachia, what he deemed 'unchaste' women suffered the most terrible deaths under his rule.

34. See Mitchell B. Merbeck, *The Thief, the Cross and the Wheel: Pain and the Spectacles of Punishment in Medieval and Renaissance Europe*, London: Reaktion Books, 1999, pp. 126–57.

35. Doukas [sic], *Decline and Fall of Byzantium to the Ottoman Turks: An Annotated Translation of 'Historia Turco-Byzantina'*, trans. Harry J. Magoulias, Detroit, MI: Wayne State University Press, 1975, pp. 231–5.

36. Letter of Bessarion 13 July 1453 to Doge Francesco Foscari.

37. See D. C. Munro, *Translations and Reprints from the Original Sources of European History*, Series 1, vol. 3:1, Philadelphia, PA: University of Pennsylvania Press, 1912, pp. 15–16.

38. Doukas, *Decline and Fall of Byzantium to the Ottoman Turks: An Annotated Translation of 'Historia Turco-Byzantina'*, trans. Harry J. Magoulias, Detroit, MI: Wayne State University Press, 1975, pp. 231–5.

39. Babinger is dubious about the motives for killing Notaras. He points out that Kritoboulos (a fifteenth-century historian and governor of Imbros) discounted Mehmed's sodomitical lust and replaced it with a political rationale. See Franz Babinger, *Mehmed the Conqueror and His Life*, ed. William C. Hickman, Princeton, NJ: Princeton University Press, pp. 96–7.

40. Some, like ardent enthusiast for the war against the infidel Philippe de Mézières, came to blame the sinful schismatics, the Orthodox, for the triumph of Islam. See Petkov, 'The Rotten Apple'.

41. Cited Robert A. Kann, *A Study of Austrian Intellectual History from the Late Baroque to Romanticism*, London: Thames and Hudson, 1960, pp. 74–5.

42. On some of its nineteenth-century forms see Elizabeth Siberry, *The New Crusaders: Images of the Crusades in the Nineteenth and Early Twentieth Centuries*, Aldershot: Ashgate, 2000.

43. Over 170 million copies of *Hymns Ancient and Modern* were sold over a period of 120 years.

44. These were processions that accompanied the traditional Whit Monday festivals in Yorkshire.

45. Thus Thomas Jefferson's 'crusade against ignorance' of 1786 eventually becomes the Presidential 'Crusade in the Classroom' in the first year of the third millennium. This was the title of a school test volume in the United States. The description read: ' "Crusade in the Classroom" is a practical non-partisan guide to the changes and choices you can expect from the Bush administration. In clear, jargon-free language, Dr. Douglas Reeves explains the Bush policies for school reform, predicts how these new programs will change our schools, and helps parents understand their options.' Captest catalogue, 2001, @ http://www.Captest.com

46. Midian was, like Ishmael, a son of Abraham, but born to Keturah. However, the Ishmaelites were elided with the Midianites, as in Judges 7: 12, where 'all the children of the east lay along in the valley as numerous as locusts'. Later 'Midianites' became for Christians another term for the desert Arabs, like Agarenes.

47. Thomas Moore's hymn of 1816:
    Come, ask the infidel what boon he brings us,
    What charm for aching hearts he can reveal,
    Sweet is that heavenly promise Hope sings us –
    'Earth has no sorrow that God cannot heal.'
    was given a new concluding verse in 1831:
    Here see the bread of life, see waters flowing
    Forth from the throne of God, pure from above.
    Come to the feast of love; come, ever knowing
    Earth has no sorrow but heaven can remove.

48. There were numerous Protestant and Catholic missions – English, Scottish, French, German, Italian, American and Austrian – to Palestine but they concen-

trated on winning over the Orthodox and did not seek to convert Muslims, which could have endangered convert and missionary alike.

49. The 'King's Cross Victory Crusade' has reported with pride that between 1976 and 2001 it has delivered more than one million Bibles to India. The nature of the victory was not specified. See Bibles for India campaign @ http://victorynetwork.org/VictoryIndia.html

50. *al'Akhbar al-saniyya fi'il-hurub al-salibiyya*, Cairo, 1899. See Emanuel Sivan, 'Modern Arab Historiography of the Crusades', *Asian and African Studies: Journal of the Israel Oriental Society* 8 (1972), pp. 124–5.

51. The Archbishop of Beirut wrote of the *al-Ifranj al-Salibiyyun* in the sixth volume of his *History of Syria* in 1901.

52. Especially in the works of Sayyid al-Qutb.

53. Joseph-François Michaud, *Histoire des Croisades* (4th edn, Paris, 1825, vol. 1, p. 510) cited and translated in Kim Munholland, 'Michaud's *History of the Crusades* and the French Crusade in Algeria under Louis Philippe', in Chu and Weisberg (eds), *Popularization*, p. 150.

54. Ibid., p. 154.

55. Ibid., p. 164, citing the Salle de Constantine in 'Versailles et son Musée Historique'.

56. The Congregatio de Propaganda Fide was established in Rome by Pope Gregory XV in 1622. It was charged with supporting missionary activity and was at the centre of a large system of colleges and other educational institutions.

57. Reissued in the 1920s and twice more in the 1950s.

58. Even today, the high passes are a severe challenge to an ill-prepared automobile.

59. In 1537, the Tyrolese cartographer Johann Putsch produced a map of Europe called 'Queen of Europe'. It was subsequently reproduced in the 1588 edition of Sebastian Munster's famous *Cosmographia*. In Putsch's design, the Balkans are on the fringe of Europe, the queen's 'skirt', but with Greece, 'Scythia' and Muscovy, they are unquestionably 'Europe'. 'Tartary' to the east is conveniently separated by a river from Europe proper, and Constantinople is depicted as a Western city on the hem of the queen's garment.

60. John Hale, *The Civilisation of Europe in the Renaissance*, London: HarperCollins, 1993, pp. 5–6. Hale is citing Denys Hay, *Europe: The Emergence of an Idea*, Edinburgh: Edinburgh University Press, 1957, p. 109.

Chapter 9

1. Jephson, *With the Colours*, pp. 158–62.
2. In some sources it is the Landstraße.
3. Robert D. Kaplan, *Balkan Ghosts: A Journey through History*, New York, NY: Vintage, 1994, p. 32.
4. Ibid., p. 227.
5. See Immanuel Wallerstein, 'The Time of Space and the Space of Time: The Future of Social Science', Tyneside Geographical Society Lecture, University of Newcastle upon Tyne, 1996, *Political Geography* XVII, 1, 1998.
6. Ibid.: 'They are arguing in terms of episodic geopolitical TimeSpace . . . the

Serbians [asserted that] current population figures and current boundaries are simply irrelevant; Kosovo was part of Serbia morally because of things that happened in the fourteenth century. These are arguments using structural TimeSpace. Kosovo's location in Serbia was said to be structurally given. There is no way of resolving such a debate intellectually. Neither side can demonstrate that it is right, if by demonstrating it we mean that the arguments are sustained by the weight of the evidence in some scientific puzzle.'

7. Ibid.: 'It was assumed (and one has to underline the verb "assumed") that, if they were "primitive" in the present, there could have been no historical evolution, and therefore that their behaviour in the past must have been the same as their behaviour in the present. They were therefore "peoples without history". For this reason, ethnographies were written in what was called "the anthropological present."' The anthropological present has produced one important study on the differential concepts of time, by Johannes Fabian, and a notable spat with another anthropologist, Maurice Bloch. But both Fabian and Bloch operate within the same spectrum, both accepting that time is relative, to varying degrees, depending on the character of an individual culture. See Fabian, *Time and the Other*, and Maurice Bloch, 'The Past and the Present in the Present' in his *Ritual, History and Power*, pp. 1–18. His Foreword describes his disagreement with Fabian. Both these approaches are extremely important in the kind of myth-history with its own time structures that emerged in the Balkans.

8. See Franjo Tudjman, *Horrors of War: Historical Reality and Philosophy*, New York: M. Evans and Company, 1996. The original version was entitled *Bespuća povisjesne zbiljnosti: Rasprava o povijesti i filozofiji zlosija (Wastelands of Historical Reality: Discussion on History and Philosophy of Aggressive Violence)* and was published in May 1989, and the second edition in November 1989, then a third and fourth in April and October 1990. On each occasion, Tudjman changed the emphasis of the book, often using his own neologisms to present his ideas. The English-language text published in 1996 was, in the words of his translator, 'substantially revised' to appeal to a US audience. I am very grateful to my colleague Dr Dejan Jović for talking to me in detail on the issues embodied in this chapter, and letting me see the text of his own book prior to publication.

9. See Vesna Goldsworthy, *Inventing Ruritania*. The Balkans' relationship to Europe was essentially detached, sandwiched between West and East, or even between the West and Africa.

10. Harry de Windt, *Through Savage Europe, Being a Narrative of a Journey Undertaken as Special Correspondent of the 'Westminster Gazette' throughout the Balkan States and European Russia*, London: T. Fisher Unwin, 1907, pp. 15–16. His book was a considerable success, with the first edition sold out in less than a month.

11. Robert D. Kaplan, *Balkan Ghosts: A Journey through History*, New York, NY: Vintage, 1994, pp. 33–4.

12. Creagh observed that the 'very pretty girl of about nineteen' who came to his room at Neusatz 'was not the least abashed at my Highland costume'. See Creagh, *Over the Borders*, p. 52.

13. Ibid., p. 15.

14. Ibid., p. 38.

15. Ibid., p. 82.

16. Ibid., p. 88.

17. Ibid., pp. 124–5.

18. Ibid., pp. 274–5.

19. Ibid., p. 276. Creagh misunderstood or misread a Montenegrin tradition. It was considered among the mountain warriors dishonourable to die 'in bed like a woman'. To the news of a tribesman's death the proper response was, 'Who killed him?' If he had not died honourably at the hands of an enemy, the euphemism was 'God, the old executioner'. See Alan Ferguson, 'Montenegrin Society 1800–1830', in Clogg (ed.), *Balkan Society*, p. 209.

20. Sam Vaknin, banner line @ www.balkanland.com/index.html, 20 December 2001.

21. From the German *Balkanhalbeiland*, used by the German geographer August Zeune in the first decade of the nineteenth century. See Todorova, *Imagining*, pp. 25–6.

22. In *Imagining the Balkans*, Maria Todorova cites Jobus Veratius, who believed that mountains stretched in a chain from Mesembria on the Black Sea to the Pyrenees. See ibid., pp. 26–7.

23. Four-fifths of Italy is taken up by mountains or hills. See Stuart Woolf, *A History of Italy 1700–1860: The Social Constraints of Political Change*, London: Methuen, 1986, p. 15.

24. W. G. Blackie, *The Comprehensive Atlas and Geography of the World*, London: Blackie and Son, 1882.

25. Cited Todorova, *Imagining*, p. 22.

26. See Linda Colley, *Britons: Forging the Nation 1707–1837*, New Haven, CT and London: Yale University Press, 1992, p. 15.

27. The Scottish wilderness where John Buchan set his novel *The 39 Steps* was not some barren northern glen but the bare and desolate mountains of Galloway, just north of the English border.

28. *Armatoli* were a form of occasional militia; *hajduks* were bandits.

29. Cited Anzulović, *Heavenly Serbia*.

30. For example, Spain's bloodthirsty 'El Cid', or the murderous Celtic anger of Rob Roy Macgregor's vengeful wife, as described by Sir Walter Scott in his novel *Rob Roy*, or the folk tales of Sicily and Calabria.

31. Albanians took pride in the roots of both dialects (*Gegë* and *Töske/Arvanitika*) in the ancient Illyrian language. From the latter dialect name came the title 'Arnauts', by which they were usually known. It was a Latinate tongue, as was the language of the Vlachs, a people displaced by the advance of the Slavs from the sixth century onwards.

32. The majority of Orthodox believers used the Cyrillic script, brought by missionaries dispatched by Bulgarian rulers after their nation had abandoned pagan beliefs.

33. A further element of linguistic diversity was that the Bulgars, with a different ethnic origin, adopted Slavic speech.

34. See, for example, the catalogue of claims for Bulgaria in Stephanove, *Bulgarians*. The construction of unitary nationalism owed much to R. W. Seton-Watson,

both in his academic writing and as advisor to the 1919 Peace Conference. See H. Seton-Watson et al. (eds), *R. W. Seton-Watson and the Yugoslavs: Correspondence 1906–1941*, 2 vols, London: British Academy, 1976.

35. Also as *Poturice*. On identity, see Ivo Banac, 'Bosnian Muslims: From Religious Community to Socialist Nationhood and Post-Communist Statehood 1918–2002', in Pinson (ed.), *Muslims*, pp. 132–3.

36. I have adapted some of the ideas developed by Mark Patton in *Islands*, pp. 179–90. These same concepts can also be applied, I believe, to the stages of Balkan development. Banac, *National Question*, also uses the 'island' or 'pocket' vocabulary and it is implicit in his analysis; pp. 43 sq.

37. Durham, *Burden*, p. 153.

38. Individualism was also ascribed to many other groups elsewhere: Highlanders in Scotland, fishermen in the Adriatic, muleteers in Iberia. But outsiders were certainly strongly conscious of this quality in South-eastern Europe.

39. See Hitchins, *Romanians*, p. 1.

40. Depicted in Mraz, *Maria Theresia*, p. 315. The cartoon was widely circulated, especially in Austria and Germany.

41. The status of Russia was ambivalent. In this context she was part of the West, and not of Slavic 'barbarism'. Russia showed what could be achieved from the raw material by the application of the values of the Enlightenment.

42. Translated in Davies, *God's Playground*, p. 419.

43. His second chapter in *Inventing Eastern Europe* is entitled 'Possessing Eastern Europe: Sexuality, Slavery and Corporal Punishment'.

44. For Ségur and Coxe, see Wolff, *Inventing*, Chapter 1.

45. This is my interpretation. Larry Wolff, in correspondence, was cautious about taking it too far.

46. *Macbeth* (1606), act 4, scene 1, line 26.

47. St Louis of France in 1270: 'Either we shall push them back into Tartarus whence they came or they will bring us all into heaven.' Cited in *OED* under 'Tartar'.

48. Cited and translated in Wolff, *Inventing*, p. 318. Wolff sees the role of the Tartars as seminal: 'The most overwhelming eastern vector of influence upon Russia, viewed unequivocally as a force of barbarism, was that of Tartary and the Tartars. China, Persia and Turkey could be regarded in the age of Enlightenment as possessing their own Oriental civilisations, but the Tartars received no such concession. If Russia belonged to the Tartar empire in the age of Batu Khan, Tartary belonged to the Russian empire in the age of Peter [the Great], but the relation, even reversed, still weighed in the balance between Europe and Asia, civilisation and barbarism'; pp. 190–91. Conversely, the Spaniards had always regarded the Tartars as Noble Savages by comparison with the greater evil of the Ottomans. See Bunes Ibarra, *Imagen*, pp. 91–2.

49. Cited Wolff, *Inventing*, pp. 192–3.

50. Abbé Fortis cited and translated in Wolff, *Venice*, pp. 126–7.

51. Ibid., pp. 152–3.

52. Cited Bracewell, *Uskoks*, p. 1887.

53. Gordon, *History*, vol. 1, p. 31.

Chapter 10

1. 'Relationi di Petro Foscarini', in Nicolò Barozzi and Guglielmo Bercht (eds), *Le Relazioni degli stati europei lette al Senato dagli ambasciatori veneziani nel secolo decimosettino 5th series: Turchia* (Venice 1866), part 2, pp. 89–90; cited and translated in Lucette Valensi, *Venice and the Sublime Porte: The Birth of the Despot*, trans. Arthur Denner, Ithaca, NY: Cornell University Press, 1993, pp. 1–2.
2. Cited Mary Lucille Shay, *The Ottoman Empire from 1720–1734 as Revealed by the Dispatches of the Venetian Baili*, Urbana, IL: University of Illinois Press, 1944, p. 34.
3. For example, successful plays on the London stage included *The Christian Hero* (1735), *Zoraida* (1780) and *The Siege of Belgrade* (1791), all of which deployed these themes.
4. The writer of these words, Nicolas-Antoine Boulanger, was a sceptical young French civil engineer and savant much admired by Diderot. He died at the age of thirty-seven in 1759, but one of his last works, published secretly after his death, tackled the controversial topic of despotism. His treatise *Recherches sur l'origine du despotisme oriental* was considered seditious in France, and so was published in the Netherlands in 1761. Although Boulanger considered that Europe had its own share of despotisms, and despite his well-honed critical sensibilities, nonetheless he held to the traditional and unquestioning view about the East, which included the Near East as well as the Far East. My text source can be found @ http://www.vc.unipmn.it/~mori/e-texts/
5. See Lewis, *Discovery*.
6. See *A British Resident*, p. 308.
7. With so many young women dying in childbirth or from disease, many Western widowers made a series of marriages. (Thus the wicked stepmother became a literary stereotype.)
8. Possibly Skene's experience of many years had not been with Constantinople sophisticates like the general, but with more traditionally minded provincials.
9. Skene was the British Consul in Aleppo.
10. The concept of 'recovered memory' was developed in the 1990s as a means of enabling children and adults to recall memories of events they had forgotten or repressed. The use of these powerful psycho-therapeutic methods also elicited recollections of events that had never taken place, or manipulated recollection to produce a desired outcome. While most of the research has focused on sexual abuse in childhood the wider implication of this research sheds light on the process of generating social 'memories' about the distant past. See Elizabeth F. Loftus, 'Imagining the Past', *The Psychologist* 14 (November 2001) 11, pp. 584–7. Moreover, 'memories that have had time to fade are particularly susceptible to distortion' by imprinting ideas; see Kathryn A. Braun, Rhiannon Ellis and Elizabeth F. Loftus, 'Make My Memory: How Advertising Can Change Our Memories of the Past', *Psychology and Marketing* 19 (January 2002), pp. 1–23.
11. The number who actually migrated is, like most other elements of this history, still violently contested. For a reasoned revisionist view, see Malcolm, *Kosovo*, pp. 139–40.

12. 'An Abbreviated Biography of Prince Lazar', translated and cited in Emmert, *Serbian Golgotha*, pp. 62–3.

13. The Serbian capacity to transmute disaster into victory had deep cultural roots and carried through into the twentieth century. The retreat of the Serbian army through Montenegro before the Austrian army in 1915, losing 100,000 killed or wounded, was followed at the end of the war with the creation of a South Slav kingdom.

14. *Il regno degli Slavi hoggi corrottamente detti schiauoni historia di Don Macro Orbini in Peso*: Appraise Girolamo Concordia, 1601.

15. The translator was a native of Herzegovina named Sava Vladislavic; see Ante Zadic, 'Strossmayer y los Búlgaros', *Studia Croatica* 1971, No. 42–3.

16. Emmert observes that the Austrian authorities tried without success to prevent copies entering the Habsburg domains.

17. See Bringa, *Being Muslim*, p. 165. Her fine book encapsulates the tragedy of modern Bosnia.

18. Thomson, *The Outgoing Turk*, p. 156.

19. Balkan Muslim cultural traditions were expressed in almost all the languages of the region, for most of the Muslim communities used an Albanian, Slavic or Greek dialect, although some of the Tartar and Anatolian migrants used Turkish among themselves. Greek and Albanian were more or less interchangeable in many areas. At the court of the most successful (and certainly best-known) local Ottoman ruler in the Balkans – Ali, Pasha of Janina – Greek was the official language, not Ottoman Turkish; Ali himself preferred his native Albanian. Indeed, it is uncertain that he was at all proficient in the complexities of Ottoman, for when he made corrections to documents, he used the Greek script. See Fleming, *The Muslim Bonaparte*, pp. 24–5.

20. Albert B. Lord, 'The Effect of the Turkish Conquest on Balkan Epic Tradition' in Birnbaum and Vryonis (eds), *Aspects*, pp. 298–9.

21. The Albanian traditional hero Skendarbeg was shared by both Muslim and Christian communities, but each tribal group constructed 'its' hero in different ways.

22. See Banac, *National Question*, pp. 46–9.

23. I have found Lawrence Stone's categories – Presuppositions, Preconditions, Precipitants, Triggers – a very useful matrix for tracing a way through the complex history of events in the Balkans. See Lawrence Stone, *The Causes of the English Revolution 1529–1642* (2nd edn), London and New York: Routledge, 2002.

24. See Davison, 'Turkish Attitudes'.

25. The Muslim communities had their own local officials who were likewise responsible for the good order of their own community.

26. Halil Inalcik discussed some of the long-term causes of the deteriorating position of the *raya* in 'The Ottoman Decline and its Effects on the Reaya' in Birnbaum and Vryonis, *Aspects*, pp. 338–53.

27. One parallel in the West is how accusations of witchcraft or heresy were eventually found to be rooted in wholly secular causes.

28. There was a literature about the horror of the *devshirme* as though it took place

within living memory, rather than centuries before. The *devshirme* was the forced recruitment of non-Muslims into Imperial service. The males were taken as soldiers (janissaries) and some were trained as officials and administrators. It did not extent, at the latest, beyond the early eighteenth century. Most converted to Islam but often retained a loyalty to their native communities and kept contact with their families. Apart from the element of religious conversion, so abhorrent to Christians, it did not differ very greatly from military recruitment in Russia or the Habsburg lands.

29. They governed Bosnia and Herzegovina with about 120 officials; the bureaucratic Austrians who took over from them in 1878 employed 600 by 1881. By 1897 this had risen to 7,379. See Sugar, *Industrialization*, p. 29.

30. See Irwin T. Sanders, 'Balkan Rural Society and War', cited in Rhoads Murphy, *Ottoman Warfare 1500–1700*, London: UCL Press, 1999.

31. See Ralston, *Importing*, pp. 43–68.

32. Britain replaced the French in the Ionian Islands.

33. At some points they sought to ally with the Ottomans, at other times to work against them. However, the French presence, their revolutionary ideology and activist government contrasted profoundly with Ottoman torpor, and undermined the Turkish position in the eyes of Christian subjects. The border was permeable and Greeks, Albanians and Serbs were well aware of what was taking place in the Ionian Islands and, later, in the Illyrian Provinces.

34. J. Savant, 'Napoléon et la libération de la Grèce' in *L'Hellénisme contemporain*, July–October 1950, p. 321. Cited and translated in Stavrianos, *Balkans*, p. 211.

35. Perhaps the best and most succinct statement of the libertarian viewpoint came much later, not from a left-wing ideologue, but from a conservative: 'Extremism in the defence of liberty is no vice!' Barry Goldwater, US Republican Presidential candidate, 16 July 1964.

36. In the case of the Greek Revolution, I do not intend to discuss the uprising in Moldavia and Wallachia, or the later conduct of the war, but to focus on the events of 1821–2.

37. As they could in other clan societies – the feud between the Campbells and the Macdonalds in Scotland originated in 1297.

38. This too had its echo in local customary law, which assumed collective and clan responsibility for any act. This could be found just as readily among the Arabs of Jordan and the Arabian peninsula, in the Druze and Maronite Christian communities of Lebanon, and in Italy and Spain.

39. See Petrovich, *History*, vol. 1, p. 84.

40. See Stevan Pavlowitch, 'Society in Serbia 1791–1830', in Clogg (ed.), *Balkan Society*, p. 144.

41. Gordon, *History*, vol. 1, pp. i–ii.

42. He gave many examples of individual Turks who had behaved with a great sense of honour, better than the Greeks.

43. Gordon, *History*, vol. 1, p. 143.

44. See W. Alison Phillips, *The War of Greek Independence 1821 to 1833*, London: Smith Elder, 1897, p. 48.

45. Gordon, *History*, vol. 1, p. 149.

46. At Patras, on Palm Sunday, the Turks 'amused themselves at their leisure in impaling or beheading prisoners and circumcising Christian children'; ibid., p. 156.

47. Ibid., pp. 244–5.

48. 'Their [the Greeks'] insatiable cruelty knew no bounds, and seemed to inspire them with a superhuman energy for evil . . . Every corner was ransacked to discover new victims and the unhappy Jewish population (even more than the Turks an object of fanatical hatred) expired amid torments which we dare not describe. During the sack of the city, the air was close, dull and oppressively hot'; ibid.

49. 'Never were firmans obeyed with more alacrity; intelligence of the revolt of Scio [Chios] excited very strong feeling throughout Asia Minor, detachments of troops covered the roads, and the ancient fervour of Islamism seemed to revive. Old and young flew to arms, and a regiment composed entirely of Imams was seen to march through the streets of Smyrna'; ibid., p. 356.

50. Ibid., p. 192.

51. 'Those who are best acquainted with the Greeks cannot fail to remark the numerous and striking features of resemblance that connect them with their ancestors . . . The Grecian character was, however, long tried in the furnace of misfortune, that the sterling metal had mostly evaporated and little but dross remained; having obliterated whatever was laudable in the institutions of their forefathers, their recent masters had taught them only evil'; ibid., p. 32. It was the 'worthiest' of the Athenians who sought to prevent the deliberate massacre of the civilian Turks in the city, while 'the system of the worst and most degraded Greeks, of exterminating, *per fas et nefas* [by fair means and foul] every disciple of Islam who fell into their hands'; ibid., pp. 414–15.

52. Ibid., p. 4.

53. Ibid., p. 231.

54. Ibid., p. 84.

55. Ibid., p. 57.

56. For a new insight into Byron's attitudes, see Makdisi, *Romantic Imperialism*, pp. 136–7. He notes Byron's: 'the Ottomans are not a people to be despised. Equal, at least, to the Spaniards, they are superior to the Portuguese. If it be difficult to pronounce what they are, we can at least say what they are *not*: they are *not* treacherous, they are *not* cowardly, they do *not* burn heretics, they are *not* assassins . . .'

57. On the pamphlet literature see St Clair, *That Greece*, pp. 372–3. At that time the publications in English and German diminished. He also noted how there was a flood of books on Greece after Byron's death, and in a number of these Byron and Missolonghi were mentioned in the title; see ibid., pp. 386–7.

58. The stronghold of the revolution was not in Greece itself, but in the Danubian Provinces of the Ottoman Empire, where the ruling class was made up of Greeks from Constantinople, many of whom patronized secret Hellenic patriotic societies. The role of the Greek secret society, or 'Friendly Association' (*Filiki Etairia*) is still unclear. At most individual members orchestrated, rather than provided a detailed plan for the killings in the Peloponnese in 1821.

59. See Athanassoglou-Kallmyer, *French Images*, pp. 11–12.
60. Nina Athanassoglou-Kallmyer draws a strong connection between the two: 'By joining regular to irregular, and classical to expressive, Delacroix's cartoons reveal a balanced dualism – sublime and grotesque . . . the prints are significant as early exemplars of similar solutions observed in Delacroix's painting. In . . . *Massacres on Chios* for example conventionally constructed scenes are punctuated by elements of the grotesque . . . possibly derived from graphic satire.' Part of the success of this picture was that it appealed to 'the street'. See Athanassoglou-Kallmyer, *Eugène Delacroix*, p. 112.
61. *Massacre of the Greeks at Missolonghi* (1827).
62. François-Emile de Lansac, *Scene from the Siege of Missolonghi* (1828) in Athanassoglou-Kallmyer, *French Images*, p. 81.

Chapter 11

1. The words are Gladstone's in *Bulgarian Horrors*.
2. Skene describes how this was decreed for the Ottoman navy, but in theory to be extended more generally: 'Everything had, however, been done to eradicate these apprehensions [Christian fears of Muslims], even to the prohibition of the terms *Raya* and *Ghiaur*, which were made punishable offences in the navy, where Christians and Turks were thrown together, and it can now only be the effect of time.' The legislation was not effective. See Skene, *A British Resident*, vol. 2, p. 332.
3. Perhaps 'Turcophilia' implies too much amity. Most of those who sympathized with the Turks were also fierce critics of what they considered their deep and inherent weaknesses.
4. I suggest that through most of the eighteenth century attraction rather than repulsion was the rule, while the balance shifted early in the nineteenth century; but in the second half a degree of attraction had returned.
5. Gladstone, *Bulgarian Horrors*, p. 15.
6. Ussama Makdisi has convincingly shown how the traditional acceptance by Druze, Maronite Christians and Muslims of their neighbours of other faiths was overthrown by the external pressures of Ottoman modernization and Western missionaries (with the consuls and navies ever present in the background). See Ussama Makdisi, *The Culture of Sectarianism*.
7. See Kamil S. Salibi, 'The 1860 Upheaval in Damascus' in William R. Polk and Richard L. Chambers (eds), *The Beginnings of Modernization in the Middle East: The Nineteenth Century*, Chicago, IL: University of Chicago Press, 1968, pp. 185–202. The Ottomans held Arab Muslim notables responsible in exactly the same way that they had Christians and Jews in other incidents. Sixty-one were hanged and 111 shot in a meadow outside the city. Other leading Damascenes were exiled. Others complained that after 1860 'Christians and Europeans, patriarchs and bishops were given undue precedence.'
8. See Magris, *Danube*, p. 327.
9. See Engin Akarli, *The Long Peace*.
10. Public Record Office FO 78/1520, 'Report of Cyril Graham Esq., on the

Conditions of the Christians in the Districts of Hasbeya and Rasheya', in Brant (Consulate, Damascus) to Russell (London), 13 August 1860.

11. Shannon, *Gladstone*, p. 22. Shannon's book is an exemplary study of the process by which publications generate political actions and attitudes.

12. E. A. Freeman, 'The English People in Relation to the Eastern Question', *Contemporary Review*, February 1877, cited in Shannon, *Gladstone*, p. 14.

13. In a letter from Stuart Poole to Henry Liddon, 4 February 1877; cited in Shannon, *Gladstone*, p. 33.

14. See Jane Robinson, *Angels of Albion: Women of the Indian Mutiny*, London: Penguin, 1997. The official investigation after the Mutiny produced no evidence of sexual violation. Copulation with an Englishman would have caused a catastrophic loss of caste for a Hindu, and there is no record of Muslims raping Christian women in India. However, the implication of sexual molestation was omnipresent, in both text and image.

15. The revolutionary group that organized the uprising south of the Danube on 3 May 1876 at Panagurishte was disorganized and ill-coordinated. Apart from persuading a woman teacher who had learned embroidery to make them a flag, showing a yellow lion with his paw on the crescent and the motto 'Liberty or Death', and holding a public meeting, they seemed to have no coherent plan. Nevertheless, the excited crowd that listened to fierce speeches and sang revolutionary songs went on to murder all the Turks they could find in the vicinity. These seem to have totalled about 1,000; see Stavrianos, *Balkans*, pp. 377–80. Mark Mazower suggests they found little support among the peasants who had proved utterly resistant to the clarion call of Bulgarian nationality; see Mazower, *Balkans*, pp. 88–95. However, Justin Macarthy suggests that they deliberately targeted Circassian villages so as to engender reprisals; see Macarthy, *Death*, p. 60.

16. The excuse that the murders were committed by forces outside the control of the Ottoman authorities is unconvincing. The authorities in Constantinople were wont to use terror by whatever means came easily to hand.

17. Malcolm, *Bosnia*, pp. 131–3.

18. Cited and translated in Stavrianos, *Balkans*, p. 379.

19. Cited and translated in Harold Temperley, *The Bulgarian and Other Atrocities 1875–8; The Light of Historical Criticism*, London: Humphrey Milford, 1931, pp. 7–8.

20. Ibid., p. 9.

21. Eugene Schuyler (1840–90) was both a scholar and a diplomat. His biography of Peter the Great was the first in English based on Russian sources. His longest and most fruitful period were his years in Russia during the 1860s and 1870s. The book of his journeys through Turkestan is a classic work of travel literature.

22. MacGahan remarks that its prosperity had excited the envy and jealousy of its Muslim neighbours. 'I elsewhere remark that, in all the Moslem atrocities, Chiot, Bulgarian, and Armenian, the principal incentive has been the larger prosperity of the Christian population'; from Sir Edwin Pears, *Forty Years in Constantinople 1873–1915* (New York: D. Appleton and Co., 1916), pp. 16–19. I have used the text from the Internet Modern History Sourcebook in which

the spelling has been modernized. Pears's own report outlining the atrocities was sent to London in June 1876.

23. News began to appear in the *Manchester Guardian* and in reports to *The Times* from Gallenga, its correspondent in Constantinople.

24. For the composition of the pamphlet see Shannon, *Gladstone*, pp. 106–9.

25. A second and wholly new pamphlet appeared in the following year.

26. Gladstone, *Bulgarian Horrors*, pp. 12–13.

27. Gladstone's Diaries, 2 February 1859. I have taken this account of Gladstone's attitudes and presuppositions about the Ottomans both from Mark Nixon's unpublished paper on the topic, and from conversations. I am extremely grateful to him for allowing me to use his material.

28. Gladstone was preoccupied, as were many of his contemporaries, with the cruel eroticism of the Turks. Six pages of J. L. Farley's pamphlet *Cross or Crescent* dealt in prurient detail with the ravishment and massacre of Christian women by the bestial Turks. Much of Gladstone's copy of this text was, according to Mark Nixon, underlined or highlighted with marginal notes.

29. His second pamphlet, *Lessons in Massacre or, The Conduct of the Turkish Government in and about Bulgaria, since May, 1876*, published in the Spring of 1877, was vintage (and slightly sententious) Gladstone.

30. See Shannon, *Gladstone*, p. 110.

31. 28 October 1876.

32. 5 May 1877.

33. See Fabian, *Time and the Other*, pp. 80–87.

34. On the Balkan past, Mazower, *Balkans*, and Todorova, *Imagining*, provide the best introductions.

35. Banac, *National Question*, pp. 202–14.

36. Emmert, *Serbian Golgotha*, p. 132, citing and translating Duško Kečkemet, *Ivan Meštrovic*, Zagreb: 1970, pp. 1–3.

37. For the position of the Turks of Bulgaria or Pomaks, see Karpat (ed.), *Turks*.

38. In my view, population transfer as practised in the 1920s (and subsequently) exists along the same spectrum as ethnic cleansing by extermination. But they are not identical. For a good discussion of these issues see McGarry and O'Leary (eds), *Politics*. The Ottomans practised forced resettlement, but the aim was usually to create colonies that would strengthen their hold on a region. For the origins of the term 'ethnic cleansing', Dražen Petrović writes in 'An Attempt at Methodology', *European Journal of International Law* 1994: 'Ethnic cleansing is a literal translation of the expression *etnicko ciscenje* in Serbo-Croatian/ Croato-Serbian. The origin of this term . . . is difficult to establish . . . Analysis of ethnic cleansing should not be limited to the specific case of former Yugoslavia. This policy can occur and have terrible consequences in all territories with mixed populations, especially in attempts to redefine frontiers and rights over given territories. There is a new logic of conflict that relies on violent actions against "enemy" civilian population on a large scale, rather than on war in the traditional sense, i.e. between armed forces. Examples of this logic and policy abound today (the extreme case being Rwanda).' The original use of the term was applied by Serbs to Albanian attacks on Serbs in Kosovo and only

later was it used (by Croats and Bosnians) to describe actions taken by Serbs. I am grateful to Dejan Jović for explaining this complex etymology. Only Slovenia has been largely exempt, but the Slovenes suffered a great deal of suspicion and pressure from the Habsburg authorities and later from the new Austrian state in the 1920s.

39. See Sugar, *Industrialization*.

40. Incorporated in the Slav state the Bosnian Muslims had an ambivalent status. It was only in the 1960s, when Bosnian Muslims were recognized as a national group by Tito, that their collective position began to improve. The appeal of a 'Yugoslav' identity rather than Serb or Croat affiliation proved seductive. See Friedman, *Bosnian Muslims*.

41. See Andrić, *Development*.

42. 'At the most critical stage of its spiritual development, at the time that the fermentation of [Bosnia's] spiritual forces had reached a culmination, invasion by an Asian warrior people whose social institutions and customs meant the negation of Christian culture and whose faith – created under different climatic and social conditions and unfit for any kind of adjustment – interrupted the spiritual life of a country, degenerated it and created something quite strange out of it.' Cited and translated by Tomislav Z. Longinović, 'East within the West: Bosnian Cultural Identity in the Works of Ivo Andrić', in Wayne S. Vucinich (ed.), *Ivo Andrić Revisited: 'The Bridge Still Stands'*, Berkeley, CA: University of California Press, 1995, p. 124.

43. Vuk Stefanović Karadžić was born in 1787. The bulk of his active life was spent in Vienna. Petar Petrović Njegoš was born in Montenegro in 1813. His four main books of poetry were *The Voice of Mountaineers* (1833), *The Cure for Turkish Fury* (1834), *The Song of Freedom* (1835, published 1854), and *The Serbian Mirror* (1845). His major work *The Mountain Wreath* was published in Serbian in Vienna in 1847.

44. Tomislav Z. Longinović, 'East within the West: Bosnian Cultural Identity in the Works of Ivo Andrić', in Wayne S. Vucinich (ed.), *Ivo Andrić Revisited: 'The Bridge Still Stands'*, Berkeley, CA: University of California Press, 1995, p. 126.

45. See Andrić, *Bosnian Chronicle*, pp. 262–3.

46. Emmert, *Serbian Golgotha*, p. 141. The famed 'blackbirds' of Kosovo Polje were no doubt crows or similar scavengers.

47. See Wachtel, *Making*, pp. 129–34.

48. Cited and translated in Tanner, *Croatia*, p. 75.

49. Cited and translated in Banac, *National Question*, p. 59.

50. Mary Shelley, *Frankenstein*, Chapter 4. It is curious how Frankenstein, set in the original in Switzerland, was moved in one of the first filmic treatments (1931) to Bavaria. Then in *Frankenstein Created Woman* (1967), Frankenstein had moved east (into 'Dracula territory'?) to a 'nineteenth-century Balkan village'.

51. Njegoš's *Mountain Wreath*; see http://www.rastko.org.yu/knjizevnost/umetnicka/njegos/mountain_wreath.html (the *gusle* is a traditional folk instrument).

52. In Lady Wilde, *'Speranza', Ancient Legends, Mystic Charms & Superstitions of Ireland with Sketches of the Irish Past, to which is Appended a Chapter on 'The Ancient Race of Ireland' by the Late Sir William Wilde*, London: Ward and Lock, 1888.

53. See Mertus, *Kosovo*.
54. Ibid., p. 100.
55. Andrić is quite specific that those who impaled the victim, the peasant Radisav, were gypsies. Martus cites the source as M. Jankovic, '*Zlocin kao u vreme Turaka*', ('Crimes Like in the Time of the Turks') *Politika Ekspres*, 14 January 1991, see Martus, *Kosovo*, p. 119. The most moving account of the continuing plight of the Balkan gypsies is Isabel Fonseca's fine book, *Bury Me Standing: The Gypsies and their Journey*, New York, NY: Vintage, 1996.
56. Mertus cites the author as Žirovad Mihajlović.
57. Mertus, *Kosovo*, p. 112.
58. Weine, *When History*, pp. 107–9. Weine was an American psychiatrist who spent five years interviewing in Bosnia on memories of ethnic cleansing.
59. He liked to carry the *gusle*, with which Njegoš and other poets are often depicted. One of his colleagues in the Kosovo Day Hospital at Sarajevo described how 'I heard his first talks in the villages and on television. He was very familiar with the language. He was making jokes . . . He used much more his knowledge of the culture, of the spiritual archetypal needs of the Serbian people than psychiatry to seduce them. He was using stories, legends, *gusle* and religion'; Weine, *When History*, pp. 114–15.
60. Robert Browning, 'The Pied Piper of Hamlin', in Browning, *Poetry and Prose*, selected by Simon Nowell-Smith, London: Rupert Hart-Davis, 1950, p. 110.

Chapter 12

1. The Russian critic Mikhail Bakhtin, writing with V. N. Volosinov in the aftermath of the Russian Revolution of 1917, looked at the emblems of their own day. A hammer and a sickle were just tools. But put them together, and they become a symbol, the insignia of the nascent Soviet Union. 'Any consumer good', Bakhtin and Volosinov observed, 'can likewise be made into an ideological sign. For instance, bread and wine become religious symbols in the Christian sacrament.' There is a long-running debate as to whether this was written by Volosinov or by Mikhail Bakhtin under Volosinov's name, or by them jointly. I have given them both credit. See Morris (ed.), *Bakhtin Reader*, p. 50.
2. It was first published in a large Latin folio at Basel in 1559, and in English in 1563. It went through four editions in Foxe's lifetime: there was a corrected edition in 1570 and two more in 1576 and 1583. Six further editions appeared in 1596, 1610, 1632, 1641, 1684 and 1784. Further versions came out in 1837–41 and 1877, growing larger and more weighty. The edition of 1684 was published in three folio volumes of 895, 682, and 863 pages. In 1571, the Convocation of Bishops ordered copies to be placed in every cathedral in England alongside the Bible, and many parish churches followed suit.
3. I suggest that impalement was a significant and evolving trope in Western depictions of the Muslim East. In Jean de Thévenot, *Voyages de M. de Thévenot tant en Europe qu'en Asie et en Afrique*, Paris: Charles Angot, 1689, vol. 2, there is an image of impalement in Ottoman Egypt. It depicts an Arab on a camel with burning brands strapped to his arms (so that boiling fat would drip down

and burn his skin). In the background are two pyramids, and in front of these two impaled men, one smoking a pipe. The text in Chapter LXXIX, 'The Punishments', criticized Egypt. However, in the Dutch edition of 1723, illustrated by Jan Luyken, the image is changed. It now depicts a European or Anatolian setting (the dominant camel has vanished and the extraordinarily brutal visual details of the impalement appear in the foreground). See *Alle de gedenkwaardige en zeer naauwkeurige reizen van den heere de Thevenot*, trans. by G. van Broekhuizen, 2nd impression, Amsterdam: N. ten Hoorn, 1723, p. 441.

4. The image is in *Les Chroniques de France ou de St. Denis*, British Library, MS Roy. 16 G VI. f. 412. In some pictures, Muslims are distinguished by Phrygian-style helmets.

5. See the cartouche in Window 11, of the Saracens climbing the walls of Assisi reproduced in Marcel Beck, Peter Felder, Emil Maurer and Dietrich Schearz, *Königsfelden: Geschichte, Bauten, Glasgemälde, Kunstschätze*, Freiburg im Breisgau: Walter-Verlag, 1983.

6. A fifteenth-century French image distinguished Arabs from Crusaders by presenting the former as half-naked savages. The image is in *Les Chroniques de France ou de St. Denis*, British Library, MS Add. 21143. f. 90.

7. As can be seen in the crest of the medieval Lords Audley, whose ancestors came to England with William the Conqueror in 1066. Their arms, in the quaint language of heraldry, consisted of: an arm couped at the shoulder, embowed, and resting the elbow on the wreath, holding a sword in pale, enfiled with a Saracen's head. The crest depicts a hand holding a sword on which is spiked the head of a bearded man of 'Eastern' appearance. The motto given below the crest, *Mors ad inimicus* (death to the oppressor), makes the point clear.

8. A. W. Kinglake, *Eothen*, London: J. Ollivier, 1847, p. 180.

9. Moreover, the relationship between image and text is rarely noted. Hélène Desmet-Grégoire classifies the eighteenth-century popular literature in France and reproduces the *Historie de Melusine*; the images of the armies are Western and not Oriental. It contains none of the Eastern stereotypes. However, the broadsheet designed to raise support for ransoming of captives *does* depict all the tortures, including impalements, inflicted on captives. The purpose is to horrify and so raise more money. See Hélène Desmet-Grégoire, *Divan magique*.

10. The *OED* gives the first usage as Edward Hall's in *The Union of the Two Noble and Illustrate Famelies of Lancastre and Yorke*, published in 1548: 'Aparaled after Turkey fashion . . . girded with two swords called cimitaries.' It cites Christophorus Richerius, *De rebus turcarum*, published in Paris in 1540, for the statement that the Janissaries called their swords 'cymitharra'. Adolphe Hatzfeld and Arsène Darmesteter in their *Dictionnaire général de la langue française du commencement du XVIIe siècle jusqu'à nos jours, précédé d'un traité de la formation de la langue*, Paris: Librairie Delagrave, 1890–1900 say it has a fifteenth-century origin but are not specific.

11. The Turkish incident was inserted at the personal insistence of Louis XIV, who had become entranced with the Ottomans after an embassy to Paris in 1669. See Fatma Müge Göçek, *East Encounters West: France and the Ottoman Empire in the Eighteenth Century*, New York, NY: Oxford University Press, 1987,

pp. 72–3. Göçek gives a full account of the mutual effects of the links between France and the Ottoman Empire.

12. G. Horton, *The Blight of Asia*, 1922, chapter 19, @ www.hri.org/docs/Horton/hb-29.html

13. 'Outlandish' moved from its late medieval usage – meaning 'external' – to the later use which had become a term of abuse. See *OED*.

14. That is, it seemed to represent the stereotypical medieval Christian view of the Jew.

15. These included an edition printed by Mikulas Bakalar in Pilsen; a Lyons edition of 1488 printed by Martin Huss (freely adapted with new illustrations); another by Anton Sorg in Augsburg also in 1488; another brought out by Pablo Hurus as *Viaje de la Tierra Sancta* in Saragossa in 1498; see Clair, *History*, and Lucien Febvre and Henri-Jean Martin, *The Coming of the Book: The Impact of Printing 1450–1800*, trans. David Gerard, London: Verso, 1976.

16. Samuel Purchas, *Purchas, His Pilgrimes in Five Books*, London: William Stainsby for Henry Fetherstone, 1625. The copy I have used is British Library BL 984 h.5.

17. One, Lithgow, opined that 'the nature of the Arabs was not unlike the jackals', decried the 'villainy of the Armenians' while noting 'the constancy of the Turks', ibid., p. 1846. 'Sir John Mandeville' was the author of the most famous (and widely read) medieval travel narrative. Mandeville – supposedly an English knight, but this was probably a pseudonym – made his 'travels' in the first half of the fourteenth century. He plainly did go east, but much of his book is the purest fantasy.

18. *Othello*, act 5, scene 2, lines 357–61.
    'In Aleppo once,
    Where a malignant and a turbaned Turk
    Beat a Venetian and traduced the state,
    I took by the throat the circumcised dog
    And smote him thus.'

19. On Beham, see M. Geisberg, *The German Single-leaf Woodcut: 1500–1550*, vol. 1, New York, NY: Hacker Art Books, 1974, pp. 268–75.

20. *Türcken Biechlin*, which is written in a south German dialect; see Bohnstedt, 'The Infidel Scourge', pp. 10–11.

21. This topic is not well covered, but I have found useful elements in the chapter on 'Towards an Emblematic Rhetoric' in Manning, *The Emblem*, pp. 85–109.

22. See Certeau, *Writing*, p. 94: 'We admit as historiographical discourse that which can "include" its other – chronicle, archive, document – in other words, discourse that is organised in a laminated text in which one continuous half is based on another disseminated half.' The 'dissemination' of an image is implicit in the multiplicity and coordination of its visual elements, arranged in predetermined order.

23. See Anna Pavord, *The Tulip*, London: Bloomsbury, 1999, p. 80.

24. Ibid., pp. 48–52.

25. See Dufrenoy, *L'Orient Romanesque*, vol. 3, p. 687.

26. See Marquis de Sade, *120 days of Sodom*, London: Arena, 1989, pp. 263 sqq.

27. The figure was given in a paper by Professor Gary Schwarz at a colloquium led by Professor John Brewer at the European University Institute, Florence.

28. The text volumes, with their 72,000 articles by 140 contributors, were often held up by censorship. But the plates did not seem to interest the censors and were published at the rate of about one volume a year from 1761. Many of the 2,569 pages of plates showed images on a double-page spread.

29. The 1783 Amsterdam and Paris edition was enlarged to eleven volumes, in a '*Nouvelle édition, enrichie de toutes les figures comprises dans l'ancienne édition en sept volumes, & dans les quatre publiés par forme de supplément par une société des gens de lettres* [A new edition, enriched with all the images in the old edition in seven volumes and the additional four published in the form of supplements by a group of literary gentlemen]'.

30. 'Let the Protestant burin of Bernard Picard exert itself as it will in tracing to us hideous representations of real or imaginary tortures inflicted by the judges of the Inquisition; it signifies nothing, or can only be addressed to the king of Spain.' Cited in Richard Lebrun, 'Joseph de Maistre's Defence of the Spanish Inquisition' @ www.umanitoba.ca/faculties/arts/history/spanishinquisition.html

31. On the development of the frontispiece see Corbett and Lightbown, *Comely Frontispiece*, pp. 1–47.

32. Part of the caption reads: the 'successor of Mahomet, Ali, explained the Alcoran to the many people who make up the Mahometan Religion', translated from 'Le Tableau des Principales Religions du Monde' in Bernard Picard, *Cérémonies et coutumes religieuses de tous les peuples du monde, représentées par des figures dessinées de la main de Bernard Picard avec une Explication Historique, et quelques Dissertations curieuses*, Amsterdam: J. F. Bernard, 1733–43.

33. He went back in 1691–2.

34. Marsigli had created his own institute in Bologna and a printing house to prepare his published works. However, he had a number of them published in Amsterdam. See Stoye, *Marsigli's Europe*, p. 309.

35. Copy in the Library of Congress listed as *Voennoe sostianie Ottomanskiia Imperii s eia prirascheniem I ipadkom. Vse ukrasheno grydorovanrlistami*, St Petersburg: Imp. Akademii nauk, 1737. I have not yet seen this text.

36. Ogier Ghislain de Busbecq, *Travels into Turkey . . . Containing the Most Accurate Account of the Turks, and Neighbouring Nations, Translated from the Original Latin of the Learned A. G. Busbequius*, London: J. Robinson and W. Payne, 1744. This was successful enough to reissue in 1774. The first edition of Busbecq in English had been edited by Nahum Tate and printed by J. Taylor and F. Wyat in London in 1694. It was published as 'The four epistles of A. G. Busbequius concerning his embassy into Turkey; being remarks upon the religion, customs, riches, strength and government of that people. As also as a description of their chief cities and places of trade and commerce. To which is added his advice how to manage war against the Turks. Done into English Epistolae quatuor.' However, Latin editions of Busbecq were also still being published – for example an Oxford edition of 1771.

37. Cited and translated in Findley, 'Ebu Bekir Ratib', p. 48.

38. The page size of an elephant folio volume is twenty-three by fourteen inches.

39. My historical data on D'Ohsson is taken from the extended version of Findley's paper 'A Quixotic Author'. I am extremely grateful to Carter Findley for letting me use his impressive work, which deserves a much wider audience.

40. Cited Çirakman, 'From Tyranny to Despotism', p. 58. Dominique Carnoy presents a rather different picture in her study of French images in *Représentations*.

41. Gladstone, *Bulgarian Horrors*, pp. 12–13. By his second pamphlet of the following year, Gladstone was less violent and more circumspect in his utterances. See *Lessons in Massacre or, The Conduct of the Turkish Government in and about Bulgaria since May 1876*, London: John Murray, 1877.

42. And, as Joseph Conrad observed at the beginning of his Eastern novel *Under Western Eyes* (1911), 'This is not a story of the West of Europe.'

Chapter 13

1. The history of print is in a state of rapid transformation. New theories and objectives have become dominant. In my view, apart from key texts such as those of Elizabeth Eisenstein, Lucien Febvre and Henri-Jean Martin, Robert Darnton, Rudolf Hirsch, and most recently Adrian Johns, the most helpful restatement has come from Gérard Genette in his construct of the 'paratexte'. This connects the physical forms of the text to its audiences, potential and actual. However, even Genette himself gracefully demurred from discussing the issue which concerns me here – the role and effect of images. 'I have likewise left out three practices whose paratextual relevance seems to me undeniable, but investigating each one might demand as much work as was required here in treating this subject as a whole . . . [the third] constitutes an immense continent: that of illustration.' I can here only allude to the issues involved but I am taking the topic up in more detail in a forthcoming work. See Genette, *Paratexts*, pp. 405–6.

2. This appears in 'The Marriage of Heaven and Hell'; see William Blake, *Poetry and Prose of William Blake*, ed. Geoffrey Keynes, London: The Nonesuch Library, 1961, p. 187.

3. See Çirakman, 'From the "Terror of the World"'.

4. Volney, *Travels*, vol. 2, pp. 177–9. Volney is in error in one small particular: Arabic letters change in terms of where they come in the word rather than in the sentence.

5. He wrote *On the Simplification of Oriental Languages* in 1795, and *The European Alphabet Applied to the Languages of Asia* in 1819.

6. See C. F. de Volney, *The Ruins, or, Meditations on the Revolutions of Empire and the Law of Nature*, rep. New York, NY: Twentieth Century Publishing Company, 1890, p. 81.

7. Ibid., p. 76.

8. I find the whole idea of counterfactual history, of which Simon Schama's *Dead Certainties* (1991) was a pioneering approach (and unjustly criticized when it first appeared), an invaluable critical tool. The collection edited by Niall Ferguson, *Virtual History* (1997), makes the case for the approach, especially Ferguson's long Introduction, pp. 1–91.

9. Jonathan Bloom in his sparkling survey of paper in the Islamic world (*Paper before Print*) can cite only one book: Dard Hunter's *Papermaking: The History and Technique of an Ancient Craft*, first published by Knopf in 1943, revised and republished in 1947, and reissued in 1978. Hunter's is still the sole general overview available in English.

10. A short-lived mill was set up in France at Troyes a little earlier.

11. Little is known of this first paper mill, while much more is known of the eighteenth-century mill set up at Yalova, on the southern (Asian) side of the Sea of Marmara in 1744. This spa town has a constant supply of high-quality water necessary for any volume of production. See Fatma Müge Göçek, *East Encounters West: France and the Ottoman Empire in the Eighteenth Century*, New York, NY: Oxford University Press, 1987, pp. 114–15.

12. Most of the Ottoman sources are not contemporary with the first fifteenth- and sixteenth-century prohibitions. See ibid., pp. 110–11.

13. Thevet's life of Gutenberg, in *Histoire des plus illustres et savans hommes de leurs siècles*, Paris: Manger, 1671, vol. VII, p. 111, cited by Gdoura, *Début*, pp. 86–7.

14. The Taliban's and the 'Islamic Emirate' of Afghanistan's attitude towards images was notoriously aniconistic. Comparisons have been drawn with Byzantine iconoclasm as state policy, and it is hard to find so radical and coordinated an Islamic equivalent in modern times. Even the murderous excesses of the Ikhwan in the capture of Mecca and Medina (and the destruction of tombs and images) were not acts of state. The Taliban's policy plainly was. The supreme leader Mullah Mohammed Omar ordered the destruction of all statues in the country, which resulted in the notorious and highly public blowing-up of the ancient Buddhist statues at Bamiyan. The official statement made through the AP agency stated that 'in view of the *fatwa* [religious edict] of prominent Afghan scholars and the verdict of the Afghan Supreme Court it has been decided to break down all statues/idols present in different parts of the country. This is because these idols have been gods of the infidels, who worshipped them, and these are respected even now and perhaps maybe turned into gods again. The real God is only Allah, and all other false gods should be removed.' It was also asserted that photographs and electronic images were likewise forbidden, but Taliban officials themselves photographed the destruction of the statues. Many Taliban leaders allowed their photographs to be taken, and it has been suggested that their 'image policy' was religious in theory but selectively political in practice.

15. See David Talbot Rice, *Islamic Painting: A Survey*, Edinburgh: Edinburgh University Press, 1971, pp. 21–6. For the Abbasids see Richard Ettinghausen, *Arab Painting*, New York, NY: Rizzoli, 1977, p. 41–53. The classic statement is Arnold, *Painting in Islam*.

16. Iconoclasm in Reformation Europe was directed not so much at images, but at art used in a religious context. See, for example, Philips, *Reformation*.

17. See Goffman, *Ottoman Empire*, p. 91. This short book, which is innovative both in its structure and in its insights, is a mature and compelling correction to a long tradition of misrepresentation. I am extremely grateful to Virginia Aksan for drawing it to my attention.

18. See Lewis, *Discovery*, especially his account of the Egyptian scholar Sheikh Rifaa Rafi al-Tahtawi's five-year stay in Paris.

19. The stage of final reading, when a written text is read out loud, is still an essential part of the legislative process in the United States and the United Kingdom.

20. Cardinal Ferdinando di Medici financed the establishment of the Typographia Medicea Linguarum Externum by Raimondi in 1585.

21. The first book to be printed in Ottoman Turkish was George Seaman's translation of the New Testament. He was the interpreter to Sir Peter Wyche, English Ambassador to Constantinople, and the book was printed at Oxford in 1606. In 1734 William Caslon was commissioned by the Society for the Promotion of Christian Literature to cut an Arabic fount for a New Testament to be used in missionary work.

22. See Bloom, *Paper*, p. 116.

23. For the prevalence (and design) of libraries see Godfrey Goodwin, *A History of Ottoman Architecture*, London: Thames and Hudson, 1971.

24. See Dov Shidorsky, 'Libraries in Late Ottoman Palestine between the Orient and the Occident', *Libraries & Culture* 33, 3, (summer 1998), pp. 260–76. See also Hitzel (ed.), *Livres*.

25. Müteferrika had already begun to print by 1719. He sent a map of the Sea of Marmara to the Grand Vizier Damad Ibrahim Pasha, with a note to the effect that 'if your Excellency so commands, larger ones can be produced.' For the document from the Sultan setting up the printing press in Constantinople, see 'The Firman of Ahmed III, given in 1727 authorizing Said Effendi and Ibrahim Müteferrika to open a printing house using Arabic script', trans. Christopher Murphy in Atiyah (ed.), *Book*, pp. 284–92.

26. He was by then himself the Ambassador to the Court of France.

27. It has been estimated that from 1455 to 1500 between 6 and 20 million copies of publications were printed in Europe. Six million is a very cautious estimate, and probably about 12–15 million might be a good working figure. Between 30,000 and 35,000 separate editions of books from this half-century still survive, representing various versions and reprints of some 10,000 to 15,000 different texts. See the estimates for editions in Europe and the useful analyses of content in southern and northern Europe in Gerulaitis, *Printing*, pp. 17–18 and 57–129. Hirsch, *Printing*, pp. 133–5, uses J. M. Lenart's figures from *Pre-Reformation Printed Books* (New York: 1935). Assuming that about 500 copies (on average) of each edition were produced, then printing in aggregate 15 million copies is reasonable. So who read or bought all these books? This question has never been answered satisfactorily. The calculations of copies printed are of necessity approximate, hence the wild discrepancies. See also Lucien Febvre and Henri-Jean Martin, *The Coming of the Book: The Impact of Printing 1450–1800*, trans. David Gerard, London: Verso, 1976, p. 248.

28. There had been several attempts to set up printers' workshops in the Balkan lands, all of which failed. In the centuries of Ottoman rule, only a handful of books were produced in the southern Slav lands. The first were printed in Cetinje in Montenegro in the 1490s by a monk named Makarije. Eight other

short-lived presses were later set up, but their total output was eleven slender titles. From the sixteenth century Slavic books were produced in other lands and brought across the frontier. Many were printed by a succession of specialist printers in Venice, beginning with the Vuković family from Montenegro in the early sixteenth century. Another major centre developed at the same time in Wallachia; but it was not until the 1770s, when recognizing the demand for texts for the Serbian market, that printers in Vienna, St Petersburg and Leipzig competed to supply Serbs both in the Vojvodina and in the lands under Ottoman rule. However, supplies were irregular and many printers could not be bothered with the effort of sending them south of the Danube, where trade was erratic and often risky. See Michel Lassithiotakis, 'Le Role du livre imprimé dans la formation et le développement de la littérature en grec vulgaire XVIe–XVIIe siècles', and Nathalie Clayer, 'Le Goût de fruit défendu ou, La Lecture de l'albanais dans l'Empire ottoman finissant', both in Hitzel (ed.), *Livres.*

29. A modern analogy is the way in which the People's Republic of China has (as of 2002) modernized its publishing industry while at the same time maintaining government supervision. I owe this analogy to a number of my Chinese students, notably Xiaoyang Chen whose help I gratefully acknowledge on this topic.

30. See Daniel Roche, 'Censorship and the Publishing Industry' in Darnton and Roche (eds), *Revolution in Print*, pp. 3–28, and Jean-Pierre Levandier, *Le Livre au temps de Marie-Thérèse: Code des lois de censure pour les pays austro-bohémiens (1740–1780)*, Berne: Peter Lang, 1993, and *Le Livre au temps de Joseph II et de Léopold II: Code des lois de censure pour les pays austro-bohémiens (1780–1792)*, Berne: Peter Lang, 1995.

31. Marie-Elisabeth Ducreux's frightening narrative of how Jiri Janda, a Czech peasant, was executed for reading a forbidden book shows that the printed word was still reckoned as a deadly threat in the Habsburg domains in 1761; see '"Reading unto Death": Books and Readers in Eighteenth-century Bohemia', in Chartier (ed.), *Culture of Print*, pp. 191–229.

32. Klaus Kreiser citing Jale Baysal, *Müteferrika'dan Birinci Meşrutiyet'e kadar Osmanlı Türklerinin bastıkları kitaplar*, Istanbul: Univertesi Edebiyat Facültesi, 1968, in Lehrstuhl, *Beginnings*, pp. 15–16.

33. Although there were few books, printed religious images played an important role in the Christian communities in the Balkans. Religious images were a strong focus of Christian belief. The devout would brave the perils of travel to visit a monastery and see its icons. Famous icons had long been copied in monasteries and simple woodblocks of these were produced and sold to the faithful. But by the eighteenth century, much more elaborate work emerged. Skilled monks in the Orthodox monasteries of Mount Athos and Mount Sinai engraved plates for printing, or sometimes drew master copies of the holy images. These would be sent to Vienna, Warsaw, Moscow or Rome, where local Greeks would pay for their reproduction. Some of the images were obviously produced for a predominantly Slav audience because they bore both Slavic and Greek captions. The printed sheets would be returned to the monasteries, where they were given to travelling monks who distributed them

to the Orthodox faithful in villages throughout the Balkans. Catholic religious texts and pictures circulated widely in the Catholic districts. By these means – word of mouth, written texts and visual images – the Christians of the Balkans preserved their sense of social and religious identity under Ottoman rule. Details are taken from the exhibition notes for 'Orthodox Religious Engravings 18th and 19th Centuries' at the University of Toronto Art Centre, and from the records of the Hellenic Ministry of Culture on Athonite paper icons @ www.culture.gr/2/21/218/218ad/e218ad00. A study of books published in Greek between 1749 and 1821 suggests that only about 7 per cent were bought by Greek-speakers within the lands that eventually formed the independent Greek state. Most of these works were prepared for a highly literate audience, and although there were schools on Patmos and Chios, in the large Greek community of Smyrna, as well as on Mount Athos and in Thessaly, there were not many readers in the southern Greek lands. See Philipos Iliou, 'Pour une étude quantitative du public des lecteurs grecs à l'époque des Lumières et de la Révolution' in *Association d'études du Sud-Est européen* IV (Sofia: 1969), pp. 475–80, cited by Peter Mackridge, 'The Greek Intelligentsia 1780–1830: A Balkan Perspective', in Clogg (ed.), *Balkan Society*, pp. 68–9.

34. There was a subculture of printed books from the outside world even before local printing got under way. In the Ottoman lands Christians and Jews had access to imported liturgical texts printed in Arabic from an early date. A Greek Orthodox Metropolitan established the printing house that printed in Arabic script in Aleppo in 1707. A generation later the Maronite monastery at Al-Shuwayr in Lebanon began to print books for their community. Printing religious books in the Armenian script began in Constantinople, also in the 1730s. But all this activity was invisible to the majority Muslim population, which had no interest in the liturgical texts of other faiths. The Christian and Jewish printers were careful to do nothing to anger the Ottoman authorities by printing work of a more contentious nature. But Armenian commercial printers, who until the nineteenth century were printing in a script incomprehensible to Arabic-readers, by then had the equipment and the skills to take a major role in the general printing market.

35. Mehmed Ali had sent Nikola Masabki to Italy in about 1811 to learn the craft of printing. He set up the new government press at Bulaq, with Arabic and Persian founts.

36. On the Cayols, see Johann Strauss, 'Le Livre français d'Istanbul (1730–1908)' in Hitzel (ed.), *Livres*, pp. 276–301.

37. See Messick, *Calligraphic State*.

38. This oral system also constituted a very active (and controlling) form of the interpretative community proposed by Stanley Fish. There was much less of the individual forming his or her own singular ideas, as Kevin Sharpe describes in his study of the reading habits of Sir William Drake in seventeenth-century England. As Sharpe put it, Drake 'constituted himself . . . as a thinking and feeling entity, an ego, a "conscious self", and as an entity to be so conceived; and he did so through writing and reading.' In the 'calligraphic state', texts were formed communally and more often than not reinforced collective views.

Other ways of reading came later, with the greater profusion of printed texts. See Stanley Eugene Fish, *Is There a Text in this Class? The Authority of Interpretive Communities*, Cambridge, MA: Harvard University Press, 1980, and Kevin Sharpe, *Reading Revolutions: The Politics of Reading in Early Modern England*, New Haven, CT: Yale University Press, 2000, p. 340.

39. I find Madigan's *The Qur'an's Self-Image* very persuasive on this topic.

40. See Esin Atil, 'The Art of the Book', in Esin Atil (ed.), *Turkish Art*, Washington, DC: Smithsonian Institution Press, 1980, pp. 138–238. This remains an essential introduction, but much work has been done in the last twenty years. Many of these books were state art, and the collective volume *The Sultan's Portrait: Picturing the House of Osman*, Istanbul: Isbank, 2000, has contributions by all the main specialists in the field.

41. See *The Rescue of Nigbolu by Sultan Bayezid*, in Lokman, *Hunername*, vol. 1, 1584–5, Istanbul: Topkapı Saray H.1523. fol.108b.

42. Private citizens also commissioned pictorial art but, like the ruler, kept it out of sight.

43. De Hamel, *The Book*.

44. See Manguel, *History*, p. 95.

45. For 'vectors and forces', see Kress and Van Leeuwen, *Reading Images*. For 'icontexts', see Alain Montandon (ed.), *Icontextes*, Paris: Ophrys, 1990, and Peter Wagner, *Reading Icontexts*.

46. James Elkins writes of a Renaissance engraving that it 'evokes writing, it has the feeling of writing, or language, not because of some nebulous or unrecognised habits of seeing, but on account of a dozen or so specific qualities that are also shared by writing.' The engraving (from a picture by Mantegna) 'is an image that evokes pictures as it evokes writing . . . Whatever narrative we might want to see here will be the result of a certain reading of the relation of signs.' See Elkins, *On Pictures*, pp. 160–61.

47. See Gilbert, *Reading Images*.

48. On the use of images in Protestant propaganda, the work of R. W. Scribner is the basic source. See, especially, Scribner, *For the Sake*.

49. See Madigan, *The Qur'an's Self-Image*.

50. A very good description of this process of learning a language of faith, Arabic, in a culture where the national script is Roman, can be found in Baker, 'Presence', pp. 102–122.

51. See Fabian, *Time and the Other*.

52. See Gerhard Dohrn-van Rossum, *History of the Hour: Clocks and Modern Temporal Order*, translated by Thomas Dunlap, Chicago, IL: University of Chicago Press, 1996, pp. 251–8.

53. See Henry C. Barkley, *Bulgaria before the War during Seven Years' Experience of European Turkey and Its Inhabitants*, London: John Murray, 1877, p. 181.

Chapter 14

1. David Crystal, *The Cambridge Encyclopaedia of Language* (2nd edition), Cambridge: Cambridge University Press, 1997, p. 145.

2. Andrić, *Bosnian Chronicle*, pp. 20–21.

3. The act of speaking is described by linguists as possessing three phases. All speech is a dialogue, even if you are only listening to your own interior voice. The first 'speech act' is a locution: something is being said. The second is the intention that may be embedded in the utterance. This is described as the 'illocution'. The third is the consequence that the locution has on the hearer or 'perlocution'. So, a statement like 'Go to the Devil' has a clear illocutionary force; it is unlikely that the listener will oblige. The perlocutionary outcome might more likely be anger, contempt or amusement. The relationship between illocution and perlocution is uncertain and unstable. Moreover, even when the exact verbal content of the speech act is not understood the same process of communication applies.

4. The Russian critic Mikhail Bakhtin (writing with V. N. Volosinov) described 'spreading ripples of verbal responses and resonances around each and every ideological sign'. See Morris (ed.), *Bakhtin Reader*, p. 52. There is an animated debate as to whether Bakhtin or Volosinov wrote this, or whether both were involved. For the sake of clarity, I have put Bakhtin's role first.

5. The italics are my addition, for clarity. See Michael Holquist's paraphrase of Bakhtin in *Dialogism: Bakhtin and His World*, London: Routledge, 1990, pp. 21–2. The fable is explained at greater length in Clark and Holquist, *Mikhail Bakhtin*, pp. 68–9.

6. Bakhtin, despite his preoccupation with Dostoyevsky and Rabelais, always regarded himself not as a literary critic but, following a line of thought in Kant, as a 'philosophical anthropologist'. This seems to me to express very well his preoccupation with the world-as-perceived, and not the remote fastnesses of theory. See Clark and Holquist, *Mikhail Bakhtin*, pp. 277–8. 'Enemies in the mirror' is the central theme of Ron Barkai's remarkable *Cristianos y musulmanes*.

7. This 'never-meeting' is also a central theme of both E. M. Forster's novel *A Passage to India* (1924) and of Paul Scott's novel sequence *The Raj Quartet* (1966–74). But both suggest that 'never-meeting', although replete with dangers of violence and hatred, does not inevitably lead to hatred.

8. Morris, *Bakhtin Reader*, pp. 86–9, quoting *Speech Genres and other Late Essays*, ed. V. W. McGee, trans. C. Emerson and M. Holquist, Austin, TX: University of Texas Press, 1986.

9. 'Language Used as Shield and Weapon' is the subtitle of a valuable study by Allan and Burridge, *Euphemism and Dysphemism*. I am grateful to Dr Judy Delin for drawing my attention to this approach.

10. These are terms used in the contemporary Middle East. In 1983 an Israeli General, Rafael Eitan, famously described the Palestinians as 'drugged cockroaches'. More recently another senior figure, Rabbi Ovadia Yosef, called Palestinians 'snakes'. More recently still (1997) a senior Palestinian, Mufti Ikrama Sabri, described Israeli settlers in the West Bank lands as 'sons of monkeys and pigs'. The Iraqi official Izzat Ibrahim used the same terminology in August 2001. For Eitan and Yosef, see American-Arab Anti-Discrimination Committee, News Update Message @ mvki2jkv1@nnrp1.deja.com 11 August 2001. For Sabri, see Jay Bushinsky, *Jerusalem Post*, 14 July 1997. For

Ibrahim, see *Irish Times*, 2 April 2002. For pariah communalism, see Ernest Gellner, *Language and Solitude: Wittgenstein, Malinowski and the Habsburg Dilemma*, Cambridge: Cambridge University Press, 1998, pp. 100–106.

11. We should not forget that in Rwanda it was Radio and Television of the Thousand Hills (Radio télévision libre des mille collines) – RTLM – that promoted the idea that the Tutsi caste were 'cockroaches' ('*inyenzi*'). This message contributed powerfully to the subsequent genocide, the most disgusting of the twentieth century, post 1945. See Linda Malvern, *A People Betrayed: The Role of the West in Rwanda's Genocide*, London: Zed, 2000.

12. 8 December 1986.

13. 'Satan' and *Shaitan* sound the same but their meaning is not identical. See the *Light of Islam*, 'The Infallibles', Chapter 4 @ http://home.swipnet.se/islam/imamsajjad.htm

14. Khomeini had always viewed his revolution as all-Islamic, transcending Sunni–Shi'i historical divergences and directed against the common enemy – namely, the twin forces of modernity and secularization and their nominally Muslim admirers, the 'Westoxicated' (*gharbzada* in Persian; *mustaghribun* in Arabic). Hopes for such a Pan-Islamic revolution were high in Tehran at the beginning of the 1980s. See Emmanuel Sivan, 'The Holy War Tradition in Islam', *Orbis* Spring 1998.

15. For a brief statement of these ideas, see *Understanding the Evil of Innovation*, Bid'ah, Riyadh: International Islamic Publishing House, 1997.

16. This was much more akin to Christian traditions of disputation and argument, as in the Spanish debates over the *Moriscos* in the sixteenth century.

17. See Edward Mortimer, *Faith and Power: The Politics of Islam*, London: Faber, 1982, pp. 113–17.

18. See Shahin, *Through Muslim Eyes*.

19. See Hiro, *Holy Wars*, pp. 60–87.

20. Cited John L. Esposito, *Islamic Threat*, p. 135.

21. See Jansen, *Neglected*, p. 193.

22. Johannes J. G. Jansen, 'Tafsir, Ijma and Modern Muslim Extremism', *Orient* vol. 27, no. 4, 1986. See also Jansen, *Neglected Duty*.

23. Jansen stated in an interview, 'I don't know when it was written: probably in the spring preceding the murder of Sadat. Five hundred copies were printed. The group started to distribute and sell the book, but then realized that the Egyptian secret police would be able to locate the group by tracing these copies. So they burned 450 copies. Fifty copies survived, and photocopies of these are bound in libraries all over the world. After the murder of Sadat, the prosecutor added the document to the case file, so the lawyer of the accused also got a copy. He gave it away to an Egyptian newspaper, *Al Ahram*, which printed it. The article appeared in December 1981. It was sold out within hours and was never reprinted in that form. If people are sentenced to death, the Egyptian State Mufti has to condone the sentence. The Mufti gave a long *fatwa* explaining why the murderers of Sadat were wrong. But as a footnote to this *fatwa*, he added the full text of the document *The Neglected Duty*. That appeared in a series of thousands of pages, but the fascicule in which that document was

reprinted sold out quicker than the rest of the volume. Then there was a third edition which was made probably in Jordan or Israel: it made use of the newspaper text, but left out a number of things that may have been sensitive in the context of an Islamic kingdom, as Jordan is'; *Religioscope* (Fribourg, Switzerland), 8 February 2002.

24. Osama bin Laden extended the doctrine still further in his pronouncement of February 1998: 'These crimes and sins committed by the Americans are a clear declaration of war on God, his messenger and Muslims. And *ulema* [Muslim scholars] have throughout Islamic history unanimously agreed that the *jihad* [Holy War] is an individual duty if the enemy destroys the Muslim countries.

   'On that basis, and in compliance with God's order, we issue the following fatwa to all Muslims:

   > The ruling is that to kill the Americans and their allies is an individual duty for every Muslim who can do it, in order to liberate the Al-Aqsa Mosque [Jerusalem] and the Holy Mosque [Mecca] . . . This is in accordance with the words of Almighty God . . . We call on every Muslim who believes in God and wishes to be rewarded to comply with God's order to kill the Americans and plunder their money wherever and whenever they find it.'

   Bin Laden's interpretation is false and misleading. The tradition of *jihad* is as a collective and not an individual duty, to be imposed only through proper authority. Even then it has to be carried out within limits so as to be lawful. His interpretation sets aside all constraints.

25. Jefferson wrote to the Virginian George Wythe, who held the first chair in law in the United States, on 13 August 1786, 'Preach, my dear Sir, a crusade against ignorance; establish & improve the law for educating the common people.' See Gordon C. Lee (ed.), *Crusade Against Ignorance: Thomas Jefferson on Education*, New York, NY: Columbia University Press, 1961.

26. Pastor Dino Andreadis, the Senior Pastor of Park Road Church, Brantford, Ontario, @ http://www.brokenhearted.org/india.html

27. He is based at the First Church of the Gospel Ministry, Wooster, Ohio.

28. @ http://www.victorynetwork.org/VictoryIndia.html

29. @ http://members.aol.com/indiacoc/

30. *Wall Street Journal*, 'WSJ Opinion: Bernard Lewis, *Jihad* vs. Crusade: A Historian's Guide to the New War', Thursday, 27 September 2001. See http://www.opinionjournal.com/extra/?id=95001224

   Here, as he often does, Lewis begins with the combative statement, and then goes on in a more contemplative vein. However, the printed responses to his piece, which reflected a wide range of differing opinions, did not suggest any acceptance of his view that crusades were now only 'a vigorous campaign in a good cause'.

31. At Princeton University in April 1999, where Professor Lewis was once a luminary, the president of the university Christian group, Phil Belin, was widely quoted as saying, 'We know the negative connotations associated with crusades turns people away from associating with us and listening to the gospel message.' The context of Belin's observation was reported in the *Yale Daily*

News, 8 April 1999: the Yale Chapter of the Campus Crusade for Christ had changed its name to Yale Students for Christ. The reason, as its president, Dave Mung, observed was, 'We wanted to have a name that more accurately reflected the nature of our group. Sometimes the CCC name connotes preconceived negative notions.' Belin was commenting on this change.

32. There is good reason for this. In Indonesia and elsewhere, civil strife between Muslims and Christians is often termed a *jihad* by Muslim groups, even if its causes are largely political and economic.

33. The term 'fundamentalism' is often used in a very broad sense, but I believe it should only be applied to those Christian communities and communicators which root their thinking in the literal truth of the Bible. It derives from the twelve short books, collectively entitled *The Fundamentals*, that were published between 1910 and 1915. Each had a print of 3 million copies, with a free copy sent to every pastor, every teacher of Christian religion, and every theology student in the United States. Many more were sold to the general public. See Nancy T. Ammerman, 'North American Protestant Fundamentalism', in Martin E. Marty and R. Scott Appleby, *Fundamentalisms Observed: The Fundamentalism Project*, vol. 1, Chicago, IL: University of Chicago Press, 1991.

34. In 1919, the World Christian Fundamentals Association was founded to advance the cause of a pure Biblical Christianity. One of its progenitors was A. C. Dixon, an editor of *The Fundamentals*. Like the new *jihadists*, the Christian 'fundamentalists' (a term which they applied to themselves after 1920) were linked by a chain of personal connections, discipleship, Bible colleges, Bible-study institutes, seminaries and 'crusades'. The name was coined by Curtis Lee Laws, editor of the *Baptist Watchman-Examiner*. Details of current crusades can be found @ http://www.christianitytoday.com/crusades

35. These details are drawn from the Faith Defenders website @ http://www.faithdefenders.com/

36. It still has a modern resonance. Recently the curse was turned into an art object. It was carved on a large stone and placed in the centre of Carlisle, the last city in England before the Scottish Border. In the Foot and Mouth outbreak of 2001, it was publicly suggested that the disease was a result of the ancient curse, and the current archbishop was asked to lift it. The whole curse extends to some 1,500 words. The powerful General Commination remains in the repertoire of the Church of England and is still occasionally pronounced. See http://www.cathtelecom.com/news/111/29-php. For the text, see http://www.geocities.com/~betapisces/academy/glasgow.htm

37. In 1989, Monsignor Philip Reilly set up his movement, Helpers Of God's Precious Infants, based on peaceful and prayerful public witness at the abortion sites – or 'Calvary' sites as he calls them. See http://www.iol.ie/~hlii/helpers_of_infants.html. Reilly's movement was non-violent, but for the wider range of activities by anti-abortion groups, violent and non-violent, see http://www.fyleserva.com/cgnews/

38. See, for example, townhall.com, which calls it the Evil Empire Speech, but the words were *not* used in the text. See http://www.townhall.com/hall_of_fame/reagan/speech/empire/html. For the address to the British Parliament, see

University of Texas Presidential Archive Website, @ http://www.reagan.
utexas.edu/resource/speeches/1982/60882a.htm

39. Reagan address to the National Association of Evangelicals @ http://www.
reagan.utexas.edu/resource/speeches/1983/30883b.htm

40. Reagan did quote Schiller – 'The most pious man can't stay in peace if it doesn't
please his evil neighbour.' – in his speech to the Bundestag on 9 June 1982. This
appears in a footnote in *The Public Papers of the Presidents of the United States: Ronald
Reagan 1981–1989*, Washington, DC: Government Printing Office, 1982–90.
See also http://www.usembassy.de/usa/etexts/ga5-820609.htm

41. Many of his mis-speakings related to memory, which may well have been the
early manifestations of Alzheimer's Disease. Thus he forgot Princess Diana's
name and called her 'Princess David'. But when working from a script he gave
reliable performances.

42. The term was first coined of Reagan.

43. He had some connections. In 1970, five members of the Full Gospel Business
Men's Fellowship, prayed with then-California Governor Reagan at his home
in Sacramento. One, a former Lear executive, was overcome with the Spirit
and began to speak in the voice of God. He compared Reagan to a king, and
prophesied that Reagan would 'reside at 1600 Pennsylvania Avenue' if he
continued to walk in God's way. It was suggested that Reagan took the
prophecy very seriously. See http://www.pir.org/gw/fgbmfi.txt. Clinton had
his 'spiritual advisers' and was rooted in a Southern Baptist heritage. See http://
www.llano.net/baptist/presidentsadvisers.htm During the Monica Lewinsky
crisis he turned to the Revd Jesse Jackson for spiritual support.

44. See *Religion and Ethics Newsweekly: The Spirituality of President Bush* @ http://
www.pbs.org/wnet/religionandethics/week421/news.html

45. Woodward, *Bush at War*, p. 16.

46. Ibid., p. 38.

47. *Washington Post*, 31 May 2000.

48. This text was subsequently massaged to change the text as delivered. At a
commonly used website, Quoteworld, the word crusade does not appear in the
transcript of the speech. See http://www.quoteworld.org/docs/gbrem926.php

49. 'This President regards words as unusually binding . . . The President likes a
language of very clear moral meaning. He thought the word "evil" was the
word he wanted to use'; Eddie Mair Interview with David Frum, a Bush
speechwriter, BBC Radio 4, *Broadcasting House*, 23 June 2002.

50. *Presidential News and Speeches*, 16 September 2001, @ http://www.whitehouse.
gov/news/releases/2001/09/20010916-2.a.ram. On 26 January 2003, at the
World Economic Forum in Davos, the US Secretary of State again used
'crusade' to describe US activity, saying that 'as we generate wealth, as we
create wealth, we recognize that ultimately the purpose of that wealth has to
be to touch the lives of every one of God's children. Let that be our solemn
obligation and let that be our charge today. And in that great crusade, the
United States is aligned with each and every country and institution represented
in this room.' Here Colin Powell used the word in its 'Jeffersonian' form, but
the deliberate choice of 'crusade' in this context, rather than, say, 'struggle', is

notable, given the new political context of the term after the president's controversial use of the word. For the text of the Secretary of State's speech, transcribed by the State Department, see http://www.startribune.com/stories/484/3615273.html

51. The linguistic technique of conversational analysis (CA) suggests that seeking the word in this way indicates that it is problematical. Nowhere else in the press conference does Bush use the same pattern of phrasing. On the practice and potential for CA, see Paul ten Have, *Doing Conversational Analysis*, London: Sage, 1999, pp. 28–34. I am grateful to Bethan Benwell for introducing me to this form of analysis and for helping me through its complexities.

52. Mark Twain, *Tom Sawyer Abroad* (1894), Chapter 1.

53. See http://www.whitehouse.gov/news/releases/2002/01/20020129-11.html

54. Humpty Dumpty, Lewis Carroll's articulate Giant Egg, invented the 'portmanteau phrase': 'You see, it's like a portmanteau [two-part suitcase] – there are two meanings packed up into one word'; *Through the Looking-Glass* (1872), Chapter 6. Humpty Dumpty 'in a rather scornful tone' also observed on this occasion that 'When I use a word . . . it means just what I choose it to mean – neither more nor less.'

55. The person who first coined the phrase 'the Rome–Berlin Axis' was the Hungarian General Gombos. The current *Webster's Dictionary* defines 'Axis' as meaning 'relating to the three powers, [Nazi] Germany, [Fascist] Italy and [Imperial] Japan', engaged against the Allied nations in World War II. These states were (and are still) considered an embodiment of evil. Hendrik Hertzberg, in the *New Yorker* ' "Talk of the Town" '; Grinding the Axis', 11 February 2002, also alluded to the connection between the phrases, and to the Reagan connection, but did not set that speech into its wider context.

56. David Frum, one of the president's speechwriters, was closely involved with the phrase 'the Axis of Hate'. Frum himself said it was 'the Axis of Hatred'; BBC Radio 4, *Broadcasting House*, 23 June 2002. Moreover, speaking to Christopher Hitchens on a BBC4 television programme, *Profile: President G. W. Bush*, Frum said that the president found the right language to describe the new context. He also said that the president was 'at home with the language of good and evil'. See http://www.bbc.co.uk/bbcfour/documentaries/profiles/george_w_bush.shtml. Frum spoke at great length to Eddie Mair on *Broadcasting House*. Frum has now published an account of the Bush administration: David Frum, *The Right Man: The Surprise Presidency of George W. Bush*, New York, NY: Random House, 2003. However it was published too late for me to use.

57. Woodward, *Bush at War*, pp. 141–3.

58. Ibid., pp. 52–3.

59. 'The Evildoers and the Misled', 6 December 2001. See http://www.ariannaonline.com/columns/files/120601.html

60. See Jonathan Swift, *Gulliver's Travels*, London: Folio Society, 1965 (1997 edn), pp. 220–21.

61. Ibid. It is now generally held that the world of the Houyhnhnms was Reason without Humanity and the world of the Yahoos, Humanity without Reason. As a consequence, the Houyhnhnm world was undesirable. This, in my view, is ana-

chronistic. Swift and his ilk sincerely found little to fear in the society of Reason.

62. Ibid., p. 261.

63. Mark 5:9.

64. Dr Ralph F. Wilson, 'The Six Simple Principles of Viral Marketing', *Web Marketing Today*, 70, 1 February 2000. See http://www.wilsonweb.com/wmt5/viral-principles.htm

65. For the debate on the pursuit of happiness, see the convenient collection @ http://www.lexrex.com/enlightened/AmericanIdeal/yardstick/pr8_quotes.html – for example: 'Kings or parliaments could not give the rights essential to happiness . . . We claim them from a higher source – from the King of kings, and Lord of all the earth. They are not annexed to us by parchments and seals. They are created in us by the decrees of Providence . . . It would be an insult on the divine Majesty to say, that he has given or allowed any man or body of men a right to make me miserable. If no man or body of men has such a right, I have a right to be happy. If there can be no happiness without freedom, I have a right to be free. If I cannot enjoy freedom without security of property, I have a right to be thus secured'; John Dickinson (Reply to a Committee in Barbados, 1766).

66. See http://www/bartleby.com/124/pres16.html

67. The 'extremism' statement is from Senator Barry Goldwater's acceptance speech for the Republican presidential nomination on 16 July 1964. But the position he advances has a long pedigree. The Bible provides justification for no contact or no compromise with the forces of evil. In the book of Nehemiah the prophet rejects the invitation of Sanballat, Tobiah and, significantly, 'Geshem the Arabian' to meet on the plain of Ono. They have malign intent, and he rejects their appeal for negotiation, saying, 'I am doing a great work, so that I cannot come down: why should the work cease whilst I leave it and come down to you?' See Nehemiah 6: 1–4.

68. Fereydoun Hoveyda, Iran's ambassador to the United Nations from 1971 to 1978, wrote in 'Pursuit of Happiness: Iran and the American Revolution', *The Iranian*, 11 February 2002: 'A decade or so back in Manhattan, I listened to a very interesting talk given by V. S. Naipaul . . . about what he dubbed the "Universal Civilization". He concluded his remarks with an apology of the idea of "pursuit of happiness". I wrote down some of his comments which I offer here as a conclusion to this short paper: "This idea . . . fits all men. It implies a certain kind of society, a certain kind of awakened spirit. I don't imagine my father's Hindu parents would have been able to understand the idea. So much is contained in it: the idea of the individual, responsibility, choice, the life of the intellect, the idea of vocation and perfectibility and achievement. It is an immense human idea. It cannot be reduced to a fixed system. It cannot generate fanaticism. But it is known to exist, and because of that, other more rigid systems in the end will blow away."'

Of course, Naipaul himself has written more than once in the crabbed language of *maledicta* about Islam, but his ideas here as remembered by Hoveyda have a general application. See http://www.iranian.com/FereydounHoveyda/2002/February/Revolution/

Sources and Select Bibliography

With a topic ranging over many different geographical areas, and over such a long time span, the range of material is virtually endless. My notes and database record over 2,000 books that I have used in writing *Infidels*. I have selected those that I found most useful, or provoking. Others are fully referenced in the notes to each chapter but do not feature here.

Unpublished Manuscript Sources, Granada

DOCUMENTS

1. Archivo de la Real Cancilleria de Granada
   Auto del Real Concejo para que el Presidente y oidores de la Cancilleria de Granada no den a nadie para que llevar armas; S. 5, Legajo 12, Pieza 42, 23 de Marzo (1518).

2. Archivo de la Real Cancilleria de Granada
   El Alguacil del campo de la Ciudad de Malaga con Juan Gaitán, morisco, vecinos de la villa de Comares, sobre llevar armas contra las leyes; S. 3, Legajo 1198, Pieza 8 (1549).

3. Archivo del Alhambra
   Armas prohibidas, Legajo A-20, Pieza 14 (1558).

4. Archivo del Alhambra
   Causa contra Diego y Francisco Lopez, christianos nuevos, vecinos de Guadix, sobre llevar armas prohibidas; Legajo A-64, Pieza 90 (1560).

5. Archivo del Alhambra
   Armas prohibidas y heridas; Legajo A-34, Pieza 5 (1561).

6. Archivo del Alhambra
   Causa contra Antín de Cardenas, morisco, por llevar armas prohibidas; Legajo A-64, Pieza 38 (1561).

7. Archivo del Alhambra
   Copia de Cédula Real sobre los muertes que habían hecho los moriscos en la Cuesta de Cebada; Legajo A-119, Pieza 18 (1562).

8. Archivo del Alhambra
   Causa contra Gabriel de Baeza sobre llevar armas prohibidas; Legajo A-64, Pieza 52 (1563).

9. Archivo del Alhambra
    Causa sobre armas contra Iñigo Antirafe, vecinos del Albaicin; Legajo A-118 (1564).

10. Archivo del Alhambra
    Justificación contra monfies, moriscos de la tierra de habián asaltado las jabegas en la playa de Velez Malaga; Legajo A-65, Pieza 2 (1564).

11. Archivo del Alhambra
    Privilegio de traer armas por ser christiano viejo y su padre haberse convertidos antes de la conversion general; Legajo A-118, Pieza 11 (1565).

12. Archivo del Alhambra
    Auto sobe hacer cautivadao unos monfies varios cristianos; Legajo A-60, Pieza 4 (1566).

13. Archivo del Alhambra
    Copia de Real Cédula por que Su Majestad le hizo merced a Hernando Manchel de poder de llevar armas; Legajo A-118, Pieza s.n. (1567).

14. Archivo del Alhambra
    Privilegio de llevar armas y que se prive a los cristianos nuevos de llevarlas; Legajo A-118, Pieza 58 (1568).

15. Archivo del Alhambra
    Sobre que no se permite a los cristianos nuevos de Casarabonela el llevarlas; Legajo A-118, Pieza 59 (1568).

16. Archivo del Alhambra
    Visita que se hizo a las casas del Albaicin con nota de las que tenían armas; Legajo A-118, Pieza 64 (1569).

17. Archivo del Alhambra
    Interrogatorio para el pleito de Andrés Jenin (Henil) sobre el privilegio de llevar armas, Legajo A-118, Pieza 65 (1569).

18. Archivo del Alhambra
    Bando para que todos los moriscos que viven en Granada salgan de ella dentro de quatro días; Legajo A-4, Pieza 19 (1569).

19. Archivo del Alhambra
    Causa contra Diego Hernandez sobre transfugia en Berberia; Legajo A-63, Pieza 6 (1569).

20. Archivo del Alhambra
    Causa contra Miguel Zoli y consortes, vecinos de Nortaez que los fueron condenados a muerte y ejecutados en justicia en la Puerta de Elvira, sobre paso a Berberia; Legajo A-64, Pieza 44 (1562).

21. Archivo del Ayuntamiento de Granada
    Real provisión mandada que en los bautismos y casamientos de los nuevamente convertidos sean padrinos cristianos viejos; Indiferentes, Legajo 2003 (1511).

22. Archivo del Ayuntamiento de Granada
    Legajo 1861 (1513).

23. Archivo del Catedral de Granada
    Apuntes sobre la manera de enseñar la doctrina a los moriscos; S.1, Legajo 36, Pieza 2.

Published Sources

'A British Resident of Twenty Years in the East' [J. H. Skene], *The Frontier Lands of the Christian and the Turk; Comprising the Travels in the Regions of the Lower Danube in 1850 and 1851*, London: Richard Bentley, 1853

'A Syrian', *Personal Collections of Turkish Misrule and Corruption in Syria* (with an introduction by the Rev. Wm Denton, MA), London: The Eastern Question Association, 1877

'*Images of the Orient': Photography and Tourism 1860–1900*, Rotterdam: Museum voor Volkerkunde, 1986

'*The Turkish Atrocities of Bulgaria': Letter of the Special Commissioner of the 'Daily News' J. A. MacGahan Esq., with an Introduction and Mr. Schuyler's Preliminary Report*, London: Bradbury, Agnew, 1876

'*Veritatis Vindex': That Unconscionable Turk and What to Do with Him*, London: Richard Bentley and Son, 1877

Abbott, George Frederick, *Under the Turk in Constantinople: A Record of Sir John Finch's Embassy 1674–1681*, London: Macmillan, 1920

Abou-El-Haj, Rifaat Ali, *Formation of the Modern State: The Ottoman Empire, Sixteenth to Eighteenth Centuries*, Albany, NY: State University of New York Press, 1991

Abu-Lughod, Ibrahim, *The Arab Rediscovery of Europe: A Study in Cultural Encounters*, Princeton, NJ: Princeton University Press, 1963

Abu-Lughod, Lila, *Veiled Sentiments: Honour and Poetry in a Bedouin Society*, Berkeley, CA: University of California Press, 1986

Agnew, Hugh LeCaine, *Origins of the Czech National Renascence*, Pittsburgh, PA: University of Pittsburgh Press, 1993

Akarli, Engin, *The Long Peace: Ottoman Lebanon 1861–1920*, London: I. B. Tauris, 1993

Akbar, M. J., *The Shade of Swords: Jihad and the Conflict between Islam and Christianity*, London: Routledge, 2002

Al-Azmeh, Aziz, 'Barbarians in Arab Eyes', *Past and Present* 134 (February 1992), 3–18

Allan, Keith and Burridge, Kate, *Euphemism and Dysphemism: Language Used as Shield and Weapon*, Oxford: Oxford University Press, 1991

Allen, Beverley, *Rape Warfare: The Hidden Genocide in Bosnia Herzegovina*, Minneapolis, MN: University of Minnesota Press, 1996

Alloua, Malek, *The Colonial Harem*, trans. Myrna Godzich and Wlad Godzich, Minneapolis, MN: University of Minnesota Press, 1986

Amades i Gelats, Joan, *Las Danzas de moros cristianos*, Valencia: Instituto de Estudios Ibéricos y Etnología Valenciana, 1966

Anderson, Benedict, *Imagined Communities: Reflections on the Origins and Spread of Nationalism*, (rev. edn) London: Verso, 1991

Anderson, M. S., *The Eastern Question 1774–1923: A Study in International Relations*, London: Macmillan, 1966

Anderson, Patricia, *The Printed Image and the Transformation of Popular Culture 1790–1860*, Oxford: Clarendon Press, 1991

Anderson, Perry, *Lineages of the Absolutist State*, London: Verso, 1984

Anderson, Roger Charles, *Naval Wars in the Levant 1559–1853*, Liverpool: Liverpool University Press, 1952

——, *Oared Fighting Ships*, Kings Langley: Argus Books, 1976

Andrić, Ivo, *The Development of Spiritual Life in Bosnia Under the Influence of Turkish Rule*, trans. and ed. Želimir B. Juričić and John F. Loud, Durham, NC: Duke University Press, 1990

——, *The Bridge Over the Drina*, trans. Lovett F. Edwards, London: Harvill, 1995

——, *Bosnian Chronicle* or, *The Days of the Consuls*, trans. Celia Hawkesworth with Bogdan Rakić, London: Harvill, 1996

Anzulović, Branimir, *Heavenly Serbia: From Myth to Genocide*, London: Hurst and Company, 1999

Arat, Zehra F. (ed.), *Deconstructing Images of 'the Turkish Woman'*, New York, NY: St. Martin's Press, 1998

Armstrong, Karen, *The Battle for God: Fundamentalism in Judaism, Christianity and Islam*, London: HarperCollins, 2000

Arnold, Thomas W., *Painting in Islam: A Study of the Place of Pictorial Art in Muslim Culture*, New York, NY: Dover Publications, 1928 (rep. 1965)

Athanassoglou-Kallmyer, Nina M., *French Images from the Greek War of Independence 1821–1830: Art and Politics under the Restoration*, New Haven, CT: Yale University Press, 1989

——, *Eugène Delacroix: Prints, Politics and Satire 1814–1822*, New Haven, CT: Yale University Press, 1991

Atiya, Aziz S., *The Crusade of Nicopolis*, London: Methuen, 1934

Atiyah, George N. (ed.), *The Book in the Islamic World: The Written Word and Communication in the Middle East*, Albany, NY: State University of New York Press, 1995

Augustinos, Olga, *French Odysseys: Greece in French Travel Literature from the Renaissance to the Romantic Era*, Baltimore, MD: Johns Hopkins University Press, 1994

Ayalon, Ami, *The Press in the Middle East: A History*, Oxford: Oxford University Press, 1995

Baker, James N., 'The Presence of the Name: Reading Scripture in an Indonesian Village' in Jonathan Boyarin (ed.), *The Ethnography of Reading*, Princeton, NJ: Princeton University Press, 1992

Balagna, José, *L'Imprimerie arabe en Occident (XVIe, XVIIe et XVIIIe siècles)*, Paris: Edition Maisonneuve, 1984

Banac, Ivo, *The National Question in Yugoslavia: Origins, History, Politics*, Ithaca, NY: Cornell University Press, 1974

Barber, Malcolm, *The New Knighthood: A History of the Order of the Temple*, Cambridge: Cambridge University Press, 1994

Barbir, Karl K., *Ottoman Rule in Damascus 1708–1758*, Princeton, NJ: Princeton University Press, 1980

Barkai, Ron, *Cristianos y musulmanes en la España medieval: El enemigo en el espejo*, Madrid: Rialp, 1984

—— (ed.), *Chrétiens, musulmans et juifs dans l'Espagne mediévale de la convergence à l'expulsion*, Paris: Editions du Cerf, 1994

Barrios Aguilera, Manuel, *Moriscos y repoblación en las postrimerias de la Granada Islamica*, Granada: Diputación Provincial de Granada, 1993

Bartlett, Robert and MacKay, Angus (eds), *Medieval Frontier Societies*, Oxford: Clarendon Press, 1989

Beaugé, G. and Clément, J.-F. (eds), *L'Image dans le monde arabe*, Paris: CNRS Editions, 1995

Beckingham, C. F., *Between Islam and Christendom: Travellers, Facts and Legends in the Middle Ages and the Renaissance*, London: Variorum, 1983

Beeching, Jack, *The Galleys at Lepanto*, London: Hutchinson, 1982

Bell-Fialkoff, Andrew, *Ethnic Cleansing*, London: Macmillan, 1996

Benassar, Bartolomé, *The Spanish Character: Attitudes and Mentalities from the Sixteenth to the Nineteenth Century*, trans. Benjamin Keen, Berkeley, CA: University of California Press, 1979

Bennett, Clinton, *Victorian Images of Islam*, London: Grey Seal, 1992

Bernard, Yvelise, *L'Orient du XVIe siècle à travers les récits des voyageurs français: Regards portés sur la société musulmane*, Paris: Editions L'Harmattan, 1988

Binney, Edwin 3rd, *Turkish Miniature Paintings and Manuscripts from the Collection of Edwin Binney 3rd*, New York, NY: Metropolitan Museum of Art, 1973

Birnbaum, Henrik and Vryonis, Speros (eds), *Aspects of the Balkans: Continuity and Change*, The Hague: Mouton, 1972

Bitterli, Urs, *Cultures in Conflict: Encounters Between European and non-European Cultures, 1482–1800*, trans. Ritchie Robertson, Cambridge: Polity, 1989

Black-Michaud, Jacob, *Cohesive Force: Feud in the Mediterranean and the Middle East*, New York, NY: St. Martin's Press, 1975

Blanks, David (ed.), *Images of the Other: Europe and the Muslim World before 1700*, Cairo: American University Press, 1997

Blanks, David and Frassetto, Michael, *Western Views of Islam in Medieval and Early Modern Europe: Perception of Other*, Basingstoke: Macmillan Press, 1999

Bloch, Maurice, *Ritual, History and Power: Selected Papers in Anthropology*, London: The Athlone Press, 1989

Bloom, Jonathan M., *Paper Before Print: The History and Impact of Paper in the Islamic World*, New Haven, CT: Yale University Press, 2001

Bohnstedt, John W., 'The Infidel Scourge of God: The Turkish Menace as Seen by German Pamphleteers of the Reformation Era', *Transactions of the American Philosophical Society* 58–59, Philadelphia, PA: The American Philosophical Society, 1968

Bolinger, Dwight, *Language – the Loaded Weapon: The Use and Abuse of Language Today*, London: Longman, 1980

Bond, George C. and Gilliam, Angela (eds), *Social Construction of the Past: Representation as Power*, London: Routledge, 1994

Bonner, Michael, *Aristocratic Violence and Holy War: Studies in the Jihad and the Arab-Byzantine Frontier*, New Haven, CT: American Oriental Society, 1996

Boronat y Barrachina, Pascual, *Los Moriscos Españoles y su expulsión: Estudio histórico-crítico*, 2 vols, Valencia: Francisco Vives y Mora, 1901

Boswell, John, *The Royal Treasure: Muslim Communities under the Crown of Aragon in the Fourteenth Century*, New Haven, CT: Yale University Press, 1977

Bourdieu, Pierre, *Outline of a Theory of Practice* (Cambridge Studies in Social Anthropology 16), trans. Richard Nice, Cambridge: Cambridge University Press, 1977

——, 'The Field of Cultural Production' in Randal Johnson (ed.), *Essays on Art and Literature*, Cambridge: Polity Press, 1993

Bowman, Alan K. and Woolf, Gregg (eds), *Literacy and Power in the Ancient World*, Cambridge: Cambridge University Press, 1994

Bracewell, Catherine Wendy, *The Uskoks of Senj: Piracy, Banditry and Holy War in the Sixteenth-century Adriatic*, Ithaca, NY: Cornell University Press, 1992

——, 'Rape in Kosovo: Masculinity and Serbian Nationalism', *Nations and Nationalism* 6 (4) 2000

Braude, Benjamin and Lewis, Bernard (eds), *Christians and Jews in the Ottoman Empire: The Functioning of a Plural Society*, 2 vols, New York, NY: Holmes and Meier, 1982

Braudel, Fernand, *The Mediterranean and the Mediterranean World in the Age of Philip II*, trans. Sîan Reynolds, 3 vols, London: The Folio Society, 2000

Brewer, John, *The Pleasures of the Imagination: English Culture in the Eighteenth Century*, London: HarperCollins, 1997

Bringa, Tone, *Being Muslim the Bosnian Way: Identity and Community in a Central Bosnian Village*, Princeton, NJ: Princeton University Press, 1995

Brubaker, Leslie, *Vision and Meaning in Ninth-century Byzantium: Image as Exegesis in the Homilies of Gregory of Nazianus*, Cambridge: Cambridge University Press, 1999

Brummett, Palmira, *Ottoman Seapower and Levantine Diplomacy in the Age of Discovery*, Albany, NY: State University of New York Press, 1994

——, 'Dogs, Women, Cholera and Other Menaces in the Street: Cartoon Satire in the Ottoman Revolutionary Press, 1908–1911', *International Journal of Middle East Studies* 27 (1995)

——, *Image and Imperialism in the Ottoman Revolutionary Press 1908–1911*, Albany, NY: State University of New York Press, 2000

Brundage, James A., *Medieval Canon Law and the Crusader*, Madison, WI: University of Wisconsin Press, 1969

Bryson, Norman, *Word and Image: French Painting of the Ancien Regime*, Cambridge: Cambridge University Press, 1981

Bunes Ibarra, Miguel Ángel de, *Los Moriscos en el pensamiento histórico: historiografía de un grupo marginado*, Madrid: Ediciones Cátedra, 1983

——, *La Imagen de los musulmanes y del Norte de Africa en la España de los siglos XVI y XVII: Los caracteres de una hostilidad*, Madrid: CSIC, 1989

Burckhardt, Titus, *Moorish Culture in Spain*, trans. Alisa Jaffa, London: George Allen and Unwin, 1972

Burnett, Charles, *The Introduction of Arabic Learning into England: The Panizzi Lectures*, London: The British Library, 1996

Burns, R. I., *Islam under the Crusaders: Colonial Survival in the Thirteenth-century Kingdom of Valencia*, Princeton, NJ: Princeton University Press, 1973

Burshatin, Israel, 'The Moor in the Text: Metaphor, Emblem, and Silence' in

Henry Louis Gates Jr (ed.), *Race, Writing and Difference*, Chicago: University of Chicago Press, 1985

Buxó, María Jesús, 'Bilingualismo y biculturalismo' in Antonio Carreira et al., *Homenaje a Julio Caro Baroja*, Madrid: Centro de Investigaciones Sociologicas, 1978

Cabenalas Rodriguez, Dario, *El Morisco granadino: Alonso del Castillo*, Granada: Patronato del Alhambra, 1965

Cahen, Claude, *Orient et Occident au temps des Croisades*, Paris: Aubier Montagne, 1983

Campbell, Mary B., *The Witness and the Other World: Exotic European Travel Writing 400–1600*, Ithaca, NY: Cornell University Press, 1988

Campo, Juan Eduardo, *The Other Sides of Paradise: Explorations into the Religious Meanings of Domestic Space in Islam*, Columbia, SC: University of South Carolina Press, 1991

Cardaillac, Louis, *Moriscos y cristianos: Un enfrentamiento polémico, 1492–1640*, Madrid: Fondo de Cultura Económica, 1979

—— (ed.), *Tolède, XIIe–XIIIe: Musulmans, chrétiens et juifs – le savoir et la tolérance*, Paris: Editions Autrement, 1991

Carnoy, Dominique, *Représentations de l'Islam dans la France du XVIIe siècle: La ville de tentations*, Paris: L'Harmattan, 1998

Caro Baroja, Julio, *Los Moriscos del Reinado de Granada: Ensayo de historia social*, Madrid, n.p., 1957

——, *Las Formas complejas de la vida religiosa: Religión, sociedad y caracter en la España de los siglos XVI y XVII*, Madrid: Akal Editor, 1978

Carrier, James, *Occidentalism: Images of the West*, Oxford: Oxford University Press, 1995

Carruthers, Mary J., *The Book of Memory: A Study of Memory in Medieval Culture*, Cambridge: Cambridge University Press, 1990

Casas, Bartolomé de las, *Apologética historia sumaria*, ed. Edmundo O'Gorman, 2 vols, Mexico City: Universidad Nacional Autónoma de México, Instituto de Investigaciones Históricas, 1967

——, *History of the Indies*, trans. Andrée Collard, New York: Harper & Row, 1971

——, *Del único modo de atraer a todos los pueblos a la verdadera religión*, trans. Atenógenes Santamaría, Mexico City: Fondo de Cultura Económica, 1975

Cassels, Lavender, *The Struggle for the Ottoman Empire 1717–40*, London: John Murray, 1966

Castro, Américo, *The Structure of Spanish History*, trans. Edmund L. King, Princeton, NJ: Princeton University Press, 1954

Cavallo, Guglielmo and Chartier, Roger, *A History of Reading in the West*, trans. Lydia G. Cochrane, Cambridge: Polity Press, 1999

Centlivres, Pierre and Centlivres-Demont, Micheline, *Imageries populaires en Islam*, Geneva: Editions GEORG, 1997

Certeau, Michel de, *The Writing of History*, trans. Tom Conley, New York, NY: Columbia University Press, 1988

Chadwick, Henry, *The Early Church*, rev. edn, Harmondsworth: Penguin, 1993

Chartier, Roger, *Cultural History: Between Practices and Representations*, trans. Lydia G. Cochrane, Cambridge: Polity Press, 1988

—— (ed.), *The Culture of Print: Power and the Use of Print in Early Modern Europe*, trans. Lydia G. Cochrane, Cambridge: Polity Press, 1989

——, *The Order of Books: Readers, Authors, and Libraries in Europe between the Fourteenth and Eighteenth Centuries*, trans. Lydia G. Cochrane, Cambridge: Polity Press, 1994

Chazan, Robert, *Medieval Stereotypes and Modern Antisemitism*, Berkeley, CA: University of California Press, 1997

Chebel, Malek, *L'Imaginaire arabo-musulman*, Paris: Presses Universitaires de France, 1993

Chejne, Anwar G., *The Arabic Language: Its Role in History*, Minneapolis, MN: University of Minnesota Press, 1969

——, *Muslim Spain: Its History and Culture*, Minneapolis, MN: University of Minnesota Press, 1974

——, *Islam and the West: The Moriscos – A Cultural and Social History*, Albany, NY: State University of New York Press, 1983

Chelli, Moncef, *La Parole arabe: Une théorie de la rélativité des cultures*, Paris: Sindbad, 1980

Chew, Samuel C., *The Crescent and the Rose: Islam and England during the Renaissance*, Oxford: Oxford University Press, 1937

Chirot, Daniel (ed.), *The Origins of Backwardness in Eastern Europe: Economics and Politics from the Middle Ages until the Early Twentieth Century*, Berkeley, CA: University of California Press, 1989

Choueiri, Youssef, *Islamic Fundamentalism*, rev. edn, London: Pinter, 1997

Christades, V., 'Arabs as "Barbaroi" before the Rise of Islam', *Balkan Studies* 10 (1969)

Christiansen, E., *The Northern Crusade: The Baltic and the Catholic Frontier of Christendom 1100–1525*, London: Macmillan, 1980

Chu, Petra ten-Doesschate and Weisberg, Gabriel P. (eds), *The Popularization of Images: Visual Culture under the July Monarchy*, Princeton, NJ: Princeton University Press, 1994

Çirakman, Asli, 'From the "Terror of the World" to the "Sick Man of Europe": European Images of Ottoman Empire and Society from the Sixteenth Century to the Nineteenth', unpublished PhD thesis, Queens University, Ontario, 1996

——, 'From Tyranny to Despotism: The Enlightenment's Unenlightened Image of the Turks', *International Journal of Middle East Studies* 33 (2001)

Clair, Colin, *A History of European Printing*, London: Academic Press, 1976

Clark, Colin, *A Chronology of Printing*, London: Cassell, 1969

Clark, Harry, 'The Publication of the Koran in Latin: A Reformation Dilemma', *The Sixteenth Century Journal* 15. 1 (Spring 1984) 3–12

Clark, Katerina and Holquist, Michael, *Mikhail Bakhtin*, Cambridge, MA: Harvard University Press, 1984

Clogg, Richard (ed.), *The Movement for Greek Independence 1770–1821: A Collection of Documents*, London: Macmillan, 1976

—— (ed.), *Balkan Society in the Age of Greek Independence*, London: Macmillan, 1981

Coe, Penny, ' "O God, the heathen have come into your inheritance" (Psalm 78.1): The Theme of Religious Pollution in Crusade Documents 1095–1188' in

M. Shatzmiller, *Crusaders and Muslims in Twelfth-Century Syria*, Leiden: E. J. Brill, 1993

Cohen, Jeffrey Jerome, *Of Giants: Sex, Monsters and the Middle Ages*, Minneapolis, MN: University of Minnesota Press, 1999

Cohen, Mark R., *Under Crescent and Cross: The Jews in the Middle Ages*, Princeton, NJ: Princeton University Press, 1994

Cohn, Norman, *The Pursuit of the Millennium: Revolutionary Millenarians and Mystical Anarchists of the Middle Ages*, rev. edn, London: Pimlico, 1993

Colbert, E. P., *The Martyrs of Cordoba 850–859*, Washington, DC: Catholic University of America Press, 1962

Collins, Roger, *Early Medieval Spain: Unity in Diversity 400–1000*, London: Macmillan, 1983

——, *The Arab Conquest of Spain 710–797*, Oxford: Basil Blackwell, 1989

Constantelos, D. J., 'The Moslem Conquests of the Near East as Revealed in the Greek Sources of the Seventh and Eighth Centuries', *Byzantion* 42 (1972)

Coope, Jessica A., *The Martyrs of Córdoba: Community and Family Conflict in an Age of Mass Conversion*, Lincoln, NE: University of Nebraska Press, 1995

Corbett, Margery and Lightbown, R. W., *The Comely Frontispiece: The Emblematic Title Page in England 1550–1660*, London: Routledge and Kegan Paul, 1979

Courbage, Youssef and Fargues, Philippe, *Christians and Jews under Islam*, trans. Judy Mabro, London: I. B. Tauris, 1998

Crampton, R. J., *Eastern Europe in the Twentieth Century*, London: Routledge, 1994

Creagh, James, *Over the Borders of Christendom and Eslamiah: A Journey through Hungary, Slavonia, Serbia, Bosnia, Herzegovina, Dalmatia, and Montenegro, to the North of Albania in the Summer of 1875*, 2 vols, London: Samuel Tinsley, 1876

Cruz, Anne and Perry, Mary Elizabeth (eds), *Culture and Control in Counter-Reformation Spain*, Minneapolis, MN: University of Minnesota Press, 1992

Curtis, William Elroy, *The Turk and His Lost Provinces*, Chicago: Fleming H. Revell Co., 1903

Cutler, Allan Harris and Cutler, Helen Elmquist, *The Jew as the Ally of the Muslim: Mediaeval Roots of Anti-Semitism*, Notre Dame, IN: University of Notre Dame Press, 1986

Daftary, Farhad, *The Assassin Legends: Myths of the Ismailis*, London: I. B. Tauris, 1994

Damiani, Anita, *Enlightened Observers: British Travellers to the Near East 1750–1850*, Beirut: American University of Beirut, 1979

Daniel, Norman, *The Arabs and Mediaeval Europe*, Beirut: Longman Librairie du Liban, 1975

——, *Islam and the West: The Making of an Image*, Edinburgh: Edinburgh University Press, 1980

——, *Heroes and Saracens: An Interpretation of the Chansons de Geste*, Edinburgh: Edinburgh University Press, 1984

Darnton, Robert and Roche, Daniel (eds), *Revolution in Print: The Press in France 1775–1800*, Berkeley, CA: University of California Press, 1989

Davies, Norman, *God's Playground: A History of Poland: The Origins to 1795*, Oxford: Clarendon Press, 1981

Davis, James C., *Pursuit of Power: Venetian Ambassadors' Reports on Turkey, France and Spain in the Age of Philip II*, New York, NY: Harper Torchbooks, 1970

Davison, Roderic H., 'Turkish Attitudes Concerning Christian-Muslim Equality in the Nineteenth Century', *American Historical Review* 59:4 (1954), 844–64

De Hamel, Christopher, *The Book: A History of the Bible*, London: Phaidon, 2001

Delbruck, Hans, *Medieval Warfare*, trans. Walter J. Renfroe, Jr, Lincoln, NB: University of Nebraska Press, 1982

Deringil, Selim, *The Well Protected Domains: Ideology and the Legitimation of Power in the Ottoman Empire 1876–1909*, London: I. B. Tauris, 1998

Derrida, Jacques, *Dissemination*, trans. Barbara Johnson, London: The Athlone Press, 1993

Desmet-Grégoire, Hélène, *Le Divan Magique: L'Orient turc en France au XVIIIe siècle*, Paris: Le Sycomore, 1980

de Zayas, Rodrigo, *Les Morisques et le racisme d'état: Les voies du Sud*, Paris: Editorial La Différence, 1992

Diamandouros, Nikiforos P., Anton, John P., Petropulos, John A. and Topping, Peter (eds), *Hellenism and the First Greek War of Liberation (1821–1930): Continuity and Change*, Thessaloniki: Institute for Balkan Studies, 1976

Djait, Hichem, *Europe and Islam*, trans. Peter Heinegg, Berkeley, CA: University of California Press, 1985

Dodds, Jerrilynn D., *Architecture and Ideology in Early Medieval Spain*, University Park, PA: Pennsylvania State University Press, 1990

Domínguez Ortiz, Antonio and Vincent, Bernard, *Historia de los Moriscos: Vida y tragedia de una minoria*, Madrid: Biblioteca de la Revista de Occidente, 1978

Douglas, Mary, *Purity and Danger: An Analysis of the Concepts of Pollution and Taboo*, London: Routledge and Kegan Paul, 1966

Douglas, Roy, 'Britain and the Armenian Question 1894–7', *The Historical Journal* 19.1. (1976)

Dozy, Reinhart, *Spanish Islam: A History of the Moslems in Spain* (1913), trans. Francis Griffin Stokes, London: Frank Cass, 1972

Drucker, Johanna, *The Alphabetic Labyrinth: The Letters in History and Imagination*, London: Thames and Hudson, 1995

Dubler, C. E., 'Sobre la crónica arábigo-bizantina de 741', *Al Andalus* 11 (1946), 298–322

Ducellier, Alain, *Chrétiens d'Orient et Islam au Moyen-Age, VIIe–XVe siècle*, Paris: Armand Colin, 1996

Dufrenoy, Marie-Louise, *L'Orient Romanesque en France 1704–1789: Etude d'histoire et de critique littéraires*, 3 vols, vols 1 and 2, Montreal: Editions Beauchemin, 1946; vol. 3, Amsterdam: Rodopi, 1975

Dupront, Alphonse, *Le Mythe de croisade*, 4 vols, Paris: Editions Gallimard, 1997

Durham, M. Edith, *The Burden of the Balkans*, London: Thomas Nelson, 1905 (1912 reprint)

Earle, Peter, *The Corsairs of Malta and Barbary*, London: Sidgwick and Jackson, 1970

Echevarria, Ana, *The Fortress of Faith: The Attitude towards Muslims in Fifteenth-Century Spain*, Leiden: E. J. Brill, 1999

Eco, Umberto, *The Search for the Perfect Language*, trans. James Fentress, London: Fontana Press, 1997

——, *Serendipities: Language and Lunacy*, trans. William Weaver, New York, NY: Columbia University Press, 1998

Edwards, Holly, *Noble Dreams Wicked Pleasures: Orientalism in America 1870–1930*, Princeton, NJ: Princeton University Press, 2000

Edwards, John, *Christian Córdoba: The City and Its Region in the Late Middle Ages*, Cambridge: Cambridge University Press, 1982

——, *Religion and Society in Spain c. 1492*, Aldershot: Variorum, 1996

——, *The Spain of the Catholic Monarchs 1474–1520*, Oxford: Basil Blackwell, 2000

Eickelman, Dale F. and Piscatori, James (eds), *Muslim Travellers: Pilgrimage, Migration and the Religious Imagination*, Berkeley, CA: University of California Press, 1990

Eisenstein, Elizabeth L., *The Printing Press as an Agent of Change: Communications and Cultural Transformations in Early Modern Europe*, 2 vols, Cambridge: Cambridge University Press, 1976

——, *The Printing Revolution in Early Modern Europe*, Cambridge: Cambridge University Press, 1983

Elkins, James, *On Pictures and the Words That Fail Them*, Cambridge: Cambridge University Press, 1998

Emmerson, Richard Kenneth, *Antichrist in the Middle Ages: A Study of Medieval Apocalyptism, Art and Literature*, Seattle, WA: University of Washington Press, 1981

Emmert, Thomas A., *Serbian Golgotha: Kosovo 1389*, New York, NY: Eastern European Monographs, 1990

Epalza, Mikel de, *Los Moriscos antes y despues de la expulsion*, Madrid: Editorial Mapfre, 1992

Erbstosser, Martin, *The Crusades*, trans. C. S. V. Sal, Newton Abbot: David & Charles, 1978

Erdmann, Carl, *The Origin of the Idea of Crusade*, trans. Marshall W. Baldwin and Walter Goffart, Princeton, NJ: Princeton University Press, 1977

Esposito, John L., *The Islamic Threat: Myth or Reality?*, Oxford: Oxford University Press, 1995

Fabian, Johannes, *Time and the Other: How Anthropology Makes Its Object*, New York, NY: Columbia University Press, 1983

Fabre-Vassas, Claudine, *The Singular Beast: Jews, Christians and the Pig*, trans. Carol Volk, New York, NY: Columbia University Press, 1997

Faroqhi, Suraiya, *Subjects of the Sultan: Culture and Daily Life in the Ottoman Empire*, London: I. B. Tauris, 2000

Fentress, James and Wickham, Chris, *Social Memory: New Perspectives on the Past*, Oxford: Blackwell, 1992

Ferguson, Niall (ed.), *Virtual History: Alternatives and Counterfactuals*, London: Picador, 1997

Findley, Carter Vaughn, 'Ebu Bekir Ratib's Vienna Embassy Narrative: Discovering Austria or Propagandising for Reform in Istanbul', *Wiener Zeitschrift fur die Kunde des Morgenlandes* LXXXV (1995)

——, 'A Quixotic Author and his Great Taxonomy: Mouradgea d'Ohsson and his

Tableau général de l'empire othoman', paper presented at the 19th International Congress of Historical Sciences Conference, Oslo 2000

Fine, John V. A., *The Late Medieval Balkans: A Critical Survey from the Late Twelfth Century to the Ottoman Conquest*, Ann Arbor, MI: University of Michigan Press, 1987

Fischer-Galati, Stephen, *Ottoman Imperialism and German Protestantism 1521–1555*, Cambridge, MA: Harvard University Press, 1959

Fleming, K. E., *The Muslim Bonaparte: Diplomacy and Orientalism in Ali Pasha's Greece*, Princeton, NJ: Princeton University Press, 1999

Fletcher, R. [Richard] A., 'Reconquest and Crusade in Spain c. 1050–1150', *Transactions of the Royal Historical Society*, 5th series 37 (1987)

Fletcher, Richard, *The Quest for El Cid*, New York, NY: Oxford University Press, 1990

France, John, *Victory in the East: A Military History of the First Crusade*, Cambridge: Cambridge University Press, 1994

Franolic, Branko, *A Short History of Literary Croatian*, Paris: Nouvelles Editions Latines, 1980

Frazee, C. A., *Catholics and Sultans: The Church and the Ottoman Empire, 1453–1923*, Cambridge: Cambridge University Press, 1983

Freedberg, David, *The Power of Images: Studies in the History and Theory of Response*, Chicago, IL: University of Chicago Press, 1989

Freedman, Paul, *Images of the Medieval Peasant*, Stanford, CA: Stanford University Press, 1999

Friedman, Francine, *The Bosnian Muslims: Denial of a Nation*, Boulder, CO: Westview Press, 1996

Friedman, J. B., *The Monstrous Races in Medieval Art and Thought*, Cambridge, MA: Harvard University Press, 1981

Friedman, Jerome, 'Jewish conversion, the Spanish Pure Blood Laws and Reformation: A Revisionist View of Racial and Religious Anti-Semitism', *The Sixteenth Century Journal* 18 1 (Spring 1987)

Fuchs, Barbara, *Mimesis and Empire: The New World, Islam and European Identities*, Cambridge: Cambridge University Press, 2001

Gabrieli, Francisco, *Arab Historians of the Crusade*, trans. E. J. Costello, London: Routledge and Kegan Paul, 1969

——, 'Islam in the Mediterranean World' in J. Schacht and C. E. Bosworth (eds), *The Legacy of Islam*, 2nd edn, Oxford: Oxford University Press, 1974

Gaignard, Catherine, *Maures et Chrétiens à Grenade 1492–1570*, Paris: L'Harmattan, 1997

Galán Sánchez, Angel, *Una visión de la 'decadencia española': La historiografía anglosajona sobre mudéjares y moriscos (siglos xviii–xx)*, Malaga: Servicio de Publicaciones, Diputación Provincial de Malaga, 1991

Gallego y Burín, Antonio and Gámir Sandoval, Alfonso, *Los Moriscos del reino de Granada según el Sínodo de Gaudax de 1554*, Granada: Universidad de Granada, 1996

Gandelman, Claude, *Reading Pictures, Viewing Texts*, Bloomington, IN: Indiana University Press, 1990

García Arenal, Mercedes (ed.), *Los Moriscos*, Madrid: Editorial Nacional, 1975

García Cárcel, R., 'La Historiografía sobre los moriscos españoles: approximación a un estado de la cuestión', *Estudis* VI (1977), 73–4

Garrad, K., 'The Causes of the Second Rebellion of the Alpujarras 1568–71', unpublished Cambridge PhD thesis, 1955

Garrido Aranda, Antonio, *Moriscos e Indios: Precedentes hispanicos de la evangelizacion en Mexico*, Mexico City: Universidad Nacional Autonoma de Mexico, 1980

Garrido Athena, M., *Las Capitulaciones para la entrega de Granada*, n.p., 1910

Gaskell, Philip, *A New Introduction to Bibliography*, Oxford: Oxford University Press, 1972

Gdoura, Wahid, *Le Début de l'imprimé arabe à Istanbul et en Syrie: Evolution de l'environnement culturel (1706–1787)*, Tunis: Institut Supérieur de Documentation, 1985

Geertz, Clifford, *Islam Observed: Religious Development in Morocco and Indonesia*, New Haven, CT: Yale University Press, 1982

——, *Local Knowledge*, New York, NY: Basic Books, 1983

——, *The Interpretation of Cultures*, London: Fontana Press, 1993

Geertz, Clifford, Geertz, Hildred and Rosen, Lawrence, *Meaning and Order in Moroccan Society: Three Essays in Cultural Analysis*, Cambridge: Cambridge University Press, 1979

Gellner, Ernest, 'A Pendulum Swing Theory of Islam', *The Philosophical Forum* 2:2 (Winter 1970–71)

Genette, Gérard, *Paratexts: Thresholds of Interpretation*, trans. Jane E. Lewin, Cambridge: Cambridge University Press, 1997

Gerulaitis, Leonardas Vytautas, *Printing and Publishing in Fifteenth-century Venice*, London: Mansell Information Publishers, 1976

Gibb, H. A. R. and Bowen, H., *Islamic Society and the West*, 2 vols, Oxford: Oxford University Press, 1950–57

Gibbon, Edward, *The History of the Decline and Fall of the Roman Empire*, ed. J. B. Bury, 7 vols, London: Methuen, 1911

Gil, Moshe, *A History of Palestine 634–1099*, trans. Ethel Broido, Cambridge: Cambridge University Press, 1997

Gilbert, Suzanne, *Reading Images: Narrative Discourse and Reception in the Thirteenth-century Illuminated Apocalypse*, Cambridge: Cambridge University Press, 1995

Gilmont, Jean-François (ed.), *The Reformation and the Book*, trans. Karin Maag, Aldershot: Ashgate, 1998

Gilsenan, Michael, *Recognizing Islam: Religion and Society in the Modern Middle East*, London: I. B. Tauris, 1990

Gladstone, W. E., *The Bulgarian Horrors and the Question of the East*, London: John Murray, 1876

Glick, T. F., 'The Ethnic Systems of Pre-Modern Spain', *Comparative Studies in Society and Sociology*, I (1977)

Glick, Thomas F., *Islamic and Christian Spain in the Early Middle Ages: Comparative Perspectives on Social and Cultural Formation*, Princeton, NJ: Princeton University Press, 1979

Glubb, Sir John Bagot, *The Empire of the Arabs*, London: Hodder and Stoughton, 1963

——, *The Great Arab Conquests*, London: Hodder and Stoughton, 1963

Goffman, Daniel, *The Ottoman Empire and Early Modern Europe*, Cambridge: Cambridge University Press, 2002

Goitein, S. D., *Jews and Arabs: Their Contacts through the Ages*, New York: Schocken Books, 1964

——, *Studies in Islamic History and Institutions*, Leiden: E. J. Brill, 1966

——, *A Mediterranean Society: The Jewish Communities of the Arab World as Portrayed by the Documents of the Cairo Geniza*, 5 vols, index vol., Berkeley, CA: University of California Press, 1967–99

Goldsworthy, Vesna, *Inventing Ruritania: The Imperialism of the Imagination*, New Haven, CT: Yale University Press, 1998

Göllner, Carl, *Turcica: Die europäischen Turkendrucke des XVI Jahrhunderts*, 3 vols, Bucharest: Academiei Republicii Socialiste România, 1961–78

Goodwin, Geoffrey, *The Janissaries*, London: Saqi Books, 1994

Goody, Jack, *The Logic of Writing and the Organisation of Society*, Cambridge: Cambridge University Press, 1986

——, *The East in the West*, Cambridge: Cambridge University Press, 1996

——, *The Power of the Written Tradition*, Washington, DC: Smithsonian Institution Press, 2000

Gordon, Thomas, *History of the Greek Revolution*, 2 vols, Edinburgh: William Blackwood, 1832

Grabar, Oleg, *The Formation of Islamic Art*, 2nd edn, New Haven, CT: Yale University Press, 1983

Graham, William A., *Beyond the Written Word: Oral Aspects of Scripture in the History of Religion*, Cambridge: Cambridge University Press, 1987

Greene, Molly, *A Shared World: Christians and Muslims in the Early Modern Mediterranean*, Princeton, NJ: Princeton University Press, 2000

Grothaus, Maximilian, 'Die "Erbfeindt christlichen Nahmens": Studien zum Türken-Feindbild in der Kultur der Habsburgermonarchie zwischen 16 und 18 Jahrhunderts', University of Graz, unpublished PhD thesis, 1986

Guanos, Pascal de, *A History of the Mohammedan Dynasties of Spain*, London: Oriental Translation Fund of Great Britain and Ireland, 1840–43

Guichard, Pierre, *Al-Andalus 711–1492*, Paris: Hachette, 2000

Guilmartin, John Francis Jr., *Gunpowder and Galleys: Changing Technology and Mediterranean Warfare at Sea in the Sixteenth Century*, Cambridge: Cambridge University Press, 1974

Gutmann, Joseph, *The Image and the Word: Confrontations in Judaism, Christianity and Islam*, Missoula, MO: Scholars Press for the American Academy of Religion, 1977

Göçek, Fatma Müge, *East Encounters West: France and the Ottoman Empire in the Eighteenth Century*, Oxford: Oxford University Press, 1987

——, *Rise of the Bourgeoisie, Demise of Empire: Ottoman Westernisation and Social Change*, Oxford: Oxford University Press, 1996

Haddad, Yvonne Yazback and Haddad, Wadi Zaidan, *Christian-Muslim Encounters*, Gainesville, FL: University Press of Florida, 1995

Haliczer, Stephen, *The Inquisition and Society in the Kingdom of Valencia 1478–1834*, Berkeley, CA: University of California Press, 1990

Hall, Kim F., *Things of Darkness: Economies of Race and Gender in Early Modern England*, Ithaca, NY: Cornell University Press, 1996

Harris, Marvin, *The Rise of Anthropological Theory: A History of Theories of Culture*, London: Routledge and Kegan Paul, 1969

Harris, Max, *Aztecs, Moors and Christians: Festivals of Reconquest in Mexico and Spain*, Austin, TX: University of Texas Press, 2000

Harvey, L. P., *Islamic Spain 1250–1500*, Chicago, IL: University of Chicago Press, 1990

Haskell, Francis, *History and Its Images: Art and the Interpretation of the Past*, New Haven, CT: Yale University Press, 1993

Haywood, John A., *Arabic Lexicography: Its History and Its Place in the General History of Lexicography*, Leiden: E. J. Brill, 1960

Healey, John F., *The Early Alphabet*, London: British Museum Press, 1990

Henderson, Frank Stewart, *Honor*, Chicago, IL: University of Chicago Press, 1994

Hendricks, Margo and Barker, Patricia (eds), *Women, 'Race' and Writing in the Early Modern Period*, London: Routledge, 1994

Hentsch, Thierry, *Imagining the Middle East*, trans. Fred A. Reed, Montreal: Black Rose Books, 1992

Hernández Juberías, J., *La Península imaginaria: mitos y leyendas sobre al-Andalus*, Madrid: CSIC, 1996

Hertog, François, *The Representation of the Other in the Writing of History*, trans. Janet Lloyd, Berkeley, CA: University of California Press, 1988

Hess, Andrew, 'The Moriscos: An Ottoman Fifth Column in Sixteenth-century Spain', *American Historical Review* LXXIV (Oct. 1968)

——, 'The Evolution of the Ottoman Seaborne Empire in the Age of the Oceanic Discoveries 1453–1525', *American Historical Review* LXXV (Dec. 1970)

——, 'The Battle of Lepanto and Its Place in Mediterranean History', *Past and Present* 57 (Nov. 1972)

——, *The Forgotten Frontier: A History of the Sixteenth-century Ibero-African Frontier*, Chicago, IL: University of Chicago Press, 1978

Hillenbrand, Carole, *The Crusades: Islamic Perspectives*, Edinburgh: Edinburgh University Press, 1997

Hillgarth, J. N., *The Spanish Kingdoms 1250–1516*, 2 vols, Oxford: Clarendon Press, 1976–8

——, *The Mirror of Spain 1500–1700: The Formation of a Myth*, Ann Arbor, MI: University of Michigan Press, 2000

Hindman, Sandra (ed.), *Printing and the Written Word: A Social History of Books c. 1450–1520*, Ithaca, NY: Cornell University Press, 1991

Hiro, Dilip, *Holy Wars: The Rise of Islamic Fundamentalism*, London: Routledge, 1989

Hirsch, Rudolf, *Printing, Selling and Reading 1450–1550*, Wiesbaden: Otto Harassowitz, 1967

Hiskett, Mervyn, *The Course of Islam in Africa*, Edinburgh: Edinburgh University Press, 1994

Hitchins, Keith, *The Romanians 1774–1866*, Oxford: Clarendon Press, 1996

Hitzel, Frédéric (ed.), *Livres et lecture dans le monde ottoman*, Aix-en-Provence: Edisud/Revue des Mondes Musulmans, 1999

Hodcraft, F. W., et al. (eds), *Mediaeval and Renaissance Studies on Spain and Portugal in Honour of P. E. Russell*, Oxford: The Society for the Study of Mediaeval Languages and Literature, 1981

Hodge, Robert and Kress, Gunther, *Language as Ideology*, 2nd edn, London: Routledge, 1993

Hodgen, Margaret T., *Early Anthropology in the Sixteenth and Seventeenth Centuries*, Philadelphia, PA: University of Pennsylvania Press, 1964

Hodgson, Marshall G. S., *The Venture of Islam, Vol. 1: The Classical Age of Islam*, Chicago, IL: Chicago University Press, 1974

Hourani, Albert, *Arabic Thought in the Liberal Age: 1798–1939*, Cambridge: Cambridge University Press, 1970

——, *Europe and the Middle East*, London: Macmillan, 1980

——, *The Emergence of the Modern Middle East*, Berkeley, CA: University of California Press, 1981

——, *A History of the Arab Peoples*, Cambridge, MA: Harvard University Press, 1991

——, *Islam in European Thought*, Cambridge: Cambridge University Press, 1991

Housley, Norman, *The Later Crusades: From Lyons to Alcazar 1274–1580*, Oxford: Oxford University Press, 1992

Houston, R. A., *Literacy in Early Modern Europe: Culture and Education 1500–1800*, Harlow: Longman, 2002

Howard, Deborah, *Venice and the East*, New Haven, CT: Yale University Press, 2000

Hyatt Major, A., *People and Prints: A Social History of Printed Pictures*, Princeton, NJ: Princeton University Press, 1971

Ibn Khaldun, *The Muqaddimah, An Introduction to History*, trans. Franz Rosenthal, Princeton, NJ: Princeton University Press, 1958

Irving, Washington, *Chronicle of the Conquest of Granada from the mss. of Fray Antonio Agapida*, (author's rev. edn), Philadelphia, PA: David McKay, 1894

Isaevych, Iaroslav, 'The Book Trade in Eastern Europe in the Seventeenth and Early Eighteenth Centuries' in John Brewer and Roy Porter, *Consumption and the World of Goods*, vol. 1, London: Routledge, 1993

Itzkovitz, Norman, 'Eighteenth Century: The Ottoman Realities', *Studia Islamica* XVI (1962)

——, *The Ottoman Empire and Islamic Tradition*, Chicago, IL: University of Chicago Press, 1980

Ivanoff, J., *Les Bulgares devant le Congrès de la Paix: Documents historiques, ethnographiques et diplomatiques*, 2nd edn, Berne: Paul Haupt, 1919

Ivic, Pavle and Pesikan, Mitar, *'Serbian Printing' in the History of Serbian Culture*, Edgware: Porthill Publishers, 1999

Ivins, W. M. Jr., *Prints and Visual Communication*, London: Routledge and Kegan Paul, 1953

Jackson, Gabriel, *The Making of Medieval Spain*, London: Thames and Hudson, 1972

Jandara, J. W., 'Developments in Islamic Warfare: The Early Islamic Conquests', *Studia Islamica* 64 (1986)

Jankowski, James and Gershoni, Israel (eds), *Rethinking Nationalism in the Arab Middle East*, New York, NY: Columbia University Press, 1997

Jansen, Johannes, *The Neglected Duty: The Creed of Sadat's Assassins and Islamic Resurgence in the Middle East*, New York, NY: Macmillan, 1986

Jardine, Lisa, *Worldly Goods: A New History of the Renaissance*, London: Macmillan, 1996

Jelavich, Barbara, *History of the Balkans: Eighteenth and Nineteenth Centuries*, 2 vols, Cambridge: Cambridge University Press, 1983

Jephson, R. Mountjoy, *With the Colours or The Piping Times of Peace*, London: George Routledge and Sons, 1880

Johns, Adrian, *The Nature of the Book: Print and Knowledge in the Making*, Chicago, IL: University of Chicago Press, 1998

Johnson, J. T., *The Holy War Idea in Western and Islamic Traditions*, University Park, PA: Pennsylvania State University Press, 1997

Johnson, J. T. and Kelsay, John (eds), *Cross, Crescent and Sword: The Justification and Limitations of War in Western and Islamic Tradition*, New York, NY: Greenwood, 1990

——, *Just War and Jihad: Historical and Theoretical Perspectives on War and Peace in Western and Islamic Traditions*, New York NY: Greenwood, 1991

Jones, W. R., 'The Image of the Barbarian in Medieval Europe', *Comparative Studies in Society and History* 13 (1971)

Joseph, John E. and Taylor, Talbot J. (eds), *Ideologies of Language*, London: Routledge, 1990

Justice, David, *The Semantics of Form in Arabic, in the Mirror of European Languages*, Amsterdam and Philadelphia, PA: John Benjamins Publishing Company, 1987

Kabbani, Rana, *Europe's Myths of Orient: Devise and Rule*, Basingstoke: Macmillan, 1986

Kaegi, Walter E., *Byzantium and the Early Islamic Conquests*, Cambridge: Cambridge University Press, 1992

Kafader, Cemal, *Between Two Worlds: The Construction of the Ottoman State*, Berkeley, CA: University of California Press, 1995

Kahf, Mohja, *Western Representations of the Muslim Woman: From Termagant to Odalisque*, Austin, TX: University of Texas Press, 1999

Karpat, K. H. (ed.), *The Turks of Bulgaria: The History, Culture and Political Fate of Minority*, Istanbul: Isis Press, 1990

Kedar, Benjamin Z., *Crusade and Mission: European Approaches towards the Muslims*, Princeton, NJ: Princeton University Press, 1984

Kedar, B. Z., Mayer, H. E. and Smail, R. C., *Outremer: Studies in the History of the Crusading Kingdom of Jerusalem*, Jerusalem: Yad Izhak, 1982

Keen, M. H., *The Laws of War in the Late Middle Ages*, London: Routledge and Kegan Paul, 1965

Kelsay, John, *Islam and War: A Study in Comparative Ethics*, Louisville, KY: John Knox Press, 1993

Kennedy, Hugh, *Muslim Spain and Portugal: A Political History*, Harlow: Longman, 1996

Kepel, Gilles, *The Revenge of God: The Resurgence of Islam, Christianity and Judaism in the Modern World*, trans. Alan Braley, Cambridge: Polity Press, 1994

Khalidi, Tarif, *Arabic Historical Thought in the Classical Period*, Cambridge: Cambridge University Press, 1994

Khan, Gabriel Mandel, *Arabic Script: Styles, Variants and Calligraphic Adaptations*, trans. Rosanna M. Giammanco Fronghia, New York, NY: Abbeville Press, 2001

Khoury, Adel-Théodore, *Polémique byzantine contre l'Islam: VIIIe–XIIIe siècles*, Leiden: E. J. Brill, 1972

Kiernan, V. G., *The Lords of Human Kind: European Attitudes to the Outside World in the Imperial Age*, London: Weidenfeld and Nicolson, 1969

Kiraly, Bela K. and Stokes, Gale (eds), *Insurrections, Wars and the Eastern European Crisis in the 1870s*, Boulder, CO: Social Science Monographs, 1985

Kleinlogel, Cornelia, *Exotik-Erotik: Zur Geschichte des Türkenbildes in der deutschen Literatur der frühen Neuzeit (1453–1800)*, Frankfurt am Main: Peter Lang, 1989

Kortepeter, C. M., *Ottoman Imperialism during the Reformation: Europe and the Caucasus*, New York, NY: New York University Press, 1972

Kress, Gunther and van Leeuwen, Theo, *Reading Images: The Grammar of Visual Design*, London: Routledge, 1996

Kritzeck, James, *Peter the Venerable and Islam*, Princeton, NJ: Princeton University Press, 1964

Kunt, Metin and Woodhead, Christine (eds), *Suleyman the Magnificent and His Age: The Ottoman Empire and the Early Modern World*, London: Longman, 1995

Lacan, Jacques, *Ecrits*, trans. Alan Sheridan, London: Routledge, 2001

Ladero Quesada, Miguel Angel, *Los Mudéjares de Castilla en tiempos de Isabel I*, Valladolid: Instituto 'Isabel la Católica' de Historia Eclesiástica, 1969

——, *Granada: Historia de un país islámico (1232–1571)*, 2nd edn, Madrid: Editorial Gredos, 1979

——, *Los Reyes Católicos: La corona y la unidad de España*, Madrid: Asociación Francisco López de Gomara, 1989

——, 'El Islam, realidad e imaginación en la Baja edad Media castellana' in *Las Utopias*, Madrid: Casa de Velásquez, 1990

Lambert, Malcolm, *Mediaeval Heresy: Popular Movements from the Gregorian Reform to the Reformation*, Oxford: Blackwell, 1992

Lambton, A. K. S., 'A Nineteenth Century View of Jihad', *Studia Islamica* xxxii (1970)

Lampe, John R., *Yugoslavia as History: Twice there was a Country*, Cambridge: Cambridge University Press, 2000

Landau, Jacob M., *The Politics of Pan-Islam: Ideology and Organisation*, Oxford: Clarendon Press, 1994

Lane Poole, Stanley, *The Moors in Spain*, New York, NY, G. P. Putnam's Sons, 1911

Lapeyre, Henri, *Géographie de l'Espagne morisque*, Paris: SEVPEN, 1959

Lapidus, Ira M., *A History of Islamic Societies*, Cambridge: Cambridge University Press, 1988

Lapiedra Gutiérrez, Eva, *Como los musulmanes llamaban a los cristianos hispanicos*, Alicante: Instituto de Cultura 'Juan Gil-Albert', 1997

Laufer, Roger, 'L'Espace visuel du livre ancien', *Revue Française du Livre* 16 (1977)

Laursen, John Christian and Nederman, Cary J., *Beyond the Persecuting Society: Religious Toleration before the Enlightenment*, Philadelphia, PA: University of Pennsylvania Press, 1998

Lea, Henry Charles, *The Moriscos of Spain: Their Conversion and Expulsion*, London: Bernard Quaritch, 1901

Lehrstuhl für Türkische Sprache, Geschichte und Kultur (ed.), *The Beginnings of Printing in the Near and Middle East: Jews, Christians, and Muslims*, Wiesbaden: Harassowitz Verlag, 2001

Lévi-Provencal, E., *La Civilizacion Arabe en España*, 4th edn, Madrid: Espasa Calpe, 1977

Lewis, A. R., *Nomads and Crusaders 1000–1368*, Bloomington, IN: Indiana University Press, 1988

Lewis, Bernard, 'Ottoman Observers of Ottoman Decline', *Islamic Studies* 1 (March 1962)

——, *Istanbul and the Civilization of the Ottoman Empire*, Norman, OK: University of Oklahoma Press, 1963

——, *The Muslim Discovery of Europe*, New York, NY: W. W. Norton, 1982

——, *The Political Language of Islam*, Chicago, IL: University of Chicago Press, 1988

——, *Islam in History: Ideas, People and Events in the Middle East*, Chicago, IL: Open Court, 1993

——, *The Multiple Identities of the Middle East*, London: Weidenfeld and Nicolson, 1998

Liss, Peggy K., *Isabel the Queen*, Oxford: Oxford University Press, 1992

Lobrichon, Guy, *1099: Jérusalem conquise*, Paris: Editions du Seuil, 1998

Lomax, Derek W., *The Reconquest of Spain*, London: Longman, 1978

Lourie, Elena, *Crusade and Colonisation: Muslims, Christians and Jews in Medieval Aragon*, Aldershot: Variorum, 1990

Lovell, Mary S., *Rebel Heart: The Scandalous Life of Jane Digby*, New York, NY: W. W. Norton, 1995

Lowe, Lisa, *Critical Terrains: French and British Orientalisms*, Ithaca, NY: Cornell University Press, 1991

Lynch, John, *Spain 1516–1598: From Nation State to World Empire*, Oxford: Blackwell, 1991

Lyons, Malcolm C., 'The Crusading Stratum in the Arabic Hero Cycles' in M. Shatzmiller (ed.), *Crusaders and Muslims in Twelfth-Century Syria*, Leiden: E. J. Brill, 1993

——, 'The Land of War: Europe in the Arab Hero Cycles' in Angeliki E. Laiou and Roy Parviz Mottahedeh (eds), *The Crusades from the Perspective of Byzantium and the Muslim World*, Washington, DC: Dumbarton Oaks, 2001

Mabro, Judy, *Veiled Half-Truths: Western Travellers' Perceptions of Middle Eastern Women*, London: I. B. Tauris, 1991

Macarthy, Justin, *Death and Exile: The Ethnic Cleansing of Ottoman Muslims 1821–1922*, Princeton, NJ: Darwin Press, 1995

MacKay, Angus, *Spain in the Middle Ages: From Frontier to Empire 1000-1500*, London: Macmillan, 1977

Mackenzie, G. Muir and Irby, A. P., *Travels in the Slavonic Provinces of Turkey in Europe with a Preface by the Right Honourable W. E. Gladstone, MP*, 2 vols, 2nd edn rev., London: Daldy Isbister and Co., 1877

Madigan, Daniel A., *The Qur'an's Self-Image: Writing and Authority in Islam's Scripture*, Princeton, NJ: Princeton University Press, 2001

Magris, Claudio, *Danube: A Sentimental Journey from the Source to the Black Sea*, trans. Patrick Creagh, London: HarperCollins, 1990

Maier, Christopher T., *Crusade Propaganda and Ideology: Model Sermons for the Preaching of the Cross*, Cambridge: Cambridge University Press, 2000

Makdisi, Saree, *Romantic Imperialism: Universal Empire and the Culture of Modernity*, Cambridge: Cambridge University Press, 1998

Makdisi, Ussama, *The Culture of Sectarianism: Community, History and Violence in Nineteenth-Century Lebanon*, Berkeley, CA: University of California Press, 2000

Malcolm, Noel, *Bosnia: A Short History*, London: Macmillan, 1994

——, *Kosovo: A Short History*, London: Macmillan, 1998

Manguel, Alberto, *A History of Reading*, London: HarperCollins, 1996

Mann, Vivian B. and Glick, Thomas F., *Convivencia: Jews, Muslims and Christians in Medieval Spain*, New York: George Braziller in association with The Jewish Museum, New York, 1992

Manning, John, *The Emblem*, London: Reaktion Books, 2002

Marcus, George E. and Fischer, Michael M. J., *Anthropology as Cultural Critique: An Experimental Moment in the Human Sciences*, Chicago, IL: University of Chicago Press, 1986

Marker, Gary, *Publishing, Printing and the Origins of Intellectual Life in Russia 1700–1800*, Princeton, NJ: Princeton University Press, 1985

Marshall, Christopher, *Warfare in the Latin East 1192–1291*, Cambridge: Cambridge University Press, 1992

Martin, Henri-Jean, *The French Book: Religion, Absolutism and Readership 1585–1715*, Baltimore, MD: Johns Hopkins University Press, 1996

Martinez-Gros, Gabriel, *Identité Andalouse*, Paris: Sindbad, 1997

Marx, Robert F., *The Battle of Lepanto 1571*, Cleveland, OH: World Publishing Company, 1966

Mas, Albert, *Les Turcs dans la littérature espagnole du Siècle d'Or*, 2 vols, Paris: Centre de recherches hispaniques, Institut d'études hispaniques, 1967

Masters, Bruce, *Christians and Jews in the Ottoman Arab World: The Roots of Sectarianism*, Cambridge: Cambridge University Press, 2001

Matar, Nabil, *Turks, Moors and Englishmen in the Age of Discovery*, New York, NY: Columbia University Press, 1999

Matvejevic, Predrag, *Mediterranean: A Cultural Landscape*, trans. Michael Henry Heim, Berkeley, CA: University of California Press, 1999

Mazower, Mark, *The Balkans*, London: Weidenfeld and Nicolson, 2000

McGarry, J. and O'Leary, B. (eds), *The Politics of Ethnic Conflict Regulation*, London: Routledge, 1993

Mellinkoff, Ruth, *The Mark of Cain*, Berkeley, CA: University of California Press, 1981

——, *Outcasts: Signs of Otherness in Northern European Art of the Late Middle Ages*, 2 vols, Berkeley, CA: University of California Press, 1994

Mertus, Julie A., *Kosovo: How Myths and Truths Started a War*, Berkeley, CA: University of California Press, 1999

Meserve, Margaret, 'The Origin of the Turks: A Problem in Renaissance Historiography', The Warburg Institute, University of London, unpublished PhD dissertation, 2001

Messick, Brinkley, *The Calligraphic State: Textual Domination and History in a Muslim Society*, Berkeley, CA: University of California Press, 1993

Metlitzki, Dorothee, *The Matter of Araby in Medieval England*, New Haven, CT: Yale University Press, 1977

Meyerson, Mark D., *The Muslims of Valencia in the Age of Fernando and Isabel: Between Co-existence and Crusade*, Berkeley, CA: University of California Press, 1991

Michel, Christian, 'Une Entreprise de gravure à la veille de la révolution: Le Tableau général de l'empire Othoman', *Nouvelles de l'Estampe*, 84 (1985)

——, *Charles-Nicolas Cochin et le livre illustré au XVIIIe siècle, avec un catalogue raisonné des livres illustrés par Cochin 1735–1790*, Geneva: Librairie Droz, 1987

Miller, Susan Gilson (ed. and trans.), *Disorientating Encounters: Travels of a Moroccan scholar in France in 1845–1846, The Voyage of Muhammad As-Saffar*, Berkeley, CA: University of California Press, 1992

Miquel, André, *Du Monde et de l'étranger: Orient, an 1000*, Paris: Sindbad, 2001

Mishew, Dimitur, *The Bulgarians in the Past: Pages from Bulgarian Cultural History*, Lausanne: Librairie Centrale des Nationalités, 1919

Mitchell, Timothy, *Colonising Egypt*, Cambridge: Cambridge University Press, 1988

Mitchell, W. J. T., *Iconology: Image, Text, Ideology*, Chicago, IL: University of Chicago Press, 1986

——, *Picture Theory*, Chicago, IL: University of Chicago Press, 1994

—— (ed.), *The Language of Images*, Chicago, IL: University of Chicago Press, 1980

Monroe, James T., *Islam and the Arabs in Spanish Scholarship*, Leiden: E. J. Brill, 1979

Moore, R. I., *The Formation of a Persecuting Society: Power and Deviance in Western Europe 950–1250*, Oxford: Basil Blackwell, 1987

Morris, Pam (ed.), *The Bakhtin Reader: Selected Writings of Bakhtin, Medvedev, Voloshinov*, London: Arnold, 1994

Moser, Stephanie, *Ancestral Images: The Iconography of Human Origins*, Stroud: Sutton Publishing, 1998

Mraz, Gerda and Mraz, Gottfried, *Maria Theresia: Ihr Leben und ihre Zeit in Bilden und Dokumenten*, Munich: Süddeutsche Verlag, 1979

Muldoon, J., *Popes, Lawyers and Infidels: The Church and the Non-Christian World 1250–1550*, Liverpool: Liverpool University Press, 1979

Musée de la Corse, *Moresca: Images et mémoires du Maure*, Ajaccio: Musée de la Corse, 1998

Musper, Heinrich T., 'Xylographic Books' in Hendrik D. L. Verlievet (ed.), *The Book Through Five Thousand Years*, London: Phaidon, 1972

Nancy, Jean-Luc and Lacoue-Lebarthe, Philippe, *The Title of the Letter: A Reading of Lacan*, Albany, NY: State University of New York Press, 1992

Naphy, William G. and Roberts, Penny, *Fear in Early Modern Society*, Manchester: Manchester University Press, 1997

Necipoglu, G., *Architecture, Ceremonial and Power: The Topkapi Palace in the Fifteenth and Sixteenth Centuries*, Boston, MA: MIT Press, 1991

Neill, Michael, ' "Mullattos", "Blacks" and "Indian Moors": Othello and Early

Modern Constructions of Human Difference', *Shakespeare Quarterly* 49 (Winter 1998)

Nirenberg, David, *Communities of Violence: Persecution of Minorities in the Middle Ages*, Princeton, NJ: Princeton University Press, 1996

Norris, David A., *In the Wake of the Balkan Myth: Questions of Identity and Modernity*, Basingstoke: Macmillan, 1999

Norris, H. T., *Islam in the Balkans: Religion and Society between Europe and the Arab World*, London: Hurst and Company, 1993

Norwich, John Julius, *A History of Venice*, Harmondsworth: Penguin, 1983

——, *A Short History of Byzantium*, Harmondsworth: Penguin, 1998

O'Callaghan, Joseph F., *A History of Medieval Spain*, Ithaca, NY: Cornell University Press, 1975

Olson, David R., *The World on Paper: The Conceptual and Cognitive Implications of Writing and Reading*, Cambridge: Cambridge University Press, 1996

Ong, Walter J., *Orality and Literacy: The Technologizing of the Word*, London: Routledge, 1982

Parker, Geoffrey, *The Military Revolution: Military Innovation and the Rise of the West 1500–1800*, 2nd edn, Cambridge: Cambridge University Press, 1996

Patton, Mark, *Islands in Time: Island Sociogeography and Mediterranean Prehistory*, London: Routledge, 1996

Pedersen, Johanes, *The Arabic Book*, trans. Geoffrey French, Princeton, NJ: Princeton University Press, 1984

Peirce, Leslie P., *The Imperial Harem: Women and Sovereignty in the Ottoman Empire*, New York, NY: Oxford University Press, 1993

Peristiany, J. G. (ed.), *Honour and Shame*, Chicago, IL: University of Chicago Press, 1965

Peters, Edward (ed.), *Christian Society and the Crusades 1198–1229*, Philadelphia, PA: University of Pennsylvania Press, 1971

Peters, Rudolph, *Islam and Colonialism: The Doctrine of Jihad in Modern History*, The Hague: Mouton, 1979

Petkov, Kiril, *Infidels, Turks and Women: The South Slavs in the German Mind c. 1400–1600*, Frankfurt am Main: Peter Lang, 1997

——, 'The Rotten Apple and the Good Articles: Orthodox, Catholics, and Turks in Philippe de Mézières' Crusading Propaganda', *Journal of Medieval History* 23, 3 (1997) 255–70

Petrovich, Michael Boro, *A History of Modern Serbia 1804–1918*, 2 vols, New York, NY: Harcourt Brace Jovanovich, 1976

Philips, John, *The Reformation of Images: Destruction of Art in England 1535–1660*, Berkeley, CA: University of California Press, 1973

Philips, Jonathan (ed.), *The First Crusade*, Manchester: Manchester University Press, 1997

Pi-Sunyer, Orio, 'The Historiography of Américo Castro: An Anthropological Explanation', *Bulletin of Hispanic Studies* 49 (1972)

Pinson, Mark (ed.), *The Muslims of Bosnia Herzegovina: Their Historic Development from the Middle Ages to the Dissolution of Yugoslavia*, Cambridge, MA: Harvard University Press, 1996

Planhol, Xavier de, *Minorités en Islam: Géographie politique et société*, Paris: Flammarion, 1997

Porch, Douglas, *The Conquest of Morocco*, New York, NY: Knopf, 1983

——, *The Conquest of the Sahara*, London: Jonathan Cape, 1985

Porterfield, Todd, *The Allure of Empire: Art in the Service of French Imperialism*, Princeton, NJ: Princeton University Press, 1998

Powell, J. M. (ed.), *Muslims under Latin Rule 1100–1300*, Princeton, NJ: Princeton University Press, 1990

Power, Daniel and Standen, Naomi (eds), *Frontiers in Question: Eurasian Borderlands 700–1700*, Basingstoke: Macmillan Press, 1999

Prawer, Joshua, *The Crusaders' Kingdom: European Colonialism in the Middle Ages*, New York, NY: Praeger, 1972

——, *The World of the Crusaders*, London: Weidenfeld and Nicolson, 1972

Prescott, William H., *The History of the Reign of Ferdinand and Isabella the Catholic*, London: Swan Sonnenschein, Le Bas and Lowrey, 1886

Preston, Cathy Lynn and Preston, Michael J., *The Other Print Tradition: Essays on Chapbooks, Broadsides and Related Ephemera*, New York, NY: Garland Publishing, 1995

Quataert, Donald, 'Clothing, Laws, State, and Society in the Ottoman Empire', *International Journal of Middle East Studies* 29:3 (1997)

——, *The Ottoman Empire 1700–1922*, Cambridge: Cambridge University Press, 2000

Rabbah, Saddek, *L'Islam dans l'imaginaire occidental: Aux sources des discours*, Beirut: Les Editions Al-Bouraq, 1998

Ralston, David B., *Importing the European Army: The Introduction of European Military Techniques and Institutions into the Extra-European World 1600–1914*, Chicago, IL: University of Chicago Press, 1996

Read, Jan, *The Moors in Spain and Portugal*, London: Faber, 1974

Reglá, Juan, *Estudios sobre los moriscos*, Valencia: Universidad de Valencia, 1971

Reilly, Bernard F., *The Contest of Christian and Muslim Spain 1031–1157*, Oxford: Basil Blackwell, 1995

Renard, John, *Islam and the Heroic Image: Themes in Literature and the Visual Arts*, Columbia, SC: University of South Carolina Press, 1993

Rhodes, Neil and Sawday, Jonathan (eds), *The Renaissance Computer*, London: Routledge, 2000

Riches, David (ed.), *The Anthropology of Violence*, Oxford: Basil Blackwell, 1986

Riley-Smith, Jonathan, *The Crusades: A Short History*, New Haven, CT: Yale University Press, 1987

——, *What were the Crusades?* 2nd edn, Basingstoke: Macmillan, 1992

——, *The First Crusade and the Idea of Crusading*, London: Athlone Press, 1993

——, *The First Crusaders 1095–1131*, Cambridge: Cambridge University Press, 1997

—— (ed.), *The Crusades: Idea and Reality 1095–1274*, London: Edward Arnold, 1981

Rodgers, William L., *Naval Warfare under Oars, 4th to 16th Centuries: A Study of Strategy, Tactics and Ship Design*, Annapolis, MD: United States Naval Institute, 1939

Rodinson, Maxime, 'The Western Image and Western Studies of Islam' in J. Schacht and C. E. Bosworth (eds), *The Legacy of Islam*, 2nd edn, Oxford: Oxford University Press, 1974

——, *Europe and the Mystique of Islam*, trans. Roger Veinus, Seattle, WA: University of Washington Press, 1987

Roland, A., 'Secrecy, Technology and War: Greek Fire and the Defense of Byzantium 678–1204', *Technology and Culture* 33 (1992)

Rosell, Cayetano, *Historia de combate naval de Lepanto y juicio de la importancia y consecuencias de aquel suceso* (1853), rep. Madrid: Editora Nacional, 1971

Rotter, Ekkehart, *Abendland und Sarazenen: Das okzidentale Araberbild und seine Entstehung im Frühmittelalter*, Berlin: Walter de Gruyter, 1986

Rouillard, Clarence Dana, *The Turk in French History, Thought and Literature 1520–1660*, Paris: Bouvin, 1941

Rubia Barcia, José (ed.), *Américo Castro and the Meaning of Spanish Civilization*, Berkeley, CA: University of California Press, 1976

Rubin, Uri and Wasserstein, David S. (eds), *Dhimmis and Others: Jews and Christians and the World of Classical Islam*, Winona Lake, IN: Eisenbrauns, 1997

Runciman, Steven, *A History of the Crusades*, 2 vols, Cambridge: Cambridge University Press, 1951

——, *Byzantine Civilization*, (1933) London: Methuen, 1961

Russell, F. H., *The Just War in the Middle Ages*, Cambridge: Cambridge University Press, 1975

Safran, Janina, 'Identity and Differentiation in Ninth-Century Al-Andalus', *Speculum* 76 (2001), 573–98

Sahas, Daniel J., *John of Damascus on Islam: 'The Heresy of the Ishmaelites'*, Leiden: E. J. Brill, 1972

Said, Edward W., *Orientalism*, London: Routledge and Kegan Paul, 1978

Said, Edward, *Covering Islam: How the Media and the Experts Determine how We See the Rest of the World*, London: Routledge and Kegan Paul, 1981

Sanchez-Albornóz, Claudio, *El Islam de España y el Occidente*, Madrid: Espasa Calpe, 1974

——, *Spain: A Historical Enigma*, trans. Colette Joly Dees and David Sven Reher, 2 vols, Madrid: Fundación Universitaria Española, 1975

Saunders, J. J., *A History of Medieval Islam*, London: Routledge, 1965

——, *Aspects of the Crusades*, Christchurch, NZ: Whitcombe and Tombs, 1968

Schama, Simon, *Dead Certainties: Unwarranted Speculations*, London: Granta, 1991

Schein, Sylvia, *Fideles Crucis: The Papacy, the West, and the Recovery of the Holy Land 1274–1314*, Oxford: Clarendon Press, 1991

Schimmel, Annemarie, *Calligraphy and Islamic Culture*, New York, NY: New York University Press, 1984

——, *Islamic Names*, Edinburgh: Edinburgh University Press, 1989

Schwartz, Stuart B. (ed.), *Implicit Understandings: Observing, Reporting and Reflecting on the Encounters between Europeans and Other Peoples in the Early Modern Era*, Cambridge: Cambridge University Press, 1994

Scribner, R. W., *For the Sake of the Simple Folk: Popular Propaganda for the German Reformation*, Cambridge: Cambridge University Press, 1981

Sells, Michael A., *The Bridge Betrayed: Religion and Genocide in Bosnia*, Berkeley, CA: University of California Press, 1998

Semaan, Khalil I. (ed.), *Islam and the Medieval West: Aspects of Intercultural Relations*, Albany, NY: State University of New York Press, 1980

Sénac, Philippe, *L'Occident médiéval face à l'Islam: L'Image de l'autre* (2nd edn), Paris: Flammarion, 2000

Setton, Kenneth M., 'Lutheranism and the Turkish Peril', *Balkan Studies* 3 (1962)

——, *Venice, Austria and the Turks in the Seventeenth Century*, Philadelphia, PA: American Philosophical Society, 1991

——, *Western Hostility to Islam and Prophecies of Turkish Doom*, Philadelphia, PA: American Philosophical Society, 1992

—— (ed.), *A History of the Crusades* (vol. 1, *The First Hundred Years*, ed. M. W. Baldwin, 1955; vol. 2, *The Later Crusades*, ed. R. L. Wolff, 1962; vol. 3, *The Fourteenth and Fifteenth Centuries*, ed. H. W. Hazard, 1975; vol. 4, *The Art and Architecture of the Crusader States*, ed. H. W. Hazard, 1977), 2nd edn, Madison, WI: University of Wisconsin Press 1969–89

Shaheen, Jack G., *Reel Bad Arabs: How Hollywood Vilifies a People*, Northampton, MA: Interlink, 2001

Shahin, Emad Eldin, *Through Muslim Eyes: M. Rashid Rida and the West*, Herndon, VA: International Institute of Islamic Thought, 1993

Shannon, Richard, *Gladstone and the Bulgarian Agitation 1876*, London: Thomas Nelson, 1963

Sharafuddin, Mohammed, *Islam and Romantic Orientalism: Literary Encounters with the Orient*, London: I. B. Tauris, 1996

Sherrard, Philip, *Constantinople: Iconography of a Sacred City*, Oxford: Oxford University Press, 1965

Sherwin-White, A. N., *Racial Prejudice in the Roman Empire*, Cambridge: Cambridge University Press, 1967

Shlain, Leonard, *The Alphabet and the Goddess – Male Words and Female Images: The Conflict Between Word and Image*, London: Allen Lane, 1998

Shouby, E., 'The Influence of the Arabic Language on the Psychology of the Arabs', *Middle East Journal* 5 (1951)

Siberry, Elizabeth, *Criticism of Crusading: 1095–1274*, Oxford: Clarendon Press, 1985

Sicroff, Albert A., *Les Controverses des statuts de 'Pureté de Sang' en Espagne du XVe au XVIIe siècle*, Paris: Didier, 1960

Sievernich, Gereon and Budde, Hendrik (eds), *Europa und der Orient 800–1900*, Berlin: Bertelsmann, 1989

Sivan, Emmanuel, *Islam et la croisade: Idéologie et la croisade dans les réactions musulmanes aux croisades*, Paris: Librairie d'Amérique et d'Orient Adrien Maisonneuve, 1968

Small, R. C., *Crusading Warfare 1097–1193*, Cambridge: Cambridge University Press, 1956

Smith, Colin (and Melville, C. H.), *Christians and Moors in Spain*, 3 vols, Warminster: Aris and Phillips, 1988

Smyth, Warington W. MA, *A Year with The Turks: Or Sketches of Travel in the European and Asiatic Dominions of the Sultan*, New York, NY: Redfield, 1854

Southern, Richard, *Western Views of Islam in the Middle Ages*, Cambridge, MA: Harvard University Press, 1962

Stavrianos, L. S., *The Balkans since 1453*, New York: Holt Rhinehart and Winston, 1958

St Clair, S. G. B. and Brophy, Charles A., *Twelve Years' Study of the Eastern Question in Bulgaria, Being a Revised Edition of 'A Residence in Bulgaria'*, London: Chapman and Hall, 1877

St Clair, William, *That Greece Might Still be Free: The Philhellenes in the War of Independence*, London: Oxford University Press, 1972

Stephanove, Constantine, *Bulgarians and Anglo-Saxondom*, Berne: Paul Haupt, 1919

Stirling-Maxwell, William, *Don John of Austria, or Passages from the History of the Sixteenth Century 1547–1578*, 2 vols, London: Longmans and Co., 1883

Stocchi, Sergio, *L'Islam nelle stampe*, Milan: BE-MA Editore, 1988

Stoianovich, Traian, *Balkan Worlds: The First and Last Europe*, Armonk, NY: M. E. Sharpe, 1994

Stoye, John, *Marsigli's Europe 1680–1730: The Life and Times of Luigi Fernandino Marsigli, Soldier and Virtuoso*, New Haven, CT: Yale University Press, 1994

——, *The Siege of Vienna* (rev. edn), Edinburgh: Birlinn, 2000

Sugar, Peter F., *Industrialization of Bosnia Hercegovina 1878–1918*, Seattle, WA: University of Washington Press, 1963

——, *South Eastern Europe under Ottoman Rule 1354–1804*, Seattle, WA: University of Washington Press, 1977

Tanner, Marcus, *Croatia: A Nation Forged in War*, New Haven, CT: Yale University Press, 1997

Temimi, Abdejelil (ed.), *Las Prácticas musulmanas de los moriscos Andaluces 1492–1609*, Zaghouan: Centre d'Etudes et de Recherches Ottomanes, Morisques, de Documentation et d'Information, 1989

Tenenti, Alberto, *Piracy and the Decline of Venice 1580–1615*, trans. Janet Pullan and Brian Pullan, Berkeley, CA: University of California Press, 1967

Thompson, James Westfall (ed.), *The Frankfort Book Fair: The Francofordense Emporium of Henri Estienne* (1911), New York, NY: Burt Franklin, 1968

Thomson, H. C., *The Outgoing Turk: Impressions of a Journey through the Western Balkans*, London: William Heinemann, 1897

Throop, Palmer A., *Criticism of the Crusade: A Study of Public Opinion and Crusade Propaganda*, Philadelphia, PA: Porcupine Press, 1975

Todorov, Tzvetan, *Mikhail Bakhtin: The Dialogical Principle*, trans. Wlad Godzich, Minneapolis, MN: University of Minnesota Press, 1984

——, *The Conquest of America: The Question of the Other*, trans. Richard Howard, New York: HarperPerennial, 1987

——, *The Morals of History*, trans. Alyson Waters, Minneapolis, MN: University of Minnesota Press, 1995

Todorova, Maria, *Imagining the Balkans*, Oxford: Oxford University Press, 1997

Toomer, G. J., *Eastern Wisdom and Learning: The Study of Arabic in Seventeenth-century England*, Oxford: Clarendon Press, 1996

Twyman, Michael, *The British Library Guide to Printing: History and Techniques*, London: The British Library, 1998

Unamuno, Miguel de, *En torno al casticismo*, Madrid: Biblioteca Nueva, 1996

Usamah ibn-Munqidh, *An Arab-Syrian Gentleman and Warrior in the Period of the Crusades: Memoirs of Usamah ibn-Munqidh (Kitab al-itibar)*, trans. Philip K. Hitti, New York, NY: Columbia University Press, 2000

van Gelder, Geert Jan and de Moor, Ed, 'The Middle East and Europe: Encounters and Exchanges', *Orientations* 1, Amsterdam: Rodopi, 1992

Van Sertima, Ivan (ed.), *The Golden Age of the Moor*, New Brunswick, NJ: Transaction Books, 1992

Vaughan, Dorothy, *Europe and the Turk: A Pattern of Alliances 1350–1700*, Liverpool: Liverpool University Press, 1954

Versteegh, Kees, *The Arabic Language*, Edinburgh: Edinburgh University Press, 1998

Vervliet, Hendrik D. L., *Post Incunabula and their Publishers in the Low Countries*, The Hague: Martinus Nijhoff, 1978

Vespertino Rodriguez, Antonio (ed.), *Leyendas aljamiadas y moriscos sobre personajes biblicos*, Madrid: Gredos, 1983

Veyne, Paul, *Writing History*, trans. Mina Moore-Rinvolucri, Middletown, CT: Wesleyan University Press, 1984

Voet, Leon, *The Golden Compasses: A History and Evaluation of the Printing and Publishing Activities of the Oficina Plantina at Antwerp*, 2 vols, London: Routledge and Kegan Paul, 1972

Volney, C. F., *Travels in Syria and Egypt during the Years 1783, 1784, and 1785*, 2 vols, Perth: 1801

Vryonis, Speros Jr, *Byzantium: Its Internal History and Relations with the Muslim World*, London: Variorum, 1971

—— (ed.), *Islam and Cultural Change in the Middle Ages*, Wiesbaden: Otto Harassowitz, 1975

Wachtel, Andrew Baruch, *Making a Nation, Breaking a Nation: Cultural Politics in Yugoslavia*, Stanford, CA: Stanford University Press, 1998

Wagner, Peter, *Reading Icontexts: From Swift to the French Revolution*, London: Reaktion, 1995

Wagner, Roy, *Symbols that Stand for Themselves*, Chicago, IL: University of Chicago Press, 1986

Walsh, Robert, *Narrative of a Journey from Constantinople to England*, London: F. Westley and A. H. Davis, 1828

Wandel, Lee Palmer, *Voracious Idols and Violent Hands: Iconoclasm in Reformation Zurich, Strasbourg and Basel*, Cambridge: Cambridge University Press, 1995

Watt, Tessa, *Cheap Print and Popular Piety 1550–1640*, Cambridge: Cambridge University Press, 1991

Watt, W. M., *The Influence of Islam on Medieval Europe*, Edinburgh: Edinburgh University Press, 1972

——, *Muslim–Christian Encounters: Perceptions and Misperceptions*, London: Routledge, 1991

Weine, Stevan M., *When History is a Nightmare: Lives and Memories of Ethnic Cleansing in Bosnia Herzegovina*, New Brunswick, NJ: Rutgers University Press, 1999

Wheatcroft, Andrew, *The Ottomans: Dissolving Images*, London: Penguin, 1995

Whittrow, Mark, *The Making of Orthodox Byzantium 600–1025*, Basingstoke: Macmillan Press, 1996

Wilken, Robert L., *The Land called Holy: Palestine in Christian History and Thought*, New Haven, CT: Yale University Press, 1992

Wolf, Eric R., *Europe and the People Without History*, Berkeley, CA: University of California Press, 1990

Wolf, Kenneth Baxter, *Christian Martyrs in Muslim Spain*, Cambridge: Cambridge University Press, 1988

——, (ed. and trans.), *Conquerors and Chroniclers of Early Mediaeval Spain*, Liverpool: Liverpool University Press, 1990

Wolff, Larry, *Inventing Eastern Europe: The Map of Civilisation on the Mind of the Enlightenment*, Stanford, CA: Stanford University Press, 1994

——, *Venice and the Slavs: The Discovery of Dalmatia in the Age of Enlightenment*, Stanford, CA: Stanford University Press, 2001

Wolff, Philippe, *Western Languages AD 100–1500*, London: Weidenfeld and Nicolson, 1971

Woodward, Bob, *Bush at War*, New York, NY: Simon and Schuster, 2002

Wortman, Richard S., *Scenarios of Power: Myth and Ceremony in Russian Monarchy*, Princeton, NJ: Princeton University Press, 1995

Yapp, M. E., 'Europe in the Turkish Mirror', *Past and Present*, 137 (Nov. 1992)

Yared, Nazik Saba, *Arab Travellers and Western Civilization*, trans. Sumayya Damluji Shahbandar, rev. and ed. Tony P. Naufal and Jana Gough, London: Saqi Books, 1996

Yates, Timothy, *Christian Mission in the Twentieth Century*, Cambridge: Cambridge University Press, 1994

Yeazell, Ruth Bernard, *Harems of the Mind: Passages of Western Art and Literature*, New Haven, CT: Yale University Press, 2000

Ye'or, Bat, *The Dhimmi: Jews and Christians under Islam*, trans. David Maisel, Paul Fenton and David Littmann, Madison, NJ: Fairleigh Dickinson University Press, 1985

——, *The Decline of Eastern Christianity under Islam. From Jihad to Dhimmitude, Seventh–Twentieth Century*, London: Associated University Presses, 1996

Yerushalmi, Yosef Hayim, *Assimilation and Racial Anti-Semitism: The Iberian and German Models*, New York, NY: Leo Baeck Institute, 1982

Young, Robert, *White Mythologies: Writing History and the West*, London: Routledge, 1990

Zernov, Nicolas, *Eastern Christendom: A Study of the Origin and Development of the Eastern Orthodox Church*, London: Weidenfeld and Nicolson, 1961

Zygulski, Zdzislaw Jr, *Ottoman Art in the Service of the Empire*, New York, NY: New York University Press, 1992

Index

n denotes notes